THE HARBRACE GUIDE TO WRITING

CHERYL GLENN
The Pennsylvania State University

WADSWORTH
CENGAGE Learning

Australia • Brazil • Japan • Korea • Mexico • Singapore • Spain • United Kingdom • United States

WADSWORTH
CENGAGE Learning

The Harbrace Guide to Writing
Cheryl Glenn

Publisher: Lyn Uhl

Senior Development Editor: Stephanie
Pelkowski Carpenter

Assistant Editor: Lindsey Veautour

Technology Project Manager: Stephanie
Gregoire

Executive Marketing Manager: Mandee
Eckersley

Senior Marketing Communications
Manager: Stacey Purviance

Senior Content Project Manager:
Lianne Ames

Senior Art Director: Cate Rickard Barr

Senior Print Buyer: Betsy Donaghey

Permissions Editor: Bob Kauser

Permissions Researcher: Sue Howard

Production Service: Lifland et al.,
Bookmakers

Text Designer: Jeanne Calabrese

Photo Manager: Sheri Blaney

Photo Researcher: Marcy Lunetta

Cover Designer: Cabbage Design
Company

Cover Image: © Digital Vision/VEER

Compositor: Graphic World, Inc.

For product information and technology assistance, contact us at:
Cengage Learning Academic Resource Center, 1-800-423-0563

For permission to use material from this text or product, submit all
requests online at **www.cengage.com/permissions**.
Further permissions questions can be e-mailed to
permissionrequest@cengage.com.

Library of Congress Control Number: 2008924960

ISBN-13: 978-0-495-80351-5

ISBN-10: 0-495-80351-0

Wadsworth
20 Channel Center Street
Boston, MA 02210
USA

Cengage Learning products are represented in Canada by
Nelson Education, Ltd.

For your course and learning solutions, visit **www.cengage.com**.

Purchase any of our products at your local college store or at our preferred
online store **www.ichapters.com**.

Printed in Canada
1 2 3 4 5 6 7 13 12 11 10 09

CONTENTS

PART 3 THE AVAILABLE MEANS: STRATEGIES FOR DEVELOPING IDEAS 401

PART 5 A RHETORICAL GUIDE TO GRAMMAR AND SENTENCE STYLE 621

PREFACE

We live in a world of conflict: school boards and community members argue bitterly over whether to build a new high school; U.S. Supreme Court judges read opinions that call their peers' judgment into question; Palestine and Israel continue to bomb each other's country, while our own country continues to bomb Iraq and Afghanistan.

Fortunately, we also live in a world of resolution and possibility, often contingent on the appropriate words being delivered to the appropriate person. Thus, more than ever before, we need to learn how to use language ethically, effectively, and appropriately to address and ultimately resolve conflict—allowing us to move ahead together and make our world a better place. We need to learn how to use rhetoric purposefully.

The Harbrace Guide to Writing helps students do just that: it helps them use rhetoric to move forward by addressing and resolving problems, whether those problems are social, academic, or workplace. A comprehensive and richly flexible guide for first-year writers—and their teachers—*The Harbrace Guide to Writing* includes a rhetoric, a reader, a research manual, and a punctuation and mechanics handbook. *The Harbrace Guide to Writing* distinguishes itself from all the other comprehensive writing guides on the market by its sustained focus on the rhetorical situation and on the specific rhetorical techniques that allow writers to shape their ideas into language that is best suited for their audience and most appropriate for their situation. Students will see writing and speaking—using language purposefully—as an integral part of daily life, in and out of school. Thus, *The Harbrace Guide to Writing* is theoretically sophisticated yet not at all complicated.

In each of the five parts, *The Harbrace Guide to Writing* translates rhetorical theory into easy-to-follow (and easy-to-teach) techniques that help sharpen the ability to observe—to observe what words, assertions, or opinions might work best with a particular audience in a specific situation.

Aristotle was the first to coin a definition for *rhetoric,* referring to it as "the faculty of observing in any given situation the available means of persuasion." Notice that Aristotle does not call for overpowering an audience (readers or listeners) with words or images, nor does he push for winning an argument. Instead, he encourages rhetors, or users of rhetoric, to observe. For Aristotle, and all of the rhetorical thinkers who have followed, observation is primary. Before rhetors do or say something, they need to observe, to take the time to figure out what kind of rhetorical situation they're entering. Rhetors must ask themselves: "Who am I speaking to? What is my relationship to that person or group of people? What is the occasion? Who else is listening? What do I want my language to accomplish?" By answering these questions, rhetors establish the elements of "any given situation."

How Does the Book Work?

Rhetorical principles . . .

First, the three chapters in **Entering the Conversation: The Rhetorical Situation** (part 1) introduce students to the rhetorical principles that underlie all writing situations and provide them with a basic method for using those principles:

▮ To recognize when writing is the best response (or when speaking—or remaining silent—might be more effective)
▮ To consider strategically their audience and their purpose
▮ To plan, draft, and revise their language so that it fits the context and delivers the intended message

. . . applied to real situations . . .

Second, the eight writing project chapters in **Rhetorical Situations for Writers** (part 2) engage students in real situations that invite response:

▮ A mini photo essay begins each chapter, relating the chapter's theme to students' own lives.
▮ A selection of readings illustrates how others have responded to the same subjects.
▮ Two responses within a familiar genre (such as memoirs, investigative reports, or critical analyses) demonstrate how the genre frames an appropriate response to many similar situations.
▮ A step-by-step guide to writing helps students bring it all together: students establish the elements of their rhetorical situation and work within a genre to create a fitting response.

. . . using a catalog of available means . . .

The Available Means: Strategies for Developing Ideas (part 3) presents the common methods of rhetorical development (definition, description, narration, and so on) not as ends in and of themselves but as means available to students as they analyze, develop, and present ideas. A conscious knowledge of these means will trigger students' thinking and writing, making part 3 a handy reference as students work through their projects in part 2.

. . . and with rhetorical reference materials

Additionally, a research manual and a grammatical handbook comprise parts 4 and 5, respectively, and provide the essential reference material students need.

- **Research manual.** Rather than present a series of lock-step procedures for students to follow as they approach a research project, the research manual in **A Guide to Research** (part 4) draws students into research as a rhetorical activity. Students will learn to see research assignments not as a set of rules and requirements but as an effective way of responding to certain rhetorical exigencies.
- **Handbook. A Rhetorical Guide to Grammar and Sentence Style** (part 5) has been constructed from the ground up to reflect an awareness at every turn that students always make grammatical choices in response to their rhetorical situation.

Benefits of Using *The Harbrace Guide to Writing*

- **Flexible organization.** Instructors can use this textbook in the order it's arranged or skip around. It's that flexible. Five simple parts each have a clear purpose and organization. Part 1 provides an overview of rhetorical principles and applications to which students will return throughout the semester. Part 2 consists of eight writing projects, from which the bulk of students' assignments can be chosen. Parts 3, 4, and 5 act as reference materials for students as they work on their projects.
- **Concise introduction to the rhetorical situation.** The three brief chapters in part 1 offer an introduction to rhetoric that is both adaptable to any composition classroom and transferable to students' other writing tasks. On its own, part 1 serves as a quick reference to help students in any writing context across the curriculum and beyond; together with the rest of *The Harbrace Guide to Writing*, it provides strategies and opportunities for thinking and writing.
- **Manageable approach to writing projects.** Step-by-step writing guides in each chapter in part 2 help students through the processes outlined in part 1: understanding the rhetorical situation (by identifying an exigence and locating an audience), identifying a fitting response, and working with the available means. In this way, manageable tasks build toward the completion of a larger writing project in direct, incremental ways.
- **Activities for thinking rhetorically and acting locally.** Activities called **Community Connections** link students to their campus or hometown communities; others—**Your Writing Experiences** and **Write for Five**, for example—connect their everyday writing with more extensive writing projects. Additionally, numerous activities called **Analyzing the Rhetorical Situation** help students understand the elements of a response to a rhetorical situation.
- **View of research as a response.** Rather than offer a series of lock-step procedures for students to follow as they approach a research project, the research manual, **A Guide to Research** (part 4), draws students into research as a rhetorical activity. Students will learn to see each research assignment not as a set of rules and requirements but as an effective way of responding to a specific rhetorical exigence. Because different research

questions require different methods, the research guide includes information on library, online, and field research.

■ **Explanation of grammar in context.** Part 5, **A Rhetorical Guide to Grammar and Sentence Style,** has been constructed from the ground up to reflect an awareness at every turn that students always make grammatical choices in response to their rhetorical situation.

The Harbrace Guide to Writing Flexfiles: Your Available Means

Far more complete than the typical instructor's manual, *The Harbrace Guide to Writing* **Flexfiles: Your Available Means** includes these components and more:

■ **Detailed syllabi.** One of three annotated course plans can be followed or consulted when teaching this text in programs that focus on academic writing, writing in the disciplines, or service learning. Activities, exercises, and journal-writing prompts are provided for each class meeting, along with suggested goals, materials for instructors to review, and so on.

■ **Sample syllabi.** If your course is organized around genres, themes, or rhetorical methods or is integrated with English21, you'll find syllabi and journal-writing prompts to address those as well—all created for *The Harbrace Guide to Writing.*

■ **Instructor's Manual and Answer Key.** Chapters follow the organization of *The Harbrace Guide to Writing,* including an overview of each chapter in the book, suggestions for teaching difficult concepts, and sample responses and guidance for all exercises and assignments.

CengageNOW for Writing

This powerful and assignable online teaching and learning system contains diagnostic quizzing and multimedia tutorials that help students build personalized study strategies and master the basic concepts of writing. It features reliable solutions for delivering your course content and assignments, along with time-saving ways to grade and provide feedback.

CengageNOW provides one-click-away results: the most common reporting tasks that instructors perform every day are always just one click away in the CengageNOW gradebook. For students, CengageNOW provides a diagnostic self-assessment and a personalized study plan that enable them to focus on what they need to learn and guide them in selecting activities that best match their learning styles. Visit academic.cengage.com/now to view a demonstration. To package access to CengageNOW for Writing with every new copy of this text, contact your Wadsworth representative.

Turnitin®

This proven online plagiarism-prevention software promotes fairness in the classroom by helping students learn to cite sources correctly and allowing instructors to check for originality before reading and grading papers. Visit academic.cengage.com/turnitin to view a demonstration.

InSite for Writing and Research™

This online writing and research tool includes electronic peer review, an originality checker, an assignment library, help with common grammar and writing errors, and access to InfoTrac® College Edition. Portfolio management gives you the ability to grade papers, run originality reports, and offer feedback in an easy-to-use online course management system. Using InSite's peer review feature, students can easily review and respond to their classmates' work. Other features include fully integrated discussion boards, streamlined assignment creation, and more. Visit academic.cengage.com/insite to view a demonstration.

Book Companion Web Site

In addition to a great selection of password-protected instructor resources, the free book companion Web site contains many interactive resources for students, including model student papers, links to useful sites, and animated tutorials on researching, revising, grammar usage, and more. The instructor's password-protected part of the site also provides access to the Flexfiles components, including electronic versions of the Instructor's Manual and syllabi.

Acknowledgments

First editions demand time, talent, and plenty of hard work. For that reason, I could not have produced this textbook without the help and support of a number of colleagues and friends. I found myself calling on their expertise at various times throughout the creation of this book. Scott Wible, Stacey Sheriff, and Loretta Gray gave generously of their time and wisdom as teachers, scholars, and writers, working with me to create assignments and exercises to which students will want to respond. Students from campuses across the country have been inspired by those prompts, and I thank them for allowing me to share their individual responses with you: Anna Seitz, Matthew Glasgow, Kelly McNeil, Adair Rispoli, Rupali Kumar, Alexis Walker, Courtney Mullen, Matthew Marusak, and Bethanie Orban. I must also thank Matthew Marusak for his careful attention to the research chapters. He is the best proofreader I've ever known—and the youngest. Those in some lucky graduate program will soon have him in their midst.

I want to thank Rebecca Wilson Lundin, research assistant extraordinaire, and Magdalena Radovic Moreno, gifted and reliable undergraduate intern. Rosalyn Collings-Eves, Susan Miller-Cochran, William Carpenter, Scott Wible, Dawn Hubbell-Staeble, and Amy Azul—all amazing instructors—have worked extremely hard to provide first-rate instructional support materials (available to you as Instructor's Flexfiles). Cynthia Selfe and Richard Selfe, the best of their kind, generously helped me connect writing with technology in brilliantly productive ways.

I also want to thank my editors: Dickson Musslewhite, who entreated me to write this book; Aron Keesbury, who guided the project along as development and then acquisitions editor; Leslie Taggart, a crucial voice in early stages of development; Jane Hoover, to whom I entrust my words; and Stephanie Carpenter, my constant intellectual companion and out-of-this-world development editor.

None of this could have happened without my dedicated team at Wadsworth: PJ Boardman, a pro, a visionary, and a trusted colleague; Mandee Eckersley, a stunningly effective executive marketing manager who inhabits professionalism and creativity with skill, grace, and good humor; Lyn Uhl, whose arrival has been continuously appreciated; Lindsey Veautour, one of the fastest studies I've ever met; Lianne Ames, who made the production wheels turn smoothly; Stacey Purviance, who managed marketing materials splendidly; Marcy Lunetta and Sue Howard, who worked hard to clear permissions; and Jeanne Calabrese, who created a beautiful and gripping page design.

Finally, I have learned from a phenomenal group of reviewers, including the following instructors:

Kathryn Abajian, *Diablo Valley College*
Jeffrey Andelora, *Mesa Community College*
Marshall Armintor, *University of North Texas*
LeAnn Athey, *Eastern Illinois University*
Amy Eskew Azul, *Chaffey College*
Anthony Baker, *Tennessee Technical University*
Evan Balkan, *Community College of Baltimore County–Cantons*
Jerry Ball, *Arkansas State University*
Stuart Barbier, *Delta College-University Center*
Sally Bennett, *Johnson County Community College*
Kris Bigalk, *Normandale Community College*
Jose Blanco, *Miami Dade Community College–Kendall*
Melody Bowdon, *University of Central Florida*
Barbara Brown, *San Jacinto College–Central*
Kermit Campbell, *Colgate University*
William Carpenter, *University of Illinois–Springfield*
Cynthia Cox, *Belmont University*
Linda Dick, *Western Michigan University*
Stephanie Downie Hummer, *University of Georgia*

Steven Elmore, *Crafton Hills Community College*
Karen Fitts, *West Chester University*
Clint Gardner, *Salt Lake Community College*
Paula Gillespie, *Marquette University*
Barbara Gleason, *CUNY (CCNY)*
Dawn Graziani, *Santa Fe Community College–Gainesville*
Deborah Hawhee, *University of Illinois*
William Hearell, *Stephen F. Austin State University*
Joel Henderson, *Chattanooga State Technical Community College*
Andrea Hills, *Portland Community College*
Becky Howard, *Syracuse University*
Dawn Hubbel-Staeble, *Bowling Green State University*
Melissa Ianetta, *University of Delaware*
Lauren Ingraham, *University of Tennessee–Chattanooga*
Katherine Jackson, *Old Dominion University*
Cynthia Jeney, *Missouri Western State University*
Peggy Jolly, *University of Alabama–Birmingham*
Kathryn Kleypas, *Queensborough Community College*
James Kroger, *Lynchburg College*
Marsha Kruger, *Univeristy of Nebraska–Omaha*
Bonnie Kyburz, *Utah Valley State College*
Martha Marinara, *University of Central Florida*
Susan Miller-Cochran, *North Carolina State University*
Kate Mohler, *Mesa Community College*
Jessie Moore Kapper, *Purdue University*
Michael Morris, *Eastfield College*
Julie Nash, *University of Massachusetts–Lowell*
Kathleen Nelson, *Palomar College*
Dana Nkana, *Illinois Central College*
Vorris Nunley, *University of Carolina–Riverside*
Heather Palmer, *University of Tennessee–Knoxville*
Betsey Pender, *Florida Community College*
Doreen Piano, *Georgia Institute of Technology–Atlanta*
Jeff Pruchnic, *Wayne State University*
Krista Ratcliffe, *Marquette University*
Vicki Russell, *Duke University*
Kelly Ryan Schendel, *Orange Coast College*
Scarlett Saavedra, *Mt. Hood Community College*
Jordan Sanderson, *University of Southern Mississippi*
Deborah Scally, *University of Texas–Dallas*
Matthew Schmeer, *Johnson County Community College*
Jacqueline Sears, *Mountain View College*
Nancy Shaffer, *University of Texas–El Paso*
Wendy Sharer, *East Carolina University*
Renee Shea, *Bowie State University*
Marcus Slease, *University of North Carolina–Greensboro*
James Sodon, *St. Louis Community College*

Sylvia Stacey, *Oakton Community College*
Srividhya Swaminathan, *Long Island University–Brooklyn*
Sharyn Talbert, *Ohio State University–Columbus*
Deborah Teague, *Florida State University*
Patricia Teel, *Victor Valley College*
Kaye Temanson, *North Dakota State University*
Debra Thomas, *Harrisburg Area Community College*
Honni van Rijswijk, *University of Washington*
Ben Varner, *University of Northern Colorado*
Helen (Lyn) Ward Page, *Oakton Community College*
Marian Wernicke, *Pensacola Junior College*
Natasha Whitton, *Southeastern Los Angeles University*
Arnold Wood, *Florida Community College*

Cheryl Glenn
May 2008

PART 1

ENTERING THE CONVERSATION: THE RHETORICAL SITUATION

Too often, the word *rhetoric* refers to empty words, implying manipulation, deception, or persuasion at any cost. But as you'll learn in this book, rhetoric and rhetorical situations are not negative and not manipulative. They are everywhere—as pervasive as the air we breathe—and play an essential role in our daily life as we work to get things done efficiently and ethically. The following three chapters define rhetoric and the rhetorical situation and show you how such situations shape the writing process. You'll begin to develop your rhetorical skills as you work through these chapters, but you'll continue to sharpen them all through your college career and into the workplace. The important point to remember is this: you're probably already pretty good at using rhetoric. So let's build on what you know—and go from there.

UNDERSTANDING THE RHETORICAL SITUATION

1

Rhetoric Surrounds Us

Every day, you use rhetoric. You use it as you read course syllabi and assignments, the directions for hooking up your stereo system, and your mail, as well as emails, newsgroup postings, and instant messages. You also use it as you write: when you submit written assignments, answer quiz questions in class, leave notes for your roommate, and send text messages to your friends. Every day, you are surrounded by rhetoric and rhetorical opportunities. In fact, you've been participating in rhetorical situations for most of your life.

WRITE FOR FIVE

1. Take a few minutes to list the kinds of writing you do every day. Include all instances when you write down information (whether on paper, white board, chalk board, or computer screen). Beside each entry, jot down the reason for that type of writing. Be prepared to share your answers with the rest of the class.

2. Consider five of the types of writing you identified in the first activity. Who is your audience for these different kinds of writing? In other words, to whom or for whom are you writing? What is your purpose for each kind of writing? What do you hope to achieve?

3

The Purposeful Use of Language and Images

Rhetoric is the purposeful use of language and images. That definition covers a great deal of territory—practically every word and visual element you encounter any day. But it's the word *purposeful* that will guide you through the maze of words and images that saturate your life. When you use words or images to achieve a specific purpose (such as explaining to your supervisor why you need next weekend off), you are speaking, writing, or conveying images rhetorically.

The Greek philosopher Aristotle coined an authoritative definition of *rhetoric* over 2,500 years ago: "rhetoric is the faculty of observing in any given situation the available means of persuasion." Let's take this definition apart and examine its constituent parts.

The faculty of observing in any given situation . . .

"Rhetoric is the faculty [or ability] of observing." Notice that Aristotle does not call for you to overpower your audience (your readers or listeners) with words or images, nor does he push for winning an argument. Instead, he encourages you (as a **rhetor,** or user of rhetoric) to observe. For Aristotle, and all of the rhetorical thinkers who have followed, observation is primary. Before you say or write something, you need to observe, to take the time to figure out what kind of rhetorical situation you're entering. To whom are you speaking or writing? What is your relationship to that person or group of people? What is the occasion? Who else is listening? What do you want your language to accomplish? By answering these questions, you are establishing the elements of the "given situation."

. . . the available means . . .

When you consider "the available means," you evaluate the possible methods of communication you might use. You want to choose the one that will best accomplish your purpose. In other words, should you deliver your message orally (in person or over the telephone), in writing (using email, instant messaging, paper, or a Web page), or via film, video, still images, other visuals, or music?

The spoken word is sometimes most appropriate. If you and a good friend have had an argument, you might not want to put your feelings into writing; it might be better if you simply pick up the telephone and say, "I'm sorry." If you're attending a funeral, you'll want to offer your condolences directly to the bereaved, even if you've already sent a card or flowers. However, if your professor expects you to submit a three-page essay recounting your experiences with technology (a technology autobiography), you cannot announce that you'd rather "tell her" your story. The only means available in this situation is the written word. Or is it? She might be impressed if you prepared an electronic presentation. An essay exam calls for a written response, as do most applications. When you applied to college, you most likely filled out pages of forms, wrote at least one short essay, and took at least one written aptitude exam. If you applied to a performing arts program, chances are that you had to submit a video or audio recording along with your written application. And you may even have had to perform live before faculty members. When you want to invite friends and relatives to celebrate an event, such as a birthday or bat mitzvah, you might telephone them, email them, write them a note, or send out formal invitations, depending on the circumstances. Whatever your daily life brings, you employ a seemingly endless variety of available means of communicating.

. . . of persuasion

The last phrase in Aristotle's definition of *rhetoric* is "the available means of persuasion." Persuasion is not a zero-sum game, with the winner taking all. Think of persuasion as a coming together, a meeting of the minds. Ideally, persuasion results in both you and your audience being changed by the experience. When both parties are changed, however slightly, the rhetorical interaction isn't one-sided: both sides are heard, and a decision is made that benefits the sender and the receiver(s) of the original message.

Aristotle tells us that rhetoric's function is not simply successful persuasion; rather, it is to "discover the means of coming as near such success as the circumstances of each particular case allow." If your purpose is to get your way, you'll sometimes succeed. But if getting your way is your only persuasive purpose, you're in for a long string of disappointments. Thinking about persuasion in broader terms will not only make you a better writer and speaker but also encourage you to use what you know about rhetoric to achieve a wide range of goals.

Persuasive writers (and speakers) have a clear sense of the rhetorical situation, the context in which they are communicating. No two situations are ever exactly the same. Every situation has both resources (positive influences) and constraints (obstacles) that affect the rhetorical transaction. Those resources and constraints include whatever else has already been said on the subject; when, where, and through what medium the transaction between writer and audience takes place; and the writer's relationship with the audience, the writer's credibility (or believability), and the appropriateness of the message in terms of both content and delivery. Thus, every rhetorical situation calls for you to observe the available means of persuasion as well as the contextual resources and constraints that will affect your persuasive success.

ANALYZING THE RHETORICAL SITUATION

Choose two of the following situations and note their similarities and differences in terms of speaker or writer, purpose, audience, and available means. Be prepared to share your answers with the rest of the class.

1. It's time for you to bring your spouse and children together to discuss the destination for next summer's family vacation.

2. For the first time, your rent check will be late. You need to explain the reason to your landlord in order to avoid the usual late fee.

3. Your manager needs you to draft a letter to customers explaining a price increase.

4. Your professor has assigned a three-page technology autobiography for Monday.

5. You and your fiancé need to show proof of citizenship to obtain a marriage license.

Recognizing and Analyzing the Rhetorical Situation

You encounter rhetoric—and rhetorical situations—throughout every day, from the minute you turn on the morning news to the moment you close your textbook and turn off the light. To develop your skills of persuasion, you need to be able to recognize the elements of rhetorical situations and gauge your rhetoric accordingly.

A **rhetorical situation** is the context a rhetor enters in order to shape an effective message that can resolve an exigence and reach an intended audience. A rhetorical situation creates a call for change (an exigence), but that change can be brought about only through the use of language, whether visual, written, or spoken text. For instance, by asking a question, your instructor creates a call for change in the classroom. The question just hangs there—until someone provides a fitting response. If the company you work for loses online business because its Web site is outdated, that problem can be resolved only through appropriate use of text and visuals. Once the fitting response comes into being, the call for change ("I need an answer" or "We need to update our Web site") is either partially removed or disappears altogether; then it is satisfied.

Often, a rhetor quickly recognizes the inherent exigence of the rhetorical situation; it may be as obvious as a teacher's question. At other times, the rhetor needs to examine all the factors and decide exactly what constitutes the rhetorical situation and then the exigence. If a company is losing online business, the reason may well be that its Web site is outdated. But the problem could also be that employees aren't responding in a timely fashion to Web-based inquiries or orders. It could be that competing products have taken business away. Or there may have been a slump in the economy, causing a drop in online business in general. Correctly pinpointing the exigence is crucial to a successful response.

ANALYZING THE RHETORICAL SITUATION

Working with several classmates, create a narrative based on the rhetorical situation diagram on the facing page. First, you'll need to think of an exigence, a rhetor, a message, and an audience. Then, you'll embody these elements in the context of a story told either graphically (through photos or images clipped from magazines or newspapers, graphics from other sources, or your own drawings) or verbally (through words). Be prepared to share your graphical or verbal narrative with the rest of the class and to explain it in terms of the elements of the rhetorical situation diagram.

Sample analysis of a rhetorical situation

If the idea of a rhetorical situation still seems unfamiliar, consider wedding announcements (or invitations). You've probably received or seen announcements of weddings or commitment ceremonies that are some variation on the one

RHETOR The rhetor (also called speaker, writer, or sender) is the person who identifies (or creates) the exigence and prepares a fitting rhetorical response, a response that forwards his or her purpose.

MESSAGE The rhetor uses language and the available means of communication to shape and send a message that is appropriate to the rhetorical situation and that will fulfill his or her purpose.

AUDIENCE The rhetor also needs to consider the nature and disposition of the audience, the person(s) who will read, hear, or see the message within a specific context. The audience may be able to act on the message to resolve the exigence; therefore, the audience may be able to help the rhetor achieve his or her rhetorical purpose.

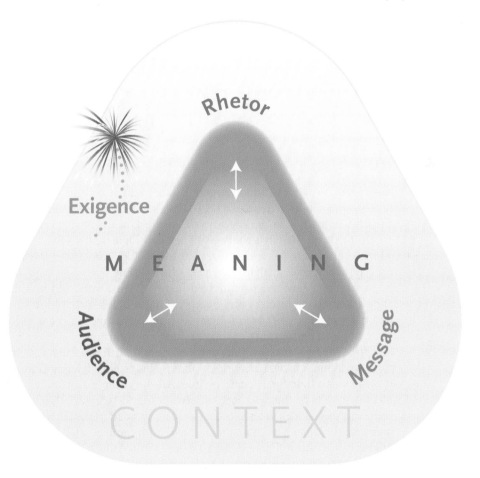

EXIGENCE To shape a fitting response to a rhetorical situation, the rhetor identifies a call for change, the exigence. In a rhetorical situation, that exigence can be resolved only through a response using language.

CONTEXT The context (the setting in which the rhetorical transaction takes place) can affect the success of any communication. The context for a rhetorical situation includes resources (positive influences and available means that contribute to the rhetor's message) and constraints (obstacles that could inhibit the resolution).

All wedding announcements embody the elements of the rhetorical situation.

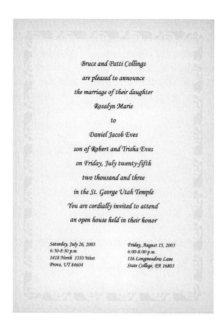

Bruce and Patti Collings
are pleased to announce
the marriage of their daughter
Rosalyn Marie
to
Daniel Jacob Eves
son of Robert and Trisha Eves
on Friday, July twenty-fifth
two thousand and three
in the St. George Utah Temple
You are cordially invited to attend
an open house held in their honor

Saturday, July 26, 2003
6:30-8:30 p.m.
1418 North 1350 West
Provo, UT 84604

Friday, August 15, 2003
6:00-8:00 p.m.
116 Longmeadow Lane
State College, PA 16803

shown here. Such an announcement is rhetorical: it conveys a purposeful message from a sender to a receiver. In doing so, it embodies every element of the rhetorical situation: exigence, purpose, sender, message, receiver, and context.

In this case, Rosalyn Marie Collings and Daniel Jacob Eves were married, which created an exigence. Bruce and Patti Collings, Rosalyn's parents, felt a need to respond to that exigence, so they sent out a message announcing the marriage. Their message arrived in two forms, print and visual: a formal announcement and a color photograph of the couple. And Bruce and Patti clarified the rhetorical purpose of their message by inviting people to a celebratory open house. The meaning of this wedding announcement, like the meaning of any message, resonates within a specific context. First, the announcement is for a wedding, a joyous celebration that includes gift giving and food. Second, it's a joyous affair for specific people. All the receivers of the message know the newlyweds or their parents; otherwise, they'd be puzzled to receive it. The context also includes the two open houses. Intended receivers will know that the marriage took place in Utah, the home of both families, and that the couple are graduate students in Pennsylvania, where many of their friends live. Having two open houses allows receivers in each state to attend the one more conveniently located for them.

ANALYZING THE RHETORICAL SITUATION

For each of the rhetorical situations below, try to identify the exigence, rhetor, audience, message, and context.

1. You've just received an email from a guy you met at summer camp several years ago, and you want to catch up with him.

2. You have won a full scholarship to college, and you need to ask your mom and dad for a car loan.

3. You've been asked to make a toast at a reception celebrating your parents' or grandparents' wedding anniversary.

4. You need to request permission to enroll in a class that is required for your field of study but is already full.

The decision to engage

Rhetorical situations may call for your attention, as when you receive a wedding announcement, or they may arise from your interpretation of some event. For instance, if you're in the market for a new car, you might be tantalized by an advertised price for a car that interests you, only to arrive at the dealership and discover that the marked price is different. If the price discrepancy catches your attention—so much so that you want to enter the rhetorical situation—then that's your exigence.

You'll next have to decide if you want to attempt to change the situation rhetorically. If you choose to say something about the discrepancy, you'll have to decide on your purpose, the type of message you want to send, how to send it, and to whom. You'll also need to take into consideration the constraints on your message: perhaps the advertised car had higher mileage than the one on the dealer's lot, or perhaps the advertised price had a time limit. If you want to enter the rhetorical situation, you'll need to shape it in a way that allows you to send a message. If you're annoyed by the price discrepancy but walk away because you don't want to negotiate with the car dealer, then you've actively perceived the rhetorical situation and been an audience for a message. But you have chosen not to act rhetorically.

As you go through your daily life, you'll encounter rhetorical situations that you'll decide to enter—and some that you'll decide to pass by. You may be a witness to an accident (someone who perceives a rhetorical situation) and volunteer to testify (an active rhetor); you might identify an old friend from a newspaper photograph (an active audience) and decide to email him (an active rhetor); you might hear a song on the radio (an active audience) and decide to perform it (an active rhetor); or you might begin introducing yourself to people in an online chat room (active perceiver, audience, and rhetor). Whatever the situations are, whether they are spoken, printed, online, or delivered in some other way, it will be up to you to decide how or whether you want to act on them.

As a responsible rhetor, you need to understand the elements and the limits of any rhetorical situation you decide to enter.

▌ You identify or establish the exigence that impels you to enter the situation: What is it that tugs at me? Why do I feel the need to speak, write, take a photo, share an image?

▌ You connect the exigence with your purpose, asking yourself: What is it that I want to and can accomplish with rhetoric? How can words or visuals alleviate or eliminate that exigence? For example, if you want the car dealer to sell you the car at the lower price, you need to discuss the lower, advertised price.

▌ Knowing that the purpose depends also on the nature and disposition of the audience, you carefully consider the composition of that audience: Who is the audience? What are they like? What opinions do they hold? What are their feelings about this exigence? How will they react to my message? In terms of the sale price of the car, will you be dealing with the dealership's owner, who wrote the newspaper ad, or with a salesperson, who works on commission? Different audiences have different needs and expectations, some of which can be met by a responsible rhetor.

▌ You also want to keep in mind whatever else has already been said on the subject. For example, if the local newspaper has recently run a story on bait-and-switch advertising, you'll want to keep that in mind. If the car dealership runs a series of television commercials, bragging that it guarantees the lowest prices or that it stands by its advertising, then, as a responsible rhetor, you'll want to use this information.

▌ You know that you should shape a fitting response to the situation, whether that fitting response is spoken, written, or sent electronically. Coloring the text of the message will be your tone, which projects an attitude to the intended audience. For example, a positive declaration of belief in the car dealer's written or televised guarantees might be the most fitting and productive way to respond to the car pricing exigence. When shaping a fitting response, you need to be fully aware that you can come only as close to persuasion as the rhetorical situation allows. A responsible rhetor cannot do or expect more.

YOUR WRITING EXPERIENCES

1. When was the last time you felt compelled to write to someone? Write for five minutes about what you wrote, to whom, and why. Also identify the means of communication you used: handwriting or word processing, sent through the mail or electronically (email or text messaging). As you look back on it, what were the elements of that rhetorical situation? How did you make your response a fitting one, even if you did so unconsciously?

2. Think of a time you identified an exigence but didn't respond. Write for five minutes, describing that exigence and explaining why you didn't write or speak in response to it. If you could do it over, how might you respond? How would you take into consideration each element of the rhetorical situation, coming as close to persuasion as conditions allowed?

3. What have you learned from reading this section that you didn't know when you started? How might the information given about the rhetorical situation help you? Is there a rhetorical situation that is tugging at you now? If you decide to enter that rhetorical situation, how will you do so? How will you take into consideration each element of the rhetorical situation?

Identifying and Shaping Reasons to Write

The photograph records a moment in the women's suffrage movement. In 1917, a group of women stood in front of the White House, holding banners that urged President Woodrow Wilson to support their cause. These women, representing all the women and men active in the nation's suffrage movement, sent the following message to a specific audience (the president): "Mr. President, how long must women wait for liberty?" That message was an authentic response to a rhetorical exigence: women did not have the right to vote. The purpose of the message was to win that right to vote—a right African American men had gained in 1870 but American Indian men and women would not gain until 1924.

What is exigence?

A **rhetorical exigence** is a problem that can be resolved or changed by discourse (or language). The problem of women not having the right to vote was eventually addressed in 1920, by the Nineteenth Amendment to the U.S. Constitution: "The right of citizens of the United States to vote shall not be denied or abridged by the United States or by any State on account of sex." Clearly, resolution of this problem came about through written discourse. The women in the suffrage movement worked successfully within the constraints of a rhetorical situation.

All effective discourse arises from a reason to use words or visuals. All successful rhetoric (whether verbal or visual) is an authentic response to an exigence, a real reason to send a message. You've undoubtedly had many real reasons to write. You, too, have set out to resolve a problem, using words or visuals. Maybe you and your partner have had an argument, and now you're both angry.

An e-greeting can be an appropriate response to an emotional exigence.

That's a problem. To resolve that problem, you might compose an email, plan what you'll say over the phone, put together a visual apology of some sort, maybe even send an e-greeting. Your audience is your partner, and your purpose is to restore your good relationship. The medium through which you deliver your message—spoken or written words, prose or poetry, original or borrowed visuals—is up to you. You'll want to deliver your message in a way that seems most appropriate. However, if you're not close to a computer, chances are you won't be able to send an e-greeting. If you and your partner are too angry to speak, you're probably better off using written words or visuals. It all depends on the elements of the specific rhetorical situation.

An exigence is a problem . . .

A rhetorical exigence is a problem. Exigencies can be political or social problems, such as the denial of voting rights to women. Exigencies can also be emotional problems, such as an argument with your partner. But exigencies are not limited to the political, social, or emotional realm; they can also be financial, religious, educational, or psychological. As long as a problem can be resolved only through discourse, it is a rhetorical exigence.

Every day, people respond to problems that can be resolved only through the use of words or images. Exigencies for writing (or speaking or creating visuals) extend far beyond those created by academic assignments. In fact, every time you respond to (or consider responding to) a rhetorical problem, you've recognized or created an exigence. Whether you're texting in a chat room, following newspaper reports of your city council's spending patterns, listening to your children arguing, or reading personal ads, you can recognize a call for a rhetorical response.

A personal ad represents a social exigence in need of a response.

. . . that can be resolved . . .

The second distinguishing characteristic of a rhetorical exigence is that the rhetor believes that it can be resolved. The women who demonstrated to gain the right to vote, the couple who were arguing, the individuals who advertised for a partner—all believed that their problems could be resolved. If any of these problems were *certain* to be resolved, however, there would have been no need to craft a response. If a problem could never be resolved, there would also be no point in responding.

. . . through discourse

Only discourse can resolve or change a rhetorical exigence. It took a law—the series of words that constitute the Nineteenth Amendment—to resolve the problem of women's not having the right to vote. It might take a visual and words—in the form of a Yahoo! e-greeting—to bring an arguing couple back together. It might require a number of phone calls to match up "Santa Fe Blonde" and "Ojitos Bonitos" from the personal ads with the partner of their dreams. Every successful phone call will need to address the specifics of the ad. "Santa Fe Blonde," for instance, is seeking a single male, between the ages of 57 and 67, who shares her interests: the outdoors, museums, ballet, traveling, concerts, and being with friends. Only words to that effect will solve the problem. "Ojitos Bonitos," on the other hand, is seeking a "humorous SPM 47–59, who is attractive, bilingual, and financially secure, for companionship." He, too, has posed a specific exigence that calls for a specific response. The better speaker and writer you are, the better you'll be able to use discourse to resolve the rhetorical problems that you'll face nearly every day in college.

ANALYZING THE RHETORICAL SITUATION

Decide whether each problem listed below is also a rhetorical exigence. Be prepared to share the reasoning behind your five responses with the rest of the class.

1. The Internal Revenue Service is charging you $2,000 in back taxes, asserting that you neglected to declare the income from your summer job.

2. Your college library has just sent you a letter fining you for several overdue books, all of which you returned several weeks ago.

3. During Eid-al-Fitr, the celebratory feast after Ramadan, your brothers and father resume their ongoing argument about the political situation in the Middle East.

4. In the student seating at the football stadium, some fans throw empty soda cans, toss beach balls, boo the opposing team, and stand during most of the game. You're quickly losing interest in attending the games.

5. If the university's child care center (so conveniently located that attending school is possible for you) raises its rates again this year, you will have to look elsewhere for affordable child care.

YOUR WRITING EXPERIENCES

1. Write for five minutes about a specific school-related assignment that created an exigence for you. In other words, try to remember an assignment that posed a problem to which you *wanted* to respond and *felt a need* to respond with spoken or written words or visuals. Be prepared to share your memory of this assignment with the rest of the class.

2. Consider a school-related assignment that you're currently thinking about. In your own words (and to the best of your memory), write out the assignment, paying careful attention to the problem (you think) the assignment is asking you to resolve with discourse. Does this assignment establish an exigence that you *want* to address? If so, explain why. If not, explain how the assignment could be rewritten in such a way that you would feel an authentic reason to write. Be prepared to share your ideas with the rest of the class.

Reading a text for rhetorical exigence The following essay, "Why I Want a Wife," by Judy Brady, was first published more than thirty years ago, in the inaugural issue of *Ms.* It remains one of the most widely anthologized essays in the United States. As you read this short essay, try to imagine American domestic life thirty years ago. What specific details does the author provide to feed your imagination? Try to determine Brady's reason for writing this essay. What might have been the exigence that stimulated her written response?

JUDY BRADY
Why I Want a Wife

I belong to that classification of people known as wives. I am a Wife. And, not altogether incidentally, I am a mother.

Not too long ago a male friend of mine appeared on the scene from the Midwest fresh from a recent divorce. He had one child, who is, of course, with his ex-wife. He is obviously looking for another wife. As I thought about him while I was ironing one evening, it suddenly occurred to me that I, too, would like to have a wife. Why do I want a wife?

I would like to go back to school, so that I can become economically independent, support myself, and, if need be, support those dependent upon me. I want a wife who will work and send me to school. And while I am going to school I want a wife to take care of my children. I want a wife to keep track of the children's doctor and dentist appointments. And to keep track of mine, too. I want a wife to make sure my children eat properly and are kept clean. I want a wife who will wash the children's clothes and keep them mended. I want a wife who is a good nurturant attendant to my children, arranges for their schooling, makes sure that they have an adequate social life with their peers, takes them to the park, the zoo, etc. I want a wife who takes care of the children when they are sick, a wife who arranges to be around when the children need special care, because, of course, I cannot miss classes at school. My wife must arrange to lose time at work and not lose the job. It may mean a small cut in my wife's income from time to time, but I guess I can tolerate that. Needless to say, my wife will arrange and pay for the care of the children while my wife is working.

I want a wife who will take care of my physical needs. I want a wife who will keep my house clean. A wife who will pick up after my children, a wife who will pick up after me. I want a wife who will keep my clothes clean, ironed, mended, replaced when need be, and who will see to it that my personal things are kept in their proper place so that I can find what I need the minute I need it. I want a wife who cooks the meals, a wife who is a good cook. I want a wife who will plan the menus, do the necessary grocery shopping, prepare the meals, serve them pleasantly, and then do the cleaning up while I do my studying. I want a wife who will care for me when I am sick and sympathize with my pain and loss of time from school. I want a wife to go along when our family takes a vacation so that someone can continue to care for me and my children when I need a rest and a change of scene.

I want a wife who will take care of details of my social life. When my wife and I are invited out by my friends, I want a wife who will take care of the babysitting arrangements. When I meet people at school that I like and want to entertain, I want a wife who will have the house clean, will prepare a special meal, serve it to me and my friends, and not interrupt when I talk about the things that interest me and my friends. I want a wife who will have arranged that the children are fed and ready for bed before my guests arrive so that the children do not bother us. I want a wife who takes care of the needs of my guests so that they feel comfortable, who makes sure that they have an ashtray, that they are passed the hors d'oeuvres, that they are offered a second helping of the food, that their wine glasses are replenished when necessary, that their coffee is served to them as they like it. And I want a wife who knows that sometimes I need a night out by myself.

I want a wife who is sensitive to my sexual needs, a wife who makes love passionately and eagerly when I feel like it, a wife who makes sure that I am satisfied. And, of course, I want a wife who will not demand sexual attention when I am not in the mood for it. I want a wife who assumes the complete responsibility for birth control, because I do not want more children. I want a wife who will remain sexually faithful to me so that I do not have to clutter up my intellectual life with jealousies. And I want a wife who understands that my sexual needs may entail more than strict adherence to monogamy. I must, after all, be able to relate to people as fully as possible.

If, by chance, I find another person more suitable as a wife than the wife I already have, I want the liberty to replace my present wife with another one. Naturally, I will expect a fresh, new life; my wife will take the children and be solely responsible for them so that I am left free.

When I am through with school and have acquired a job, I want my wife to quit working and remain at home so that my wife can more fully and completely take care of a wife's duties.

My God, why wouldn't I want a wife?

After reading Brady's essay, you may want to spend some class time discussing the merits of her argument, for the 1970s and for today. You may also want to consider her pervasive use of irony (her tongue-in-cheek attitude toward her subject), the extent to which she's being serious, and the potential sexism of the essay. Few readers of this essay can resist registering their agreement or disagreement with its author; this may be something you'll want to do as well.

Whether or not you agree with Brady, it's important for you to be able to analyze her rhetorical situation, starting with the reason she may have written this essay in the first place. Why would she keep repeating "I want a wife …"? Why would she write from the husband's point of view? Why would she describe a wife who does all the "heavy lifting" in a marriage? What kind of husband does she evoke? What effects do her rhetorical choices have on you as a reader?

Write your responses to the following questions (which constitute a rhetorical analysis) to identify the exigence for Brady's essay:

1. *What does this essay say?* Compile the details of a wife's daily life and describe the writer's feelings about a husband's expectations; then write one sentence that conveys Brady's main argument.
2. *Why does the essay say that?* Drawing on your previous answer, write three or four assertions that support Brady's argument.
3. *Who composed this message?* What information does the writer supply about her identity?
4. *What is the exigence that sparked the writing of this essay?* State the exigence in one sentence.
5. *How does the essay resolve the exigence?*

Adbusters' version of the U.S. flag is a visual response to an exigence.

Reading an image for rhetorical exigence Responses to exigencies are not limited to verbal ones. Visual responses to various exigencies constantly bombard us—from advertisements and promotions to personal communications and political stances. If you think the flag image is illustrating the "problem" of capitalism or the power of corporations in the United States, then you are considering it as a response to an exigence. In thinking about this image in terms of a rhetorical response, you are "reading" it more exhaustively than you might have otherwise.

Reading for exigence helps you develop your skills as an active, informed reader and as a rhetorical analyst. Respond to the same questions you answered about "Why I Want a Wife," but this time focus on the visual of the flag:

1. *What does the visual "say"—and how?* Describe the visual in one sentence, paying attention to the corporate logos that have replaced the state-signifying stars.

2. *Why does the visual say that?* Consider what the stars and stripes have traditionally represented. Compare that representation with this one.

3. *Who composed this message?* It was composed by Adbusters, a media foundation that describes itself as being "concerned about the erosion of our physical and cultural environments by commercial forces." If you don't already know about Adbusters, go online to find out about its series of campaigns.

4. *What is the exigence?* Using the information you've amassed from questions 1, 2, and 3, identify the exigence to which this visual is responding.

5. *How does the visual resolve the exigence?* What message does this visual send to viewers? How might this visual work to change the exigence you described in the previous answer?

Whether you're reading an essay, listening to a speech, or viewing a visual, you'll better understand the message if you begin your analysis by determining what rhetorical exigence those words or visuals are responding to. Very often, the responses you're "reading" create an exigence you want to respond to. You may, for example, feel a strong urge to respond to "Why I Want a Wife" or to the logo-laden version of the U.S. flag. Whether your response is spoken, written, or composed visually, its power lies in your understanding of the exigence.

The power of exigence

Unless you perceive an exigence, you cannot respond. This fact is obvious, but you may not know why a response is so difficult—if not impossible—to formulate in certain situations. In other words, *something* needs to provoke or stimulate your interest and response. For instance, when you take an essay examination for an American history midterm, you might be given the choice of answering one of three questions:

1. Some historians have argued that the great increase in size and power of the federal government since the Civil War is one of the dominant themes of American history. Trace the growth of the federal government since 1865, paying particular attention to its evolving involvement in world affairs and the domestic economy. Be sure to support your argument with relevant historical details.

2. Some historians have referred to the modern civil rights movement as the "Second Reconstruction." Do you think the comparison between the first era of reconstruction (post–Civil War years to the early twentieth century) and the so-called second era of reconstruction (1950s to the 1970s) is accurate? Compare and contrast the attempts to create and safeguard African American civil rights in these two periods. Your answer should consider government policies, African American strategies, and white responses.

3. "The United States has never entered a war for purely idealistic reasons. Its primary goal has always been the defense of vital national interests." Assess the accuracy of this statement with reference to any three of the following: the Spanish-American War, World War I, World War II, the Cold War, and the Vietnam War. Be sure to explain what you mean by "idealistic reasons" and "national interests." Remember to support your argument with relevant historical details.

Your selection will depend on which question seems to you to present the most compelling exigence. Which question do you care the most about? Which one do you know the most about? Which one can you write most successfully about? In this case, you can ignore the two questions that you don't want to answer and turn your energies to the one you choose. Similarly, when an instructor supplies a number of different topics for a research project, you choose the one that sparks your interest.

You might consider the entire essay examination or any other college-writing situation as an exigence for a written response. But, more accurately, it's each question or topic that provides a rhetorical exigence by posing a problem that can be modified through discourse. Some questions or topics pique your interest; others do not. And you make decisions every day about whether to respond.

Exigence online

If you've ever participated in an online chat room, you already know how people in that context recognize or shape exigencies to which to respond. In fact, most people log on to chat rooms in order to locate a topic or a person whose presence creates an exigence. You might participate in chat rooms that discuss novels because you have questions about them or wonder what other readers are thinking (*The Da Vinci Code*, for example, is the focus of several elaborate Web

A Web site with many potential exigencies.

Hyun Jong Song
MPCCN Case File: 1529F00

Above Images: Song, circa 2001

Vital Statistics at Time of Disappearance

- **Missing Since:** November 1, 2001 from State College, Pennsylvania
- **Classification:** Endangered Missing
- **Date Of Birth:** February 25, 1980
- **Age:** 21 years old
- **Height and Weight:** 5'1-5'3, 110-130 pounds
- **Distinguishing Characteristics:** Black hair, brown eyes. Song is of Korean descent. Her ears and navel are pierced. Song's nickname is Cindy. Her middle name may be spelled "Jung." Song's first name may be spelled "Hyunjong" or "Hyunjung."

Details of Disappearance

Song was raised in Seoul, South Korea. She moved to the United States in 1995 to live with relatives in Springfield, Virginia near Alexandria. Song graduated from high school and enrolled in Pennsylvania State University, where she majored in integrated arts. She was scheduled to graduate during the spring of 2002.

Song attended a Halloween party during the early morning hours of November 1, 2001 at the *Player's Nite Club* in the 110 block of West College Avenue. She departed from the party at 2:00 a.m., then stopped by a friend's home for two hours. Another friend dropped Song off outside of her residence in *State College Park Apartments* in the 340 block of West Clinton Avenue at approximately 4:00 a.m. She had been drinking that evening and was mildly intoxicated when taken to her apartment. She was last seen wearing her costume, which consisted of a pink sleeveless shirt with a rabbit design imprinted on the front, rabbit ears, a white tennis skirt with a cotton bunny tail attached to the back, brown suede leather knee-

sites that include chat rooms). You might enter a chat room to share your views on the 2007 World Series, the movie *Juno*, or games such as *World of Warcraft*. A quick Web search will lead you to pertinent chat rooms—and potential exigencies—for every interest.

If you're familiar with the Web site myspace.com, for example, you'll immediately see the ways it has been designed to present tantalizing exigencies. Not every visitor to this site will want to respond to any of the individuals featured under "Cool New People," but some will. Others will navigate their way to the pages of MySpace friends with whom they want to communicate. In other words, different people recognize different exigencies—and exigencies exist nearly everywhere you look.

College student Cindy Song disappeared on Halloween 2001. Despite an extended, intensive search, an ongoing FBI investigation, and a feature on the TV series *Unsolved Mysteries*, she remains missing. Like the flyers that still hang all over my university campus, this Web site asks anyone who knows anything about the missing woman to come forward. Each of these flyers, as well as the Web site, creates an exigence. Every time I walk by a flyer, I wish I could respond—but I cannot. I have no information about this missing woman. Therefore, despite the glaring exigence, I don't respond, even though I wish I could.

Web sites such as this one for missing persons try to create an exigence to which viewers want to respond.

Exigence in everyday life

A disappearance like Song's is tragic, but tragedies and troubles are part of daily life, which offers exigencies on a regular basis. If your best friend has moved away, the distance between the two of you creates an exigence that you might address with daily emails, a phone call, or a letter. When someone dies, their death creates an exigence that you might address with a letter to the family or a bouquet of flowers and an accompanying condolence note. A friend's illness, an unexpected increase in child care expenses or tuition, an essay exam, a list of questions from the IRS, a sales presentation, a job interview, a sorority rush, a deposition, or arguing children—these are all situations that provide possible exigencies for response. In other words, these situations pose problems that could be resolved or changed through spoken or written words or through visuals.

Whether you choose to recognize, let alone address, any exigence is usually up to you. Whether your response is elaborate or simple is usually up to you, too. How you deliver your message may be your choice as well—whether you choose to write a letter to the editor of the campus newspaper, make a phone call to your state representative's office, prepare a PowerPoint presentation, create a fact sheet, or interrupt someone else and speak. You often have a choice, but not always. Sometimes you're forced to respond and to do so in a particular manner.

4. How might the response to your exigence resolve it? In other words, what might the response do to relieve or resolve the exigence in your life? Add your answer to this question to what you've already written. Be prepared to share your overall analysis with the rest of the class.

5. In class, listen carefully to your classmates' analyses, and take notes. Be prepared to provide suggestions for improving their concept of exigence, response, and resolution.

Selecting a Rhetorical Audience and Purpose

Many of you have, no doubt, received mail and email that was targeted to you based on your interests and purchases. The message shown here was sent via email by Barnes & Noble in anticipation of the last installment in the Harry Potter series. The invitation was sent to many people—but not to everyone—for one purpose: to persuade the receivers to come to a celebration at a Barnes & Noble bookstore and to buy a copy of *Harry Potter and the Deathly Hallows* there, too.

Of course, not everyone is interested in Harry Potter books, let alone attending a late night party in costume, just to be among the first to get a copy of the newest one. So Barnes & Noble sent this email message to people who had purchased other Harry Potter books or calendars, notebooks, and so on, anticipating that they would be receptive to the tradition of arriving at a store hours ahead of time ("Join us … as you count down the final moments to Harry's arrival!"). Additionally, because Barnes & Noble is reaching these people through

You are targeted as a rhetorical audience by many businesses.

the medium of email, the message also includes information about ordering the book online—just a click away for those already reading email. Thus, the specific audience (people who have purchased Harry Potter items in the past) for the email was closely related to the purpose (enticing these people to purchase Harry Potter items in the near future).

Rain can't hit what rain can't catch.

Introducing the all new turbocharged Saab 9-3 Convertible.

SAAB 9-3

Thrills start at $39,995*

Saab 93 Convertible

Welcome to the state of independence

SAAB

1 800 SAAB USA · www.saabusa.com

A magazine advertisement has a particular rhetorical audience.

Audience versus rhetorical audience

Audience is a key component of any rhetorical situation. After all, you'll direct your writing, speaking, or visual display to a specific audience in an attempt to change some opinion or action. But even as you tailor your verbal or visual discourse to a specific audience, you must keep in mind that that person or group may not be a rhetorical audience. A **rhetorical audience** consists of *only* those persons who are capable of being influenced by verbal or visual discourse and of bringing about change, either by acting themselves or by influencing others who can create change. The following examples will help clarify the concept of rhetorical audience.

Not every person who receives the invitation to come to the Harry Potter party will necessarily be persuaded to do so. No matter how enticing the invitation might be, some people will not even open the email: they are not capable of being influenced by the message. Others might look it over quickly, consider the offer, and *then* delete it. Still others might wait to discuss the invitation with their friends before deciding whether to attend. Those who do accept the invitation are capable of bringing about a change—adding to the number of guests at the party.

Now consider the Saab advertisement. Clearly, the purpose of all advertising is to sell a product, so every advertiser must keep a buying audience in mind. The Saab ad tantalizes readers with visual and verbal details, including the $39,995 price tag. The audience for this ad consists of people who appreciate Saabs and perhaps admire (or even envy) Saab owners. Some of them might even yearn for a Saab themselves but feel they cannot afford one. The rhetorical audience for this ad, however, consists of those people who can either buy a Saab or influence someone else to buy one. These people can use words to negotiate specific features (color, engine, wheel design, model, and so on) and price. Or they can use words to influence someone else to purchase a Saab. Either way, theirs is a fitting response to the exigence of not owning a Saab.

Not every group of people who listens to a presidential hopeful's speech, watches court television, or reads about impending tuition hikes constitutes a rhetorical audience. After all, not every person is capable of being influenced by the discourse and bringing about change or influencing those who can make a change. But some people *are* capable of those things. The delegates at the Republican National Convention are a rhetorical audience: they listen to speeches and cast their votes. When the delegates choose the presidential and vice presidential candidate, they eliminate all the other Republican candidates, thereby influencing the voting options of millions of Americans.

Judge Joe Brown: a rhetorical audience.

Judge Joe Brown is the rhetorical audience on court television. He listens to both sides of the case, asks questions, and then makes a judgment. Whether he rules that the former girlfriend must pay the former boyfriend $3,000 in damages, or that a renter did indeed break his lease, or that a borrowed car is not a stolen car, Judge Joe Brown is shaping a fitting response to the rhetorical exigence presented by each case. And although many more people are upset—and affected—by tuition hikes than those who actually try to do something about them, those in the rhetorical audience write or telephone their state representative, their university's board of trustees, and the university administration to protest tuition hikes. They feel empowered as agents of change, that their words can change the minds of the people who determine tuition rates.

A rhetorical audience can be influenced by discourse . . .

The message—whether verbal or visual—can influence a rhetorical audience. You apply this knowledge every time you stand in front of a large display of greeting cards and spend what seems like more time choosing "just the right" card than you spent choosing the gift. You consider each visual and each greeting, considering and rejecting cards in rapid succession until you find the one that best suits your rhetorical audience, the person who can be influenced by the discourse of your selection. Because you want your influence to be positive, you spend time matching up the features of the card with the interests of the recipient. Whether you choose a card with a Bible verse for your Christian friend, a picture of a black lab catching a Frisbee for your dog-loving roommate, or a romantic greeting for your sweetheart, your choice reflects the message you want to send to your audience, the person who is capable of being influenced by the words and pictures that you choose.

Even when choosing a birthday card, you're considering a rhetorical audience.

Consider the pile of holiday cards you receive each winter. Some may be celebrating Christmas, Hanukkah, or Kwanzaa; some may be reminders of lesser-known holidays: Winter Solstice, Yule, or Ásatrú. Others may just be wishing you "Happy Holidays" or hoping for "Peace on Earth." Whatever the greeting and visual, you are the audience for all the cards you receive. You are capable of being influenced by any of them. But, in actuality, you'll be influenced by only a few: those that give you especial pleasure, motivate you to call the sender, surprise you because you don't celebrate that particular holiday, or make you feel sentimental about the holiday at hand.

When you're part of the rhetorical audience, you're capable of being influenced by the rhetorical situation, of being moved in some way by the words or visuals.

. . . and is capable of bringing about change

As a member of a rhetorical audience, you're not only capable of being influenced (or changed) by the situation but also capable of bringing about change as a result of the situation. You can bring about change on your own, or you can influence the people who can make the change.

You are bringing about change yourself, for example, when you pick up the phone and heal a long-standing misunderstanding after you read a former friend's moving handwritten message at the bottom of a "Peace on Earth" card. After receiving a "Happy Holidays" card from your brother announcing that he'll be home from Iraq for the holidays, you might recruit all his old buddies for a surprise welcome. Both decisions render you part of the rhetorical audience. When your English instructor writes comments on your drafts, you can become part of her rhetorical audience by following her instructions and writing better essays.

Not everyone in the viewing audience is a member of Dr. Phil's rhetorical audience, but those who follow the steps in his Weight Loss Challenge—begin to exercise, watch their eating habits, and lose weight—indicate that they are not only capable of being influenced by his discourse but also capable of bringing about change. And if those same people decide to support a friend or family member in a weight-loss program, then they are influencing other people who can make a change.

So you're part of the rhetorical audience when you're capable of making or influencing change. Sometimes, you can do both at once. For instance, you might respond to public outcry against U.S. intervention in the Middle East by joining a protest march in Washington, DC. You might participate in an anti-racism or AIDS-prevention program in order to inform others about the negative consequences of racist behaviors or unsafe sex practices. Your life situation might find you best served by Al Anon, Alcoholics Anonymous, or any of the other twelve-step programs that help people make or support positive changes. Even if you're a star athlete, you might need to listen carefully to the coach so that you can help influence the attitudes of your teammates—and the same goes for strong members of writing, study, therapy, and exercise groups.

Considering purpose in terms of rhetorical audience

Many writers equate purpose with their reason for writing: they're fulfilling an assignment or meeting a deadline; they want a good grade or want to see their essay in print; they want to make money or win a contest. When you're writing with a **rhetorical purpose**, however, you move beyond such goals to one of influencing your rhetorical audience. In order to achieve this influence, you'll need to keep in mind the nature of your audience (their control, power, and status) and their disposition (sympathetic or unsympathetic to, opposed to or in favor of your message).

You already know that rhetorical audience and purpose cannot be separated. You always try to send your message to someone who can do something about it, someone who can be influenced by your discourse to change or resolve something. For example, when you enter a department store to return defective merchandise, you know that you need to speak to a salesperson or maybe go to the service desk. You don't want to waste your time talking with people who cannot help you.

Once you reach your rhetorical audience, you try to shape your message in terms of information, tone, and language so that it successfully influences that audience. Whether you're talking to your instructor, one of your parents, or your physician, you try to keep in mind the kind of information you should deliver—and how best to deliver it. You already know that audience and purpose cannot be separated, but balancing audience and purpose is a skill you can work to improve.

Reading a comic strip for rhetorical audience and purpose The ongoing war in Iraq continues to be a controversial topic in the United States. Whether they support it or not, U.S. citizens tend to equate the wisdom of the war with the character of President George W. Bush. Supporters believe that this war will go down in the annals of military history as a superb act of liberation. They believe that Saddam Hussein was a brutal tyrant, whose country harbored and trained terrorists and provided them access to weapons of mass destruction. To them, Bush's foreign policy signifies the moral high ground of a righteous leader, as well as the altruism of a great country willing to rebuild the political, educational, and economic infrastructure of a smaller one.

Detractors of the war in Iraq believe that Bush is an empty-headed publicity hound, whose road to Washington was paved by his father and whose political decisions are masterminded by others. His decision to invade Iraq has been blamed on industrialists who have dark designs on Iraq's oil, as well as on financiers who are covertly helping Israel.

The comic strip represents President Bush's surprise Thanksgiving visit to U.S. troops in Iraq. Some say he visited the troops to mitigate criticism that he hadn't attended any of the funerals of fallen soldiers. Others say that visiting the troops was a perfect way to raise their spirits at holiday time. Everyone agreed, however, that the photo of the president holding up the beautiful table decoration made a picturesque scene.

DOONESBURY

This comic strip responds to a political exigence.

ANALYZING THE RHETORICAL SITUATION

1. Reread the comic strip, and then write for five minutes about it. List all the information you can possibly glean from the visual and verbal details of the strip.

2. Working with one or two classmates, compare your answers from question 1 and write a joint account of the visual and verbal details of the strip and its overall impact.

3. What is the exigence for the comic strip? How does it fulfill the definition of a rhetorical exigence?

4. Who is the rhetorical audience for the comic strip? In what ways does that audience fulfill the definition of a rhetorical audience?

5. Account for your response to the comic strip. Are you a member of the rhetorical audience? If so, list the ways you fulfill the role of a rhetorical audience. Be prepared to share your answer with the rest of the class.

6. What specific visual or verbal details reveal something about the character of the cartoonist? Appeal to your emotions (positively or negatively)? Shape an argument, even if it's one you don't agree with?

Reading a letter for rhetorical audience and purpose Racism has long been an exigence in the United States, appearing most boldly in language that diminishes others. Martin Luther King, Jr., believed in the power of language to overcome racism. As his 1963 "Letter from Birmingham Jail" indicates, King also believed that discourse could be used to influence a rhetorical audience, explaining a situation to them until they agreed to be agents of change or to influence those who could make change. For King, then, language provided the means for black and white people to work together to overcome racism and achieve justice.

When King sent the following letter (excerpted here), he believed that it was a fitting response to the moderate white clergymen who had issued a public statement criticizing King's nonviolent civil disobedience. As you read the selection, circle all references to the rhetorical audience and underline all references to King's purpose.

MARTIN LUTHER KING, JR.
Excerpt from Letter from Birmingham Jail

April 16, 1963

MY DEAR FELLOW CLERGYMEN:

While confined here in the Birmingham city jail, I came across your recent statement calling my present activities "unwise and untimely." Seldom do I pause to answer criticism of my work and ideas. If I sought to answer all the criticisms that cross my desk, my secretaries would have little time for anything other than such correspondence in the course of the day, and I would have no time for constructive work. But since I feel that you are men of genuine good will and that your criticisms are sincerely set forth, I want to try to answer your statements in what I hope will be patient and reasonable terms. . . .

You deplore the demonstrations taking place in Birmingham. But your statement, I am sorry to say, fails to express a similar concern for the conditions that brought about the demonstrations. I am sure that none of you would want to rest content with the su-

perficial kind of social analysis that deals merely with effects and does not grapple with underlying causes. It is unfortunate that demonstrations are taking place in Birmingham, but it is even more unfortunate that the city's white power structure left the Negro community with no alternative. . . .

You may well ask: "Why direct action? Why sit-ins, marches and so forth? Isn't negotiation a better path?" You are quite right in calling for negotiation. Indeed, this is the very purpose of direct action. Nonviolent direct action seeks to create such a crisis and foster such a tension that a community which has constantly refused to negotiate is forced to confront the issue. It seeks so to dramatize the issue that it can no longer be ignored. My citing the creation of tension as part of the work of the nonviolent-resister may sound rather shocking. But I must confess that I am not afraid of the word "tension." I have earnestly opposed violent tension, but there is a type of constructive, nonviolent tension which is necessary for growth. Just as Socrates felt that it was necessary to create a tension in the mind so that individuals could rise from the bondage of myths and half-truths to the unfettered realm of creative analysis and objective appraisal, so must we see the need for nonviolent gadflies to create the kind of tension in society that will help men rise from the dark depths of prejudice and racism to the majestic heights of understanding and brotherhood. . . .

I must make two honest confessions to you, my Christian and Jewish brothers. First, I must confess that over the past few years I have been gravely disappointed with the white moderate. I have almost reached the regrettable conclusion that the Negro's great stumbling block in his stride toward freedom is not the White Citi-

zen's Counciler or the Ku Klux Klanner, but the white moderate, who is more devoted to "order" than to justice; who prefers a negative peace which is the absence of tension to a positive peace which is the presence of justice; who constantly says: "I agree with you in the goal you seek, but I cannot agree with your methods of direct action"; who paternalistically believes he can set the timetable for another man's freedom; who lives by a mythical concept of time and who constantly advises the Negro to wait for a "more convenient season." Shallow understanding from people of good will is more frustrating than absolute misunderstanding from people of ill will. Lukewarm acceptance is much more bewildering than outright rejection.

I had hoped that the white moderate would understand that law and order exist for the purpose of establishing justice and that when they fail in this purpose they become the dangerously structured dams that block the flow of social progress. I had hoped that the white moderate would understand that the present tension in the South is a necessary phase of the transition from an obnoxious negative peace, in which the Negro passively accepted his unjust plight, to a substantive and positive peace, in which all men will respect the dignity and worth of human personality. Actually, we who engage in nonviolent direct action are not the creators of tension. We merely bring to the surface the hidden tension that is already alive. We bring it out in the open, where it can be seen and dealt with. Like a boil that can never be cured so long as it is covered up but must be opened with all its ugliness to the natural medicines of air and light, injustice must be exposed, with all the tension its exposure creates, to the light of human conscience and the air of national opinion before it can be cured. . . .

You speak of our activity in Birmingham as extreme. At first I was rather disappointed that fellow clergymen would see my nonviolent efforts as those of an extremist. I began thinking about the fact that I stand in the middle of two opposing forces in the Negro community. One is a force of complacency, made up in part of Negroes who, as a result of long years of oppression, are so drained of self-respect and a sense of "somebodiness" that they have adjusted to segregation; and in part of a few middle class Negroes who, because of a degree of academic and economic security and because in some ways they profit by segregation, have become

continued

insensitive to the problems of the masses. The other force is one of bitterness and hatred, and it comes perilously close to advocating violence. It is expressed in the various black nationalist groups that are springing up across the nation, the largest and best-known being Elijah Muhammad's Muslim movement. Nourished by the Negro's frustration over the continued existence of racial discrimination, this movement is made up of people who have lost faith in America, who have absolutely repudiated Christianity, and who have concluded that the white man is an incorrigible "devil."

I have tried to stand between these two forces, saying that we need emulate neither the "do-nothingism" of the complacent nor the hatred and despair of the black nationalist. For there is the more excellent way of love and nonviolent protest. I am grateful to God that, through the influence of the Negro church, the way of nonviolence became an integral part of our struggle. . . .

Oppressed people cannot remain oppressed forever. The yearning for freedom eventually manifests itself, and that is what has happened to the American Negro. Something within has reminded him of his birthright of freedom, and something without has reminded him that it can be gained. Consciously or unconsciously, he has been caught up by the Zeitgeist, and with his black brothers of Africa and his brown and yellow brothers of Asia, South America and the Caribbean, the United States Negro is moving with a sense of great urgency toward the promised land of racial justice. If one recognizes this vital urge that has engulfed the Negro community, one should readily understand why public demonstrations are taking place. The Negro has many pent-up resentments and latent frustrations, and he must release them. So let him march; let him make prayer pilgrimages to the city hall; let him go on freedom rides—and try to understand why he must do so. If his repressed emotions are not released in nonviolent ways, they will seek expression through violence; this is not a threat but a fact of history. So I have not said to my people: "Get rid of your discontent." Rather, I have tried to say that this normal and healthy discontent can be channeled into the creative outlet of nonviolent direct action. And now this approach is being termed extremist.

But though I was initially disappointed at being categorized as an extremist, as I continued to think about the matter I gradually gained a measure of satisfaction from the label. Was not Jesus an extremist for love: "Love your enemies, bless them that curse you, do good to them that hate you, and pray for them which despitefully use you, and persecute you." Was not Amos an extremist for justice: "Let justice roll down like waters and righteousness like an ever-flowing stream." Was not Paul an extremist for the Christian gospel: "I bear in my body the marks of the Lord Jesus." Was not Martin Luther an extremist: "Here I stand; I cannot do otherwise, so help me God." And John Bunyan: "I will stay in jail to the end of my days before I make a butchery of my conscience." And Abraham Lincoln: "This nation cannot survive half slave and half free." And Thomas Jefferson: "We hold these truths to be self-evident, that all men are created equal. . . ." So the question is not whether we will be extremists, but what kind of extremists we will be. Will we be extremists for hate or for love? Will we be extremists for the preservation of injustice or for the extension of justice? In that dramatic scene on Calvary's hill three men were crucified. We must never forget that all three were crucified for the same crime—the crime of extremism. Two were extremists for immorality, and thus fell below their environment. The other, Jesus Christ, was an extremist for love, truth and goodness, and thereby rose above his environment. Perhaps the South, the nation and the world are in dire need of creative extremists.

I had hoped that the white moderate would see this need. Perhaps I was too optimistic; perhaps I expected too much. I suppose I should have realized that few members of the oppressor race can understand the deep groans and passionate yearnings of the oppressed race, and still fewer have the vision to see that injustice must be rooted out by strong, persistent and determined action. I am thankful, however, that some of our white brothers in the South have grasped the meaning of this social revolution and committed themselves to it. They are still too few in quantity, but they are big in quality. Some—such as Ralph McGill, Lillian Smith, Harry Golden, James McBride Dabbs, Ann Braden and Sarah Patton Boyle—have written about our struggle in eloquent and prophetic terms. Others have marched with us down nameless streets of the South. They have languished in filthy, roach-infested jails, suffering the abuse and brutality of policemen who view them as "dirty nigger lovers."

Unlike so many of their moderate brothers and sisters, they have recognized the urgency of the moment and sensed the need for powerful "action" antidotes to combat the disease of segregation. . . .

Before closing I feel impelled to mention one other point in your statement that has troubled me profoundly. You warmly commended the Birmingham police force for keeping "order" and "preventing violence." I doubt that you would have so warmly commended the police force if you had seen its dogs sinking their teeth into unarmed, nonviolent Negroes. I doubt that you would so quickly commend the policemen if you were to observe their ugly and inhumane treatment of Negroes here in the city jail; if you were to watch them push and curse old Negro women and young Negro girls; if you were to see them slap and kick old Negro men and young boys; if you were to observe them, as they did on two occasions, refuse to give us food because we wanted to sing our grace together. I cannot join you in your praise of the Birmingham police department.

It is true that the police have exercised a degree of discipline in handling the demonstrators. In this sense they have conducted themselves rather "nonviolently" in public. But for what purpose? To preserve the evil system of segregation. Over the past few years I have consistently preached that nonviolence demands that the means we use must be as pure as the ends we seek. I have tried to make clear that it is wrong to use immoral means to attain moral ends. But now I must affirm that it is just as wrong, or perhaps even more so, to use moral means to preserve immoral ends. Perhaps Mr. Connor and his policemen have been rather nonviolent in public, as was Chief Pritchett in Albany, Georgia, but they have used the moral means of nonviolence to maintain the immoral end of racial injustice. As T. S. Eliot has said: "The last temptation is the greatest treason: To do the right deed for the wrong reason."

I wish you had commended the Negro sit-inners and demonstrators of Birmingham for their sublime courage, their willingness to suffer and their amazing discipline in the midst of great provocation. One day the South will recognize its real heroes. They will be the James Merediths, with the noble sense of purpose that enables them to face jeering and hostile mobs, and with the agonizing loneliness that characterizes the life of the pioneer. They will be old, oppressed, battered Negro women, symbolized in a seventy-two-year-old woman in Montgomery, Alabama, who rose up with a sense of dignity and with her people decided not to ride segregated buses, and who responded with ungrammatical profundity to one who inquired about her weariness: "My feets is tired, but my soul is at rest." They will be the young high school and college students, the young ministers of the gospel and a host of their elders, courageously and nonviolently sitting in at lunch counters and willingly going to jail for conscience' sake. One day the South will know that when these disinherited children of God sat down at lunch counters, they were in reality standing up for what is best in the American dream and for the most sacred values in our Judaeo-Christian heritage, thereby bringing our nation back to those great wells of democracy which were dug deep by the founding fathers in their formulation of the Constitution and the Declaration of Independence.

Never before have I written so long a letter. I'm afraid it is much too long to take your precious time. I can assure you that it would have been much shorter if I had been writing from a comfortable desk, but what else can one do when he is alone in a narrow jail cell, other than write long letters, think long thoughts and pray long prayers?

If I have said anything in this letter that overstates the truth and indicates an unreasonable impatience, I beg you to forgive me. If I have said anything that understates the truth and indicates my having a patience that allows me to settle for anything less than brotherhood, I beg God to forgive me.

I hope this letter finds you strong in the faith. I also hope that circumstances will soon make it possible for me to meet each of you, not as an integrationist or a civil rights leader but as a fellow clergyman and a Christian brother. Let us all hope that the dark clouds of racial prejudice will soon pass away and the deep fog of misunderstanding will be lifted from our fear-drenched communities, and in some not too distant tomorrow the radiant stars of love and brotherhood will shine over our great nation with all their scintillating beauty.

Yours for the cause of Peace and Brotherhood,
Martin Luther King, Jr.

ANALYZING THE RHETORICAL SITUATION

Respond to the following questions about Martin Luther King's letter.

1. To what exigence is King responding? How does the problem fulfill the definition of exigence?

2. Who is King's intended audience? What specific information can you glean about them from King's letter?

3. How does King's audience fulfill—or fall short of—the definition of a rhetorical audience? Provide specific examples from the letter.

4. Account for the specific ways in which King's rhetorical audience could be capable of effecting change or of influencing others who could make change.

5. Do you consider King's letter to be a fitting response to the rhetorical situation? Why or why not?

The power of a rhetorical audience—and a purpose

When we speak and write, we often hope that our words will reach a rhetorical audience. Whether we want our words to influence members of that audience in terms of their relaxation, imagination, reflection, curiosity, enjoyment, or questioning, our purpose is to change the way they think about, behave in terms of, or act in response to some idea, person, or action. In that way, we are no different from a U.S. president making an appearance at an army installation in Iraq or a civil rights leader writing to his detractors from a jail cell. Just like us, public figures send out (visual and verbal) messages in the great hope that those messages will reach—and influence—an audience.

Among the many impressive features of King's "Letter from Birmingham Jail" is the author's ability to include both his detractors and his supporters in his rhetorical audience. King's skill in reaching a wide rhetorical audience is one reason that his is a rich intellectual and political legacy. Over forty years later, intellectual and political leaders continue to respond as part of King's rhetorical audience. Michael Eric Dyson is such an intellectual leader. Author of many books, including *I May Not Get There with You: The True Martin Luther King, Jr.*, and a frequent radio, television, and print media commentator, Dyson spoke at length about King's legacy during a 2001 interview with Frank A. Thomas.

MICHAEL ERIC DYSON
Speech Is My Hammer

The genius of Martin Luther King, Jr. is that he is a vitalizing and energizing force—and I use the present tense here because his words still live in our memories—through which millions of people continue to experience the richness and sublime character of religious commitment. King felt that we can't experi- ence the fullness of our religious passions and gospel beliefs until they are translated into social action. If anything motivated Martin Luther King's career, it was this ethic of translation. He translated the work of philosophical theologians who advocated personal- ism, like Henry Nelson Wieman, into principles that

© Lisa Godfrey/*Penn Arts & Sciences*, 2003

ordinary people could comprehend. Besides his genius for translating ideas and beliefs, King also possessed the gift to translate love into concrete political action. As I've argued in a couple of my books, Martin Luther King, Jr. believed that justice is what love sounds like when it speaks in public. In King's mind—and in the critical reflections of Paul Tillich, whose philosophy King examined in his doctoral dissertation—justice, love, and power could hardly be divorced. King believed that power exercised without the mediating forces of love and justice was ruthless; that justice without power and love was weak because it was empty of vision; and that love without power and justice was mere sentimentality.

King's social activism grew from his extensive study of Christian ethics and liberal theology, and his intuitive grasp of the black religious tradition. For King, black religion at its best was concerned with how we speak the truth of the gospel to brothers and sisters who are worried about rent payments, keeping the lights on, getting an equal education, reducing economic suffering, and achieving racial justice. Because he cared about these things, Martin Luther King, Jr. spent his life translating the philosophical tenets and ethical demands of the gospel into concrete social resistance to interlocking oppressions.

Finally, what's absolutely critical about King's genius is his ability to change his mind and methodology. Although Malcolm X is credited with transforming his life in the last year of his life, King is rarely given his due in embracing a thoroughgoing radicalism in regard to the aims and means of nonviolent social change. King initially desired to appeal to the white conscience to effect racial progress, but later he contended that social change must be forced in more dramatic fashion. He began to advocate a more aggressive version of nonviolence that focused on blocking the flow of traffic and commerce in local municipalities as a sign of severe displeasure with the status quo. King also began to articulate his belief about the inextricable link between militarism, racism, and materialism.

King's theology near the end of his life was radically incarnational, insofar as he was fairly obsessed with making the gospel of Jesus come alive off the biblical page and thrive in our nation's cities, especially among the broke and brokenhearted. King was committed to pushing the black church to become much more intentional about directing its social, political, and economic resources to enable social revolution and to ameliorate the plight of the poor. If the gospel of Jesus is concerned with impressing God's identity on the human psyche and with imprinting it in human community, then the church must expand the boundaries of social intervention in seeking to render service and to improve the chances of social redemption. We have by and large failed to embody King's ethic of translation and his theology of radical incarnationalism, and I think American Christianity and the black church are the worse for it.

ANALYZING THE RHETORICAL SITUATION

Once you've carefully read Dyson's analysis of King's legacy, work with one or two other classmates to answer the following questions. Be prepared to share your answers with the rest of the class.

1. What exigencies does Dyson describe that can be resolved through verbal or visual discourse? In other words, what exigence does King respond to? What is the exigence of his legacy?

2. What are the responses to these exigencies?

3. Describe the rhetorical audience for each response. How do you know who comprises the audience in each case?

4. Describe the power of targeting—and reaching—a rhetorical audience, in terms of Dyson's analysis.

5. What is the rhetor's overarching purpose for targeting this audience? (Note that there is more than one rhetor in Dyson's essay, including Dyson himself.)

Dyson's analysis describes the continuing exigence of King's legacy, an exigence that must be addressed if the United States is to guarantee civil rights to every citizen. As you compare your small group's responses with those of the rest of your class, discuss Dyson's purpose, especially in terms of his rhetorical audience. Also discuss whether and how Dyson's response is fitting to the rhetorical situation.

COMMUNITY CONNECTIONS

1. Bring a copy of your local or campus newspaper to class. Spend time with a classmate looking over the cartoons, columns, and letters on the editorial page. Choose one of the editorials or cartoons and determine the exigence it addresses or presents. Who is the rhetorical audience for the editorial or cartoon? In what specific ways can that audience be influenced or changed? What is the purpose of the editorial writer or artist? What does the artist or writer want the rhetorical audience to do with the information? Be prepared to share your answers with the rest of the class.

2. As you reconsider the legacy of Martin Luther King, Jr., work with one or two other classmates to consider someone with influence in your school or community (whether in politics, education, sports, medicine, or the arts) in terms of an exigence he or she has addressed. Describe the rhetorical exigence and the details of the person's response to that exigence. What group of people comprise the rhetorical audience for that response? What would that person have his or her rhetorical audience do? Be prepared to share your answers with the rest of the class.

3. What problem do you face today? How might that problem best be resolved? What is a possible fitting response to your problem? Who is the rhetorical audience for the response? How would you like them to be influenced or changed? Write for a few minutes, describing the elements of this rhetorical situation.

4. Consider yourself as a rhetorical audience. For whom do you function as such? In what ways are you considered capable of being influenced by discourse? Capable of implementing change? Capable of influencing those who can make change? Write for five minutes, describing yourself as a rhetorical audience. Prepare to discuss your answer with the rest of the class.

IDENTIFYING A FITTING RESPONSE | 2

Establishing a Fitting Response

Confronted with the exigence of bird extinction, amateur birdwatcher and professor of English Christopher Cokinos began researching and writing his book *Hope Is the Thing with Feathers*. The problem he had identified was that people knew nothing about important North American birds. Knowing that he couldn't undo the extinction of the Carolina parakeet (shown on the opposite page), he concentrated instead on making "certain that we never again forget this species nor the others" of which he writes. These six bird species were hastened into extinction by logging, the millinery trade, unregulated hunting, and bird collecting. He couldn't "restore" the birds, he writes, but he could "restory" the lives of these lost beings to human consciousness while energizing conservation efforts for other endangered nonhuman species.

> On an afternoon in late September, in a brisk prairie wind, I watched a bird I'd never seen before, a bird that had strayed far from its usual skies a continent away. Nearly epic in memory, that day began my journey, though I didn't know it then. The journey would take years and retrieve many things: first among them the name of the bird I had watched and didn't know—an escaped parrot that didn't "belong" in Kansas.
>
> Seeing this bird led me to learn of—and revere—America's forgotten Carolina Parakeet, which once colored the sky "like an atmosphere of gems," as one pioneer wrote. The more I learned of the Carolina Parakeet's life, its extinction and its erasure from our memory, the more I wondered: How could we have lost and then forgotten so beautiful a bird? This book is, in part, an attempt to answer those questions and an effort to make certain that we never again forget this species nor the others of which I write.
>
> —**Christopher Cokinos**, from *Hope Is the Thing with Feathers*

WRITE FOR FIVE

In writing answers to the following questions, think back to a time when you responded to a problem through some form of writing.

1. In what ways did your response reach and satisfy your intended audience?
2. In what ways was it an appropriate response to the problem you identified?
3. What other appropriate responses would have been possible?

What is a fitting response?

Chapter 1 stressed the importance of identifying the elements of a rhetorical situation (exigence, purpose, sender, message, receiver, and context). Now that you can identify these elements, you can begin evaluating the wide range of possible responses you can offer. The goal of every person who responds rhetorically to a situation is to shape a **fitting response**, a visual or verbal (written or spoken) response that addresses the problem (exigence), is delivered in an appropriate medium and genre that reach the audience, and successfully satisfies the intended (rhetorical) audience.

Was Christopher Cokinos's book on the extinction of bird species a fitting response? Yes.

Was his the *only* fitting response? No.

Had Cokinos been a different sort of person, with different resources and interests and imagining different rhetorical audiences, he might have made a feature film about these birds, one starring Clive Owen and Nicole Kidman as either hunters or conservationists. He might have put together a public television special, underwritten by the U.S. Department of the Interior. Or maybe he could have induced PIXAR Studios to make an animated children's movie about these birds, with voiceovers by Michelle Pfeiffer, Sylvester Stallone, and Bernie Mac. Depending on the problem, responses in different media may reach and satisfy the rhetorical audience.

A fitting response suits the problem . . .

In September 2005, the United States government commissioned a small group of educational leaders to develop a "comprehensive national strategy" for higher education. In a speech a year later, Secretary of Education Margaret Spellings described the exigence for the charge:

> The country is encountering a significant change to its economic structure, resulting in unmet workforce needs. This is particularly true with respect to highly skilled workers and in the fields of mathematics and science. The need is clear and unavoidable: only 68 out of 100 entering 9th graders graduate from high school on time. Yet, 80 percent of our fastest-growing jobs will require some higher education.

In addition, countries that once lagged behind the United States "are now educating more of their citizens to more advanced levels than we are. Worse, they are passing us by at a time when education is more important to our collective prosperity than ever."

To respond to what Spellings called "an urgent need for change," the Department of Education, together with the newly appointed commission, took immediate action, reassuring businesspeople, parents, and students that a new strategy would be quickly implemented, one that confronted the issues that had been identified as hurting higher education. The Spellings Report, as it came to be known, was made available online as a PDF document, but the actual findings and recommendations of the commission were even more widely distributed immediately after Spellings gave a talk to the National Press Club on September 26, 2006 (excerpted here). Her remarks serve as a direct response to the rhetorical exigence, a nation's anxiety about the future of postsecondary education.

MARGARET SPELLINGS
An Action Plan for Higher Education

A year ago, I formed a bipartisan Commission on the Future of Higher Education. Its purpose: to launch a robust national dialogue on the vital issues of accessibility, affordability, and accountability.

Some of our best and brightest came together from across many sectors to examine these issues. Not from the standpoint of the government, but from that of consumers, employers, and academics.

Their report . . . offers keen insights into the changes that must be made for us to remain the world's leader in higher education providing wider opportunities for more Americans.

Higher education has long been one of the undeniable strength[s] of our nation. In quality, diversity, and character, it's the envy of the world.

American universities have been the incubators of great ideas, the birthplaces of great inventions, and the testing grounds of great individuals.

For generations, a college education has meant the difference between a life lived on the edge of promise and one lived in the full embrace of the American Dream. A system so intrinsically linked to the future success of our children and our nation should be one of our highest priorities.

So, I ask: In our changing . . . world has higher education kept pace? Is it accessible to students of all backgrounds, including minorities, low-income students, and adults? Is it affordable? And accountable to the students, parents, and taxpayers who foot the bill?

Our universities are known as the best in the world. And a lot of people will tell you things are going just fine. But when 90 percent of the fastest-growing jobs require post-secondary education—are we satisfied with "just" fine?

Is it "fine" that college tuition has outpaced inflation, family income, even doubling the cost of health care?

Is it "fine" that only half of our students graduate on time?

Is it "fine" that students often graduate so saddled with debt they can't buy a home or start a family?

None of this seems "fine" to me. Not as a policymaker, not as a taxpayer, and certainly not as the mother of a college sophomore. The Commission drew a similar conclusion. In their words, ". . . higher education has become . . . at times self-satisfied and unduly expensive."

In fact, times have changed. Nearly two-thirds of all high-growth, high-wage jobs created in the next decade will require a college degree, a degree only one-third of Americans have.

Where we once were leaders, now other nations educate more of their young adults to more advanced levels than we do!

This makes families anxious, and I understand why. We know higher education is the key to our children's future. We want more than anything to provide it. Yet, it's becoming difficult to do so and still make ends meet.

And like many parents, I'm wondering—will my daughter graduate equipped with skills for a career, or is she going to move back home with me?

continued

AN ACTION PLAN FOR HIGHER EDUCATION (CONTINUED)

Colleges and universities are the keepers of the flame of intellectual discourse. Well then, let's have some discourse! Let's have some debate on how to make higher education available and attainable for more Americans.

I'm not the first to grapple with these issues. States, local leaders, the business community and many in higher education are already hard at work tackling challenges from affordability to measuring student learning. They need and deserve our help and support.

This is an issue that touches us all. Parents, students, and taxpayers pick up the majority of the tab for higher education. Over the years, we've invested tens of billions of dollars in taxpayer money and just hoped for the best. We deserve better.

So, today I'm announcing my immediate plans to address the issues of accessibility, affordability and accountability raised by the Commission.

First: how do we make college more accessible?

There are far too many Americans who want to go to college but can't—either because they're not prepared or can't afford it. To expand access to higher education we must better prepare our students—starting with high standards and accountability in our public schools.

These principles are the pillars of *No Child Left Behind*. And let me assure you—NCLB is going strong.

We've made great progress towards our goal of every child reading and doing math at grade level by 2014—and that's not too much to ask!

Thanks to this law our youngest students have made more academic gains in the last 5 years than the previous 28 combined. But, at the high school level, it's a different story.

A million kids drop out every single year. And those who do graduate often aren't prepared for college.

As a result, colleges, students, and taxpayers spend over a billion dollars a year on remedial classes after graduation. Ultimately, we pay the bill twice, because students don't get what they need in high school.

A high school diploma should be a ticket to success—including success in college. That's why President Bush proposed a plan to increase academic rigor in our high schools and prepare more students to succeed.

ACTION ONE under my plan is to build on this by expanding the effective principles of *No Child Left Behind* and holding high schools accountable for results.

And we will continue efforts to align high school standards with college work by increasing access to college-prep classes such as Advanced Placement.

Next, how do we make college more affordable?

Higher education's escalating sticker price has many parents facing the tough choice—whether to save for college or their own retirement. In the past five years alone, tuition at four-year colleges has skyrocketed by 40 percent. I want to know why . . . and I know other parents do too!

As the Commission noted, the entire financial aid system is in urgent need of reform. At the federal level, it's a maze of 60 Web sites, dozens of toll-free numbers, and 17 different programs. Just to give a comparison, the main federal student aid form is longer and more complicated than the federal tax form!

The Commission recommends Congress scrap the system and start over with one that's more user-friendly and effective.

In the meantime, ACTION TWO under my plan is for my Department to streamline the process, cut the application time in half, and notify students of their aid eligibility earlier than Spring of their senior year to help families plan.

The reality is no matter the costs, the wealthy can pay. But for low-income, mostly minority students, college is becoming virtually unattainable. Chuck Vest, former MIT President and Commission member, put it this way: "In this country, you are better off being rich and dumb than poor and smart."

Lately, increases in institutional and state aid for low-income families have not kept pace with assistance for more affluent families. In a recent report card, 43 states were given an "F" for failing on affordability.

We must increase need-based aid. We've worked with Congress to strengthen financial aid and we've made progress. This includes making available four and a half billion dollars in scholarships for low-income students who take challenging courses in high school and study fields such as math and science.

I look forward to teaming up with Congress again to improve the financial aid process and help the students who need it most. But more money isn't going to make a difference if states and institutions don't do their part to keep costs in line.

We, at the federal level, can do our part, too. As the Commission pointed out, a big part of the cost burden on higher education is complying with the more than 200 federal regulations currently on the books. We can help lift that burden.

But even so, there are still too many who will say "just give us more money." Money's important. But we're going to keep chasing our tail on price until we realize that a good deal of the solution comes down to information. Like any other investment or enterprise, meaningful data is critical to better manage the system.

My daughter's college costs went up this year . . . for what? And, this is not unique to me. For most families, this is one of the most expensive investments we make. Yet there is little to no information on why costs are so high and what we're getting in return.

Which brings me to my final point. How are we going to make college more accountable for results?

I, too, experienced the confusion and frustration many parents face with the college selection process. I found it almost impossible to get the answers I needed. And I'm the Secretary of Education!

We live in the "Information Age." If you want to buy a new car, you go online and compare a full range of models, makes, and pricing options. And when you're done, you'll know everything from how well each car holds its value down to wheel size and number of cupholders.

The same transparency and ease should be the case when students and families shop for colleges, especially when one year of college can cost a lot more than a car!

That's why I support the Commission's recommendation on this issue. ACTION THREE under my plan will work to pull together the same kind of privacy-protected student-level data we already have for K through 12 students. And use that data to create a higher education information system.

More than 40 states already have a system like this in place, but that's 40 islands unto themselves.

That kind of localized system may work when you're dealing with kindergarten through 12th grade, but it's not helpful when it comes to college and you're trying to compare options: in state versus out of state, public versus private, community college versus four-year.

We want to work with Congress, states, and institutions to build a system that's more useful and widely available to every student.

The information would be closely protected. It would not identify individual students or be tied to personal information. It wouldn't enable you to go online and find out how Margaret Spellings did in her political science class.

Armed with this information, we can redesign my Department's existing college search Web site and make it much more useful—capable of addressing concerns such as: How much is this school really going to cost me? How long will it take to get my degree?

Believe it or not, we can't answer these basic questions. That's unacceptable. And I challenge states and universities to provide the information to make this system a reality.

Information will not only help with decision-making; it will also hold schools accountable for quality. As the Commission wrote: "higher education must change from a system primarily based on reputation to one based on performance."

No current ranking system of colleges and universities directly measures the most critical point—student performance and learning.

You'd never buy a house without an inspection, take a vacation without researching your destination, or these days, buy groceries without reading the nutritional label. And in almost every area of our government we expect transparency and accountability: from prescription drug programs to housing to K–12 education.

If we're that particular in those areas, shouldn't we do the same with higher education? Something so critical to our future success and quality of life?

We absolutely should! And ACTION FOUR under my plan will provide matching funds to colleges, universities, and states that collect and publicly report student learning outcomes.

Right now, accreditation is the system we use to put a stamp of approval on higher education quality. It's largely focused on inputs, more on how many books are in a college library than on whether students can actually understand them. Institutions are asked, "Are you measuring student learning?" And they check yes or no.

That must change. Whether students are learning is not a yes or no question. . . . It's how? How much? And to what effect?

To that end, ACTION FIVE under my plan will convene members of the accrediting community this

continued

November to move toward measures that place more emphasis on learning.

I realize after what I've just said, commencement speaker invitations may suddenly get lost in the mail. But the urgent need to spark this debate and engage on these issues is worth the risk.

As I've outlined, we need to make higher education more accessible by better preparing our students in high school. We need to make higher education more affordable by increasing need-based aid, simplifying the financial aid process, and holding costs in line.

And we need to make higher education more accountable by opening up the ivory towers and putting information at the fingertips of students and families.

This course will not, should not, and cannot be charted by the federal government alone. Just as the Commission reflected a cross-section of higher education stakeholders, finding the right solutions will take a similar partnership.

Today, I've touched on some of the main recommendations, but the Commission has done a comprehensive examination of a whole host of other issues from adult learning to innovation to information technology.

This Spring, I'll convene a Summit and bring these many sectors together to discuss the full slate of recommendations, our progress, and specific responsibilities going forward.

This is the beginning of a process of long overdue reform. And let me be clear: at the end of it we neither envision, nor want, a national system of higher education. On the contrary, one of the greatest assets of our system is its diversity—something we must protect and preserve.

Our aim is simply to make sure the countless opportunities a college education provides are a reality for every American who chooses to pursue it. The Commission's report is rightly titled "A Test of Leadership," and for the sake of our students and our future, this is one test we must not fail!

Thank you.

. . . is delivered in a medium and genre that reach the audience . . .

In addition to comprising a fitting response to the problem at hand, the Spellings Report and detailed supporting documents were delivered through an easily accessed electronic medium that immediately reached a wide audience: the World Wide Web. College instructors, high school teachers, students, and citizens alike could read the online PDF documents—or they could order print copies by writing directly to the U.S. government.

The chosen medium hardly limited the **genres**—the kinds of writing—available to the Spellings Commission. The World Wide Web could have delivered anything from a blog entry to streaming video. But the exigence (the need to develop a comprehensive national strategy for higher education) and other elements of the rhetorical situation called for a kind of writing that featured research and documentation. It's no surprise, then, that the genre the commission chose for its informative writing was the report.

Like any genre, the report has a history, one which no doubt played into the commission's choice. Consider reports that you have seen or read: book reports, status reports, credit reports, or even articles in *Consumer Reports*. All examples of this genre employ formal language, a serious tone, and careful documentation of research to reach their goal of conveying information. (Even the satirical *Colbert Report* on Comedy Central displays many of these characteristics—the spoof of the report genre is part of what makes the show so humorous.) It's not a coincidence that reports share these characteristics. Rather, the genre developed in this way in response to common rhetorical situations. Because elements of the commission's rhetorical situation were similar enough to those of other situations to which reports are suited, the commission's audience had an expectation that a report—not streaming video, a blog entry, or a memoir—would be the chosen genre.

. . . and successfully satisfies the intended audience

The report and its supporting documents—fitting responses that they are— work on at least two levels to satisfy a worried American public and to do so using a genre that meets that audience's expectations. On the most obvious level is the attempt to link the government's economic and educational policies with the values of U.S. citizens. But on a more urgent level is the attempt to galvanize the support of the American public in terms of the government's influence on education. Interestingly, these government documents shaped another rhetorical situation that developed around another exigence. Because these documents didn't please every U.S. citizen, they created another rhetorical problem, one that would need to be changed by yet another fitting response.

ANALYZING THE RHETORICAL SITUATION

For each of the following problems, decide whether you could shape a response that fulfills the three-part requirement for being fitting: discourse that fits the problem, is delivered in an appropriate medium and genre, and successfully satisfies the intended audience. Be prepared to share your answers with the rest of the class.

1. Your university's football coach, whom you have long admired, is receiving a great deal of negative press because the football team is losing.

2. When you and your friends get together, they always try to persuade you to join their church.

3. Your history instructor has assigned a research paper that is due on the same day as your biology midterm.

4. After taking your LSATs, you receive mailings from more than twenty law schools.

5. For security reasons, U.S. Immigration Services has not allowed your Middle Eastern friend to return to the United States and resume his college education.

Recognizing a fitting response

The Spellings Report provoked a sharp reply from the Association of American Colleges and Universities (AAC&U). But that fitting response to the government documents was not arrived at easily or instantly: university administrators and professors from all over the nation and from all kinds of schools came together on numerous occasions to discuss, investigate, research—and respond to—the facts, reasoning, and sometimes unexamined beliefs that underpin the commission's report.

In their online reply, "AAC&U Statement on Spellings Commission Draft Report," the authors criticize the report for combining a "hollow concern for quality in undergraduate education with a practical encouragement of a cafeteria-style college curriculum." The AAC&U statement finds promise in the "main recommendations in the third part of the report," especially the discussion of "college access and preparation," "enhancing the role of the Fund for the Improvement of Postsecondary Education," and making "new investments in science, technology, engineering, and mathematics." But, the authors write, "the devil is in the details." And the details of the Spellings Report "chart a dismal direction for undergraduate learning in the United States."

In addition, the authors of the AAC&U statement write that the Spellings Commission's report implicitly dismisses faculty, despite the fact (proved by "abundant evidence") that "close interaction between faculty and students is one of the most important predictors of college completion and achievement." And in a genuine effort to speak to policy makers, university and college faculty, and U.S. citizens, the AAC&U authors close their response with this admonishment: "It is very important that . . . when the final report is released, AAC&U presidents and trustees take the lead—in partnership with their faculty—and call for a vision of college learning that is worthy of a great democracy. College admission is important—and so too is college completion. But the key to America's future is what happens in between." The purpose of AAC&U's online statement is to clarify the organization's values and goals in response to the disparaging commission report.

AAC&U's response to the Spellings Report.

Because they were responding to the controlling exigence of a rhetorical situation, the AAC&U authors came up with *a* fitting response, but not the only possible one. Whether their response can be considered the best—or not—depends on the occasion, the audience, the purpose, the constitution of the writing committee, and so on. Even if their response was (or was not) the best, it was nevertheless a well-researched and well-executed response, one that called for a cascade of responses from other interested citizens' groups, professors, and university and college administrators.

All through your life, you have been and will continue to be faced with rhetorical exigencies that call for a fitting response of some kind. Right now, as a college student, you are asked on a regular basis to shape fitting responses to exigencies, many of which come in the form of assignments, social dilemmas, and political or religious challenges. In your first-year writing class, your instructor will direct you to a number of exigencies that you'll need to analyze and then address in writing. It's doubtful that only one person in your class will shape the perfect resolution to any exigence; more than likely, a number of students will shape fitting responses to each assignment, succeeding even as the responses vary from person to person.

The following list of questions can help you evaluate responses to determine whether or not they are fitting.

What Makes It a Fitting Response?

If any of the following conditions are not met, you have a problem that is not a rhetorical exigence or a response that is not fitting.

1. Is the problem an exigence that can be modified through verbal (spoken or written) or visual discourse?
2. Is the response either verbal or visual discourse?
3. Does the response fit the problem?
4. Is this response delivered in an appropriate medium and genre that reach its intended audience?
5. Is the intended audience also a rhetorical audience (see chapter 1)?
6. Does this response successfully satisfy the intended audience?

Your Writing Experiences

1. Think back on your writing experiences—academic and otherwise—and try to recall a fitting response you've received. What characterized the response? What made it fitting?
2. When you submit a piece of writing to your instructor, what kind of response do you like most to receive (other than praise, of course)? Answer the following questions to formulate a description of a fitting response to your academic writing: (a) In what medium (or media) do

continued

you like to receive responses to your writing? Verbally, in a conference? In an email message or online course discussion list? Handwritten in ink on your printed page? (b) Do you like comments throughout your text, or just at the end? Do you like your instructor to correct mechanical errors for you, point them out, or allude to them in a final comment? (c) What do you want to learn from your instructor's comments and markings?

3. Think of a time when you gave a fitting response to someone else's writing. In what ways did it fit the problem, get delivered in an appropriate medium and genre, and successfully satisfy the intended audience?

Reading a resolution as a fitting response As you already know, people shape different responses to the same exigence. Some responses may seem to you more fitting than others, but you may not know exactly why that is the case. Next, you'll read closely several responses to the 1992 Rodney King verdict and determine which meet the criteria for a fitting response.

You might remember hearing about the Rodney King verdict: the Los Angeles police officers who had beaten King for 19 seconds—recorded on an 81-second videotape—were initially exonerated. (In a later trial, the two officers who had struck King were found guilty and served time in prison.) Commentators, news analysts, and race-relations experts rushed to the airwaves, the printed page, and cyberspace to provide what they thought were fitting responses to the verdict. The Academic Senate at San Francisco State University, for example, posted a public resolution, questioning "whether the American system of justice treats people equitably under the law." As you read this resolution, which follows, consider how fitting a response it is.

ACADEMIC SENATE OF SAN FRANCISCO STATE UNIVERSITY
Resolution Regarding the Rodney King Verdict

At its meeting of May 5, 1992, the Academic Senate approved the following resolution regarding the Rodney King verdict:

WHEREAS The April 29, 1992, verdict in the case of the officers charged with beating Rodney King has raised questions about whether the American system of justice treats people equitably under the law; and

WHEREAS The powerlessness born of having an unequal voice and inadequate representation begets frustration sometimes leading to violence; and

WHEREAS San Francisco State University, through the efforts of its Commission on Human Relations, Working Committee on Multicultural Perspectives in the Curriculum, and other projects has placed a high priority on implementing the principles embodied in its recently adopted statement, "Principles for a Multicultural University"; and

WHEREAS The hostile climate generated by the verdict in this case imperils the foundations of reason, common sense, morality, and compassion which underlie the academic enterprise as well as the larger society which this enterprise serves and is inimical to the equity and diversity goals of this campus; therefore be it

RESOLVED That the San Francisco State University Academic Senate decry the verdict in the case of the officers charged with beating Rodney King; and be it further

RESOLVED That the San Francisco State University Academic Senate reaffirm its commitment to a governance process which actively encourages the participation of all members of the academic community; and be it further

RESOLVED That the San Francisco State University Academic Senate reaffirm its commitment, and redouble its efforts, to provide an academic environment which promotes the empowerment, embraces the diverse viewpoints, and celebrates the contributions of all members of the community which the University serves; and be it further

RESOLVED That this resolution be distributed to the SFSU Campus community, the Chair of the Academic Senate, CSU and to the Chairs of the CSU Campus Senates.

Reading the L.A. riots as a fitting response Although dramatic by academic standards, the preceding resolution pales in comparison to the most powerful response of all: the three-day riots that began in Los Angeles shortly after the Rodney King verdict was announced. With arson, looting, and fighting, the riots spread throughout South Central Los Angeles and to several other cities, as far away as Atlanta, Georgia. By the end of the rioting, which lasted for several days, more than 50 people had been killed, over 4,000 injured, and over 12,000 arrested in Los Angeles alone. Many participants in the riots as well as some onlookers felt that the riots were, indeed, a fitting resolution to the exigence of the verdict. What do you think?

One response to the Rodney King verdict.

ANALYZING THE RHETORICAL SITUATION

1. Use the questions in the "What Makes It a Fitting Response?" box (on page 43) to determine whether the L.A. riots and the SFSU Academic Senate's resolution were fitting responses to the Rodney King verdict. Be sure to consider all questions for each of the responses.

2. Which response(s) do you consider fitting? If both are fitting, why do you think such different responses can both be fitting? If only one response is fitting, what makes it more fitting than the other?

Reading political commentary as a fitting response If you argue that the L.A. riots were, in and of themselves, a kind of visual rhetoric, you might believe them to be the most fitting of all the various responses to the Rodney King verdict. Columnist and activist Barbara Smith believed that the riots were the most fitting response to a terrible verdict. In fact, as the flames of the riots were reduced to embers, Smith commented on the political potential of those riots: "the insurrection in Los Angeles will galvanize unprecedented organizing." She also wrote about her own simmering fury. Recounting King's beating and a catalogue of brutalities that preceded it, Smith forged her fury into a verbal response that she felt fit the occasion.

BARBARA SMITH
Excerpt from The Truth That Never Hurts

What I felt at the King verdict and its aftermath was all too familiar. I felt the same gnawing in the pit of my stomach and in my chest when sixteen-year-old Yusuk Hawkins was gunned down on the streets of Bensonhurst, Brooklyn, in 1989. I felt the same impotent rage when the police murdered sixty-seven-year-old Eleanor Bumpurs with a shotgun in the process of evicting her from her Bronx apartment in 1984. I choked back the same bitter tears when I heard the verdict in the 1991 rape case involving a Black woman student and several white male students at St. John's University on Long Island. I was just as terrified when they murdered four Black school girls (my age peers) by bombing a church in Birmingham, Alabama, in 1963. And even though I was too young to understand its meaning, I learned Emmett Till's name in 1955 because of witnessing my family's anguish over his lynching in Mississippi.

So what do we do with all this fury besides burn down our own communities and hurt or kill anyone, white, Black, brown, or yellow, who gets in our way? Figuring out what to do next is the incredibly difficult challenge that lies before us.

Above all, the events in Los Angeles have made it perfectly obvious why we need a revolution in this country. Nothing short of a revolution will work. Gross inequalities are built into the current system and Band-Aids, even big ones, won't cure capitalism's fundamental injustice and exploitation.

We need, however, to build analysis, practice, and movements that accurately address the specific ways that racism, capitalism, and all the major systems of oppression interconnect in the United States. It's not a coincidence that the most dramatic political changes have so often been catalyzed by race. In the United States, racism has shaped the nature of capitalism and race relations.

It is our responsibility as Black activists, radicals, and socialists to create vibrant new leadership that offers a real alternative to the tired civil rights establishment and to the bankrupt "two-party" system. It is our responsibility as we build autonomous Black organizations to make the connections between all of the oppressions and to work in coalition with the movements that have arisen to challenge them.

Recognizing the leadership of radical women of color, feminists, and lesbians is absolutely critical from this moment forward. Women of color are already building a movement that makes the connections between race, class, gender, and sexual identity, a movement that has the potential to win liberation for all of us.

It is past the time to talk. I really want to know how the white left, the white feminist, and the white lesbian and gay movements are going to change now that Los Angeles is burned. It's not enough to say what a shame all of this is or to have a perfect intellectual understanding of what has occurred. It's time for all the white people who say they're committed to freedom to figure out what useful antiracist organizing is and to put it into practice.

Smith says, "Figuring out what to do next is the incredibly difficult challenge that lies before us." You might think of "figuring out what to do next" as the challenge of shaping a fitting response to the exigence of any rhetorical situation. Smith, a socialist, explores a number of options, all of which are "fitting" and some of which are more revolutionary than others.

Look again at Smith's final sentence: "It's time for all the white people who say they're committed to freedom to figure out what useful antiracist organizing is and to put it into practice." That sentence, the last one in her fitting response, opens up another rhetorical exigence that invites yet another response. In fact, like Secretary Spellings's address regarding higher education, Smith's writing actually prescribes a response, going so far as to dictate the form that response should take.

ANALYZING THE RHETORICAL SITUATION

1. Is the problem to which Barbara Smith is responding a rhetorical exigence?
2. Is the response verbal or visual discourse?
3. Does the response fit the problem?
4. Is this response delivered in a medium and genre that reach its intended audience?
5. Does this response successfully satisfy the intended audience?

Compare your answers with those of your classmates, and then decide, as a class, if Smith's response is fitting to the rhetorical situation. You may also want to consider what result Smith hopes to achieve through her writing.

COMMUNITY CONNECTIONS

1. Your campus or town undoubtedly has unrest (or even upheaval) of some kind, strong dissatisfaction related to economics, employment, politics, justice, race, athletics, or gender. Look through your local newspaper and identify one such incident of unrest. What rhetorical exigence does this incident present? What is one possible fitting response to that exigence? Be prepared to share your answer with the rest of the class.

2. Celebrations—birthdays, engagements, weddings, commitment ceremonies, graduations, family reunions, athletic victories, and holiday gatherings—invite fitting responses. These responses take the form of letters, cards, songs, speeches, and toasts. For an event that you're going to attend soon, draft a fitting response.

3. Think about the fitting response you drafted for question 2. Choose a different kind of event and explain how you would need to alter your response in order to make it a fitting one for that event. Would you need to change the medium in which you plan to deliver your response? Its length? The specific kind of language used?

Using the Available Means of Persuasion

In chapter 1, you learned that Aristotle defined *rhetoric* as "the faculty of observing in any given situation the available means of persuasion." When you consider the available means, you think about the possible methods of communication you might use, whether those are oral (speaking person to person, over the telephone), written (using email, instant messaging, paper, a Web page), or visual (using film, video, still images, and so on).

You've already had years of experience in using your critical judgment to identify available means of persuasion, means that are dependent on the rhetorical situation, including the specific audience you're trying to reach. Whatever the rhetorical situation and whoever the audience, you select from the available means of persuasion. Humans were doing just that long before Aristotle wrote his *Rhetoric*. In fact, one of the earliest examples of humans tapping an available means of persuasion can be found in cave paintings, such as the ones in Lascaux, France, which depict stories of hunting expeditions that took place between 15,000 and 10,000 BCE. Using sharpened tools, iron and manganese oxides, and charcoal, Paleolithic humans recorded incidents from their daily life for the edification of others. From 400 BCE to 1300 CE, people living in what is now the southwestern part of the United States also recorded the stories, events, beliefs, fears, and characters of their daily life by carving their representations on stone faces of various kinds. Using the available means at their disposal (sharpened tools and stones), these First Americans composed stories that continue to speak to and intrigue us.

The contemporary rhetorical scene also offers many varieties of available means—from electronic and printed to visual and spoken—for delivering as well as shaping potentially effective information for a specific audience. Let's

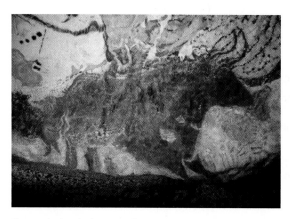

Cave painting in Lascaux, France.

Early stone carvings from the American Southwest.

review some of those means so that you can optimize your choices in order to succeed as a rhetor.

What is the available means?

Every rhetorical situation depends on delivering a fitting response by some available means of persuasion. **Available means** can be defined as the physical material used for delivering the information, the place from which the author creates and sends the information, and the elements of the presentation itself, such as the rhetorical appeals, the use of evidence or authority, the conventions of style, and the rhetorical methods of development. Each rhetor naturally chooses from among the available means, basing choices on the context, the audience, and the **constraints** (negative obstacles) and **resources** (positive influences) of the rhetorical situation.

Instinctively, we all know how to make rhetorical choices. Still, we can all improve, especially when we become more aware of the choices we're making and the effects of those choices. Rhetorical consciousness (and success) comes with recognizing the vast array of options at our disposal, including those already in existence and those we can create as we attempt to negotiate the constraints of our rhetorical situation and thereby successfully reach our intended audience.

If you think about your writing class, for instance, you'll see that information is being delivered to you by all sorts of available means: textbooks, lectures, discussions, computer programs, listservs, in-class activities, and homework assignments. This textbook, *The Harbrace Guide to Writing*, is one available means for helping you learn how to write for your college courses. Your instructor's classroom presentations and activities are another available means. Whether delivering lectures, leading class discussions, working with you through various in-class exercises, or supervising writing workshops, your instructor is tapping all possible available means to teach you and the other members of your class.

The available means delivers information . . .

In the weeks following the September 11, 2001 attacks on the World Trade Center, many Americans responded to the exigence by extending their condolences, regardless of whether they knew any of the dead and missing personally. The range of fitting responses to the exigence varied widely: for instance, those whose loved ones were missing contributed to memory walls, filling them with bouquets of flowers and photographs. Others wrote essays and newspaper columns, decrying the terrorists, mourning the victims, and extolling the rescue efforts. Some people presented television and radio programs focusing on what happened on that day and how the United States was responding. Still others created online memorial boards and chat rooms. And one inventive rhetor went so far as to hire a skywriter, posting a message that spoke for and to millions of Americans: "We miss you." Each of these rhetors chose a different physical means of delivering a message.

Photo © Suzi Altman

A September 11
memory wall.

These rhetors worked within the constraints and resources of their individual rhetorical situations, whether those constraints and resources were physical ("What passerby or hospital worker may have seen my missing loved one?"), geographical ("How can I reach the survivors in New York City?"), or financial ("I'm going to spend money broadcasting my message in skywriting"). The means of delivery each rhetor used depended on the rhetor's expertise, intended audience, and contextual constraints and resources.

. . . is anchored to the rhetor's place . . .

Every time a rhetor sends a message, he or she does so from a physical place. Whether the rhetor is writing at a desk, talking on a telephone, preaching from a pulpit, speaking from a podium, keyboarding at a laptop, or conversing in a coffee shop, the message itself is constituted by the constraints and resources of that specific place. For instance, when you write a letter to someone, you assume that person can read the language in which you're writing. You may be writing a letter because the person isn't within speaking distance and doesn't have access to email. You may choose writing over telephoning because your message needs to be phrased carefully so as to not upset or confuse the person. If you're sending a message electronically, you may use your cell phone to text message, in which case the message is likely to be shorter than if you were typing it on a full-size keyboard.

Bill Richardson for President Web site.

When New Mexico's governor Bill Richardson entered the race for his party's presidential nomination in 2007, a contextual constraint was financial: he didn't have as much funding as his better-known competitors, Senators Barack Obama and Hillary Clinton. Richardson realized he could tap the resources of electronic communication to reach a wide audience on the Internet, rapidly and relatively cheaply (so the Internet became a contextual resource). In his **blog** (or Web log, an interactive online journal), he may have found the best available means for exploiting the resources of electronic communication, especially given the blog's various links to relevant news updates, articles, Web sites, official campaign entries, reader comments, and even video clips, such as YouTube's clip of the governor's appearance on Jon Stewart's *The Daily Show*. Richardson's choice of blogging as an available means of reaching the American public was a practical choice, influenced by various resources and constraints. But it was also a political choice, anchored in his right to speak.

Not all rhetors, however, have access to all of the available means of persuasion. Many groups of people throughout American history have been denied the right to education, the right to speak publicly, and the right to participate in politics on grounds of their gender, race, ethnicity, physical ability, or lack of property. For example, when you consider voting as an available means of persuasion, of sending a message to a specific rhetorical audience, you see how oppressive the lack of voting rights has been for many groups. In 1776, only white Protestant men who owned land had the right to vote. By 1847, all white men could vote, including Catholics and non-Christians. In 1870, black males were given the right to vote, but only under certain conditions, including proof of their literacy and ability to pay a poll tax. Women were not granted voting rights until 1920, and American Indians not until 1924. Thus, the means of persuasion available to these groups were fewer than those available to white men.

Those who are not educated, don't have access to computers and books, cannot read and write well, and don't speak publicly (whether their speaking is at a podium, over a telephone, or on the radio) simply don't have access to as many means of persuasion as those who have such opportunities. In fact, the right to speak publicly has been a rhetorical constraint for members of these groups for centuries. The delegates at the 1848 Seneca Falls Convention demanded that women be permitted to speak in public without the ill grace of their audience. After all, women—just like men—have thoughts and opinions that should be heard. For some groups facing discrimination, then, declaring themselves as worthy of speaking has been the first step toward overcoming the constraints of their rhetorical situation.

. . . and includes the rhetorical elements of the message itself

When a rhetor considers the available means for sending a purposeful message to a particular audience, he or she considers the rhetorical elements of the message. Because human beings are not persuaded to believe or act in a certain way based on facts alone, because we don't believe only that which can be proved, rhetors use **rhetorical appeals**, which arose from the truly human nature of persuasion. These three persuasive strategies are **ethos**, the ethical appeal of the rhetor's credibility and trustworthiness; **logos**, the logical appeal of a reasonable, well-supported argument; and **pathos**, the emotional appeal of language and examples that stir the audience's feelings (within a reasonable limit). The use of these appeals is reliably balanced in most successful messages, for to exaggerate any one of these appeals is to risk losing the audience and thereby failing to achieve the rhetorical purpose.

Many successful messages emphasize each of these appeals separately, but doing so is not the same as exaggerating any one of them. Consider the following excerpts from a speech given at the 1851 Women's Rights Convention in Akron, Ohio. During a time when white women were rarely permitted to speak in public, especially to a "promiscuous assembly" of men and women, former slave Sojourner Truth (b. Isabella Baumfree, 1787–1883) faced an audience of educated white Northerners, mostly women, to speak about the importance of women's rights for black women as well as white women. Truth negotiated the constraints and resources of her rhetorical situation to reach her audience.

According to tradition, Truth, the only black person in attendance, had been listening carefully to the various speeches, many of which denounced the rights of women. Truth was constrained by being illiterate, black, a Southerner, and a woman, and her spoken ideas (recorded and later published in multiple versions by white people) would be met with resistance, if not outright objection. Some of her constraints, however, proved to be her richest resources. The minute she ascended the platform to address the audience, Truth transgressed all the social norms of the educated Northern white "lady."

In her opening paragraphs, Truth set out the circumference of the struggle for women's rights as she saw it, establishing her ethos. Notice how her first paragraph establishes common ground with the white women in her audience: both speaker and audience subscribe to the idea that both Northern and Southern women, white and black, share a concern over women's rights. Truth continues to burnish her ethos by demonstrating her goodwill toward her audience, her good sense and knowledge of the subject at hand, and her good character:

Sojourner Truth.

> Well, children, where there is so much racket there must be something out of kilter. I think that 'twixt the Negroes of the South and the women of the North, all talking about rights, the white men will be in a fix pretty soon. But what's all this here talking about?
>
> That man over there says that women need to be helped into carriages and lifted over ditches, and to have the best place everywhere. Nobody ever helps me into carriages, or over mud puddles, or gives me any best place! And ain't I a woman? Look at me! Look at my arm! I could have ploughed and planted, and gathered into barns, and no man could head me! And ain't I a woman? I could work as much and eat as much as a man—when I could get it—and bear the lash as well! And ain't I a woman? I have borne thirteen children, and seen them most all sold off to slavery, and when I cried out with my mother's grief, none but Jesus heard me! And ain't I a woman?

A speaker in Truth's position had to devote most of her words to establishing her ethos; after all, she needed to be heard and believed as the black woman she was. But like many successful rhetors, Truth spent the body of her speech emphasizing logos, the shape of her reasoning, particularly her response to arguments against women's rights:

> Then they talk about this thing in the head; what's this they call it? ["Intellect," somebody whispers.] That's it, honey. What's that got to do with women's rights or Negro's rights? If my cup won't hold but a pint, and yours holds a quart, wouldn't you be mean not to let me have my little half measure-full?
>
> Then that little man in black there, he says women can't have as much rights as men, 'cause Christ wasn't a woman! Where did your Christ come from? Where did your Christ come from? From God and a woman! Man had nothing to do with Him.
>
> If the first woman God ever made was strong enough to turn the world upside down all alone, these women together ought to be able to turn it back, and get it right side up again! And now they is asking to do it, the men better let them.

The closing of her speech emphasizes pathos. Her gratitude translates into an emotional appeal to her audience:

> Obliged to you for hearing me, and now old Sojourner ain't got nothing more to say.

Ethos, logos, and pathos are often distributed among three sections of any piece of powerful writing in both separate and overlapping forms. Once you start looking for them, you'll discover that these rhetorical appeals appear in much of the reading and writing you do.

Within a message itself, the available means also include the rhetor's use of evidence or authority. You can see for yourself how Truth used the example of her own hardworking life as evidence that women were just as suited for voting rights as men. In fact, her example carried far more authority than that offered by any of the well-educated white women who shared the speaker's platform with her. And for authority, Truth wisely went straight to the Bible, the ultimate authority for all her listeners, whether they were Northern or Southern, black or white, male or female, educated or uneducated.

In addition to the rhetorical appeals and the use of evidence or authority, conventions of style constitute yet another aspect of the available means. Truth's 1851 speech circulated in at least four versions, all of them recorded by white people, all of them resorting to some version of dialect. The most prominent use of dialect is the word *ain't*, but it's not the only one. Later, allegedly "cleaned-up" versions of the speech included the phrases *out o' kilter, a-talking, be in a fix*, and *aren't I a woman*. No version of her speech has appeared in **Standardized English**, the style of writing and speaking expected in most academic and business settings, which would dictate *Am I not a woman?* as the refrain. The use of dialect authenticates Truth as an uneducated former slave speaking to an educated white Northern audience.

Finally, rhetors choose the most appropriate of the rhetorical methods of development (description, narration, exemplification, classification and division, comparison and contrast, process analysis, cause-and-consequence analysis, and definition). In her speech, Truth used definition and narration in the second paragraph: she defined herself as a woman, just not the kind of woman that opponents to women's rights have in mind, and she narrated several incidents from her life that supported her self-definition. In the body of her speech, she used cause-and-consequence analysis to bring home her point that women have already set a powerful precedent, one supported by scripture.

Truth's speech, no matter which version is examined, offers a clear textual context for examining the available means of persuasion.

ANALYZING THE RHETORICAL SITUATION

For two or three of the following situations, identify available means of persuasion that take into consideration (a) the physical means of delivering the information, (b) the place from which the author creates and sends the information, and (c) the rhetorical elements (including the rhetorical appeals) of the message itself. Be prepared to share your answers with the class.

1. You want to support your favorite recording artist, who is under scrutiny for criticizing the current government of the United States.

2. Your family wants to help some neighbors, who have lost all of their worldly possessions in a house fire.

3. You want to change majors, from communications to international business, but your grade-point average is slightly below the necessary minimum for acceptance to the School of Business.

4. Your spouse wants to relocate in order to further his or her career, but you're making good progress on your undergraduate degree in your current school.

5. Your economics professor has assigned you a research project: you are to evaluate the kinds of jobs that are appropriate for high school students.

Recognizing available means

When Boston University's School of Public Health created Join Together to provide information to individuals and communities interested in fighting and preventing underage drinking and substance abuse, it needed to tap the available means for distributing that information. One of the available means chosen was a Web site. On its site, the group mentions specific means: coalitions, leadership training for community-based efforts, public education and media, and public policy initiatives—all of which can be realized through print, oral, visual, and electronic means of delivery.

This Web site is an available means of communication for the organization Join Together.

This Web page has links to additional available means of response.

www.jointogether.com

In addition, Join Together's Web site contains links to many other available means. As you analyze Join Together's Web site, you'll see that it uses the rhetorical appeals, evidence and authority, a specific style, and various rhetorical methods of development. In fact, the site argues for the importance of its existence not only by recounting specific evidence and leveraging the rhetorical appeals of pathos and logos but also by sending the reader to relevant links to find out how to take further action.

No matter what document, Web site, or television program you're reading or viewing (and analyzing rhetorically), you need to keep in mind that the creators of those communications have tried to choose the best from among all means of communication available to them. As you read and view, then, you'll want to remain alert to the specific choices rhetors have made as well as whether those choices are the most fruitful ones.

Rarely will two rhetors make identical choices in response to a rhetorical exigence. Each rhetor's physical place of composing and status in terms of the situation often complicate those choices. Each rhetor must negotiate a unique set of rhetorical constraints and resources in order to determine the best available means.

YOUR WRITING EXPERIENCES

1. Chances are you may not know very many people, if anyone, in your writing class. Your instructor may not know anyone either. Describe the available means you could use to remedy this situation. How exactly would you do so, and what would be the substance of your message?

2. What means are available to you for letting your writing instructor know what kind of person, student, and writer you are? Write for ten minutes, describing the available means in terms of three constituent parts: (a) the physical means of delivering the information, (b) the place from which you could create and send the information, and (c) the rhetorical elements of the message itself. How might you use the rhetorical appeals (ethos, pathos, and logos) to convey an impression of yourself to your instructor?

3. After you receive a marked and graded piece of writing from your instructor, what are the means available to you for responding? In terms of the three constituents of available means, describe how you usually respond. How might you more profitably respond? Write for five minutes and be prepared to share your answer with the rest of the class.

4. Reconsider the answers you wrote for questions 1, 2, and 3. Carefully translate your three answers into one that takes advantage of the available means of persuasion. Consider your rhetorical constraints and resources (including the rhetorical appeals) as you introduce yourself as a college writer to the rest of your class, including your instructor. Be prepared to share your fitting response with the rest of the class.

Reading an essay for available means   Acclaimed author Susan Orlean has established her career by writing about the ordinary things in life. After spending the early part of her career writing profiles of famous people (actors, musicians, politicians, businesspeople) that were published in popular magazines (*Rolling Stone, Vogue, Esquire, The New Yorker*), Orlean now writes from a different perspective altogether: she writes profiles of ordinary people, most of whom wonder why she wants to talk to them. In an interview at University of Oregon, Orlean said that she's drawn to the extraordinary in the ordinary: "There's no question in my mind that being a writer is a moral occupation and one that requires an awareness all the time of what that means morally and philosophically." As you read the following excerpt from her essay "The American Man, Age Ten," locate the extraordinary features of this ten-year-old's daily existence that Orlean identifies.

SUSAN ORLEAN

Excerpt from The American Man, Age Ten

If Colin Duffy and I were to get married, we would have matching superhero notebooks. We would wear shorts, big sneakers, and long, baggy T-shirts depicting famous athletes every single day, even in the winter. We would sleep in our clothes. We would both be good at Nintendo Street Fighter II, but Colin would be better than me. We would have some homework, but it would never be too hard and we would always have just finished it. We would eat pizza and candy for all of our meals. We wouldn't have sex, but we would have crushes on each other and, magically, babies would appear in our home. We would win the lottery and then buy land in Wyoming, where we would have one of every kind of cute animal. All the while, Colin would be working in law enforcement—probably the FBI. Our favorite movie star, Morgan Freeman, would visit us occasionally. We would listen to the same Eurythmics song ("Here Comes the Rain Again") over and over again and watch two hours of television every Friday night. We would both be good at football, have best friends, and know how to drive; we would cure AIDS and the garbage problem and everything that hurts animals. We would hang out a lot with Colin's dad. For fun, we would load a slingshot with dog food and shoot it at my butt. We would have a very good life. . . .

Here are the particulars about Colin Duffy: He is ten years old, on the nose. He is four feet eight inches high, weighs seventy-five pounds, and appears to be mostly leg and shoulder blade. He is a handsome kid. He has a broad forehead, dark eyes with dense lashes, and a sharp, dimply smile. I have rarely seen him without a baseball cap. He owns several, but favors a University of Michigan Wolverines model, on account of its pleasing colors. The hat styles his hair into wild disarray. If you ever managed to get the hat off his head, you would see a boy with a nimbus of golden-brown hair, dented in the back, where the hat hits him.

Colin lives with his mother, Elaine; his father, Jim; his older sister, Megan; and his little brother, Chris, in a pretty pale blue Victorian house on a bosky street in Glen Ridge, New Jersey. Glen Ridge is a serene and civilized old town twenty miles west of New York City. It does not have much of a commercial district, but it is a town of amazing lawns. Most of the houses were built around the turn of the century and are set back a gracious, green distance from the street. The rest of the town seems to consist of parks and playing fields and sidewalks and backyards—in other words, it is a far cry from South-Central Los Angeles and from Bedford-Stuyvesant and other, grimmer parts of the country where a very different ten-year-old American man is growing up today.

There is a fine school system in Glen Ridge, but Elaine and Jim, who are both schoolteachers, choose to send their children to a parents' cooperative elementary school in Montclair, a neighboring suburb. Currently Colin is in fifth grade. He is a good student. He plans to go to college, to a place he says is called Oklahoma City State College University. OCSCU satisfies his desire to live out west, to attend a small college, and to study law enforcement, which OCSCU apparently offers as a major. After four years at Oklahoma City State College University, he plans to work for the FBI. He says that getting to be a police officer involves tons of hard work, but working for the FBI will be a cinch, because all you have to do is fill out one form, which he has already gotten from the head FBI office. Colin is quiet in class but loud on the playground. He has a great throwing arm, significant foot speed, and a lot of physical confidence. He is also brave. Huge wild cats with rabies and gross stuff dripping from their teeth, which he says run rampant throughout his neighborhood, do not scare him. Otherwise, he is slightly bashful. This combination of athletic grace and valor and personal reserve accounts for considerable popularity. He has a fluid relationship to many social groups, including the superbright nerds, the ultrajocks, the flashy kids who will someday become extremely popular and socially successful juvenile delinquents, and the kids who will be elected president of the student body. In his opinion, the most popular boy in his class is Christian, who happens to be black, and Colin's favorite television character is Steve Urkel on *Family Matters*, who is black, too, but otherwise he seems uninterested in or oblivious to race. Until this year, he was a Boy Scout. Now he is planning to begin karate lessons. His favorite schoolyard game is football, followed closely by prison dodgeball, blob tag, and bombardo. He's crazy about athletes, although sometimes it isn't clear if he is absolutely sure of the difference between human athletes and Marvel Comics action figures. His current best friend is named Japeth. He used to have another best friend named Ozzie. According to Colin, Ozzie was found on a doorstep, then changed his name to Michael and moved to Massachusetts, and then Colin never saw him or heard from him again.

He has had other losses in his life. He is old enough to know people who have died and to know things about the world that are worrisome. When he dreams, he dreams about moving to Wyoming, which he has visited with his family. His plan is to buy land there and have some sort of ranch that would definitely include horses.

Sometimes when he talks about this, it sounds as ordinary and hard-boiled as a real estate appraisal; other times it can sound fantastical and wifty and achingly naïve, informed by the last inklings of childhood—the musings of a balmy real estate appraiser assaying a wonderful and magical landscape that erodes from memory a little bit every day. The collision in his mind of what he understands, what he hears, what he figures out, what popular culture pours into him, what he knows, what he pretends to know, and what he imagines makes an interesting mess. The mess often has the form of what he will probably think like when he is a grown man, but the content of what he is like as a little boy.

He is old enough to begin imagining that he will someday get married, but at ten he is still convinced that the best thing about being married will be that he will be allowed to sleep in his clothes.

The physical means Orlean uses to deliver her information is print, for the most part, although one of her books and one of her essays have been made into films (*The Orchid Thief* and *Blue Crush*) and she's a regular on the lecture circuit. The place in which she composes and from which she sends her message is transitory: she travels around to conduct research and interviews; then she writes about them. All of her writing, however, tends to be tethered to other people, the ones she observes and interviews. The most distinctive feature of her prose is its substance: her use of rhetorical appeals, evidence and authority, style, and rhetorical methods of development.

ANALYZING THE RHETORICAL SITUATION

1. If Susan Orlean's purpose is to find the extraordinary in the ordinary, what is the exigence for her essay?

2. How does she work to respond to that exigence through her verbal discourse? How does her verbal discourse fit the problem?

3. What are the available means she taps to form her discourse? Where and how does she use the rhetorical appeals of ethos, pathos, and logos?

4. Whom or what does she use as evidence or authority?

5. What stylistic choices does Orlean make that enhance her response as a fitting one?

6. Which of the rhetorical methods of development (see page 54) does she use to shape her response? Which passages are built on those identifiable rhetorical methods?

7. Who might be Orlean's audience? How does her choice of available means suit her intended audience?

1. Some feature of college life is no doubt a source of dissatisfaction: living conditions, roommates, the commute, lack of family time, cost, instructors, or course offerings. Choose one of these features that is problematic for you and identify the means available to you for resolving that problem. Make sure that your available means reflect the three parts: (a) the physical means of delivering the information, (b) the place from which the information is created and sent, and (c) the rhetorical elements (including the rhetorical appeals) of the message itself. Be prepared to share your response with the rest of the class.

2. Consider a trial being held in your own town (a case involving murder, embezzlement, theft, assault, or arson, for example). As you keep up with local news (print, electronic, visual, gossip), try to determine the available means of persuasion being used by the prosecution and the defense. Also identify the means of persuasion that remain either unavailable to or untapped by either the defense or the prosecution. Make a list of possible reasons those specific means are not being used. Be prepared to share your findings with the rest of the class.

Reading a book introduction for available means English professor Michael Bérubé publishes widely about academic matters: curriculum, teaching loads, classroom management, and cultural studies. But with the birth of his second son, James (Jamie), Bérubé ventured into another kind of writing, writing aimed at a wider audience. The following excerpt is from the introduction to his chronicle of his family's experiences with Jamie, who has Down syndrome.

MICHAEL BÉRUBÉ
Excerpt from Life as We Know It

My little Jamie loves lists: foods, colors, animals, numbers, letters, states, classmates, parts of the body, days of the week, modes of transportation, characters who live on Sesame Street, and the names of the people who love him. Early last summer, I hoped his love of lists—and his ability to catalogue things *into* lists—would stand him in good stead during what would undoubtedly be a difficult "vacation" for anyone, let alone a three-year-old child with Down syndrome: a three-hour drive to Chicago, a rush-hour flight to La-Guardia, a cab to Grand Central, a train to Connecti-cut—and *then* smaller trips to New York, Boston, and Old Orchard Beach, Maine. Even accomplishing the first of these mission objectives—arriving safely at O'Hare—required a precision and teamwork I do not always associate with my family. I dropped off Janet and nine-year-old Nick at the terminal with the baggage, then took Jamie to long-term parking with me while they checked in, and then entertained Jamie all the way back to the terminal, via bus and shuttle train. We sang about the driver on the bus, and we counted all the escalator steps and train stops, and when we finally got to our plane, I told Jamie, *Look, there's Mommy and Nick at the gate! They're yelling that we're going to lose our seats! They want to know why it took us forty-five minutes to park the car!*

All went well from that point on, though, and in the end, I suppose you could say Jamie got as much out of his vacation as might any toddler being whisked up and down New England. He's a seasoned traveler, and he thrives on shorelines, family gatherings, and New Haven pizza. And he's good with faces and names.

Then again, as we learned toward the end of our brief stay in Maine, he doesn't care much for amusement parks. Not that Nick did either, at three. But apparently one of the attractions of Old Orchard Beach, for my wife and her siblings, was the small beachfront arcade and amusement park in town, which they associated with their own childhoods. It was an endearing strip, with a roller coaster just the right size for Nick—exciting, mildly scary, but with no loop-the-loops, rings of fire, or oppressive G forces. We strolled among bumper cars, cotton candy, games of chance and skill, and a striking number of French-Canadian tourists: perhaps the first time our two little boys had ever seen more than one Bérubé family in one place. James, however, wanted nothing to do with any of the rides, and though he loves to pretend-drive and has been on bumper cars before, he squalled so industriously before the ride began as to induce the bumper cars operator to let him out of the car and refund his two tickets.

Jamie finally settled in next to a train ride designed for children five and under or thereabouts, which, for two tickets, took its passengers around an oval layout and over a bridge four times. I found out quickly enough that Jamie didn't want to *ride* the ride; he merely wanted to stand at its perimeter, grasping the partition with both hands and counting the cars—one, two, three, four, five, six—as they went by. Sometimes, when the train traversed the bridge, James would punctuate it with tiny jumps, saying, "Up! Up! Up!" But for the most part, he was content to hang onto the metal bars of the partition, grinning and counting—and, when the train came to a stop, pulling my sleeve and saying, "More, again."

This went on for about half an hour, well past the point at which I could convincingly share Jamie's enthusiasm for tracking the train's progress. As it went on my spirits began to sink in a way I do not recall having felt before. Occasionally it will occur to Janet or to me that Jamie will always be "disabled," that his adult and adolescent years will undoubtedly be more difficult emotionally—for him and for us—than his early childhood, that we will never *not* worry about his future, his quality of life, whether we're doing enough for him. But usually these moments occur in the relative comfort of abstraction, when Janet and I are lying in bed at night and wondering what will become of us all. When I'm *with* Jamie, by contrast, I'm almost always fully occupied by taking care of his present needs rather than by worrying about his future. When he asks to hear the Beatles because he loves their cover of Little Richard's "Long Tall Sally," I just play the song, sing along, and watch him dance with delight; I do not concern myself with extraneous questions such as whether he'll ever distinguish early Beatles from late Beatles, Paul's songs from John's, originals from covers. These questions are now central to Nick's enjoyment of the Beatles, but that's Nick for you. Jamie is entirely *sui generis*, and as long as I'm with him I can't think of him as anything but Jamie.

I have tried. Almost as a form of emotional exercise, I have tried, on occasion, to step back and see him as others might see him, as an instance of a category, one item on the long list of human subgroups. *This is a child with Down syndrome*, I say to myself. *This is a child with a developmental disability.* It never works: Jamie remains Jamie to me. I have even tried to imagine him as he would have been seen in other eras, other places: *This is a retarded child.* And even: *This is a Mongoloid child.* This makes for unbearable cognitive dissonance. I can imagine that people might think such things, but I cannot imagine how they might think them in a way that prevents them from seeing Jamie *as* Jamie. I try to recall how I saw such children when I was a child, but here I guiltily draw a blank: I don't remember seeing them at all, which very likely means that I never quite saw them *as* children. Instead I remember a famous passage from Ludwig Wittgenstein's *Philosophical Investigations:* "'Seeing-as' is not part of perception. And for this reason it is *like* seeing, and then again *not* like." Reading Wittgenstein, I often think, is something like listening to a brilliant and cantankerous uncle with an annoying fondness for koans. But on this one, I know exactly what he means.

ANALYZING THE RHETORICAL SITUATION

1. Michael Bérubé is writing to an audience of general readers, not the academic audience for whom he regularly writes. Who might these general readers be? Think of specific people you know who might be interested in *Life as We Know It*.

2. What are the specific means available to Bérubé for reaching a general audience?

3. Working on your own or with a classmate, analyze the available means that Bérubé employs. What are the physical means by which he delivers his information? What is the place (physical, social, academic, and/or economic) from which he creates and sends his message?

4. As you continue to analyze the available means, consider the rhetorical elements of the message itself. In other words, account for Bérubé's use of the rhetorical appeals (ethos, pathos, and logos), evidence and authority, distinctive style, and rhetorical methods of development. Write for five to ten minutes, taking all of these elements into account. Be prepared to share your analysis with the rest of the class.

5. If you were writing an essay about a remarkable person, whom would you choose to write about? Who would make up your audience? What exigence might you create or perceive in order to shape a fitting response? What would be your purpose? What means would you use to deliver your message? Freewrite for ten minutes and be prepared to share your thoughts with the rest of the class.

Writing a Rhetorical Analysis

Now that you are familiar with the features of the rhetorical situation and the ways those features can be employed to shape a fitting response, you can use your knowledge to analyze the rhetoric of someone else.

Your task is to select and then analyze a written or visual text, one that appears to be a fitting response. You can choose from the texts presented in this or the previous chapter or find something else in print or online. What you are looking for is a piece of writing or a visual produced by a person or group with a vested interest in the effect of the words or image. The following two questions will help you determine if your selection is appropriate for a rhetorical analysis:

1. Is the text responding to an exigence that can be modified through verbal or visual discourse?

2. Is the response verbal (spoken or written) or visual discourse?

After you have selected a text, read it carefully, keeping in mind that the ultimate goal of a rhetorical analysis is twofold: to analyze how well the rhetorical elements work together to create a fitting response, and to assess the overall effectiveness of that response. Then, write answers to the following questions, using textual or visual evidence to support each answer:

1. Who is the author (or rhetor)? What credentials or expertise does the author have? What opinions or biases did the author bring to the text?

2. What is the exigence? How is it identified? Why is the author engaged with this exigence? Is this an exigence that can be modified through discourse?

3. Who is the audience for the message? What opinions or biases might the audience hold? How does the audience feel about this exigence? What relationship is the author trying to establish with the audience? And most important, can this audience modify or bring about a modification of the exigence? How?

4. Identify the rhetorical elements of the message itself. In other words, where and how does the author employ the rhetorical appeals of ethos, pathos, and logos? How does the author invoke credentials, goodwill, or good sense to establish ethos? How does the author use evidence (examples, statistics, data, and so forth) to establish logos? And how does the author create an emotional connection to establish pathos? Keep in mind that the rhetorical appeals can sometimes overlap.

5. What kind of language does the author use—plain or specialized, slang or formal? How does the language reveal the author's view of the intended audience?

6. What is the place (physical, social, academic, economic, and so on) from which the author creates and sends the response? What are the resources of that place? What are its constraints (or limitations)?

7. How does the author send the response to the audience? What medium does the author use? How private or public, accessible or inaccessible is the medium? What are the resources and the constraints of that medium?

The next part of your job is to consider whether the response is fitting and successful. To achieve that goal, respond in writing to this list of questions:

1. Is the author's intended audience a rhetorical audience? Draw on evidence from the text to support your answer.

2. If the audience is a rhetorical one, what can it do to resolve the exigence?

3. Does the response address and fit the exigence? How exactly? If not, how might the author reshape the response so that it does fit the exigence?

4. Is the response delivered in an appropriate medium that reaches its intended audience? If so, describe why the medium is appropriate. If not, explain how it could be adjusted so that it would be appropriate.

5. Can you think of other responses to similar rhetorical situations? What genre is commonly used to respond to these situations? Does the author of this piece use that genre? If not, what is the effect of going against an audience's expectations?

Now that you have carefully read the text and answered all of the questions, you are ready to write your rhetorical analysis. As you begin, search your answers for an idea that can serve as the basis for your thesis statement. For example, you might focus on the author's declared goal—if there is one—and whether it has been achieved. You might speak to how successfully the author has identified the rhetorical audience, shaped a fitting response, or employed the best available means. Or you might focus on the use of the rhetorical appeals and the overall success of that use. Whether you agree with the author—or not—is beside the point. Your job is to analyze—in a two- or three-page essay built on a clear thesis statement—how or how well the author has accomplished his or her purpose.

WORKING WITH YOUR AVAILABLE MEANS

Writing Processes: From Tentative Idea to Finished Product

Responsible rhetors always consider the rhetorical situation as they write; they know the importance of responding to an exigence with a purposeful message directed at a specific audience and delivered by the most appropriate means available. By paying careful attention to their audience, to the available means of delivery, as well as to the steps in their composing process, effective rhetors adjust their message until it comes as close to fulfilling their rhetorical purpose as conditions (resources and constraints) allow. In short, they know that successful communication takes time and effort—and often more than one draft. As you develop into a responsible and effective writer and speaker (rhetor), you'll want to reconsider your own writing processes and work to improve them.

In this chapter, you'll move through the three general steps of the writing process: planning, drafting, and revising. As you read about each of these steps, you'll learn when it's necessary to consider the components of the rhetorical situation covered in chapters 1 and 2 (exigence, sender, purpose, message, receiver, and context) and when to ignore them and just write. This chapter features an example of student writing, from the initial idea to the final draft. As you read the various versions of Anastasia "Stacy" Simkanin's work, you'll see how she took advantage of planning strategies, how she drafted and used feedback from peers to revise, and how she prepared her final draft for submission.

WRITE FOR FIVE.

Write for five minutes in response to each of the following questions. Be prepared to share your answers with the rest of the class.

1. When you receive a writing assignment, what is usually your first reaction? What do you look for in the assignment? What kinds of information are important for you to have before you get started?

2. What kinds of writing do you do regularly? Which of them seem to be work- or school-related? Which of them are personal? Which of the means of delivery available to you do you use most often? Make a list of the kinds of writing you do, categorizing them as work- or school-related or personal.

3. Compare your responses to questions 1 and 2 with those of two classmates. What surprised you about their responses? Pick two things a classmate wrote that made you rethink your answers; then rewrite those answers.

Finding Pleasure in Writing

Whether you realize it or not, you've been writing almost all your life. When you were a small child, you grabbed crayons, felt-tip markers, or chalk and wrote on whatever surfaces you could find: paper, coloring books, sidewalks, chalk boards, table tops, walls, lampshades. You might not yet have been talking fluently, but you were already "writing" words and images as well as your fine motor skills and developing linguistic expertise would allow. Like the human animal you are, you were marking your territory—leaving messages for the people who entered your world. When you learned to write cursive, with all its up and down strokes, loops, and ties, you may have felt the same kind of satisfaction that you felt when you scribbled on the sidewalk. You were moving forward into the adult world of writing, a world that feeds our primitive human need to make marks as well as to communicate with others.

As you think back on your earliest memories of writing (whether it was scribbling, printing, drawing, or cursive), keep in mind the process of writing that you practiced then. You gathered up your materials and set to work. The final result was pleasing and the entire process usually joyously simple—unless, of course, your fine motor skills hadn't developed enough to support a textbook cursive that your teacher approved. Many of you have been writing—and enjoying it—for years. One award-winning author cannot recall a time when she wasn't writing:

What do you remember about early writing experiences?

> Before I could write what might be called human words in the English language, I eagerly emulated grown-ups' handwriting in pencil scribbles. My first "novels" . . . were tablets of inspired scribbles illustrated by line drawings of chickens, horses and upright cats.
>
> —Joyce Carol Oates,
> "To Invigorate Literary Mind,
> Start Moving Literary Feet"

Like the writing you happily did as a child, college writing can also be satisfying, but that is not to say that it will *always* be joyous, let alone easy. The process might at times seem grueling, but the results can often be exhilarating, something you're proud of. If that weren't the case, then you wouldn't worry about writing well or care what your teacher thinks of your writing.

Perhaps the best way to make writing a pleasurable activity is to build on what you already do well and enjoy as you write. If you're a person who likes to explore a topic, you may already have a collection of special notebooks in which you jot down notes and observations, write freely about interesting topics, copy delicious phrases or sentences you've heard or read, and make rough outlines.

You may be a writer who especially likes composing the first draft—by hand or keyboard. Maybe you enjoy the tactile sensation of writing with a gel pen on a yellow legal pad or the friction of moving a felt-tipped pen across pulpy paper. Maybe you always draft with a word processor, entertaining yourself by connecting particular fonts with particular ideas in your draft. The word processor offers you the opportunity to rewrite phrase after phrase, sentence after sentence, tinkering that may be especially comforting and pleasurable for you.

Or maybe you're one of those writers who are relieved when they finish a draft so that they can use their energy to work with and against that draft. You may like to print out your piece, sit back in a comfortable chair, and read it line by line, penciling in new sentences, cutting out entire sections, fiddling with your word choice, drawing arrows for reorganizing your thinking. You might have a thesaurus, dictionary, and handbook in a stack nearby—maybe one of your special notebooks, too, so that you can work in some of your favorite phrases or thoughts. Writers who enjoy this final part of the writing process feel that the hardest part is over. These writers especially enjoy polishing their writing until they're proud to submit it. As internationally known writer Susan Sontag put it:

> You write in order to read what you've written and see if it's OK and, since of course it never is, to rewrite it—once, twice, as many times as it takes to get it to be something you can bear to reread.   —**Susan Sontag**, *Writers on Writing*

For writers like this, the enjoyment they get from rereading their revised work is the best part, whether or not they send it on to someone else to read.

Regardless of which parts of the process they enjoy most, all good writers move through a general, three-step writing process: planning, drafting, and revising. Each of these general steps has smaller steps within it, which is probably why no two writers move through these three basic stages in exactly the same way. Still, most experienced writers use some variation of the general writing process that we'll review in the rest of this chapter. Before we begin, take a few minutes to jot down answers to the following questions, which will reveal what parts of the writing process you already do well and already enjoy.

YOUR WRITING EXPERIENCES

1. What kind of writing do you do that gives you the most pleasure? Is it handwritten or keyboarded? Is it instant messages or planned, drafted, and revised essays? Why do you do this kind of writing?

2. Which of the means available to you for writing gives you the most pleasure? Makes you feel most confident?

3. How would you describe the process you go through to accomplish this pleasurable writing?

4. What part(s) of your writing process do you most enjoy? Find most difficult? Can you imagine any ways to make the difficult part easier or more enjoyable?

Recognizing an Exigence

Writing most often begins with an exigence, a reason to write, as you learned in chapter 1. The exigence may be as obvious as a due date for a written assignment, or it might be more subtle—a tug on you to respond. After attending a school board meeting and listening to the discussion of budget cuts, you may feel the need to write a letter to the editor of your local newspaper about the importance of music classes to schoolchildren. At the movie theater, you might find yourself wanting to speak to the manager when you see the sorry state of the restrooms. When you open your credit card statement and discover two mysterious charges on it, you are likely to call the 800 number to clear up the matter. Or you may be bothered by a controversy—such as that surrounding Pete Rose's nomination to the Baseball Hall of Fame—and feel the need to post your opinion online. Whatever your exigence, that's where you'll start. Your exigence is the answer to this question: what has prompted you to enter the conversation about this topic?

Responding to an Exigence through Planning, Drafting, and Revising

Much of the writing you do is writing that you initiate for personal reasons. But in college, you'll do a great deal of writing that has been assigned. If you're like Stacy Simkanin, you're entering the conversation about a particular topic because your teacher has asked you to. Stacy, an English major, discovered on the first day of the semester that she'd be expected to write an essay about technology for her writing and technology course. As she considered the exigence—an assignment—Stacy moved through the three basic steps of the writing process: planning, drafting, and revising.

What Happens during Planning?

Planning to write usually involves two steps: exploration and organization. Experienced writers employ a variety of methods for exploring a topic, or inventing things to say about it.

Planning involves exploration . . .

The most commonly used methods of exploration are listing, keeping a journal, freewriting, and questioning. But experienced writers also regularly use conversation, meditation, reading, and listening as ways to discover good ideas; they know that good ideas can come to them in all sorts of settings. In fact, many writers keep a pen and notebook by their bed because ideas often come to them just as they're falling asleep. They grab the notebook, scribble down their idea, and sleep soundly, no longer worried that they'll forget the idea.

As you plan your college writing assignments, you'll probably continue to rely on the methods that have worked for you in the past. When you're stuck, however, you'll probably try out a new method, if only as a way to jump-start your writing.

Listing As soon as you get some idea of what you'll be expected to write formally about, you may want to start—and keep up—a list of possibilities. Look over some of the lists you made in response to the questions in Write for Five. These are the kinds of lists that can propel your writing, as Stacy's list will demonstrate.

During the first week of school, Stacy jotted down a few ideas, with the hope that, as time went by, she'd keep adding possibilities for her formal essay. You can follow Stacy's example and keep your list going over a course of a few days. Or you can jot down all your ideas at one sitting, a kind of listing often referred to as **brainstorming**. What follows is the list Stacy made and kept adding to:

computers	Web searches	online concordance
chat rooms	Statistical Universe	downloadable essays
visual culture class	plagiarism	forum discussions
photo essays	convenience	electronic requests
quality	online databases	Internet
constantly developing	online course notes	time saver
full-length journal articles	classroom computers	Google

Keeping a journal Some writing instructors expect you to keep a weekly journal, either print or online, and submit it to the class every week. And that's a good idea: the more you write, the more you'll have to say. When you're writing in your journal, you don't need to be concerned with punctuation, grammar, spelling, and other mechanical features. If you write three pages a week for a journal or as part of your online class discussion, you may not be able to lift a ready-to-submit essay directly from your work, but you will have accumulated a pool of ideas from which to draw. But even more important, you will have been practicing getting thoughts into words.

In addition to writing journal entries to explore your topic, you might also use your journal to write out what you understand about your course assignments, along with your reactions to your reading or to class discussions or lectures. As Stacy considered her own upcoming assignment, she wrote in her ongoing electronic journal:

> I think I tend to take modern advances for granted, but when I look at how
>
> much more I use technology as a college student than I did, say, eight years ago
>
> as a junior high student, it's amazing to think of how much my studies have
>
> become dependent on it. I need computer access for almost everything anymore,
>
> from writing papers to sending emails to doing research on the Web. Not only

that, but some of my favorite classes have been those that incorporated some form of technology into the course format. I think this is one of technology's major advantages--turning learning into something new and interactive, which gets students involved. I've had courses that used technology in basic ways, like my Biological Science class, in which the class lectures were recorded and saved online for students to listen to later. Some of my other courses, though, have used it in lots of interesting ways. In one of my English classes, for instance, we took a day to hold class in a chat room, and we all signed into the room from our computers at home. It was great as part of our discussions about literacy, because experimenting with computer literacy allowed us all to see how people communicate differently when they're not face to face. Of course, some people would argue that kids my age spend way too much time "chatting," and that Instant Messenger is one of a student's biggest distracters. I guess, like any good thing, technology also carries with it some disadvantages.

Freewriting Freewriting means just what it says: it's the writing you do that costs you nothing. You don't have to worry about spelling or grammar; you don't even have to worry about writing complete sentences, because no one is going to grade it. In fact, no one (except you, of course) may ever even read it. It's the kind of writing you do to loosen up your thinking and your fingers; it's the kind of no-pressure writing that can, nevertheless, yield an explosion of ideas.

When Stacy's teacher asked everyone in class to write for five minutes about the connection between technology and their college success, Stacy wrote:

> Spanish 3: used chat room discussion.
>
> English 202: used chat room discussion to analyze Internet communication as it relates to literacy.
>
> English 202 and Phil 197: used ANGEL's online forums.

Being an English major, I tend to see the biggest advantages of modern technology as those that have most helped my writing. My courses require hours of writing from me each week, and I know that, without access to all the Web resources that have been available to me, the amount of time I have to spend working on a paper would probably double. For instance, technology helps me write a research paper before I've even typed the first word, because I can research my topic so much faster by first consulting the online catalogues, instead of going to the library and getting lost in the stacks. If there is material I need that this library doesn't have, I simply have it sent to me through interlibrary loan. Then, when I actually start writing, the process is made easier through referencing certain Web sites that I can't live without. I don't think I've written a single paper as a college student without consulting an online dictionary, thesaurus, reference page, or concordance . . . and sometimes I use all four resources in the course of writing a single paper. And once I'm finished writing my paper, I can use any one of a number of Web pages that are designed to show the proper way to cite any resources I may have used. Of course, there are also some things that students get from the Web that they'd be better to stay away from, such as downloadable essays and book notes that help you skip out of actually reading a text. With technology being so accessible, so fast, so convenient, so easy to use, so full of information, etc., it can be hard to make sure you don't rely on it *too much*. For instance, I don't think it's a good idea to always use information from the Internet as a replacement for going to the library, because sometimes I've found that the perfect resource for a paper I'm writing is sitting on a shelf in the University Library. I think the best way for students to make use of modern advances is to draw on them to help build their own ideas and abilities, and not use them as a means of avoiding any real work.

Notice how Stacy starts with a list of some courses that used technology. She doesn't seem to be heading in any one direction. Then—she's off and running about how the use of technology affects her life as an English major.

After trying several methods of exploration (listing, keeping a journal, and freewriting), Stacy found that she was starting to repeat herself. She didn't yet have a point she wanted to make, let alone a **thesis**, a controlling idea for her essay. She needed to try a new tack.

Questioning Sometimes when you're in a conversation, someone will ask you a question that takes you by surprise—and then forces you to rethink your position or think about the topic in a new way. By using structured questioning, you can push yourself to explore your topic more deeply.

There are two sets of questions that can readily serve your purpose: journalists' questions and the pentad. You're probably already familiar with the **journalists' questions**: *Who? What? Where? When? Why? How?* As Stacy answered these questions, she began to form an opinion about her topic.

<u>Who</u> is using technology? Teachers, students, librarians--everyone on campus, it seems. But I'm going to talk about how it affects me.

<u>What</u> technology is being used, and what is it being used for? All kinds of technology, from email and Web searches to PowerPoint presentations and voice mail, is being used, for instruction, homework, student-to-student communication, student-and-teacher communication, and research. I'm going to concentrate on my use of computer technology, mostly access to the Web.

<u>Where</u> is technology being used? At the library, in the classroom, but most often in my bedroom, where my computer is.

<u>When</u> is technology being used? Usually at night, after I come home from classes and am doing my homework.

<u>Why</u> do students use or not use technology? I use it because it's more convenient than walking over to the library and searching. Not all students have Internet access in their apartments; others may not know all the online research techniques that I know.

<u>How</u> are students using it? Some students are using it to advance their educations; others are using it to subvert it (like downloading essays and cheating schemes).

Rhetorician and philosopher Kenneth Burke.

Kenneth Burke's **pentad** offers you another way to explore your topic, your thoughts on that topic, and what you've already written about it. Often referred to as the **dramatistic pentad**, this method leads you to analyze relationships among the *act*, *actor*, *scene*, *agency*, and *purpose*. Stacy needed to consider each of these five components of the pentad in terms of the question it raised:

- *Act.* What is happening?
- *Actor.* Who is doing it?
- *Scene.* What are the time, place, and conditions in which the act occurred?
- *Agency.* How was the act accomplished?
- *Purpose.* How and why did the act, actor, scene, and agency come together?

Considered this way, the relationship between technology and learning began to take on more definite meaning for Stacy:

What is the relationship between using technology (the act) at school and me

(the actor)?

Where (the scene) and why (the purpose) do I use technology at school?

How (the agency) do I use technology?

How did I come to be reliant on technology (again, the purpose)?

As Stacy answered these questions, she realized that she conducts most of her research and does most of her writing in her bedroom. Although she thinks she should spend more time in the library to see what she might discover there, she rarely goes. Instead, she conducts research online, drafts and revises online, and emails her instructor a final, ready-to-be-graded essay.

Stacy didn't need to think about the genre in which she would write: her instructor had already determined that fitting responses would take the form of an academic essay. But situations will arise when you need to determine which genre is most appropriate. The genre you choose should fulfill your purpose and be deliverable through a medium that will reach your intended audience. In other words, picking the most effective genre is key to making the best use of your available means.

Here are some other tips for determining which genre is appropriate to your rhetorical situation:

- Consider who else has been faced with a similar rhetorical situation and what genre(s) they used in response.
- Locate one or more examples to identify common characteristics of a genre, such as the kind of language used (formal or informal, for example), where and how the rhetorical appeals of ethos, logos, and pathos are used, and what kind of evidence is used and how it is presented.
- Ask yourself whether it is most appropriate to use a genre that has been used in similar situations or whether an unexpected genre would have the effect you want. Similarly, you can ask whether your response should employ all the characteristics of others in that genre or if there is a good reason for it to diverge in some ways.
- Finally, consider your available means. To what means of delivery do you have access? If you're writing in an academic context, what means of delivery are you expected to use and what kinds of specialized audiences are you addressing? How do these factors influence your choice of genre?

. . . and planning involves organization

Once you've explored your topic as thoroughly as you can, it's time to begin organizing your essay. Two simple methods can help you get started: clustering and outlining.

Clustering **Clustering** is a visual method for connecting ideas that go together. You might start with words and phrases from a list you compiled or brainstormed and link them with arrows, circles, or lines, the way Stacy does. Notice

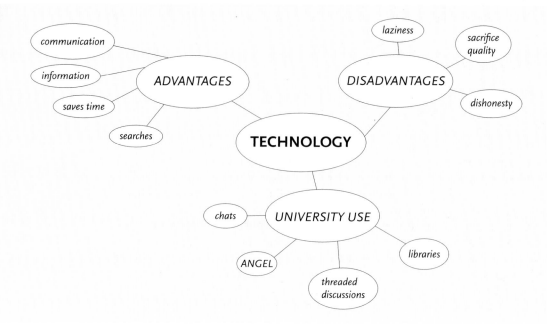

Stacy's clustering.

how Stacy uses different fonts and sizes of type to accentuate the connections she wants to make between technology and learning. (You might want to use color as well to help you make connections.) Interestingly, she hasn't yet put herself into the essay's plan.

Outlining An outline establishes the limits of your topic at the same time as it lists the main parts. Outlining is a good way to plan, but only if you allow yourself to add and delete points and move things around, if you consider yours a rough outline, not a formal one. Like clustering, outlining helps you visualize how things relate to one another. Stacy's outline shows a close relationship to her clustering, but she's added details and a general title:

Technology and Learning

I. Advantages

    Information

        fast and convenient

        online catalogues

        eBay's First Edition or Rare Books page

        online concordances

        databases

Communication

    ANGEL

    online forums

    new forms of interaction

    chat rooms

II. Disadvantages

    Academic laziness

        ignore traditional forms of research

        quality vs. convenience

        lose the value of a trip to the library

    Dishonesty

        free online book notes

        downloadable essays

        plagiarism

Notice that Stacy started out using Roman numerals for her main sections, the way we were taught to outline in elementary school. But she switched to simply listing subpoints, thereby making her outline easier to put together and work with.

WRITE FOR FIVE

Write for five minutes in response to each of the following questions. Be prepared to share your answers with the rest of the class.

1. What was the last exigence you responded to in writing? Why did you choose to respond to it?

2. How did you go about exploring possible responses? Which of the invention strategies did you employ?

3. How did you begin organizing your response? What organizational methods did you explore? How was your response organized in its final form? Did you use chronological, emphatic, or some other system of ordering?

4. What means did you use to deliver your response? Was it the only means available to you, or did you choose it from several available means?

5. Compare your answers with those of two classmates. What surprised you about their answers? List two things a classmate wrote that made you rethink your own answers. Then rewrite those answers.

What Happens during Drafting?

After you've explored your topic and loosely organized your paper, you'll begin drafting, another two-step process that includes writing the first draft (or several drafts) and evaluating that draft. During the drafting stage you begin weighing more heavily all the elements of the rhetorical situation (see chapter 1). For some writers, that first draft is the toughest part of the process. For others, however, the joy of putting words onto a surface is exhilarating; for them, the first draft is a combination of an outline and a freewrite. A first draft is just that—you'll revisit it to evaluate and adjust your message to fit your rhetorical situation.

Up until this point, Stacy was writing for herself (she was both sender and receiver of her message), and her lists, outlines, and so forth were casual and exploratory. Some of them were handwritten or drawn, others keyboarded. Some were short, others long. What they all had in common was that none of them were graded or judged.

A writer begins to (re)consider audience . . .

Next, Stacy needed to begin a draft that her instructor would read and respond to. Stacy approached her instructor, asking him if he might give her some direction. Specifically, she wanted to know how she might most productively write an essay that addressed the requirements of the course. Here's what her teacher proposed:

> Consider me your audience as you write a three- to four-page essay in which you describe the ways the campus computer system does (or could) support your learning. In this essay, you'll need to describe the current system, explain its beneficial consequences, and perhaps provide recommendations for how it could be improved. Your paper is due two weeks from today.

This assignment provides Stacy with a firm exigence for writing: she has an assignment with a due date. It also supplies her with a receiver of her paper (her message): her instructor is her audience. Now that she knows to whom she is writing, she can gauge the amount of detail and information she needs to use. After all, her instructor knows a good deal about technology and writing, but he may not know what technological services are available to his students, let alone how good students like Stacy use these services.

. . . context, including constraints, . . .

The context seems to be the course, Writing and Technology. The assignment also provides some constraints on Stacy's writing: her message must be at least three pages long and no more than four; it must include a description of the technology she's referring to, or a list of consequences (how the system *does* support her learning), and perhaps some recommendations (how the system *could* support her learning); and it is due in two weeks.

. . . and other elements of the rhetorical situation

Given these constraints, Stacy doesn't know whether her purpose will be to inform, explain, or analyze; she will have to wait and see what her first draft reveals, which parts of the assignment take root and thrive.

By thinking of her assignment as a rhetorical situation, Stacy has a better idea of how to approach her draft. In fact, when an instructor doesn't write out an assignment, you should feel free to ask him or her to explain it in terms of the rhetorical situation—that is, ask your instructor specific questions about purpose, audience (or receiver), context, and constraints.

Here is Stacy's first draft.

Technology for teaching and learning is especially strong here at State. It provides many advantages for students and teachers alike, but it also brings with it some disadvantages. In this essay, I'm going to talk about my experiences with technology, the advantages I've experienced and the disadvantages I feel. I'll draw upon my experiences in Spanish 3, English 202, Philosophy 197, Biological Sciences, Art History, and my internship.

Technology is rapidly becoming increasingly advanced, and much of it is used to enhance learning and writing. Not only does it increase the amount of information available, but it allows for stronger writing. I can search libraries around the world, use eBay to find rare manuscripts, use interlibrary loan, and file electronic requests for needed items.

Technology also makes the writing process faster, more convenient. I often access online concordances, view library books on my PC, email librarians, and read full-text journal articles online. This technology is also allowing for more ways to develop ideas and new forms of written communication. For instance, I'm now experienced with chat room communication, forum discussions, and photo essays.

But at the same time that technology brings these advantages, it also inhibits learning and writing. I know that when I'm conducting online research I may be missing out on information or lowering the quality of information because I'm limiting my searching to electronic sources. Nowadays, students don't really have to learn to use the library, where often more information can be found than what appears on an online search. I fear that students are placing convenience over quality. I know I do sometimes. The information online isn't always reliable, either. Students don't often take the time to investigate sources.

For these reasons, campus technology may be promoting academic laziness in some students, and dishonesty as well. So much information is available that you can practically write a book report without ever reading the book. And online papers make plagiarism easy.

In conclusion . . .

Stacy's first draft begins to address the components of the rhetorical situation: she understands that she needs to talk about her own experiences with technology and describe the technology that she uses. As she gets her thoughts down, she's beginning to sketch out an organizational structure that starts with the advantages of this technology and ends with the disadvantages. She makes certain to add that some students take advantage of technology only in a way that cheapens their learning experience. Notice that she hasn't begun to shape a strong thesis yet, let alone a conclusion. Still, she's ready to begin revising.

WRITE FOR FIVE

1. What methods do you use to launch your first draft?
2. What's the easiest part of drafting for you? The most difficult? Why?
3. How does having a specific sense of audience help or hinder you?
4. Many writers concentrate on the big picture when drafting; others find themselves slowing down and filling in some details as well. How would you describe your process of producing a first draft? Be prepared to share your answers with the rest of the class.
5. How does your means of delivery affect your process? In other words, which means of delivery help or hinder you?

What Happens during Revision?

Revision means evaluating and rethinking your writing in terms of the rhetorical situation. Writers use several techniques during revision. Some put the draft aside for 24 hours or more in order to return to it with fresh ideas and a more objective viewpoint. Others like to print out the draft and actually cut it into different sections so that they can experiment with organization. One of the most popular—and most effective—revision techniques is called peer evaluation.

A writer evaluates and rethinks a draft . . .

After composing her first draft, it was time for Stacy to begin evaluating her draft and think about revising, rethinking her writing in terms of her rhetorical situation. Naturally, she read through her draft and evaluated it herself, but she also took advantage of **peer evaluation**, a form of collaboration that provides productive advice and response from a fellow student writer. If the thought of letting a peer (a classmate or friend) read your first draft makes you uncomfortable, if you've tried peer evaluation before and it didn't work, or if you're worried that you won't receive good advice, please reconsider. All effective writing is the result of some measure of collaboration, whether between colleagues, editors and writers, publishers and writers, actors and writers, students and teachers, or friends. Just consider for a moment all the writing you read, hear, and see every day—newspapers, magazines, online chat, billboards, commercials, sitcoms, newscasts. All of the words that you experience on a daily basis come to you as a result of collaboration and peer evaluation. Every day, experienced writers are showing their first drafts to someone else in order to get another point of view, advice, and evaluation.

Peer evaluation is a valuable step in the writing process that you, too, will want to experience. No matter how good a writer you are, you'll benefit from hearing what one or more real receivers have to say about your message. They may ask you questions so that you clarify the points you want to make, nudge you to provide more examples so that your prose comes alive, or point out attention-getting passages. When you respond to a peer's first draft, you'll not only be helping that writer, but you'll also strengthen your own skills as a reader and writer. As you discover strengths and weaknesses in someone else's writing, you can also look for them in your own. Most important, the successful writing of a peer will energize your own writing in ways that the successful writing of a professional might not. A peer can show you how attainable good writing can be.

. . . in terms of a rhetorical situation

Although it is sometimes helpful to get pointers on things like grammar and word choice, you'll usually want a peer reviewer to focus first on how well your draft responds to your rhetorical situation. The following set of ten questions can help guide a peer reviewer:

PEER EVALUATION QUESTIONS

1. What is the exigence for this essay?
2. What is the topic of this essay? What is the main idea the writer wants to make about this topic?
3. What can you tell about the writer of this essay? What is his or her relationship to this topic?
4. Who is the audience? What information in the essay reveals the audience to you? What do you imagine are the needs and concerns of this audience?
5. What seems to be the relationship between the writer and the audience? How is the writer meeting the needs and concerns of this audience? What specific passages demonstrate the writer's use of the rhetorical appeals (ethos, pathos, and logos)?
6. What is the purpose of the writer's message? What is the relationship among the writer, the audience, and the writer's purpose? Do you have any other comments about the purpose?
7. What means is the writer using to deliver this message? How is this means appropriate to the situation?

8. What constraints are on the writer and this message?
9. What idea or passage in the essay is handled most successfully? Least successfully?
10. What are two questions you have for this writer?

These questions can be answered fairly quickly. Although you might be tempted to go through them quickly and orally, you'll be better served if you ask the peer reviewer to write his or her answers either on a separate piece of paper or directly on your draft. When it's your turn to evaluate a peer's draft, you may well come away from the experience surprised at how much you learned about your own writing. There's no better way to improve your own understanding than to explain it to someone else.

The peer reviewer of Stacy's paper offered her a good deal of advice, most of which had to do with large-scale revising, as you can see from his responses to questions 6 and 9:

6. I cannot tell for sure what your purpose is in writing this essay. You describe technology, but I'm not sure why. Do you want to explain the opportunities, or do you want to show how bad it can be for students? And I cannot tell who you're writing to--maybe just any reader? Still, I think you have a good start on a strong essay because you know so much neat stuff about all the technology here at school. I didn't know half this stuff.

9. The beginning of your essay is the least successful part; I can't tell by reading it where you're headed with your topic, so I think you're going to want to revise with a stronger purpose in mind. But like I said earlier, the strongest part of your essay is all the specific information you already know about using technology. No wonder you get such good grades. Oh, you don't have any conclusion yet. I think if you get a better start on your introduction that you can pull together your overall argument in your conclusion. Maybe talk about how technology is always thought of as being better, an improvement, but that it's not always, not really.

The peer reviewer confirmed what Stacy already thought: the beginning of her essay needed work. She knew that now would be the time to focus on her thesis statement. Earlier in this chapter, a **thesis** was defined as a controlling idea. More specifically, a **thesis statement** is a central idea stated in the form of an assertion, or **claim**, which indicates what you believe to be true, interesting, or valuable about your topic. A thesis statement also gives readers a clear idea of your purpose in writing, and it sometimes outlines the approach you'll take.

Although it is often phrased as a single sentence, it doesn't need to be. Here is Stacy's first attempt at a thesis statement:

> Technology provides many advantages for students and teachers alike, but it also brings with it some disadvantages. In this essay, I'm going to talk about my experiences with technology, the advantages I've experienced and the disadvantages I feel.

This is a fine start, as Stacy identifies her topic—technology (and its use by students and teachers)—and forecasts that she will be talking about both advantages and disadvantages. Given that the peer reviewer was unclear about her purpose in writing, Stacy knows that she will want to think about her purpose and audience to create a thesis statement that narrows her topic and makes a comment on that topic.

Editing and Proofreading

Although the peer reviewer focused on Stacy's approach to the rhetorical situation, other evaluative responses had to do with smaller issues related to **editing**: improving word choice, adding specific details, and structuring sentences more effectively.

> I think the easiest way for you to get started with your revision is to go through what you've already written and add specific details throughout. You might not use all this information, but at least you'll have it to choose from. For instance, when you talk about the way technology makes writing more convenient, you list some library and online tools. But you don't show your reader (who is your audience?) exactly why you'd use these tools. If you've already used them successfully, then tell the rest of us how you did it--and why.

The peer review didn't harm Stacy's confidence as she moved forward with her essay. Fortunately, she's already a good college writer. And some of that confidence comes from being a good proofreader and editor. After all, her rough draft didn't have any small-scale problems of punctuation, grammar, spelling, or mechanics, the errors you focus on when you're proofreading.

Although revising, editing, and proofreading are often done simultaneously, you might be better off focusing on revising first—getting the big issues taken care of—before you focus on editing and proofreading, which can often be done at the same time, or one right after the other.

After the peer reviewer finished responding to Stacy's essay (and she to his), Stacy took his advice, wrote two more drafts, and edited and proofread her way to her final draft. Like most writers, Stacy stopped revising because she'd run out of time—not because she thought her essay was perfect in every way.

WRITE FOR FIVE

1. How do you define *revision?*
2. When do you revise? Can you name the last piece of writing that you revised? Why did you choose to revise that particular piece?
3. What are your strengths as a reviser? Your weaknesses?
4. What features of revision do you like to have help with?
5. What features of proofreading and editing are your strengths? Which could you use help with? Be prepared to share your answers with the rest of the class.

A Final Draft

Stacy's final draft appears on the following pages. She formatted her paper according to Modern Language Association (MLA) guidelines (see chapter 21).

Anastasia Simkanin

Professor Glenn

Writing and Technology, English 270

October 22, 2006

Technology and the Learning Process: One Student's View

Could today's college student survive without a microwave to heat Easy Mac in her dorm room, a computer to send instant messages to her friends down the hall, and a DVD player to escape the tedium of *another* evening spent doing homework? The answer is debatable. What's *not* debatable, however, is that though technology of various forms has brought a certain ease to the life of today's youths, it has also allowed the modern college student to embark on serious academic pursuits that would not be possible without technological innovation. [1]

The Internet, for instance, offers students a wealth of advanced search engines and online library databases. Many students find that such tools open up a world of information, allowing for more expedient research and, in turn, stronger student essays. But some people argue that the ease of computer-searching and the availability of almost anything over the Internet exposes students to the dangers of academic laziness and dishonesty. Which side is right? The incorporation of technology into the learning process is a complex matter and, as with any powerful innovation, poses possible setbacks alongside its advances. Perhaps the best way to approach both sides of the issue is to draw a clear picture of the pros and cons, thereby assessing the different ways that technology has revolutionized learning in today's universities. [2]

[1] The thesis statement makes a comment on a narrowed topic.

[2] Stacy forecasts her approach, which involves looking at both pros and cons of technology. This sentence also clarifies her purpose: to assess technology's dynamic effect on learning.

One major way that modern advances have facilitated the learning process is by supplying students with a wealth of information that could not be obtained without Internet resources. Online catalogues such as WorldCat, for instance, allow users to search libraries anywhere in the world for books, articles, serials, and more in a single step. Borrow Direct allows students to simultaneously search all Ivy League university libraries, and the CIC Virtual Electronic Library allows the same type of search within Big 10 schools. [3] Alternatively, students can opt to go to a specific library Web page, such as Oxford University libraries' online catalogue, and begin their search there. With such a vast array of resources available, only very rarely is a student unable to find the information he or she wants. Once a patron has located a needed item, she can file an electronic request through interlibrary loan and have it delivered to a location of her choosing. A State U student who needs a rare manuscript located only at the University of Cambridge can view important pages online. Whereas once a student's research was limited to the resources in her own neighborhood, technology now allows a student access to information in libraries across the Atlantic.

[3] This is one of the many places where Stacy takes the peer reviewer's suggestion to include specific details about using resources.

[4] This transition sentence links this paragraph to the preceding paragraph.

[4] Not only does the Internet allow users to find information that is hard to obtain because it's held in distant locations, but it also allows access to information that is hard to obtain for a variety of other reasons. On those rare occasions that students are unable to find a needed item by searching the library catalogues, they can look through sites such as eBay's First Edition or Rare Books page and possibly locate a volume that is to be found only in someone's living room.

Besides searching *for* books, technology has simplified searching *through* them as well. Writing a paper on *Great Expectations* and want to know the exact spot where Pip admits Biddy is "immeasurably better than Estella"? Web resources such as the Concordance of Great Books allow users to type in a word or phrase and instantly see all the occurrences of those words in a book, along with the surrounding text and chapter numbers. The above quote, by the way, is found in chapter 17 of the Penguin edition.

Even with all the time it can save a student, the average dot-com site is not necessarily the top rung when it comes to the ladder of searching expediency. Today's students can easily write stronger, more persuasive papers by taking advantage of the information that online databases place at their fingertips. Compare, for instance, the effect of saying "State U conferred many doctoral degrees in the year 2000" with the effect of saying "State University conferred 513 doctoral degrees in the year 2000." **[5]** Including statistics in a paper can make one's points sharper and more vivid, and databases such as Statistical Universe allow students to achieve this result. Other databases, such as JSTOR and MUSE, let students sort through full-length journal articles simply by moving their mouse. With libraries containing thousands of volumes of journals and periodicals, the amount of time saved through computer searches is invaluable. And, of course, consulting Statistical Universe is a lot faster than surveying the 6,165 graduate students who were enrolled at State U in the year 2000.

Not only is technology improving traditional methods of research and writing, but it's also providing students with new ways to communicate and

[5] Stacy uses another specific detail that makes the essay more persuasive.

develop ideas. State U's ANGEL page is designed to give professors and students online space for managing their courses. By accessing the page, students can click on the link for a course and view daily reminders, weekly assignments, selected lecture notes, and more. A favorite feature of the ANGEL site is its threaded discussion board. Online forums allow students to carry on the one-on-one discussion that is precluded by large class size and limited lecture time. As an additional step in carrying course discussion beyond the classroom setting, some instructors at State U--especially those who teach language classes--have experimented with "holding class" in a chat room. Online chats allow students to carry on multiple conversations at once, which gives them more opportunities to share and develop ideas. The fact that most students enjoy chat room discussion is an added bonus, as the appeal of what's "new" and "fun" can go a long way in keeping students interested and eager to learn.

With all the ways that technology is changing life for students, it's to be expected that some of the effects will be less welcome than others. One possible downfall of relying on technology is that, ironically, ignoring more traditional ways of research can sometimes cause students to lose information, or at least information quality. Searching a library's database from home while a stereo plays in the background is more appealing to most students than taking a trip to the stacks, but what many don't realize is that, though online catalogues are a great place to start, they may not be enough to give students all they need to know. Finding the approximate spot where a needed item is located and then perusing those shelves will almost always turn up more results than would an online catalogue search alone. When it comes to finding that approximate location, however, the catalogues are indeed the place to begin. The danger lies in falling into the trap of placing convenience over quality. What many students find to be most convenient are simple online searches using an engine like Google, but this method carries its own set of problems. Anyone can create a page on the Internet, meaning that my 14-year-old brother could post his paper on how Jane Eyre's inheritance reveals Brontë's secret obsession with the power of money. Would such a paper help a college student write a sophomore-level essay? Probably not. Being lured into the convenience of Web searches, students can sometimes forget to investigate the reliability of their sources, thus compromising the quality of their own work.

Perhaps the most serious dangers of depending too much on technology are the possibilities of academic laziness and dishonesty. There is *so* much information available online today that a student can practically write a paper on a book without even opening it. Sites like SparkNotes.com are great when you're running late for class and need to quickly find out what happens in a particular chapter of a text, or when you want to refresh your memory of what you've read earlier, but a student will never get as much out of summary notes as she will out of reading the book herself. But with free online literature notes replacing $5.99-a-copy *Cliffs Notes*, the temptation to skip out on one's assignments is becoming all the more pervasive.

More serious than simply consulting book notes is another issue that no one likes to approach: plagiarism. Not only are notes on books available online, but so are entire essays on them. Whole sites are devoted to selling papers to students who are looking to avoid writing an essay themselves, and papers are sometimes available for free. Every college student knows the feeling of sitting at a computer screen late at night, trying to write a paper but having little success doing so because it's 2 a.m. Times like these are when the temptation to abuse modern advances sets in, and a student might think of how easy it would be to simply download someone else's essay, hand it in as her own, and get some sleep. While having an abundance of information available is usually a wonderful thing, today's college students especially need to be wary of letting technology do their work *for* them, rather than just help it along.

With technology affecting the learning process in so many ways, it's hard to say that it's wholly positive or wholly negative. Perhaps it wouldn't be fair to say either, and to agree, instead, that though the value of Web content depends upon how one uses it, the dramatic changes that have been brought on by recent advances are amazing. Technology is changing the way we learn and the way we write. Visual Culture, a 400-level State U English course, encourages students to "write" essays in new ways, using images instead of words. Many students choose to obtain their images off the Net, or to present their photo essay in the form of a PowerPoint presentation. With "writing an essay" no longer requiring actual *writing*, there's little--if any--room to doubt that education today is being constantly shaped and molded as technology continues to progress. **[6]** Let's wait and see what the future brings.

[6] Closing the essay with a focus on a course at her school demonstrates Stacy's awareness of her audience, her instructor.

YOUR WRITING EXPERIENCES

1. Where does your best writing appear? What qualities of this writing help you judge it to be your best?

2. What writing do you feel most proud of? Why does this writing make you feel proud?

3. On the occasions when you write especially well, what is the exigence? Who is your audience? What is your purpose? What is the context? What is your medium for writing?

4. After reading this chapter and studying Stacy's writing process, describe two specific ways in which you could improve your writing process. Be prepared to share your improvements with the rest of the class.

2

RHETORICAL SITUATIONS FOR WRITERS

You already know how to engage in rhetorical situations that call for your response; after all, for most of your life, you've been observing the elements of the situation (exigence, audience, message, purpose, and context) in order to shape your purposeful message into the most fitting response. The following eight chapters will help you become more familiar with types of writing you've likely already practiced, even if you don't know them by the names used here. You'll come to understand how memoirs, profiles, investigative reports, position arguments, proposals, critical reviews, critical analyses, and literary analyses can serve as appropriate responses to rhetorical situations. As you work through the chapters, you'll recognize the everyday nature of rhetorical theory and practice. In addition, you'll understand how well you're already using rhetorical techniques, how you resort to these kinds of writing as your response, and how you can quickly become even more skillful in their use.

4 | SHARING THE EXPERIENCE OF TASTE: RESPONDING WITH MEMOIRS

Many college students—and former students—have had highly animated conversations about the cafeteria food at their schools. Legends have been passed down through the generations about the quality of the food and the havoc it could wreak on unsuspecting students. *Boston Globe* reporter Taryn Plumb interviewed University of New Hampshire students who "expressed unease about the long-standing rumor—common to many college campuses—that servers mix laxatives into recipes to safeguard against food poisoning or botulism." In his January 2000 article "Fond Memories of a Congenital Glutton," on the Web site epinions.com, Jonathan Kibera offered a different rumor, which circulated among the students

at Harvard University: "We used to joke that there was one chicken dish at Harvard, the left-overs of which were reheated under different names throughout the week. General Wong's chicken on Monday had morphed into some greasy Kung Pao derivative by Wednesday, and could well have been the Soup du Jour by Friday."

Chances are that more than once during your times in the college cafeteria you've longed for a home-cooked meal. Some alumni, though, carry fond memories of the food they enjoyed while relaxing with their friends after a long day of classes. Readers of the food-related Web site Chowhound.com, which its creators describe as being "for those who live to eat," were asked to post stories about their college dining experiences in order to determine which college has the best food. Sixty responses were posted. One University of Southern California graduate remembered:

> The dorms had a great selection of hot and cold food, a salad and fruit bar and a grill with chicken sandwiches, hamburgers and hotdogs that were pretty good. They had international stations with make your own pasta bars and asian fast food. As for the rest of campus. . . . Wolfgang Puck's Cafe, Betty Crocker baked goods, a sushi/asian bar with full time sushi chef, asian and mexican fast food (not taco bell) and they even have a sit down restaurant called "Upstairs Commons" (not sure of the actual name, but that was what everybody called it) where you could order a real sit down meal with linen, menus and waiters.

Other contributors to the online discussion expressed longing for their school's unique delicacies. "Lidi B" of Penn State University opined, "Oh, to have a grilled sticky from the Ye Olde College Diner a la mode with Penn State Creamery ice cream . . . that would just about be heaven . . . ," and "Quick" from Cornell University admitted, "I still remember the great reuben and chicken salad sandwiches from Cascadeli, the Dijon burger and roast chicken from Ivy room, and the awesome breakfasts from Hughes." For each of these contributors, the thoughts of college food brought back pleasant memories—not only of the food itself but also of fun and relaxation with friends.

Memoirs are a kind of writing used to narrate and analyze significant experiences in our lives, including those concerning certain foods. Food-related memoirs, which are appearing in greater numbers on bookshelves around the world, present past experiences with food that resonate with a larger historical, psychological, or social meaning. Diana Abu-Jaber's memoir of her childhood in upstate New York and Jordan, for example, centers on food but is also a reflection on living between two cultures. In other words, a good food-related memoir, like any memoir, is a kind of history that captures distinctive moments in the life of the writer and the larger society. Food memories are primarily sensory, starting with an aroma, a texture, or a visual delight but then encompassing an event, an occasion, or an interaction.

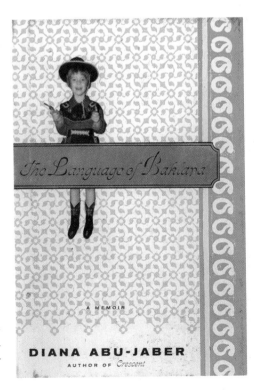

This food truck at UCLA will no doubt become part of many students' memories.

Real Situations

Many food memories, like the ones the three alumni posted online at Chowhound.com, are positive. On a discussion forum for Roadfood's Web site, "Mosca" reminisced similarly about a food truck just off Cornell's campus: "After 30 years I can still taste the (great) heartburn from the Ithaca hot truck, which was the source of my personal 'freshman 15.'" That hot truck is just one of numerous food trucks serving college campuses today or in the past, such as the "Chinese Kitchen" at Harvard, the grease trucks at Rutgers, "Chuck's" at the University of Miami, and the enchilada trucks at the University of Arizona.

Here's an example of another delightful food memory that involves the candy that brings many positive memories for people of all ages—chocolate. Clotilde Dusoulier, the author of the blog "Chocolate & Zucchini," prefers to enjoy high-quality chocolate with fresh coffee because for her, together they simply make for happiness.

What Clotilde Dusoulier sees as a recipe for happiness.

On a Sunday afternoon, after a copious lunch, wait for your next-door neighbor Patricia to knock on your window with a wooden spoon. Agree to come over to their place for coffee. From the special chocolate cabinet in your kitchen (surely you must have one) grab what's left of the excellent dark chocolate with fragments of roasted cocoa beans that your friend Marie-Laure brought you last time she came for dinner. Walk next door in your socks. Leave Maxence and Stéphan to chat about Mac OS-X and guitar tuners in the living room, while you watch Patricia brew coffee on their espresso machine. When asked, opt for the designer coffee cups. Bring the four cups to the table on a metal tray. Take a cup, break a square of the chocolate, sit down, relax. Have a bite of chocolate, then a sip of coffee. —**Clotilde Dusoulier**, "Happiness (A Recipe)"

Some food memories are negative—yet still entertaining, as shown by the following excerpt from Ruth Reichl's food memoir:

> This is a true story.
>
> Imagine a New York City apartment at six in the morning. It is a modest apartment in Greenwich Village. Coffee is bubbling in an electric percolator. On the table is a basket of rye bread, an entire coffee cake, a few cheeses, a platter of cold cuts. My mother has been making breakfast—a major meal in our house, one where we sit down to fresh orange juice every morning, clink our glasses as if they held wine, and toast each other with "Cheerio. Have a nice day."
>
> Right now she is the only one awake, but she is getting impatient for the day to begin and she cranks WQXR up a little louder on the radio, hoping that the noise will rouse everyone else. But Dad and I are good sleepers, and when the sounds of martial music have no effect she barges into the bedroom and shakes my father awake.
>
> "Darling," she says, "I need you. Get up and come into the kitchen."

Ruth Reichl, editor-in-chief of *Gourmet* magazine.

> My father, a sweet and accommodating person, shuffles sleepily down the hall. He is wearing loose pajamas, and the strand of hair he combs over his bald spot stands straight up. He leans against the sink, holding on to it a little, and obediently opens his mouth when my mother says, "Try this."
>
> Later, when he told the story, he attempted to convey the awfulness of what she had given him. The first time he said that it tasted like cat toes and rotted barley, but over the years the description got better. Two years later it had turned into pigs' snouts and mud and five years later he had refined the flavor into a mixture of antique anchovies and moldy chocolate.
>
> Whatever it tasted like, he said it was the worst thing he had ever had in his mouth, so terrible that it was impossible to swallow, so terrible that he leaned over and spit it into the sink and then grabbed the coffeepot, put the spout into his mouth, and tried to eradicate the flavor.
>
> My mother stood there watching all this. When my father finally put the coffeepot down she smiled and said, "Just as I thought. Spoiled."
>
> And then she threw the mess into the garbage can and sat down to drink her orange juice.   —**Ruth Reichl**, "The Queen of Mold"

As Reichl makes clear in her memoir, Americans are not known for their appreciation of fine food. In fact, internationally, Americans are better known for their love of junk food and fast food. Eric Schlosser captures the fast food experience in the following excerpt:

> Pull open the glass door, feel the rush of cool air, walk in, get in line, study the backlit color photographs above the counter, place your order, hand over a few dollars. Watch teenagers in uniforms pushing various buttons, and moments later take hold of a plastic tray full of food wrapped in colored paper and cardboard. The whole experience of buying fast food has become so routine, so thoroughly

A typical fast food meal, at the heart of many recent debates.

unexceptional and mundane, that it is now taken for granted, like brushing your teeth or stopping for a red light. It has become a social custom as American as a small, rectangular, hand-held, frozen and reheated apple pie.

—Eric Schlosser, *Fast Food Nation*

In recent years, the American culture of food has been the focus of books, movies, countless newspaper and television features—plus a good deal of criticism. You've no doubt seen articles about the obesity epidemic in the United States, an epidemic linked directly to overconsumption of fast food. With 65.4 percent of Americans either overweight or obese, the detrimental effects of fast-food consumption have been well publicized in books and movies such as *Fast Food Nation* and *Super Size Me,* public debates, and even lawsuits.

In industrialized, developed nations like the United States, the culture of food is increasingly characterized by an overabundance of choices—from dozens of ethnic cuisines and hundreds of snack and frozen food products to fresh fruits, vegetables, and fish imported from around the globe. The once strong connection between eating and ritual, represented by Clotilde Dusoulier's chocolate-and-espresso routine, is weakening in the United States. On-the-go eating habits and reliance on fast food don't necessarily lend themselves to meaningful experiences with nourishment, but many people still have vivid and personally significant memories of their experiences with food.

DESCRIBING THE CULTURE OF FOOD

1. What kinds of food best represent your childhood? In other words, what foods did you eat at home and with your family? Of those foods, which ones were your personal favorites? If you are now living away from home at college, what kind of memories and emotions do thoughts of this food bring to mind?

2. Identify a key moment when you were first introduced to an unfamiliar kind of food. How did that event affect you?

3. Our food experiences are often shaped just as much by our visual sense as by smell or taste. We might think a food looks disgusting without even tasting it, or we might favor a particular restaurant as much for its hip décor as for its food. Choose one of the images in this chapter and write for five minutes about what it suggests to you.

4. Working with a classmate, make a list of ways in which the eating habits of current college students differ from those of past generations of students. Explain how, when, and where you learned about these differences.

5. Recall a negative stereotype about food on your college campus, the ill effects of a particular food on campus, or the students who eat that specific food.

COMMUNITY CONNECTIONS

1. What types of food experiences, positive or negative, have been most significant to you, either while growing up or during college life? Describe these specific experiences in as much detail as possible. Why have the experiences been memorable to you?

2. What locations and foods make up the culture of food on your campus or in your community? Think about the restaurants, dining halls, convenience stores, snacks, take-out meals, and cafeteria offerings that make your school's or community's culture of food unique. Describe each of these locations and foods in as much detail as possible.

3. Select the location or food from the preceding question that you find most significant, most memorable, or most satisfying. Write for five minutes about the experiences you've had in this location or with this food or the memories that it brings to mind for you. Be as specific as possible when describing your experiences or memories.

Real Responses to Real Situations

Telling the stories of their kitchens

With the proliferation of cable television channels such as The Food Network and Fine Living, specialty magazines such as *Cooking Light* and *Everyday Food,* and online discussion boards such as "Slow Food Forum" and "Plate of the Day Food Forum," food lovers now have more ways than ever to satisfy their appetite for new recipe ideas, reviews of exotic dining destinations, descriptions of how their favorite foods are made, and stories about food industry personalities.

One particularly noteworthy contribution that the cooking and dining community has made to the entertainment industry has been the food memoir. Many good family recipes have interesting stories behind them, from Grandma and Grandpa's ill-fated experimentation with prune-filled pierogies on Christmas Eve in 1953 to a father's tale of picking onions in the blazing hot Texas summers, the same kind of onions his children are now piling high on top of their chili. The food memoir brings those narratives from the realm of family folklore

MFK Fisher

THE GASTRONOMICAL ME

M. F. K. Fisher's autobiographical writings, including *The Gastronomical Me*, were key precursors of contemporary food memoirs.

and the margins of cookbooks to the *New York Times* bestseller list. One newspaper reporter described the development of the food memoir in this way:

Food memoirs were once the sole province of such confirmed culinary superstars as M. F. K. Fisher, whose prose was filled with tantalizing descriptions of summer picnics and late night tete-a-tetes over cheese and figs.

But these days, as the American obsession with all things free-range, organic, grass-fed and locally harvested spreads from coast-to-coast, the food memoir has become a genre unto itself, with recipes where pictures used to be. Some of the efforts emanate from those who have made a career of food, such as *Gourmet* editor Ruth Reichl, whose new *Garlic and Sapphires* is the third in her series of memoirs about a life spent in the kitchen and the dining room. Some are thinly disguised as diet books, such as Mireille Guiliano's *French Women Don't Get Fat*. Others, though, originate from writers who grew up in homes where food was the center of the day, an instrument to coax and infuriate, to flatter and to fatten—such as Diana Abu-Jaber, whose childhood, it is clear from her new memoir, *The Language of Baklava*, smelled and tasted like lamb.

—**Julia Silverman**, "Abu-Jaber Finally Pens Food Novel"

Indeed, the type of writing called the "food memoir" has grown to the point that as Katherine Powers argued in her November 2006 column in the *Boston Globe*, "I know that this business of writing memoirs of food has been going on for a long time, but it seems to me that it has now raged out of control." Despite such criticisms, however, the increasing popularity of cooking shows such as The Food Network's *30 Minute Meals* with Rachael Ray and Bravo's *Top Chef* and of cookbooks such as Bobby Flay's *Boy Meets Grill* and Moosewood Kitchen's *Moosewood Cookbook* suggests that our appetite for food memoirs has not been satisfied yet.

In her memoir *Julie & Julia: 365 Days, 524 Recipes, 1 Tiny Apartment Kitchen*, Julie Powell narrates a year-long effort to pull herself out of a rut of living in a run-down New York apartment, working in dead-end secretarial jobs, and approaching her thirtieth birthday without a clear direction in her life. Her recovery came in the form of her mother's battered copy of Julia Child's classic *Mastering the Art of French Cooking*. Powell cooked every recipe in Child's influential cookbook, from Filets de Poisson Bercy aux Champignons and Poulet Rôti to Carottes à la Concierge and Crème Brûlée, and recorded her reflections on these cooking ventures on her blog, which she titled "The Julie/Julia Project." This blog became wildly popular; her daily posts regularly attracted forty, fifty, sometimes even eighty comments from readers interested in her culinary and personal journey. In Powell's blog and memoir, Julia Child becomes a model not just for aspiring cooks, but for anyone who wants to know how to grow older and how to learn.

Recipe blogs are one popular kind of food blog.

JULIE POWELL
Excerpt from The Julie/Julia Project

Working with the book, one comes to know Julia as a teacher—a brilliant one, with a spark of humor, a passion for her subject, and an unfailing intuition for how to create a feeling of comfort in the midst of chaotic striving. But in her shows, and particularly her later ones, "Cooking with Master Chefs," . . . Julia proves an exemplary, and inspirational, student. She is endlessly curious—every time she sticks her big, curled paws into a pot of boiling water, or right under the flying knife of a chef forty years her junior, to pick up some bit of something to taste, the tiny bit of my soul that still harbors a belief in a higher power squeezes its eyes shut and crosses its fingers and prays as hard as it can that when I am her age, I'll be just like Julia. She asks endless questions—in the episode PBS is so obsessed with that they show it about once a week, it's the anti-flatulence properties of epazote that holds her attention, to a rather unseemly degree—and always seems glad to learn from the people she brings on to the show, often wet-

> "As a student, on these shows, she's teaching us all how to learn."

eared young whippersnappers who treat her like she's some dotty old biddy until I want to grab them by the shoulders and shake them— "Show some respect, kid, this is *Julia,* and you wouldn't be here if it wasn't for her!!!" But she never seems to feel slighted or disrespected—really, in the end, how could she? She is Julia— always changing, but always, utterly, herself. As a student, on these shows, she's teaching us all how to learn.

She has a wonderful aside in [the] endlessly repeated episode about lard—when she gets off the epazote for a minute. "We should talk about this," she warbles, as Rick dumps a nice big scoop of lard into a frying pan, "because everyone's so *afraid* of lard." They discuss the pros and cons of the stuff—less cholesterol than butter, but more saturated fats, the authenticity lard lends to Latin American dishes, etc. . . ., and Julia says, "The point is, if you don't want to make something right, *don't make it.* Choose something else. Like making tamales with olive oil, it's *TERRIBLE!"*

continued

And her voice swoops briefly up into the stratosphere, and you feel this passion in her, and yes, she's probably had a glass or two of wine, which God love her she deserves, but to me the wonderful thing is the hint that there's yet another Julia, another face. I've learned from the teacher and I've learned again from the student, but when she talks of lard, Julia hints that there is another, wilder, Julia beneath it all, a rebellious, passionate, dare I say *dangerous* individual. Was it this Julia who joined [the] OSS and created shark repellent? Or maybe just this Julia who walked into a cooking school in France—no longer a spring chicken herself, but with an unquenchable fire in her that she herself didn't quite understand. That's the Julia I'm striving toward, the Julia that I hope someday to be like.

In the following *Boston Globe* article, Jessica Thomson describes the increasing popularity of food- and cooking-related blogs, a cultural trend that Julie Powell no doubt energized with "The Julie/Julia Project." Thomson, who authors her own cooking blog, "Hogwash," provides a glimpse into how blogs and the World Wide Web have helped to support the increasing interest in food and cooking in many demographics of American society.

JESSICA THOMSON
Blogs Add a New Ingredient to Food Writing

Blogging is the latest trend in food writing. Just about anyone who likes to cook and has an Internet connection can use free online software to create a weblog, or blog, that allows them to publish stories, recipes, photographs, and videos. Some blogs are edgy, some sassy, and some, like Julie Powell's The Julie/Julia Project—in which a young New Yorker cooked her way through Julia Child's *Mastering the Art of French Cooking*—are hilarious recordings of successes and mishaps. The blog became a book.

Since Powell's 2002 blog, which was required reading in some circles, blogs have become wildly popular. Food writing expert and book coach Dianne Jacob, author of *Will Write for Food*, recently calculated that there are now at least 200,000 food blogs. On her website diannej.com, she writes that publishers scan blogs for up-and-coming authors, and periodicals now pursue bloggers to write cookbook reviews. Although many blogs, like The Julie/Julia Project, are narratives, a growing number publish recipes, providing readers with a constant stream of free kitchen material. As a result, the way people find and use recipes is changing; some wonder if the role of cookbooks may change, too.

"The way people find and use recipes is changing . . ."

Earlier this month, the Well Fed Network, an online compilation of food blogs, announced its annual food blog awards. This year's winner for best blog overall is Simply Recipes, started about five years ago by Elise Bauer to record her family's food. Simply Recipes isn't funny, and it isn't storytelling at its greatest. . . . Before dismissing Simply Recipes as lightweight, consider this: Bauer is posting new recipes continually, most recently roasted parsnip puree, roast chicken with carrots, and butter pecan ice cream. She gets many recipes from her family, who have clipped from newspapers, magazines, and cookbooks for years. Recipes come with a professional-quality photo and often a series of how-to photos. The database, which now holds more than 500 recipes, is searchable. Readers can also post comments or ask for clarification from the writer.

As appealing as that seems, an online database will never replace cookbooks, say industry insiders. For some, the heft and comfort of holding a book, combined with the fact that most ordinary cooks don't use computers in their kitchens (yet) are enough to keep books on shelves for now. Molly Wizenberg, author of the blog Orangette, thinks cookbooks have a certain amount of prestige that blogs have yet to acquire. Cookbook recipes go through a unique and rigorous editorial and testing process, she says, which blogs don't. Orangette was last year's Well Fed Network winning overall blog.

In fact, many bloggers like to refer to cookbooks and authors when they write. Wizenberg, who often publishes recipes on Orangette based on those in her favorite cookbooks, thinks recipe blogs and cookbooks have a positive symbiotic relationship. "Blogs are increasing interest in cooking in general," she says, "which has to be good for the publishing world." Wizenberg's first cookbook, tentatively titled "Orangette: The Stories My Kitchen Tells Me," is slated for release in 2008. Sydny Miner, vice president and senior editor at Simon & Schuster—and the editor of Wizenberg's book—insists cookbooks serve a much different purpose than blogs. "Blogs record what their authors are thinking in the moment, and they are wonderful for immediate inspiration," says Miner. But while blogs are most often fragmented and unpredictable, she says, a good cookbook offers a unified vision and allows the reader to expect a certain type of recipe. . . .

On the phone from Carmichael, California, where she lives and is a partner in Pacifica Group, a technology consulting firm, blogger Bauer says that online recipe writing is reshaping the way people cook. Free recipes have been available on the Internet for years,

through large Web sites like epicurious.com, but until recipe blogs became popular, interaction between authors and users was less common. Bauer thinks that unless cookbook authors create blogs to support their cookbooks, an author can't offer the same sense of community that a blogger can.

Book-bound recipes have always suffered from a phenomenon that Matthew Amster-Burton, author of the blog Roots and Grubs, calls "recipe rot," meaning that something in a book can seem to get stale on the shelf while new recipes are far more exciting.

Ultimately, a blog's success depends on the quality of the recipes, writing, and photographs, and whether the author has your taste. This aspect of blogging is similar to cookbooks. But cookbook authors test themselves or hire recipe testers, and they also have editors. Bad bloggers can publish poor recipes repeatedly, regardless of how much traffic their sites see. That means there are many new recipes online that don't work—a common complaint among Web browsers. I tested Parmesan chicken, baked in a hot oven with breadcrumbs and cheese, from Simply Recipes, which was homey, simple, and kid-friendly. Winter-into-spring salad, made with radicchio, radishes, and endive, from Orangette was fresh-tasting and season-celebrating. Both were well-written and easy to follow.

It's clear that recipe blogs and cookbooks are going to be compatible for some time. How large a niche recipe blogs find in the food world may just depend on who's writing them—and whether you're in the mood for what they're offering.

Real Responses

While Thomson doesn't precisely predict how blogs and the World Wide Web will affect the future of recipes and cookbooks, she does acknowledge that blogs are undoubtedly shaping the American culture of food by giving more people access to forums for not only swapping recipes but also sharing their opinions about and memories of food.

ANALYZING THE RHETORICAL SITUATION

The readings in this section suggest that food memoirs have great appeal for many people in America. The following questions ask you to consider this kind of writing in terms of the elements of the rhetorical situation. You'll want to reread the excerpts in this section carefully before answering. *continued*

1. Who might be the intended audience of Julie Powell's food blog "The Julie/Julia Project"? What textual evidence can you provide for your answer? Be prepared to share your answers with the rest of the class.

2. Who might be the intended audiences for Julia Silverman's and Jessica Thomson's articles on food memoirs and food blogs? How do these audiences differ, and what textual evidence leads you to these conclusions?

3. Is the purpose of each excerpt in this section evident? If so, what is it? What are the differences among the excerpts in terms of purpose? And how does each purpose relate to the writer's intended audience? Again, be prepared to share your answers with the rest of the class.

4. Keeping in mind that the publication of each of the pieces in this section occurred in the past, to what exigence might each writer be responding? How does the piece of writing work to resolve or address that exigence?

5. How does each writer draw on the rhetorical appeals of ethos, logos, and pathos to fulfill the purpose? Cite passages from the texts to support your answer.

The changing significance of food

Food memoirists share their experiences tasting the fresh winter-into-spring salad or their first failed attempts at flipping omelets; other writers have focused their attention on better understanding people's relationship to food and the consequences of that relationship. Indeed, the growing popularity of food writing and programming within the entertainment industry suggests that Americans connect food more with pleasure and fun than with nourishment and sustenance. Newspaper headlines over the past few years have begun to warn readers about scientific findings that link the growing health epidemics to problematic obsessions with food. However, this evolving relationship with food has been a topic that some anthropologists and sociologists have been writing about over the course of the past three decades.

Margaret Mead (1901–1978) was the most influential and the most persistent explorer of the American culture of food. A psychology graduate of Barnard College, Mead went on to earn a PhD in anthropology at Columbia University, believing that understanding human behavior held great promise for the future. After graduate school, Mead conducted research among adolescents in Samoa, which culminated in the 1928 publication of the now classic *Coming of Age in Samoa*. In another of her studies, Mead argued that the biological differences between men and women should not preclude women's full participation in the world. All of Mead's anthropological work—whether on indigenous cultures, social roles, or family structure—advanced the idea that human traits are primarily social, not biological.

Mead's observations on the social influences on human traits were continued in her sociological studies of Americans' eating habits. During World War II (1939–1945), for instance, she focused her research agenda on the culture of food in the United States. At that time, she was one of the scientists and social scientists recruited by the U.S. government to conduct various "national character" studies and then to give public policy advice. An anthropologist already versed in the interconnectedness of all aspects of human life, Mead understood the connections among the elements of national character, including ritual, belief, and identity—and the ways those elements linked up with the culture of food.

Mead remained interested in food and nutrition throughout the tremendous social and cultural changes of the 1960s in America. As a skilled writer and observer of human behavior and social structures, she continued to study both domestic and international changes in the availability of food and the consequences of the increased efficiency, automation, and industrialization of the food industry. She had good reason to be concerned: famine struck India and Pakistan in the late 1960s. And despite the great progress of U.S. agriculture during that same time, hunger was a major American problem as well, as Marion Nestle, author of *Food Politics,* points out. Even today, despite agricultural advances, hunger affects 36 million Americans, or one-eighth of the nation's population, with children and the elderly at the greatest risk, according to the organization Food First.

Margaret Mead holds a baby on Admiralty Island, Papua New Guinea, in 1954.

When President Lyndon Baines Johnson took office in 1963, poverty and hunger affected one-fifth of all Americans. He declared a war on poverty and established food assistance programs, some of which still remain. Around that same time, Margaret Mead dedicated herself to updating the World War II–era findings of the National Research Council's Committee for the Study of Food Habits, believing that social and technological developments had significantly altered the way people ate in the United States. In a section of her update, Mead observes the following:

> In the United States, within the lifetime of one generation, there has been a dramatic shift from malnutrition as a significant nutritional state on a national scale, to overnutrition as one of the principal dangers to the nation's health. Overnutrition, in the United States, may be attributed to food habits carried over from a situation of relative scarcity to one of plenty and to the development of food vending methods which continually expose people to an extreme amount and variety of foods. . . . Today we may distinguish an increasing number of affluent industrialized countries in which it is essential to develop an educational system within which children can learn self-regulation in the face of tremendous variety. Conditions in these countries contrast sharply with those which prevail—and may be expected to continue to prevail—in the underdeveloped areas of the world, where children must still be taught a rather rigid adherence to a diet that is only just sufficient for survival.
>
> —**Margaret Mead,** *Food Habits Research: Problems of the 1960s*

Prepackaged and highly processed foods are often consumed along with entertainment today.

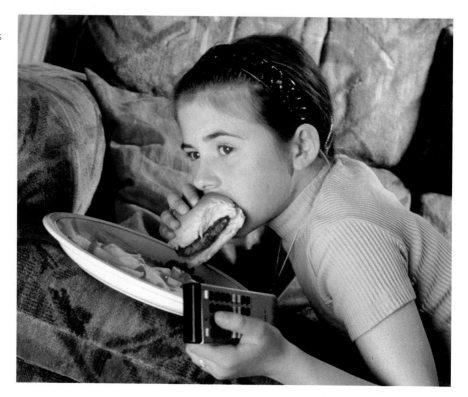

Mead's observations about Americans' eating habits led her to consider the changing significance of food in people's lives. No longer was food being used to commemorate special events or traditions; instead, it was used for easy consumption or quick entertainment, with little thought for its nutritional value. In her update, Mead also noted dramatic alterations in the way food was produced (mass), prepared (breaded and fried), and distributed (frozen and canned). Given the current debates over American diets and eating habits—as well as over widespread hunger in America—Mead's writing now seems prophetic. She brought national attention to the split between food as nourishment and food as a commercial commodity as well as to the profound postwar changes in the foods produced by industrialized nations and their distribution (or lack thereof).

In 1970, Mead published what would become one of her most famous essays, "The Changing Significance of Food," which appeared in the magazine *American Scientist*. Mead argued that despite all the national attention, the United States remained dangerously ignorant of its food-related challenges and capabilities. "Today, for the first time in the history of mankind," she asserts, "we have the productive capacity to feed everyone in the world." But the United States was not feeding every American, let alone everyone else in the world. World hunger and food scarcity simply had not yet been properly addressed. She used this essay, then, to single out conditions that had contributed to this refusal or inability to recognize the severity of the situation. In the following passage, Mead describes one such condition— "the increase in the diseases of affluence."

MARGARET MEAD
Excerpt from The Changing Significance of Food

In a country pronounced only twenty years before to be one-third ill-fed, we suddenly began to have pronouncements from nutritional specialists that the major nutritional disease of the American people was over-nutrition. If this had simply meant overeating, the old puritan ethics might have been more easily invoked, but it was over-nutrition that was at stake. And this in a country where our ideas of nutrition had been dominated by a dichotomy which distinguished food that was "good for you, but not good" from food that was "good, but not good for you." This split in man's needs, into our cultural conception of the need for nourishment and the search for pleasure, originally symbolized the rewards for eating spinach or finishing what was on one's plate if one wanted to have dessert, lay back of the movement to produce, commercially, nonnourishing foods. Beverages and snacks came in particularly for this demand, as it was the addition of between-meal eating to the three square, nutritionally adequate meals a day that was responsible for much of the trouble.

> **"How can the country be over-nourished and undernourished at the same time?"**

We began manufacturing, on a terrifying scale, foods and beverages that were guaranteed not to nourish. The resources and the ingenuity of industry were diverted from the preparation of foods necessary for life and growth to foods non-expensive to prepare, expensive to buy. And every label reassuring the buyer that the product was not nourishing increased our sense that the trouble with Americans was that they were too well nourished. The diseases of affluence, represented by new forms of death in middle-age, had appeared before we had . . . conquered the diseases of poverty—the ill-fed pregnant women and lactating women, sometimes resulting in irreversible damage to the ill-weaned children, the school children so poorly fed that they could not learn. . . .

It was hard for the average American to believe that while he struggled, and paid, so as not to be over-nourished, other people, several millions, right in this country, were hungry and near starvation. The contradiction was too great. . . . How can the country be over-nourished and undernourished at the same time?

For Mead, the increased availability of highly processed snack foods and drinks and American businesses' focus on these products was proof that the United States had a problem with over-nutrition and food abundance. The boom in consumer goods and prepared foods—from TV dinners to baby formula—rendered nearly invisible the millions of Americans who were not benefiting from food surpluses. Mead warned that once food became an international commodity, a product separated entirely from its cultural and nutritional significance, its production, distribution, and consumption would become a huge international problem.

Margaret Mead warned in the 1970s about the trend toward easy-to-make, prepackaged foods that were believed to be a solution to the world's nutrition problems because they seemed easier to distribute and consume. You likely have experienced the end results of this trend in the school cafeterias where you went to grade school, high school, and college. These facilities have long struggled to balance the need to provide students with nourishing foods with the constraint of a limited budget, while keeping students happy that they're eating something that tastes good. If you're like many college students, you may be more than a little skeptical about or resistant to some of the culinary offerings in your college cafeteria, and you may even buy into

In a cafeteria at Kenyon University in Ohio, the word *Local* on the salad bar sneeze guard tells diners that the food came from a nearby family farm.

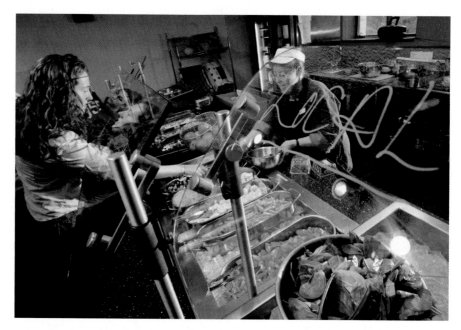

the rumors about what the cooks may be stirring into your dinner. Indeed, for many college graduates, the memories they have of their college dining experiences have more to do with the people they were with and the stories that were told than with the food they happened to be eating.

Many college dining facilities are seeking to change this negative impression and to assume ecological and nutritional responsibility for their students and their communities at the same time. And while they're at it, these new-and-improved cafeterias are trying to leverage their weight in the college recruiting process. The following excerpt from an article in the *Atlantic Monthly* describes two recent developments at Yale University to provide students with delicious foods while also teaching them the value of producing foods in locally sustainable ways.

CORBY KUMMER
Excerpt from Good-bye Cryovac

I recently washed up after a supper consisting of four kinds of vegetables from the farmers' market—all four of them vegetables I usually buy at the local right-minded supermarket. As I considered the vivid, distinctive flavor of every bite, I thought, What is that stuff I've been eating the rest of the year?

One of the twelve residential colleges at Yale University is trying to give students that kind of summertime epiphany at every meal, by serving dishes made from

> "Not long ago a college would never have thought to mention food in a brochure or on a school tour . . ."

produce raised as close to New Haven as possible. In just two years the Yale Sustainable Food Project has launched two ambitious initiatives to bridge the distance from farm to table: the complete revamping of menus in Berkeley College's dining hall to respect seasonality and simplicity, and the conversion of an overgrown lot near campus to an Edenic organic garden. The garden does not supply the dining hall—it couldn't. Rather, it serves as a kind of Greenwich Mean Time, suggesting what is best to serve, and when, by illustrating what grows in the southern New England climate in any given week. The goal of the project is to sell students on the superior flavor of food raised locally in environmentally responsible (but not always organic) ways, so that they will seek it the rest of their lives.

A few dishes I tasted last summer during a pre-term recipe-testing marathon in Berkeley's kitchen convinced me that this goal is within reach for any college meals program willing to make an initial outlay for staff training and an ongoing investment in fewer but better ingredients. I would be happy to eat pasta with parsnips once a week, for example, the candy-sweet roots sharpened by fresh parsley and Parmesan. In fact, I demanded the recipe. Any restaurant would be pleased to serve fresh asparagus roasted with a subtle seasoning of balsamic vinegar and olive oil alongside, say, filet of beef. Even the chicken breasts, coated with black pepper, grilled, and served with a shallot, garlic, and white-wine sauce, tasted like chicken.

Not long ago a college would never have thought to mention food in a brochure or on a school tour—except, perhaps, in a deprecating aside. Now food is a competitive marketing tool, and by the second or third stop on the college circuit parents and students practically expect to be shown the organic salad bar and told about the vegan options and the menus resulting directly from student surveys. Yale has gone these colleges what I consider to be a giant step further, showing students what they should want and making them want it.

As caring about food has become interwoven with caring about the environment, enjoying good food has lost some of the elitist, hedonistic taint that long barred gourmets from the ranks of the politically correct. The challenge, as with any political movement, is to bring about practical institutional change that incorporates ideals.

It's a very big challenge with college food, almost all of which is provided by enormous catering companies like Sodexho, Chartwells, and Aramark, the company that has run Yale's dining services since 1998. These companies have long offered vegetarian, organic, and vegan choices. But none of those options—not even, sadly, going organic—necessarily supports local farmers and local economies, or shows students how much better food tastes when it's made from scratch with what's fresh. Vegetarian, organic, and vegan foods can all be processed, overseasoned, and generally gunked up, and in the hands of institutional food-service providers they usually are. . . .

Whatever the argument for spending more money on food . . . , the practical successes at Yale should encourage other schools to consider similar changes. [Associate Director of the Yale Sustainable Food Project Josh] Viertel gives the example of granola, a simple seduction tool. At the beginning of this year the Food Project's formula of organic oats, almonds, and raisins, a local honey, and New England maple syrup was so popular that Commons had to take over making it for every college. And the project's recipe is actually cheaper than buying pre-made granola in bulk. Viertel recently began a composting program; the first step is asking students to scrape their own plates, which shows close up the waste involved when they take, say, just one bite of cheese lasagne. Other schools ought to take that same step, even if they stop there. . . .

Kummer's description of this new food project at Yale University illustrates the kinds of efforts going on at some colleges to combat the disturbing trend toward "over-nourishment" that Mead saw over three decades ago as Americans moved more and more toward foods that were easy to produce and consume yet nutritionally empty. While Mead emphasizes the social and, elsewhere in her writings, the environmental benefits that would follow from producing more local-based diets, Kummer adds the element of economic gain that colleges and universities would achieve as they enticed more students to their respective schools. Indeed, we can all imagine that such locally oriented dining experiences might someday leave all of us longing for the days in college cafeterias not only because we experienced such great times relaxing and telling stories with friends but also because we were eating such delicious, inventive foods.

ANALYZING THE RHETORICAL SITUATION

1. What is "over-nutrition," and how does Mead argue that it came to be a problem?

2. What evidence does Mead provide to demonstrate that diseases of affluence result not just from biological traits but also from social traits? Who is the audience for this argument?

3. What problems (or exigencies) does Mead address? What arguments does she make about the roots of these problems? What evidence does she provide to support these claims about the sources of the problems?

4. What are Mead's proposals for solving these problems? What actions does she want her readers to take?

5. How does Mead use the rhetorical appeals of ethos, pathos, and logos to build the arguments in her two pieces? Provide textual evidence to support your answer. Which of the rhetorical appeals does she rely on most? Be prepared to share your answer with the rest of the class.

6. What exigence prompted Kummer's piece on the Sustainable Food Project at Yale University? How would you characterize the relationship between his work and Mead's theories? In what ways is he helping to develop the conversation about the culture of food in the United States?

COMMUNITY CONNECTIONS

1. How do the reflections and descriptions by Powell and Thomson coincide with or diverge from your experiences with cooking and with food? Take about ten minutes to write your response.

2. Now do the same for the pieces by Mead and Kummer: how do their analyses coincide with or diverge from your experiences or observations about the culture of food in the United States?

3. Is it true, as Mead argues, that "ideas of nutrition [in the United States have] been dominated by a dichotomy which distinguished food that was 'good for you, but not good' from food that was 'good, but not good for you'"? Draw on your childhood experiences, education, or independent living at college, to support your answer.

4. Now that you have considered various arguments made about humans and their relationships with food, how would you describe the culture of food on your campus or in your community? What key aspects of food options or eating habits seem most significant to you? What economic, political, social, cultural, or biological forces have shaped the culture of food?

Memoirs: A Fitting Response

Two memoirs on food and culture

Food triggers vivid memories for all of us—some joyous or satisfying, others painful or awkward. Food can also serve to define our relationships with family, friends, and even complete strangers. Many writers have discussed their experiences with food in their memoirs precisely to trigger reflections on defining moments in their lives or to crystallize the perceptions of people and cultures that they have developed. Pooja Makhijani provides one such reflective memoir in her essay "School Lunch." As you read, notice the rich details that Makhijani provides to help readers visualize, smell, taste, and even feel the food that her mother packed for her each day before she left for school. As you take pleasure in these descriptions, though, see how Makhijani uses her descriptions of food to illustrate a larger point about her relationship with her mother and with the American culture in which she wants to immerse herself.

Pooja Makhijani
School Lunch

Mom says she is being "sensible" about what I eat and she likes to pack "sensible" lunches. Plastic sandwich bags filled with blood-red pomegranate seeds. Fresh raisin bread wrapped in foil. Homemade vegetable biryani made with brown rice and lima beans. Yellow pressed rice with potatoes and onions. A silver thermos full of warm tamarind-infused lentil soup. Blue and white Tupperware containers that can be reused. Lunch sacks that have to be brought home every day. Silverware. [1]

I don't want her lunches. [2] I want to touch a cold, red Coca-Cola can that will hiss when I open it. I want to pull out a yellow Lunchables box so I can assemble bite-size sandwiches with Ritz crackers and smoked turkey. I want to smell tuna salad with mayonnaise and pickles. I want bologna on white bread, Capri Sun Fruit Punch, and Cool Ranch Doritos in a brown paper bag. I want plastic forks that I can throw away when I am done eating. But I am too scared to ask her. I know she will say, "No."

[3] "Why don't you invite Chrissy over this Friday after school?" Mom ladles a spoonful of sweetened, homemade yogurt into a white ceramic bowl. "You've already been to her house twice." I hoist myself onto one of the high chairs at my kitchen table and pull my breakfast toward me. I tear the hot masala roti into eight irregular pieces and dip the largest one into the cold yogurt.

"I will, I will." I rub my fingers on the paper towel in my lap. The last time I went to Chrissy's house, Mrs. Pizarro gave us mini–hot dogs wrapped in pastry topped with a squirt of mustard, and tall glasses of Hawaiian Punch as an after-school snack. I can't imagine Chrissy coming to our house and munching on cauliflower and broccoli florets while gulping down chilled milk. [4] I don't want to think about all the questions she will ask. When she sees the bronze Ganesh idol on the wooden stool near the sofa, she will inquire, *What is that elephant-headed statue in your living room?* When she sniffs the odor of spices that permeates the

[1] The writer provides examples with details to help readers visualize the contents of the lunches she totes to school.

[2] With the short first sentence of the second paragraph, the writer creates tension between her and her mother, tension that will give momentum to the rest of the memoir.

[3] The jumps from scene to scene signal one important feature of memoirs—rather than narrating every event of a character's life, they focus on those experiences or events that carry the most significance for shaping who the writer is and his or her perspective on the world.

[4] The writer provides a vivid description of the snacks served at Chrissy's house and her own house in order to help readers visualize the cultural differences she believes are keeping her distanced from friends at school.

bedrooms, she will question, *What's the smell?* And when she accidentally touches my mother's henna colored sari, she will query, *What's your mom wearing?*

"I will," I say between bites so Mom won't ask me again. "Just not this week."

She glances at the clock on the oven. "Hurry up with your food, beti. Nishaat Aunty will be here any second." She grabs the rest of the roti, dunks it into the yogurt, and shovels it into my mouth. Thick globs of yogurt slide in rivulets down her palms and she licks it off once I am done eating. She wipes her hands on her red gingham apron and hands me a bulging brown paper bag. "Your lunch," she says.

"What did you pack today?" I ask as I shove the bag into my purple canvas backpack alongside my spelling and math textbooks.

"Aloo tikkis. Left over from last night."

"Oh." I part the curtains of the kitchen window and look for Nishaat Aunty's midnight-blue station wagon. "Chrissy brought Coke with her to school yesterday." I look into her eyes, hoping she will understand.

"Coca-Cola! During school?" she says. "Of course, that's what those American parents do. That's why their children are so hyper and don't concentrate on their studies." [5] I am not allowed to drink soda, except on Saturdays when Mom makes fried fish. Recently, I've been drinking lots of apple juice because she is worried that there is too much acidity in orange juice.

[5] The writer uses dialogue strategically. Each line of dialogue between herself and her mother helps to reveal their opinions or characteristics and to underscore the different perspectives each one holds toward Indian and American cultures.

"Okay, class, time for lunch." Miss Brown, my fifth-grade teacher, puts down the piece of chalk and rubs her hands on her chocolate-brown pleated pants, leaving behind ghostly prints. She grabs her cardigan off her chair and heads to the teachers' lounge near the gym.

Our lunch aide, Ms. Bauer, walks into the classroom. Her long silver hair cascades over her shoulders and down her back, hiding her ears.

"Row One, you can go to the closets and get your money or your food," Ms. Bauer's raspy voice instructs the five students in the front of the room. I wait for her to call "Row Four" so I can run to the back of the classroom and yank my sack off the top shelf of the closet. Every day, I take my food out of my sack and slide it into my desk. I leave it there until the end of the day so I can throw it away in the large garbage bin next to Principal Ward's office before I head home.

"Row Two." I look out the window. I see the rusty swing set in the front of Washington School. Before Christmas, there were three wooden planks attached to the bar. This spring, only one remains and it sways, lonely, in an early April breeze. [6]

"Row Three." By now, several of my classmates have lined up near the globes in front of the room. They will wait there until everyone whose parents gave them a dollar and two quarters this morning have lined up. Ms. Bauer will walk them down the hall to the temporary lunch stations and they will bring back compartmentalized Styrofoam trays loaded with food.

[6] The writer builds the readers' sense of anticipation: what's she going to do once Ms. Bauer calls "Row Four"?

"Row Four." I bolt. As I reach for my sack, I feel someone tug on my pink turtleneck. I turn around to see who tapped me on the shoulder.

"Aisha." She reintroduces herself.

It's the new girl. Mr. Ward brought her to our classroom on Monday, right after we had finished the Pledge of Allegiance. "Aisha's family just came from Pakistan two days ago," he said. "Please make her feel welcome."

Miss Brown rearranged our desks a bit, and put Aisha in the center of the room. Then she pulled down the world map and gave everyone a quick geography lesson. "Now, who can find Pakistan?" she asked. Even though I knew, I didn't raise my hand. Months before, we'd studied India and Pakistan and Bangladesh in our South Asia unit in social studies. As we took turns reading aloud paragraphs, Miss Brown asked me to read the longest section on topography of the subcontinent. "And in the northeast, Nepal is separated from Tibet by the mighty Himalayan Mountains." I concluded as I heard snickers behind me. [7]

"Hima-aa-layan," Eddie whispered to no one in particular.

"It's Him-a-lay-an." Miss Brown corrected me at the same time. An accent of the first syllable. Short 'a' sounds. Four quick strokes and not the drawn-out vowels that had rolled off my tongue.

I wasn't going to pronounce "Pakistan" the way I knew how to—with a hissing "st" sound not heard in the English language.

"Will you have lunch at my desk today?" she asks. Today, just like yesterday, she wears her fanciest salwaar khameez to school. Yesterday, she wore a blue kurta over a satin white churidaar, and today she wears a shimmery lavender top decorated with clusters of pearls along the edges. She slings her dupatta over her left shoulder. It is longer in the front than in the back and the end gets caught in the heel of her white chappal.

I look down at my cuffed jeans and wonder if she wants to wear sneakers. Will everyone ask Aisha questions about what she is wearing, why she has an accent, or where she comes from? I have always said "No, thank you" when Chrissy or Heather have asked me to eat with them because I don't want to explain anything that makes me different from them. Will I have to explain things about Aisha too? I don't know whether to say yes and be nice, or say no, and read a book while waiting for recess.

"Sure, I'll eat with you," I say finally. I know she has asked me to sit at her desk because I am the only person in the classroom who looks somewhat like her.

She looks relieved. "I have to go buy some food." She rummages through her fleece-lined jacket and takes out $1.50. "Pull your chair up to my desk. I will be back in ten minutes." I watch her get into the lunch line that Ms. Bauer directs out the door.

I drag my chair over to the front of the room. I haven't had a chance to stuff my lunch into my desk, so I peer inside my bag.

I see Mom's aloo tikkis. She's stuffed the leftover potato patties inside a hard roll from La Bonbonniere bakery. The deep-fried flattened ball of potato is spiked with garam masala and shoved into a bun slathered with fresh coriander chutney, which Mom makes with coarsely ground almonds that crunch in my mouth when I least expect it. Below the sandwich are a bunch of grapes in a Ziplock bag. No dripping-wet can of Sprite. No Little Debbie apple pie. No Hostess chocolate cupcakes filled with vanilla cream. No strawberry Pop-Tarts. [8]

I zip up my bag again and wait for Aisha to return. She brings back her tray and places it on her desk. Today's lunch is six chicken nuggets, a spoonful of corn, sticky peach halves floating in sugar syrup, and a tough dinner roll.

"I thought you would have started eating by now." Aisha pierces her chocolate milk carton with a straw.

[7] This event has little to do with the writer's lunch, but it serves an important purpose in the story; it continues to deepen readers' sense of her feelings of frustration and awkwardness as she tries to blend into her cultural surroundings, even as she reads aloud about the geography of her cultural homeland.

[8] The writer doesn't stop at describing the food that's in her lunch bag; she describes the food that's not there, too, in order to continue reinforcing her desire to connect with American culture.

Guide to Memoirs

"I am not that hungry." My stomach growls. I am used to ignoring the sounds. I can usually get through the day on the normal, easily-explainable-if-anyone-sees food. Carrot sticks, apple slices, or Saltines.

"But you brought your lunch. I saw you take something out of the bag. What is it?" she insists.

I reach inside my bag and feel the crusty bread. I draw it out, pressing it between my fingers and thumb, flattening it into a tiny Frisbee, mashing the roll into the soft potatoes.

"See, it is just bread." The disk is so flat that you can't see the tikki inside.

"No, there's something inside it." Aisha peers at the sandwich. "Is that an aloo tikki in a bun? I wish my mother would pack them in my lunch for me. Yesterday, I bought peanut-butter-and-jelly sandwiches. I've never had peanut butter before. It's such a funny food. It stuck to the back of my teeth and I could taste it for the rest of the day."

I look at the flattened mess in my hands and think about licking peanut butter from the crevices in my mouth. I gaze at Aisha's chicken nuggets.

"Wanna trade?" I ask.

"Are you sure? If I were you, I'd keep my food." She cocks her head and her eyes dart between the multicolored array in front of her and the earth-tone concoction just a few inches away from her.

"If you want it, you can have it." My fingers inch over to her side of the desk.

"You can have everything except the corn. I like that." She passes her plate to me and I hand my lunch to her.

"How long have you been here?" I devour all the chicken nuggets before Aisha changes her mind.

"We just got here last weekend. We are living in Edison Village, right near the train station." She nibbles her way around the entire circumference of the bun. "You've probably been here longer than that. You sound American."

I realize she is commenting on the way I pronounce words. Her accent sounds like my mother's. "I was born in New York. I've lived in Edison as long as I can remember."

"Then why don't you eat the school lunch?" Aisha spoons the corn into her mouth.

I don't have an answer for Aisha. I know it's not because it's too expensive or that Styrofoam trays are environmentally unsound. It's because Mom thinks her deep-fried aloo tikkis and freshly ground masalas are what good Indian parents give their daughters. She doesn't understand that good Indian daughters just want to become American. **[9]**

It's too complicated an issue to explain. Like my mother, Aisha won't understand it.

"Time for recess." Ms. Bauer claps her hands three times. I throw the tray and the plastic utensils in the garbage can in the front of the room, and Aisha walks with me back to the closets to put my lunch sack back on the shelf. I race back towards the front of the line that is heading out the door, a few steps behind Chrissy and Heather, following them to the asphalt playground. The boys bolt off to play kickball, their four bases taking up most of the space on the grounds. The girls congregate near the fence around Ms. Bauer as she pulls multicolored jump ropes out of her tote bags.

[9] All good memoir writers pause in their narration of events to reflect on the significance of those events to their personal development and worldview.

"Cookies, candies in a dish. How many pieces do you wish?" Chrissy and Heather both jump into the twirling rope. "One, two, three, four," twenty-five girls chant. "Twelve, thirteen . . ." The rope gets caught under Heather's sneaker.

"Aisha, would you like to try?" Ms. Bauer turns to Aisha and me, who both watch intently.

"Okay." She kicks off her chappals and ties her dupatta round her waist. "But I don't know any of the songs."

"Don't worry. I will pick one for you." Aisha stands between the two lunch ladies, the rope swaying in the wind against her bare feet. I collapse down onto the ground and sit, legs crossed, as I usually do, singing along, but never joining in. "Cinderella, dressed in yella. Went upstairs to see her fella. How many kisses did she get?" Aisha is jumping furiously in time with the music. "Twenty-eight, twenty-nine, thirty, thirty . . ." Aisha missteps and stumbles.

"That was fun." She sits down next to me.

I smile. "You are very good."

"There is a new girl in our class," I tell Mom after school as I peel the tangerine she's given me. "She's from Pakistan." I pull the segments apart and arrange them in a circle on the napkin.

"When did they come?"

"Last weekend." I tell her all the stories Aisha told me at lunch—about her all-girls school in Islamabad, her two younger brothers, and how busy her parents are trying to find a job in New Jersey. I pick up a single slice of the tangerine and glide it between my teeth. "She even wore Indian—I mean, Pakastani—clothes to school every day this week."

"You should do that too." She sweeps the discarded peel with her hands.

I sink my incisors into the fruit. A burst of juice fills my mouth. "She just came from there. That's why she does it," I rationalize to her. "She doesn't have American clothes. And she eats the school lunch." I hope that she picks up on my second subtle hint of the day.

"I am sure once they are all settled in, Aisha's mother will be giving her biryani as well." She wipes the tangerine juice that's dribbled out of my mouth onto my chin, and I lower myself from the chair. "They'll want to hold onto that in this country. **[10]** Don't you want your banana today?"

"No, I am not hungry. I ate lunch."

Aisha and I continue to exchange meals for the rest of the school year. I give her more of my mom's aloo tikkis, and she hands over her pizza bagels. I demolish her macaroni and cheese, and she inhales my masala rice. Aisha starts to wear jeans by June. She always takes off her sneakers and socks before jumping rope, though; she says it's easier that way.

Every day, at 3:15, as I jump into our ice-blue Dodge Caravan, Mom asks me, "Did you finish the lunch I packed you for today?"

"Yes, Mom," I lie. I am not about to spoil my arrangement.

In the following excerpt from his memoir, Abe Opincar sees in the eggs that soothe his mother through pregnancy reflections of her careful, loving ways with her husband and sons.

[10] Again, the writer uses dialogue to good effect—this line succinctly captures the mother's perspective on the importance of continuing to cook Indian food in their adopted homeland and to pass on such cultural touchstones to her children.

[1] In just one paragraph, the writer has already helped readers **begin** visualizing his mother by putting numerous sensory details into the description.

[2] The writer uses the research study as a way to connect his personal experiences with the world and to establish his theme about the connection between himself and his mother.

[3] The writer continues to develop the character of his mother by providing specific details that describe her daily work and her role within the family.

[4] Once again the writer connects his personal observations of his mother to the wider world by describing the qualities of a familiar, everyday object—something that she ate to soothe her stomach while pregnant with him.

[5] As the writer extends this comparison by describing the delicate care required for eggs, readers begin to learn about his character, as well.

[6] The phrase *Even today* at the beginning of this sentence signals a time shift from the writer's childhood to the present.

[7] The writer quotes his mother's speech sparingly but purposefully—to reveal specific aspects of her personality or to deepen readers' understanding of his relationship with her.

Abe Opincar

Excerpt from Fried Butter

When my mother was pregnant with me, her eyes became light sensitive. Cloudless August made her head throb. Sunlight off our bright white garage gave her vertigo. Eggs, she says, fried sunny-side up, barely firm, soothed her stomach. She pulled down all the shades, closed all the curtains. All summer long she sat in the dark kitchen, eating eggs, their yolks shining like little suns on her plate. While she was carrying me, she says, the kitchen smelled always of fried butter. **[1]**

This past summer the European Centre for Taste Science in Dijon, France, published a study in which pregnant mothers who ate anise seed gave birth to babies, who, in their first four days of life, turned toward anise odor. Babies whose mothers didn't eat anise turned away from the odor or ignored it. There are few foods I enjoy more than sunny-side up or soft-boiled eggs, their yolks hot, smooth, and runny. **[2]**

My mother's job was to care for my brother, father, and me. My retrograde childhood was privileged. My mother made my bed, washed the sheets and pillow cases. She woke me in the morning. I put on clothes she had bought, washed, and ironed. I sat at the breakfast table and she placed before me a plate of eggs cooked just as I liked them. She made the lunch I took to school. She made my after-school snack. She never complained. Once when I was very young she was standing at the kitchen sink washing dishes. I said I wanted to go outside and play. She said, "I'm lonely. Please stay with me and talk." I didn't. **[3]**

Some foods we take from the world by force. Others, like eggs, seem freely given. Humans, forever hungry, always looking for a handout from brutal stingy nature, concentrate not upon the hen, but the egg. The hen clucks and blinks and deposits yet another in her nest. Her selflessness is inexplicable, almost comical. The egg is revered as a symbol of eternal life. Its roundness, the endless regularity of its production, suggest the cycle of birth and death. Its brittle shell suggests life's fragility. **[4]**

That eggs are a feminine food is made obvious in their preparation, which often requires maternal care. Milk is churned and scaled, but eggs, like babies, are "coddled." When discussing soufflés, cookbooks sound like Dr. Spock's *Baby Book*. Kitchen becomes nursery. Whites and yolks must be *carefully* separated. Egg whites must be *gently* folded. Once the soufflé goes into the oven, no loud noises or heavy footsteps! *Shh. Be quiet. Baby's sleeping.* **[5]**

My mother never taught me to cook. She never let me, my brother, or father, so much as wash dishes. (She feared we wouldn't do it right, that we wouldn't rinse them properly. There was also a generalized fear of germs, and we, she felt, were careless about them.) Even today she regards my cooking as a reckless habit, something I'd be wise to leave in the hands of a wife, if only I were sensible enough to remarry. **[6]** When she visits she disinfects my sink, scrubs my cutting boards with bactericidal soap. She eyes my refrigerator as if it were booby-trapped. "Have you checked any expiration dates lately?" **[7]**

When she visits, she cooks for me. I get up in the morning, I smell coffee. I get out of the shower, I smell eggs. I sit at the table, she watches me eat. "You're slumping," she says. Or, "Your nose and forehead look like your father's." I kiss her cheek. She smiles and sighs. She tells me that she'll wash the dishes.

Later in the day she goes out for a while. She returns heavy-laden with groceries. Organic fruit. Organic milk. Whole wheat bread. Organic eggs from free-range hens. She says they have "more vitamins." I tell her I'm not malnourished. She shrugs. She puts the groceries away. She wipes each egg with a damp paper towel and places it in the refrigerator's special holder. [8]

In the fourth grade I had my first course in, as it was called back then, sex education. [9] In the darkened classroom, the movie projector stuttered and chattered, dust motes shining in its unsteady beam. *The Miracle of Life* was revealed to us. Sperm, their tails whipping jerkily, mechanically, looked like insects. When the most valiant sperm, twitching in spasms, drilled its way into the passive egg, I felt numb. How could it be that these stupid, speechless, bug-like things, acting only on instinct, produced human beings? How could a miracle be so ugly?

Every year on my birthday my mother calls early early in the morning to say, "This is the exact time when you were born." Her tone is cheerful, but she sounds like she can't half believe it. That it happened. That so many years have passed so quickly. I ask if it was all worth it. The pain, the diapers, the breakfasts, the laundry. "I didn't do any of it because I enjoyed it," she says. "I did it out of love." [10]

The writers of the preceding memoirs use food to highlight particular aspects of their relationships with their mothers. Both memoirs include sensory details to describe the food and make judicious use of quoted dialogue or speech to reveal the mother's character. Both memoirs focus on specific events that show key dimensions of the writers' relationships with their mothers. Finally, both memoirs complement descriptions of events and characters with analysis that helps readers understand the significance of the food to the writers' relationships with their mothers and their relationship to the wider world.

[8] Through this description of his mother's actions, the writer creates an image that finally connects the mother, the object of the egg, and the characteristic of maternal care that each one connotes for him.

[9] *In the fourth grade* alerts readers to the fact that the author is flashing back in time in order to tell a story.

[10] The writer allows his mother the last word in the story, giving weight to her own explanation of her role within the family.

WHAT MAKES IT A MEMOIR?

The following questions are ones you should consider when thinking critically about any memoir. For now, try applying them to the memoirs by Pooja Makhijani and Abe Opincar to determine how closely those writers followed the conventions for memoirs.

1. Does the writer focus on significant events in his or her life rather than trying to narrate his or her entire life's story?

2. Do the descriptions of the characters or important objects in the memoirs include sensory details that help readers to visualize, hear, smell, or feel them?

3. Has the writer quoted speech or dialogue so as to reveal some important aspect of a character's personality?

4. Does the writer narrate or describe events in a way that allows readers to connect them to experiences or relationships in their own lives?

5. Has the writer explained the significance of the people, events, places, or objects in shaping who he or she has become? Does this explanation make sense in relation to the events, people, places, and things described throughout the memoir?

Understanding the Rhetorical Situation

Identifying an exigence

In the excerpt from his food memoir, *Fried Butter,* Abe Opincar identifies a unique, meaningful relationship in his life and explores significant experiences that helped to shape that relationship. He undoubtedly sees food at the heart of his relationship with his mother, a relationship through which he enjoyed privilege as a child and maturing adult. And his reflection on the interconnections among himself, his mother, and food leads him to a telling discovery—the eggs that eased his mother's sick stomach while she was pregnant with him require the type of delicate care and attention that his mother gave to him throughout his childhood. Opincar's memoir, then, suggests how we can use our experiences with food to explore the significance of special events and relationships in our lives.

Think about special foods or special meals in your life, those you've eaten at holiday celebrations, campus eateries, or ethnic or cultural events. Are any of these foods or meals a source of pride for you, your family, or friends? Have any of these foods or meals helped you better understand your values and your relationships with others? Are some of these foods or meals ones that a classmate needs to hear more about in order to better understand you as a person? Did your experiences in making or eating these foods or meals ever cause any tension between you and family members, friends, or outsiders? Have any of these foods or meals taken on a special significance in your life that they didn't have when you first ate them or participated in them?

You might, for example, think back to a time when a parent or other relative calmed your anxieties about a bad result on an exam, a devastating break-up, or a tough loss with a comforting meal. You might reflect on the candies and snacks in the care package that a friend sent you to help motivate and energize you for finals' week. You might remember the specific details of a meal at your favorite diner or coffee shop in your hometown, the one where you and your friends still congregate when you are all home for semester break. Or you might recall your first experience eating a unique food on your campus that, once you had tasted it, confirmed that you were now an official member of the campus community.

As you consider the foods, the recipes, and the dining spots that you find most familiar and most comforting—or, conversely, most alien and most disturbing—you are beginning the process of thinking about how the culture of food has shaped who you are as a daughter or son, brother or sister, niece or nephew, friend or colleague. What you are searching for here is an experience or event or relationship within which food has played a vital role—and helped you to understand something about life that you want other people to know.

1. Make a list of the foods that are most pleasurable, most memorable, or most meaningful to you. For each food, describe at least one experience that you have had with it. Explain why the experiences were positive or negative, providing as many details as possible. If anything could have made the bad experiences better, explain what and how. For each experience, include as many contributing factors as you can: the people you were with when you were eating the food, the place where you were eating the food, the occasion for eating the food, the events that had led up to the moment or that followed immediately after it, and so forth.

2. Choosing one or two foods, sketch pictures of the food, the location where you ate it, or the occasion on which you ate it. Or take photos of the food, the event, or the location from different vantage points, paying particular attention to the details and features that you find most intriguing about the experience of eating the food.

3. Choose the food you want to write about and compose four or five descriptions of the significance that food has for you. Vary the ways you describe the significance by emphasizing different aspects of the situation in which you have eaten or most often eat the food. For example, one description might emphasize your pleasant or unpleasant memories of the first time you ate the food. Another description might emphasize a particular person the food reminds you of, and yet another might deal with the sense of belonging or alienation that eating this food has created in you.

Locating an audience

For her blog and her memoir, Julie Powell had to consider two audiences: those readers who were most interested in hearing specific details about how she made and adapted recipes from Julia Child's classic *Mastering the Art of French Cooking* and those readers who were more interested in hearing her tell humorous stories and give interesting details about her experiences in the kitchen. The structure and the language of her writing, then, conformed to the demands of critics who expected to see her demonstrate her culinary abilities as well as the interests of readers who wanted to laugh their way through her cooking journey.

Which audiences should you consider for your writing? First, think about the type of food-related experience that you'll be describing; then, ask yourself who would be most interested or engaged in reading about that experience. For instance, if you're going to write about how the local diner's grilled sticky buns sustained you through many long nights of essay writing, perhaps your school's alumni would be interested in reminiscing about—and longing for—that tasty dessert. Or if you'll be writing about a particular traditional food that's unique to your family, perhaps your classmates, teachers, and friends should read about this in order to learn more about you and your family's unique culinary contribution. Or if your memoir is going to be about your delicious discoveries at the downtown farmers' market, perhaps you could write it for the community magazine or local newspaper. Whatever food-related experience you choose to write about, you'll want to think about the message you want to convey about it and yourself and then decide who would be a receptive audience for this story—or an adversarial audience that you want to persuade to a new way of thinking about a food.

The following questions will help you locate your rhetorical audience as well as identify their relationship to the food-related experience you've decided to write about. Having identified your audience, you'll be able to choose the most descriptive details to include and the best way to deliver the message you want that audience to receive.

1. List the names of the persons or groups who might be most interested in hearing about your experiences with this particular food or who might be most resistant to your story but need to hear about it anyway.

2. Next to the name of each potential audience, write reasons that audience could have for acknowledging the significance of your experience. In other words, what would convince these audiences that you have a unique and interesting story to tell—a story they need to hear more about in order to think more deeply about the food experiences in their own lives?

3. What kinds of responses to your writing could you reasonably expect each of these audiences to have? Think here about similar experiences that the audience might have had as well as the openness to new perspectives or the desire for familiar experiences that the audience likely possesses.

4. With your audience's interests, experiences, and perspectives in mind, look again at the descriptions of food experiences and their significance that you composed in the preceding section on identifying an exigence. Decide which descriptions will engage your audience most forcefully and help your audience to understand something about their own food-related experiences. At this point, it is probably necessary to revise your best descriptions to tailor them to your audience.

Identifying a Fitting Response

Finding a purpose and shaping a fitting response

You have now explored various food-related experiences that have been significant in your life. You have written specific details describing those experiences to bring them to life for readers and considered who your audience might be and how your writing would resonate with them. But what specifically do you want to accomplish? Next, you need to define your purpose, which in turn will inform the specific type of text you create.

As you've been learning throughout this book, different purposes and different audiences require different kinds of texts. For example, the desire to recount your temptations and traumas at the college cafeteria's dessert table might prompt you to write a humorous column for the school's alumni magazine. Your narrative describing how your grandfather taught you to cook his delicious stir-fry recipe might find a place in your family's scrapbook. The point here is that once you identify your exigence, audience, and purpose, you need to determine what kind of text will best respond to the rhetorical situation.

Use the following questions to help you narrow your purpose and shape your response:

1. What specific message do you want to convey about your food-related experience?
2. What kind of reaction do you want from your audience? Are you asking the audience to be more thoughtful about the experiences that have shaped their own lives? Are you asking the audience to reconsider foods that they tend to think of as "different" or "bad"? Or are you asking the audience to perform a particular action?
3. What is the best way to connect with your audience? That is, what kind of text is this audience most likely to have access to and most likely to respond to?

Your instructor (or your rhetorical situation) may prompt you to write a letter, a review, or some other form of written response. Anna Seitz's lesson on killing a chicken, for instance, which begins on page 122, could have been relayed in any of several genres. If her purpose had been to inform other novices, she could have written a how-to guide using the rhetorical strategy of process analysis (see chapter 14). If she wanted her somewhat gory descriptions to make a direct argument against eating meat, she could have written a position argument. A letter tucked inside a birthday card to her cousin would have conveyed a funny anecdote about the perils of animal husbandry. Instead, Anna wanted her readers to feel the conflict she had experienced, and she knew that to replicate those feelings, she would need to appeal to her readers' physical senses and to pay particular attention to the ethos she was creating for herself. She also knew that her experience was about more than just chickens—and that she could describe it in a way that made clear its larger significance. Thus, Anna knew a memoir was appropriate for her rhetorical situation. If, like Anna, you are prompted to write a memoir, continue with the following assignment as a guide.

Writing a Memoir: Working with Your Available Means

Shaping your memoir

As you have probably figured out by now, a memoir is a genre arranged much like a fictional work such as a novel or short story. The **introduction** hooks readers by dropping them right in the middle of an interesting situation or by presenting them with an especially vivid description. This introduction announces the focal point of your memoir, whether that be a specific food or a significant culinary experience, or a particular aspect of your present personality that was shaped by a food or eating experience earlier in your life. Pooja Makhijani, for example, opens her memoir with descriptions of what her mother packs in her lunch bag and what she yearns for instead—what would be on her classmates' lunch trays that day. In so doing, she introduces the tension between herself and her mother, which manifests itself in their different ideas about what is appropriate or desirable food. But Makhijani also begins to build a conflict for the rest of her memoir by leaving this tension unspoken. Rather than being open about her desire to eat bologna on white bread and Cool Ranch Doritos like her classmates, she says nothing. In short, Makhijani, like all good memoir writers, creates effective pathos appeals through the introduction of her piece—she describes the characters and their actions in such a way as to get readers emotionally invested in her topic.

The **body** of a memoir presents the narrative, the plot or the major sequence of events. As you've learned in this chapter, a memoir focuses on a specific event or series of events that is significant rather than narrating each and every event in a person's life. The events or experiences that you choose to include should be those that have proven to be most meaningful for you, that best illustrate the point you want to make, or that best convey the message you want to send. As you describe the specific events, choose concrete, precise verbs that reveal the actions taken by the different characters and use transitional phrases such as *by that time* and *later in the day* to show the sequence of events and help readers see how the events relate to one another in time.

In addition, the body of a memoir provides specific sensory details. You'll want to describe the food you ate, the place where you ate it, and the other people (the characters in your memoir) you were with. Makhijani helps readers to understand the care with which her mother made those school lunches by describing each piece of food in mouth-watering detail; she contrasts these homemade lunches with the bland mass-produced foods on her classmates' lunch trays. Such sensory details are important for helping readers to imagine the events, the foods, and the characters at the heart of your memoir; they also help you to deliver the specific message you want to convey to readers. Vivid descriptions invite readers to emotionally connect with and invest themselves in the lives and activities of the major characters. In Makhijani's memoir, her vivid details help readers feel just how strong her desire to assimilate is, so strong that she would rather eat peaches from a can than her mother's deep-fried potato patties "spiked with garam masala" and "slathered with fresh coriander chutney."

The body of a memoir also develops the various characters. You'll certainly want to use sensory details to help readers visualize the key features and actions of each character. Equally important, you'll want to create dialogue between the characters to reveal important aspects about their personalities and relationship to one another. For example, Makhijani never directly asks her mother if she can buy school lunches. Instead, because she fears what her mother will say, she speaks indirectly about what her classmates do and eat ("Chrissy brought Coke with her to school yesterday") in the hope that her mother will get her point. It's important to use dialogue or quoted speech purposefully, to help readers get deeper insight into the thoughts and emotions of your characters.

One more element to incorporate into the body of your memoir is reflection on or analysis of the events that you're narrating. Reflection and analysis encourage readers to notice particular details or help them understand the significance of a particular experience for a character's self-development. Drawing on the methods of critical analysis allows you to craft compelling rhetorical appeals. In the case of logos, you may try to convince readers that your analysis is the best way to interpret the significance of certain events in the memoir. In terms of ethos, you may present an analysis that seems to consider the perspectives of all characters involved in order to cast yourself as an open-minded, well-reasoned observer of events. For example, look again at the paragraph that comes immediately after Aisha asks, "Then why don't you eat the school lunch?" Makhijani's reflection not only gives dramatic pause but also reveals her perception of herself: "I know it's not because it's too expensive or that Styrofoam trays are environmentally unsound. It's because Mom thinks her deep-fried aloo tikkis and freshly ground masalas are what good Indian parents give their daughters. She doesn't understand that good Indian daughters just want to become American." This allows readers to see how Makhijani's relationship to her mother's food was directly connected to her desire to identify herself as an "American." As you narrate the events in your memoir, look for places where you can help readers to understand the significance of specific details or events by stopping the action and providing a few sentences of reflection or analysis.

The **conclusion** of a memoir reinforces the message, or the point of the story. The important consideration here is to be sure the events you've narrated, the details you've provided, and the reflection or analysis you've composed all work together to deliver a clear, coherent message. You might, as Makhijani does, conclude your memoir with a scene that perfectly captures the mood you want readers to experience or the image you want them to remember. Or you might decide to conclude your memoir with a more traditional paragraph that, like your reflective components, speaks fairly explicitly about the point of the events that you've described. Either way, your readers will respond favorably to your conclusion if it helps them to see how the events have significance both for you as the writer and for them as your readers.

CHECKING OVER A MEMOIR

✓ The memoir focuses on a particularly significant experience or series of experiences in the writer's life.

✓ The memoir contains ample sensory details to help readers visualize, hear, smell, taste, or feel the key events, characters, experiences, and objects.

✓ The memoir includes selected bits of dialogue or quoted speech that reveal something unique about or central to a character or the character's relationship with other people, events, or objects in the story.

✓ The memoir includes clear transitional phrases to show how events relate to one another in time and how the action of the narrative unfolds.

✓ The memoir provides reflection on or analysis of the key narrative events in order to help readers understand their significance for the writer's development and his or her perspective on everyday life.

Student paper

The following student essay is a memoir about a food-related event. Because the memoir uses the narrative form, it includes a setting, characters, dialogue, and a sequence of events—all of which enrich the text.

Anna Seitz

English 260

Professor Lundin

November 20, 2007

Herb's Chicken

Last year, my husband Bill and I, fueled by farmers' market fantasies, decided we wanted to keep some backyard chickens. Since we had to wait until spring to order birds, we spent the winter getting our coop, and ourselves, ready. We read stacks of books and magazines on raising chickens, and we decided to ask our friend Herb to teach us to "process" them.

When we pulled into Herb's driveway on the big day, he was already hanging out the back door, gesturing to the cane at the bottom of the steps. He's 87 years old and has been a poultry farmer since he got back from the war. He shuffles slowly, hunched over. He can't hear much of what we say. When he can hear, he usually just rolls his eyes. Bill handed him the cane, and Herb led us to the last of his coops that still has chickens. His farm of 6,000 birds is down to 75. "Well, how many you want?" Herb asks.

"I don't know," said my husband. "Got one that's not layin'?"

"Get that one there," said Herb. He pointed his finger in the direction of a group of three birds, and my husband, appearing to know which one Herb meant, took a couple of steps toward them. They immediately dispersed.

Herb grabbed a long handle with a hook at the end, resembling the sort of wand I've used to roast weenies over a campfire, and handed it to Bill. He pointed again. "There," he said. Bill grabbed the tool and managed to at least tangle up the bird's feet. Herb snapped up the bird with the efficient movement of someone who has snapped up tens of thousands of birds, and handed the bird, upside-down, to me.

I held it carefully by the ankles and got a little shiver. It flapped its wings a few times, but it didn't really try to fight me. It actually looked pretty pitiful hanging there. Herb was already walking back to the house.

"Pull up that bird feeder, Billy," barked Herb, in his thin voice.

My husband had worked digging graves with Herb since he was fifteen, and he was used to taking orders. "Yup," he said. He walked up to a bird feeder on a stake and pulled it up from the ground.

Herb unhooked a metal cone which he'd been using on the stake as a squirrel deterrent and slid it off the bottom. "For the chicken," he told me as I caught up to them. "I'll open the cellar."

Bill and I waited outside the bulkhead for Herb. He opened it up still holding the metal cone in his hand. "Come on," he instructed. We made our way down into the dark. The chicken tried to arch its head up to peck me. I handed it over to Bill.

In the cellar, Herb hooked the cone to a beam. "Give me that," he said to me, gesturing at a dusty bucket on the floor next to me. I pushed it with my foot until it was under the cone.

"All right!" said my husband brightly. I stiffened. He pushed the chicken head-first into the cone, until her head poked through the opening at the bottom and her feet stuck out the top. The chicken got one wing free, but my husband put a rubber band around her feet and hooked it on the nail that held the cone. She was stuck.

Herb fished through his pocket for his knife, and my eyelids started to wrinkle. I held my lips tightly closed. "You just need to go through the roof of the mouth and get them right in the brain," said Herb. "It's better than chopping the head off because they don't tense up. Makes it easier to get the feathers off."

"Won't it bite you?" I asked.

"So what if it does?" answered Herb. "Last thing it'll ever do." Herb easily pried the mouth open with his left hand, and with his right, he pushed the knife into its brain and turned it. It was over. I furrowed my brow.

"Then you gotta bleed it," he said. Herb pulled the knife down, and in one quick motion, cut the chicken's throat from the inside. Blood spilled from its open beak into the bucket. My husband watched with interest, offering the same occasional "Yup" or "Uh-huh" that he uses when listening to any good story. I watched with my eyes squinted and my face half turned away.

Herb rinsed the knife in the washbasin and announced, "Gotta get the water. Anna, it's on the stove. Hot but not boiling." I went up to the kitchen and fiddled with the temperature under a big soup pot. It looked about right, I guessed.

By the time I got the water down to the cellar, Herb and Bill had already pulled the chicken out of the cone and tossed the head into the bloody bucket. It looked more like food when I couldn't see the eyes. Herb told my husband to dip the bird in the hot water a few times, and he did, holding it by the rubber-banded legs. When he pulled it out, some of the feathers on its chest started to drop off.

From under the stairs, Herb pulled out a large plastic drum, the sides dotted with rubber fingers. He put the chicken inside and switched it on. After a few minutes, he pulled out a mostly featherless chicken. The feathers stuck to the sides of the drum. "Get that," he said to Bill. While Bill pulled feathers out of the plucker, Herb held the chicken by the feet and pulled off the remaining feathers—mostly large wing and tail feathers, and a few small pin feathers. By now there really wasn't any blood left, and the chicken looked pretty close to what you might get in the store, except skinnier.

Bill brought the chicken and the bucket up to the kitchen, and Herb and I followed. Herb took the bird and dropped it down into the sink with a smack. "Now, you cut out the crop," Herb said. He pointed to something I couldn't see, then cut into the throat and showed us a little sack full of stones and grain. "It's how they chew, I guess," he added. He tugged on it, and it brought with it a large section of the windpipe. "To get the rest of the guts out you gotta cut in the back."

Herb made an incision and stuck in his hand, making a squishy sound. He pulled out a handful of guts and dropped most of it into the bucket. He cut off one section and held it toward Bill. "You got the wrong bird," he said. The slimy tube was sort of transparent, and through it we could see a string of about eight little eggs of increasing size, beginning with a tiny yolk, and ending with an almost full-sized egg.

"Can you eat 'em?" I asked.

"Guess you could," said Herb, throwing the whole mess into the bucket, "but I got eggs." He turned the chicken, lopped off the feet, and tossed them into the bucket. They landed toes up, like a grotesque garnish. "Well, want a plastic bag?"

I accepted the grocery bag and some plastic wrap and wrapped the carcass up while Herb and Bill took the bucket outside. They talked for a while, and then Herb directed Bill up onto a ladder to check a gutter. I stood with my back to the carcass, examining Herb's wife's display of whimsical salt and pepper shakers.

When my husband and I got back in the car, I put the carcass at my feet. "That was great!" said my husband. "Think we can do it on our own?"

I thought through the steps in my mind. "I think I can," I chirped. I thought of the bucket and the toe garnish. "But I'm not eating it."

Now that you have read the successful memoir by Anna Seitz, think about other options she might have considered as a fitting response to her rhetorical situation.

1. Have you recently had a satisfying dining-out experience, on campus or off, that you want your friends and classmates to enjoy as well? Or have you suffered through a restaurant meal that you would not wish on your worst enemy? What were the aspects of your experience that made it satisfying and enjoyable or unfulfilling and unpleasant? In an essay of three to four pages, critically review that dining experience. Be sure to specify the criteria on which you're basing your evaluation and to provide specific examples that show how the food, the service, and the atmosphere contributed to the overall dining experience.

2. In *Fast Food Nation,* Eric Schlosser notes a disturbing trend in the culture of food in industrialized nations, and he analyzes both the causes and the consequences of this problem. In a three- or four-page essay, analyze the causes and consequences of a positive or negative aspect of the culture of food on your campus or in your community. Be sure to provide concrete evidence and details to support your analysis.

3. Margaret Mead identified a particular problem in the American culture of food and offered a difficult solution for that problem. Identify a problem concerning the culture of food on your campus or in your community and write a proposal in which you outline in three or four pages a plan for solving that problem. Be sure to identify the rhetorical audience for your proposal (that is, some person or group in a position to put your solution into action) and to describe the problem in a way that emphasizes the importance of addressing it right away. Present your solution in specific detail and include analysis that shows its appropriateness and feasibility.

Guide to Responding

5 | PORTRAYING SUCCESSFUL RHETORS: RESPONDING WITH PROFILES

What thoughts come to your mind when you see the famous image of the Reverend Dr. Martin Luther King, Jr., speaking at the March on Washington for Jobs and Freedom, on August 28, 1963? Perhaps you think about the values in which King believed and the civil rights for which he fought. Perhaps you think of his nonviolent resistance to the oppression faced by African Americans in the 1950s and 1960s. Perhaps you remember other images from the civil rights movement—marchers beaten back by powerful streams of water or sit-ins at once-segregated lunch counters. Chances are, though, that this image brings to your mind the famous words spoken on that day in 1963 on the steps of the Lincoln Memorial:

So even though we face the difficulties of today and tomorrow, I still have a dream. I have a dream that one day this nation will rise up and live out the true meaning of its creed . . . that all men are created equal. I have a dream that one day even the state of Mississippi, a state sweltering with the heat of oppression, will be transformed into an oasis of freedom and justice. I have a dream that my four little children will one day live in a nation where they will not be judged by the color of their skin but by the content of their character. I have a dream today. And if America is to be a great nation, this must become true.

—**Martin Luther King, Jr.,** "I Have a Dream"

King's legacy in U.S. history centers on his great victories in the civil rights movement. This legacy was shaped, though, by his enviable ability to put his message into words. He could create moving narratives, vivid images, and logical arguments. He employed a host of rhetorical tools to persuade Americans of the need to act in ensuring universal civil rights.

There have been times in all of our lives that we have been moved to tears or to action or have been angered by the words of a public figure. What makes language move us in this way? How does the speaker or the writer craft language that can move us in this way? As curious human beings, we often want to learn about what motivates a person to say or write the things that he or she does or to learn when, where, and how the person learned to use language as effectively and as powerfully as he or she does. In pursuing answers to these questions, we often learn that how a person comes to craft a speech or a piece of writing is just as interesting as what any particular passage might say.

Every bit as important as how a person crafts the message is how those words are delivered. Given our multimodal world, you may already have a great deal of experience—maybe even expertise—in delivering your ideas electronically. But how much do you know about delivering information orally? Few of us deliver our ideas orally as well as we do in other ways. Great speakers, though, gauge perfectly the relationship between the content of their message and the expectations of their intended audience. They seem to be able to understand the context perfectly, adjusting their words and the delivery of those words accordingly. Finally, they usually have very appealing voices, which they

modulate with artistry. Most of the successful rhetors profiled in this chapter, like Martin Luther King, Jr., for instance, say good things—and say those good things very well.

Writers have used **profiles**—biographical sketches—to help others better understand how the most eloquent writers and politicians have honed their skills and how they have deployed them to effective ends. As readers of a profile, we gain glimpses into a person's private life and see how personal experiences affect the very visible work that the person does. A profile of Dr. Martin Luther King, Jr., for example, might help us to better understand how his daily life experiences as a black man and as a father affected his ideas about the value

of words in public life. A profile might also help us to better understand how King viewed his public speaking in relation to his actions, whether boycotting, marching, or conducting acts of civil disobedience such as those that landed him in the Birmingham Jail.

Writers create profiles to help readers gain a deeper understanding of a public figure—or of a person their readers might not otherwise have heard of. Writers create profiles to analyze the individuals who have shaped history. Writers create profiles to paint portraits with words, to describe a person in detail and to show how the pieces fit together to form the whole person. Quite simply, writers create profiles to better understand people in the world in which we live.

Dale Carnegie in Warrensburg, Missouri, on Dale Carnegie Day.

Real Situations

Many Americans believe that their ability to succeed in their personal and professional lives can be greatly enhanced by learning to be more effective public speakers. In 1912, Dale Carnegie taught his first public speaking courses at the 125th Street YMCA in New York City. By the early 1930s, Carnegie's approach had become so successful that he was teaching public speaking courses throughout New York. Carnegie persuaded many people who took courses that "despite what many school texts would lead us to believe, public speaking is not a closed art, to be mastered only after years of perfecting the voice and struggling with mysteries of rhetoric." Carnegie tapped into many Americans' beliefs about the importance of effective speaking—his book *Public Speaking and Influencing Men in Business* went through more than fifty printings and was translated into twenty languages, and more than three and a half million people have graduated from Dale Carnegie courses in many corners of the globe. Carnegie's success speaks to the belief of many people that, in radio broadcaster Lowell Thomas's words, "the ability to speak is a shortcut to distinction."

A public speaking class.

Organizations such as Toastmasters International have also tapped into this belief. The Toastmasters program branched off from Carnegie courses being conducted at a YMCA in Santa Ana, California, in 1924, and the organization today boasts nearly 211,000 members in 10,500 clubs in ninety countries. Participants gain a foundation in public speaking by working through a series of ten speaking assignments in a supportive atmosphere.

Your college or university may require you to take a public speaking course. Such a requirement, much like the requirement that all students take at least one writing course, is grounded in the belief that professionals need to possess more than the technical knowledge at the heart of their field or discipline—they need to be able to communicate this knowledge to others, as well. Moreover, your experiences in your public speaking course are meant to instill in you the ability to appreciate and engage in debates in your other courses and in your community. Many colleges and universities also give their students extra-curricular opportunities to improve their abilities in public speaking through participation in debate teams. Students on these teams learn to generate arguments in response to challenging ethical, legal, and political questions and to present their positions in a logically reasoned and stylistically polished way. Many students use their experiences on college debate teams as preparation for future careers in the law, business, or politics.

A member of the Irvine Valley College debate team makes an argument.

The Dale Carnegie courses, Toastmasters programs, and college public speaking courses are premised on the belief that anyone can become an effective wielder of words by learning to apply some basic skills. Most people, however, are somewhat awed by public figures who, like King, possess a powerful ability to move people through words. Where did they gain this ability? Were they born with it? Did they learn it? What motivates their work, and how do they approach their tasks?

In this chapter, you'll gain insight into some successful and effective rhetors. Just as important, you'll learn about the profile, a kind of writing that can give readers a fuller understanding of how public figures have come to their lives' work, how they have learned to use words effectively, and what motivates them to wield this power in their professional lives.

DESCRIBING SUCCESSFUL RHETORS

1. What do you know about Dr. Martin Luther King, Jr.'s abilities with words? What skills did he use most effectively or most often? Where did he acquire those skills? What motivated him to use words in the ways that he did? After freewriting in response to these questions for several minutes, conduct online research to learn what others have said about King's ability to achieve things with words.

2. Conduct online research on the topic of effective public speaking. What do your searches reveal about common beliefs and attitudes concerning the importance of wielding words effectively?

3. What do the images in this chapter suggest to you about successful rhetors?

1. Do you think effective public speakers are born with their ability, or can it be learned?

2. When have you listened to someone you consider to have achieved success through his or her ability with words? What were your impressions of your encounter with this person's words? What qualities or characteristics did this person possess that made him or her an effective rhetor?

3. Do you consider yourself to be good with words? If so, where did that ability come from? Did you learn it? When or how did you first discover that you did or did not have this skill?

4. What would you like to accomplish with words in your personal, professional, or civic life? What skills do you need to accomplish these things? When, where, or how might you learn them?

Real Responses to Real Situations

Persuasion from the presidential podium

President Lyndon B. Johnson's historical legacy has been tied to his creation of domestic social policies that shaped The Great Society as well as to U.S. struggles abroad in the Vietnam War. He was a consummate political professional, having served the country in numerous elected offices during his career. He first came to Washington in 1938 as a U.S. Representative from Texas's Tenth Congressional District. He had become a well-known Washington insider by the time he was elected to the U.S. Senate in 1948. He assumed the position of Democratic leader of the Senate in January 1953 and became the Senate majority leader two years later. During his time in this position, Johnson gained a reputation as being effective at wheeling and dealing, exercising his personal influence to get his colleagues to follow his lead and to drive legislation through the Senate. According to biographer Robert Dallek, he said, in 1960, "The only real power available to the [majority] leader is the power of persuasion. There is no patronage; no power to discipline; no authority to fire senators like a President can fire [Cabinet] members."

By the time Johnson was elected vice president in 1960, he had become so effective in his persuasive skills that President John F. Kennedy felt he had to be very careful in assigning Johnson duties. As Dallek explains, Kennedy did not want Johnson "managing [the administration's] legislative program and creating the impression that the President was following the lead of his Vice President, a more experienced legislator." Instead, Kennedy designated Johnson, among numerous responsibilities, to head the new Committee on Equal Employment Opportunity (CEEO) and to represent the nation abroad. Kennedy knew that civil rights issues were going to be central to his domestic agenda during the course of his four-year term. He also knew, however, that a conservative Congress was unlikely to move quickly to pass significant legislation in this area. He saw Johnson playing a key role as head of the CEEO in efforts to pass legislation

prohibiting discriminatory hiring practices by federal agencies and private businesses with federal contracts. As Dallek explains, Johnson was a southern moderate who guided the 1957 Civil Rights Act through Congress and maintained that "the national well-being required equal treatment for blacks." Kennedy believed that Johnson could use his skills of persuasion to see that legislation on this emotionally charged topic would become law.

Johnson was sworn in as president in November 1963, immediately after Kennedy's assassination. He rode the wave of popular sentiment and political support that followed the assassination and saw Congress pass significant laws aimed at fighting the War on Poverty. Then, in his 1964 presidential campaign, he promoted a sweeping domestic agenda to create a Great Society. After winning the election, he devoted much of his attention to passing Kennedy's civil rights bill. He made repeated public appeals to gather support for the legislation but eventually had to broker compromises that allowed the bill to pass with reluctant agreement from many Southern legislators. Even with the passage of this bill—or, more likely, because of its passage and the compromises that brought it into being—civil rights were forced onto the top of Johnson's agenda for the next several months. His skills in persuasion were never more needed to achieve social progress on such a volatile issue.

Johnson enjoyed renown for persuasive and political skills as he rose to power, and he also exerted tremendous power in shaping his public persona. Biographer Robert Caro noted that Johnson made it hard for others to understand his private and public selves: "Enlisting all his energy and all his cunning in a lifelong attempt to obscure not only the true facts of his rise to power and his use of power but even of his youth, he succeeded well." Caro set out to write a profile of Johnson as a means for better understanding not only what facts Johnson had obscured but also why he felt compelled to guard these details and stories so closely. As he slowly, painstakingly began to uncover these facts by reading over 650,000 pages of documents from the Johnson Presidential Library and conducting countless interviews, Caro began to see that Johnson employed his rhetorical skills for more than passing progressive social legislation and

persuading the American people of the need for ensuring equal rights and opportunities. Caro writes: "The more one thus [chronologically] follows his life,
the more apparent it becomes that alongside the thread of achievement running
through it runs another thread, as dark as the other is bright, and as fraught
with consequences for history: a hunger for power in its most naked form, for
power not to improve the lives of others, but to manipulate and dominate them,
to bend them to his will."

In the following excerpt, Caro provides a profile of Johnson's persuasive
abilities and strategies while president. This profile opens the second book,
Means of Ascent, in Caro's three-volume *The Years of Lyndon Johnson*. This scene
centers on President Johnson's speech on March 15, 1965, before a special joint
session of Congress, which Johnson used to introduce a bill that would bring
significant civil rights legislation into federal law.

ROBERT CARO
Excerpt from The Years of Lyndon Johnson: Means of Ascent

During the sixteen months since he had taken the oath
of office as thirty-sixth President of the United States,
Lyndon Johnson had done much for civil rights—
including pushing through to passage a civil rights bill
in 1964—but, in the view of most of the movement, he
hadn't done nearly as much as he should have.

. . . Very few of the tens of thousands—hundreds of
thousands—of men and women, black and white, in
the American civil rights movement believed Lyndon
Johnson was wholeheartedly on their side. So now, on
Monday, March 15, 1965, pickets had been marching

in front of the White House for the eight days since the
Edmund Pettus Bridge, walking in a long oval formation
along the sidewalk outside the tall black wrought-iron
fence that guarded the broad lawn that led to the Executive Mansion, carrying signs demanding that Lyndon Johnson take action, and singing. And the previous
day, a Sunday on which churches across the country
held services in memory of Reverend Reeb, fifteen
thousand protesters had held a rally in Lafayette Park,
across Pennsylvania Avenue from the White House, to
protest "federal inaction"—Johnson's inaction, ulti-

mately—"in the Alabama racial crisis." The rally end-ed with the singing of "We Shall Overcome." On the White House lawn, 350 Washington policemen formed a human wall reinforcing the wrought-iron wall, with White House guards and Secret Service men deployed behind them, but the mighty hymn could be heard clearly inside the White House, as could the words of a chant the protesters had adopted: "LBJ, you just wait / See what happens in '68." Speakers at the rally assailed his promises—"President Johnson's words are good, but they remain just that: words," one said—and his performance. His Administration, another speaker said, "has told the same old story in the Selma crisis. The minute there's violence, the Administration announces it's powerless to deal with it." There was little feeling in that crowd that Lyndon Johnson had any deeper commitment to this cause than he had shown in the past, so that the words "We shall overcome," sung outside the White House, were saying, in effect, that the cause would manage to win even without him. And now, on the evening the limousines were pulling away from the White House, the pickets were singing "We Shall Overcome."

Inside the fourth in the line of long, black vehicles that headed for the South gates, away from the pickets, a long double line of motorcycle outriders moving out ahead, Lyndon Johnson sat in the back seat, facing three of his assistants, his huge ears, outsized nose and jutting jaw accentuated by the light from the reading lamp behind him as he bent over a black looseleaf notebook containing the speech he was about to give to Congress. His massive bulk—he was more than six feet three inches tall, and weighed about 230 pounds—and the fierceness of the concentration with which he bent over the notebook and of the way his big hands snatched for the next page while he was still reading the one before it seemed to fill the car. He had entered the limousine without a word of greeting, and had immediately opened the notebook for a last-minute study of the speech. He said not a word during the ride to the Capitol. His eyes didn't look up from the notebook as the limousine passed the White House gates—with the pickets singing "We Shall Overcome" as if to tell him to his face, "If you won't help us, we'll win without you." But one of the assistants riding with him had worked for him for almost twenty years, and saw his

expression, and knew what it meant. "He heard," Horace Busby recalls.

With almost the first words of his speech, the audience—the congressmen and Senators with whom he had served, the Cabinet members he had appointed, the black-robed Justices of the Supreme Court, the Ambassadors of other nations, a few in robes of far-off countries as if to dramatize that the world as well as America was listening, the packed galleries rimming him above—knew that Lyndon Johnson intended to take the cause of civil rights further than it had ever gone before. "At times history and fate meet at a single time in a single place to shape a turning point in man's unending search for freedom," the President said. "So it was at Lexington and Concord. So it was a century ago at Appomattox. So it was last week in Selma, Alabama."

He would submit a new civil rights bill, Johnson said—the Congress would have it before them that week—and it would be far stronger than the bills of the past. The strength of those bills had been diluted by compromise, he said, by compromise and delay; in the case of the last bill, just a year before, by a Southern filibuster which it took liberal forces eight months to overcome. In the minds of many in his audience as he spoke was the fact that he himself, on the previous bill, had often led the forces of compromise. "This time, on this issue," he said now, "there must be no delay, no hesitation and no compromise." But still no one among those Senators, congressmen, Justices, Ambassadors, not even the most perceptive, knew how far he was really going to go—for none of them could have predicted the words to come.

By submitting the bill, Johnson said, he was fulfilling the formal purpose of his appearance before them, but it was not merely a bill that he wanted to talk about. "Even if we pass this bill," the President said, "the battle will not be over. What happened in Selma is part of a far larger movement which reaches into every section and state of America. It is the effort of American Negroes to secure for themselves the full blessings of American life."

There was the briefest pause, as if he were gathering himself, and over his face came a look that the public, thus far in his presidency, had seldom seen, so careful had he been to wear a mask he considered statesmanlike and dignified. The eyes narrowed a little, and the jaw

continued

> "The next four words fell like sledgehammers."

jutted, and the mouth, barely keeping itself from a snarl, hinted at it, and the tens of millions of people watching on television were looking into a face that many of those in the audience in the Capitol knew already—the face of a Lyndon Johnson determined to win.

"Their cause must be our cause, too," Lyndon Johnson said. "Because it is not just Negroes, but really it is all of us, who must overcome the crippling legacy of bigotry and injustice."

Briefly, he paused again. He always had so much trouble in his speeches with the emphasis on the words, but he got it right this time. The next four words fell like sledgehammers.

"And we shall overcome."

There was a moment of silence, as if, one observer was to say, it took a moment for the audience to realize that the President had adopted the rallying cry of black protest as his own, had joined his voice to the voices of the men and women who had sung that mighty hymn. And then the applause rolled across the Chamber.

And there were testimonies to the power of that speech even more eloquent than that applause. One took place in the living room of a local family in Selma, Alabama, where Martin Luther King and several of his aides were watching the speech on television. During all the years of struggle, none of his aides had ever seen Dr. King cry. When Johnson said, "We shall overcome," they looked over to their leader to see his reaction. So they were looking when Martin Luther King began to cry.

Another testimony took place on the motorcade's return to the White House. As the limousines slowed to turn into the White House gates, the turn was made in silence.

The pickets were gone.

This profile gives readers a sense of how the social and political context shaped Johnson's presentation of the Voting Rights Act. More broadly, Caro writes this profile in a way that shows readers how Johnson employed his vast arsenal of rhetorical skills to persuade Congress and the nation of his vision and his capacity to lead.

Peggy Noonan worked as a speechwriter for U.S. Presidents Ronald Reagan and George H. W. Bush. She also authored *What I Saw at the Revolution: A Political Life in the Reagan Era*. In the following excerpt from that book, she describes her craft. As you read, consider how this passage might deepen your understanding of Robert Caro's profile of Lyndon Baines Johnson's March 15, 1965 speech in which he introduced the Voting Rights Act.

PEGGY NOONAN
Excerpt from What I Saw at the Revolution: A Political Life in the Reagan Era

All speechwriters have things they think of when they write. I think of being a child in my family at the dinner table, with seven kids and hubbub and parents distracted by worries and responsibilities. Before I would say anything at the table, before I would approach my parents, I would plan what I would say. I would map out the narrative, sharpen the details, add color, plan momentum. This way I could hold their attention. This way I became a writer.

The American people too are distracted by worries and responsibilities and the demands of daily life, and you have to know that and respect it—and plan the narrative, sharpen the details, add color and momentum.

I work with an image: the child in the mall. When candidates for president are on the campaign trail they always go by a mall and walk through followed by a pack of minicams and reporters. They go by Colonel Sanders and have their picture taken eating a piece of

Peggy Noonan with President Ronald Reagan.

Real Responses

chicken, they josh around with the lady in the mall information booth, they shake hands with the shoppers. But watch: Always there is a child, a ten-year-old girl, perhaps, in an inexpensive, tired-looking jacket. Perhaps she is by herself, perhaps with a friend. But she stands back, afraid of the lights, and as the candidate comes she runs away. She is afraid of his fame, afraid of the way the lights make his wire-rim glasses shine, afraid of dramatic moments, dense moments. When you are a speech writer you should think of her when you write, and of her parents. They are Americans. They are good people for whom life has not been easy. Show them respect and be honest and logical in your approach and they will understand every word you say and hear—and know—that you thought of them.

The irony of modern speeches is that as our ability to disseminate them has exploded (an American president can speak live not only to America but to Europe, to most of the world), their quality has declined.

Why? Lots of reasons, including that we as a nation no longer learn the rhythms of public utterance from Shakespeare and the Bible. When young Lincoln was sprawled in front of the fireplace reading *Julius Caesar*—"Th' abuse of greatness is, when it disjoins remorse from power"—he was, unconsciously, learning to be a poet. You say, "That was Lincoln, not the common man." But the common man was flocking to the docks to get the latest installment of Dickens off the ship from England.

The modern egalitarian impulse has made politicians leery of flaunting high rhetoric; attempts to reach, to find the right if sometimes esoteric quote or allusion seem pretentious. They don't really know what "the common man" knows anymore; they forget that we've all had at least some education and a number of us read on our own and read certain classics in junior high and high school. The guy at the gas station read *Call of the Wild* when he was fourteen, and sometimes thinks about it. Moreover, he has imagination. Politicians forget. They go in for the lowest common denominator—like a newscaster.

People say the problem is soundbites. But no it isn't. . . .

Soundbites in themselves are not bad. "We have nothing to fear . . ." is a soundbite. "Ask not . . ." is a soundbite. So are "You shall not crucify mankind upon a cross of gold," and "With malice toward none; with charity for all . . ."

Great speeches have always had great soundbites. The problem is that the young technicians who put together speeches are paying attention only to the soundbite, not to the text as a whole, not realizing that all great soundbites happen by accident, which is to say, all great soundbites are yielded up inevitably, as part of the natural expression of the text. They are part of the tapestry, they aren't a little flower somebody sewed on.

They sum up a point, or make a point in language that is pithy or profound. They are what the politician is saying! They are not separate and discrete little one-liners that a bright young speechwriter just promoted out of the press office and two years out of business school slaps on.

But that is what they've become. Young speechwriters forget the speech and write the soundbite, plop down a hunk of porridge and stick on what they think

> "The irony of modern speeches is that as our ability to disseminate them has exploded . . . , their quality has declined."

continued

is a raisin. (In the Dukakis campaign they underlined them in the text.)

The problem is not the soundbitization of rhetoric, it's the Where's-the-beef-ization. The good news: Everyone in America is catching on to the game, and it's beginning not to work anymore. A modest hope: Politicians will stop hiring communications majors to write their speeches and go to history majors, literature majors, writers—people who can translate the candidate's impulses into literature that is alive, and true.

Noonan gives readers a glimpse into the process of crafting presidential rhetoric and helps them to evaluate how it works and achieves—or fails to achieve—its desired ends. Her reflections on her own writing process also help readers to understand the ways all good communicators envision their audiences as a means toward connecting with them through the spoken or written word.

ANALYZING THE RHETORICAL SITUATION

1. Who do you think might be the intended audience of each of these profiles? Do the audiences differ from one to the next? If so, in what ways? What textual evidence have you analyzed that leads you to these conclusions? Be prepared to share your answers with the rest of the class.

2. What is the purpose of each profile? What opinions does each writer want readers to leave with? What are the specific differences in the purposes of these two excerpts? How does the purpose of each intersect with the writer's intended audience? Again, be prepared to share your answers with the rest of the class.

3. To what exigence might each writer be responding? How does the piece of writing work to resolve that exigence?

4. How does each writer marshal the rhetorical appeals of ethos, logos, and pathos to support an opinion on presidential rhetoric? Draw on passages from the texts to support your answer.

5. Robert Caro's profile introduced *Means of Ascent*, the second book of a three-volume biography. What do you learn about President Lyndon Johnson in this passage, and why might Caro have decided to use this profile as the first image that his readers encounter about Johnson in this book?

Rhetorical success in the African American pulpit

Like many people in the United States, you've likely been introduced to African American preaching in the form of public speeches made by Dr. Martin Luther King, Jr., the Reverend Jesse Jackson, or the Reverend Al Sharpton. All three of these speakers undoubtedly draw on their religious and rhetorical training in their efforts to influence the course of public events. Indeed, the story of Dr. King's youth has been well told, as he sat in the pew at Ebenezer Baptist Church in Atlanta. Throughout his career as a public servant of the civil rights movement, King often said, "In the quiet recesses of my heart, I am fundamentally a clergyman, a Baptist preacher." Scholars and political commentators have thoroughly analyzed how King, Jackson, and Sharpton draw on the rich traditions of both European American and African American sermonic traditions in making their public appeals for justice and freedom for marginalized peoples. Even as they tap into these rhetorical traditions, however, the public oratory of Reverends King, Jackson, and Sharpton, according to Michael Eric Dyson, has been informed "by a mission to translate the aspirations of black Americans to the larger secular society." Dyson explains that as a result, they have emphasized certain elements and themes that mark African American preaching styles, but they have also submerged other rhetorical strategies and styles.

King, Jackson, and Sharpton have attracted the attention of mainstream U.S. society both through their actions, leading sit-ins and marches labeled as "newsworthy" by the popular press, and through their oratory, which has brought the religious pulpit to the public podium. Much less is known by mainstream society about prominent African American religious leaders who spend their entire lives and careers serving their local congregations and teaching and inspiring them through their words. One of these is the Reverend Dr. Gardner Taylor, the man *Time* magazine in 1980 called "the dean of the nation's black preachers."

Taylor's preaching skill was revered by King, and the two became close friends as Taylor worked actively for the civil rights movement in New York. In a 1993 survey for *Ebony* magazine, Taylor's peers voted him the greatest black preacher and one of America's greatest preachers. In *Ebony*'s accompany-

Reverend Gardner Taylor, "the dean of the nation's black preachers."

ing article, James H. Costen, who was then president of the Interdenominational Theological Center, echoed *Time*'s 1980 declaration, saying that Taylor "stands alone" as "the president, dean, provost and master artisan of Black preaching. . . . Hearing him preach gives one the impression that he has a direct pipeline to God." In 2000, Taylor received the Presidential Medal of Freedom. President Bill Clinton said, as he bestowed the award on Taylor, "For those of us who heard him preach, and those of us whom he has counseled in his private wisdom, we know we have been in the presence of not only a man of God, but a great American citizen."

Michael Eric Dyson wrote the following profile of Taylor in 1995. Dyson is University Professor at Georgetown University, the author of more than a dozen books, and an ordained Baptist minister. He wrote the profile for *Christian Century*, where he was a contributing editor.

MICHAEL ERIC DYSON
Excerpt from Gardner Taylor: The Poet Laureate of the American Pulpit

"Gardner Taylor is the greatest preacher living, dead or unborn," Wyatt Tee Walker proclaimed as he introduced Taylor at a service marking Walker's 25th anniversary as pastor of Harlem's Canaan Baptist Church. Among black Baptists, the pastoral anniversary is an often lavishly orchestrated event, joining praise and pocketbook in feting a congregation's spiritual head. But on the crisp October morning of his celebration, Walker shared the spotlight with the man *Time* magazine in 1980 dubbed "the dean of the nation's black preachers." David Dinkins, then mayor of New York, also spoke at the service, and declared that Taylor's preaching could be described in only two ways: "good and better."

These free-flowing encomiums might seem the natural excesses of a feel-good service. But they mirror the sentiments of many—black and white, religious and secular, preaching authorities and laypeople—who have been entranced, even transformed, by Taylor's oratorical gifts.

Taylor himself is more modest. When I mentioned *Time*'s declaration he deflected the tribute with characteristic humor. "You know what they say a dean is, at least of eastern schools?" he asked. "Somebody too smart to be president, but not smart enough to teach." He smiled, shrugged his shoulders in self-deprecation and deadpanned, "So much for being dean."

His humor and lack of hubris, combined with his preaching genius, have won the energetic 74-year-old Taylor a legion of admirers during his half century of ministry. Most of his career has been spent as pastor of Brooklyn's 14,000-member Concord Baptist Church of Christ. He made that pulpit perhaps the most prestigious in black Christendom before retiring in 1990 after 42 years of service. The imposing, block-long gray brick church is a massive monument to black Christianity's continuing vitality. Under Taylor's leadership, Concord built a home for the aged, organized a fully accredited grade school (headed for over 30 years by Taylor's wife, Laura), and developed the Christ Fund, a million-dollar endowment for investing in the Brooklyn community.

For Taylor, his success is an example of how God works in human life. "It is as if God said 'I'm going to take this unlikely person from the Deep South and I'm going to open opportunities for him to show [the world] what I can do,'" he says.

Taylor was born in Baton Rouge, Louisiana, in 1918, the only son of the Rev. Washington and Selina Taylor.

Michael Eric Dyson.

"My father was a huge, tall ebony man who had no trace of anything but Africa in him," Taylor says. "And he was extraordinarily arrogant about it." By contrast, his mother "looked white." After her husband's death, Selina Taylor attended "normal school" to become a teacher, later earning a degree from Southern University through extension courses. In one of his four books of sermons, Taylor writes that despite his parents' lack of formal education, they "had a natural feel for the essential music of the English language wedded to an intimate and emotional affection for the great transactions of the scriptures." The same is true of their son. . . .

Despite his father's influence, Taylor had hopes of becoming a lawyer. With that in mind he attended Louisiana's Leland College. "Clarence Darrow fascinated me," he says. And because an aunt who helped raise him held the ministry in contempt, Taylor confesses that his view of religion wasn't exalted. "I thought preaching was a foolish way for people of normal intelligence to waste their lives."

But Taylor's plans changed dramatically when he survived a deadly automobile accident in which two men died. Taylor experienced his "call" in that event, discerning God's claim on his life: "I thought that God must want me to be his lawyer." Instead of enrolling at the University of Michigan Law School where he had been admitted, Taylor went to the now-defunct Oberlin School of Theology. At Oberlin he read avidly, following writers ranging from Heywood Broun to Walter Lippmann. Their "literary styles affected me," he says. He also served as pastor of a church in nearby Elyria, Ohio, and after graduation he pastored one in Baton Rouge, before being summoned at the tender age of 30 to Brooklyn's Concord Baptist Church, then with a membership of more than 5,000.

In New York Taylor joined an elite fellowship. "I don't think ever in the history of these two millennia have so many pulpit geniuses come together in one setting as I found in New York in the early 50s. . . . My God, it was unbelievable," he says. Taylor's multiracial aggregate included such preaching luminaries as Adam Clayton Powell Jr., George Buttrick, Paul Scherer, Robert McCracken, Sandy Ray and Fulton J. Sheen. . . .

Taylor's unique blend of gifts may place him at the forefront of even this great cadre of preachers. His mastery of the technical aspects of preaching is remarkable. He brilliantly uses metaphor, and he has an uncanny sense of rhythmic timing put to dramatic but not crassly theatrical effect. He condenses profound biblical truths into elegantly memorable phrases. He makes keen use of parallels to layer and reinforce the purpose of his sermons. His stunning control of narrative flow seamlessly weaves his thoughts together. His adroit mix and shift of cadences reflects the various dimensions of religious emotion. He superbly uses stories to illustrate profound intellectual truths and subtle repetition to unify sermons. And his control of his resonant voice allows him to pliantly whisper or prophetically thunder the truths of the gospel. What was once alleged of Southern Baptist preacher Carlyle Marney may equally be said of Taylor: he has a voice like God's—only deeper.

Taylor's commanding physical presence, hinged on a solid 6'1" frame, suggests the regal bearing of pulpit royalty. His broad face reveals seasoned character. His wide set eyes are alive to the world around him. Taylor's forehead is an artistic work of chiseled complexity. Furrows furiously cross-hatch his bronze brow,

"He condenses profound biblical truths into elegantly memorable phrases."

extending to the receded areas of his exposed, upper cranium where a shock of grey hair fastidiously obeys its combed direction. Taylor's massive hands are like finely etched soft leather. They function as dual promontories that stab the air in the broad sweep of pulpit gesture or clasp each other in the steadied self-containment of quiet reflection.

Taylor's snappy sartorial habits, though, hint more at Wall Street executive than Baptist preacher. For a class on homiletics [conversational preaching, as opposed to more formal sermonizing] that he occasionally teaches at Princeton Theological Seminary, Taylor wore a dark-blue, double-breasted wool suit with a windowpane design, a burgundy-striped shirt, and a paisley tie. And at Wyatt Walker's pastoral anniversary, he wore a charcoal-gray pin-striped suit, with a white shirt and burgundy tie.

But it is not his sharp dressing which draws most attention to Taylor. The preacher's magnetism lies in his intimate and unequalled command of the language and literature of the English-speaking pulpit.

James Earl Massey, himself a noted preacher, professor of homiletics and dean of Anderson School of Theology in Indiana, contends that the gifts such figures as Harry Emerson Fosdick, Phillips Brooks, and Henry Ward Beecher brought to the American pulpit scene, "Taylor has brought in one person." Taylor possesses Beecher's "prolix ability to spin words," Brooks's "earnestness of style and breadth of learning," and Fosdick's "ability to appeal to the masses and yet maintain a dignity in doing so."

Preaching authority Henry H. Mitchell, author of the widely cited *Black Preaching*, agrees. He points to Taylor's familiarity with the preaching tradition as a key to his appeal. "He's not only master of black preaching as such. He knows all the great white preachers and quotes them [as well]."

Carolyn Knight, a professor of preaching at Union Theological Seminary and pastor of a New York church, recalls a conversation she had with Taylor that displayed his endless pursuit of preaching excellence. "He told me last year—and he advised me to do it—that in preparation for his Beecher Lectures, he went into the stacks of Union's library and read every set of published Beecher Lectures."

continued

Taylor's reputation as the "poet laureate of American Protestantism" is a considerable achievement. Throughout its history, black preaching has been widely viewed as a form of public address brimming with passion but lacking intellectual substance. Like black religion in general, black preaching is often seen as the cathartic expression of pent-up emotion, a verbal outpouring that supposedly compensates for low self-esteem or oppressed racial status. Not only are such stereotypes developed in ignorance of the variety of black preaching styles, but they don't take into account the black churches that boast a long history of educated clergy.

James Weldon Johnson's classic poem "God's Trombones" provides a literary glimpse of the art and imagination of the black folk preacher, while C. L. Franklin's recorded sermons, available in 60 albums put out by Chess records, brings the vigor of the black chanted sermon—dubbed in black church circles as "the whoop"—to the American public. By and large, however, Americans have remained insulated from the greatest rhetorical artists of the black pulpit.

Of course, broad segments of American society have sampled the richness of black preaching through the brilliant political oratory of Martin Luther King, Jr. and Jesse Jackson. Both King's and Jackson's styles of public speech—their impassioned phrasing, intellectual acuity and imaginative metaphors—reflect their roots in the black church. And their involvement in civil rights and politics extends the venerable tradition of black preachers serving as social critics and activists.

But their oratory—like that of preacher-politicians from Adam Clayton Powell to William Gray—has been shaped by the demands of public life and informed by a mission to make known the aspirations of black Americans to the larger society. This has led them to emphasize certain elements of the black preaching and church tradition, such as social justice, the institutional nature of sin and the redistribution of wealth, while leaving aside such others as the cultivation of the spiritual life, the nurturing of church growth and the development of pastoral theology. Such varying emphases are usually framed as the difference between "prophetic" and "priestly" religion. If the former has been most visible to American society in the guise of church-based civil rights activists, the latter has been closer to the heart of the religious experience of most black Christians.

Though Taylor has combined both approaches—he was active in the civil rights movement in New York, and was a close friend and preaching idol of Martin Luther King, Jr.—he realizes that his life work has ruled out the kind of visibility that comes from high-profile activism. "I recognized early that the [kind of] work I do is not attention-grabbing. . . . When I came along . . . college presidents were the lords of black America. Later, it became civil rights [leaders]. Still later, it became [holders of] political office." As James Massey maintains, "Taylor has stuck with the church. He has been busy handling the themes of the gospel and seeking to affect society in ways that are consonant with the gospel purpose. This is not newsworthy, like leading a sit-in."

Don Matthews of Washington's First Baptist Church, the church of fellow Baptists Bill Clinton and Al Gore, agrees. "We're in a time when the pulpit and the church in general are not particularly admired by anybody that isn't in it. The only place it is perceived as powerful is in the political world. . . . But the people who have the spiritual word to speak aren't paid much attention by the *New York Times* or the *Washington Post*."

William Augustus Jones, noted pastor of Brooklyn's Bethany Baptist Church, contends that Christians are resident aliens who have a radically different perspective on the world than secular citizens. "For a preacher to be regarded as popular means that his faithfulness to the word is not what it ought to be." . . .

It is above all Taylor's unsurpassed ability to preach to preachers—his keen sense of the preaching mission and its encumbrances and opportunities—that make him a popular presence among seminarians and seasoned preachers alike. In his homiletics class at Princeton, Taylor ranges through the history of the English pulpit with formidable ease, sharing stories of history's great divines. He whips out tattered pieces of newspaper, whose margins are covered with notes drawn from a massive and virtually infallible memory bank of preaching lore and legend.

On one of the days I attend his class, Taylor produces a snatch of paper ripped from the previous Sunday's *New York Times Book Review*, which he reads religiously, along with the *New Republic* ("I despise almost every word in it, but it gives me good targets to shoot at," he says), the *New York Review of Books*, and the daily *New York Times* and *Newsday*. Taylor reads the class a review listing the ingredients of a great novel—from its descriptive power to its presentation of a made view of humanity without losing its link to individual characters. He reminds them that great preaching contains the same elements. . . .

Taylor wrestles with some of the inevitable sadness that life brings—for instance, the suffering that comes with aging. "I have reached a very unflattering and un-enviable time. I have more money than I have time. And that's not good. It was much better the other way. But then I'll take it—what can I do?" As we discussed his 52 years of marriage to Laura, he said, "I sometimes see her lying in repose now, and a great sadness comes over me because I know one of us must leave the other. But what can we do?" One suspects that Taylor will do what he has always done, whether life has favored or assaulted him. He will, as long as he is able, preach the word of God.

Reverend Gardner Taylor's influence on his congregation and the broader African American community has been profound, in both material and spiritual ways. Dyson's profile helps readers to understand the experiences that have motivated Reverend Taylor in his religious commitments and convictions as well as the cultural and professional sources that have helped him to shape his influential sermons.

In his profile of Gardner Taylor, Michael Eric Dyson notes, "By and large, . . . Americans have remained insulated from the greatest rhetorical artists of the black pulpit." One of the most significant reasons for this lack of attention, Dyson suggests, is that mainstream white America, and particularly the mainstream press, considers African American preachers as contributing much in the way of rhetorical flourishes but little in the way of keen spiritual insight. Dyson writes,

> Like black religion in general, black preaching is often seen as the cathartic expres-sion of pent-up emotion, a verbal outpouring that supposedly compensates for low self-esteem or oppressed racial status. . . . Such stereotypes developed in ignorance of the variety of . . . black churches that boast a long history of educated clergy.

Dyson's profile of Gardner Taylor, then, can be seen as one means for changing mainstream society's understanding of and attitudes toward the value of Afri-can American pulpit oratory.

Geneva Smitherman, a linguist at Michigan State University, has also done much throughout her career to introduce to mainstream audiences the rhetorical variety of African American verbal practices, including sermons. In her landmark 1977 book *Talkin and Testifyin: The Language of Black Amer-ica*, Smitherman describes the grammar and syntax of what she then called Black English (but now refers to as African American Vernacular Language). Equally important, she also analyzes how this language both reflects and shapes black culture and lifestyle. The following excerpt from her book dis-mantles the notion mentioned by Dyson, that black preaching is "brimming with passion but lacking intellectual substance." Smitherman describes how the African American preacher analyzes the rhetorical situation and strategi-cally crafts a sermon that meets his or her goals as well as the audience's expectations and needs. Smitherman also describes how African American preachers use the rhetorical practice of testifying to help their congregants understand the meaning of specific biblical passages.

Smitherman wants readers to understand that African American sermons are not improvised, off-the-cuff performances fueled by emotion and lacking intellectual content. The rhetorical situation taxes the preacher's imagination and communicative ability "to the max." Still, "most come through" as they deftly explicate the meaning of biblical passages and help congregants to apply these lessons as they live their daily lives.

GENEVA SMITHERMAN
Excerpt from Talkin and Testifyin: The Language of Black America

To testify is to tell the truth through "story." In the sacred context, the subject of testifying includes such matters as visions, prophetic experiences, the experience of being saved, and testimony to the power and goodness of God. In the secular context, the subject matter includes such matters as blues changes caused by yo man or yo woman, and conversely, the Dr. FEEL-GOOD power of yo man or yo woman; experiences attesting to the racist power of the white oppressor; testimonials to the power of a gifted musician or singer. The retelling of these occurrences in lifelike fashion recreates the spiritual reality for others who at that moment vicariously experience what the testifier has gone through. The content of testifying, then, is not plain and simple commentary but a dramatic narration and a communal reenactment of one's feelings and experiences. Thus one's humanity is reaffirmed by the group and his or her sense of isolation diminished.

The rendering of sermons in the traditional black church nearly always involves extended narration as a device to convey a theme. Rarely will black preachers expound their message in the linear fashion of a lecture. Rather, the thematic motif is dramatized with gestures, movement, plot, real-life characterization, and circumlocutory rhetorical flourishes. The preacher thus becomes an actor and story-teller in the best sense of the word. When he makes reference to Peter "building the church on solid rock" rather than "on

"The preacher . . . becomes an actor and story-teller in the best sense of the word."

shifting sand," the preacher will lift his foot in the air and put it back down firmly to symbolize Peter placing the church on solid ground. When the preacher alludes to the crucifixion, he will throw his handkerchief over his shoulder, to symbolize the cross, and then walk up and down the aisle or across the floor in a stooped position to re-create for his congregation the image of Jesus climbing Mount Calvary. If he refers to the experience of being saved, he may say that "God put running in my feet" and do a kind of slow run across the floor.

The preacher knows that his congregation needs guidance in the conduct of daily affairs, as well as spiritual inspiration to keep on pushin, but the interactive communication process puts on him constraints and demands that he must fulfill. The orchestration of the sermon requires that Biblical persons be brought to life and the events recast into present-day context. Yet, no matter how contemporary the theme, the congregation expects the message of the sermon to be grounded in Biblical textual reference. At the same time, despite the narration of events far removed from their present world and experience, they expect the preacher to make them feel the Spirit. (You ain done no preachin if don't nobody shout!) Since the preacher is the one who must bring it all together—the story, the message, Scriptural clarity, and the Spirit—his imagination and communicative ability is taxed to the max. But most come through. In fact, some sermon-stories are so vividly and dynamically narrated that they become popular and widely known throughout the church community in a given city or town.

ANALYZING THE RHETORICAL SITUATION

1. Why is Reverend Gardner Taylor a person that Michael Eric Dyson's audience would be interested in learning more about? How does Dyson help his readers see Taylor as an important figure worthy of their interest?

2. Select an interesting anecdote from Dyson's profile. What do you learn from this anecdote? How does it bring Taylor to life for readers?

3. What does Dyson say about Reverend Taylor's physical appearance? What were your first impressions as you read those details? Why do you think Dyson provides this description?

4. Besides interviewing Taylor, what else has Dyson done to learn about him? How did his sources of information influence Dyson's writing of the profile? How does the information—and Dyson's way of writing about it—affect you as a reader?

5. Who was Geneva Smitherman's audience? What makes you think so? What is her purpose in writing about her topic for this specific audience? What specific strategies does she employ in the excerpt to achieve this purpose?

COMMUNITY CONNECTIONS

1. Spend several minutes freewriting about your response to Lyndon B. Johnson's speech. Why was this speech important? Next, spend several minutes freewriting about whether Peggy Noonan's description of speechwriting made you think differently about the effectiveness, purpose, or value of Johnson's speech. Why or why not? Refer to specific passages from the text as you compose your response.

2. What reasons does Noonan offer for the importance of political speeches? What is your opinion of each of these reasons? In what ways have technological innovations since 1990, when Noonan presented her ideas, affected political speeches?

3. Write for several minutes about your responses to the following two statements: (a) Dyson: "Throughout its history, black preaching has been widely viewed as a form of public address brimming with passion but lacking intellectual substance." (b) Smitherman: "You ain done no preachin if don't nobody shout!" At first glance, Smitherman's statement might seem to support the widely held misunderstanding that Dyson wants to disrupt. How, though, does Smitherman's analysis support Dyson's wider claim?

4. Identify two or three speeches—formal or informal—that you've heard in the past year. Of these, choose one that you consider a "success," and explain what made it successful.

Profiles: A Fitting Response

Two profiles of professionals who shape their worlds with words

We seem to be fascinated by people who have demonstrated unique abilities to establish a character, connect with our emotions, and move others to action through words. Profiles serve as a means through which readers can understand what motivates these rhetors and what experiences have helped them develop their abilities with words.

Mike Allen's 2002 *Washington Post* article profiles Michael J. Gerson, a speechwriter for President George W. Bush, whose speeches steered the nation following the terrorist attacks of September 11, 2001. Allen's profile helped readers learn about the man responsible for the president's words and, ultimately, for the nation's course of action. As you read this profile, notice how Allen provides a glimpse into the daily life and political influence of a president's speechwriter. He also gives readers a clear idea of the personality and personal history that shaped Gerson's vision for his job and for the nation's future.

Mike Allen

For Bush's Speechwriter, Job Grows Beyond Words; "Scribe" Helps Shape, Set Tone for Evolving Foreign Policy

Within days of the Sept. 11 attacks, the White House upgraded the security clearance of Michael J. Gerson, President Bush's wordsmith, for the dramatic change that lay ahead for his job. Gerson, a 38-year-old with Armani horn-rims, was hired as Bush's chief speechwriter for his fluency in the strain of Republican education and welfare policy known as compassionate conservatism. Now, he is playing a growing role in preparing the nation for war. **[1]** Like Bush, Gerson is learning on the job, helping convert a presidency that was all about tax cuts and faith-based social programs into one that hopes to transform the nation's defense and foreign policies for the first time since the aftermath of World War II.

Gerson is often invited into the Situation Room to soak in the discussion before addresses on terrorism or the Middle East. For Bush's speech to the United Nations last month, Gerson helped establish the just-the-facts tone for the litany of complaints against Iraq's Saddam Hussein. "We wanted to create an impression, which was justified by the evidence, of inevitability," Gerson said as he worked alfresco at one of the coffeehouses near the White House where he often jots, unrecognized, on legal pads. **[2]** "The president likes to outline clear and blunt alternatives. This is an organization which is not all that accustomed to that, which added to the drama of the moment."

Indeed, Bush has shelved the "humble foreign policy" he promoted during his campaign and instead plans to use American might to preempt what he considers budding terrorist threats throughout the world. Domestic policy clearly will

---

[1] These opening sentences tell readers why Gerson is important. The writer communicates clearly to readers that this person is making a difference in the political life of the United States.

[2] The writer provides details about how Gerson does his work; these details signal to the reader that the writer has tried to learn more about Gerson than simply what he writes.

not be Bush's legacy, or Gerson's. "All these other things remain important," Gerson said. "But you do realize that there's a broader story you're a part of."

Aides to Bush's father recall that he responded to his discomfort with words by distancing himself from his speechwriters, denying them perks and ignoring their advice. White House officials said his son, who saw the disappointing result, learned from his father's mistake and has embraced his writers.

Formal speeches have been so crucial to building Bush's credibility after a gaffe-prone candidacy that scholars are calling Gerson the most influential presidential speechwriter since Theodore C. Sorensen, confidant and muse of President John F. Kennedy. Anthony R. Dolan, who coined "evil empire" as chief speechwriter to President Ronald Reagan [3], said Bush's address to Congress nine days after the Sept. 11 attacks and his Sept. 14, 2001, remarks at the National Cathedral ("Our responsibility to history is already clear") will become two of the most memorable presidential speeches in history. "FDR's 'infamy' line is remembered, but the speech itself is not that distinguished," Dolan said. "Bush's are, and it started before September 11th."

[3] This attributive tag establishes the credibility of the source making the subsequent assertion.

White House officials said Gerson's clout has increased even more now that Bush's longtime adviser Karen P. Hughes is no longer at the White House on a daily basis, even though she remains deeply involved in shaping Bush's image. "Mike has become the arbiter of what Bush would want," said a person who has sat in hundreds of meetings with him. "When he says, 'It's not going to happen,' there's nobody in the room who's going to say, 'Well, yeah, maybe it might.'" **[4]**

[4] The preceding two paragraphs provide comments on Gerson's work from several of his colleagues, not just from one. Readers also learn about how he interacts with his colleagues.

Two Mondays ago, Gerson was assigned to write an address that would offer vivid evidence to the American public of the risk posed by Hussein, yet try to convince voters that Bush would not attack Iraq rashly. He had to scare people and reassure them at the same time. As he began the 29-minute speech that Bush delivered Monday in Cincinnati, Gerson wrote that the Iraqi leader was building a fleet of small planes for dispersing chemical and biological weapons. CIA agents reviewing the draft said "small planes" was misleading. Bush wound up warning of "unmanned aerial vehicles," which he later referred to as "UAVs." Bush remembered from some conversation or briefing that Hussein could make a nuclear weapon with a softball-sized batch of uranium. Gerson checked into that and the government's atomic energy experts finally agreed to "a little larger than a single softball."

Although finessing language to protect intelligence sources and methods is a part of the job that no one had envisioned, **[5]** Gerson's role has extended well beyond polished rhetoric ever since he joined the Bush campaign a year and a half before the election. Bush formalized that in July, 10 days after Hughes moved out, by elevating Gerson's title to assistant to the president for speechwriting and policy adviser, from deputy assistant to the president and director of presidential speechwriting.

[5] The two examples in the preceding paragraph, along with this transitional phrase, help to bring the subject to life, in that readers see how he thinks through challenges in his job.

The White House speechwriting office includes eight writers and researchers. Gerson has a West Wing office, an upgrade from his predecessors' quarters in the adjacent Eisenhower Executive Office Building. He attends the 7:30 a.m. senior staff meeting, and often speaks up at the 8:30 a.m. communication meeting, where Bush's daily message is shaped. **[6]**

[6] Again, the writer captures details about the subject's daily work life.

Gerson's style is less conversational than his boss's, favoring flourishes and classical devices. "Flowery," the Texans call it. Bush and Hughes have made Gerson adapt to the president's plain-spokenness, which Hughes believes connects with average voters. The hallmark of Gerson's speeches is the invocation of the vocabulary and literature of faith, and that only increased after Sept. 11, 2001. Gerson, an evangelical Episcopalian who said he is reading a biography of the Apostle Paul for "escape," shares Bush's willingness to talk publicly about the centrality of Christian faith to his life. **[7]** The result is a president whose public words are laced with biblical undertones. At Bush's inauguration, he vowed that when Americans "see that wounded traveler on the road to Jericho, we will not pass to the other side." After the terrorist attacks, he told a skittish nation, "God's signs are not always the ones we look for." **[8]**

Gerson said the White House found that America's broad faith tradition helped foster healing. "We have tried to employ religious language in a way that unites people," he said. "Martin Luther King did it all the time during the civil rights movement. He was in this long tradition, going back to Old Testament prophets, that says God is active in history and, eventually, he's on the side of justice." **[9]**

Bush can be harsh with aides who could crowd his spotlight, but people close to Bush say he has only grown more comfortable with the scholarly man whose presidential nickname is "Scribe" or more often "Gerson!" **[10]**

Gerson had planned a career in teaching and had been accepted at the interdenominational Fuller Theological Seminary in Pasadena, Calif. Instead, he went to work for Charles W. Colson, the Nixon aide turned prison minister, who had seen a column Gerson wrote about Mother Teresa in the college newspaper at Wheaton College in Wheaton, Ill. **[11]** Gerson began incubating the notion of compassionate conservatism as policy director for former senator Daniel R. Coats (R-Ind.), now Bush's ambassador to Germany. Gerson caught the presidential-candidate bug and wrote for Jack F. Kemp and Robert J. Dole, then took a two-year detour into journalism when James Fallows, then editor of *U.S. News & World Report*, recruited him to cover philanthropy.

In 1999, Bush summoned Gerson to his Washington hotel suite during a National Governors Association meeting and hired him on the spot to help develop domestic policy, including an education message that included a federal role. **[12]**

Gerson rarely watches Bush perform in person—he caught Monday's speech from his den in Alexandria. But he took Air Force One to West Point, N.Y., in June when the president announced his new military doctrine of preemptive strikes against nations that harbor terrorists or weapons of mass destruction.

Gerson said he knew it would be one of the most important speeches Bush had ever given, and he just wanted to be there. "It only falls to a few presidents in our history to create a new strategic approach for our country that's going to be influential for decades," he said. "We've been forced to think about these things and to articulate them."

[7] These sentences show readers a unique aspect of Gerson's personality that has also significantly shaped the public persona of President Bush.

[8] The writer doesn't just *tell* readers but really *shows* them how Gerson's—and President Bush's—faith has manifested itself within Bush's speeches.

[9] This paragraph helps readers to gain further insight into the motivations and worldview that shape the subject's work.

[10] Readers learn how the subject interacts with his boss, President Bush.

[11] Readers learn how faith had been a motivating force in Gerson's professional life even before he became a speechwriter for President Bush.

[12] The two preceding paragraphs trace Gerson's career path to show readers how he's gotten to the position of influence he holds.

In the following profile, Marisa Lagos examines Tommie Lindsey's efforts to help students at Logan High School in California improve their abilities in public speaking and debate.

Marisa Lagos
Successes Speak Well for Debate Coach

Logan High School forensics coach Tommie Lindsey's classroom says a thing or two about his success: It's crowded with banners, trophies and kids. On this morning, Lindsey is just minutes from loading 38 high school students into buses and heading to Long Beach, where they will compete in the Jack Howe Invitational. More than 60 schools from across the nation would participate in the three-day forensics challenge, competing in public speaking, presentation and debate. The Logan High team would take the grand sweepstakes award as well as six individual first-place awards. [1]

Lindsey, a 15-year teacher at the Bay Area school, was recently named one of 23 recipients of the MacArthur Foundation's annual $500,000 award—a so-called "genius grant" the foundation disburses over a five-year period with no strings attached. [2] Meant to underscore "the importance of a creative individual in society," according to the foundation, "fellows are selected for their originality, creativity, and the potential to do more in the future."

Recipients of the grants are nominated anonymously, but Lindsey's qualifications are obvious. Logan High, a public school in a middle- to low-income area, has claimed four state forensics titles and many other awards in a type of academic competition usually more suited for prep schools than public schools. [3] Typically, the 16 forensic categories include speech, interpretation and acting.

Lindsey, 53, a Mississippi transplant, is known for his dedication. He usually works seven days and up to 150 hours a week. If he's not practicing with the 300-plus-member team—most schools have about 40 members and as many as eight coaches—he's attending weekend tournaments from 6 a.m. to 11 p.m. [4] "I think every teacher does a lot," said Alphonso Thompson, Lindsey's substitute teacher and former student, "but what Lindsey does goes above and beyond the call of duty a million times over. I don't know where I would be if it wasn't for Mr. Lindsey." He has had numerous offers, mostly from private schools, to bring his expertise, and his assistant coach, Tim Campbell, elsewhere, and says he has entertained some of those offers seriously, especially since learning that the program's funding for next year is threatened. For now, Lindsey is still at Logan, where he has taught public speaking and debate to about 3,000 students, many of them from poor and/or single-parent homes.

When Lindsey started at Logan in 1989 there were many skeptics. "Even the principal didn't think we would be able to do forensics at Logan," he said.

[1] The writer shows that she not only interviewed her subject but spent time with him engaged in activity that has made him newsworthy.

[2] The writer explains why the subject is interesting and important—he's a prestigious award winner (a "genius," no less).

[3] The writer gives details about how the subject is making a difference in his community.

[4] The writer gives readers a sense of the specific types of work that the subject does as well as the attitude with which the subject approaches his job.

So Lindsey began recruiting athletes, whom he believed would take to competition. "I went out and started getting athletes and putting them to the challenge. I would say, 'I don't think you can do this.' . . . Finally, they would come out and find that they love it."

It's that mix of tough love, confidence and intuition that makes Lindsey both a friend and a foe. But most of all, it's what sparks his students. Varun Mitra, a senior at Logan, started on the team as a freshman. "Mr. Lindsey sacrifices a lot," Mitra said. "He never gives up on you if you say no to him. . . . He'll keep going after you to the point where you realize he was right, until he molds you into a better life." Before forensics, Mitra had planned to go to a University of California campus because his parents encouraged it. Now, he has even grander plans: after a bachelor's degree, law school. "Four years ago when I came in, I wasn't able to speak in front of anyone. . . . This program made me want to pursue a career in public speaking—as a lawyer, in politics," he said. "This program has helped me decide what I want to do in life." **[5]**

Not all of Logan's students fit the typical mold for a forensics team, however. Many have been diagnosed with learning disabilities; others have never made academics their focus. And half the team members are female, still somewhat unusual in forensics.

But what really sets Lindsey's program apart is that its popularity has made being smart cool, mainly because the students see each other getting good grades. "When you join the program it creates expectations that you're going to further your education in college," said Mike Joshi, a senior. He plans to apply to several Ivy League colleges this year. **[6]** "There are kids in honors classes that need the intellectual outlet," Lindsey said, "but many of the kids may not fit into standard academics. Some have been labeled special ed, and they come in and we find a place for them. . . . It's a matter of believing in a kid and finding a special something the kid does." **[7]**

It's also about pushing students to do what they never thought possible: More than 90% of them go on to attend college. "I presently have a kid living in a two-bedroom apartment with five people. He sleeps on the couch. . . . But he wants to be able to do forensics, because it's an outlet," Lindsey said. "Once you're involved in this group, you start thinking about four-year colleges. Not if, but when." Lindsey moved to west Oakland as a child and graduated from Castelmont High School. He received a bachelor of arts degree from the University of San Francisco—where he was the school's first African American valedictorian—and went on to get a bachelor of science degree and secondary teaching certificate there. **[8]** Lindsey then went to law school for a year and simultaneously began teaching to "pay the bills." He was hooked, and after five years teaching at Alameda County's Juvenile Hall, Lindsey landed a full-time teaching job at El Rancho Verde High School, where he stayed until moving to Logan.

He is the father of two Logan students—Terrence, a junior at the school, and Erica, 21, now a student at UCLA. It was his children he thought of first when he was awarded the grant last month, he said. "With this money, we're finally going to get some relief here. Most important is my daughter and son's educations." **[9]** That help is well-deserved, say Lindsey's colleagues and students, who are pleased that the money is for him alone.

[5] The writer doesn't simply tell readers that Lindsey "sparks his students"; she lets one student's experiences serve as an example to show how Lindsey motivates students.

[6] Again, the writer provides an example of one student's experiences to illustrate a characteristic of the subject.

[7] The writer has consulted more than one source in putting together this profile: the subject himself and several students.

[8] The profile turns to Lindsey's past to show how his experiences have informed his present-day efforts to motivate students to attend college.

[9] The writer shows readers how the concerns Lindsey has for his family also shape his encouraging of his students.

Lindsey said he was surprised and happy when he got the call. "It's great, not just because I was honored, but because teachers are not respected as they should be. Teaching changes lives and builds kids up. . . . They should be given more recognition than they receive," he said. "I was so happy the MacArthur Foundation is now looking at public school teachers, because it's very different. You have to be loyal to work in a public setting. I was shocked, and very appreciative."

Lindsey said he ended up in forensics because he was always fascinated by oration—including listening as a child to sermons at the Baptist churches he attended and to civil rights speeches by the Rev. Martin Luther King, Jr. **[10]** While in high school, Lindsey decided he wanted to speak at the graduation ceremony. Though his teacher doubted him, she said he could try, then handed him his topic: "Investing in Learning to Cultivate the Intellect." After his initial frustration melted away, Lindsey sat down with a neighbor and hashed out a speech—one that got him a standing ovation at the ceremony. **[11]** "I took that negative energy and propelled it," he said, adding that he still looks after that neighbor, who is now 102. The students at Logan are not the only ones to gain something, however. Logan journalism teacher Patrick Hannigan said: "At the end of my career, what I will remember is that I worked with Tommie Lindsey."

[10] The writer helps readers see what motivates the subject.

[11] The anecdote reveals how the subject's own experiences showed him the power and possibilities of effective public speaking; it also helps to bring the subject to life.

The preceding profiles allow readers to see how the subjects' perspectives toward their work and their worlds influenced their use of words. Each writer provides a clear statement of the subject's significance to society. Both profiles describe and analyze concrete details of the individual's life and work. Both profiles offer specific anecdotes that reveal important aspects of the subject's character. And both writers include direct quotes from people close to the subject to explain the significance of the individual in others' lives.

WHAT MAKES IT A PROFILE?

The following questions are ones you should consider when thinking critically about any profile. For now, try applying them to the profiles by Mike Allen and Marisa Lagos to determine how closely those writers followed the conventions for profiles.

1. Does the writer explain why the subject is an interesting person? Is the subject someone readers will want to learn about?

2. Does the writer's description of the subject and his or her work make a specific point about the subject's personality or character?

3. Has the writer helped readers to understand what motivates the subject in his or her professional and public life?

4. Has the writer drawn on a variety of sources (personal observations, interviews, and research as well as comments from friends and colleagues) for concrete details about the individual?

5. Does the profile ask readers to think about this subject in a specific way?

Understanding the Rhetorical Situation

Identifying an exigence

Marisa Lagos describes Tommie Lindsey's efforts to prepare his students for success through developing their skills in public speaking and debate. Her article draws on the perspectives of Lindsey's students, his colleagues, and Lindsey himself to create a richly detailed portrait of what motivates Lindsey to teach his students to be successful rhetors. Lagos wrote a profile on Lindsey not just because Logan High School's debate team was about to compete in the Jack Howe Invitational forensics competition; even more compelling for her readers was the fact that Lindsey, a high school teacher, had been recognized as a "genius" by the MacArthur Foundation and awarded one of its prestigious grants.

Consider the people who work or study in the community around you. Are there any fellow students who have inspired others to action through their words? Are there any local business owners or political activists who have used their eloquence to shape the community? Are there any teachers who have inspired students to develop their own voices in their writing and project these voices into the important conversations on campus? Are there any people in the local community who capture the interest and attention of others through their unique way with words? Are there any poets, rappers, or writers pushing the boundaries of how words are used in our everyday lives? Are there speechwriters, communications directors, or publicists working behind the scenes to compose the public presentations of local political leaders? You might listen to those individuals on campus whose voices have shaped the dialogue about pressing concerns. Or you might listen attentively to others whose voices influence the people in your community, such as the preachers who craft their messages with deft rhetorical styles or the teachers and debate coaches who create learning opportunities for students to develop writing and speaking skills they can put to use as active civic participants both now and in the future.

1. Make a list of the interesting writers you've read or the inspiring speakers you've heard over the past few weeks or months. For each one, write a few sentences describing your initial impressions of the rhetor. Write down as many details about the writer's presentation or the speaker's performance as you can to help explain your impressions.
2. For one or two of the writers or speakers that you wrote about in response to question 1, locate images—or, if the opportunity presents itself, take photos—that capture some aspects of the individual's personality. Then spend several minutes writing about what the visuals convey about the person's ability to inject life and energy into his or her words.

3. Choose the writer or speaker that you would like to profile and compose four or five sentences that describe the ways in which that person has succeeded as a rhetor. Then spend several minutes freewriting about the contexts in which this person's words have influence and the specific ways in which they move people: What is the purpose of the person's writing or speeches? When and where do this person's words have the most influence, and who has been the audience for these words? Describe what you know about the person's background and analyze how this background might be influencing the person's public success with words. If your profile will feature a particular text or speech, describe how you interpreted it when you initially encountered it and after you thought about it.

Locating an audience

For his profile of Michael J. Gerson, Mike Allen had to consider the range of perspectives and opinions that *Washington Post* readers might hold on the office of the president in general and on George W. Bush in particular. He had to write his profile in a way that acknowledged those various positions while also presenting a clear, richly detailed portrait of how Gerson has helped to shape the president's public positions. Ultimately, Allen wanted his readers to have a clearer understanding of the personal experiences and the social, political, and cultural forces that have influenced Gerson's work and have helped him to create the themes guiding Bush's administration.

What audience should you consider for your profile of a campus or community member who has achieved success through words? First, you have to determine who has—or should have—an investment in the future direction of your school or community as it relates to the issue your subject has spoken or written about. Then, you'll need to consider how to convince that audience to read your profile and accept the importance of learning what life experiences and personal convictions have motivated the rhetor you've chosen as your subject. For instance, if you believe that the entire student body needs to appreciate the rhetorical sophistication of a campus environmental activist who has succeeded in drawing the administration's attention to green alternatives for energy use, you'll need to think about the attitudes that most students hold toward public debates, political activism, and environmental issues.

The following questions will help you identify your rhetorical audience for your profile of the rhetor. Your answers will also help you describe and analyze your subject's effective way with words.

1. List the names of the persons or groups (students, faculty, administrators, community members, or alumni) likely to be engaged—positively or negatively—by the work your subject has done through words.
2. Next to the name of each potential audience, write reasons that audience could have for appreciating the subject's rhetorical prowess. In other words, what would persuade these audiences that they need to learn about this rhetor's experiences, perspectives, and motivations in greater detail?

3. How could each of these audiences be influenced by a profile of this individual? In other words, what emotional responses or logical conclusions could you expect your profile of this successful rhetor to lead to? Consider the implications of these emotional responses or logical conclusions for each audience and the motivations each audience might have for learning more about the personal experiences, values, and worldview that have affected your subject.

4. With these different audiences' interests and motivations in mind, return to the descriptions of the subject's speaking or writing that you composed in the preceding section on identifying an exigence. Add descriptive details or compelling quotes (you may need to do some research) that will enable your readers to feel invested in exploring the life of this person who has shaped the campus or local community with his or her words. A good description helps your audience more clearly visualize the person at work, hear how he or she has moved people to action through speeches or writing, and understand how this individual has affected the school or community. Tailor your best description to connect it closely to your audience's needs and interests.

Identifying a Fitting Response

Finding a purpose and shaping a fitting response

You have reflected on how a particular individual uses words to influence your school or local community. You have described the speeches or written texts that best illustrate your subject's ability to project his or her ideas through words, and you have considered what the audience needs to hear about this individual's activities, motivations, and experiences. But what do you want to accomplish through your profile? What specific emotional or logical response do you want your audience to have? What in particular do you want your readers to understand about the individual you're profiling? Your answers to these types of questions should help you identify your purpose for writing, which in turn affects the kind of text you'll create.

As you've been learning throughout this book, different purposes and different audiences require different kinds of texts. For example, if you're writing about a student leader on campus, you might want to compose a feature article to appear in the student newspaper, the alumni magazine, or on the Web site of the Office of Student Life. If you're writing about a community activist, your profile could take the form of a creative piece for a local zine. Your profile of a community business or political leader could be the centerpiece of a program for an awards banquet honoring that person for effectiveness in charting the town's future. You could draft a profile of an inspiring professor as a letter written to a friend encouraging her to take this professor's writing or public speaking course next semester. The point is that once you identify your exigence, locate your audience, and find your purpose, you will want to determine what kind of text will best respond to the rhetorical situation.

Use the following questions to help you narrow your purpose and shape your response:

1. What kinds of facts and details do you need to provide in order to create a vivid picture of your subject and his or her success?
2. What past experiences or current activities and actions make your subject compelling to your audience?
3. What do your readers need to know in order to understand what motivates this speaker or writer and to appreciate the significance of this person's words for the school or community?
4. Are you asking the audience to adopt a new perspective on this individual? Or do you, perhaps like the subject himself or herself, want to prompt the audience to take a specific action in response to your writing?
5. What is the best way to reach this audience? That is, to what kind of text—in terms of its genre, its visual design, and its format—will this audience most likely respond?

Your instructor (or your rhetorical situation) may prompt you to write a magazine article, create a Web page, or compose a letter or some other type of document. Matthew Glasgow, whose profile begins on page 160, could have worked in various genres to present his professor's skills as a rhetor. If his purpose had been to persuade his fellow education majors of the power of particular teaching practices, he could have written a position argument; if he wanted to nominate his professor for a teaching award, he could have drafted a formal letter to the nominating committee; or if he wanted to share his musings on why some people are so good with words, he could have composed a blog entry. Matthew knew that his subject was someone that his audience—his English instructor—didn't know well but would find compelling. He also knew that he had several anecdotes based on experiences in and out of the classsroom that he could combine with observations and direct quotations to provide a well-rounded picture of his subject—in a word, a profile. If, like Matthew, you are prompted to write a profile of a person who has succeeded with words, continue with the following assignment as a guide.

Writing a Profile: Working with Your Available Means

Shaping your profile

One major reason writers create profiles is to let others know more about the people who shape the world in which we live. A writer using this genre often uses the rhetorical appeal of pathos in the introduction to connect the subject to the readers' emotions and values. In short, the introduction to a profile needs to show readers that the subject is someone they need to know more about—right now. Mike Allen, for example, starts with a brief anecdote to underscore Michael J. Gerson's increasing importance in national and international affairs. Specifically, Allen tells readers that Gerson's security clear-

ance was upgraded immediately after the September 11, 2001 terrorist attacks so that he could assume "a growing role in preparing the nation for
war." By the end of the first paragraph, readers know that Allen's profile will
explore the work of a person who is doing much to affect U.S. politics. Writers also use the introduction of a profile to highlight some key aspect of the
subject's personality, character, or values; Allen draws attention to Gerson's
"fluency in the strain of Republican education and welfare policy known as
compassionate conservatism."

After capturing readers' attention with a brief image of the subject, the
writer may begin the body of the profile by presenting a fuller description of
the subject and his or her life's work. Marisa Lagos, for example, lets readers
know that Tommie Lindsey possesses "obvious" credentials for the MacArthur
Foundation's grant because of his work in helping students from a middle- to
low-income area win several state titles "in a type of academic competition usually more suited for prep schools than public schools." Lagos uses the rhetorical
appeal of pathos as she describes Lindsey as a "genius." This appeal to the
emotions of the readers—who's not fascinated by geniuses and interested in
learning how they see the world?—helps convince them that Lindsey is worth
learning more about.

The body paragraphs of a profile also include descriptive details that help
readers to visualize the subject's actions and to hear the subject's words. Readers
of Allen's profile, for example, can see Gerson working "alfresco at one of the coffeehouses near the White House where he often jots, unrecognized, on legal pads."
They hear George W. Bush hailing his primary speechwriter as "Scribe" or "Gerson!" And they can sense the ways Gerson works "the vocabulary and literature
of faith" into his speeches for the president. Allen incorporates these and other
details into his profile in order to draw readers closer to the subject and to let them
feel they're learning about aspects of Gerson's personality that make him unique
and influence the ways in which he works with words.

Writers also use the body of a profile to provide logical appeals in the form
of numerous examples that show that the subject is indeed making a difference
in the community. The crux of the logical appeal, in fact, is the explanation of
how the individual's work affects the lives of people like the readers themselves.
Lagos, for example, presents the story of Varun Mitra, a senior at Logan High
School whose participation on Lindsey's forensics team has inspired him to
work toward a law degree. Readers see from examples such as this one that
Lindsey has indeed helped to inspire many students to continue their education. Lagos has connected the details supporting Lindsey's status of "genius"—
he's found a way to improve the lives of students often ignored and marginalized in public education—with a value her readers no doubt hold, the
importance of all students having equal access to quality education and equal
opportunities to succeed in life.

Lagos strengthens this logical appeal by providing quotations from Varun
Mitra and Lindsey's colleague, Patrick Hannigan. These quotations lend support to Lagos's assertions about Lindsey's significance to his community.
Moreover, they lend insight into the ways that those closest to Lindsey have
been affected and influenced by his work. Readers learn from Mitra, for example, that Lindsey "never gives up on you if you say no to him. . . . He'll keep

going after you to the point where you realize he was right, until he molds you into a better life." These eloquent comments speak to Lindsey's ability to affect people in positive ways. The strength of Lagos's logical appeal ultimately rests on the fact that her readers value people who expend the energy and effort necessary to make this kind of contribution to their communities. The quotations from Lindsey's students and colleague, as well as quotations from Lindsey himself, also help Lagos create an ethical appeal. That Lagos talked directly with several people before composing the profile strengthens the credibility of her claims about Lindsey's abilities to motivate his students as well as to inspire his fellow teachers.

Finally, the conclusion of a profile often contains one final quote or anecdote that nicely captures the essence of the individual. Allen, for example, leaves readers with an image of Gerson, who rarely watches Bush deliver his speeches, flying on Air Force One to West Point to listen as the president announces a new military doctrine. This image, as well as the quotes from Gerson that follow it, reinforces the significance of this individual.

Many engaging profiles include visuals. As you draft your profile, you may want to consider whether a visual or two will make your subject more vivid or more memorable for readers. Consider taking a photograph of the individual at work drafting a speech or scanning an interesting page from a public document that the individual wrote.

CHECKING OVER A PROFILE

✓ The subject of the profile is someone many readers will find compelling or interesting.
✓ The profile provides descriptive details to help readers imagine what the subject looks like, sounds like, or acts like.
✓ The profile includes several direct quotations from the subject or others that give readers an opportunity to understand directly the person's opinions and perspectives.
✓ The profile draws on evidence and insights from a variety of sources, such as personal observations, interviews, and research.
✓ The profile presents several anecdotes about the subject that show readers the background and experiences that have shaped the subject.
✓ The profile leads readers to a particular emotional response or logical conclusion about the subject.

Student paper

In the following profile, student writer Matthew Glasgow addresses the rhetorical exigence of capturing a classroom experience.

Matthew Glasgow

Professor Goldthwaite

English 215

November 20, 2007

The Liberating Mind

Colloquially speaking, he's rad. He entered the lecture hall donning his sleek black-rimmed glasses, in one hand a notebook and a text, our first reading, Plato's *Five Dialogues*. Bookmarks jutted out on all sides, drawing attention to the annotated pages within, which he had no doubt read upwards of twenty times throughout his relatively young lifetime. In the other hand he carried a cup of coffee, envied by most students, particularly myself, at 8:30 a.m. on that first Tuesday of the fall semester at Saint Joseph's University. After placing each item on the table, Dr. Arnold Farr began to read off the names listed on his roster, thus launching his course The Human Person, which, for many of us, served as our first experience in the realm of philosophy.

Though quickly impressed with the subtleties of Dr. Farr's professional mien, I soon came to increasingly respect the process behind his work and the way he successfully communicated with his students and colleagues. Throughout the course he was able to identify with his students by relating the texts to topics that a college student might be more prone to understand. The first of these many connections occurred during our studies of Sigmund Freud and Herbert Marcuse.

When discussing Marcuse's interpretation of the Freudian Performance Principle, Dr. Farr informed us that he does not carry a cell phone. The principle refers to how socially and historically created structures serve as guidelines for what societies should desire. Marcuse believed that such a standard of behavior functioned as a subtle form of oppression, isolating those who differed from the societal norm.

"If you don't have a cell phone, people look at you funny," Farr explained, yet he found his life simplified by using only his office and home phones when necessary. This example shows how he not only explains philosophy in more readily understood terms, but also the way in which he himself manifests his philosophical beliefs in his own life.

Another clarifying example came from the music industry. During our study of Marcuse's "Dialectic of Civilization," we considered culture's influence on communities. Marcuse identified Eros as a pleasure-seeking and creative principle, which finds itself in conflict with the death instinct. This death instinct also seeks pleasure; however, its qualities are more destructive and produce aggression. To help us understand the relationship between Eros and the death instinct, Dr. Farr explained that the history of music and the music industry have a similar relationship. Originally musicians wrote songs and melodies as a means of personal, social, and cultural expression, but as record labels emerged as major corporations seeking greater profits, artists' music became increasingly formulaic. By repressing musicians' freedom of expression, the music industry destroyed what the art of music was meant to achieve.

Farr's explanations in his course lectures provided guidance for his students; however, in several functions on campus, Dr. Farr also identified with people of various walks of life. "In a way I am still the same kid from years ago, while a part of me has also matured as well," Farr said of this ability to speak several forms of English, which proved vital when he lectured to students, fellow professors, and members of the local community simultaneously.

As part of the celebration of Black History in February, he organized multiple events, including an African-American Read-In and a campus visit by actress Ruby Dee Davis. Farr spoke at both events, sharing a passage by Dr. Cornel West at the read-in and providing an introduction for Ms. Davis, to audiences of students, professors, and many residents of the Philadelphia area. With such a range of people, most of whom spoke to Farr prior to or following the festivities, it was not hard to notice the appreciation and respect he had earned over the years through his cordial nature and stimulating intellectual activities.

In yet another significant contribution to the community, Dr. Farr organized the Alain Locke Conference, an event celebrating and discussing the work of the praised African-American philosopher. Through Farr's efforts, several of the top Lockeian experts from across the country joined together to present their own essays interpreting and expanding upon Locke's philosophies. In addition to hosting and organizing the conference,

Dr. Farr presented his essay entitled "Beyond Repressive Tolerance: Alain Locke's Hermeneutics of Democracy as a Response to Herbert Marcuse's Deconstruction of the Same."

Though the extensive title of his work appeared to be slightly intimidating, Dr. Farr provided a clear lecture to ensure clarity for all persons present. He examined the extent to which tolerance serves as a democratic value, specifically questioning the tolerance of harmful views and ideas. When misunderstood by a colleague, Farr clarified his thesis by explaining the need for a struggle and potential for change. Interpreting values as contingent rather than dogmatic, Farr stated that one's ability to change or legitimate his views over time allowed for a greater chance for true tolerance.

After Dr. Farr's thoughts on "the problem of tolerance as a democratic value" were clarified, the man replied, "if that is what you are saying, then I understand and I agree with you." Once again, Farr's communication through his essay and his words following its presentation revealed the ease with which he can educate both young and old, scholar and student.

As the semester progressed, we reached one of the more sensitive subjects-- race and its prevalence in the philosophical realm. Race, in itself, arose as an intriguing medium through which to consider the philosophies of liberation, criminalization, and dialectics of past and present human relations.

For this subject we turned to the writings of Angela Davis, who had made a much publicized visit to the campus the previous year, tainted by unfair assaults

Guide to Responding

on her character. Prior to her visit, flyers produced by a select group of students and faculty were posted labeling Davis as a "lesbian, communist, and black panther" among other things. As a friend of Davis and the administrator who had invited her to speak, Dr. Farr quickly came to her defense and even emailed a colleague who had been involved with the flyers and negative articles in the newspapers. He simply asked his co-worker if he had ever taken the time to read any of Davis's work, which his colleague, coincidentally, had not.

A student later posted on a Web site created to rate professors that Dr. Farr's class was aimed at making white people feel bad about slavery and the oppression of African-Americans. Upon discovering this accusation, Farr decided to incorporate a question on his final exam asking his students to agree with or deny this statement based upon the readings and class focus. The responses overwhelmingly disproved the allegation, primarily discussing the calls by Davis for change and liberation in the future, rather than sympathy for slavery.

Strangely enough, the attacks were manifestations of many of the philosophies in Davis's texts and discussed by Farr during course lectures. Due to the events surrounding his friend's visit and the need for greater understanding of the role of race in philosophy, Dr. Farr committed himself to teaching Davis's texts in every semester of The Human Person. His professional and humorous responses to these unfortunate claims emphasize his clever use of language to resolve conflict and succeed at his position as teacher, philosopher, and friend.

"I have always advocated the ability to think critically," Farr has said, careful to differentiate between critique and criticism. Farr referred to social critique in philosophy as a means of improving injustices and liberating individuals in the future, while criticism offers only negative responses without any means of progress.

"I also take into account the historical context which gave birth to all these ideas. It is important to understand how language has come to be in itself," Farr said of his appreciation of the history of both the philosophical ideologies and the language by which they are communicated.

At the conclusion of the semester, I interviewed Dr. Farr concerning a documentary I had been crafting entitled "War and Peace." Hundreds of texts lined the walls of his office, all surely consolidated in the man before me who spoke of Immanuel Kant's "Perpetual Peace" and mankind's current inability to reconcile differences without violence.

"We have to be careful to not always assume we are the 'good guy'," he told me. "You cannot force democracy on people, and we have not yet completed our democratic experiment here." These words were not spoken with spite, like many in the political realm, but rather were grounded in reason and conscientious thought.

These words were a product of his extensive studies at Carson-Newman College and the University of Kentucky, where he received his master's and doctoral degrees. He remembers those years at the University of Kentucky as ones that changed and matured his way of thinking, providing a constant value for education.

And now, as the educator, Dr. Arnold Farr recognizes himself as one person attempting to inspire many young people, but realizes his students have the same opportunities he once did. "Teaching is difficult when students have no interest," he says, "but I hope that by the end of the semester some lights go on." And though those lights may be sparse in a world where philosophy seems to be fading, each new gleam sheds hope on the future.

Matthew Glasgow's essay provides an opportunity to consider the option of writing a profile. The following questions will stimulate your ideas about other options.

ALTERNATIVE ASSIGNMENTS

1. What have you accomplished through the persuasive or inventive use of language? What specific events exemplify your ability to get things done or to move people to action through words? What life experiences propelled you to this success? Write a three- to four-page memoir that describes how you succeeded with spoken or written words. Be sure to include details and quotations to help your readers imagine what that experience must have been like, as well as a concise analysis of the insights you gained through that experience.

2. You learned in Robert Caro's profile of Lyndon B. Johnson that the president's March 15, 1965 speech spurred Congress to pass the Voting Rights Act. Elsewhere in *Means of Ascent*, Caro implies that Johnson's forceful interactions with congressional representatives proved equally important in prompting this legislative success. How effective are eloquent, rhetorically powerful speeches? What political, cultural, or social consequences have followed from them? In a three- to four-page analytical essay, trace the consequences of one public address that many people claim to be historically significant or even timeless. As you allow this analysis to unfold, consider the extent to which this speech contributed to the actions that followed.

3. Write a three- to four-page critical review of a speech or public document that addressed an issue of particular importance to your campus or your community. Identify the criteria that you will use to evaluate the effectiveness of the speech or text and then evaluate the extent to which it did or did not meet those criteria. Be sure to provide specific evidence and details from the speech or public document in order to support your conclusion.

6 INVESTIGATING CORPORATIONS ON CAMPUS: RESPONDING WITH REPORTS

Chances are that you have viewed a scene like the one shown in the photo on your college campus—a table set up by a credit card company in the student union or another high-traffic location to solicit new customers. Like the University of Michigan grad student seen here, students can sign up for a card in a few short minutes. After providing their names, addresses, and average yearly income, they often walk away with promotional T-shirts, frisbees, or tote bags emblazoned with the school's logo and the credit card company's name.

Some colleges and universities have signed marketing deals with credit card companies to give them exclusive rights to sell credit cards with the school's logo or some image associated with the school, such as the University of Colorado at Boulder's buffalo logo or a photo of Pennsylvania State University's football coach Joe Paterno, to alumni, students, and employees. In exchange for these rights and the names and addresses of alumni, employees, and students, the cooperating colleges and universities often receive millions of dollars in revenue. The University of Tennessee, for example, signed a seven-year, $16.5 million contract with Bank One to market an affinity card featuring the school's logo, while the University of Oklahoma has a ten-year,

$13 million contract with FirstUSA that includes exclusive rights to set up tables at the school's football games in order to market a special Visa/Oklahoma Sooners credit card.

Credit card companies have also established a presence on college and university campuses through purchasing the naming rights to buildings. MBNA donated $25 million to finance the MBNA Student Center at Columbia University in 1996 and $7 million for the MBNA Performing Arts Center at Georgetown University in 1999. At the MBNA Career Services Center (now the Bank of America Career Services

Center) on the main campus of the Pennsylvania State University, for which the company donated $4 million in 1999, students can attend workshops in job hunting, résumé writing, and interviewing; research career paths and potential employers; and network with alumni who visit the campus as job recruiters. MBNA's funding of the Career Services Center enabled Penn State to build the facility and pay for the balance of its cost with public funds. In exchange for its funding, MBNA gained public recognition and marketed its brand name to a large student body.

The increasing presence of credit card companies on campuses reflects a larger trend of corporations in general becoming involved in the day-to-day operations of universities and colleges and, in some instances, shaping schools' teaching and research missions. Yet it's not always clear to students and faculty—or the larger community—what the exact nature of corporate involvement on a campus is. This lack of knowledge was an exigence for Robert Cwiklik, who reported in a June 1998 *Wall Street Journal* article ("Ivory Tower Inc.: When Research and Lobbying Mesh") on an attempt by UPS to buy an academic chair and, with it, considerable influence at the University of Washington. Investigative reports like Cwiklik's are commonly used when a writer wants to present the results of research.

In this chapter, you'll look further into the corporate presence on college campuses. As you learn more about what's at stake, you'll have opportunities to identify or create exigences in your own surroundings and to examine ways of responding rhetorically.

Real Situations

Even if you attend a school such as the University of Memphis or Simon Fraser College, both of which have effectively banned credit card companies from soliciting on campus, you might still see the presence of corporations. Corporate advertisements might line bulletin boards in your student union or fill the pages of your student newspaper. They might be featured prominently in sports arenas or stadiums, as seen on the scoreboard at the University of Arizona. Or you might note that corporations provide basic services on your campus, from food and hospitality to selling books. For example, Sodexho-Marriott Services has been awarded contracts to supply food services for more than 500 campuses. Coke and Pepsi routinely battle for campus "pouring rights," a battle that began when Pepsi and Penn State entered a ten-year, $14 million agreement in 1992, according to which "The University agrees during the term of the Agreement to purchase its total requirements of soft drink products from Pepsi." Meanwhile, at the University of Pennsylvania and more than 340 other universities and colleges, Barnes & Noble manages the campus bookstore.

Furthermore, some prominent media outlets, from MTV and ESPN to *Sports Illustrated,* have extended their reach onto campuses by producing cable television channels and magazines specifically for college students. *Sports Illustrated,* for example, publishes *SI on Campus,* a biweekly sports news magazine that, before it went completely online in December 2005, was distributed free to students at approximately 150 U.S. campuses. *SI on Campus* has also gotten involved with student unions, recreation centers, and athletic departments at various schools "to increase *SI*'s participation in daily campus life."

A scoreboard at the University of Arizona displays advertising for a number of corporate sponsors.

The practice of enmeshing itself in daily campus life helps a corporation create customers who will continue to show brand loyalty long after graduation. One advertising agency, Alloy Media + Marketing, has explained the demographic appeal of college students for corporations: "Away from the influence of home, college students make hundreds of first-time, independent buying decisions . . . decisions that will influence their preferences and purchasing habits for years to come."

At several institutions of higher education, however, students, faculty, and staff members have resisted this encroachment of corporations onto campuses. Student newspapers and groups have investigated the business practices of corporations with which universities have made agreements and, in several instances, have found that the business

Barnes & Noble's bookstore at Georgia Institute of Technology is one of hundreds of campus bookstores run by that chain.

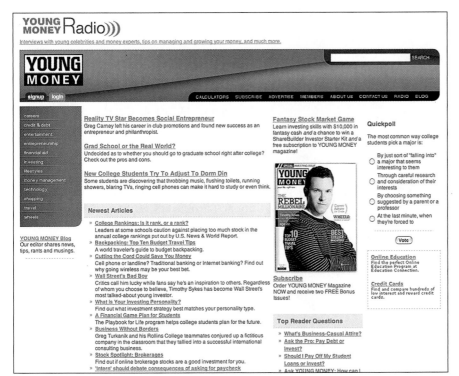

The magazine *Young Money* and its Web site directly target college students and recent graduates.

practices of specific corporations have run counter to the university's educational and social missions.

In 1998, the Union of Needletrades, Industrial and Textile Employees (UNITE) published a report on the BJ&B factory in the Dominican Republic, which made the baseball hats for at least nine large American universities, including Cornell, Duke, Georgetown, Harvard, and the University of Michigan. As Naomi Klein explains in her book *No Logo: No Space, No Choice, No Jobs,* UNITE's report showed that workers at the BJ&B factory were subjected to "long hours of forced overtime, fierce union busting (including layoffs of organizers), short-term contracts, paychecks insufficient to feed a family, pregnancy tests, sexual harassment, abusive management, unsafe drinking water and huge markups (while the hats sold, on average, for $19.95, workers saw only 8 cents of that)." These reports spurred several student groups into action, calling for university administrators to award clothing licenses only to businesses that use fair labor practices. Students at Duke University, for example, a school that sells approximately $25 million worth of clothing associated with its men's basketball team each year, pressured university administrators to review the university's 700 licensees that contract production work to hundreds of plants in the United States and ten other countries. In March 1998, public arguments by student groups led Duke University to create a policy requiring that every university licensee agree to follow clear labor standards in the production of Duke apparel. As Klein explains, "The code required that contractors pay the legal minimum wage, maintain safe working conditions and allow workers to form unions, no matter where the factories were located." Two months later, Brown University passed a similar licensing code, and the following September students at Georgetown, Wisconsin, North Carolina, Arizona, Michigan, Princeton, Harvard, Cornell, and University of California at Berkeley held conferences, teach-ins, protests, and sit-ins to draw attention to the labor practices that their schools were tacitly approving through their licensing arrangements with athletic apparel producers. At many of these schools and others, school administrators have developed policies requiring that all of their licensees agree to higher labor standards in the production of clothing bearing the school's name and logo.

Students' investigative reports on colleges' and universities' corporate partners have extended to other types of goods and services as well. As Liza Featherstone explains in a May 15, 2000 article in *The Na-*

Wanisha Smith of the Duke University women's basketball team, which has a licensing agreement with Nike.

tion, students on ten college campuses that year launched a boycott against Sodexho-Marriott, trying to draw attention to the facts that the company was the nation's largest investor in U.S. private prisons and had been censured by the National Labor Relations Board. Three years earlier, students and faculty took action in response to the California State University (CSU) system's planned partnership with four corporations—Microsoft, Fujitsu, GET, and Hughes Electronics—which was to provide a telecommunications infrastructure for CSU in exchange for the right to provide related services to the state schools at a profit. Several investigative reports in student newspapers, such as San Francisco State University's *Golden Gater,* explored the implications of the partnership for the CSU system's academic and financial integrity, focusing particularly on how the partnership would enable the four corporations to create a new generation of students familiar with their technological products and thus more likely to buy them after graduation. By April 1997, Microsoft and Hughes Electronics had pulled out of the partnership under pressure from faculty and student groups; two months later, the other two corporations withdrew as well.

United Students Against Sweatshops protest at the Niketown store in New York City.

DESCRIBING THE CORPORATE PRESENCE ON CAMPUS

1. How do you define a corporation? Make a list of all the things you think define a corporation. How do you define a college or university? Make a list of all the things you think define a college or university. In what ways do these definitions overlap? Where do they diverge?

2. Working on your own or with a classmate or two, describe when and where you have seen or experienced any corporate presence on your college or university campus. Describe these experiences in as much detail as you can.

3. What kinds of questions might an investigator hope to answer about corporations' presence on campuses? How would someone likely go about trying to find answers to these questions?

continued

4.   What groups, both on campus and off campus, might have a stake in the findings of investigative reports on relationships of corporations with colleges or universities? What might investigative reports about corporations' presence on campus uncover? Make a list of the things such a report might uncover.

Community Connections

1.   Which forms of the corporate presence on campus have you had experience with—in the dorm, the student union, the bookstore, or the classroom? Describe a specific experience in as much detail as possible. What corporations have established the most visible presence on your campus? In what ways have they made their presence known? Where and when have they made their presence known?

2.   Which of these types of corporate presence would be most likely to affect your day-to-day life on campus?

3.   Select the particular corporate-campus relationship that most interests you and that you would like to explore in greater detail. If you could know at least one specific thing about how a corporation influences the activities on your campus, what would that be? Be as specific as possible.

Real Responses to Real Situations

In the pages that follow, writers use their available means to respond to exigencies they have identified related to the investment of corporations on university and college campuses. As you explore their responses to situations that may be unfamiliar to you, ask yourself if what they have to say relates in any way to the corporate presence on your campus.

Investigating corporations in student unions and classrooms

Perhaps the most obvious ways in which corporations create a presence in any particular demographic group are through marketing their brands and advertising their services. Corporations and other businesses place print ads in newspapers, run commercials on radio and television, and sponsor special events both on campus and off. Nevertheless, corporations historically have had a difficult time reaching college students through traditional media outlets such as national newspapers and magazines. They have therefore researched and tested alternative methods of marketing and advertising that allow them to reach this attractive market.

Businesses and corporations increasingly seek to target college students with their advertising messages, seeing this group as possessing a largely untapped buying power, especially in light of their new independence often combined with generous parental support. However, there are some difficulties inherent in targeting college students, given that they come and go so often and so quickly. To meet these challenges, advertising and marketing agencies have developed some innovative practices to effectively market corporations' brands to college students.

One company that has developed new approaches to help corporations target college students is EdVenture Partners. EdVenture Partners runs a variety of marketing programs that bring corporations' advertising inside the college classroom. The various programs that EdVenture Partners offers to corporations and universities tap into corporations' need to market their products as efficiently and effectively as possible as well as college students' desire for real-world work experiences to supplement their classroom learning. In the following March 31, 2006 article from the *Pittsburgh Post-Gazette*, journalist Don Hammonds describes the participation of a group of University of Pittsburgh marketing students in one such marketing model.

DON HAMMONDS
Honda Challenges Students to Market Its Latest Car to Younger Buyers

---

Honda is counting on a group of University of Pittsburgh students to size up the Fit, its all-new entry-level subcompact. Pros in Motion, a student organization within the College of Business Administration, is developing a marketing campaign aimed at buyers just like themselves—both on and off campus. The students' project is part of the Honda Fit Marketing Challenge, a competition among 18 universities. Honda supplied students at each of the schools an operating budget of $2,500. The Fit goes on sale at the end of April, with prices starting at around $14,500.

"It's a really definite win-win-win for us," said Tom Peyton, senior manager–marketing support for Honda. "First and foremost, we love the energy and ideas that the students come up with in regard to marketing our products. There's only so many ideas in this world and taking this to the campuses is a big help with that."

The students recognize the campaign is a rare opportunity for them, too. "It's significant for us because in class, it's a lot of theory and not a lot of practice. It's almost like having an internship because you are arguing a campaign that affects a company and the new products they are coming with," said Lindsay Livorio, a senior

> "The sky's the limit on how the ideas generated by the students could be used by Honda . . . "

marketing major who is working on the public relations segment of the Fit campaign. "And in job searching, in some of the interviews I've gone on, our campaign has been a huge topic of conversation because it's doing something that not a lot of students get to do," she added.

The students are competing for a top prize of $5,000, a second place prize of $3,000 and a third place prize of $1,000.

The top three teams will be flown, all-expenses paid, to Honda headquarters in Torrance, Calif., on June 1 to present their campaigns to top executives from Honda and RPA, Honda's advertising agency. Teams from Honda and RPA will visit the Pitt campus on April 21 for a presentation on the campaign, and the finalists will be selected based on both quantitative factors—such as the number of hits on Web sites, results from surveys and other items—and qualitative factors, Ms. Livorio said. She expects to find out whether Pitt made the final cut in early May.

The sky's the limit on how the ideas generated by the students could be used by Honda, Ms. Livorio said. "For all we know, Honda could totally love the whole campaign and use all of it, or they could use a certain part of our campaign, or perhaps a slogan.

continued

Or they could use something from our campaign and something from the other schools' campaigns, too," Ms. Livorio said. "If they like what they see when we get to California it's definitely possible it could be used in a national Fit campaign."

Regardless of the outcome of the national competition, Pros in Motion's ideas will be used for the promotion of the Fit in Pittsburgh through early May when Pitt's classes and the advertising campaign end. "Our campaign is based solely on a new product that has not been seen here yet," said Lauren Feintuch, coordinator of Pros in Motion's project. "It's all up to us. There's nothing on television about it yet. It's just our little class that's introducing it to the school and to Pittsburgh. Better us to market it than some corporate person who doesn't really know us. We know what we want. Who better to market to our peers than us because we know what they want," Ms. Feintuch said.

"We also are at the age where we want new things, including new cars, not old, used ones—and the Honda Fit is priced just right for us," said Erin Conlon, senior marketing major, who heads the public relations group of the campaign.

As part of the campaign, the students already have come up with a number of ads that will be published in the *Pitt News* and have been distributed as fliers in the South Side and Oakland. Each calls attention to the Bigelow Bash from 10 a.m. to 6 p.m. tomorrow at the William Pitt Union, which will be the main marketing event for the car to the students. The event will include break dancers, inflatable jousting, food and prizes for participants, including a contest to see how many people can fit into the Honda Fit in 30 seconds. One advertisement features a kindergarten-style picture of the Fit in which color is scribbled all over the surface. The ad says, "You couldn't stay in the lines then. Why change now?" Another is a play on words for the well-known game show "The Price is Right"—"It's a new car! Come on down!" A third calls attention to the Fit's many features and calls them a "Blueprint for fun."

In a contest handbook, Honda urges students to do something the automaker would not ordinarily do in its ad campaigns—to push the envelope. "Since they're looking for something different, we can do whatever we want. They're looking for people who think a little different, and that makes it easy for us," said Mike Jack, a senior marketing student who is working on the ad campaign. Other students are working on public relations events and market research.

Regardless of how the student group finishes in the contest, the experience that they are getting is invaluable, said Bob Gilbert, an associate professor at Katz Graduate School of Management. The campaign contest is sponsored by EdVenture Partners, a company that specializes in industry-education partnerships. Shadyside Honda also is assisting. "We're really committed to this program. It gives them real-world experience and it looks great on the resume. The research that we are doing here is first-class research and the advertising is quite well done, too," he added.

And the students are learning the ins and outs of the advertising industry. Just listen to how Ms. Feintuch, the coordinator of the project, talks about the Fit: "First, it doesn't look like any other car out there. And it's small and very well built. And I was really surprised how many of us could actually fit into it. It's really ingenious." Spoken like a seasoned advertising executive.

Another significant feature of the corporate presence on campus has been the formal agreements that corporations—particularly those in the fields of science, engineering, and business—have created with various institutions to fund research projects. In the following excerpt from an investigative report that appeared in the *Atlantic Monthly,* Eyal Press and Jennifer Washburn define what they see as a new category among institutions of higher education: the kept university. This category, they explain, consists of schools where corporations exert significant control over the direction of research, teaching, and service.

Press and Washburn see the kept university illustrated most clearly in a November 1998 business agreement between the University of California–Berkeley's College of Natural Resources and Novartis, a Swiss pharmaceutical company and producer of genetically engineered crops. Through this agreement, Novartis agreed to pay $25 million to fund basic research in the college's Department of Plant and Microbial Biology. In exchange, the college granted the Novartis

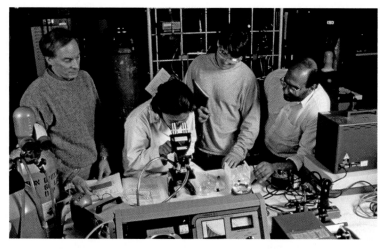

Graduate student Johann Leveau (standing at center) works in a plant and microbial lab at Berkeley.

Agricultural Discovery Institute (NADI) the licensing rights to a portion of the discoveries made by the department as well as two-fifths representation on the department's research committee, which makes decisions about how research money will be allocated. Several faculty members and student groups argued that this business deal threatened to undermine the college's mission to serve the public interest; others maintained that the agreement provided the money and technology necessary to fulfill this mission. Press and Washburn explored such corporate sponsorships of academic research in order to better understand their implications for the future of higher education and the nation's social, political, and economic vitality.

EYAL PRESS AND JENNIFER WASHBURN
Excerpt from The Kept University

. . . Gordon Rausser, the chief architect of the Novartis deal, believes that faculty concerns about the alliance reflect ignorance about both the Novartis deal and the changing economic realities of higher education. When we met with Rausser last year, in his spacious office in the ornate neoclassical Giannini Hall, he insisted that the deal, far from violating Berkeley's public mission, would help to perpetuate the university's status as a top-flight research institution. An economist who served on the President's Council of Economic Advisors in the 1980s and now operates a sideline consulting business, Rausser contends that Berkeley's value is "enhanced, not diminished, when we work creatively in collaboration with other institutions, including private companies." In a recent article in the Berkeley alumni magazine Rausser argues, "Without modern laboratory facilities and access to commercially developed propri-

etary databases . . . we can neither provide first-rate graduate education nor perform the fundamental research that is part of the University's mission."

Rausser's view is more and more the norm, as academic administrators throughout the country turn to the private sector for an increasing percentage of their research dollars, in part because public support for education has been dropping. Although the federal government still supplies most of the funding for academic research (it provided $14.3 billion, or 60 percent, in 1997, the latest year for which figures are available), the rate of growth in federal support has fallen steadily over the past twelve years, as the cost of doing research, particularly in the cutting-

"... universities, once wary beneficiaries of corporate largesse, have become eager co-capitalists ..."

continued

edge fields of computer engineering and molecular biology, has risen sharply. State spending has also declined. Berkeley Chancellor Robert Berdahl says that California now supplies just 34 percent of Berkeley's overall budget, as compared with 50 percent twelve years ago, and he claims that other state universities have suffered similar cuts.

Meanwhile, corporate giving is on the rise, growing from $850 million in 1985 to $4.25 billion less than a decade later—and increasingly the money comes with strings attached. One marked trend is a boom in industry-endowed chairs. Kmart has endowed a chair in the management school at West Virginia University which requires its holder to spend up to thirty days a year training assistant store managers. Freeport-McMoRan, a mining company embroiled in allegations of environmental misconduct in Indonesia, has created a chair in environmental studies at Tulane. In its series on privatization at Berkeley, *The Daily Californian* noted that buildings throughout the Haas School of Business were "plastered with corporate logos." One major contributor to the school is Don Fisher, the owner of The Gap, whose company also happens to be featured as a case study in an introductory business-administration course. Laura D'Andrea Tyson, formerly one of President Clinton's top economic advisers, is now officially known as the BankAmerica Dean of Haas. . . .

In an age when ideas are central to the economy, universities will inevitably play a role in fostering growth. But should we allow commercial forces to determine the university's educational mission and academic ideals? In higher education today corporations not only sponsor a growing amount of research—they frequently dictate the terms under which it is conducted. Professors, their image as unbiased truth-seekers notwithstanding, often own stock in the companies that fund their work. And universities themselves are exhibiting a markedly more commercial bent. Most now operate technology-licensing offices to manage their patent portfolios, often guarding their intellectual property as aggressively as any business would. Schools with limited budgets are pouring money into commercially oriented fields of research, while downsizing humanities departments and curbing expenditures on teaching. Occasional reports on these developments, including a recent *60 Minutes* segment on corporate-sponsored research, have begun to surface beyond the university. But the larger picture has yet to be filled out. It is this: universities, once wary beneficiaries of corporate largesse, have become eager co-capitalists, embracing market values as never before.

Through their investigation of the agreement between Novartis and the University of California–Berkeley, Press and Washburn concluded that opportunities for free intellectual exploration were in danger. They called for university administrators and academic researchers to disclose their connections to sponsoring corporations, and they called for scholars and teachers to follow their own instincts about the types of topics that should be explored in the public interest.

Several corporations have bypassed marketing courses and research labs and directly hired undergraduate students to market their products and imprint their brand within the student body. Like the EdVenture Partners' programs, these corporate initiatives seek to tap into college students' general openness to messages that come from their peers. In the following article, which first appeared in the *Boston Globe* on October 24, 2005, Sarah Schweitzer investigates the corporations' use of student "ambassadors" on college campuses.

SARAH SCHWEITZER
Excerpt from Building a Buzz on Campus

During lunch at Boston University, five girls ogled a 6-foot-7 blond senior with a winning smile and high cool-quotient as he approached their table. He was cute, they agreed. But equally intriguing was his pitch.

"I heard this is amazing!" Pam Spuehler, a sophomore in general studies, said as she read a postcard touting the OneNote software program that Cody Gossett had handed her.

"It is," Gossett said. "You should check it out!"

"I will!" Spuehler said, adding as she eyed the phrase "Save Trees. Use OneNote" on his chest, "How do I get one of those T-shirts?"

The exchange was a corporate marketer's dream—and one, in this case, come true for Microsoft, which hired Gossett to peddle its notes-organizing software on campus. Microsoft is among a growing number of companies seeking to reach the elusive but critical college market by hiring students to be ambassadors—or, in more traditional terms, door-to-door salesmen. In an age when the college demographic is no longer easily reached via television, radio, or newspapers—as TiVo, satellite radio, iPods, and the Internet crowd out the traditional advertising venues—a microindustry of campus marketing has emerged. Niche firms have sprung [up] to act as recruiters of students, who then market products on campus for companies such as Microsoft, JetBlue Airways, The Cartoon Network, and Victoria's Secret. "There is a paradigm shift in the way that corporations are marketing to college students," said Matt Britton, a managing partner of Mr. Youth, a New York-based firm that specializes in college student marketing. "The student ambassador tactic embraces all the elements that corporations find most effective: It's peer-to-peer, it's word of mouth, it's flexible, and it breaks through the clutter of other media. For all that, it's growing very quickly."

By the estimate of leading youth marketing firms, tens of thousands of students work as campus ambassadors nationwide, with many in the college-rich Bos-

> "... you don't feel like they are just pushing a product on you—it's more like they're sharing their opinion."

ton region. The students selected tend to be campus leaders with large social networks that can be tapped for marketing. Good looks and charm tend to follow. Many are specially trained, sometimes at corporate headquarters, Gossett said, as in the case with Microsoft. They are expected to devote about 10 to 15 hours a week talking up the products to friends, securing corporate sponsorship of campus events, and lobbying student newspaper reporters to mention products in articles. They also must plaster bulletin boards with posters and chalk sidewalks—tactics known as "guerilla marketing," which, marketing firms acknowledge, intentionally skirt the boundaries of campus rules.

Students are compensated with the products they hawk, and some are paid a small stipend. The bigger attraction appears to be the resume-worthy experience and a possible inside track for a job with a company after graduation. The companies generally track the work through self-reporting: Mr. Youth maintains an online portal where students log their numbers of fliers posted, e-mail addresses collected, and the like. Microsoft, Gossett said, monitors the work by counting the number of student downloads by school.

Colleges and universities say they have little say over student marketers on campus and are often unaware they exist. While many schools bar companies from setting up shop or sending nonstudent representatives to approach students on campus property, administrators say many campus spaces are difficult to restrict to students. "We are not in a position to tell people that they can't talk to people," said Bruce Reitman, dean of student affairs at Tufts University. . . .

College students are, however, a tough crowd for marketers. Wired as the generation may be, its members not only tend to ignore traditional media—television, radio, and newspapers—but, studies show, they are no more likely to click open an Internet ad than older adults are. They do, however, listen to one another. Gary Colen, an executive vice president of marketing at Alloy, said telecommunication compa-

continued

nies were early users of campus ambassadors, but, increasingly, retail and consumer goods firms are relying on them to counter the cacophony of corporate messages.

The method is a blend of other emerging tactics: buzz marketing, in which people talk up a product to friends and family without necessarily revealing corporate representation; and street teams, young people who hand out stickers, fliers, and products. But the use of campus ambassadors differs, specialists say, in that it is not cold-call salesmanship, used by street groups, and it is more forthcoming than buzz marketing. Campus ambassadors generally are not required to state their corporate affiliation, but most companies instruct them not to try to obscure it.

At BU, Gossett, 22, and his co-worker, Trevor Guthrie, 21, also a senior majoring in advertising, did not announce their corporate ties—allowing their logo-bearing T-shirts to do the work. Students they approached said, in interviews after listening to the pitch, they did not understand the students' relationship with Microsoft, but that it mattered little. "I probably listened to Trevor more because he's a friend," said Kelsey Henager, a sophomore studying public relations. "Students come from your level, and you don't feel like they are just pushing a product on you—it's more like they're sharing their opinion." Youth marketing firms say that sentiment is echoed in their research, which indicates that students have a growing mistrust of corporate messages—both because of the number of them and [because of] the recent string of corporate scandals. . . .

Boston University senior Trevor Guthrie sells his fellow students on Microsoft products.

[Josh] Velasquez, who heard about the JetBlue job though the career services center at [MIT's] Sloan School of Management, said his marketing methods have focused on filling campus bulletin boards with company posters, placing flight schedule booklets on computer consoles at the campus computing center, and securing corporate sponsorship of MIT's fall festival. The website for the festival now includes the JetBlue logo. Velasquez said he is continually brainstorming new ways of getting his message out. His latest: preprinted Post-it notes, the better for sticking to computing center monitors. "We're supposed to break the rules a little bit," he said. "Traditional media doesn't work, so you have to go out and be creative."

Student ambassadors have proved effective at helping corporations strengthen their brand identity and market new products and services to the college market; the ambassadors' already established and ever expanding connections with friends and classmates enable corporations to tap directly into college social networks. The ambassador positions have also proved attractive to college students because they offer income, sales experience, and potential postgraduate employment. As some colleges and universities establish policies and rules that limit corporations' advertising on campus, use of student ambassadors gives the companies access to the college market through more informal—and, they hope, more authentic—means.

ANALYZING THE RHETORICAL SITUATION

1. What specific feature of the corporate presence on college campuses does each report in this section investigate?

2. Who is the specific audience for each of the three reports? For what purpose was each report written? How does that purpose affect the audience for each report?

3. What kinds of facts and evidence does each report present to help readers better understand corporations' presence and activity on college campuses? What kinds of research did the writers likely do to find these types of facts and evidence?

4. What exigencies prompted the reports in this section? How would you characterize their responses to the corporate presence on college and university campuses?

5. How do the writers of these reports draw on the rhetorical appeals of ethos, logos, and pathos to support their opinions on corporations' proper role on college campuses? Cite passages from the texts to support your answer.

The University of Oregon's football uniforms clearly display the school's Nike affiliation.

Investigating corporations' involvement in collegiate athletics

On many college and university campuses in the United States, the most visible corporate presence can be seen on the football field, basketball court, and soccer pitch. Major college athletic programs have signed multimillion-dollar deals in which an athletic apparel company such as Nike, Adidas, or Reebok produces the athletes' uniforms and the fans' T-shirts, hats, and sweatshirts—all of which are emblazoned with the corporation's logo. Corporate leaders have also made large financial contributions to the athletic departments of their alma maters, such as Nike CEO Phil Knight's donations to upgrade the athletic facilities at the University of Oregon, where he competed in cross-country running and track and field as an undergraduate, and T. Boone Pickens's $165 million donation to the athletic

program at Oklahoma State University. Sponsorship deals and alumni donations like these have served as another advertising medium for corporations, and several corporate executives have successfully wielded significant influence in athletic departments at colleges and universities. As investigative journalist Mike Fish explains in the story that he filed for ESPN.com, an affinity for college athletics can run beyond a CEO's alma mater.

MIKE FISH
Excerpt from Riding the Trojan Horse

Not all boosters run around town singing their school's fight song. Or dressing like colorful clowns on football Saturdays. Some like Joe Malugen, current sugar daddy to Troy University's upstart Division I-A squad, never set foot in a class on campus. His roots, in fact, trace to the University of Missouri (Class of '73). So here, in a rural southeast Alabama town of about 15,000, boosterism has nothing to with emotional ties and everything to do with smart business.

And let it be noted the dough isn't coming out of Malugen's pocket, but the coffers of his video rental company, Movie Gallery—No. 2 in the business behind only Blockbuster. Two years ago, Malugen signed a $5 million marketing deal with Troy to name its freshly renovated stadium Movie Gallery Veterans Stadium. Malugen fancied it as a way to tie the company's name to a sports team—a Trojan program flush with a pair of

NCAA Division II national titles that aspired to tee it up with the big boys—and also curry favor in the local community, where Movie Gallery is headquartered just an hour down Highway 231 in Dothan.

Years ago, Syracuse kicked off the football naming rights deals with the Carrier Dome, followed by Louisville and Papa John's Stadium and Texas Tech's SBC Stadium. And now comes Troy. "We sort of rolled the dice and did the deal, and what we found was the impact was greater than we anticipated," says Malugen, the Movie Gallery chairman and CEO. "And I think that is probably due to the TV coverage we have gotten of the stadium. And, of course, one of the good things is we picked a good horse to ride. Troy University is kind of a Cinderella-type team. They have had some great successes beating Marshall and beating Missouri [in 2004]. They sort of delivered in doing what they said they were going to try and do. Obviously if they'd gotten blown out in every game I probably would be less excited about it. They've been on national and regional TV quite often, so that Movie Gallery Stadium, logos and all, has certainly gotten around the southeast."

This fall's 4-7 Troy squad didn't prove quite the entertainment buy, yet Malugen can't say much after a steeper-than-anticipated downturn in the movie rental business resulted in $12.5 million third-quarter losses for Movie Gallery. Both sides are in this for the long haul anyway, thanks to the 20-year naming rights deal.

So what does Movie Gallery get for Malugen signing on? For starters, Suite 509, a 20-seat skybox perched squarely above the 50-yard line, outfitted with movie theater seats and posters from "Radio" and "Re-

> **"People don't sit around . . . very often and talk about what is happening at the University of Missouri's School of Business."**

Joe Malugen at Troy University.

member the Titans" hanging on the walls. The company this fall leased a larger, 40-seat skybox that's near the 25-yard line. Malugen also sits on the Troy University Foundation's Board of Directors, the major fundraising arm of the university. According to the most recent IRS Form 990 filed last year, the foundation has $32 million in net assets after having issued cash grants of almost $5.5 million—$3.4 million of it going to the athletic department. When Troy went looking for an athletic director last fall, Malugen was called to serve on the eight-person search committee . . . .

Malugen says he doesn't meddle in the day-to-day affairs of the athletic department, and by all accounts that's true. When he does offer an occasional thought, it's usually about scheduling—Troy has an ambitious, if not downright silly nonconference road stretch next season at Florida State, Georgia Tech and Nebraska—and down the road perhaps upgrading its Sun Belt Conference affiliation. "He gives money, offers his opinions, but doesn't dictate," [Troy's Senior Associate Athletic Director Scott] Farmer explains.

Troy chancellor Jack Hawkins Jr. says the university has no trepidation dealing with outside corporate types such as Malugen and Richard Scrushy, [HealthSouth founder and former] CEO. Hawkins buys into the grander sports profile as a vehicle to bring name recognition and push his vision for a global campus; Troy currently has a physical presence in 13 countries.

Perhaps even more pressing is the necessity to find and attract diverse revenue streams to keep the university running, which is true of most universities not named Harvard or Yale. When Hawkins came to Troy almost two decades ago, he says 43 percent of his budget was derived from the state. Today, the number is only 23 percent. So there'd be no big-time ath-

letics if not for corporate checks signed by Malugen and Scrushy. And, as an acknowledgement, displayed prominently on a wall in the athletic department offices are enlargements of the original checks they wrote.

Scrushy—who still faces civil claims after a June acquittal on federal fraud charges in the $2.7 billion overstatement of earnings at HealthSouth, the chain of rehabilitation hospitals he helped found—provided the seed money spawning Troy's move to I-A. Hawkins had personally lobbied Alabama Gov. Fob James for Scrushy's appointment to the Troy board of trustees. And you find the football field still bears his name, if you look hard enough. It was at a 1998 meeting at the HealthSouth headquarters in Birmingham that Scrushy pushed Troy trustees to take the sports teams to the next level. "We were wrestling with, 'Do we go I-A?'" Hawkins recalls. "Right in the middle of the meeting, Richard slapped the table and he said, 'I'm good for a million dollars.' And the hands went up and we went I-A."

In Scrushy's case, there was an emotional attachment because his wife and an uncle graduated from Troy. For Malugen, at least initially, it was bottom-line business. "I see the athletic programs as really the marketing department for the university," Malugen offers. "I feel like these universities are really a brand. Just like a Movie Gallery brand or the Hollywood Video brand. Just like the ESPN brand. Like I tell them at Missouri, 'People don't sit around on any given day very often and talk about what is happening at the University of Missouri's School of Business. They sit around and talk about what is happening with the Mizzou football team.' It is just branding." With rare exceptions, more and more schools are happy to play the game.

Joe Malugen understands that athletic teams are often what gives a college or university visibility in the mass media. Tapping into the marketing potential of this visibility just makes good business sense to Malugen, and administrators at Troy University and other schools seem willing to accept the financial windfall that comes from such corporate support.

Columnist Paul Boyer addresses concerns about how corporate sponsorship of higher education engendered problematic conceptions of the relative value of different activities in colleges and universities. His column appeared in

December 1995, shortly after the University of Wisconsin–Madison announced a five-year deal with Reebok that would provide $6.7 million to the school's athletic department and $1.2 million to finance academic scholarships and sports programs in the Madison area. As the editors of the *Wisconsin State Journal* noted, Boyer's column was a satire inspired by that deal.

PAUL BOYER
Corporate America Takes on the Care and Clothing of Public Education

Situations for Writers

At a news conference in New York City today, top executives of Time Warner Corp. announced that the media giant had signed a multiyear contract to become official shoe supplier to members of the UW-Madison history department. Unveiling details of the plan, the Time Warner spokesperson explained that all full-time members of the history faculty, tenured or untenured, will be presented with a booklet of vouchers which they can then use to purchase new shoes at Famous Footwear or any other Madison shoe store. Depending on how many historians take advantage of the plan, the spokesperson commented, the deal could amount to as much as several hundred dollars a year.

When asked about Time Warner's motivation for this innovative step, the spokesperson commented: "Basically, we just wanted to show our support for American higher education as it faces severe budget cutbacks. Of course, if a historian who is wearing a pair of shoes paid for by Time Warner chooses to mention in his or her lecture that regular reading of *Time Magazine* can provide valuable depth and perspective on history and current events, we will be most pleased." Still, he added with a chuckle, "these shoes come with no strings attached."

History department chairman James S. Donnelly Jr., reached at his suburban Oregon home, responded enthusiastically to the news. "We've been working on the details of this arrangement for a long time," he commented, "and it's just great to see it come to fruition. My Irish heart is overflowing with joy." Donnelly added that he had noticed at recent department meetings that faculty members' shoes were showing considerable wear, so this corporate gesture is most welcome.

Donnelly denied any impropriety in this form of corporate subsidy for professors at a public university. "Things are getting so tough we'll take help wherever we can find it," he said; "I know my colleagues well, and I'm confident that having their shoes paid for by Time Warner will not diminish their independence or integrity in any way. The athletic department has been getting corporate subsidies like this for years, and now the shoe is on the other foot."

Members of the history department reacted positively to the news. Historian Robert M. Kingdon, reached at his office at the university's Institute for Research in the Humanities, said: "I've been thinking about buying a new pair of shoes for some time, so this announcement comes at just the right moment for me." Other historians, particularly some of the younger ones, were equally grateful in their praise of Time Warner's generosity.

Only a few malcontents and well-known radicals in the department insisted that they would continue to buy their own shoes. The idea appears to be spreading. UW-Madison Chancellor David Ward, who is a member of the geography department, is reported to be in high-level but still secret telephone negotiations with the publisher of *National Geographic* magazine, working on an arrangement by which this much-loved and very profitable publication would become the official supplier of chino trousers to members of the geography department.

Wisconsin Gov. Tommy Thompson, who flew to New York to participate in the news conference, warmly endorsed the new arrangement. Said Thompson: "Coming in the wake of the $6 million Reebok deal with the athletic department, this is further encouraging evidence of creative privatization at the university. Now that corporate America is stepping in to provide shoes and other necessities for professors, we can look for further cuts in the university budget for the next biennium." Continued Thompson: "The business of Wisconsin is business, and it's good to see that some of those big-government, big-spending Democrat liberals at the other end of State Street are beginning to understand what the '90s are all about."

> "... the deal could amount to as much as several hundred dollars a year."

Paul Boyer uses satire to make a point about the priorities of corporations and college administrators in this era of big-time college athletics as well as to highlight the relatively low value given the humanities. Boyer seems to warn that directing university activities according to bottom-line concerns undermines the traditional conception that intellectual freedom is at the heart of education in general and the university in particular.

ANALYZING THE RHETORICAL SITUATION

1. What specific problem does Mike Fish explore in his investigative article? What specific argument does he appear to be making in his article? What does Fish see as the ideal relationship between corporations and universities?

2. What specific conclusions does Fish want his audience to reach? What rhetorical appeals of ethos, logos, and pathos does Fish use to try to produce this response?

3. What specific problem does Paul Boyer address? Who is the audience for his column? What action does Boyer want this audience to take?

4. How does Boyer use ethos, pathos, and logos to build the argument in his column? (Provide textual evidence to support your answer.) Which of the rhetorical appeals does he rely on most?

5. What would Boyer propose as the proper relationship between corporations and universities? What actions does he want corporations or universities to take?

6. How do you characterize Boyer's response to Reebok's agreement with the University of Wisconsin–Madison? In what ways is he helping to develop the conversation about the corporate presence on campuses?

COMMUNITY CONNECTIONS

1. Write for ten minutes responding to one of the five reports you've just read about the corporate presence on campus. How do the various activities described by these writers coincide with or diverge from your experiences on your campus?

2. What specific corporate advertising and marketing activities can you identify on your campus? List several examples. Who likely made the various decisions leading to these instances of corporate presence on your campus?

3. Write for ten minutes about the causes or the consequences of one specific instance of corporate presence on your college or university campus.

4. Based on your experiences, what is your definition of the ideal relationship between corporations and institutions of higher education? Write for ten minutes and be prepared to share your answer.

Investigative Reports: A Fitting Response

As the readings in this chapter illustrate, corporations have created a presence on many college and university campuses. Some corporations advertise their products and services in the campus newspaper; others sponsor classroom projects and athletic programs; still others provide financial resources to fuel and, in some cases, shape the direction of academic research. Each of the investigative reports precisely defines the nature of a corporate-academic partnership, clarifies the various perspectives and motivations that gave rise to this partnership, and illustrates how this partnership affects various stakeholders.

Two reports investigating the corporate presence on campus

The two investigative reports that follow continue this chapter's exploration of the corporate presence on campus. As you read these reports, notice the ways in which Robert Cwiklik and Kate Fitzgerald address these elements of their rhetorical situation: exigence, audience and purpose, and context. Notice, too, how they meet the requirements for an investigative report: they (1) define in precise terms the issue they are exploring, suggest why the issue is one that needs to be investigated immediately, and articulate a specific conclusion that they want readers to reach; (2) provide convincing facts and details to help readers understand how the issue affects different groups with a connection to or an interest in the issue; and (3) include direct quotations that vividly convey perspectives of various groups with a stake in the issue.

Robert Cwiklik

How UPS Tried to Buy into the Ivory Tower

[1] Here the writer defines the scope of his investigation: he will explore how the UPS offer to the University of Washington went "beyond the now-routine corporate practice."

[2] Cwiklik identifies the exigence for his investigation: academic prerogatives could be endangered if corporations continue to encroach with deals of this sort.

Closer financial ties between corporations and universities have raised many troubling questions in recent years, and a United Parcel Service of America Inc. offer to the University of Washington managed to stir up just about all of them. More than two years ago, UPS offered the university's medical school $2.5 million to establish a research chair in occupational orthopedics. But the Atlanta-based shipping giant wanted to go beyond the now-routine corporate practice of specifying a subject area for a bequest. [1] UPS asked that a particular researcher at the school, Stanley J. Bigos, be appointed to the chair and granted tenure. Both demands trespass on academic prerogatives traditionally considered off-limits to corporate sponsors. [2]

Although the two-year negotiations between UPS and the University of Washington ended unsuccessfully, the paper trail they left illustrates how aggressively corporations wield their supposedly philanthropic dollars. About 20%, or $2.8 billion, of total contributions to higher education came from companies in 1996, according to the Council for Aid to Education, a New York nonprofit group. [3] Today, corporations increasingly "want something back" for their gifts, says John Coy, head of Consulting Network, a Vienna, Va., firm that advises big companies on their financial relationships with universities.

It's understandable that UPS would want to endow a chair for Dr. Bigos, an orthopedic surgeon and professor. His research has suggested that workers' back-injury claims may relate more to poor attitudes than ergonomic factors on the job. UPS has opposed recent government efforts to impose workplace ergonomics standards. [4] Dr. Bigos says UPS's proposal never struck him as a threat to academic independence. Instead, he says, the company's money would have helped him to do the kind of research he was doing "before I even knew who UPS was."

Cuts in government support for higher education have turned universities into scavengers for private funds, and schools now routinely permit corporate donors not only to name endowed professorships and chairs, but also to select their subject areas. [5] That ensures that "issues related to their core business" will be studied, says Mr. Coy. Thus, there's a Coca-Cola Professor of Marketing at the University of Georgia, a Lego Professor of Learning Research at the Massachusetts Institute of Technology (who is also a Disney fellow) and a La Quinta Motor Inns Professor of Business at the University of Texas.

Critics of these relationships say they erode academic independence. Derek Bok, former president of Harvard University, says in cases when a company wants to sponsor a particular scholar, universities should submit the matter to an independent panel. Otherwise, he says, "you're making what are essentially tough academic judgments with a thumb on the scale."

University of Washington officials concede that corporations get something back for their gifts. "But only in the sense of receiving visibility for their generosity," says a spokesman. In its negotiations with the University of Washington, UPS hoped to establish the "Stanley J. Bigos Endowed Chair of Occupational Orthopedics." Today UPS officials say they would have settled for sponsoring another researcher, had the university insisted. But documents exchanged among participants in the negotiations show that Dr. Bigos was UPS's clear choice. The documents were obtained through a state freedom-of-information law by a researcher for the Teamsters union, which represents UPS employees. The researcher made them available for this article. [6] The university's first contact from UPS came from an outside attorney representing an unidentified "potential benefactor." In a second letter, the attorney frankly stated that the donor's proposed bequest of "at least" $1.5 million—the medical school's minimum for endowing a chair—was "principally intended" to support a "specific individual" in the school and only "secondarily" for the university. Typically, endowments for chairs are invested by the university, and the generated income pays for the salary and staff of the chair holder, as well as overhead for the university itself. Mr. Coy says that the amounts allocated for such purposes are generally negotiable. But UPS's attorney went further. He asked questions that "the benefactor considers critical," including whether endowment funds would be "mobile" should the faculty member move to another school, and whether "a tenured position" would be offered. In response to the attorney's

[3] The writer includes an essential element of all investigative reports—attribution of evidence to specific sources.

[4] Cwiklik spells out the specific motivation behind UPS's support of Dr. Bigos.

[5] The writer provides some historical context for understanding the present issue: colleges and universities have been more open to corporate funding as government support for higher education has grown smaller.

[6] This paragraph and the preceding one present opposing views on the issue under consideration. Providing both perspectives helps the writer convey to readers that he has conducted a fair, balanced investigation.

letter, Krista Mattox, then executive director of development for the university's medical school, said the university did not establish chairs for specific individuals. The donor's candidate could be considered, she wrote, but any appointment had to clear internal reviews. She also said that endowment funds "must remain at the university." [7]

UPS was undaunted. Shedding its cloak of anonymity, the company identified itself as the benefactor in a memo to the university and named Dr. Bigos as the researcher it wanted to support. UPS also repeated its request that the chair holder be tenured. And it raised its offer to $2.5 million—$1 million above the minimum—"in hopes of assuring our intentions." S. John Goodwin, then assistant vice president for development at the university, responded by asking UPS for the time to develop a proposal that's "as detailed and well thought-out as your generous offer deserves." He said university officials would try to incorporate UPS's goals into the endowment, "subject (of course) to reasonable limits of academic freedom." Mr. Goodwin's letter mentioned Dr. Bigos by name, citing the medical school dean's support for Dr. Bigos's research. He didn't mention the school's policies prohibiting donors from aiding specific individuals.

Dr. Bigos had excellent credentials for an endowed chair. A full professor since 1990, he had served as chairman of a panel of experts that developed guidelines for the treatment of lower-back pain, which were released in 1994 by the Association for Health Care Policy and Research, a federal agency. He had also gained notice for leading a 1991 study of back-injury claims filed by workers at a Boeing Co. plant in Washington. The study found that "psychosocial factors," such as life distress, outweighed working conditions in explaining back-injury claims. [8]

UPS data for 1996 show that its employees suffer on-the-job injuries at levels well above those in comparable industries tracked by the Labor Department. And the Occupational Safety and Health Administration (OSHA) says that in the past 12 years, more worker complaints have been filed against UPS than against any other company. Employee complaints declined in the past couple of years, says Bob Godlewski, a UPS spokesman who notes that the company is implementing programs to reduce its injury levels. While its injury rate is still "not where we want it to be," he says comparisons with companies where workers may face dissimilar conditions are unfair. [9] In 1995, when OSHA's work on ergonomics standards was gathering steam, UPS lobbyists argued that scientific evidence that such rules would reduce injuries was scanty and that they would cost businesses billions. Later that year, Congress ordered OSHA to halt work on the rules, a ban that won't be fully lifted until fiscal 1999. "Ergonomics is not a medical science," says Thomas Walsh, UPS health and safety officer. "It's engineering." Dr. Bigos's work, on the other hand, is "sound science," Mr. Walsh says.

In May 1996, University of Washington officials sent a proposed endowment agreement to UPS. "It is the university's desire that Dr. Stanley J. Bigos be the initial holder" of the chair, the university said. The document goes on to note that the appointment would be made by the medical-school dean "in accordance with university policies and procedures and subject to approval by

[7] Cwiklik provides direct quotations from primary sources to give readers a clearer sense of the issue.

[8] Cwiklik creates an effective ethical appeal—he provides Dr. Bigos's credentials as a counter-statement to those readers who might conclude that the professor has been overly influenced by UPS's support of his research.

[9] Cwiklik continues to provide historical context for understanding the issue under investigation.

the Board of Regents." [10] In an accompanying letter, Philip J. Fialkow, dean of the medical school, promised to support the proposed tenure for Dr. Bigos, though again "in accordance with university policies." University officials say that such policies call for a search committee to choose the chair holder, regardless of the fact that Dr. Bigos was named in the agreement. UPS's interest in ergonomics "of course" would have been weighed in the approval process, says L. G. Blanchard, a spokesman for the medical school. (Dr. Fialkow died in an accident in October 1996.)

Although the university and UPS seemed to be nearing an accord, in March of last year, Mr. Walsh of UPS wrote to the school that "for reasons having nothing to do with the merits" of the proposal, "UPS is not in a position this year to endow the Bigos chair." Mr. Walsh says the bequest was scuttled because the UPS Foundation, the company's charitable arm, no longer endows academic chairs. It hasn't done so since the 1970s, says foundation director Gary Lee. Allowing companies to request a particular professor for an endowed chair is "against academic freedom," Mr. Lee adds. Mr. Walsh, however, says he sees nothing "inappropriate" about the company's negotiations with the university. "I don't think we're at all embarrassed that we wanted Stan Bigos to get the chair," he says. [11]

[10] Again, the writer provides direct quotations from pertinent documents so that readers can understand as precisely as possible the specific details of the issue under investigation.

[11] Cwiklik concludes his investigative report by allowing both sides to voice their perspectives. This conclusion shows readers that he has approached and investigated the issue with an open mind.

In her investigative report, which appeared in June 2003 in the journal *Credit Card Management*, Kate Fitzgerald explores new activities that some credit card companies are undertaking in order to market their services to college students. Her report provides an audience of business executives with an overview of how those corporations are pursuing such activities.

Kate Fitzgerald

They're Baaaaack: Card Marketers on Campus

It wasn't so long ago that many college administrators threw credit card marketers off campus. But now, restrictions on campus credit card solicitation are loosening up. In fact, a growing number of issuers are starting to invade campuses through the classroom, as well as through application sign-up tables. Increasingly, colleges and universities are inviting card marketers onto campuses to sponsor education programs. At a growing number of universities, credit card marketers are being allowed to develop classroom curricula. Card-industry firms recently expanding activity in this area include MasterCard International, Citigroup Inc.'s Citibank, J. P. Morgan Chase & Co., and Capital One Financial Corp.

The caveat: the credit card brand name moves into the background, and credit card applications are not part of classroom educational activities.

But issuers are jumping at the opportunity to reach college students on this level and with the approval of institutions, even if their brand marketing must be somewhat subdued. "College students are among the very toughest people to target, because they don't watch much TV, their media tastes change constantly, and they're very savvy about brands," says Ann Brown, vice president of business development for US Concepts, a New York City–based company that specializes in youth and mobile marketing. [1] "The most powerful way to reach kids is through experiences." US Concepts has had credit card clients in the past, and is in talks with one now.

Policies barring credit card marketers from on-campus solicitation are gradually relaxing in many areas, to the relief of card marketers. The shift follows a widespread movement among school administrators in the late 1990s to shut card marketers out as a reaction to students' growing debt burdens and perceived exploitation by marketers. Hundreds of campuses banned card marketers, according to credit card marketing sources. Talk of legislation to prevent credit card marketers from exploiting college students also has died down. But plenty of on-campus card solicitation continues, and controversy about it smolders in some circles.

Robert Manning, a professor at the Rochester (N.Y.) Institute of Technology, has emerged as a widely quoted opponent of direct solicitation of students by credit card marketers, which he claims leads to thousands of students going bankrupt and failing at school each year. [2] "It's clear that students are carrying more cards each year, and are getting into debt at an earlier age than ever," he says. "And with the tough economic climate we're in, it's only going to get worse." His chief complaint is the fact that although many of the nation's largest universities claim to have banned the credit card marketers as a whole from campus, these same schools have inked marketing contracts with top issuers such as MBNA Corp. and Bank One Corp., both of which have long tenure in campus marketing. The deals generally provide exclusive credit card marketing access to students, faculty and alumni, including tabling at campus events. "The universities say they are restricting campus marketing of credit cards to students, but their policies are only keeping out rival marketers," says Manning. "The preferred issuer is still doing big business with students on campus." [3]

The University of Tennessee reportedly has a seven-year, $16.5 million contract with Bank One to market an affinity credit card featuring the school's logo. [4] Manning says students are caught in Bank One's marketing net on many levels, particularly at popular sporting events, where tabling is widespread. Other universities with Chicago-based Bank One affinity card programs that also claim to have banned on-campus marketing include the University of Louisville and San Diego State University.

A Bank One spokesperson counters that although some students may be exposed to card solicitations through tabling at college events, they are not the primary target of its marketing initiatives, and represent only a "tiny fraction" of cardholders. "College students tend to have very low credit limits and low balances, and they are not the focus of our university-affiliated cards," says the

[1] Here and throughout the report, the writer provides attribution for each direct quotation, telling readers not only the person's name but also his or her affiliation or perspective.

[2] The writer shows how the source is qualified to speak to the issue at hand—and reveals something about the person's relationship to or stake in the issue.

[3] Fitzgerald provides readers with Manning's key point.

[4] The preceding sentence provides an example to illustrate Manning's point—that universities increasingly are signing big contracts with credit card companies.

spokesperson. "Our main thrust is in reaching alumni, who are far more profitable to us than college students, with low credit limits and low usage volume, would be." . . . [5]

REAL CAMPAIGN [6]

Meanwhile, the opportunity to integrate credit card information into the university experience is relatively new and growing fast, say college marketing experts. Examples now include the "Citibank Credit Education Program," which is integrated with university marketing courses, usually in the business department. Each participating college class receives a budget of $2,500 from Citibank to create a marketing campaign aimed at helping to educate other students with key facts about the need for credit cards and how to use them responsibly. The program, in its third year, involves five schools annually. This fall it will be introduced at the University of Akron and at Temple University in Philadelphia. A Citibank executive visits each participating class to provide real-life information about the credit card industry. Students then gather market research from their peers about credit card awareness, while studying credit card competition and the marketing strategies used by various issuers.

The students' data are used to create on-campus advertising and public-relations programs about credit cards in general and not specifically to promote Citibank's cards. A competition among five universities in the program last year resulted in a real-life credit card awareness public-service publicity campaign developed by a class at Portland State University that Citi used in several markets. The campaign was themed, "Paper or Plastic?"

EdVenture Partners, Orinda, Calif., developed the program and executes it for Citibank, which offers additional credit-awareness and credit card responsibility materials through colleges and online. "Citibank is the supporter, not the subject, of the marketing campaign, but when the students have contact with an actual Citibank executive, there is a definite connection to the brand during the program," says Tony Sgro, chief executive of EdVenture Partners. "Generation Y is very focused on firsthand experience, and this program introduces college students to the brand at a deep level, which helps build general loyalty." [7]

Capital One tested college classroom channels for the first time last fall, offering credit card education programs for credit at Washington State University, Texas A&M University and the University of South Florida, says a Capital One spokesperson. Relying primarily on credit card education materials provided by Visa, Capital One also offered grass-roots training about credit card responsibility throughout the campuses, including workshops in dormitories and athletic departments, says the spokesperson. The issuer plans to continue the program this fall at the same universities.

TOOLS

Larry Chiang, chairman of Oak Brook, Ill.-based United College Marketing Services, says his credit card marketing agency offers seminars for new students to explain the advantages and risks of credit cards. Schools have become more

[5] This quotation from a Bank One spokesperson creates balance in the writer's presentation of the issue by allowing readers to hear the voices of different individuals and groups invested in the issue.

[6] With section headings, the writer effectively highlights the smaller issues that make up the larger issue of credit cards on campus.

[7] The writer shows readers how one credit card company, Citibank, works to educate potential card users—simultaneously creating a loyal customer base.

[8] Notice throughout this section that the writer provides a range of examples to show that different groups are invested in this issue, to create a balanced discussion of the credit card industry's tactics, and to help readers visualize more clearly how credit card companies are marketing themselves on college campuses.

interested in such programs in recent years as a way of helping students head off credit problems early, he says. [8]

Issuers are allowed the opportunity to promote their brands in conjunction with the seminars, which usually last about 20 minutes, and occasionally the colleges allow applications to be offered as well. "Colleges know that students are getting credit cards and using them, so they want to give students as many tools as possible for coping," says Chiang. MasterCard, according to a spokesperson, has reached "thousands" of college students over the past several years with its campus education program, introduced in 1999, called "Are You Credit Wise?" The program offers paid internships for college credit to one student on each of 15 different university campuses. Each year more than 100 students compete for the internships, through which students hold seminars and workshops for other students using MasterCard-developed materials about credit usage and smart money management.

Chase joined the program last year by sponsoring two interns and plans to continue next year, says James Taylor, vice president of marketing for Chase Cardmember Services. Chase also promotes responsible credit card usage by delivering credit education information to student customers via monthly statement inserts that focus on topics determined by which stage of the school year students are in, according to Taylor.

Visa U.S.A. also offers an assortment of credit and financial-services educational materials for students and teachers, from preschool through college, under its "Visa Practical Money Skills for Life" program, which is available online. The site offers lesson plans and guidance for teachers. Visa is mentioned as the presenter of the information but its products are not promoted in the text.

For MasterCard, reaching college students in peer-to-peer settings with relevant information is effective, even without the opportunity to push its brand heavily. "Even without having a big sales effort, simply having students see MasterCard's name at the end of a presentation is a very powerful one-on-one association when it's presented by another student," says Catherine Cummings, MasterCard's vice president of consumer affairs.

WHAT MAKES IT AN INVESTIGATIVE REPORT?

The following questions are ones you should consider when thinking critically about any investigative report. For now, try applying them to the preceding reports by Robert Cwiklik and Kate Fitzgerald to determine how closely the authors follow the conventions of writing investigative reports.

1. Does the writer define the issue in terms that will make sense to the audience for the report?

2. What reasons are given for why the issue needs to be investigated immediately?

3. Are facts and details given to explain how the issue affects different groups that might have an interest in or connection to the issue?

4. Whom does the writer quote? Whose perspectives are represented in direct quotations? Whose perspectives are not represented through the use of quotations?

5. What specific conclusion about the issue does the writer want readers to reach?

Understanding the Rhetorical Situation

Identifying an exigence

Are there any corporations with a highly visible presence on your campus? Are there any corporations that have a less visible presence but some significant relationship to your college or university? Is anything about this corporate presence a source of contention among groups at your school? Are any aspects of this corporate presence unclear or seemingly innocuous to you? Are some features of this corporate presence more acceptable than others to you or other students? Are there any unrealized opportunities for advantageous corporate-academic partnerships on your campus?

You might survey the walls in your student union, the pages of your campus newspaper, the walkways outside stadiums or arenas on game days, or the list of investments that fund the school's endowment. Maybe there are few visible signs of corporate advertising and marketing on your campus. Or maybe it seems as if corporations have permeated almost every aspect of campus life, from determining what soft drinks you can buy in the vending machines to limiting the selection of texts available in the bookstore to shaping the curricula in your business courses or science labs.

1. Make a list of experiences you have had that were either directly or indirectly shaped by a corporate presence on campus. If the experiences were positive, explain why, providing as many details as possible. If the experiences were negative, identify the factors that contributed to that outcome. Write down details about the factors that might have shaped your experiences: the place and time (both during the day and during the semester) the experience occurred, the number of people involved in or affected by the experience, the school policies affecting this corporate presence on campus, and so forth.
2. Choosing one or two of the experiences that you wrote about for question 1, take photos documenting the corporate presence on your campus. Pay particular attention to documenting how this corporate presence shapes students' activities on campus.
3. Choose which corporate presence on campus you would like to write about and compose four or five sentences that describe the various groups that seem to be affected by this presence. Describe what you understand to be the college or university's mission to the student body, to its employees, to the citizens of surrounding communities, to its corporate partners, and to the public at large. Describe policies that you think the school might have established or should establish to determine the particular activities that corporations are able to pursue on campus.

Locating an audience

For his investigative report on UPS's proposal to establish a research chair in occupational orthopedics, Robert Cwiklik had to consider two audiences who might be reading the *Wall Street Journal* article: (1) corporate executives and (2) school administrators and faculty members. The report, then, had to account for the perspectives and motivations of members of these different audiences, as well as the personal and academic concerns of the student body and the general public.

What audience do you need to consider for your investigative report? First, you have to determine who is affected by the particular corporate presence on campus that you've decided to write about. Then, you'll need to consider how to make that audience (or audiences) understand the various ways in which this corporate presence affects their academic and personal activities. For instance, if you think the student body needs to know more about the presence of one or more corporate executives on your university's board of trustees, you'll need to think about the attitudes that students hold toward the university's mission, its responsibility to the public interest, and the means by which it goes about fulfilling this mission.

The following questions will help you identify the rhetorical audience for your investigative report on the corporate presence on your campus. Having identified your audience, you'll be able to choose the best way to deliver your message about corporate-academic relationships.

1. List the names of the persons or groups who are affected by or have a stake in the particular corporate-academic relationship you're going to explore. This step may require some research.
2. Next to the name of each potential audience, write possible reasons that audience could have for acknowledging the importance of this corporate presence. In other words, what would convince them that this particular corporate-academic relationship is something that needs to be investigated in more detail?
3. How could these audiences reasonably be influenced by an investigative report? In other words, what emotional responses or logical conclusions could they be expected to reach through reading your investigative report? What actions could these audiences reasonably be expected to perform in response to your report? Consider what motivations each audience might have for learning more about the particular corporate-academic relationship.
4. With these different audiences' interests and motivations in mind, look again at the descriptions of the corporate presence on campus that you composed in the preceding section on identifying an exigence. Decide which descriptions will enable your audiences to feel invested in exploring this particular corporate presence in greater depth and will help them understand why and how it affects them. At this point, it is probably necessary to revise your best descriptions to tailor them to the audiences.

Identifying a Fitting Response

Finding a purpose and shaping a fitting response

You have now identified a particular corporate presence on your own college or university campus and considered the audience or audiences that need to hear more about this particular relationship. But what do you want to accomplish with your writing? What particular response do you want an audience to have when reading your investigative report? Your answers to these questions should provide you with your purpose, which in turn will inform the kind of text you create.

As you know, different purposes and different audiences require different kinds of texts. For example, university investments in corporations that have questionable labor or environmental practices might prompt you to write a pamphlet you could distribute in the student union to raise awareness of those practices and their implications for university life. On the other hand, an interest in having more real-world experiences in the classroom might prompt you to draft a letter to your faculty advisor, in which you describe corporate involvement in business and marketing classes at colleges and universities. The point here is that once you identify your exigence, audience, and purpose, you need to determine what kind of text will best respond to the rhetorical situation.

Use the following questions to help you narrow your purpose and shape your response:

1. What kind of facts and details do you need to provide in order to precisely define the nature of this corporate presence on campus?
2. What perspectives on this corporate presence do you need to acknowledge?
3. Are you asking the audience to adopt a new perspective, or do you want the audience to perform a particular action in response to your writing?
4. What is the best way to reach this audience? That is, to what kind of text is this audience most likely to respond?

Your instructor (or your rhetorical situation) may prompt you to create a pamphlet or write a letter or some other kind of document. A letter to the editor of the campus newspaper would have been an appropriate genre for West Virginia University student Kelly McNeil to use in writing up her findings about Red Bull's marketing campaign on campus—if her main purpose had been to urge fellow students or the administration to take a particular action. She also could have written a case study if her rhetorical context was a business course. But she knew that her extensive research and her surprising finding—that Red Bull is somehow able to maintain a presence on campuses where Coca-Cola products are the drinks "officially" sold—lent themselves to a genre she had encountered in journalism classes, the investigative report. (Her report begins on page 199.) If, like Kelly, you are prompted to write an investigative report, use the following assignment as a guide.

Writing an Investigative Report: Working with Your Available Means

Shaping your investigative report

You are no doubt familiar with investigative reports because you have read many of them in newspapers and magazines, both for personal reasons and for research projects. Like many other genres, investigative reports take advantage of the power of the rhetorical appeals. At the same time as it establishes the writer's ethos, the introduction of an investigative report provides readers with a specific description or definition of the issue to be explored. Kate Fitzgerald, for example, opens her investigative report by explaining that credit card companies have returned to college campuses after being away from them for several years. In so doing, Fitzgerald encourages readers to see that this issue is one that needs to be explored immediately; after all, it's a problem they all share. The introduction to an investigative report also states the writer's thesis, which conveys the essence of his or her stance on the issue being investigated. Robert Cwiklik's thesis claims that UPS's proposal to the University of Washington raised many "troubling questions" because it would have gone "beyond the now-routine corporate practice of specifying a subject area for a bequest." By stressing the ethical aspect of this issue, Cwiklik begins to establish his good will, good sense, and good moral character. Of course, good sense is also exemplified in the body of a report, where the writer establishes logos.

The body of an investigative report provides many facts, details, and direct quotations in order to further clarify the issue under question—while shaping the logic of the writer's argument. A successful investigative report is one in which the writer displays good sense in the presentation and analysis of evidence. At every turn, the writer uses attributive tags to show where each piece of evidence came from and how each source of information is credible and possesses authority to speak to this issue. For example, Fitzgerald quotes Larry Chiang, chairman of United College Marketing Services; Robert Manning, a professor who has conducted extensive research on credit card marketing techniques and student credit card debt; and spokespersons from several credit card companies. With each attributive tag, Fitzgerald helps readers understand the motivations and qualifications of the various sources of facts and opinions that she incorporates into her investigative report.

The body of an investigative report also traces the effects that the issue has on various groups. Cwiklik, for example, describes the procedures that most universities put into place in order to ensure that researchers can pursue their projects independent of undue influence from outside organizations. Writers of investigative reports need to trace the various effects that a particular issue might have on different groups, particularly those groups that are not in a position of power. For just that reason, Fitzgerald provides insight from Robert Manning about the increasing dangers that students face from credit card debt. Every use of examples, statistics, and other data accentuates the good sense of the writer and also establishes the appeal of logos.

The body of an investigative report also attempts to characterize fairly the positions and motivations of the various stakeholders in the issue, another way for the writer to establish ethos and logos simultaneously. As you can see, all the rhetorical appeals must continually overlap, even if one appeal is emphasized at certain points. In a successful investigative report, the writer presents different perspectives in a fair, even-handed way, balancing the ethical appeal of good sense with the logical appeal of supporting information. The writer attends carefully to the connotations of words used to describe the different perspectives of groups involved in the issue and gives voice to members of these different groups by quoting them directly.

Finally, the conclusion of an investigative report brings together the various perspectives on the issue and sometimes makes a final appeal for readers to adopt a specific attitude or opinion, using the emotional appeal (of pathos) by connecting the writer's cause with the interests of the readers. Cwiklik wants readers to be attentive to the limits on academic freedom that could follow from undue corporate influence on research in the university. At the same time, Cwiklik wants readers to judge each case of corporate involvement in university activities on its own basis rather than to make immediate assumptions that all corporate activity on university campuses corrupts some idealized version of academic inquiry. As readers of the *Wall Street Journal,* his audience may have an interest in how corporate-academic relationships work out for all parties.

Many influential investigative reports include visuals. As you consider your available means of delivering your report, you may want to think about whether a visual or two will make it more effective and memorable. Consider scanning an advertisement you've seen in the school newspaper or in a building's common area to document a particular corporation's presence on campus. Or you might take a photograph that illustrates how the corporation's presence on campus influences the daily activities of students.

CHECKING OVER AN INVESTIGATIVE REPORT

✓ The report defines the issue in precise terms.
✓ It is clear why the issue is one that needs to be investigated by this report.
✓ The report provides convincing facts and details to help readers understand how the issue affects different groups that have some stake in the situation.
✓ Direct quotations are used to vividly convey the perspectives of various groups with a stake in the issue.
✓ There is a clear, identifiable conclusion readers should reach about the issue.

Student paper

In the following essay, student writer Kelly McNeil investigates the presence of a corporation on her campus. Like all investigative reports, this one involved careful research and reasoned analysis.

Kelly McNeil

Professor Harmon

English 210

October 23, 2007

Red Bull: Out-Marketing the Campus Competition

One Energy Drinker at a Time

"Red Bull gives you wings," according to its tagline. It's no mystery why: each 8.3-ounce can of Red Bull contains 80 milligrams of caffeine, about the same amount as a cup of coffee and more than twice as much as a 12-ounce can of Coke, giving consumers a feeling of immediate alertness and an energy high. What is more mystifying, at a Coca-Cola campus such as West Virginia University (WVU), is how Red Bull has become the preferred study buddy, chosen by eleven out of twelve students over Coke-distributed Full Throttle, RockStar, Tab Energy, and Vault, according to the results of a focus group study conducted by my advertising class. After all, Coke products are the only drinks sold in campus stores. What makes Red Bull such a presence on a campus limited to Coke is a relatively new kind of marketing strategy that is well suited to its college-aged audience, a strategy that relies on grass-roots, or person-to-person, marketing.

College students born in or around the 1980s are known as the Echo Boomers, the Millennium Generation, and, more formidably, Generation Y. Typically considered a more diverse and socially conscious group than their predecessors, Generation Y has grown up in a media-saturated and brand-conscious world, consequently keeping advertisers on their toes. This age group tends to be increasingly skeptical of traditional advertising, such as commercials and print ads, and more receptive to nontraditional marketing methods, including grassroots marketing. Unfortunately for Coca-Cola, Red Bull's grassroots marketing tactics are truly some of the most innovative and successful around.

Unlike Coca-Cola with its classic multimillion-dollar advertising campaigns, Red Bull focuses its time on saturating the everyday lives of the Generation Y consumers aged eighteen to twenty-four. In addition to the company's popular sponsorship of extreme sporting events and video games, Red Bull has a significant presence on college and university campuses nationwide. The company employs brand representatives for its Mobile Energy Team (MET). These MET Members are the face of the brand on campuses. Driving around in specially designed Red Bull "Racers" topped with an oversized can of Red Bull, the MET Members, in Red Bull logoed shirts, complete daily missions that include bringing energy where it is needed.

From an advertising perspective, the Red Bull company is ingenious. Not only is the company reaching the Generation Y population, its target audience, but it is doing so on their turf--the college campus. This allows the company to build a trusting relationship with the consumers. Red Bull hopes that this relationship will be long term and will carry over into their adult, post-graduation lives.

The Coca-Cola Company may have had the same long-term goals in mind in 2002, when it signed a marketing and sponsorship agreement with WVU. Under this ten-year contract, only Coke products are available in on-campus vending machines, eateries, convenience stores, and athletic concessions. Product logos also appear on the front of WVU vending machines, at athletic promotions, and in other university-oriented retail sites. In exchange, WVU receives "significant annual revenues for academic initiatives targeted by the University-wide budget committee," according to Chief Procurement Officer Ed Ames in a May 2002 press release ("Life Tastes Good").

Not surprisingly, the MET is not always welcomed at campus events. Recently, the MET was kicked out of a study abroad fair in the Mountainlair, the WVU student union, by the school administrators. This was not the first time something like this happened. Much to the chagrin of the student population, the MET has often been banned from on-campus activities. Many students, including two student body leaders who wish to remain anonymous, presume that the reason is simply because WVU is a Coke campus; thus, the administration will not condone solicitation for any competitors' products for fear of retaliation by The Coca-Cola Company, which extensively contributes products and funding to the school.

WVU administrators have also been working hard to relieve the campus of Red Bull Energy Drink due to the negative press surrounding the substance on an international level. In Europe, a number of young people have died after consuming the beverage after exercise or after mixing the drink with alcohol, a popular combination for the party crowd, despite company warnings. However, there has been no finding that directly correlates the product with these deaths. The Austria-made product is now banned in France and has been considered a medicine in other European countries.

While a Red Bull cooler filled with the energy drink is prominently displayed in bars up and down High Street, Morgantown's bar-lined district, the MET discourages students from making, ordering, or drinking Red Bull cocktails and advises them to drink a lot of water in addition to the beverage to prevent dehydration. Thus, Generation Y still considers Red Bull to be a consumer-friendly and socially conscious company.

On the other hand, it seems that The Coca-Cola Company has far worse social troubles to combat. Between 1990 and 2002 thousands of Coke workers lost jobs and many communities were forced to give up land and water resources to the corporate giant (Wendland). An international campaign, the Campaign to Stop Killer Coke (killercoke.org), was created to reduce the Coca-Cola market share and to punish the company for its ongoing involvement in environmental, human, and workers' rights abuses in several South American countries. According to a June 2006 article in *Political Affairs Magazine*, the major organizer of this campaign is working with students from universities around the country, including Harvard, Yale, and, yes, West Virginia University, to block Coke's access to college campuses and other venues (Wendland). The WVU administration has not commented on this campaign. Five months after the article was published, WVU is still a Coke campus, and the continued partnership prompts some students to wonder whether WVU values money more than social responsibility.

Despite some negative viewpoints on the company's campus presence, Red Bull is not deterred. On a daily basis, the friendly MET is seen zooming around campus in the Red Bull Racer, a moving advertisement in its own right, and handing out chilled cans of the syrupy energy-boosting substance to its unassuming audience. The company could not have dreamed up a more effective or affordable marketing method. While it might not taste as good as a mouth-watering Coca-Cola beverage, the student enthusiasts at WVU will continue to choose Red Bull, over its competitors, for an energy jolt. Thus, the corporate presence of Red Bull on the West Virginia University campus, welcome or not, seems to be there to stay.

Works Cited

"Generation Y Defined." *OnPoint Marketing & Promotions*. OnPoint Marketing,
n.d. Web. 30 Jan. 2007.

"Life Tastes Good: WVU and Coca-Cola Launch Partnership." WVU News &
Information Services News Release. 22 May 2002. Web. 8 Feb. 2007.

"Red Bull GmbH SWOT Analysis." *Datamonitor PLC* Oct. 2004: 1-8. *Business
Source Premier Publications*. Web. 8 Feb. 2007.

Red Bull MET: Looking for a Great Job? Red Bull USA, n.d. Web. 30 Jan. 2007.

Rodgers, Anni L. "It's a (Red) Bull Market After All." *Fast Company* Sept. 2001.
Mansueto Ventures LLC, Web. 2 Feb. 2007.

Wendland, Joel. "Coca-Cola: Classic Union Buster." *Political Affairs Magazine*.
Communist Party, USA, 26 June 2006. Web. 9 Feb. 2007.

Situations for Writers

If your rhetorical situation does not call for an investigative report like Kelly McNeil's, you can consider the following other options.

ALTERNATIVE ASSIGNMENTS

1. What forms does the corporate presence take on your college campus? How does this presence affect students in their daily lives? Write a three- to four-page narrative of a day in the life of a fellow student that describes in vivid detail how the corporate presence shapes his or her personal and academic activities.

2. As you saw throughout this chapter, the corporate presence on a college or university campus can take various forms. In a three- to four-page essay, use classification and division to help the students, teachers, or administrators conceptualize the different ways in which corporations have assumed either a visible or an invisible presence on your campus.

3. Identify a particular problem on your campus that either results from the presence of a corporation or could be resolved by inviting some corporation onto campus. Write a three- to four-page proposal that describes the problem and argues for a specific solution. As you write, make sure that you consider your audience (who should be in a position to act on your solution) and the feasibility of your proposal (what would the solution cost and how might it negatively affect the institution's research, teaching, and service missions).

7

PERSUADING IN A MULTILINGUAL CONTEXT: RESPONDING WITH POSITION ARGUMENTS

As the Modern Language Association's map indicates, over 50 million people in the United States speak a language other than English in their homes. Of the more than 200 million other inhabitants who do speak English in their homes, very few claim knowledge of the rules and conventions that govern what they might call "correct" English. This is another term for **Standardized English**, the English used in schools, businesses, government, textbooks, standardized tests, entrance examinations, and other kinds of official places and documents.

In "Word Court," a feature in the *Atlantic Monthly*, Barbara Wallraff regularly settles disputes for people who concern themselves with the rules and conventions of English grammar and usage. For instance, Frederick G. Rodgers wrote asking Wallraff about the trend of "people using the word *do* as an alternative to a more fitting verb": "When I hear statements such [as] 'I often *do* French bread twice a week' and 'The mayor is not planning to *do* an investigation yet,' I automatically wonder why *bake* in the first statement and *order* in the second were not used." After pointing her finger at Nike for its successful "Just

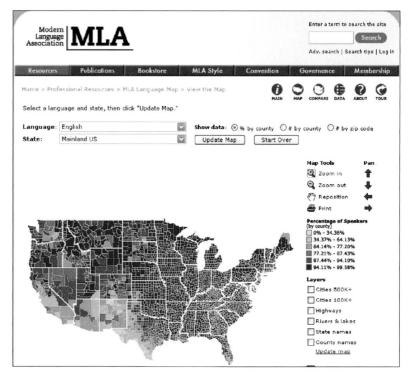

WORD COURT

BY BARBARA WALLRAFF

CAROLYN SIMON, of Tucson, Ariz., writes: "I am seeking evidence to present to the activities committee here at my retirement center. Each evening on our closed-circuit TV channel a feature film is broadcast. In the past we've had variety. Now we have a new activities director. I suggested *Babel*, and one of our members said, 'No, it has the F word!' I said that the F word is part of today's accepted vernacular and often simply means 'Omigosh!' or 'Oops!' or 'Look what I did!' Our activities director has been swayed by the puritan wing of our committee. What do you think?"

I think saying the F word, like doing the F thing, is appropriate behavior for consenting adults in private. Newspapers and many magazines are concerned mainly with the public sphere, so they (we) tend to shy away from the word unless it's part of a quotation that was uttered in public. Saying the word in public demonstrates recklessness, crassness, or both. But movies almost inevitably portray private life. Here the word, like the deed, tends to come up. Anyone who is truly shocked when he

word *dubious* where I'm certain the writer means *doubtful*. I see this error in newspapers and in books by respected writers. It upsets me every time I see it. Is *dubious* now synonymous with *doubtful*?"

Even worse: *Dubious* has been synonymous with *doubtful* for centuries. The two main definitions for *dubious* in the *Oxford English Dictionary* begin "objectively *doubtful*; fraught with doubt or uncertainty" (the supporting citations include this one, from 1548: "To abide the fortune of battayle,

f word

indifferent musical performance, *sure* of a *sure* thing. Granted, this imprecision could give rise to misunderstandings. But it hardly ever does: Does the chair feel *comfortable* or does it make us feel that way? You say that when you read *dubious*, sometimes you're "certain the writer means *doubtful*." That's about as much clarity as you can reasonably expect.

HAROLD SIMON, of Camarillo, Calif., writes: "An article in *Time* magazine, a very positive one about a popular TV personality, called her 'antisnob and utterly *nonaspirational*.' My medical background complained. *Aspiration*, medically, is the oral ingestion of a substance into the trachea instead of the esophagus, and it may have serious consequences. Am I being picky or reasonable?"

Aspiration in medical lingo is one thing; in common parlance it's something else. Though the word comes from the Latin for *breathe*, its meaning is often more nearly "desire." As for *aspirational*, time was it tended to have to do with lofty spiritual desires. In recent

do it" campaign, Wallraff maintains that beyond the world of advertising, this overuse of *do* "sabotages communication," allowing us to "express ourselves in ways that can mean anything listeners want." For many American readers, "Word Court" would feed anxieties about their use of spoken and written English, about their inability to use English "right"—neither in English class nor outside of it. Even those of us who speak English fluently freeze up the minute we have to speak or write something that other people will be judging for correctness. Paradoxically, these are the kinds of experiences that lead so many Americans to believe in the importance of Standardized English for maintaining civility and precise communication in U.S. public life.

A **position argument**—the delivery of a point of view and the use of logical, emotional, and ethical appeals to help an audience understand that point of view—is one means of asserting how and why Americans ought to use English. Given the increasing linguistic and cultural diversity of the United States, however, questions about "correctness" are increasingly complicated to address. Whether the overuse of *do* signals the decline of the English language or any similar issue is overshadowed by the larger concern of whether English is the national (i.e., official) language of the United States, especially given the public presence of Spanish, Mandarin Chinese, and Tagalog. Position arguments can serve as individuals' and groups' means for participating in debates concerning speaking and writing in this increasingly multilingual context.

Real Situations

The last page of the *Atlantic Monthly* provides a space for people to police the boundaries of "correct" English, but one hundred years ago, the magazine featured a series of articles critiquing an educational policy aimed at eradicating the languages and cultural ways of Native American tribes. In three successive issues, autobiographical essays by Zitkala-Ša argued for the end of that educational policy. Zitkala-Ša, born in 1876 on the Yankton Reservation in South Dakota and later a student and teacher at the off-reservation Indian School in Carlisle, Pennsylvania, published "Impressions of an Indian Childhood," "The School Days of an Indian Girl," and "An Indian Teacher among Indians" in 1900. She criticized the school's policy of forbidding students to use their tribal languages to communicate with teachers or to converse with fellow students. While directors at the school claimed to be freeing the students from their "savage ways" by teaching them English, Zitkala-Ša declared in "Impressions of an Indian Childhood" that, as she lost her native language, "I no longer felt free to be myself, or to voice my own feelings." She argued, in effect, that rather than dictating students' language choices and deciding what constitutes "correct" and "proper" language use, U.S. schools should give students opportunities to learn English while also maintaining the language of their cultural heritage.

Zitkala-Ša's arguments speak to the difficulties faced by thousands of Native American students at off-reservation boarding schools at the turn of the twentieth century. But those difficulties remain for many students in the twenty-first

Cover of the 1895 catalogue for the federal Indian School in Carlisle, Pennsylvania, one of many off-reservation boarding schools.

century. As you will read later in this chapter, students from language minority backgrounds continue to experience cultural tensions in their formal schooling, often being forced to leave behind the language of their friends, families, and relatives. Other groups of non-English speakers in the United States, however, live in tightly knit communities where they can thrive without using English at all, conducting their domestic life and daily business in the language with which they feel most comfortable. In still other settings, speakers of several languages encounter situations that require them to mix their languages. Such mixing sometimes helps a person express exactly something a single language could not convey; it can also, however, make a person feel uncertain about issues of identity. Puerto Rican poet Sandra Mariá Esteves uses Spanglish in her poem "Not Neither," in which she identifies herself as both "Puertorriqueña" and "Americana" but shows that she does not feel a full member of either community: "Pero ni portorra, pero sí portorra too / Pero ni que what am I?" The billboard shown here attests to one business's "strategic" mixing of Spanish and English to tap into patrons' linguistic preferences—and to make profits.

During the past forty years, arguments echoing those by Zitkala-Ša and others have helped to make the use of languages other than English more visible within the American political, educational, and journalistic arenas. According to the Voting Rights Act of 1965, when 5 percent of the voting-age citizens in any state or political subdivision are members of a single language minority group, local election boards must print ballots and other relevant materials in that language. The Federal Bilingual Education Act of 1968 allowed languages other than English to be used in schools across the nation. But that practice has since been at the center of public debate on educational policies, most notably

In parts of the United States where Spanish speakers are numerous, advertisers often use that language to appeal to consumers.

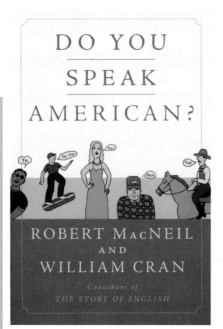

Robert MacNeil and William Cran ask, *Do You Speak American?*

concerning California's Proposition 227, whose adoption meant that all public school instruction in California had to be conducted in English only, limiting bilingual instruction to one year for students who need it. In 2002, there were 26 Spanish-language television networks in the United States, with Univision reaching 98 percent of Latino households with televisions and Telemundo reaching 91 percent. In 2003, approximately 190,000 federal court proceedings required the work of qualified translators; 96 percent of these cases involved Spanish, while the other 4 percent involved 102 other languages. The prevalence of Spanish and other languages in the U.S. political, educational, and legal arenas gives added layers of meaning to the question Robert MacNeil and William Cran pose in their title of their book, *Do You Speak American?*

As the linguistic and ethnic demographics of the U.S. population continue to change, local, state, and federal agencies have explored ways of making public services and public communications more accessible to language minority groups. For example, the city government of Minneapolis, Minnesota, posted a sign printed in four languages: English, Hmong, Spanish, and Somali. Medical service providers similarly have sought to make printed and online materials available in multiple languages in order to communicate essential health information to all the language groups in a community. The National Institutes of Health, for example, published a booklet on cholesterol levels in a side-by-side, English-Spanish format.

Public notices and government publications are increasingly multilingual or bilingual.

Some people in the United States, however, consider the visible presence of non-English languages as a threat to the English language's prominence in the nation's public affairs. These people want to halt the use of languages other than English in the public sphere. Joey Vento, a third-generation Italian American and owner of Geno's Steaks in Philadelphia, Pennsylvania, went so far as to post a sign at the counter where restaurant patrons place their orders instructing them to do so in English. This sign sparked an intense month-long debate in the local newspapers and on radio and television talk shows. The Philadelphia Commission on Human Relations even filed a discrimination complaint over the sign, arguing that it violated the city's Fair Practices Ordinance, which prohibits discrimination in public accommodation. Vento responded in several interviews, including one conducted by Neil Cavuto of Fox News, that he simply wants all Americans to learn English the way his ancestors did when they arrived in the United States.

Joey Vento with his controversial "Speak English" sign.

Members of the Dominican vocal group Voz a Voz get ready to sing in an ensemble performance of "Nuestro Himno" at Ellis Island in New York.

A similar debate centers on a Spanish-language version of the U.S. national anthem. British music producer Adam Kidron created the song in 2006 as a response to the immigration debate in the United States. The recording, entitled "Nuestro Himno" ("Our Anthem"), features Puerto Rican singers Carlos Ponce and Olga Tanon and hip-hop artists such as Wyclef Jean and Pitbull singing Spanish lyrics based on "The Star-Spangled Banner." At certain points, however, the song switches to English and directs sharp criticism at U.S. immigration policy, for example:

> These kids have no parents
> 'cause all of these mean laws . . .
> let's not start a war with all these
>   hard workers
> they can't help where they were born.

Pitbull suggested that "the American dream is in that record: struggle, freedom, opportunity, everything they are trying to shut down on us."

Despite such appeals to Americans' democratic values, countless numbers of critics have expressed outrage that the U.S. national anthem might be sung in anything but English. U.S. Senator Lamar Alexander, a Republican from Tennessee, went so far as to propose a resolution:

> . . . giving senators an opportunity to remind the country why we sing our National Anthem in English . . . . We Americans are a unique nation of immigrants united by a common language and a belief in principles expressed in our Declaration of Independence and our Constitution, not by our race, ancestry or country of origin. We are proud of the countries we have come from, but we are prouder to be Americans.

In expressing his pride in the common culture and political ideals of the United States, Alexander argues for a specific view of how citizens can and should reaffirm the nation's democratic principles.

Ironically, as calls for using only English to reaffirm the nation's political and cultural values have multiplied, the U.S. Defense Department has argued that language education plays a key role in strengthening U.S. security capabilities. The Defense Department came to see language education as a national security concern shortly after September 11, 2001, when it realized that it did not have enough linguists and translators to read the covert documents (written in Arabic, Chinese, Korean, Russian, and other less frequently taught languages) warning of the terrorists' attack. Concluding that language education is important to the military, Defense Department officials now believe that schools—and, in particular, language arts classrooms—are valuable places for securing the nation against terrorist threats.

And while the U.S. government is striving to build the nation's resources in certain foreign languages, scholars and community activists have launched campaigns to draw attention to and revitalize the nation's heritage languages (Native American, Alaska Native, and Native Hawaiian languages), those that have died out or are threatened with extinction as a result of monolingual educational policies and the use of English in the mass media. In effect, these language revitalization projects are attempting to reverse the effects of the educational legacy Zitkala-Ša warned *Atlantic Monthly* readers about in 1900. The projects bring communities together physically or virtually in order to create a meaningful context for learning and using their heritage languages. Scholars and community leaders in Hawaii, for instance, have successfully adapted Apple software to meet the needs of their language revitalization project by translating computer commands into the Leokï language. This adaptation of literacy tools helps students to see Leokï as a living language they can use to communicate with others across the Hawaiian island chain.

While revitalization advocates try to breathe life into languages that have declined because of educational, political, and technological trends that have established English's prominence in the world, others have turned their attention to what English might be like in the United States in the years to come, given immigration, the growth of the Spanish-speaking population, and technological advances that abridge the language. One thing is certain: within the next fifty years in the United States, native speakers of English will be outnumbered by nonnative speakers of English, but all Americans will use English in a multilingual context. Consequently, while some readers of the *Atlantic Monthly* hold fast to the seemingly fixed rules of Standardized English and bring cases before the "Word Court," the notion of plural "Englishes" may prove to be a more useful way of characterizing the language usage of the future.

An Apple pull-down menu translated into Leokï increases the perception of that language as a living one.

Cover of *Atlantic Monthly*, questioning the status of English as the global language.

Describing Language Use in the United States

1. Write for five to ten minutes about your experiences using, listening to, or reading languages other than English in the United States. Is your reaction to the use of these languages in public spaces positive, negative, or neutral?

2. Write for five minutes about the experiences your parents (or children) have had with languages other than English in the United States. Are their experiences like yours or different? What is their level of frustration or acceptance?

3. Finally, take five minutes to consider your viewpoint on language diversity in the United States by composing a claim (or assertion). What reason can you provide for your claim? What evidence supports that reason?

4. Does your viewpoint match that of your family members, or is it different from theirs? How do you account for that similarity or difference?

Community Connections

1. Look again at the images in the first section of the chapter. What specific argument does each visual make about the relationship between language and diversity in the United States? What details in the image lead you to those conclusions?

2. Select the particular image that resonates most strongly for you as you think about the language differences in the United States. Write for five minutes about what seems most familiar—or disorienting—in this image, what interests you the most about it.

3. What images in this section seem to support the claim about language diversity in the United States that you composed in question 3 of Describing Language Use? In what specific ways do they provide this support?

4. What images in this section seem to challenge your claim about language diversity in the United States? In what specific ways do they present an opposing perspective?

| Real Responses to Real Situations |

Should we make English the official language of the United States?

There would be no United States were it not for immigration. In fact, the history of this country is directly linked to a sequence of immigrants. The dominant image for assimilating the various national and ethnic groups has long been the melting pot. Although many people see the melting pot as a symbol of Americans' openness to immigrants, each new wave of immigrants—Irish, Italians, Eastern Europeans, Asians, or Mexicans—became an object of scorn for those who were already citizens. Throughout U.S. history, immigrants have come to this country to escape danger, poverty, or persecution and to improve their lives. Those who had the easiest time assimilating were of Northern European backgrounds, which made it easier to blend into the mainstream.

When huge numbers of Latin Americans and Asians arrived in the United States between 1970 and 1990, many joined ever-growing linguistic communities of Chinese, Korean, Japanese, and Spanish speakers who are able to live out their entire lives without learning, let alone using, English. Perceiving these non–English-speaking communities as a threat to English as the dominant U.S. language, some citizens began rallying to make English the official language of the United States. Supporters of this position argue that Americans—regardless of native language—should all speak the same language in order to work toward common national goals and participate fully in public life.

S. I. Hayakawa (1906–1992) served California as a Republican Senator from 1977 to 1983, during which time he introduced the first English language amendment to Congress in 1981. After serving his state and nation, Hayakawa, the son of immigrants and speaker of English as a second language, helped to found the organization U.S. English, whose dual missions entailed generating public support for an English language amendment to the Constitution and lobbying Congressional representatives to enact such legislation. Subcommittees of the Senate Judiciary Committee, in 1984, and the House Judiciary Committee, in 1988, conducted public hearings on the amendment. Although the U.S Congress has taken no action to add an English language amendment to the Constitution, English language amendments have been added to twenty-two state constitutions since 1981, and four states had already enacted such legislation by that time. Hayakawa outlined the vision guiding English-only supporters in his 1985 policy paper "One Nation . . . Indivisible? The English Language Amendment." According to Hayakawa, an English language amendment to the U.S. Constitution would reinforce the nation's political and cultural values.

S. I. HAYAKAWA
Excerpt from One Nation . . . Indivisible? The English Language Amendment

> "It is with a common language that we have dissolved distrust and fear."

What is it that has made a society out of the hodge-podge of nationalities, races, and colors represented in the immigrant hordes that people our nation? It is language, of course, that has made communication among all these elements possible. It is with a common language that we have dissolved distrust and fear. It is with language that we have drawn up the understandings and agreements and social contracts that make a society possible. . . .

One need not speak faultless American English to become an American. Indeed, one may continue to speak English with an appalling foreign accent. This is

continued

true of some of my friends, but they are seen as fully American because of the warmth and enthusiasm with which they enter into the life of the communities in which they live. . . .

In the past several years, strong resistance to the "melting pot" idea has arisen, especially for those who claim to speak for the Hispanic peoples. Instead of a melting pot, they say, the national ideal should be a "salad bowl," in which different elements are thrown together but not "melted," so that the original ingredients retain their distinctive character. . . .

I welcome the Hispanic—and as a Californian, I especially welcome the Mexican—influence on our culture. My wife was wise enough to insist that both our son and daughter learn Spanish as children and to keep reading Spanish as they were growing up. Consequently, my son, a newspaperman, was able to work for six months as an exchange writer for a newspaper in Costa Rica, while a Costa Rican reporter took my son's place in Oregon. My daughter, a graduate of the University of California at Santa Cruz, speaks Spanish, French, and after a year in Monterey Language School, Japanese.

The ethnic chauvinism of the present Hispanic leadership is an unhealthy trend in present-day America. It threatens a division perhaps more ominous in the long run than the division between blacks and whites. Blacks and whites have problems enough with each other, to be sure, but they quarrel with each other in one language. Even Malcolm X, in his fiery denunciation of the racial situation in America, wrote excellent and eloquent English. But the present politically ambitious "Hispanic Caucus" looks forward to a destiny for Spanish-speaking Americans separate from that of Anglo-, Italian-, Polish-, Greek-, Lebanese-, Chinese-, and Afro-Americans, and all the rest of us who rejoice in our ethnic diversity, which gives us our richness as a culture, and the English language, which keeps us in communication with each other to create a unique and vibrant culture.

The advocates of Spanish language and Hispanic culture are not at all unhappy about the fact that "bilingual education," originally instituted as the best way to teach English, often results in no English be-

ing taught at all. Nor does Hispanic leadership seem to be alarmed that large populations of Mexican Americans, Cubans, and Puerto Ricans do not speak English and have no intention of learning. Hispanic spokesmen rejoice when still another concession is made to the Spanish-speaking public, such as the Spanish-language Yellow Pages telephone directory now available in Los Angeles.

"Let's face it. We're not going to be a totally English-speaking country any more," says Aurora Helton of the governor of Oklahoma's Hispanic Advisory Committee. "Spanish should be included in commercials shown throughout America. Every American child ought to be taught both English and Spanish," says Mario Obledo, president of the League of United Latin American Citizens, which was founded more than a half-century ago to help Hispanics learn English and enter the American mainstream. "Citizenship is what makes us all American. Nowhere does the Constitution say that English is our language," says Maurice Ferré, mayor of Miami, Florida.

"Nowhere does the Constitution say that English is our language." It was to correct this omission that I introduced in April 1981 a constitutional amendment which read as follows: "The English language shall be the official language of the United States." Although there were ten cosponsors to this resolution, and some speeches were given on the Senate floor, it died without being acted upon in the 97th Congress.

But the movement to make English the official language of the nation is clearly gaining momentum. It is likely to suffer an occasional setback in state legislatures because of the doctrinaire liberals' assumption that every demand made by an ethnic minority must be yielded to. But whenever the question of English as the official language has been submitted to a popular referendum or ballot initiative, it has won by a majority of 70 percent or better.

It is not without significance that pressure against English language legislation does not come from any immigrant group other than the Hispanic: Not from the Chinese or Koreans or Filipinos or Vietnamese; nor from immigrant Iranians, Turks, Greeks, East Indians, Ghanians, Ethiopians, Italians, or Swedes. The only people who have any quarrel with the English language are the Hispanics—at least the Hispanic politicians and "bilingual" teachers and lobbying organizations. One wonders about the Hispanic rank and file. Are they all in agreement with their leadership? And what does it profit the Hispanic leadership if it gains power and fame, while 50 percent of the boys and girls of their communities, speaking little or no English, cannot make it through high school?

While the U.S. Congress has yet to ratify an English language amendment, such legislation is periodically introduced in both houses. On May 18, 2006, for example, Oklahoma Republican Senator James Inhofe introduced an amendment to an immigration policy reform bill to declare English the "national language" in order "to promote the patriotic integration of prospective U.S. citizens" (U.S. Senate, Amendment 4064). The specific language of the amendment reads as follows: "Unless specifically stated in applicable law, no person has a right, entitlement, or claim to have the Government of the United States or any of its officials or representatives act, communicate, perform or provide services, or provide materials in any language other than English." Senator Inhofe explained, "This is not just about preserving our culture and heritage, but also about bettering the odds for our nation's newest potential citizens."

From the first time an English language amendment was introduced in the U.S. Congress in 1981, the idea of this form of legislation has met significant opposition from people who argue that negative legal, social, and cultural consequences will follow such a constitutional amendment. In 1988, a diverse collection of groups (American Civil Liberties Union, American Jewish Congress, Chinese for Affirmative Action, Haitian Refugee Center, Mexican American Legal Defense and Educational Fund, Organization of Chinese Americans, and Teachers of English to Speakers of Other Languages) rallied to counter the English-only movement by forming the English Plus Information Clearinghouse (EPIC). EPIC called on the federal government to expand access to comprehensive English-language instruction and social services in order "to ensure all persons the ability to exercise the rights and responsibilities of full participation in society," a policy EPIC referred to as "English Plus." In addition, EPIC encouraged the federal government to foster multilingualism for all people in order to advance the national interest in economic and political affairs as well as to strengthen the nation's commitment to democratic and cultural pluralism.

The various ethnic groups represented in EPIC reflect a broad-based concern over official English legislation. Some critics (including Juan F. Perea, who is featured later in this chapter) have labeled the ideas of Hayakawa, U.S. English, and the entire English-only movement as anti-immigrant, even nativist; others, such as Victor Villanueva, have questioned the assumptions about language, culture, and politics on which the English-only movement builds its case. Brooklyn-born of Puerto Rican heritage (and multilingual but English-dominant), Villanueva points out the problems in trying "to cur[e] social fears with laws." In the following passage, he questions the popular myth that immigrants to the United States, particularly Latinos, increasingly refuse to learn English. He asks readers to attend more closely to the real motivations of non-English speakers and to understand how social, economic, and political pressures in many ways lead people to place different values on learning new languages.

VICTOR VILLANUEVA
On English Only

Situations for Writers

There are many ghettos in the United States full of Spanish-speaking people (never mind various Asian groups and Russians and others). And the numbers are greater than in any time past. But most Latinos and Latinas are not new immigrants; most were never immigrants at all, but natives to this country, long ago learning to move between Spanish and English. Latinos and Latinas are only partly the descendants of Spain; we are also the indigenous peoples of these lands before the Spaniards and (at least for the Caribbean Latino/Latina) of the West Africans who came to this continent as slaves. Only Native Americans have been on this continent longer than the descendants of Spain.

The New World belonged to Spain, claimed by Columbus (an Italian—which should remind us that the continent will also have to be renamed, since the A in USA represents an Italian derivative). Columbus was "Colón" to the Spaniards. Colón is still a common surname among Caribbean Latinos and Latinas. In 1513 Ponce de León discovered Florida. In 1565 the Spaniards established their first colony in St. Augustine. By 1540 Francisco Vásquez de Coronado had conquered the Aztec empire and explored what are now Arizona, Texas, Colorado, and New Mexico. In 1598 Juan de Oñate founded [San] Gabriel de los Españoles, [now Chamita, New Mexico]. In the Caribbean, the Arawak and Boricua languages of the Taino Indians of Puerto Rico and the native Indian tongues of Cubans were erased by the Spaniards. We are many groups united in having been subjected to Spanish Only mandates for four hundred years.

The numbers of Spanish-speaking ghettos may be great, but the numbers resistant to English learning are negligible. Ninety-eight percent of Latinos/

> "... way stations on the path to full participation in U.S. society."

Latinas responding to a national survey believed it essential for their children to learn to read and write "perfect" English. . . .

The fear of Hispanics/Latinos outnumbering Euro-Americans that John Tanton, former president of U.S. English, betrayed in his infamous 1986 memo is too silly, so silly that I am amazed of the need for this book [*Language Ideologies: Critical Perspectives on the Official English Movement*] at all. How does the periphery—the Third World—hope to overturn the core? If numbers alone dictated which language holds superior, English would not have been the language of the United States. English would not be the language of the globe. And yet English is the lingua franca, though the populations of the United States, Canada, England, and Australia combined do not constitute a majority of the world population. I have seen [Yassir] Arafat, the chairman of the PLO, trouble to speak to U.S. news reporters in English; I have heard the ambassador of Iraq speaking English, as well as the prime minister of Israel, who was likely elected in part for being bilingual in Hebrew and English. Years ago the PBS television series *The Story of English* noted that an Air Italia commercial jet flying over Italian air space, making a routine local run, piloted by Italians speaking to an exclusively Italian ground crew, must nevertheless speak in English. If a student in Beijing or Liberia or Mexico City recognizes the need for English, surely the American and would-be American recognizes the need. There might well be U.S. ghettos in which little English is spoken. That has been the case for most of this century, and such ghettos have proven to be way stations on the path to full participation in U.S. society.

Linguist Geoffrey Nunberg, researcher at Stanford University's Center for the Study of Language and Information, has also addressed the common perception that an increasing number of nonnative English speakers, particularly Spanish speakers, are clinging to their native languages rather than learning English. Not worried about the number of non-English speakers in the United States, Nunberg has attempted to understand the motivations of official English proponents, who continue to push for an English language amendment to the U.S. Constitution. His findings indicate that Hayakawa, U.S. English, and other English-only advocates concern themselves far more with the symbolic importance of the English language—that is, what an individual's competency in English seems to signal about his or her commitment to American ideals and values—than with the practical matters affecting bilingual education and social services.

Real Responses

GEOFFREY NUNBERG

Excerpt from The Official English Movement: Reimagining America

[L]inguistic diversity is more conspicuous than it was a century ago. To be aware of the large numbers of non-English speakers in 1900, it was necessary to live in or near one of their communities, whereas today it is only necessary to flip through a cable television dial, drive past a Spanish-language billboard, or (in many states) apply for a driver's license. As a best guess, there are fewer speakers of foreign languages in America now than there were then, in both absolute and relative numbers. But what matter symbolically [are] the widespread impressions of linguistic diversity, particularly among people who have no actual contact with speakers of languages other than English. . . .

[T]he debate is no longer concerned with the content or effect of particular programs, but the symbolic importance that people have come to attach to these matters. Official English advocates admit as much when they emphasize that their real goal is to "send a message" about the role of English in American life. From this point of view, it is immaterial whether the provision of interpreters for workers' compensation hearings or [the provision] of foreign-language nutrition information actually constitute a "disincentive" to learning English, or whether their discontinuation would work a hardship on recent immigrants. Pro-

> "What actually is the message [of the Official English Movement]?"

grams like these merely happen to be high-visibility examples of government's apparent willingness to allow the public use of languages other than English for any purpose whatsoever. In fact, one suspects that most Official English advocates are not especially concerned about specific programs per se, since they will be able to achieve their symbolic goals even if bilingual services are protected by judicial intervention or legislative inaction (as has generally been the case where Official English measures have passed). The real objective of the campaign is the "message" that it intends to send.

What actually is the message? . . . Proponents of Official English claim that they seek merely to recognize a state of affairs that has existed since the founding of the nation. After two hundred years of common-law cohabitation with English, we have simply decided to make an honest woman of her, for the sake of the children. To make the English language "official," however, is not merely to acknowledge it as the language commonly used in commerce, mass communications, and public affairs. Rather, it is to invest English with a symbolic role in national life and to endorse a cultural conception of American identity as the basis for political unity.

Nunberg sees the official English movement granting a symbolic power to language that previous generations of Americans did not. He explains that the nation's founders believed "the free institutions of the new nation would naturally lead to the formation of a new and independent culture," symbolized by an American variety of English increasingly distinct from the British variety, but today's advocates for official English legislation consider a common language to be a guarantee of the cultural sameness they believe is necessary for political unity.

Every ten years, the U.S. Census Bureau collects, distributes, and analyzes information concerning the demographics of the population, including data on race, age, sex, ancestry, income, and household types. Beginning in 1890, one hundred years after the first census, the Census Bureau has also inquired about language use. The following excerpt discusses some of the most recent findings on the daily language practices of the U.S. public.

HYON B. SHIN WITH ROSALIND BRUNO
Excerpt from Language Use and English-Speaking Ability: Census 2000 Brief

The ability to communicate with government and private service providers, schools, businesses, emergency personnel, and many other people in the United States depends on the ability to speak English. In Census 2000, as in the two previous censuses, the U.S. Census Bureau asked people aged 5 and over if they spoke a language other than English at home. Among the 262.4 million people aged 5 and over, 47.0 million (18 percent) spoke a language other than English at home. . . .

These figures were up from 14 percent (31.8 million) in 1990 and 11 percent (23.1 million) in 1980. The number of people who spoke a language other than English at home grew by 38 percent in the 1980s and by 47 percent in the 1990s. While the population aged 5 and over grew by one-fourth from 1980 to 2000, the number who spoke a language other than English at home more than doubled.

In 2000, more people who spoke a language other than English at home reported they spoke English "Very well" (55 percent, or 25.6 million people). When they are combined with those who spoke only English at home, 92 percent of the population aged 5 and over had no difficulty speaking English. The proportion of the population aged 5 and over who spoke English less than "Very well" grew from 4.8 percent in 1980, to 6.1 percent in 1990, and to 8.1 percent in 2000.

> "People who do not have a strong command of English . . . are defined here as 'linguistically isolated.'"

. . . Spanish was the largest of the four major language groups (Spanish, Other Indo-European language, Asian and Pacific Island languages, and All other languages), and just over half of the 28.1 million Spanish speakers spoke English "Very well."

Other Indo-European language speakers composed the second largest group, with 10.0 million speakers, almost two-thirds of whom spoke English "Very well." Slightly less than half of the 7.0 million Asian and Pacific Island language speakers spoke English "Very well" (3.4 million). Of the 1.9 million people who composed the All other languages category, 1.3 million spoke English "Very well."

After English and Spanish, Chinese was the most commonly spoken at home (2.0 million speakers), followed by French (1.6 million speakers) and German (1.4 million speakers . . .). Reflecting historical patterns of immigration, the numbers of Italian, Polish, and German speakers fell between 1990 and 2000, while the number of speakers of many other languages increased.

Spanish speakers grew by about 60 percent and Spanish continued to be the non-English language most frequently spoken at home in the United States. The Chinese language, however, jumped from the fifth to the second most widely spoken non-English language, as the number of Chinese speakers rose from

1.2 million to 2.0 million people. . . . The number of Vietnamese speakers doubled over the decade, from about 507,000 speakers to just over 1 million speakers.

Of the 20 non-English languages most frequently spoken at home . . . , the largest proportional increase was for Russian speakers, who nearly tripled from 242,000 to 706,000. The second largest increase was for French Creole speakers (the language group that includes Haitian Creoles), whose numbers more than doubled from 188,000 to 453,000. . . .

In the United States, the ability to speak English plays a large role in how well people can perform daily activities. How well a person speaks English may indi-cate how well he or she communicates with public of-ficials, medical personnel, and other service providers. It could also affect other activities outside the home, such as grocery shopping or banking. People who do not have a strong command of English and who do not have someone in their household to help them on a regular basis are at even more of a disadvantage. They are defined here as "linguistically isolated."

In 2000, 4.4 million households encompassing 11.9 million people were linguistically isolated. These num-bers were significantly higher than in 1990, when 2.9 million households and 7.7 million people lived in those households.

ANALYZING THE RHETORICAL SITUATION

The texts you have just read demonstrate that the issue of making English the official U.S. language is a complex one, not easily settled on the basis of a few examples or statistics. The following questions ask you to consider the writings of S. I. Hayakawa and Victor Villanueva in terms of the elements of their respective rhetorical situations. Be sure to reread each excerpt carefully before answering.

1. Who might be the intended audience of each of the two excerpts? How do the audiences differ from one excerpt to the next? What textual evidence can you provide for your answers?

2. Is the purpose of each excerpt evident? If so, what is it? What are the differences between the excerpts in terms of purpose? How does each purpose relate to the intended audience?

3. To what exigence might each writer be responding? How does the piece of writing work to resolve that exigence? Who holds the power to resolve or affect the resolution of that exigence?

4. How does each writer deploy the rhetorical appeals of ethos, pathos, and logos to support an opinion of the official English movement? Use passages from each excerpt to support your answer.

Living on the margins of English-speaking America

The official English movement has been opposed by a number of professional and public advocacy groups. In addition to the work done by EPIC, bilingual educators have argued about the cultural perspective and the sense of cultural identity that nonnative English speakers gained from having their native lan-guages valued in school. And legal scholars have criticized the legal viability of English-only laws, arguing that they constitute national-origin discrimination, which was made illegal by the Civil Rights Act of 1964.

Legal scholar Juan F. Perea may be best known for his analyses of the social consequences of English language amendments, but he has long worked to confront anti-immigration laws and attitudes as well as national-origin discrimination in the United States. In the following excerpt, Perea writes of the social and legal situations that prevent ethnic and linguistic minorities from participating fully in American society. For Perea, English language amendments give nonnative English speakers no incentive to learn English or to enter the melting pot. Perea's argument encourages his readers to think more carefully about how the language of Spanish-speaking U.S. citizens affects their public identity.

JUAN F. PEREA
Excerpt from Los Olvidados: On the Making of Invisible People

In his recent book, *Latinos*, Earl Shorris poignantly describes Bienvenida Pation, a Jewish Latino immigrant, who clings to her language and culture "as if they were life itself." When Bienvenida dies, it is "not of illness, but of English." Bienvenida dies of English when she is confined to a nursing home where no one speaks Spanish, an environment in which she cannot communicate and in which no one cares about her language and culture.

> "... denying one's own identity as a Latino is ... to begin to die of English."

"Death by English" is a death of the spirit, the slow death that occurs when one's own identity is replaced, reconfigured, overwhelmed, or rejected by a more powerful, dominant identity. For Latinos, illness by English of varying degree, even death by English, is a common affliction, without known cure. It may be identified, however, by some of its symptoms.

The mere sound of Spanish offends and frightens many English-only speakers, who sense in the language a loss of control over what they regard as "their" country. Spanish also frightens many Latinos, for it proclaims their identity as Latinos, for all to hear. The Latino's fear is rational. Spanish may subject Latinos to the harsh price of difference in the United States: the loss of a job, instant scapegoating, and identification as an outsider. Giving in to this fear and denying one's own identity as a Latino is, perhaps, to begin to die of English.

Latino invisibility is the principal cause of illness by English. When I write of Latino invisibility, I mean a relative lack of positive public identity and legitimacy. Invisibility in this sense is created in several ways. Sometimes we are rendered invisible through the absence of public recognition and portrayal. Sometimes we are silenced through prohibitions on the use of Spanish. Sometimes we are rendered politically invisible, or nearly so, through the attribution of foreignness, what I shall call "symbolic deportation." I do not maintain that Latinos are the only people rendered invisible in America. In many respects the processes of invisibility have more general application. In this chapter, however, I shall discuss only the invisibility I know best: How American culture, history, and laws make "invisible people" out of American Latinos who arrived before the English. . . .

According to its English conquerors, America was always meant to belong to white Englishmen. In 1788, John Jay, writing in the *Federalist* Number 2, declared, "Providence has been pleased to give this one connected country to one united people—a people descended from the same ancestors, speaking the same language, professing the same religion, attached to the same principles of government, very similar in their manner and customs." Although Jay's statement was wrong—early American society was remarkably diverse—his wish that America be a homogeneous, white, English-speaking Anglo society was widely shared by the Framers of the Constitution and other prominent leaders. . . .

The Framers' white America also had to be a predominantly English-speaking America in the words of John Jay and later echoes by Thomas Jefferson. Benjamin Franklin's dislike of the German language was palpable. I will use two examples to illustrate the perceived need for a white and English-speaking America.

In 1807, Jefferson proposed the resettlement, at government expense, of thirty thousand presumably English-speaking Americans in Louisiana in order to "make the majority American, [and] make it an American instead of French State." The first governor of Louisiana, William Claiborne, unsuccessfully attempted to require that all the laws of Louisiana be published in English.

The saga of New Mexico's admission to statehood also illustrates the perceived need for a white and English-speaking America. Despite repeated attempts beginning in 1850, New Mexico did not become a state until 1912, when a majority of its population was English-speaking for the first time. Statehood was withheld from New Mexico for over sixty years because of Congress's unwillingness to grant statehood to a predominantly Spanish-speaking territory populated by Mexican people.

A tremendous disparity, of course, separated the country the Framers desired and the one they came to possess. The country was composed of many groups, of different hues and speaking different languages. Several examples of governmental recognition of American multilingualism illustrate my point. The Continental Congress, hoping to communicate with and win the allegiance of American peoples whose language was different from English, published many significant documents in German and French. After the Revolutionary War, the Articles of Confederation were published in official English, German, and French editions.

Particularly during much of the nineteenth century, several states had rich legal histories of official bilingualism, by which I mean statutory or constitutional recognitions of languages other than English: Pennsylvania was officially bilingual in German and English; California and New Mexico were officially bilingual in Spanish and English; and Louisiana was officially bilingual in French and English. The implementation of official bilingualism in these several states shared common features. All of the laws of those states were required to be published in more than one language. Although this state-sponsored bilingualism mostly died out during the nineteenth century, New Mexico's official bilingualism was remarkably long-lived. New Mexico was officially bilingual between 1846 and early 1953, over one hundred years.

Most people are not aware of the existence and the extent of American multilingualism and its official, state-sponsored character. I am not aware of any United States history texts that include this material. Nor will you find it in any legal history text. . . .

continued

Latinos are made invisible and foreign . . . despite our longtime presence, substance, and citizenship. Latinos must be recognized as full and equal members of our community. This equality I describe is an equality of respect and of dignity for the full identity and personhood of Latino people. It is an equality and respect for the similarities we share with our fellow Americans. It is also an equality and respect for the differences we contribute to American identity. In 1883, Walt Whitman complained that the states "showed too much of the British and German influence." . . . "To that composite American identity of the future," Whitman wrote, "Spanish character will supply some of the most needed parts." Our Mexican and Latino character continues to supply some of our most needed parts.

In *Hunger of Memory,* Richard Rodriguez reflects on his educational experiences, particularly how his Spanish-language identity of home conflicted with the English-speaking identity he felt that he needed to succeed in public school. For him, learning the English of the classroom offered him the public identity necessary for participating in American civic life. In the following excerpt from his book, Rodriguez describes how he came to believe that English should be his "public language" and Spanish his home language. He argues from his own experience that immigrants to the United States remain invisible until they learn the public language of English.

RICHARD RODRIGUEZ
Excerpt from Hunger of Memory

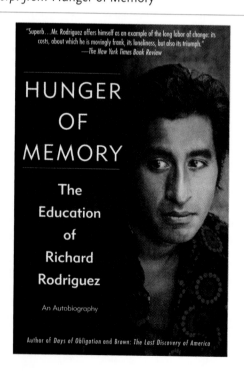

"Superb. . .Mr. Rodriguez offers himself as an example of the long labor of change: its costs, about which he is movingly frank, its loneliness, but also its triumph."
—*The New York Times Book Review*

HUNGER
OF
MEMORY

The
Education
of
Richard
Rodriguez

An Autobiography

Author of *Days of Obligation and Brown: The Last Discovery of America*

Supporters of bilingual education today imply that students like me miss a great deal by not being taught in their family's language. What they seem not to recognize is that, as a socially disadvantaged child, I considered Spanish to be a private language. What I needed to learn in school was that I had the right—and the obligation—to speak the public language of los gringos. The odd truth is that my first-grade classmates could have become bilingual, in the conventional sense of that word, more easily than I. Had they been taught (as upper-middle-class children are often taught early) a second language like Spanish or French, they could have regarded it simply as that: another public language. In my case such bilingualism could not have been so quickly achieved. What I did not believe was that I could speak a single public language.

> "... the bilingualists simplistically scorn the value and necessity of assimilation."

Without question, it would have pleased me to hear my teachers address me in Spanish when I entered the classroom. I would have felt much less afraid. I would have trusted them and responded with ease. But I would have delayed—for how long postponed?—having to learn the language of public society. I would have evaded—and for how long could I have afforded to delay?—learning the great lesson of school, that I had a public identity.

Fortunately, my teachers were unsentimental about their responsibility. What they understood was that I needed to speak a public language. So their voices would search me out, asking me questions. Each time I'd hear them, I'd look up in surprise to see a nun's face frowning at me. I'd mumble, not really meaning to answer. The nun would persist, "Richard, stand up. Don't look at the floor. Speak up. Speak to the entire class, not just to me!" But I couldn't believe that the English language was mine to use. (In part, I did not want to believe it.) I continued to mumble. I resisted the teacher's demands. (Did I somehow suspect that once I learned public language my pleasing family life would be changed?) Silent, waiting for the bell to sound, I remained dazed, diffident, afraid. . . .

Today I hear bilingual educators say that children lose a degree of "individuality" by becoming assimilated into public society. (Bilingual schooling was popularized in the seventies, that decade when middle-class ethnics began to resist the process of assimilation—the American melting pot.) But the bilingualists simplistically scorn the value and necessity of assimilation. They do not seem to realize that there are two ways a person is individualized. So they do not realize that while one suffers a diminished sense of private individuality by becoming assimilated into public society, such assimilation makes possible the achievement of public individuality.

ANALYZING THE RHETORICAL SITUATION

1. Compare the excerpts from the writings of Juan F. Perea and Richard Rodriguez. How does each writer explain the invisibility of some people in the United States? What claim does each writer make about this invisibility?

2. What reasons does each writer give for the invisibility? What evidence does each author provide to support his claim?

3. What do the two writers say about resisting or embracing assimilation into the melting pot? How does each writer evaluate the importance of public language?

4. Identify the exigence, audience, purpose, and context of Perea's and Rodriguez's rhetorical situations. What are the resources and constraints of their contexts? Be prepared to share your answers with the class.

COMMUNITY CONNECTIONS

1. Write for ten minutes about your own perspective on the English-only movement. What do you think about Hayakawa's aim of adding an English language amendment to the U.S. Constitution, or the arguments of U.S. English? What statement, or claim, can you make to summarize your position?

2. Write for five minutes about the vision of public life that Hayakawa believes an English language amendment will reflect. What positive consequences does he see arising from making English the official language of the United States? What claim might you make about such positive effects?

continued

3. Write for another five minutes about the negative consequences that might follow from making English the official language of the United States. What claim can you make? What reasons can you provide to back up your claim? What evidence can you provide?

4. Perea writes, "Most people are not aware of the existence and the extent of American multilingualism and its official, state-sponsored character." Were you aware of the multilingual history of the United States? If so, where and when did you learn about it? If not, why do you suppose you never heard of it? Write for ten minutes about your response to Perea's historical overview, including the reasons you knew—or didn't know—about the history of American multilingualism. At the end of the ten minutes, write one sentence that captures your opinion about multilingualism. If possible, make a claim about multilingualism.

5. Both Perea and Rodriguez talk about how language shapes both public and private identities. How would you characterize the language-based differences between these two identities? What are the roots of these differences? Using your own experiences or those of someone you know well, write for five to ten minutes on how a person can use language to distinguish his or her public and private selves.

6. Rodriguez argues that Latinos who push for public bilingualism think they can "have it both ways," that is, can participate in public life while retaining their cultural and ethnic identities. Drawing on your observations of life within the United States and within your community, is it possible for people to "have it both ways"? On what evidence do you base your conclusion?

7. Perea and Rodriguez have different views of the importance the mainstream culture in the United States should place on the cultural and linguistic heritages of minority communities. After writing a sentence that captures the view of each of these writers, write for ten minutes about whether that view has crucial implications for education. Provide specific evidence from both excerpts to support your claim.

Position Arguments: A Fitting Response

Two arguments about language diversity in the United States

As you have learned in this chapter, many people—from politicians and scholars to activist groups and individual language speakers—have made arguments about the political, economic, social, and cultural consequences of the use of non-English languages in the United States. Some of these arguments (those by Hayakawa and Perea, for instance) attempt to present objective analyses of how particular laws or policies will or will not bring about certain ends. Equally compelling have been the narratives (of Villanueva and Rodriguez) that argue for or against official recognition of language diversity in the United States by describing personal experiences. Let's consider two more examples: an argument from personal experience and an argument from a more public stance. First, in an editorial, Gabriela Kuntz, a retired elementary-school teacher living in Cape Girardeau, Missouri, tells why her own painful experiences of ethnic and linguistic discrimination have led her to decide not to teach her children Spanish.

Gabriela Kuntz

My Spanish Standoff

Once again my 17-year-old daughter comes home from a foreign-language fair at her high school and accusingly tells me about the pluses of being able to speak two languages. Speaker after speaker has extolled the virtues of becoming fluent in another language. My daughter is frustrated by the fact that I'm bilingual and have purposely declined to teach her to speak Spanish, my native tongue. **[1]** She is not the only one who has wondered why my children don't speak Spanish. Over the years friends, acquaintances and family have asked me the same question. Teachers have asked my children. My family, of course, has been more judgmental. **[2]**

I was born in Lima, Peru, and came to the United States for the first time in the early '50s, when I was 6 years old. At the parochial school my sister and I attended in Hollywood, Calif., there were only three Hispanic families at the time. I don't know when or how I learned English. I guess it was a matter of survival. My teacher spoke no Spanish. Neither did my classmates. All I can say is that at some point I no longer needed to translate. When I spoke in English I thought in English, and when I spoke in Spanish I thought in Spanish. I also learned about peanut-butter-and-jelly sandwiches, Halloween and Girl Scouts. **[3]**

We went to a high school in Burbank. Again, there were few Hispanic students at the time. My sister and I spoke English without an "accent." This pleased my father to no end. He would beam with pleasure when teachers, meeting him and my mother for the first time and hearing their labored English, would comment that they had no idea English was not our native tongue.

My brother was born in Los Angeles in 1959, and we would speak both English and Spanish to him. When he began to talk, he would point to an object and say its name in both languages. He was, in effect, a walking, talking English-Spanish dictionary. I have often wondered how his English would have turned out, but circumstances beyond our control prevented it. **[4]** Because of political changes in Peru in the early '60s (my father being a diplomat), we had to return to Peru. Although we had no formal schooling in Spanish, we were able to communicate in the language. I was thankful my parents had insisted that we speak

[1] Kuntz indirectly presents her position in the introduction. She alludes to the counterarguments, too, and gives readers a clear idea about how widely supported these counterarguments are.

[2] This final sentence creates the impression that the writer has thought hard about her decision and has strong reasons to support her argument.

[3] By saying that she "also learned about peanut-butter-and-jelly sandwiches, Halloween and Girl Scouts," Kuntz implicitly argues that learning English marks an important part of the process of becoming "American."

[4] Kuntz mentions that "circumstances beyond our control" kept her younger brother from developing his abilities in using English. She implicitly juxtaposes these uncontrollable circumstances and those surrounding her daughter, which Kuntz has controlled as much as possible.

[5] Kuntz concedes a point to those who disagree with her position that she's doing her own daughter a disservice. She has yet to reveal her reasons for not teaching her child Spanish.

[6] The writer signals that she is shifting to the reasons supporting her argument. Yet this paragraph does not mention the Spanish language.

[7] Kuntz uses the phrase "to be fair" to anticipate readers' objections.

[8] Kuntz presents the major reasons supporting her argument that she's doing her daughter a service by not teaching her Spanish.

[9] Kuntz anticipates readers' counterarguments with this question and then answers them in the next sentences.

[10] Kuntz begins to situate her personal decision within the context of larger public events.

Spanish at home. [5] At first our relatives said that we spoke Spanish with a slight accent. But over time the accent disappeared, and we became immersed in the culture, our culture. My brother began his schooling in Peru, and even though he attended a school in which English was taught, he speaks the language with an accent. I find that ironic because he was the one born in the United States, and my sister and I are the naturalized citizens.

In 1972 I fell in love and married an American who had been living in Peru for a number of years. Our first son was born there, but when he was 6 months old, we came back to the States. My husband was going to get his doctorate at a university in Texas.

It was in Texas that, for the first time, I lived in a community with many Hispanics in the United States. [6] I encountered them at the grocery store, the laundry, the mall, church. I also began to see how the Anglos in the community treated them. Of course, I don't mean all, but enough to make me feel uncomfortable. Because I'm dark and have dark eyes and hair, I personally experienced that look, that unspoken and spoken word expressing prejudice. If I entered a department store, one of two things was likely to happen. Either I was ignored, or I was followed closely by the salesperson. The garments I took into the changing room were carefully counted. My check at the grocery store took more scrutiny than an Anglo's. My children were complimented on how "clean" they were instead of how cute. Somehow, all Hispanics seemed to be lumped into the category of illegal immigrants, notwithstanding that many Hispanic families have lived for generations in Texas and other Southwestern states.

To be fair, I also noticed that the Latinos lived in their own enclaves, attended their own churches, and many of them spoke English with an accent. [7] And with their roots firmly established in the United States, their Spanish was not perfect either.

It was the fact that they spoke neither language well and the prejudice I experienced that prompted my husband and me to decide that English, and English only, would be spoken in our house. [8] By this time my second dark-haired, dark-eyed son had been born, and we did not want to take a chance that if I spoke Spanish to them, somehow their English would be compromised. In other words, they would have an accent. I had learned to speak English without one, but I wasn't sure they would.

When our eldest daughter was born in 1980, we were living in southeast Missouri. Again, we decided on an English-only policy. If our children were going to live in the United States, then their English should be beyond reproach. Of course, by eliminating Spanish we have also eliminated part of their heritage. Am I sorry? [9] About the culture, yes; about the language, no. In the Missouri Legislature, there are bills pending for some sort of English-only law. [10] I recently read an article in a national magazine about the Ozarks where some of the townspeople are concerned about the numbers of Hispanics who have come to work in poultry plants there. It seemed to me that their "concerns" were actually prejudice. There is a definite creeping in of anti-Hispanic sentiment in this country. Even my daughter, yes, the one who is upset over not being bilingual, admits to hearing "Hispanic jokes" said in front of her at school. You see, many don't realize, despite her looks, that she's a minority. I want to believe that her flawless English is a contributing factor.

Last summer I took my 10-year-old daughter to visit my brother, who is working in Mexico City. She picked up a few phrases and words with the facility that only the very young can. I just might teach her Spanish. You see, she is fair with light brown hair and blue eyes. [11]

[11] Kuntz ties together earlier strands of her argument in which she juxtaposed racial discrimination and linguistic discrimination.

Whereas Gabriela Kuntz composed a personal narrative to present her argument for English-only education, Agustin Garza focused on a public arena. Garza used an editorial to highlight a language-related problem he saw affecting California's lawmakers. Garza argues that California's elected Latino representatives need to be able to speak the Spanish language that is their heritage and that reflects the worldview of a significant percentage of their constituencies.

Agustin Garza

A Language Is a Terrible Thing to Lose

It almost qualifies as political farce. California has more Latino lawmakers than ever before, elected partly by an immigrant constituency anxious for a greater voice in government. But many of these new leaders can't communicate with all of the supporters who helped send them to Sacramento. Why? No hablan español.

Recently, Gov. Gray Davis invited a few of the state's 24 Latino legislators to join him on a mission to improve relations with Mexico. [1] Yet, some of these Latino ambassadors don't speak enough Spanish to comfortably address people in the country of their parents' origin.

Now that's not funny. That's embarrassing, even painful. [2]

Lt. Gov. Cruz Bustamante and other Latino officials recently completed intensive Spanish courses at a popular language school in Cuernavaca. Their mission: learn Spanish or polish up their pocho, the hybrid Spanglish developed for survival, not success, by the offspring of immigrants. [3]

Bilingual legislators, like Assembly Speaker Antonio Villaraigosa, struggled to hold on to their Spanish while growing up in the 1950s, before bilingual education. "It was an era when many of our parents, because of the discrimination they faced, were reluctant to speak to us in Spanish," said Villaraigosa, 46, who practiced his native tongue on the streets. [4] Today, he added, it's essential to speak a second language in California. Yet, it's getting harder and harder. Being bilingual may be in, but bilingual education is out, thanks to the English-only language police. [5]

Unfortunately, the pressure to assimilate forces Latinos and other immigrants to lose their native language. And language experts worry that public schools have done little to encourage language retention by native speakers. Proposition 227, which severely curtailed bilingual education in California, can only make matters worse. So while adults pay thousands of dollars trying to

[1] Garza establishes the timeliness of his argument by linking it to a recent public event.

[2] Here Garza makes his argument implicitly—Latino legislators in California need to be able to speak the Spanish language of their constituents.

[3] Garza says that Spanglish is "for survival, not success," as a way of implying that California's Latino legislators learn only enough Spanish to secure votes.

[4] The writer explains how the present condition came to be.

[5] Garza highlights a paradox: the ability to speak Spanish is valuable in public life, but only English is taught in public schools.

[6] Garza creates a contrast to get readers to think about resources in a broader sense than they normally do.

[7] Garza intersperses Spanish phrases throughout his editorial to give life to his argument that legislators need to be able to connect with constituents in their heritage language.

[8] Garza introduces and then immediately responds to a counter-argument.

[9] Garza uses authoritative voices to support his major points.

[10] Garza uses another's experience to support his analysis of his own family's situation.

[11] Garza again makes an explicit argument— foreign languages should be taught in elementary schools. At the same time, he hints at a larger, implicit argument— majority attitudes toward language difference destroy an important cultural, political, and economic resource.

learn a second language in costly crash courses, our children are being forced to forget the languages they already know. **[6]**

Que absurdo! **[7]**

On Friday, Lou Correa, the new assemblyman for Santa Ana, addressed a group of professionals volunteering at Anaheim schools, where students speak almost 50 different languages. The multitude of tongues may seem like a Tower of Babel, Correa cautioned, but it's really a solid foundation to build on. **[8]** "When these kids learn English, they are going to be the business captains of the 21st century," he told the group. Correa was raised with Spanish at home. Now, he and his wife make an effort to speak to their children in Spanish too. "Hablame en español," the Correas insist. **[9]** My parents repeated those very words a thousand times in my home, but we still grew up speaking fractured Castilian. My Spanish didn't improve until I spent a year in Mexico City after high school, enduring merciless teasing about my gringo accent.

On this side of the border, many Latinos are ashamed they've lost their native tongue. They feel cut off from their relatives and their roots. My own son finds it difficult to communicate with his family in Mexico and Peru. Miguel spoke only Spanish until he was 3. Then he started preschool and insisted on speaking English. It was easier to get him to eat his vegetables than to speak in Spanish anymore. The same thing happened to Speaker Villaraigosa, who spoke Spanish until he entered kindergarten. "At school, I lost my Spanish," he said. **[10]** That's some sad sentence. Imagine losing a language in school. What kind of backwardness is that?

Deliberate, says my old friend Luis Moll. Language is used as an instrument of colonial control, says the native Puerto Rican and professor in the department of language, reading and culture at the University of Arizona. In the United States, Luis sees the English-only movement as an extension of Manifest Destiny, that delusional American ideology that justified genocide and invasions. And Proposition 227 is a form of white supremacy, he argues, "well rehearsed with American Indian and African American children before it was applied to Latinos." In other words, first take the land, then the language.

That may sound radical, but it makes me wonder. If children learn languages best when they're little, as the proponents of English immersion argue relentlessly, why don't we teach foreign languages in the early grades? Maybe we're supposed to learn only English when the learning is easiest, then try to salvage a second language when it's too late. **[11]**

Cuernavaca anyone?

The two preceding editorials demonstrate different strategies for arguing a position on the language diversity in the United States. Both writers connected their arguments to a contemporary event. Both arguments explained how a particular problem affected a group of people. Both arguments presented supporting reasons that, wherever possible, were grounded in readers' values and beliefs. Both arguments anticipated opposing viewpoints, conceding points where necessary and providing logical rebuttals where possible.

What Makes It a Position Argument?

The following questions are ones you should consider when thinking critically about any position argument. For now, try applying them to the editorials by Gabriela Kuntz and Agustin Garza to determine how closely those writers followed the conventions for position arguments.

1. Does the writer explain how his or her argument relates to contemporary events? Does the writer show how the issue or topic affects a specific group of people about whom readers will be concerned?

2. Does the argument that the writer presents seem to address the problem he or she wants to resolve?

3. Does the writer present clear reasons to support his or her argument? Are these reasons ones that readers will find convincing?

4. How does the writer acknowledge opposing viewpoints? Does the writer explain why he or she objects to a particular counterargument or concedes a specific point?

5. Does the writer argue, either implicitly or explicitly, for a particular outcome or solution? Does the argument call for readers to adopt a new perspective on an issue or ask them to follow a specific course of action?

Understanding the Rhetorical Situation

Identifying an exigence

In his column on California's Latino legislators, Agustin Garza articulates two major concerns: some of these elected officials "don't speak enough Spanish to comfortably address" their constituents, and public schools are wasting the valuable linguistic resources many children are bringing to the classroom. Garza's argument follows from his desire to see all Americans enjoy adequate political representation and to see all children have equal opportunities to connect their education to the social and economic realities of their world. His argument, then, highlights problems with the current situation and creates a picture of how things could be different.

Even if you don't encounter arguments about English-only education on a daily basis or have the specific concerns that Garza has, you no doubt have observed how language practices distinguish various communities of which you are a member. Consider a community you are part of—whether it's academic, activist, artistic, athletic, professional, civic, ethnic, national, political, or religious. What language practices help members of this group to communicate with one another? What language practices distinguish the group from others and help its members to create a collective identity? What aspects of language use have created tension between this group and others? Is language used by certain members of the group in ways that others have not intended for it to be used? What problems do or might result from these "misuses" of language? Are any of them the result of unnecessary or misguided rules?

For example, you might study the language practices that characterize a particular online community in which you participate. What rules concerning language use have certain group members created? What steps have these members taken to generate agreement on these rules or to communicate them to the entire community? What have certain group members written that has violated the established etiquette? How have other community members addressed such situations? Did the established rules guide the communal responses to the "misuse" of language? Do the rules need to be reinforced, revised, or completely reconsidered?

Questions like these help you identify an exigence for your writing. As you consider the communities you identify with, think about the language practices or attitudes toward language that have shaped your experiences within each group.

1. Make a list of the communities with which you identify most strongly. For each group, list several significant or unique language experiences that have marked your participation in that group. If the experiences were positive, explain why, providing as many details as possible. If the experiences were negative, describe the factors that made them difficult or unpleasant. Also, write down any rules—whether written or unwritten—that influence the

ways in which you or other group members use language to participate in the community.

2. Choosing one or two of your communities, take photos or sketch pictures of group members speaking, writing, texting, blogging, or engaging in some other use of language. Or grab a screenshot illustrating a relevant example of the group's online communication. Whatever visual you choose should include details or features that make the community's language use compelling to examine.

3. Choose the community whose language practices or rules you want to write about and compose four or five descriptions of a problem related to language use in that community. Vary the ways you describe the problem. For example, one description might emphasize how some people are marginalized by an online community member's language practice, and another might emphasize the ways in which others in the community did or did not respond to this language practice. Another description might focus on the process by which rules for language use have been communicated (or not) to new group members, and yet another might describe what ideal seems to guide the community's online language use.

Locating an audience

For her editorial on her daughter's language education, Gabriela Kuntz had to consider various people in her audience who, while interested in issues of language and education, held a range of beliefs and attitudes about the aims of American schools in general and the place of non-English languages in education in particular. She suggests that English-only education will pull Latinos out of "their own enclaves," a logical appeal that may strengthen her support from readers who already agree with her decision. She concedes the point that "there is a definite creeping in of anti-Hispanic sentiment in this country" as a means of strengthening an ethical appeal to her critics. And she emphasizes her belief in giving her children opportunities to live free from discrimination as an emotional appeal that connects with a value held by all her readers; she hopes to convince the different people in her audience to understand more deeply the beliefs guiding her decision.

What audience should you consider for your position argument? First, you have to determine who is affected by, needs to know more about, or is in the best position to respond to the problem you're addressing. Then, you need to consider how to make that audience feel compelled to respond to the problem or to consider it in a new light. For instance, if you want to argue that your school needs to put more emphasis on developing students' abilities in non-English languages, you might consider several audiences. You could write directly to your fellow students encouraging them to make space in their schedules for modern language courses. You could write to professors, arguing for more material on international and cross-cultural communication in their courses. Or you could find out who makes decisions about major-level requirements at your school and learn more about how these decisions are made. Once you've identified the audience for your argument, you'll want to consider how you can best present the problem you're addressing: the college is not prioritizing students' development of language abilities.

The following questions can help you locate your rhetorical audience as well as identify the relationship they have to the problem you're addressing. Then, you'll be able to choose the best way to describe that problem.

1. List the names of the persons or groups who are affected directly or indirectly by the problem you're addressing.
2. Next to the name of each potential audience, write reasons that audience could have for acknowledging the existence of your problem. In other words, what would persuade these audiences that something needs to change or that they need to view the situation in a new way?
3. What actions could these audiences reasonably be persuaded to perform? What new perspectives could they be expected to adopt? In other words, consider what each audience would be able to do to resolve this problem.
4. With your audience's interests and capabilities in mind, look again at the descriptions of the problem that you composed in the preceding section on identifying an exigence. Decide which description will best help your audience feel connected to the situation as you've described it. Be open to revising your best description in order to tailor it to the audience's attitudes, beliefs, experiences, and values.

Identifying a Fitting Response

Finding a purpose and shaping a fitting response

You have explored issues of language use in the communities you identify with most strongly. You have identified a problem that you want people to think about more deeply, and you have considered who makes up your audience and how those readers are invested in the problem you'll be writing about. But what do you want to accomplish with your writing? What specific type of response do you want to invoke in these readers? For example, you might want to reaffirm readers' commitment to a cause they already support and provide them with further reasons to support their position. Or you might want to encourage readers to simply listen to and more carefully consider the perspectives of an overlooked and silenced group. Or you might want to help two seemingly different groups to realize they have common interests in relation to a particular issue. For any of these or some other rhetorical purpose, how could your writing help bring about such a response? Answering these types of questions should provide you with your purpose, which in turn will inform the specific kind of text you create.

Identifying a problem and getting others to recognize it as a problem is only the beginning of your response to your rhetorical situation. You need to sharpen your one-sentence statement of the argument you want to make and marshal sound reasons to support your position. The most effective supporting reasons are those that connect with the values, beliefs, and attitudes of your audience. For example, an argument for increased public funding for disseminating health information to language minorities might be strengthened with appeals to readers' interest in public safety, equal and open access to information, and long-term savings in medical costs, even as you acknowledge some readers' concerns over the short-term costs of providing such informational materials.

Different purposes and different audiences require different kinds of texts. For example, a lack of local resources for people who speak languages other than English might prompt you to create a newsletter that draws attention to the daily challenges these people face as well as argues for a greater public commitment to addressing this problem. Community debate over an English-only policy or a bilingual education program might lead you to write a letter to the county commissioners or the school board to highlight an important aspect of the issue they may be overlooking. As these two examples suggest, once you identify your problem, audience, and purpose, you need to determine what kind of text will best respond to the rhetorical situation.

Use the following questions to help you narrow your purpose and shape your response:

1. What reasons support the argument you want to make? What evidence or examples can you provide to convince readers that each supporting reason is valid?
2. Which supporting reasons are most likely to resonate with your audience? What are the audience's beliefs, attitudes, or experiences that lead you to this conclusion?
3. What specific response are you hoping to draw from your audience? Do you want the audience to feel more confident in its current position? Do you want the audience to listen to and consider an overlooked position? Or do you want the audience to take some specific action to address the problem you're trying to resolve?
4. What is the best way to present your argument to your audience? That is, what kind of text is this audience most likely to respond to?

Your instructor (or your rhetorical situation) may prompt you to write an editorial, a narrative, a letter, or some other form of written response. Alicia Williams (whose essay begins on page 239) has strong opinions about the status of American Sign Language (ASL) as a language and became interested in how the English-only movement might affect it. As a deaf individual, she knew she could write a personal narrative such as a memoir or autobiography that would shed light on her experiences and beliefs. She could also join forces with others concerned about English-only education and start a letter-writing campaign to influence the local school board. But Alicia decided that a good first step would be to further understand how ASL, like Spanish, Tagalog, or Mandarin Chinese, is a language affected by English-only policies. She could then use a position argument to help her develop and present her thoughts for others to consider. If, like Alicia, you are prompted to write a position argument, use the following assignment as a guide.

Writing a Position Argument: Working with Your Available Means

Shaping your position argument

You are likely familiar with the form and arrangement of position arguments because you come across examples of this genre in your daily life. The introduction of an argumentative essay grabs readers' attention as it describes the problem in a way that helps readers see how it concerns them as well as why the situation needs their attention right now. The introduction also states the thesis, which presents your argument in a single sentence or short string of sentences; you might also present supporting reasons in the introduction as a cluster of concise sentences following the thesis statement. In the introduction to his editorial, Agustin Garza connects his problem to a recent event and then presents a paradox meant to highlight the problem: many of California's Latino representatives have been invited by the governor to work on improving the state's political, economic, and cultural relations with Mexico, but many of these legislators "don't speak enough Spanish to comfortably address people in the country of their parents' origin." Garza then introduces his argument in a one-sentence paragraph made all the more powerful because of its brevity: this situation is "embarrassing, even painful."

The body of an argumentative essay provides the major reasons supporting the argument. Here the writer not only presents the supporting reasons but also explains how each reason strengthens his or her larger argument. And, as you have already learned, the stronger supporting reasons are those that connect to readers' beliefs, values, and attitudes. For example, Gabriela Kuntz grounds much of her argument in support of English-only education on two interrelated supporting reasons: learning to speak and write only in English improves one's ability to speak the language "without an accent"; speaking "without an accent" improves one's ability to live in the United States without facing discrimination and to fully assimilate into mainstream culture. The first of Kuntz's supporting reasons projects a logical appeal, as it reinforces readers' commonsense understanding of how we learn languages (although many bilingual educators would refute this claim). Kuntz's second supporting reason creates an emotional appeal as it connects with readers' belief that all people should have an equal opportunity to succeed in life. Ultimately, the success of most arguments depends on how well the writer has identified the audience's core beliefs and values and how successfully the writer has supported her or his argument with reasons that speak to those concerns.

In addition, writers use the body of an argumentative essay to present evidence and examples that create stronger logos and ethos appeals. Writers present facts and figures, direct quotations, and brief narratives to convince readers that each supporting reason does strengthen the larger argument. For example, Garza narrates the educational experiences of one California legislator who spoke Spanish until he entered kindergarten but then struggled to maintain this language through his years of schooling. Further along in the body of his argument, Garza supports his analysis of the U.S. educational system's approach to non-English languages by including commentary from a teacher of language, reading, and culture at the University of Arizona, Luis Moll. This commentary advances both a logical appeal, one that exposes the "backwardness" of an educational system that forces students to *lose* a language, and an ethical appeal, one that shows Garza has the good sense to draw on the knowledge and opinions of experts in order to support his argument.

The body of an argumentative essay also acknowledges and responds to counterarguments and opposing viewpoints. This rhetorical move helps writers not only create stronger logical appeals, as they address possible gaps in their arguments, but also project more convincing ethical appeals, as they show readers they are open to considering alternative perspectives on the issue. Kuntz, for example, acknowledges that "by eliminating Spanish" from her children's education, she and her husband "have also eliminated part of their heritage." She presents herself as being open to the views of English-only opponents who lament the loss of people's culture and who perceive "a definite creeping in of anti-Hispanic sentiment in this country." At the same time, though, Kuntz asserts that she's not sorry her daughter's lost the language of her heritage because, Kuntz explains, her daughter's "flawless English" has helped her to assimilate into mainstream U.S. culture. Ultimately, Kuntz shows readers she has weighed her argument against compelling counterarguments.

Finally, the conclusion of an argumentative essay reinforces the benefits that will be realized if the audience responds to the writer's argument in the intended way. Or, conversely, the conclusion may illustrate the negative situation that will result if the writer's argument is ignored. Garza, for example, concludes his editorial by making one final logical appeal to readers. He re-emphasizes that if California doesn't change its schools' approach to languages other than English, it will perpetuate a failed process by which people must "try to salvage a second language when it's too late." He punctuates this point about schools' failure to teach the language of Latin America with the question "Cuernavaca anyone?" This final sentence alludes to the Spanish-language school that many of California's Latino legislators had to attend.

Many writers include visuals in their arguments to help achieve their rhetorical purposes. As you draft your argumentative essay, you may want to consider whether a visual or two will strengthen your argument. Consider grabbing an Internet window that illustrates a particular form of online communication you're discussing. Create a customized language map that emphasizes your point about the need for more English-as-a-second-language learning opportunities in your community. Photograph signs, physical spaces, or individual interactions that illustrate your argument about the campus or community's openness toward language minority groups. You might even create a multimedia presentation that incorporates digital video and audio interviews to support your argument.

CHECKING OVER A POSITION ARGUMENT

✓ There is a vivid description of the problem or issue with which the argument is concerned.

✓ The argument is directed toward an audience with a clear connection to or investment in the problem being addressed.

✓ There is a concise statement of the writer's major argument.

✓ Reasons that support the writer's argument are provided, and each supporting reason takes into account the audience's beliefs, attitudes, and values.

✓ The argument contains specific evidence—details, examples, and direct quotations—to back each supporting reason.

✓ The argument describes the benefits that will be achieved by responding to the writer's argument in the intended way or the negative situation that will result from ignoring it.

Student paper

In the following essay, student Alicia Williams develops her position on American Sign Language, which she believes is an authentic (live and vibrant) language with a rich history and vital present.

Alicia Williams

Professor Glenn

English 275

November 20, 2007

The Ethos of American Sign Language

The termination of the Bilingual Education Act was followed by the No Child Left Behind Act (2001), thus removing a bilingual approach from the education tracks of non-English native speakers. The loss of bilingual education has caused the political group, English First, to lobby hard for an English-only education that purports to produce truly American citizens. This, in turn, produces more momentum for the group's side project: making English the official language of United States of America. Not only does this negate the melting pot of languages in America, but it diminishes the impact of a truly unique language—American Sign Language (ASL). The drive for English-only education treats the manifestations of language through a purely verbal platform, thereby perpetuating long-held prejudices and the commonly mistaken assumption that ASL is not, in fact, a language.

Only fifty years ago did American Sign Language (ASL) receive its long overdue recognition as a distinct language, rather than being perceived as a "hindrance to English," a "bastardization of English," or even a "communication disorder." By the end of the nineteenth century, during the rise of formal educational instruction in ASL for the Deaf, an oppositional camp

Guide to Responding

known as Oralists had fervently portrayed signing by the Deaf community as a pathological version of spoken language.[1] A few even preposterously correlated deafness with low intelligence. Ironically, the husband of a Deaf woman, Alexander Graham Bell, who was the inventor of the telephone and hearing aids, was a supporter of the oralists' philosophy. He endorsed "genetic counseling for the deaf, outlawing intermarriages between deaf persons, suppression of sign language, elimination of residential schools for the deaf, and the prohibition of deaf teachers of the deaf" (Stewart and Akamatsu 242).

Oralism faced counteractions by the numerous, though less famous, people who were working for the needs of the Deaf community as its educators. They understood that ASL is requisite for a deaf person's social, cultural, and lingual needs. The Deaf community managed to keep its educational programs intact without losing ASL, though not without struggle. It was not until a half-century later, in the 1960s, that William Stokoe's linguistic analysis of ASL produced the much needed equilibrium between the Deaf and hearing communities concerning the legitimacy of ASL. Even so, when most people talk about language, their thinking assumes communication through speaking: most classify as unconventional forms of language outside of a verbal modality. Native signers such as myself understand that our minority language must coexist with a dominant majority language, but the practice of reducing ASL to a type of communication disorder, or worse, obliterating it for the spoken English-only movement, ignores the historical presence of Deaf culture in America, as well as the key characteristics ASL shares with the evolution of languages.

ASL was derived from French Sign Language (FSL) in the early nineteenth century. Harlan Lane and François Grosjean, prominent ASL linguists, found supporting evidence for this date from "the establishment of the first American school for the deaf in 1817 at Hartford, Connecticut. . . . Its founders, Thomas Gallaudet and Laurent Clerc, were both educated in the use of FSL prior to 1817" (Stewart and Akamatsu 237). Historically speaking, David Stewart and C. Tane Akamatsu have determined that "approximately 60% of the signs in present-day ASL had their origin in FSL" (237). The modification of a parent language, such as FSL for the birth of ASL, is part of the process spoken language has undergone in its evolution throughout history, producing our contemporary languages. For instance, the English spoken in England during Shakespeare's lifetime is not the same English spoken in America today; nonetheless, they are both of English tradition.

Another characteristic that ASL has in common with other languages is that it changes from one generation to another. Undoubtedly, spoken languages continue to change. For instance, slang words used now may not be the same when the toddlers of today are in college. ASL also experiences these changes, which is contrary to a common misconception that the signs in ASL are concrete in nature, meaning there are no changes. For example, an obsolete sign for "will/future" is conveyed by holding your right arm bent in a ninety-degree angle with your fingertips parallel to the ground. Then you

Guide to Responding

move your entire forearm upwards to a forty-five-degree angle in one swift movement. The modern sign starts with an open palm touching the right jawline, underneath the ear; then the forearm moves forward until the arm is in a ninety-degree position, equivalent to the starting position of the arm in the old form. The evolution of signs is comparable to the changing connotations of various words found in the history of languages.

In the process of its shift to physical hand gestures and appropriate facial expressions, ASL does not discard the traditional syntax of language, maintaining its legitimacy as a distinct language. The rich complexity of ASL's syntax conveys itself through designated facial expressions and specific sign constructions, demonstrating that "ASL is governed by the same organizational principles as spoken languages . . . essential differences based on the fact that ASL is produced in three-dimensional space" (Neidle 30). As every language has a syntaxical structure, so does ASL.

Despite its similarities to languages such as English, it is a mistake to think of ASL as a pathology of spoken English. Perpetuating this myth is the misconception of ASL signs as direct translations of English. ASL has rules of its own, which are not identical to those of English syntax. In English, for instance, one says, "Who hates Smitty?" but in ASL, it is signed "Hate Smitty who?" The photos in Fig. 1 show another example of how signs in ASL are not a direct translation of English, but also show how differing hand placements denote different pronouns used with the verb *give.*

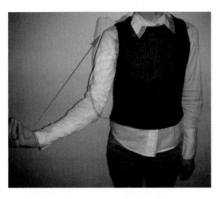

Fig. 1. The photograph on the left shows the signing of "Me give to him or her," and the photograph on the right shows that of "Me give to you." (Photographs by the author.)

Stokoe's work establishing the legitimacy of ASL spurred a movement for a bilingual approach in educating the deaf. The teaching of ASL was a top priority because of the hardship of expecting the Deaf community to acquire English as our native language, which carries a disadvantage by working on a modality inaccessible to us—hearing. In the bilingual approach, after the deaf child has attained a solid working background in ASL, some parents elect to have oral English taught as a second language. The success of English as a second language is largely subject to the individual's capabilities, which are dependent on numerous factors. My parents chose the bilingual approach in my education track at Rufus Putnam Elementary School (for the Deaf). While I maintained my fluency in ASL, I developed an efficacy at speech reading (informally known as lip reading). For instance, when I speak, I am able to convince hearing persons that I am not deaf. In my Deaf community, I always resort to my first language—ASL. All this would not be possible if Oralism or English First were successful in a push for *spoken* English only.

My bilingual background has been met with fierce opposition from hearing people who believe ASL is a crutch language and that it is an antiquated solution for the Deaf community. In other words, they believe the advances of medical technology will enable researchers to develop revolutionary digital hearing aids, while aggressively diagnosing deaf children at younger ages should cause a decreasing need for ASL, which they assume is a diminished form of English. But if ASL meets all other criteria of what linguists consider a language—with the exception of the use of a vocal apparatus—how can it be called a "crutch language"? And hearing aids only amplify whatever remaining hearing a deaf person has, if any at all; they do not compensate for hearing loss. Even if a doctor diagnoses a deaf child at birth, the severity of the child's sensorineural hearing loss may be so severe that spoken language will be impractical to acquire, whereas ASL will be a better approach for the child.[2] In rare cases, adults who become deaf later in their lives find comfort in ASL, rather than English. The naturalization associated with the visual-spatial lingual framework of ASL is uniquely characteristic of the Deaf community because it operates to their advantage, bypassing the confines of oral-aural languages. The use of a verbal apparatus in spoken languages is a natural reaction from the body possessing a functional audio-physiological system. Often this is not the case within the Deaf community; hence that is why ASL is deeply embedded in its culture and will remain the staple of its community, regardless of technology's novelty or the hearing community's desire to push for English-only education.

The most primeval function of language is to create a medium for people's desire to outwardly express themselves to others. Whatever form language may take—visually or verbally—it laid the foundation for humanity's collective identity as great storytellers. Through language we have been able to pass on stories of past heroes and enemies, warn future generations of failed philosophies, create new ideals for better living, share our aspirations and fears, even express our wonder at all that remains unknown to us. Language binds us as humans, and its diverse forms are reflected in the embodiments of its heterogeneous natives. ASL is but another paintbrush of language, and yet proof of humanity's palette of mutability.

Notes

[1]I realize the use of the term *Deaf* might seem archaic, but for the purpose of this paper, it is representative of all members who psychologically or linguistically identify themselves as members of the Deaf community through ASL as their common language, regardless of their physiological hearing capacity.

[2]There are three basic types of hearing loss: conductive hearing loss, sensorineural hearing loss, and mixed hearing loss, which is any combination of the first two. All three types can make speech hard to acquire.

Works Cited

Neidle, Carol, et al. *The Syntax of American Sign Language: Functional Categories and Hierarchical Structures.* Cambridge: MIT P, 2000. Print.

Stewart, David A., and C. Tane Akamatsu. "The Coming of Age of American Sign Language." *Anthropology & Educational Quarterly* 19.3 (Sept. 1988): 235-52. Web. 7 Nov. 2007.

If your rhetorical situation does not call for a position argument like Alicia Williams's, you can consider the following other options.

ALTERNATIVE ASSIGNMENTS

1. Compose a three- to four-page critical essay analyzing the consequences of an English language amendment. To fully understand the political, social, and cultural context in which the legislation was passed, conduct research to find print materials (newspaper articles, editorials and letters to the editor, transcripts of legislative hearings and testimony) from the time when the legislation was being considered. Use these materials to try to discern the stated and unstated goals of the advocates of the English language amendment. You also will want to conduct interviews with community leaders and local citizens as well as other primary research to determine what effects, if any, such legislation has had at the local level, such as restrictions on access to social services or implicit or explicit policies and practices in local workplaces.

2. Many supporters of English-only legislation draw attention to the costs of providing public services in languages other than English. Several opponents of English-only legislation suggest that these costs are not as significant as activists such as S. I. Hayakawa might argue; others emphasize the costs of failing to provide such services. Respond to this debate by composing a four-page investigative report that explores the specific costs associated with multilingualism in your community. Conduct research on local, state, and federal government resources in order to create strong logical and ethical appeals in your report; you might also consider interviewing local policymakers as part of your research process.

3. How do English-as-a-second-language speakers experience life on your campus or in your community? What atmosphere of linguistic diversity or homogeneity do they perceive in their daily lives, and how does this atmosphere manifest itself in their academic, professional, and extracurricular activities? Interview a student or community member who speaks English as his or her second language, and write a profile of that person that helps readers better understand how multilingual people move between languages in their daily lives and what motivates them either to maintain their abilities in their first language or to let these abilities erode.

8 WHO DECIDES?
RESPONDING WITH PROPOSALS

At Pioneer Courthouse Square, you can meet friends, buy a cup of coffee, sit and enjoy the weather, or catch the light rail. This square, in downtown Portland, Oregon, exemplifies the best kind of public space: it's centrally located, safe, beautiful, and free and open to the public. Twelve months a year, the square serves as a venue for various events, from the Senior Prom (for people 65 years and older) and Fashion Week (which previews local designers' collections) to a summer concert series and the annual Festival of Flowers. All year long, residents and visitors stand around the coffee shop, shop at the florist stand, and watch young people playing hacky sack or listen to them playing music.

Portland's Pioneer Courthouse Square is hugely successful—and it was purposefully designed to encourage the specific kinds of activities that take place there.

In fact, you could even say that the design was a top-down approach to organizing human interaction in a public space. Before the city acquired the property, it had been a department store parking lot (shown in the photo below), which served only the people shopping at a particular store and willing to pay to park their cars. In large cities such as Portland, open space like this is a precious commodity, a rarity among the tall buildings and busy streets. When such space is used to serve only a small percentage of a large population, many may wish it could be turned into something more people could use.

To transform a parking lot that served few people to a public square that serves many people, developers and city leaders first had to explain why the use of the space was somehow problematic for the city and its residents. Then, they had to propose a better use for the space, one that residents would approve. In so doing, they had to address the kinds of questions residents would be sure to ask: Who will pay for the transformation and subsequent upkeep? How will the new use of the space improve our lives? How long will the project take to complete? Where else will people be able to park? The developers and politicians had to create proposals that explained the exigence, defined the situation as problematic, offered various solutions, and explained which of those solutions were the most feasible and effective.

Proposals are a common response to this question: How can something be improved? But that simple question leads to a number of other questions: Why is something a problem in the first place? What are viable solutions to the problem? Why is one solution better than others? What will it take to enact the best solution? Who will be affected by this solution? This chapter will challenge you to respond to these questions rhetorically as you identify or create exigencies in your own surroundings.

Real Situations

You do not have to be from Portland to understand the concept of public space. Even if you are not familiar with the term, you are familiar with such places. Whether you are from a large city, a small town, or a rural environment, you are conscious of the way public space is used. You know how to use the parks, malls, streets, sidewalks, fairgrounds, stadiums, forests, game lands, beaches, river fronts, and other public spaces. You understand how human interaction is organized at those places, whether people gather to watch the sights (passersby or a scenic attraction) or experience the space individually (noon-time churchgoers, for instance, who sit quietly in a pew). Whether you use public transportation, drive your car, or walk, you know how to get to those public spaces—and home again—using means of public access: highways, streets, sidewalks, or trails.

Ever since you were a little child, you have inhabited public space. Whether you were taking turns on the playground equipment, waiting in line at the bus stop, or walking to school, you knew how to use the space, sometimes choosing to do so according to the rules for that space, sometimes not. By now, you are well accustomed to using public space of all kinds.

But not all uses of public space are planned for; no doubt, you are also aware of the ways uses emerge. From the bicycle messengers who dart between parked and moving cars and kids who take shortcuts across a school lawn to the hunters who blaze a trail through a state game land—systems of use emerge rather than conform to plans.

Take a look at the photographs on this page. Like many small college towns in the Midwest, Wooster, Ohio, has both rural and urban features. The first photograph shows a winding road through a residential section of town. The fairly narrow road provides access to driveways and a place for children to play, as the "Watch Children" sign indicates.

The photograph of downtown Wooster shows more direct planning than in the residential neighborhood. Main Street is a well-paved, two-lane street with on-street parking. It also has stoplights and streetlights. Notice, too, how much taller and closer together the buildings are.

Residential section of Wooster, Ohio.

Downtown Wooster, Ohio.

The College of Wooster is another kind of public space in Wooster, Ohio. Notice the shape and height of the various campus buildings. Notice, too, the pathways among the buildings.

The next photograph was taken on the corner of Bleecker and Sullivan Streets in New York City's Greenwich Village, which is the hometown of many people. You can see signs, traffic lights, store fronts, and parallel parking spots, all of which indicate planning of how people are supposed to use the public space. Notice that the buildings allow for higher-density living than those in downtown Wooster.

In city suburbs, public spaces have been made to look as nonurban as possible. In the photo of an apartment complex on the next page, notice how a greenbelt takes the place of asphalt. Trees line the walkway, and bushes surround the buildings. The landscaping gives the complex a peaceful, tranquil look—far different from the action seen on the New York City street. Yet, this space could be considered high density, since it houses multiple families in a relatively small area. In some ways, the occupants live as close together here as their counterparts do in Greenwich Village.

College of Wooster, Wooster, Ohio.

Corner in Greenwich Village, New York City.

Suburban apartment complex with greenbelt.

Many of us live or have lived in a suburban development, which offers yet another type of public space. The photograph below shows a well-paved street with single-family houses, a series of curbside mailboxes, and two sets of abruptly ending sidewalks. You might notice, too, the garages, the fence, the backyard deck, and the small trees—details that provide specific information about the way public space is used in the suburbs.

Suburban street with single-family residences.

DESCRIBING PUBLIC SPACES

1. Working with a classmate or two, choose two of the photographs in this section and make a list of specific details about the public space. What details can you discern that have not been mentioned in the text? Be prepared to share your answers with the rest of the class.

2. How many and what types of people use each of the spaces you chose? At what times of the day (and night) do they use that space? How long are they in that space? How do they get there? Where can they go to from that space?

3. How is each of these public spaces defined? What physical, geographical, and material boundaries define each of them? Be prepared to share your answers with the rest of the class.

4. Make a list of the things people can do in each of the spaces. Which of these uses of space seem to be encouraged by the way the space is planned?

5. What are the physical limitations on people's use of each of these spaces? What limitations are placed on children who want to play, people who want to walk for pleasure or to a destination, families who need a carton of milk and a loaf of bread, automobile drivers, people without automobiles, bicyclists, and parents with small children?

6. Translate one or more of these limitations into a one-sentence problem.

7. What solution can you imagine for the problem you stated? What specific action could be taken to resolve the problem? What money, time, or cooperative effort is necessary to the success of such an action?

COMMUNITY CONNECTIONS

1. Look again at the photographs in this section. Which of them seem familiar to you? In other words, have you ever used the kind of public space in downtown Portland, a small college campus, an urban neighborhood, an apartment complex, or a suburb? How did you use the space? And how did your use of public space change from place to place? Be prepared to share your answers with the rest of the class.

2. In which of the public spaces shown in the photographs would you most like to spend a Saturday night? How many Saturday nights would you like to spend there? Why?

3. Which of the spaces would you most like to live near? When and with whom? What are the positive and negative aspects of living in each of these settings? Be prepared to explain to the class why you prefer one of the settings.

4. Select a public space that is near where you live. If you could change just one thing about that space, what would it be? How could that space better accommodate your needs and desires? (Consider, too, the other people whose needs and desires would be accommodated as well.) Be as specific as you can about your proposal for improvement as well as the potential audience for it.

5. Account for the money, time, and cooperative effort that would be required for your proposal to be feasible.

Real Responses to Real Situations

This section features responses from four writers who used their available means to try to resolve an exigence surrounding the use of public space. As you explore their responses to situations that may be unfamiliar to you, ask yourself if what they have to say relates in any way to the public spaces you know well.

Planning the spaces where we live

One of the most powerful people of the twentieth century was Robert Moses (1888–1981), who single-handedly reshaped New York City. Son of German-Jewish parents, both of whom had fulfilled their own aspirations, Moses grew up in New Haven, Connecticut, and graduated with honors from Yale University, got a master's degree at Oxford University, and finally earned a PhD in political science from Columbia in 1914. He developed his own theory of public service, one based on merit not croneyism, a theory that helped propel his meteoric rise in a city that had tired of Boss Tweed and the Tammany Hall corruption. (William Marcy Tweed chaired the Democratic Party of New York County and headed the Tammany Society, an organization that controlled New York City politics for nearly a century.)

New York City provided Moses with a venue for pairing his strong work ethic with his aggressive progressivism, a social reform philosophy that aimed to reinstate political democracy and economic individualism and to eradicate slums and alleviate poverty. Before long, he was City Park Commissioner, City Construction Coordinator, and a member of the City Planning Commission, three powerful public service positions that would allow him to fulfill his dream of reshaping the city through a system of integrated planning. Besides creating a highway system to crisscross all five boroughs of New York City, Moses reinvigorated the city's park system, transforming rundown parks and overgrown open spaces into inviting, often beautiful spaces for families to spend time in. He and his team of engineers and architects took control of abandoned industrialized areas and trash-laden oceanfront stretches as well, replacing them with affordable housing, public parks, and decent beaches. In many ways, Moses made the city of New York accessible to people of all social ranks and ethnic backgrounds. In *Working for the People*, his first-person account of public service, Moses described the city he helped to build.

ROBERT MOSES
Excerpt from Working for the People

Here are a few examples of progress in the field of municipal construction which some visitors may overlook: They should note the emerging new neighborhood patterns along the East and Harlem rivers in Manhattan—parks, parkways, housing, the United Nations headquarters, on what was until recently a shambles, revising adjacent real estate values; the rebuilding of Astoria, across the river; the Triborough Bridge system, the Brooklyn Civic Center; Flushing Meadow Park and its burgeoning environment, with the corridors beyond it extending through Kissena and Cunningham parks to Alley Pond in Queens Borough.

We would not expect visitors to appreciate our prodigious sewage disposal systems, the pure Delaware upland water supply flowing down by gravity. Our own citizens do not fully appreciate these things or what they represent in the way of hard work on the part of little-known people in the public service. What business, industry, trade, and the arts and professions have done within this framework of municipal improvements is most impressive of all.

Local critics who refer mournfully to the exodus of industry from the city talk nonsense. They never see the new plants in the southeast Bronx, trucking in Williamsburgh, and the amazing waterborne commerce of Newtown Creek and the Gowanus Canal. We have had something of a waterfront mess, but it is being cleared up and I doubt if other ambitious ports will draw away our shipping.

We are rebuilding New York, not dispersing and abandoning it. The city spreads into the suburbs, to be sure, and that, within bounds, is what should happen. The process, however, needs no speeding up. It requires no compulsion. It demands no metropolitan supergovernment by ambitious regional planners.

Those interested in the new city that is emerging should note the vast reclamation areas in Queens, Brooklyn and Staten Island, the West Side and Henry Hudson [Parkway] renovations with their widespread repercussions and influences; the gradual reduction of slums in every borough; the salvaging of all of Jamaica Bay and its frontage; the great Soundview, Ferry Point, Whitestone, Rockaway and Clearview park projects; the many constructive achievements of the Port of New York Authority; the reconstruction of our museums; new schools and hospitals and health centers; the many modern city buildings housing courts, libraries and countless other services.

The material, psychological, sociological, and political ramifications of planning public space are many. Robert Moses was not hesitant to make decisions and live with the consequences of those decisions. He identified a problem and offered himself and his ideas as the proposed solution. One such problem was the difficulty many New York City residents had in traveling among the city's boroughs, several of which are separated by water. In the 1930s, residents in Queens who wanted to travel to The Bronx had to cross over to Manhattan first, adding to traffic congestion in the city streets. In 1932, Moses resurrected plans for the Triborough Bridge, which is actually three bridges connecting The Bronx, Manhattan, and Queens. When it opened in 1936, the Triborough Bridge ushered in a new age, making travel to the suburban parks and southern shorelines much easier for many city residents. Today, it remains a vital artery for New York City commerce.

Moses's reputation as a civic force was chronicled daily in the *New York Times* from the 1930s throughout the 1960s, but some other accounts of his career have not been celebratory. In particular, Robert A. Caro's *The Power Broker* describes Moses as a man who eventually deployed his system of integrated planning to overpower the interests of the working poor, destroying neighborhoods to serve the interests of the automobile and the upper-class people who could afford it. Although Moses repeatedly espoused uncompromising devo-

Triborough Bridge
from Manhattan,
one of Robert
Moses's projects.

tion to the lower classes, Caro writes that Moses "never forgot that the lower classes were lower."

One of Moses's most impressive accomplishments, the West Side Improvement Project (the Hudson River Parkway and Riverside Park), serves as a case in point. According to various newspaper reports cited by Caro, the project "gives the island not only a new major highway and a new shore line along part of its length but park and . . . playgrounds" and "all that has been unsightly along the Hudson—the railroad, the ash dumps, the coal yards—has been swept away or completely disguised." These reports were true—as far as they went. Like all of Moses's projects, the West Side Improvement Project benefited many people, but not the most vulnerable residents of the city.

ROBERT A. CARO
Excerpt from The Power Broker

"The railroad tracks are covered at last," an editorial said.

Not exactly.

The railroad tracks were covered until they reached 125th Street—the beginning of Harlem.

Moses had decided to economize on the section of the West Side Improvement, between 125th and 155th streets, that bordered the city's Negro community, and one of the economies was dispensing with the track cover-

ing in that section. Uncovered tracks meant a never-ending clanking, from the couplings of railroad cars, and periodic bawling, from the cows and other animals being transported south to the slaughterhouses, unless the people who lived in the apartments above kept their windows closed. And in the summer, when it was too hot to keep the windows closed, uncovered tracks meant not only noise but odors, the stench of the animals, and they meant soot and smoke that spread a coat of gritty grime, confined to windowsills in winter, over walls and furniture. Now, thanks to the genius of Robert Moses, the white people who lived along

Riverside Drive were freed from these annoyances.

But the black people weren't.

Robert Moses spent millions of dollars enlarging Riverside Park through landfill, but he did not spend a dime for that purpose between 125th and 155th streets. He added 132 acres to the parts of the park most likely to be used by white people—but not one acre to the part of the park most likely to be used by black people.

Robert Moses ruthlessly removed all commercial enterprises from the waterfront along the entire six-mile length of Riverside Park—except for those commercial enterprises (wharves, small warehouses, coal pockets, junk yards and the like) that were located in the Harlem section of Riverside Park. Those he allowed to remain—to occupy what otherwise would have been park land for Harlem.

Because he did not enlarge Riverside Park in the Harlem section, there was, really, for two-thirds of the Harlem section, the stretch between 125th and 145th streets, no Riverside Park at all. The green of lawns and trees that he laid out with such a lavish hand south of Harlem ends abruptly at 125th Street and the only green that remains is a very narrow, very steep treed slope, too steep for anything except slipping and sliding down it, that, for some of those twenty blocks, climbs from the uncovered tracks to Riverside Drive above. Except for that little ribbon of trees, pathetic when compared to the lush lawns and lavish plantings downtown, the "park" is, for these twenty blocks, only the grim steel of the tracks and the gray concrete of the parkway.

Robert Moses devoted endless ingenuity to making the Henry Hudson Parkway beautiful in and of itself. From Seventy-second to 125th Street, for example, he lined the roadway with trees and shrubs and faced the walls along its sides with granite and marble and expensive masonry. But between 125th and 145th streets, he lifted the roadway into the air—on a gaunt steel viaduct. There is not a tree or shrub on the viaduct. There is not a foot of granite or marble or masonry. The only ornamentation whatsoever on the starkly ugly steel is the starkly ugly cheap concrete aggregate with which it is paved.

And the viaduct is not only unlovely in and of itself. It makes the waterfront over which it runs even uglier

than it was before, filling its streets with its shadows and the never-ending rumble of the cars that travel along it. And its presence insures that even should New York City one day decide to give those twenty blocks of Harlem what it has given most of the other residential neighborhoods along the Hudson River, a park below Riverside Drive, the park will have to be one filled with shadow and noise.

There is at least one spot in this twenty-block stretch at which it would have been easy to create a park even without landfill operations.

At the foot of 125th and 126th streets, these mean and narrow thoroughfares slope down and, after running under Moses' viaduct, run right out into a broad wharf that juts out into the river, so that turning it into a park would have made the riverfront a part of Harlem. Of the whole Hudson River waterfront, no area was more intimately a part of the adjoining community and more suitable to be a park for it.

Moses might not have wanted to spend much money on the Harlem section of the West Side Improvement but a park here would not have cost much money. Condemning the wharf would have been cheap, as would also have been placing playground facilities on it to give the children of the neighborhood a chance to play right on the river or laying earth and sod on it to bring a touch of brightness to a neighborhood without brightness. And seeing the park possibilities of the wharf was easy; in fact, it would have been hard not to, for on every sunny day it was crowded with people fishing, staring out over the water or washing their cars in the sun.

But somehow Moses didn't see. He never made a move to turn the 125th Street wharf into a park, and in 1974 it would still be standing vacant, a monument to a city's indifference to the needs of its poorest people.

Harlem does, of course, have a section of Riverside Park, the section between 145th Street, where the Henry Hudson Parkway swings down off the viaduct, and 155th Street—a stretch of land ten blocks long, plenty long enough to provide the playgrounds, ballfields and other facilities that a recreation-starved community so desperately needed.

Robert Moses built seventeen playgrounds as part of the West Side Improvement. He built one playground in the Harlem section of the Improvement. He built five football fields as part of the Improvement. He built

continued

one in the Harlem section. He built eighteen horseshoe courts, twenty-two tennis courts, half a mile of roller-skating paths and a mile of bicycle paths in the rest of the Improvement. He did not build a single horseshoe or tennis court or a foot of roller-skating or bicycle path in the Harlem portion.

When the Improvement first opened, in fact, there was not a single recreational facility of any type in the entire "Harlem section"—not so much as a stanchion with a basketball hoop attached. The initial plans Moses had distributed to newspapers when he was persuading La Guardia to approve the Improvement had shown a recreational area between 146th and 148th streets on the river side of the parkway, but while most of the recreational areas above and below Harlem were completed when the Improvement opened, the 146th Street–148th Street area was not even begun. He did move thereafter to build it—hurriedly, because, according to one report, La Guardia suddenly realized the omission and insisted it be rectified and Moses was afraid the Mayor would make it public. But its pitifully inadequate and cheaply built facilities proved remarkably difficult to reach from the community it was supposed to serve. The only way to reach it on foot from Harlem, in fact, was by walking to Riverside Drive, walking down an incredibly long flight of steps to the New York Central tracks, crossing the tracks on a footbridge (which meant climbing up another flight of steps to get on it and climbing down a flight to get off) and then walking down another flight of steps to an underpass under the parkway which led to the recreational area. And reaching it was downhill. Getting back up to Riverside Drive was uphill. On even pleasant summer afternoons, the recreational area Moses had so generously bestowed upon Harlem would be almost empty—except for motorists from other areas who found it remarkably accessible (just pull off the parkway and there you were) by car.

Robert Moses had always displayed a genius for adorning his creations with little details that made them fit in with their setting, that made the people who used them feel at home in them. There was a little detail on the playhouse–comfort station in the Harlem section of Riverside Park that is found nowhere else in the park. The wrought-iron trellises of the park's other playhouses and comfort stations are decorated with designs like curling waves.

The wrought-iron trellises on the Harlem playhouse–comfort station are decorated with monkeys.

ANALYZING THE RHETORICAL SITUATION

As the excerpts in this section demonstrate, Robert Moses was a complex man. The following questions ask you to consider Moses and his work in terms of the elements of the rhetorical situation. You'll want to reread the excerpts carefully before answering.

1. Who might be the intended audience for each excerpt? How do the audiences for the excerpts differ? What textual evidence can you provide to support your answers? Be prepared to share your answers with the rest of the class.

2. Is the purpose of each excerpt evident? If so, what is it? How do the excerpts differ in terms of purpose? And how does each purpose correspond to the intended audience? Again, be prepared to share your answers with the rest of the class.

3. To what exigence might each writer be responding? (Keep in mind that these works were published in 1960 and 1975.) How does each piece of writing work to resolve that exigence? Who holds the power to resolve or affect the resolution of that exigence?

4. How does each writer draw on the rhetorical appeals of ethos, logos, and pathos? Cite passages from the text in order to support your answer.

Public space as emerging space

As you realize by now, Robert Moses's reputation as a city shaper ebbed and flowed. He held sway over New York City's planning for nearly thirty years, but by the middle of the twentieth century, his plans were being met with opposition, from the same people whose neighborhoods he wanted to "improve." Moses's belief that cities were created by and for traffic infuriated those who believed that cities should be planned to facilitate the intricate networks of contact, support, and diversity that neighborhoods provided. The turning point of Moses's power may have been the showdown he had with the residents of Greenwich Village in the 1960s; the opposition was led by Jane Jacobs (1916–2006), whose own theory of public space—that the city itself is more important than "moving traffic"—struck at the heart of Moses's basic theory.

In *Working for the People*, Moses wrote that "New York is too big for village intimacies, small-town fellowship and cracker-barrel town meetings." In contrast, Jacobs argued that those "village intimacies" are exactly what keep a city alive. In her response to what she considered to be short-sighted city planning, *The Death and Life of Great American Cities*, she claimed that observing how cities really function "is the only way to learn what principles of planning and what practices in rebuilding can promote social and economic vitality in cities, and what practices and principles will deaden these attributes." In what was to become a classic text of city planning, Jacobs recounted some costly and tragic decisions that were made in the name of progress, alluding to all the public works that Moses had supervised.

JANE JACOBS
Excerpt from The Death and Life of Great American Cities

There is a wistful myth that if only we had enough money to spend—the figure is usually put at a hundred billion dollars—we could wipe out all our slums in ten years, reverse decay in the great, dull, gray belts that were yesterday's and day-before-yesterday's suburbs, anchor the wandering middle class and its wandering tax money, and perhaps even solve traffic problems.

But look what we have built with the first several billions: Low-income projects that become worse centers of delinquency, vandalism and general social hopelessness than the slums they were supposed to replace. Middle-income housing projects which are truly marvels of dullness and regimentation, sealed against any buoyancy or vitality of city life. Luxury housing projects that mitigate their inanity, or try to, with a vapid vulgarity. Cultural centers that are unable to support a good bookstore. Civic centers that are avoided by everyone but bums, who have fewer choices of loitering places than others. Commercial centers that are lack-luster imitations of standard-

ized suburban chain-store shopping. Promenades that go from no place to nowhere and have no promenaders. Expressways that eviscerate great cities. This is not the rebuilding of cities. This is the sacking of cities. . . .

continued

"This is the sacking of cities."

One need ... only a pertinent specialty of some sort [to become a specialized sidewalk character]. It is easy. I am a specialized public character of sorts along our street, owing of course to the fundamental presence of the basic, anchored public characters. The way I became one started with the fact that Greenwich Village, where I live, was waging an interminable and horrendous battle to save its main park from being bisected by a highway. During the course of battle I undertook, at the behest of a committee organizer away over on the other side of Greenwich Village, to deposit in stores on a few blocks of our street supplies of petition cards protesting the proposed roadway. Customers would sign the cards while in the stores, and from time to time I would make my pickups. As a result of engaging in this messenger work, I have since become automatically the sidewalk public character on petition strategy. Before long, for instance, Mr. Fox at the liquor store was consulting me, as he wrapped up my bottle, on how we could get the city to remove a long abandoned and dangerous eyesore, a closed-up comfort station near his corner. If I would undertake to compose the petitions and find the effective way of presenting them to City Hall, he proposed, he and his partners would undertake to have them printed, circulated and picked up. Soon the stores round about had comfort station removal petitions. Our street by now has many public experts on petition tactics, including the children.

Not only do public characters spread the news and learn the news at retail, so to speak. They connect with each other and thus spread word wholesale, in effect.

Jacobs detested the so-called improvements that Moses and other planners and developers made to New York City, as well as Boston, Seattle, and other big cities. (Later in her life, however, she praised Portland, Oregon's city center, with its balance of residents, retailers, sidewalks, and public transportation.) In her response to the short-sighted, traffic-oriented city planning of New York, she wrote at length about the importance of sidewalk public contact, which carries inestimable power in counteracting segregation and racial discrimination. A well-used street, according to Jacobs, is apt to be a safe street, where people meet and greet one another, quickly send important information over an extraordinary web of contacts, assimilate children into their daily lives (and therefore protect them), and naturally sustain a system of community surveillance. Wide sidewalks, city parks, small blocks, a mix of old and new buildings (which allows both commercial use and a socioeconomic diversity of tenants), and a concentration of people—including public characters—are the ingredients for a healthy city. Diversity of every kind—not replicable parks, monotonous highways, and a sweep of new buildings—is what continually nourishes city life.

Believing that cities should bring people and buildings together, not drive them apart, Jacobs galvanized the inhabitants of several neighborhoods, leading a successful opposition to Moses's proposed expressway through Washington Square in Greenwich Village. In doing so, Jacobs became the "public character" that she argued was so crucial to the life of any city. She used the sidewalk, storefronts, and other public spaces to become familiar to all Village residents as well as a conduit of information among them. Thus, Jacobs's theory of public space highlights a bottom-up, emergent system, which evolves from the ways inhabitants already use the space. Moses's system, on the other hand, is a top-down, planned system that requires people to rethink the ways they use public space.

Adina Levin
Ants and Jane Jacobs

In "Death and Life of American Cities," Jacobs writes about the lively, crowded, haphazard streets of her Greenwich Village neighborhood, and compares them to the planned high-rise developments and efficient elevated highways of her nemesis, developer Robert Moses.

In the 50s and 60s, developers like Moses swept into run-down urban neighborhoods bearing a vision of "cities of the future," demolished the houses and stores, and replaced them with sterile projects that turned into slums worse than the neighborhoods they replaced.

Jacobs explains why the organically grown neighborhoods are better than the planned developments. The variety of newer and older structures [helps] the neighborhood support a diverse population—elderly folks on pensions, young folks starting out, families with children. The mix of commercial and residential properties helps keep the neighborhood safe, since the neighborhood is populated day and night, weekdays and weekends. The sidewalks and front porches enable people to stroll, chat, and look out for each other. By contrast, the uninviting plazas and parking lots surrounding high-rise buildings are often deserts where the ill-intentioned can prey on the unwary without being observed.

Simply by observing local norms, people extend the neighborhood by inviting their elderly parents to move in, buying and upgrading a ramshackle storefront, and sweeping their walk. These activities aren't centrally planned, individuals don't get permission to do them, and, in sum, they add up to pleasant and safe neighborhoods.

But looking at Greenwich Village as an example of ant-like emergent behavior misses a lot of the story.

There is a large substrate of social and cultural structures that enable these unplanned activities to create a pleasing and diverse order. The neighborhood has sewers and clean running water. Without these, the city neighborhood would harbor endemic infectious diseases. There is a fire department which protects the block if a single house catches fire. There are people with the technical and project-management skills required to design and repair plumbing, heating, and electrical systems.

A colony of ants couldn't create Greenwich Village. Neither could a tribe of hunter-gatherers. There are underlying levels of infrastructure—some of which require planning—in order to enable the higher-level decentralized behavior.

In order to facilitate decentralized, unplanned human systems that work, it's important to think about the ordered infrastructure patterns—like sewer systems, and ordered nodal activities—like designing an electrical system—that are needed to enable the larger unplanned pattern to emerge.

> " . . . it's important to think about the ordered infrastructure patterns . . ."

ANALYZING THE RHETORICAL SITUATION

1. What is an emergent system, and how does it relate to the development of a city, town, or neighborhood? You may want to draw on your own hometown or neighborhood for examples.

2. What evidence do Robert Moses and Jane Jacobs provide that emergent systems are good or bad? Who is the audience for each of these excerpts?

3. What problem or exigence does Jacobs address? Who can resolve or effect the resolution of that problem?

4. What is Jacobs's proposal for resolving the problem? What action does she want her audience to take?

continued

5. How does Jacobs use ethos, pathos, and logos to build the argument in her proposal? (Provide textual evidence to support your answer.) On which of the rhetorical appeals does she most rely? Be prepared to share your answer with the rest of the class.

6. How does Jacobs evaluate the feasibility of her proposal in terms of the necessary time, money, and people? Provide textual evidence to support your answer.

7. What exigence prompted Adina Levin's response to Jacobs's theories? In what ways is Levin helping to develop the conversation about city planning?

COMMUNITY CONNECTIONS

1. Write for ten minutes about your response to Jacobs's opinions. How do her arguments coincide with or diverge from your experiences in a town or city you know well?

2. Now do the same for Moses: how do his arguments coincide with or diverge from your experiences in a town or city you know well?

3. Is it true that cities are built for traffic? Draw on your experience (as a driver or pedestrian) in cities you have inhabited or visited to support your answer.

4. What infrastructure can you identify in a town or city where you have lived? Who do you think planned it? Or was it unplanned?

5. Write for ten minutes about the causes or the consequences of the infrastructure you identified in question 4. Be prepared to share your response with the rest of the class.

6. Given your experiences, what is your definition of a livable city? What elements constitute that sort of city? What are the sources of those elements? Write for ten minutes and be prepared to share your answers.

Proposals: A Fitting Response

As the readings in this chapter illustrate, public spaces, by their very nature, are of concern to more than just the individuals involved in designing them. What the spaces allow or don't allow and whom they serve or exclude are issues that create a need for conversation. To consider such issues and set forth their own visions, many writers offer proposals, which can be distributed to the intended audience in a variety of ways.

Two proposals for Ground Zero

After the terrorist attacks of September 11, 2001, Ground Zero became one of the most famous public spaces in the world. The gaping hole, former site of the World Trade Center, was an eyesore, to be sure. Worse than that, it was a constant reminder of horror, not only on the day both towers collapsed but also on the day of the bombings some eight years earlier. Private citizens and civic leaders quickly agreed that the crater in lower Manhattan was a problem calling for a solution. In other words, Ground Zero presented an exigence.

Agreeing that the site provided a problem was easy; agreeing on exactly what to do about that problem took longer. After extensive deliberation, the people of New York City decided to take specific action, to erect a memorial on the site that would meet four basic requirements: recognize each individual who was a victim of the attacks, provide space for contemplation, create a unique and powerful setting, and convey historic authenticity. In addition to honoring the dead (in lower Manhattan, Washington DC, and Shanksville, Pennsylvania) and the grieving, the memorial was also to celebrate heroism, international compassion, and the enduring values of democracy—"without establishing any hierarchies." The memorial's design would be chosen from proposals submitted to judges who would decide which was most appropriate.

Michael Arad and Peter Walker's proposal, "Reflecting Absence," was one of eight finalists, ultimately winning the competition. As you read their proposal, notice the ways in which they address each element of their rhetorical situation: exigence, audience, purpose, fitting response, and available means. Notice, too, how they meet the requirements of any proposal: they (1) define the problem and the solution; (2) supply convincing arguments to support their design; (3) account for the feasibility of their design (a more detailed feasibility report accompanies the final plan); and (4) defend their proposal from potential objections.

Artist's rendering of World Trade Center Memorial.

Michael Arad and Peter Walker

Reflecting Absence

This memorial proposes a space that resonates with the feelings of loss and absence that were generated by the destruction of the World Trade Center and the taking of thousands of lives on September 11, 2001 and February 26, 1993. [1] It is located in a field of trees that is interrupted by two large voids containing recessed pools. The pools and the ramps that surround them encompass the footprints of the twin towers. A cascade of water that describes the perimeter of each square feeds the pools with a continuous stream. They are large voids, open and visible reminders of the absence.

The surface of the memorial plaza is punctuated by the linear rhythms of rows of deciduous trees, forming informal clusters, clearings and groves. This surface consists of a composition of stone pavers, plantings and low ground cover. Through its annual cycle of rebirth, the living park extends and deepens the experience of the memorial.

Bordering each pool is a pair of ramps that lead down to the memorial spaces. Descending into the memorial, visitors are removed from the sights and sounds of the city and immersed in a cool darkness. [2] As they proceed, the sound of water falling grows louder, and more daylight filters in from below. At the bottom of their descent, they find themselves behind a thin curtain of water, staring out at an enormous pool. Surrounding this pool is a continuous ribbon of names. The enormity of this space and the multitude of names that form this endless ribbon underscore the vast scope of the destruction. Standing there at the water's edge, looking at a pool of water that is flowing away into an abyss, a visitor to the site can sense that what is beyond this curtain of water and ribbon of names is inaccessible. [3]

The names of the deceased will be arranged in no particular order around the pools. After carefully considering different arrangements, I have found that any arrangement that tries to impose meaning through physical adjacency will cause grief and anguish to people who might be excluded from that process, furthering the sense of loss that they are already suffering. [4]

The haphazard brutality of the attacks is reflected in the arrangement of names, and no attempt is made to impose order upon this suffering. The selfless sacrifices of rescue workers could be acknowledged with their agency's insignia next to their names. Visitors to the site, including family members and friends of the deceased, would be guided by on-site staff or a printed directory to the specific location of each name. For those whose deceased were never physically identified, the location of the name marks a spot that is their own.

In between the two pools is a short passageway that links them at this lower level. A single alcove is located along this passageway, containing a small dais where visitors can light a candle or leave an artifact in memory of loved ones. Across from it, in a small chamber, visitors might pause and contemplate. This space provides for gatherings, quiet reflection, and memorial services.

Along the western edge of the site, a deep fissure exposes the slurry wall from plaza level to bedrock and provides access via a stairway. Descending alongside its battered surfaces, visitors will witness the massive expanse of the original foundations. The entrance to the underground interpretive center is

[1] The problem—how to honor the grief and loss of life surrounding these two historic days—is stated.

[2] Here Arad and Walker are aware of multiple audiences: the people who will visit and interact with the World Trade Center Memorial *and* the panel of judges.

[3] In this paragraph, Arad and Walker respond directly to the primary audience of judges and the memorial guidelines published by the Lower Manhattan Development Committee—an important element of the rhetorical situation for this proposal—by indicating how their design will encourage quiet reflection while reflecting the enormity of the losses.

[4] In anticipation of possible objections to their plan of listing victims' names randomly, Arad and Walker argue that alternative arrangements of the names in a purposeful pattern or order might cause hurt to some families and survivors. Their random arrangement is in keeping with the memorial guidelines, which caution against hierarchies.

located at bedrock. Here visitors could view many preserved artifacts from the twin towers: twisted steel beams, a crushed fire truck, and personal effects. The underground interpretive center would contain exhibition areas as well as lecture halls and a research library. [5]

In contrast with the public mandate of the underground interpretive center is the very private nature of the room for unidentified remains. It is situated at bedrock at the north tower footprint. Here a large stone vessel forms a centerpiece for the unidentified remains. A large opening in the ceiling connects this space to the sky above, and the sound of water shelters the space from the city. Family members can gather here for moments of private contemplation. It is a personal space for remembrance.

The memorial plaza is designed to be a mediating space; it belongs both to the city and to the memorial. Located at street level to allow for its integration into the fabric of the city, the plaza encourages the use of this space by New Yorkers on a daily basis. The memorial grounds will not be isolated from the rest of the city; they will be a living part of it.

[5] These final paragraphs provide essential information addressing the challenges of memorializing the World Trade Center victims—and the feasibility of the design.

Paula Deitz responded to Arad and Walker's design, along with the other finalists' designs. Using the medium of a newspaper editorial, Deitz identified a problem with all of the designs and proposed a Memorial Hall, rather than another kind of space.

Paula Deitz

A More Civic Response to Loss

During a midday break in jury duty last week, I joined the stream of New Yorkers and out-of-town visitors heading for the exhibition in the Winter Garden of the World Financial Center of the eight proposed memorials for the World Trade Center site. [1] As I jostled for position around the models and the showcased visuals, I found that despite the crowds I could concentrate to the point of imagining myself in those cavernous underground spaces under the vast plaza encompassing the accentuated footprints of the Twin Towers. [2] I had two immediate reactions: One, I would be afraid to descend alone into cold empty corridors two levels down; and secondly, I observed that the windswept urban spaces that once eddied around the towers would remain as a permanent problem. Furthermore, water basins that would stay empty all winter and football-field sized lawns or gardens that would thrive only in season would add to the desolation of the site in cold weather.

But even more regrettable is the misconceived notion that these memorials should cater to private loss as if the rest of us—the public—do not share in the tragic aftermath of the terrorist attack. [3] Throughout American history, cities and towns have traditionally responded to such horrors as war by honoring their dead with a public display of individual names on plaques or monuments in central squares, community recognition of those "gone but not forgotten," a comforting message to the grieving families. When this custom reached its dignified apotheosis in Maya Lin's Vietnam Veterans Memorial, the site took on

[1] Immediately, Deitz refers to her rhetorical audience: New Yorkers and out-of-town visitors, the people who will visit the memorial.

[2] By becoming one with her audience, Deitz presumes that her experience and her assessment are the same as theirs.

[3] Deitz seems unaware of the memorial guidelines, which call for encouraging "reflection and contemplation."

a more private nature as a gathering place for mourners who felt isolated from communities because they had lost their loved ones in an unpopular war. The World Trade Center memorial proposals, as promoted by New York's memorial lobby, are all descendants of Maya Lin's work, and, I suspect that in this case the families themselves do not wish their private griefs to be forgotten.

A grander response is required that will fulfill the expectations not only of the families but of the nation, and not only of the nation but of the international community that is drawn daily to this site to pay its respects—something more than just an aimless wander through cold underground spaces. [4] There is an obvious answer, I believe: the Memorial Hall, a building of stunning architectural presence combining the functions of a performing arts center with those of a great civic auditorium for public ceremonies.

This is an original American building form. [5] Unlike the sprawling performance arts centers that succeeded them, memorial buildings were designed as civic auditoriums for a combination of uses. Part meeting house, part theater, they serve as a civilizing cultural force in the community with an architectural importance akin to that of museums, courthouses, and city halls. Anyone who has walked around Harvard University knows the weight on campus of the soaring Gothic architecture of Memorial Hall, designed in the late 1860s by Ware and Van Brunt to commemorate Harvard's Civil War dead. Henry James devoted several pages of "The Bostonians" to this "big building with the beautiful pinnacles, which you see from every point." He admired the vast refectory dining hall and the lecture and performance theater, a paneled and polychromed 1,200-seat [space] that is a venue today of the Boston Philharmonic Orchestra.

San Francisco's War Memorial and Performing Arts center, proposed after World War I, is a configuration of twin buildings, the War Memorial Opera House and the Veterans Building, designed by Arthur Brown, Jr., with G. Albert Lansburgh, in a French Renaissance style that harmonizes with the neighboring City Hall and its surrounding Beaux-Arts Civic Center. While the opera house is the permanent home of the San Francisco Opera and the San Francisco Ballet, the great stage also provided the setting for the founding of the United Nations in June 1945 when President Truman and other statesmen signed the United Nations Charter there. An actual Memorial Hall with mementos of the two World Wars is housed within the Veterans Building.

And closer at hand is Trenton's gracious War Memorial building completed in 1932 in a neo-Italian Renaissance and Art Deco style designed by Louis S. Kaplan from a preliminary plan by William A. Klemann. Early ballets by George Balanchine were performed there in the 1940s, and there is still a resident opera company and symphony. But New Jersey's gubernatorial inaugurations also take place in the 1,800-seat auditorium, as do graduation ceremonies, and in 1960 John F. Kennedy stood between the Ionic columns of its portico in an autumnal twilight and gave a stirring campaign address to thousands standing in the plaza below against a view of the Delaware River flowing in the background. [6]

A Memorial Hall at the World Trade Center site would be a dramatic and significant addition without altering the ongoing planning process since the space is already allotted for a memorial. [7] In addition, performance groups and

Situations for Writers

[4] Deitz has identified a problem (none of the proposed designs are adequate) and offers her own solution: a Memorial Hall, which offers solace to private mourners, sympathizers, and local and international visitors.

[5] According to Deitz, the public memorial hall has a rich history. She provides three distinguished examples of such halls, using them as convincing supporting arguments for her proposal.

[6] By noting the wide range of artistic, governmental, and community activities occurring in other memorial halls, Deitz supports her claim that a building of this type would "fulfill the expectations" of the many different groups interested in using this public space.

[7] In her concluding paragraph, Deitz addresses the feasibility of her proposal. The city has already set aside memorial space, various artistic groups are interested in renting space in the location, and a building dedicated to "shared cultural experiences and civic ceremonies" would be a more fitting tribute to the dead and the survivors.

arts organizations are already seeking a downtown presence. It is understandable that the city should choose not to construct another office tower on the site, but a building that would honor the dead through shared cultural experiences and civic ceremonies would be a constant and meaningful tribute to those whom we all as survivors hold most dear. And, yes, the names would be there, too, inscribed in legible bands on the walls of the public corridors, not isolated underground, but in the mainstream of community life. [8]

[8] Finally, Deitz assures her audience that the names of the dead would be memorialized, in the spirit of all fitting memorials, and makes one final distinction between her proposal and the others.

The preceding proposals demonstrate two different solutions to the problem of what to do to memorialize the victims of September 11, 2001. Both proposals identified a problem, though each defined that problem differently. Both proposals addressed an audience; both described a solution and enumerated good reasons for its feasibility; and both anticipated objections and questions by defending features of the proposal.

WHAT MAKES IT A PROPOSAL?

The following questions are ones you should consider when thinking critically about any proposal. For now, try applying them to the proposals by Michael Arad and Peter Walker and by Paula Deitz to determine how closely these writers followed the conventions for proposals.

1. Does the writer define the problem in such a way that others will recognize it as a problem? Is the problem one that affects people other than the writer?

2. Does the description of the problem have an impact on the solution offered by the writer? Does it affect how the writer deals with objections and practical concerns?

3. Has the writer demonstrated a good understanding of how the problem affects the audience and other people and of how people will be affected by the solution?

4. Does the solution seem feasible?

5. What does the solution ask of the audience? Is the requested action explicit or merely implied?

Understanding the Rhetorical Situation

Identifying an exigence

In her proposal for a Memorial Hall at the former site of the World Trade Center, Paula Deitz articulates two main objections to the chosen design: it could be unsafe for individuals visiting alone, and it focuses too much on personal, rather than community, grief. Deitz's objections stem from her desire to make the memorial accessible and meaningful to as many people as possible. Her proposal, then, suggests how that could be done.

Consider some public spaces you know: the mall, the campus, a local park, a town square, a suburban green belt, a public library, a parking lot, a train or bus station. Are any of these spaces a site of contention among different groups? Are any of them used in ways the planners likely did not intend? Are some "misuses" more acceptable than others? Are any of the public spaces underused as the result of poor design, limited accessibility, or lack of publicity? You might observe skateboarders practicing their stunts on the walkways surrounding the local courthouse, for example. Does their practice interfere with pedestrians? Do the skateboarders have access to other practice spots? Is the city or town liable for injuries, to either the skateboarders or pedestrians?

Questions like these help you identify an exigence for your writing. As you consider the public spaces familiar to you, think about the experiences you have had there. Perhaps you have witnessed skateboarders—or some other group of people—being asked to stop what they are doing or to leave. Maybe you have felt unsafe in a particular space at particular times of the day or night. Or maybe you have had a wonderful experience, and you want others to be able to enjoy it, too.

1. Make a list of public spaces with which you are familiar. For each space, list the experiences you have had there. If the experiences were positive, explain why, providing as many details as possible. If anything could have made the experiences better, explain how. If the experiences were negative, describe the factors that made them difficult or unpleasant. Write down as many contributing factors as you can: the shape of the space, the number of people in the space, the posted rules for the space, and so forth.
2. Choosing one or two of the spaces you've listed, sketch pictures of the location(s), with labels that name and describe key features. Or take photos of the location(s) from various vantage points, paying particular attention to the features you find most intriguing.
3. Choose the public space you would like to write about and compose four or five descriptions of a problem you see in the space. Vary the ways you describe the problem. For example, one description might emphasize one group of people who are affected by the problem, and another might emphasize a different group. Another description might focus on the physi-

cal dimensions of the space, and yet another might identify uses the space seems to promote or prohibit.

Locating an audience

For their proposal for the WTC memorial, Michael Arad and Peter Walker had to consider two audiences: the judges who would choose the winning proposal and the people who would eventually visit the memorial. The structure and language of their proposal, then, conformed to the guidelines established by the judges, while their design also considered the social and personal concerns of the public.

What audience should you consider for your proposal? First, you have to determine who is in the best position to help you resolve the problem you've defined. Then, you need to consider how to make that audience concerned enough about the problem to consider your solution. For instance, if you think your town needs a skatepark, you'll need to find out what government agencies or officials make decisions about park space. Once you have that information, you'll consider how you can present the problem you've identified—lack of a public skate park—to this audience.

The following questions can help you locate your rhetorical audience as well as identify the relationship they have to the problem you've identified. Then, you'll be able to choose the best way to describe that problem.

1. List the names of the persons or groups who are in the best position to help with your problem. This step may require some research and some legwork.
2. Next to the name of each potential audience, write reasons that audience could have for acknowledging the existence of your problem. In other words, what would persuade these audiences that something needs to change?
3. What actions could these audiences reasonably be persuaded to perform? In other words, consider what each audience would be able to do to address the problem.
4. With your audience's interests and capabilities in mind, look again at the descriptions of the problem that you composed in the preceding section on identifying an exigence. Decide which description will best help your audience feel connected to the public space in question and invested in improving it. At this point, it may be necessary to revise your best description to tailor it to your audience.

Identifying a Fitting Response

Finding a purpose and shaping a fitting response

You have explored features of a public space with which you are well familiar. You have identified a problem with the design or use of that public space, and you have considered who makes up your audience and how they might help solve the problem. But what do you want to accomplish with your writing? How could your writing help bring about the change you want to see? Answering these questions should provide you with your purpose, which in turn will inform the specific kind of text you create.

Identifying a problem and getting others to recognize it as a problem is only the beginning of your response to your rhetorical situation. You also need to identify and support a suitable solution to the problem. Your solution should consider the information you gathered about your audience, such as the limitations of their position. It should also be feasible in the sense that it provides an efficient and cost-effective way to go about making a positive change.

As you know, different purposes and different audiences require different kinds of texts. For example, if a local shopping center doesn't provide enough accessible parking spaces for patrons with disabilities, you might write a letter of complaint to the owner. The threatened closing of a favorite coffee shop to make way for a chain restaurant might prompt a narrative essay that describes your experiences at the old hangout and evokes feelings of nostalgia in readers. Neither of these situations calls for the kind of extended, formal proposal that Arad and Walker submitted for the Ground Zero memorial. The point is that once you identify your problem (exigence), audience, and purpose, you need to determine what kind of text will best respond to your rhetorical situation.

Use the following questions to help you narrow your purpose and shape your response:

1. How would you efficiently and effectively solve the problem you've identified?
2. What would this solution require of your audience?
3. Are you asking your audience simply to support your solution or to perform a particular action?
4. What is the best way to reach this audience? That is, what kind of text is this audience most likely to respond to?

Considering your proposal's acceptability and feasibility

The next step has to do with two concepts that are particularly important to proposals: acceptability and feasibility. Audiences are more likely to be persuaded by solutions that make responsible use of resources and that benefit some group rather than just a few individuals. Once you have identified and defined the problem for a particular audience, one that can affect the resolution of the problem by showing support or giving permission or by working on the solution, you can begin to consider the acceptability and feasibility of your proposal.

1. What resources—time, money, and human effort—are needed to accomplish the solution you're proposing? Write about each of these needs separately: time, money, and human effort.
2. What positive consequences will follow from your proposed solution? List them.
3. What examples can you provide of other instances where your proposed solution (or a similar one) has had positive results?
4. What logistical challenges does your solution face? List them.
5. What can be done to address each of these challenges?

Your instructor (or your rhetorical situation) may prompt you to write a letter or a narrative or some other form of written response. Rupali Kumar, the student whose proposal for creating a play area at her temple appears on pages 273–278, might have decided to write a letter to an appropriate person or committee in response to the child's accident that was her exigence. Given her rhetorical context, she also could have composed a prayer for the child's speedy recovery. But, as she notes, the accident pointed to a larger problem—one that affected all members of the temple community. After thinking about possible solutions and their feasibility, she decided to write a proposal that presented a specific plan and described its advantages. If, like Rupali, you are prompted to write a proposal, use the following assignment as a guide.

Writing a Proposal: Working with Your Available Means

Shaping your proposal

As you have probably figured out, a proposal is arranged much like an argument. The introduction provides enough background information to describe and define the problem (perhaps in terms of its causes or consequences), states your thesis, which conveys the essence of your proposed solution, and establishes your ethos. Paula Deitz, for example, opens her proposal for a memorial hall with her personal response to the design by Arad and Walker. In so doing, she voices the concerns of the secondary audience for Arad and Walker's proposal—the public—thereby establishing common ground with her readers. She then explains how the proposed WTC memorial carries on a tradition started with the Vietnam Memorial, the elevation of private, individual grief over that of the community. She is establishing her good will, good sense, and good moral character (essential features of ethos). Once her concerns for safety and community are articulated, she can offer her solution: "the Memorial Hall, a building of stunning architectural presence combining the functions of a performing arts center with those of a great civic auditorium for public ceremonies." Every sentence in her introduction helps build her ethos.

The body of a proposal provides supporting evidence for your proposed solution, particularly in terms of its consequences or results. The shape and content of your overall argument help establish your logos. In her proposal, Deitz describes memorial halls built in Boston, San Francisco, and Trenton. She does so to establish precedent through the use of examples and to emphasize the combination of symbolism and usefulness offered by these halls. By explaining the roles these buildings still play in the civic lives of their cities, Deitz encourages her readers to imagine the benefits of such a place at the WTC site.

In addition, the body accounts for the feasibility of the proposed solution in terms of time, money, and human effort. In other words, what resources are necessary for implementing your solution? What needs to be done first, second, and next? How much time will it take? How much will it cost? Who needs to do what? And when?

The body of a proposal also acknowledges possible objections and criticisms (whether they have to do with the disadvantages of your solution, the superiority of another alternative, or the costs) by including a point-by-point defense of the solution. Successful proposals often discuss trade-offs in this section. Arad and Walker, for example, use the body of their proposal to discuss their decision to place the names of the dead in no particular order around the memorial. Using the rhetorical method of comparing and contrasting, they tell why they do not want to use some traditional system for organizing the names (such as alphabetical or by affiliation)—because it would create a type of social hierarchy, one in which certain groups of people appeared "more important" than other groups. Thus, their solution trades convenience for egalitarianism. Although people looking for a particular name will have to consult a directory, the memorial establishes the victims' identities as human beings first and foremost.

Finally, the conclusion of a proposal predicts the positive consequences or improvements that will result from the proposed solution. Also, it's in the conclusion that you'll want to make an emotional connection with your audience, using the rhetorical appeal of pathos. Your goal is to identify your solution with the interests of your audience. In her conclusion, Deitz notes the need for a downtown cultural center in New York City and argues that the memorial hall would provide a home for "performance groups and arts organizations." She concludes that "a building that would honor the dead through shared cultural experiences and civic ceremonies would be a constant and meaningful tribute to those whom we all as survivors hold most dear." This claim speaks to her audience's desire that the dead not be forgotten, connecting her proposed solution with the interests of her audience. In her conclusion, Deitz has established pathos.

Many successful proposals include visuals. As you consider your available means, you may want to think about whether a visual or two will strengthen your argument. Consider sketching what the public space will look like after the improvement you're proposing. Graphs and charts that lay out expenses can demonstrate that you've done your research and can provide readers with a better sense of what will be expected of them or the community.

CHECKING OVER A PROPOSAL

✓ There is a clear, identifiable problem that the proposal seeks to resolve.
✓ This problem is of concern to a significant number of people.
✓ The proposed solution will resolve the problem in a way these people will find acceptable.
✓ The proposal contains specific details about the costs and benefits of the solution.
✓ The proposal is directed to the appropriate audience and demonstrates a good understanding of that audience's needs and interests.
✓ The proposal clearly explains the steps or processes required to enact the solution.

Student paper

In the following essay, student writer Rupali Kumar proposes specific improvements to the Sri Venkateswara Temple.

Rupali Kumar

Professor Enoch

English 215

29 February 2007

Baal Leela[1]

It is quite common to see Srinivas Charyulu, the very lively and animated son of our priest, running around in the Sri Venkateswara Temple (SVT) parking lot. Surely he has to expend his abundance of energy somehow! However, things took an unfortunate turn last year, when the five-year-old collided with a parked car at his top speed. The sight of tiny Srinivas in a full-leg cast is one that the temple community will not soon forget.

Srinivas's case is not an isolated one. Our temple is regularly filled with dozens of equally active children. When these small devotees are not busy in music lessons or Sunday school, they are naturally inclined to play. Inside of the SVT, I often see kids tossing footballs in the small auditorium, chasing each other through the halls, and congregating in the coat closet. When it suits them, they venture outside to engage in parking lot Frisbee games and snowball fights on unfenced hills overlooking the road.

And naturally, the children's behavior is a source of constant tension for the parents and other adults. Some complain that the kids are treating the temple as their playground; they are being too noisy, congesting the halls, breaking ceiling tiles, denting cars with their Frisbees, and disrupting prayer

Guide to Responding

services and important meetings. Most of all, many adults fear that children will suffer injuries like Srinivas's, or worse.

Therefore, many of the temple's adults are of the opinion that the children must be controlled. To prevent ruckus and injury in the temple, they believe that children's wild behavior must be stopped. They argue that parents ought to be more responsible and force their children to sit quietly, because after all, the temple is a place to pray, not a place to play.

I respectfully disagree with this opinion. Anyone well-acquainted with Sri Venkateswara Temple knows that it is more than merely a place to pray. It is a center for social interaction and therefore should allow for interaction among children as well as adults. Furthermore, it is as difficult as it is inappropriate to prohibit children from playing. In my experience with the SVT children, most of them equate being at the temple with having fun with their friends. Attempts to force children to behave contrary to their playful nature are usually unsuccessful. Thus, such an approach is ineffective in stopping the incidence of disruption and injury.

In its place, I propose an alternative solution: the creation of designated recreational areas for children in and outside of the temple. First, a portion of the temple's outdoor property must be designated for children to play on. Ideally, this area should be distant enough from the temple building to prevent children from breaking windows, yet close enough to be conveniently accessible from the building. It should be distant enough from the parking lot to prevent children from interfering with traffic flow, damaging cars, or having accidents like Srinivas's. Furthermore, this area should be fenced in or otherwise contained to avoid accidents such as those that might occur on the unfenced hills that the children currently play on.

Taking into account these factors, I find that the best place for this outdoor play area would be the region currently known as the Lower Parking Lot. The loss of those few parking spaces is sufficiently counterbalanced by the ample space in the newly constructed Upper Parking Lot. Because it is at a lower elevation, the Lower Parking Lot is set apart from the main parking lot and traffic artery while being sufficiently close to the building. The region can easily be fenced in for added security. Part of this outdoor play area could be a spacious field designated for the popular pastimes of Frisbee and football. Another part could contain safe playground equipment selected to appeal to the children's preferences.

Fig. 1. Proposed space for outdoor play area (photograph by the author).

For those times of year when Pittsburgh weather makes it unfavorable to be outdoors, an indoor children's recreational space must be designated. Such a room should be reasonably spacious to allow children to run around freely. Furthermore, the room's sole purpose should be for children to play in it. This will prevent children from playing in other places and disrupting temple happenings.

In light of recent construction developments, the creation of a children's recreational room in the body of the temple is highly feasible. New space is being added onto the building with the recently initiated Kitchen Annex Project. This project, as advertised in the temple calendar, aims to create a "modern kitchen and dining facility," a "community hall" for devotee use, and "classrooms for youth education" (*Sri Venkateswara Temple Calendar*). While all of these grand improvements to the temple are being made, the problem of inadequate safe play space can finally be solved by including a carefully designed recreational area in the final blueprint.

Once the necessity and clear benefits of creating indoor and outdoor play areas are recognized by the members of the SVT, we will need to undergo a meticulous planning process to ensure the best results. Volunteers dedicated to this project must join to form a special committee. This committee will obtain input from the temple's administrative chairs, especially the Construction Committee members, as well as parents and children. Suggestions for the play areas, regarding such details as layout, types of play equipment present, safety precautions, and supervision must be gathered, along with ample donations.

The committee's main task will be to integrate the collected input into a detailed blueprint of both recreational areas. The next step, for which community participation will also be necessary, will be to construct the recreational areas. Volunteers could be employed to do some of the work, while construction firms, perhaps including the one currently working on the Kitchen Annex Project, can be employed for more difficult tasks.

Creating areas solely for children to play in, both indoors and outdoors, will prove exceedingly beneficial to the temple community. It will give respect and approval to children interacting in their natural, playful manner. It will reduce playing children's disturbance of other temple activities. Finally, it will save children from Srinivas's fate of getting hurt playing in areas not designed for playing. With the collaborated enthusiasm and efforts of all of the temple's devotees, the most fitting play areas for our purposes can be designed and built.

It has been over a year since Srinivas's accident, and it is still common to stumble across the priest's lively little son, along with dozens of kids like him, as they dart through the halls and driveways of Sri Venkateswara Temple. Nothing has changed. Nothing is being accomplished by those who point fingers at parents for failing to suppress children's natural playful tendencies, or those who stubbornly declare playing inappropriate at the social interaction center that is our temple. Instead, disentangling ourselves from the unproductive web of petty arguments, we must collectively redirect our focus onto creating play areas for the welfare of the temple community and its children.

Note

[1]Baal Leela refers to the delightful childhood nature of Lord Krishna, one of the human incarnations of the Hindu deity Vishnu (also known as Sri Venkateswara, the presiding deity of this temple). Accounts of Krishna's childhood always mention his endearing mischief and playful nature as a child. Thus, in our faith, God has shown by example that it is children's nature and duty to be playful.

Work Cited

Sri Venkateswara Temple Calendar. Etna, PA: Schiff Printing, 2006. Print.

Situations for Writers

If your rhetorical situation does not call for a proposal like Rupali Kumar's you can consider the following other options.

ALTERNATIVE ASSIGNMENTS

1. In a public space that is familiar to you, what uses emerged, from the bottom up? Which uses were planned, from the top down? In an essay of three to four pages, describe a familiar public space in terms of its use. Various rhetorical methods of development—process analysis, comparison and contrast, cause and consequence analysis, exemplification, classification and division—may help you conceptualize and then arrange your essay.

2. Pioneer Courthouse Square in Portland, Oregon, is considered a successful example of a planned public space, with its recurring activities (flower and fashion shows, musical events), inviting amenities (public art, flowers, trees), easy access (by foot, light rail, city bus, or automobile), and comfort (comfortable seating was incorporated in the architecture itself). Identify a public space—on campus or in your community—and in an essay of three to four pages evaluate it in relation to Pioneer Courthouse Square or according to criteria of your own (function, identity or character, arrangement, access and circulation, seating, environment, food and drink, and so on). Be sure to specify the criteria on which you're basing your evaluation. As you write, consider your audience (who may or may not share your ideas about criteria), your purpose (which should align with your audience), and the constraints and resources of your rhetorical situation.

3. Consider a public space that you know well. Analyze how the space brings people together, keeps them apart, or otherwise controls how they interact. Along with this process analysis, determine whether some groups of people are encouraged to or discouraged from interacting in this space. Draft an essay of three to four pages, making certain to consider exigence, audience, purpose, constraints and resources, and available means.

9 EVALUATING VISUAL CULTURE: RESPONDING WITH CRITICAL REVIEWS

It's more than likely that your first introduction to the college or university where you're now studying came through a brochure, a booklet, or a Web site describing the school's programs, its student body, and campus life. Prospective students who visited the Web site of Colorado State University recently, for example, saw two photos of the library, which create a visual narrative highlighting the community's resilience. The inviting scene above those photos provides further evidence of a vibrant campus that has fully recovered from a natural disaster.

Students considering Lewis & Clark College in Portland, Oregon, can scroll through a host of photos and student blogs that depict "Real Life at Lewis & Clark College." Showing images of real students and presenting their accounts of college life may persuade viewers that Lewis & Clark College is the place for them to pursue their undergraduate career.

Web pages such as these—in addition to the countless brochures and pamphlets published in order to stimulate recruitment—are a means by which colleges and universities craft a recruitment message to send to prospective students and their parents. Each school wants potential students to appreciate all the available opportunities and imagine themselves as successful and satisfied at that particular school. When you were a prospective student, it was up to you to decide how you were going to evaluate these highly visual messages. As your evaluation, you explained your assessment of various schools and the criteria on which you based your assessment anytime someone asked you why you chose the one school you did.

Evaluations—spoken or written texts that argue whether something meets a particular set of criteria—are particularly useful for understanding how well individuals and groups portray themselves visually and what kinds of decisions readers or viewers make in response to that portrayal. Evaluations consider such questions as the following: What is the immediate overall effect of the visual? What are the specific parts of the visual? How are these parts pieced together? What is the overall effectiveness of the visual? These are the types of questions you will be asking and responding to in this chapter, questions that lead not only to detailed evaluations of visual images but also to thoughtful analysis of how the visual culture in which we are increasingly immersed shapes our society, often in new ways.

Real Situations

Now that you are on campus, of course, you are immersed in a sea of visual images, some that are portrayed in the official brochures, and some that are not. On your walk to class, you may step over chalk drawings urging you to attend an upcoming lecture or pass by fliers urging you to participate in an upcoming Critical Mass bike ride. While visiting your friend's dorm room, you may spend a few moments looking at the posters of abstract art or the hundreds of photos of her family and friends that she has scattered over every available inch of wall space. And, when eating lunch at the student union, you may have glanced at posters encouraging you to sell your chemistry textbook back to the bookstore during finals week. You may read advertisements in the student newspaper persuading you to spend your hard-earned money on dinner-and-drink specials at restaurants in town. All of these kinds of visual texts use images as a means of capturing a particular mood, delivering a specific message, or provoking a specific action.

As personal computers play an increasingly central role in our leisure time, we become ever more enmeshed in a world of visual images and multimedia. Many students present themselves through a careful construction of photos, videos, and text on a personal blog or sites such as Facebook and MySpace. More students than ever before read about and watch the news on visually rich online magazines and newspapers, such as Salon.com, FoxNews.com, and Yahoo! News. All of these offer visually intense environments, with photos and text situated alongside colorful banner ads, animated graphics, and links to sponsors' Web sites. And, in addition to participating in online courses, students are viewing online slideshows for Art Appreciation 101 or creating and editing a course wiki.

Fliers like this one are among the many visuals competing for attention on college campuses.

Pittsburgh Critical Mass

Who?
You and other Pittsburgh cyclists

What?
An easy group ride through senic Pittsburgh

When?
The last Friday of each month, meet at 5:00, ride at 5:30. Arrive before 5:30.

Where?
By the dinosaur by the Oakland Carnegie Library, across from the Pitt Student Union

More Info
http://www.pghcriticalmass.org

Why?
Why, indeed?
We're not an orgnaization, we're just a bunch of people who like to ride. There's no party line. Some reasons that people might want to ride in Critical Mass include:
· Raising the profile of cycling in Pittsburgh
· Campaigning for better provisions for cyclists
· Creating a car-free space in the center of our city
· Having fun
· Riding in safety
· Meeting friends
· Getting back at the drivers
· Showing off our flashy new bikes and clothes
· Creating a vision and experience of a possible better future

Many dorm rooms are visual presentations of students' interests and self-image.

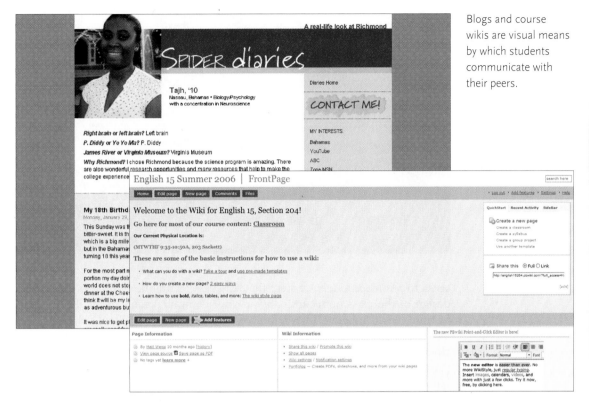

The ways in which you and your fellow students experience visual culture do not end with the more obvious forms of photographs, posters, advertisements, Web pages, and movies. The visual design of the buildings, green spaces, and monuments creates a particular atmosphere on your college or university campus. For example, the prominent Bonfire Memorial at Texas A&M University

The Bonfire Memorial at Texas A&M University.

A redesigned digital writing classroom at Stanford University allows for effective collaboration.

seeks to reinforce a deep respect for that school's unique traditions. The visual design of the classrooms and labs on your campus creates particular types of learning environments. The digital writing classrooms at Stanford University have been redesigned to foster collaboration and innovation, with computers clustered in groups of three to enable students to work on writing projects in teams. And the visual design of the chairs, tables, lights, and bookshelves in the Humanities Reading Room in Penn State University's Pattee Library creates a comfortable space in which students and faculty members are invited to focus their energy on their individual reading and writing projects.

If you look around your own campus, you'll see an environment rich in visuals. Whether or not you have thought much about it, living within this visual culture shapes the ways you seek and communicate information every day. Charles A. Hill, a professor of rhetoric and writing at the University of Wisconsin, Oshkosh, describes the effects in this way:

> [T]he students now entering our classrooms have grown up with one hundred channels of television, and the World Wide Web is no longer a novelty, but part of their social, academic, and working lives. If we include nonelectronic sources of visual communication such as billboards, print advertisements, and the ubiquitous packaging that has taken such an important place in our consumer culture, then we have to conclude that most of the information our students are exposed to is in a visual form.

For Hill, this high level of immersion in an increasingly visual culture calls for both teachers and students to know how to read what images communicate.

DESCRIBING VISUALS ON CAMPUS

1. Choose two of the photographs in this section of the chapter and list the specific details you notice about the images—for example, the way objects (people and furniture) are arranged, the lighting, or a contrast in color or sizes. Be prepared to share your answers with the rest of the class.

Humanities Reading Room in Penn State University's Pattee Library.

2. Who do you imagine designed the spaces or arranged the objects? Who produced the images themselves?

3. What might be the rhetorical audience and purpose for each image?

4. What adjectives come to mind when you consider these images? Which of the details that you used to answer question 1 illustrate each of those adjectives?

5. Translate the purposes, adjectives, and details into a single statement about each of the images. Then compose a list of criteria by which you might best evaluate each image. Be prepared to share your statement and list with the rest of the class.

COMMUNITY CONNECTIONS

1. Look again at the photographs in this section. Which of them represents a designed space or object that is familiar to you? Which ones are unfamiliar? How do you ordinarily interact with that familiar scene or object? How might you interact with the unfamiliar ones?

2. What kinds of images or designed spaces do you encounter in your everyday life? What details constitute these images or designs? How do you interact with or respond to these images or designs? Be prepared to share your answers with the rest of the class.

3. Which of the images in this section do you find especially interesting? Which ones would stimulate you to look twice or think more deeply were you to pass them on your way across campus?

4. What kinds of words would you use to describe the especially stimulating images? What specific details prompt you to think about these images in this particular way?

5. How would you describe the ways these images make you feel or the thoughts they prompt?

Real Responses to Real Situations

There is no question that visual media such as television and movies are popular, as well as being multimillion-dollar industries. In fact, this form of entertainment is the second-largest U.S. export. The United States produces an impressive variety of visual entertainment in the form of Hollywood and "indie" movies, music videos, and computer games. In 2004, the average American watched more than two thousand hours of filmed entertainment.

Thus, one good way to explore visual culture in this country is to consider one of its most common forms: movies. The evaluation of movies in the United States is a mini-industry itself. We rely on the professional assessments of Roger Ebert and Gene Shalit, on publications such as *Entertainment Weekly* and Web sites such as rottentomatoes.com, and on the regular columns in our local and school newspapers. Every day, we have easy access to evaluations of this part of our visual culture—even though we don't always think in these terms when we search online for movie reviews or read an opinion piece about the latest crop of action films.

A reasonable and insightful movie evaluation includes judgments about overall quality, strengths and weaknesses, cast, setting, and technical features. In addition, a good evaluation might include a consideration of the cultural referents of the film, such as costumes or historical references in the movie's plot line. Whatever the reviewer argues, it is paramount that he or she supply specific evidence to support that claim (for example, that a movie is ground-breaking or derivative, suspenseful or confusing).

Evaluating the visual spectacle of a Hollywood film: *The Matrix*

One film that has generated an enormous amount of critical evaluation from a variety of perspectives is *The Matrix*, written and directed by Andy and Larry Wachowski. *The Matrix* was released in 1999 and was an instant box-office hit, generating $27.8 million in its opening weekend—the biggest opening weekend of that year. Not only was *The Matrix* widely reviewed, but it soon became the subject of articles, classroom discussions, and books. *The Matrix* proved to be one of those unusual films enjoyed by both casual moviegoers of a wide variety of ages, ethnicities, and regions and devoted fans who gave it cult status.

When *The Matrix* was first released, most people had never seen anything like it. The film combined cinematic techniques from popular Hong Kong action movies, kung fu films, and Japanese anime with sophisticated digital technology. One visual, what the directors call "bullet time photography," gives key action sequences in the film a slow-motion, 360-degree view in which the characters appear to be able to halt or slow down time. This technique was combined with digital special effects and "wire" fighting scenes adapted from Asian martial arts movies to create a movie that was new and startling. As one reviewer for the *Village Voice* observed, "It's that rare sci-fi film that actually looked like it was from the future."

According to critic Joshua Clover, *The Matrix*'s story is based on two popular premises in many science fiction stories: "the war between man and machine, and the possibility that reality is a hoax." The movie is set in the twenty-second century, when intelligent machines have taken over the world, conquered humanity, and turned people into living "battery packs" farmed by the machines for energy. The plot centers around a small band of free rebels (played by Keanu Reeves, Laurence Fishburne, Carrie-Anne Moss, and Joe Pantoliano) who are searching for "The One" to help them conquer the ruling machines and end the virtual reality called "The Matrix" that they have created to fool humanity.

The Matrix won four Oscar awards: Best Visual Effects, Best Film Editing, Best Sound, and Best Sound Effects Editing. It inspired two sequel films, *The Matrix Reloaded* (2003) and *The Matrix Revolutions* (2003), which most viewers judged to be disappointing in comparison to the original. Nonetheless, more than a dozen popular books on the cinematography, philosophy, religion, and artwork—just to name a few of the most common themes—countless reviews, fan sites, a comic book series, animated movies, and an online computer game have since been published about *The Matrix*. The evaluative conversation about the meaning and merits of this movie is an active one.

In an early review of the film, professional film critic Kenneth Turan gave *The Matrix* a positive evaluation. Like many of the first reviewers, Turan praises the film primarily for its visual look and feel, energy, and action sequences. He clearly lays out all the criteria he uses to evaluate a film, and he provides vivid descriptions of scenes and characters to explain how he sees the film stacking up to these criteria. He acknowledges where *The Matrix* falls short, but he leaves readers with a strong sense that, overall, the movie's combination of interesting story line and innovative visual techniques makes it worth seeing.

KENNETH TURAN
An Apocalypse of Kinetic Joy

"Imagine you're feeling a little like Alice, tumbling down the rabbit hole," someone says in the dazzling and disorienting "The Matrix," and who has the strength to argue?

A wildly cinematic futuristic thriller that is determined to overpower the imagination, "The Matrix" combines traditional science-fiction premises with spanking new visual technology in a way that almost defies description. Like it or not, this is one movie that words don't come close to approximating.

Written and directed by the Wachowski brothers, Larry and Andy, "The Matrix" is the unlikely spiritual love child of dark futurist Philip K. Dick and the snap and dazzle of Hong Kong filmmaking, with digital technology serving as the helpful midwife.

Yet because this tale has been on the Wachowskis' minds for so long—it was written before their 1996 debut film, "Bound"—"The Matrix" never feels patched together. And its story, constructed though it is from familiar elements and pseudo-mystical musings, is nevertheless strong enough to support the film's rip-roaring visuals.

Thomas Anderson (Keanu Reeves), a software programmer in a world very much like our own who goes by his nighttime hacker moniker of Neo, has heard the Matrix whispered about his whole life, but no one knows what it is. All the beautiful Trinity (Carrie-Anne Moss of TV's "Dark Justice") can tell him is that "it's looking for you," which is certainly scary but not a great deal of help.

For that Neo has to turn to Trinity's partner, the legendary Morpheus (Laurence Fishburne), considered the most dangerous man alive by the authorities. What he says is more than frightening: What Neo thinks is the real world is no more than a computer-generated dreamscape, a virtual reality created by the artificial intelligence that really controls things to distract our human minds while our bodies are systematically plundered as an energy source to keep those nefarious machines up and running.

Sometimes those machines take human form as agents, robotic parodies of FBI men, like the chilling Agent Smith (Hugo Weaving of "Proof" and "The Adventures of Priscilla, Queen of the Desert"), who wear security earpieces, sunglasses and white shirts with ties and are terrifyingly close to indestructible.

These Matrix men have a special interest in Neo. There's a feeling in the air, one that Morpheus and his ragtag colleagues (including "Bound" veteran Joe Pantoliano) are tempted to share, that Neo might be the One, the foretold liberator who has the power to destroy the Matrix and free the human race. But only the Oracle (a fine cameo by Gloria Foster) knows for sure, and everything she says is, well, oracular.

Obviously, there's a great deal that's familiar about "The Matrix," starting with its sturdy themes of alternate realities, the deadly rivalry between men and machines, the resilient power of the human mind and the creeping dangers of conformity. And the film's fake-Zen dialogue, lines like "Don't think you are; know you are" and "There's a difference between knowing the path and walking the path," isn't going to win any ovations for originality.

On the other hand, the somber quality of the dialogue suits the apocalyptic quality of "The Matrix" story, and the gravity of the actors, especially the always magisterial Fishburne and the magnetically phlegmatic Reeves, makes the words more bemusing than bothersome.

Helping most of all are the riveting visuals shot by Bill Pope. The Wachowskis do have a taste for the bizarre (witness an electronic bug that turns into a body-piercing insect) but this tendency pays off in bravura moments like a mesmerizing vista of a body farm without end (inspired by the work of comic-book artist Geof Darrow) where humans are relentlessly harvested for energy like so many replaceable Eveready batteries.

Just as exciting are "The Matrix"'s two kinds of action sequences. One strata involves John Woo–type expenditures of massive amounts of ammunition shot in super slow-motion and the other uses both Hong Kong–style stunt work and a technique the press notes refer to as "bullet-time photography" that involved shooting film at the computer-aided equivalent of 12,000 frames per second.

"The Matrix" cast members who were involved in the film's eye-catching kung fu fight sequences also apparently committed to four months of pre-production work with Hong Kong director and stunt coordinator Yuen Wo Ping, someone who specializes in the technique, known as wire fighting, that gives H.K. films like "Drunken Master," "Once Upon a Time in China" and "Fist of Legend" their distinctive high-flying look.

Not everything in "The Matrix" makes even minimal sense, but the Wachowski brothers, said to be major fans of comic books and graphic novels, are sure-handed enough to smoothly pull us over the rough spots. When a film is as successful as this one is at hooking into the kinetic joy of adrenalized movie making, quibbling with it feels beside the point.

> "Like it or not, this is one movie that words don't come close to approximating."

Real Responses

Taking a different position from Kenneth Turan's largely positive review, Lisa Schwarzbaum, in *Entertainment Weekly,* argued that *The Matrix*'s technology doesn't create a memorable film. For her, style and look are not enough to make a great film—plot development and character growth must also be present to make a movie great.

LISA SCHWARZBAUM
Techno Prisoner

Keanu Reeves has logged more than 35 pictures on his resume, yet I still can't get him in focus as an actor. I'm not talking about his fine form, which I can clearly see and appreciate—the exotic eyes, the dancer's limbs, the characteristic expression of serene blankness hinting at either deep secrets or maybe only serene blankness. But the essence of Keanu, his own private I-dunno-ah, that is the mystery on which millions meditate: Is there a there there? *River's Edge, Bill & Ted's Excellent Adventure, My Own Private Idaho, Speed,* and *The Devil's Advocate* lead us to believe there is; *Much Ado About Nothing, Johnny Mnemonic,* and *A Walk in the Clouds* all point to No. *Little Buddha* asks, Huh?

The Matrix suggests that a computer has taken the measure of the man—now 34 and maturing into even greater, timeworn beauty—and has calculated that the most efficient use of the guy, with the least wear and tear on his dramatic abilities, is as a piece of handsome machinery, a morph of *Speed*'s action hero and *Johnny Mnemonic*'s brain-scan man. In this flashy sci-fi thriller, underwritten and overdirected by Andy and Larry Wachowski, the brothers who made the scenically kinky lesbo-noir caper *Bound,* Reeves plays a hacker called Neo, who lives in a grim future disguised as the present. It's a future in which daily life is actually an elaborate construct controlled by artificially intelligent computers, i.e., the Matrix. In classic sci-fi form, the rabble don't realize that they're blips in a global virtual-reality game. Following similar genre convention, evil, Matrix-made agents wear the dark sunglasses and suits of Secret Service men and purse their lips in ritualized expressions of humorlessness.

But a group of freedom fighters want to bust loose, like rebels in a commercial for Macintosh computers. These individualists in sexy black-leather couture (one, played

> "... cinematic advances ... diminish the impact of elegant stunt work in a story with nothing more to care about."

continued

by former model Carrie-Anne Moss, ideal for marketing as a somber Matrix Barbie doll) report to a cryptic Obi-Wanish guru, Morpheus (Laurence Fishburne). And Morpheus—a paranoid but benevolent leader—has identified Neo as The One. The One what? Handsome cyber-Buddha, I guess, who, if he accepts his fate (and acquires the right wardrobe and training), can free humanity from the tyranny of the soulless Matrix.

In fact, the real soullessness here is built into the production, a polished adaptation of Hong Kong–style filmmaking that, with its cast of depressive characters, allows for little Hong Kong–style joy. With stunt work supervised by veteran choreographer Yuen Wo Ping (whose father worked with Jackie Chan) and groundbreaking special effects, *The Matrix* sells itself as a gaudy chopsocky concoction with expensive Hollywood action details—a blast of Holly-Kong glitz that never approaches the stylistic cohesiveness of, say, John Woo's *Face/Off* or the charisma of that film's propulsive star John Travolta.

With the aid of invisible wires and nifty camera work, the cast shimmies up walls and flips through the air as bullets fly. Bodies absorb all sorts of assaults and mutilation, then reassemble themselves whole. But Fred Astaire got there first, dancing on the ceiling nearly half a century ago in *Royal Wedding*. *Terminator 2* reconstituted evil in human form over and over again. The same cinematic advances that destroyed the White House in *Independence Day* diminish the impact of elegant stunt work in a story with nothing more to care about.

Reeves and Fishburne can flip and scramble all they want. But to an audience inured to spectacle, flipping and scrambling demonstrations don't raise the pulse in this convoluted yet rudimentary yarn. The moral of *The Matrix*, I think, is that people who spend too much time staring at the computer screen and not enough time enjoying healthy physical activity like kung fu are susceptible to brainwash. Of course, if we rabble understood more about what moves Keanu Reeves to express emotion—any emotion—we wouldn't be wasting so much time jacked into the Internet, poring over Reeves Web sites, looking for clues to his Buddha-like passivity.

Like Turan, Schwarzbaum weighs various criteria in order to evaluate *The Matrix*, and she presents in clear terms how she sees the film meeting or falling short of each one. For her, the plot is "convoluted yet rudimentary," and the visual look that Turan found so stunning and difficult to put into words seems to Schwarzbaum to consist of "flipping and scrambling demonstrations" that fail to "raise the pulse." Even though she presents a completely different evaluation of *The Matrix* than does Turan, Schwarzbaum does provide evidence and examples to show how the movie stands up next to her criteria. Ultimately, both Turan and Schwarzbaum are trying to convince their readers that the criteria they use to evaluate the film are the most important ones to consider.

Joshua Clover, the author of a book about *The Matrix* published by the British Film Institute, views this film as a specific response to its times and their material conditions. Clover evaluates *The Matrix* based on what was happening economically and culturally to some people involved in the information technology industry in the United States and on its relationship to another form of visual culture: video games. His evaluation considers the ways in which the visual elements and plot lines in the movie speak to contemporary society's fear—or excitement at the possibility—of digital immersion (and finally of immersion in the virtualized and ever-expanding workplace). Despite taking such a distinctive approach in his evaluation, one that contextualizes the film, Clover too follows one of the fundamental principles underlying a clear, convincing evaluation—he provides ample evidence and examples to show how the movie fits his evaluative criteria.

JOSHUA CLOVER
Excerpt from The Matrix

I want to propose that, if there is an allegory to be found in *The Matrix*, it's not about truth. Equally, though it might concern these things, it's not about machines, nor is it about movies. It's about life as we lived it around 1999.

Long before that threshold, Marshall McLuhan proposed that there were two kinds of media: "light on" and "light through." The former included the most longstanding forms: paintings, the newspaper, street signs. The latter suggests more modern apparitions: movies, television, computer screens. This distinction is nowhere more vivid than in the wired cubicle of 1999, shaded on three sides by temporary partitions and on the fourth opening into a labyrinth of more cubicles, each with a monitor rather than a window [just like *The Matrix*'s opening office scenes]—a country in which *light through* had displaced *light on* with imperial indifference.

For the core audience of *The Matrix*, daily life bobbed near the wavefront of the tech boom, the infinitely expanding "new economy" that was always hiring, if you could write code or just punch keys. You worked in a cubicle not so different from Thomas Anderson's for a company that wanted as many of your hours as it could get, and had newer and better ways to get them. Everything was fluid but the work. The company might change every month, and the cubicle needn't be fixed. Any monitor would do, if it could connect to the system. At stake is not whether this was good or bad, but rather simply that it was, at that moment, a social fact. You sat at a workstation and worked long hours staring at a screen. When you were done, if you weren't too exhausted, maybe you went to the movies.

. . . During the last six weeks of 1998—a rather crucial earnings window for the film business—a videogame called *The Legend of Zelda: Ocarina of Time* outearned any Hollywood release. This represented an unprecedented and unexpected development; the home-console gaming world was still in its infancy, relatively speaking. Yet, in 1999 it would almost overtake Hollywood's $7.45 billion income with $6.3 billion of its own; two years later,

while Hollywood posted a record year at $8.35 billion domestic, the fledgling gamebiz waved from the passing lane en route to $9.4 billion.

These were the numbers of the times, but also the signs. The videogame's ascendancy was irrevocably written into the tech boom: it was new, it was interactive, it was a gizmo. Whether one played on a PC or a dedicated platform like PlayStation or GameCube, it was, in fact, a computer—fully digital, all code. Movies were so twentieth century, so *analog*.

Hollywood understood the challenge, as it has mostly understood such insults to its supremacy, as something to be assimilated. . . . It's possible to conceive of *The Matrix* as in many ways a response to the challenge of videogaming. It remains a movie—no joystick. But looking at, for example, bullet time, we recognize it as an explicit immersion effect. Shot from our point of view, the optical perspective swoops through three-dimensional space, fully-rendered, 360 degrees, without ever revealing the apparatus of film-making; we could be inside the synthworld of *Zelda*, except that the graphics are incomparably higher resolution. Real, more or less. And even better: we can dodge bullets.

This is the extraordinary advantage in *The Matrix*'s version of bullet time. If everything stops while the camera wheels around the scene (as in [the Gap commercial] "Khaki Swing"), we're still watching objects, still outside as analytic viewers. It's perhaps like Eadweard Muybridge's stroboscopic photos of a man running, except it's the body that's still, the camera shifting incrementally. Then again, it's something like Cubism, pictorially revealing all perspectives of a still life on a two-dimensional surface.

. . . Mediating relentlessly between the present and future, analog and digital, *The Matrix* could lay claim to being the most immersive movie ever made; it was also without question the movie most haunted by the fear of immersion. Put another way, if *The Matrix* revels in the immersive possibilities of digital pleasures, the Matrix is a terror of digital immersion; this leaves the film as an ambivalent object, shuddering between positions in a kind of delirium.

". . . a terror of digital immersion . . ."

1. State Kenneth Turan's main evaluative claim about *The Matrix* in one sentence. What reason(s) does Turan use to support his claim? What specific evidence does he provide to support his reason(s)?

2. State Lisa Schwarzbaum's main evaluative claim in one sentence. What reason(s) does Schwarzbaum use to support her claim? What specific evidence does she provide to support her reason(s)? How is some of the same evidence used by Turan used differently in this evaluation?

3. You have read both a positive review of *The Matrix* (Turan's) and a negative one (Schwarzbaum's). Which one seems more persuasive to you? Why? Be prepared to share your answer with the class.

4. Joshua Clover's evaluation is concerned with putting *The Matrix* in social context. Do you think any differently about the film now that you've read Clover's review?

5. Working with a classmate or two, identify Clover's most important evaluative claim and state it in one sentence. What historical evidence does Clover use to support his claim? What cinematographic evidence from the film? What is your group's response to Clover's claim?

COMMUNITY CONNECTIONS

1. Write for ten minutes about your response to one of the evaluations of *The Matrix*. How do the various elements of the movie that this evaluation explores coincide with or diverge from the elements that you normally consider when evaluating a movie?

2. Now write for ten minutes about each of the other two evaluations of *The Matrix*. What criteria do the respective writers use to evaluate the movie, and how are these criteria similar to or different from the criteria that you use to evaluate a film?

3. What visually compelling images on your campus or in your community have grabbed your attention over the past few weeks? Write for ten minutes about your initial impressions of one visually compelling image. Describe, with as much detail as you can, the image and the context in which you first saw it.

4. Now consider the rhetorical situation for the image you've just described: Who created this image? Who was intended to see and respond to the image? What exigence might have prompted this visual image?

5. What criteria would you use to evaluate the image you've described? On what basis would you evaluate it?

6. What do you understand to be the purpose for evaluating the visual elements in our everyday lives? What particular kinds of rhetorical situations call for evaluation, and what does evaluation allow us to do in response to those situations?

Evaluating visual culture in our everyday lives

We tend to think first of television, movies, and computers when we consider visual culture. In doing so, we overlook other visual elements we encounter every day: the façade of a classroom, a new laptop computer, and an attractive chair in the student lounge. The designers who created these objects considered not only the object's function and purpose but also how the object's aesthetic dimensions influence the users' experiences with it. Just as we can analyze and evaluate movies, we can assess the ways in which the design of everyday objects speaks to our needs for function and aesthetic pleasure.

Charles Eames (1907–1978) and Ray Kaiser Eames (1912–1988) were among the most innovative American industrial designers of the twentieth century. They created influential designs for buildings, toys, interiors, fabrics, and a host of other consumer goods, almost all of them manufactured through mass-production techniques. Their most notable contribution to American life—and one still seen in homes, businesses, and classrooms across the country—was designing furniture, especially chairs. In-deed, chances are you sat on a chair designed by Charles and Ray Eames during elementary or secondary school. The Eames molded plastic stacking chair has been used in schools everywhere because its functional design allowed several to be linked together in straight rows and, when not being used, stacked twelve chairs high.

Eames molded plastic stacking chairs.

Ray and Charles Eames working on a conceptual model for an exhibition.

Ray Kaiser Eames first worked with Charles Eames in 1940, when she assisted him and Eero Saarinen in preparing designs for the Museum of Modern Art's Organic Furniture Competition. Art historians Dung Ngo and Eric Pfeiffer explain in *Bent Ply: The Art of Plywood Furniture* that the competition was created to address the lack of suitable modern furniture on the market. Eliot Noyes, the director of the museum's department of industrial design, specifically stated the impetus for the competition: "Obviously the forms of our furniture should be determined by our way of life. Instead, for the most part, we have had to adapt ourselves uncomfortably and unreasonably to what happened to be manufactured." Charles Eames and Eero Saarinen won two first-place prizes for the designs of their chairs, which were made of molded plywood shaped into curves that fit the contours of the human body. And, because they developed a process for molding the plywood in a mass-production process, the designers created chairs that blended the visual appeal of organic design with the affordability demanded by the growing middle class of American consumers.

Charles Eames and Ray Kaiser married in 1941 and moved to California, where they continued to work with plywood molding techniques for designing and building furniture. During World War II, the U.S. Navy commissioned them to produce molded plywood splints and stretchers as well as shells for experimental gliders. Throughout all of these projects, the Eameses pursued a larger vision for evaluating design according to how the object's visual elements allowed it to meet the intended purpose.

The designs of the Eames chairs reflect the social and cultural moment in which the Eameses worked. They pursued all their work with the wholehearted belief that "design could improve people's lives." Following World War II, the middle class grew, and an increasing number of Americans achieved home ownership and had more disposable income to spend on items for filling these homes. As curators at the U.S. Library of Congress explain, "Early in their careers together, Charles and Ray identified the need for affordable, yet high-quality furniture for the average consumer—furniture that could serve a variety of uses."

Perhaps the most well-known and critically acclaimed design of Charles and Ray Eames is that of the Eames lounge chair. This chair continued the Eameses' experiments with molded plywood, but it was the first piece of furniture that the Eameses designed for the high-end consumer market. The chair consists of three curved plywood shells into which are fitted thick cushions covered in top-quality glove leather. Pat Kirkham, professor of design history at the Bard Graduate Center, explains, "Much of the Lounge Chair and Ottoman's com-

fort comes from their thick cushions (six inches deep in parts) in a mix of high-quality down and foam, the seat size sufficiently big for an adult to move around in, the semi-reclining position of the body the Chair and Ottoman allow, the natural resilience of the plywood, and the added give obtained by using rubber shock mounts to join the pieces." Kirkham continues her evaluation of the Eames lounge chair in this way: "The base of each piece adds both elegance and stability. There is a certain visual weight and solidity about the Chair that surprised those who associated the Eameses with chairs that seemed to float in space." This particular visual and material difference, though, follows from the Eameses' view of design as a means of solving problems rather than merely a matter of attending to formalist issues of a visual nature. The Eameses wanted the chair to have "the warm, receptive look of a well-used first-baseman's mitt" because they wanted it to be a piece of furniture that people did not simply contemplate but that they used both for work and for leisure in their day-to-day lives.

In 2006, the Eames lounge chair celebrated its fiftieth anniversary, an anniversary that sparked a reconsideration of the Eameses' productions and their design philosophy. Some recent reevaluations of the Eames lounge chair's design can prompt us to consider how the designs of objects in our everyday lives affect how we work and play. A visual evaluation of any object should account for the aesthetics of the piece itself as well as the ways and contexts in which it is used. In the following excerpt from a column, Rob Forbes evaluates the design elements of the Eames lounge chair that contribute to its aesthetic appeal and its functionality—and make it an object that attracts people across many generations. Forbes provides a contextual evaluation of the chair that accounts for its success in the past and the present. Through his evaluation, he helps readers better understand what makes certain designs endure across time periods and cultural shifts.

ROB FORBES
The Endurance of an Icon

The Eames Lounge Chair and Ottoman (1956) stand firmly in the world of icon status, and the pair's golden anniversary is being commemorated internationally. However, what truly makes this chair special is its exceptional comfort, even more so than its star status. Charles and Ray Eames conceived the chair as the 20th-century American answer to the Edwardian English Club Chair. In the process, they introduced the concept of a "lounge" chair to postwar America, as well as to Europe. (If you have a copy of *1000 Chairs* nearby, flip through the pages up to the Eames Lounge, and then flip through the pages that follow. Do you agree the chairs appear to relax?)

> "... stand[ing] firmly in the world of icon status ..."

At the time of the chair's debut, governments and businesses were busy ushering in a period of tremendous growth, cultural expansion and the rise of corporate America. The need for mass-produced housing was shaping architecture (11,000 Eichler homes were built between 1950 and 1974 in California alone), and roadways showcased the crisp and clean styling and performance of new automobiles. It was a time when American values were expressed through well-designed products manufactured in the U.S., and the results were recognized globally for their appeal.

Not only did these items have appeal then, but many continue to be popular today. The reason for the continuing relevance of the Eames Lounge Chair and Ottoman is simple. It's comfortable. It's at once precise and voluptuous, without sacrificing function or form. The Eameses wanted the chair to have "the warm receptive look of a well-used first-baseman's mitt" and the chair fulfills this objective, plus it has the unexpected motion from its cool swivel base. Its trim lines make this high-style lounger suited to the office as well as the study, and at the time of its introduction it was one of the first lounge chairs that appealed to women as much as it did to men. (A 1975 cover of *Business Week* had the headline "The Corporate Woman: Up the Ladder, Finally" next to a picture of a woman sitting in the Eames Lounge.) When a design offers as much as the Eames Lounge, it has the potential for longevity. If one could pick only one piece of modern furniture to use and appreciate, this would be as suitable as any.

The following brief article by The Eames Office, which is "dedicated to communicating, preserving and extending the work of Charles and Ray Eames," evaluates an Eames PKR-2 chair and describes what makes it a vintage piece of furniture. At the same time, the evaluation helps readers understand how to determine the authenticity of a vintage piece of furniture. Any visual evaluation of an everyday object requires a detailed description of that object and its constituent parts, which is found in this article. The authors use the criteria established by one dictionary definition of *vintage* as the basis for evaluating a specific piece of Eames furniture. It is clear that they consider this particular criterion—whether it is vintage or not—to be one of the most important ones to use in evaluating any piece of Eames furniture or, for that matter, any everyday object.

Ray and Charles Eames working on a chair.

Situations for Writers

THE EAMES OFFICE
Vintage Eames Chair

"vintage" • **noun** 1 the year or place in which wine was produced. 2 a wine of high quality made from the crop of a single identified district in a good year. 3 the harvesting of grapes for winemaking. 4 the grapes or wine of a particular season. 5 the time that something was produced. *"vintage"* • **adjective** 1 referring to vintage wine. 2 referring to something from the past of high quality. —From the *Oxford English Dictionary* When we say "vintage Eames" we are using the word "vintage" as an adjective, and clearly we are not talking about wine, but rather, "some things from the past of high quality."

But, we can also look at the first definition, "made from the crop of a single identified district in a good year," in reference to "vintage Eames."

"SINGLE IDENTIFIED DISTRICT." For this as well there is an EAMES vintage furniture analogy.

"A vintage Eames chair" is not only made up of "vintage parts," all from the same year; a true "vintage Eames chair" is made up of all the right parts for that chair's ultimate purpose, as the chair was configured, before leaving the factory.

The Eames Office and Herman Miller were not in the business of offering "furniture kits" with mix and match parts.

This is how the reference to "vintage Eames" relates to vintage WINE. A true true VINTAGE wine or piece of furniture is not adulterated, [it] is a unity, in all aspects.

Taking just one type of Eames furniture, Herman Miller offered over 125 different Eames fiberglass arm shell chairs, each with its own distinct features and purpose. The purpose of each piece was defined by the base, the upholstery, the shell, the screws, the glides, all put together, on the same date, inspected by one final HM factory worker, before it went out the door, as that specific, and singular chair. Here is a picture of an Eames PKR-2. This is the official "name" of a wire top, rocking chair base, with a bikini pad.

We can tell by examining the underside, that the screws have not been removed. In addition, as was often the case with early production pieces, it has the Herman Miller upholstery tag on the bikini, and we know this is a fabric that HM offered for early PKRs.

" . . . a 'true vintage Eames chair' is made up of all the right parts for that chair's ultimate purpose . . . "

The screws that secure the rockers, and the screws that secure the base to the chair, are all original. The original button which was used to fasten the bikini top to the bikini bottom is present.

This is a "vintage Eames chair" in the best sense of that word. You would not find a "Miscellaneous Side Wire chair" with matching and optional features in the Herman Miller catalogues. It is undeniable that the bases and tops are interchangeable, but this was not for the purpose of mixing and matching. That there are interchangeable bases and other parts has to do with the goal of the Eames Office, which was to offer the best product, at the lowest possible price. Standardized parts, and connecting devices made it easier and more economical for them to offer the best products.

The visual appeal of furniture and other everyday objects is often analyzed as part of a larger context that they help to create. Objects combine with others to create a particular mood in people who regularly use a particular space or to project an image of the person who created and arranged that space. Furniture certainly works to shape the look of any room, and the Eames lounge chair is no exception. In the following excerpt, Thomas Hine visually analyzes the set of the popular television series *Frasier* in order to explore how the various pieces in the main character's living room, including an Eames lounge chair, helped to communicate key aspects of his personality and character.

THOMAS HINE
Excerpt from Half a Century of Lounging: Sightings and Reflections

Situations for Writers

Since its network debut, the Eames Chair has been sighted several times on television. For example, Giles, the school librarian and counselor on magic in *Buffy the Vampire Slayer* (1997–2003), had one in his seldom-seen bachelor pad. But the Chair had its longest run on *Frasier*, which ran on NBC from 1993 to 2004. It stood for all those seasons in the background of the show's principal set—the living room of an upscale high-rise apartment in Seattle—and embodied the tensions between the tastes and lifestyles of Frasier Crane, a radio psychiatrist, and his down-to-earth, retired policeman father, Martin.

Probably no other set in history has had such a distinguished pedigree. "You know, every item here was carefully selected," Frasier tells Martin early in the first episode. "The lamp by Corbu, this chair by Eames, and this couch is an exact replica of the one Coco Chanel had in her Paris atelier." Moments later, a delivery man arrives with Martin's contribution to the apartment, a ratty-looking, duct-tape–mended reclining chair, which he insists on keeping in the living room. For eleven seasons this bilious chartreuse easy chair was the focus of the room, while the Eames Lounge Chair was exiled to the background, where it mutely expressed Frasier's resentment at his father's intrusion into what he hoped would be a perfect place.

"All of the furnishings and paintings denote a man who has money, taste, and style," said Roy Christopher, who designed *Frasier*'s set. "He's a man who likes the nicer things in life and isn't afraid to spend money on them." Frasier's living room was, as he noted in the first episode, eclectic, but it had a bias toward classic modern pieces. Production designers do not use fur-

> "Production designers … use furnishings … because they help to create character and embody situations."

nishings because they find them aesthetically pleasing, but because they help to create character and embody situations. In movies and on television, those who inhabit modern architecture or surround themselves with modern design are often people who, like Frasier, feel that they have more control over their circumstances than they actually do. They are often people who, like Frasier, are emotionally cold and need to be reminded of life's simpler truths. Christopher has said that many viewers admired the items in the *Frasier* set and he frequently answered queries on where they could be bought. But the living room—with its pedigreed objects that also included a large, genuine Dale Chihuly glass sculpture and a fake Rauschenberg canvas—was comically excessive. Martin's recliner was the comeuppance the Eames Chair and the rest of the big-name décor deserved. Frasier himself was a fussbudget and a snob, not a naturally attractive character, but one who was likable nevertheless, mostly because his insecurities were so evident. His desire to surround himself with objects he thinks will show he has refined tastes seems slightly pathetic, in contrast with his father, who is comfortable both with himself and his ugly recliner.

During the years *Frasier* was on the air, some of the objects in his apartment—including the Eames Chair—stopped looking quite so rarefied and became increasingly popular, talked about, and imitated. But the Lounge Chair went un-sat-upon until the final episode of the program aired on May 13, 2004. Finally, with Frasier moving out of his apartment, Martin, who had moved earlier, returns and tries out the chair. "Mmm, well, this is pretty comfortable," he said. "I would have been OK with this!"

Thomas Hine shows how the objects in Frasier's living room define the space where they are located and convey something about their owner. In particular, the Eames lounge chair—and, more importantly, Frasier's desire to make known that he owns such a chair—communicates that it served as more than just a solution to a particular problem, as Charles and Ray Eames originally crafted it. Rather, the Eames lounge chair was for Frasier a way of signaling his refined taste. You can use visual evaluation as a means for analyzing the ways in which furniture and other everyday objects communicate particular messages about the people who have put together spaces to serve specific ends.

ANALYZING THE RHETORICAL SITUATION

1. Look again at the photographs of Charles and Ray Eames at work. What do these images convey to you about the Eameses and their work?

2. What specific features of an Eames chair does each writer featured in this section evaluate?

3. What criteria do the writers use to evaluate the design of the Eames chair? How do they describe the Eames chair in terms of these criteria?

4. Who is the specific audience for each of the three evaluations in this section? What purpose does each writer hope to achieve? How does that purpose relate to the audience for each evaluation?

5. What kinds of specific details and evidence does each writer provide in order to evaluate the chair? What kinds of questions does the writer ask about the chair in order to draw out these types of details and evidence?

6. What exigence prompted each of the visual evaluations in this section? How would you characterize each one's contribution to the ongoing professional and public conversation about Eames designs?

COMMUNITY CONNECTIONS

1. Write for ten minutes about your response to one of the evaluations of an Eames chair. What criteria does the writer use to evaluate the design of the chair? How do the criteria used by the writer coincide with or diverge from the criteria that you would apply to evaluate a piece of furniture you use every day?

2. Write for ten minutes about each of the other two evaluations: What criteria does the writer use to evaluate the chair? How do these criteria relate to those you consider most important for evaluating a chair or other common object?

3. What object other than a chair that you use every day has a design that affects how you work or play? Who made the design decisions that shaped this object? How and why do you come into contact with this object?

4. Write for ten minutes about the design of this object. Provide as many specific visual and tactile details as you can in describing it. Then, write for five minutes about the ways in which you use this object. Be sure to specify the places in which and the times at which you use it. Finally, write for five minutes about how the visual design of this object affects your attitude toward the work or play that you do. Be prepared to share your answers.

Evaluations: A Fitting Response

The readings in this chapter illustrate the use of evaluation to understand how visual elements shape our everyday experiences. Visual effects in movies such as *The Matrix* can lead us, in the words of Morpheus, to "free our minds" and consider the limits of human thought. The visual appeal of furniture can lead us, in the manner of Charles and Ray Eames, to take pleasure in the efficient functioning of everyday objects. Clearly, evaluating visuals in our culture helps us to better understand the logical and emotional responses they produce in us.

The two articles in this section continue the exploration of visual culture that you have been pursuing throughout this chapter. As you read these evaluations, notice how Mike D'Angelo and Susan Beatty address each element of their rhetorical situation: exigence, audience, purpose, and available means. Notice, too, how they meet the requirements for any evaluation: (1) introduce the particular object or phenomenon and establish why it needs to be evaluated; (2) define in precise terms the category in which the object or phenomenon fits; (3) present the criteria against which the object or phenomenon is going to be evaluated; (4) provide concrete evidence and examples to illustrate the ways in which the object or phenomenon does or does not meet each evaluative criterion; and (5) articulate a clear argument about whether or not the object or phenomenon meets each evaluative criterion.

Two evaluations of visuals in contemporary culture

As you have seen throughout this chapter, there are many visual elements in our culture that affect the ways in which we live and work, whether we realize it or not. Critics compose evaluative essays as a means for exploring the ways in which our lives are shaped by images and design. Each of the essays in this section examines one specific feature of our visual culture: the first evaluates two movies in terms of the technique used in their creation; the second reports on some criteria developed to evaluate corporate logos.

Mike D'Angelo

Unreally, Really Cool: Stop-Motion Movies May Be Old School, But They Still Eat Other Animation for Breakfast

As a filmgoer, I have virtually no allegiances. My goal is basically to avoid things that suck. However brilliant the actor, I have no interest in watching him sort his laundry or demonstrate that even the mentally retarded can be wonderful parents, thereby teaching Michelle Pfeiffer the true meaning of family. You say your movie is about lesbian vampire Catholic schoolgirls on a submarine? It may take zero stars from every critic on the face of the planet to keep me away . . . but if it does get the pan of a lifetime, I can resist. Or at least wait for the DVD.

That said, no amount of negative buzz could keep me away from two of this season's tastiest offerings: Tim Burton's *Corpse Bride* . . . and *Wallace & Gromit: The Curse of the Were-rabbit*. . . . If there's one thing in the vast world of cinema that qualifies as inherently compelling, that thing is stop-motion animation. Almost as old as the medium itself—you can see stop motion at work in Georges Méliès's classic short *A Trip to the Moon* (1902)—the basic process has remained unchanged. The original King Kong, the dueling skeletons in Ray Harryhausen adventures, the barnyard animals in *Chicken Run*—all involve miniature puppets being painstakingly manipulated one frame at a time. [1]

Pixar may have the most consistently impressive track record since the glory days of Walt Disney, but a Pixar CG [computer-generated] movie with a mediocre script and generic voice characterizations would be . . . well, it'd be *Madagascar*. Traditional cel animation, too, no matter how beautiful, can be deadly dull. [2] Stop motion is different. There is no such thing as a stop-motion film that isn't fascinating to watch. Obviously, some are better than others—and there's reason to hope that *Corpse Bride*, a typically macabre Burton fable about a man who inadvertently marries a cadaver, and *Were-rabbit*, the long-awaited feature debut of Nick Park's beloved duo, will both be terrific. But all of them share the same singular, outré visual allure. [3] They're uncanny.

Consider Gromit. [4] (I've been waiting years to say that.) If you've seen any of Park's Oscar-winning shorts about the adventures of a cheerful English nincompoop and his faithful, tolerant canine companion, you're familiar with the character's look and temperament: big floppy ears, deep-set goggle eyes, silently unperturbable demeanor. You probably have a favorite Gromit moment, and it probably involves nothing more dynamic than a single styptic blink in response to escalating lunacy. But I submit that Gromit would not be half as funny or as endearing were he hand drawn or computer generated, no matter how expertly the animators replicated his appearance and mannerisms. Whether we're conscious of it or not, his oddball charisma is rooted in a combination of tactility and artificiality that's unique to stop motion. [5] It's a very different kind of response from the one we have to Dumbo or Buzz Lightyear. We love Gromit because he's at once real and not real.

Human beings are drawn to borders, gray areas, the mystery of the in-between. The director's favorite time of day is dusk, also known as the "magic hour": no longer light, not yet dark. Many movie stars have vaguely androgynous features (Julia Roberts looks exactly like Eric Roberts to me), and movies themselves tend to appeal to us the more they resemble our dreams, that world weirdly suspended between waking and sleeping. What makes stop motion so arresting, regardless of whether we're involved in the story or the characters, is that it pushes this dichotomy one step further, straddling the line that separates reality from imagination. [6] Cel animation and computer animation, no matter how aesthetically pleasing, never offer anything more than a simulacrum of reality; they are clearly make-believe. But when we look at one of the grandiosely morbid sets in Burton's *The Nightmare Before Christmas*, we can plainly see that those ornate tombstones and grinning jack-o'-lanterns and curlicue hills are really there, physically present. [7] (The next time you watch *Nightmare*, notice how many objects have grooves cut into them, or have surfaces that are stippled. That sort of three-dimensional detail works only in stop motion.) And there's something oddly riveting about watching puppets navigate this tactile landscape 1/24 of a second at a time.

[1] The writer provides a succinct definition of the phenomenon he will evaluate.

[2] D'Angelo mentions some characteristics that he does not apply to stop-motion films: "mediocre scripts" and "generic voice characterizations."

[3] In this passage, D'Angelo introduces one criterion he will use to evaluate animated films—"outré" suggests that an animated film ought to be evaluated according to whether it's unconventional, eccentric, or bizarre.

[4] The word "Consider" signals that the writer is going to begin providing evidence and examples to support his claim that stop-motion animated films make for entertaining viewing because they are unconventional and eccentric.

[5] Here D'Angelo introduces two more characteristics he uses to evaluate visual animation: the objects on the screen should combine tactility and artificiality.

[6] And here readers learn about one more criterion D'Angelo uses to evaluate animated films—the blurring of the line between reality and imagination.

[7] D'Angelo provides an example to show how the last criterion applies to stop-motion animation.

That's another thing about stop motion: There are no shortcuts. Cel animation is exacting work, but there are numerous ways to economize, as any *Speed Racer* fan knows all too well. Computer animation allows for endless revision. But stop motion is always and only moving everything a fraction of an inch, taking a picture, moving everything a fraction of an inch, taking a picture—day in, day out, for years and years. Screw something up and you have to do it all . . . over . . . again. It's like building a skyscraper using a pair of tweezers. Consequently, the folks who toil in this nearly moribund field tend to be perfectionists—not just when it comes to technical matters but in every aspect of filmmaking. **[8]** *Corpse Bride* and *Were-rabbit* don't have to be good. But I bet you they will be.

Susan Beatty

Logo Logic: Professors Give "A" to the "Swoosh" but Flunk Giant

Nike's logo works, but Minolta Camera's isn't as memorable. Oldsmobile's new space-age-looking choice is a definite improvement, but the Jolly Green Giant is just too much. Such are the lessons drawn from a new academic study, which tries to solve the mystery of why one corporate logo will captivate consumers while another is a turn-off. **[1]**

Logos are an elemental form of advertising, not to mention a big investment. They can cost anywhere from $100,000 to $1 million to develop, plus millions more to splash across everything from trucks to storefront signs. Yet many logos are chosen by marketing managers and chief executive officers based on little more than gut instinct. The new study seeks to give future logo-seekers more to go on. The authors are Pamela W. Henderson and Joseph A. Cote, two professors at Washington State University in Richland. They showed 195 logos to 560 college students, asking that each be rated for memorability and attractiveness. **[2]**

To help develop guidelines, the students were shown unfamiliar logos of smaller and foreign companies, and asked to measure them by three different design yardsticks: "naturalness vs. geometricality," "elaborateness vs. simplicity," and "the degree of harmony, which combines symmetry and balance." Conclusion: Logos should look natural, not overly hard-edged or abstract, and they need a dash of elaboration, though they shouldn't be photographic. **[3]**

Balance is important, but designs shouldn't be too symmetrical. Nike's "swoosh" logo, on the face of it, violates the guidelines outlined by the study. It's exceedingly simple, abstract even. It has no real detail and resembles nothing found in nature. But because of its slanted shape, it looks as if it's moving, and so it registers to the eye as much more complex. **[4]**

Previous studies have found that the Jolly Green Giant, part of Diageo's Pillsbury, and the Land O' Lakes woman aren't much liked by consumers as logos. Ms. Henderson says the study helps explain why: "They are too elaborate and go too far." The giant is "fine on your packaging, but he probably should be

[8] D'Angelo makes a final assertion to convince readers to accept his evaluation—the people who make stop-motion animated films attend to all the specific details that make an animated film great.

[1] By the end of the first paragraph, readers know the topic of Beatty's article—how can corporate logos be evaluated for their effect on consumers?

[2] Here Beatty introduces two specific criteria to use to evaluate a proposed corporate logo: "memorability" and attractiveness.

[3] This paragraph further differentiates each of the evaluative criteria.

[4] Discussing Nike's "swoosh" logo, the writer begins to provide examples to illustrate how to apply the various criteria for evaluating a corporate logo.

Situations for Writers

more stylized" as a logo, Ms. Henderson says. "You can do a Green Giant without having all the photographic detail. You don't have to do every single leaf." The same goes for the Land O' Lakes lady. But Ms. Henderson says Mr. Peanut (of RJR Nabisco Holdings' Planters unit) works as a logo, because he has been drawn with fewer lines and yet is still recognizable. [5]

[5] More examples help readers understand all of the elements deemed important for evaluating a corporate logo.

And the new logo of General Motors' Oldsmobile? "It's got more depth, and it's more active, and yet it's simple," Ms. Henderson says. It also has an abstract design, which studies show consumers generally don't respond well to. But Ms. Henderson says that because of the depth achieved by layering imperfect shapes in the design itself, "you've accomplished the goal of being more elaborate, which will make your symbol more likable and memorable."

Minolta's logo is pleasing, but because its abstract spherical shape, sliced by a series of lines, is so symmetrical, it isn't easily linked by consumers to the famous photography company it represents. [6] "Symmetry is going to get you nowhere if you don't have some naturalness or some elaborateness," Ms. Henderson says. [7]

[6] Beatty provides examples that show readers how to weigh the various criteria when evaluating logos that seem to succeed in some ways but not others.

Different types of companies want different things from logos. If you're a plumber, for example, or a business that customers locate by flipping through the Yellow Pages, the study says you want a design that creates a false sense of knowing—a logo that you think you've seen before, even if you haven't. Professionals such as doctors, lawyers and accountants want something else again. A lawyer, Ms. Henderson says, is "not after something that's memorable. All I want is something that is visually appealing and gives a finished look." Such a logo should be "moderately elaborate because it's going to be better liked" that way, Ms. Henderson says. "Most logos in the world today are too simple." [8]

[7] Direct quotations from the researchers who investigated the topic help to establish Beatty's credibility.

[8] In the final paragraph, Beatty shows that there is no single way to apply the criteria for evaluating a corporate logo.

Guide to Evaluations

WHAT MAKES IT AN EVALUATION?

The following questions are ones you should consider when thinking critically about any evaluation. For now, try applying them to the reviews by Mike D'Angelo and Susan Beatty to determine how closely those writers followed the conventions for evaluations.

1. Does the writer introduce the particular object or phenomenon he or she is exploring and suggest why it needs to be evaluated?

2. Does the writer define in precise terms the category in which the object or phenomenon fits?

3. Does the writer clearly present the criteria with which the object or phenomenon is going to be evaluated?

4. Do concrete evidence and examples illustrate the ways in which the object or phenomenon does or does not meet each evaluative criterion?

5. Does the writer articulate a clear argument about whether or not the object or phenomenon meets each criterion?

| Understanding the Rhetorical Situation |

Identifying an exigence

Consider your campus. Are there any buildings with unarguably unique architecture? Are there any pages on the school's Web site that are either visually compelling or aesthetically uninspired? Are there any advertisements in the campus newspaper, in a building stairwell, or on a campus bus that you think have particularly innovative imagery or layout? Is there any public artwork that made you do a double-take when you first walked by it? Are there any computer labs that make you feel mentally and physically exhausted—or all revved up? Are there any couches or chairs in the common area of your dormitory that seem to be particularly inviting—or just the opposite? Are any of your friends' dorm rooms creatively decorated?

You might look for interesting images or designs on the public message boards in the student union, in the campus art museum, in the computer labs, or on the sides of campus buses. Maybe you realize that the reason you work best in the library's reading room is because the dark, heavy wood of the chairs and the tables helps you move into a state of deep concentration. Or maybe you feel that the sculpture at the entrance to campus paints too plain a picture of what is a vibrant community.

1. Make a list of five interesting images or designs that you have noticed over the past week. For each one, write a few sentences describing your initial impressions. Were your impressions positive or negative? Provide as many details as you can to explain why. Also identify the contextual factors that may have shaped your impression of each image or design: the time of day and the place on campus when and where you saw it, what you were doing at that time, the emotion or response evoked.

2. Choose two of the images or designs you listed and take photos of them. Pay particular attention to documenting the physical context in which the image or design appears.

3. Choose the image or design you want to write about and compose four or five sentences that describe its visual aspects in concrete, specific detail. After composing these descriptions, spend several minutes freewriting about the context of the image or design. Respond to questions such as these: What do you think the purpose of this image or design might be? When and where do you tend to interact with it in your everyday life? If you are writing about the visual design of an everyday object, what are the purposes for which you use it? If you are writing about an image, how do you view it and in what ways do you interpret it and make sense of it?

Locating an audience

For his evaluation of stop-motion animated films, Mike D'Angelo had to consider various audiences—casual moviegoers, die-hard animation fans, serious film critics—and to account for the range of preferences and motivations that these different groups bring to the movie-watching experience. He had to present evidence and examples in such a way as to convince all of these readers to agree with his evaluation of the artistic and the technical merit of this particular movie-making style.

To what audience should you direct your evaluation of a visual element? First, you have to determine who encounters the image or design on a regular basis—or only occasionally, if that seems pertinent. Then, you need to imagine possibilities for prompting that audience to consider your evaluation. For instance, if you think that your composition class could work more productively if the computers were arranged in a fashion that fostered more collaboration, you'll need to think about the attitudes that the professors and students and information technology administrators hold about function and aesthetics in the design of classrooms.

The following questions can help you locate your rhetorical audience as well as identify the relationship they have to the visual element you're writing about. Then, you'll be able to determine the best way to present your evaluation of that image or design.

1. List the names of the persons or groups—students, faculty, administrators, community members, alumni, parents—most likely to see and be affected by the visual element you've chosen. These are potential audiences for your evaluation.
2. Next to the name of each audience, write reasons that audience might have for thinking in greater depth about this particular image or design. In other words, what would persuade these audiences that the visual element needs to be evaluated?
3. How could each of these audiences reasonably be influenced by an evaluation of this image or design? In other words, what emotional responses or logical conclusions could they be expected to have when reading your evaluative essay? Consider what motivations each group might have for analyzing the specific details that make up an object's design or an image's composition.
4. With your audience's interests and motivations in mind, look again at the descriptions of the image or design that you compared in the preceding section on identifying an exigence. Which description(s) will enable your readers to feel engaged in your evaluation and invested in exploring this image or design in greater depth? The better description not only allows readers to create a vivid mental picture of the visual element but also helps them understand why and how it affects them. At this point, it may be necessary to revise your best description to tailor it to your audience's needs and interests.

Identifying a Fitting Response

Finding a purpose and shaping a fitting response

In her *Wall Street Journal* article, Susan Beatty draws on the work of a pair of academic researchers to evaluate the visual effectiveness of corporate logos. Her article analyzes several examples and explains how specific features of each one's design evoke particular responses from potential customers. Beatty wrote about this topic not only because the research on it was timely but also because her readers—many of whom work in the corporate world—might be wondering about the effectiveness of their companies' logos. Her essay, then, provides readers with specific criteria and concrete examples to help them begin to understand what makes a corporate logo effective.

Like Beatty, you have described a visual element that many people encounter on a daily basis and have identified an audience that needs to hear more about this image or design. Now it's time to consider exactly what you want to accomplish with your evaluative writing. How might your evaluation spark the interests or motivations of this audience? What particular response do you want your audience to have when reading your evaluative essay? What should your readers gain from reflecting on specific aspects of this visual element? Answering these types of questions should provide you with your purpose, which in turn will inform the specific kind of text you create.

Indeed, different purposes and different audiences require different kinds of texts. For example, if you are evaluating an image such as a photograph or painting, you might want to compose an essay that would appear as part of a museum display or in an exhibition catalog. Your evaluation of a visually uninspiring Web page could be crafted as a letter to the staff in the admissions or alumni relations office. Your evaluation of the dysfunctional design of a computer lab could take the form of a pamphlet or flier to be distributed to other students in order to gain their support for change. The point is that once you identify your exigence, audience, and purpose, you need to determine what kind of text will best respond to your rhetorical situation.

Use the following questions to help you narrow your purpose and shape your response:

1. What kinds of facts or details about the image or design do you need to provide in order to precisely define the contexts in which it shapes or influences or interacts with people's everyday lives on campus?
2. What kinds of facts or details about the visual image or visual design make it particularly compelling?
3. What cultural, social, economic, or political details do you need to know in order to better understand the purpose of this visual design and its significance for the people who created it as well as for the people who interact with it, whether regularly or only once?
4. Are you asking the audience to adopt a new perspective on this particular object or image or do you want the audience to perform a particular action in response to your writing?

5. What is the best way to reach this audience? That is, what kind of text is this audience most likely to respond to?

Your instructor (or your rhetorical situation) may prompt you to create a pamphlet, compose a newspaper column, or write a letter or some other type of document. If Alexis Walker, the student whose essay begins on page 310, had wanted to argue against the sale of a downtown shop to Dunkin' Donuts, she could have organized her thoughts into talking points and spoken at a city council meeting. Or, if she had wanted to focus on architectural details that were obscured by the new sign, she might have written a letter to the local preservation association. As a long-time resident witnessing a shift in the aesthetics of the downtown area, Alexis wanted to evaluate the effects of this latest change in order to influence the perceptions of other residents—so that they might use the criteria she establishes in her critical review to evaluate future developments. If, like Alexis, you are prompted to write an evaluative essay, use the following assignment as a guide.

Writing an Evaluation: Working with Your Available Means

Shaping your evaluation

You are no doubt familiar with evaluation essays because you have read many examples of this genre in the form of movie reviews in newspapers and magazines and product reviews in print and online publications such as *Consumer Reports* and *PC Magazine*. What you may not have noticed, however, are the ways in which evaluation essays use the rhetorical methods of development. For instance, the introduction of an evaluative essay provides readers with a concise definition of what is to be evaluated, the reasons it merits evaluation, and the particular ways in which it is to be evaluated. By the end of the introduction, then, the writer has begun to establish his or her expertise and good sense, asserting a position as a qualified evaluator. For example, by the end of his second paragraph, Mike D'Angelo has provided a brief definition of stop-motion animation ("miniature puppets being painstakingly manipulated one frame at a time") and explained how he thinks animated films should be evaluated (by whether or not they provide compelling movie-going experiences). Writers of evaluation essays also use the introduction to show readers why they need to consider the evaluation, and D'Angelo is no exception because he tells readers that two animated movies will be released soon. By providing an in-depth explanation, D'Angelo establishes his expertise and knowledge. In other words, he establishes his ethos.

The body of an evaluation essay generally provides the criteria according to which the particular object or phenomenon will be evaluated, using appeals to logic (logos) to make—and shape—the argument. To accompany each criterion, the writer also offers facts, details, and direct quotations to show how the object or phenomenon does or does not meet it. For example, Susan Beatty presents in each body paragraph an additional criterion for evaluating whether a corporate logo is effective. As she introduces each new criterion, she describes how different logos do or do not meet it. Readers learn that consumers don't respond well to corporate logos such as the Jolly Green Giant that are "too elaborate" but look much more favorably on GM's new Oldsmobile logo because it has "more depth, and it's more active, and yet it's simple."

The body of an evaluation essay also attempts to describe the object or phenomenon in as much specific detail as possible, again maintaining the appeal to logos. Readers of D'Angelo's essay, for example, can imagine Gromit's "big floppy ears, deep-set goggle eyes, silently unperturbable demeanor" and see the grooves cut into the tombstones in *The Nightmare Before Christmas*. These details grab and maintain the readers' interest. Just as important, sensory details help the writer to convince his or her readers that the evaluation is based on a careful, complete analysis of all the elements that make up the object or phenomenon, and they provide the evidence to support the writer's argument and make the readers believe that it is based on sound reasons. Indeed, the reader of D'Angelo's essay is no doubt convinced that stop-motion animators "tend to be perfectionists—not just when it comes to technical matters but in every aspect of filmmaking."

The body of an evaluation essay often attempts to explain the political, economic, social, or cultural context that gives this object or phenomenon particular significance. D'Angelo, for example, argues that "movies themselves tend to appeal to us the more they resemble our dreams." Thus, stop-motion animation is particularly compelling because this method of composing visual imagery in a film "pushes this dichotomy [between waking and sleeping] one step further, straddling the line that separates reality from imagination." This contextual evaluation helps deepen readers' understanding of how the animated films fit into contemporary visual culture and influence their daily lives.

Finally, the conclusion of an evaluation brings together the various criteria and the collected evidence in order to make one final appeal for readers to adopt a specific attitude or opinion. Beatty wants readers to be more attentive to the corporate logos they encounter in their daily lives and to consider whether the companies they work for might benefit from evaluating how effective their own logos might be. D'Angelo appeals to his readers on an emotional level (pathos), urging them to appreciate the technical artistry of stop-motion animated movies and the "folks who toil" to create these films.

Many compelling evaluative essays include visuals. As you think about your physical means of delivering information, you may want to consider whether a visual or two will make your evaluation more vivid and more memorable for readers. Consider taking a photograph of a person working in the poorly designed computer lab or printing a bland, uninspiring page from your school's Web site. Or you might sketch the façade of a campus building or scan an advertisement you saw posted in the hallway of the student union. Depending on the constraints and resources of your rhetorical situation, you might consider creating a slide presentation that uses digital videos and audio files to support your evaluation of graffiti on campus or your friend's striking dorm room.

CHECKING OVER AN EVALUATION

✓ The evaluation describes the particular object or phenomenon in a way that the rhetorical audience will understand.

✓ The evaluation makes clear why this particular object or phenomenon should be evaluated.

✓ The evaluation identifies the precise category in which the object or phenomenon fits.

✓ The criteria by which the object or phenomenon is going to be evaluated are presented clearly.

✓ Concrete evidence and examples illustrate the ways in which the object or phenomenon does or does not meet each evaluative criterion.

✓ The evaluation articulates a clear argument about whether or not the object or phenomenon meets the criterion required of the category against which it is being evaluated.

Student paper

In the following essay, student Alexis Walker reviews what the downtown area of her hometown, Easton, Pennsylvania, has to offer, basing her evaluation on the architecture, public space, and businesses.

Alexis Walker

Prof. Davis

English 251

September 27, 2007

Donuts at Easton's Center Circle: Slam Dunk or Cycle of Deterioration?

The way a city looks--its skyline, the buildings, the streets, even the greenery--affects how we feel in that city and the perception of what it has to offer. From the hectic environment of New York to the calming quality of a rural farm, these feelings are informed by what surrounds us. With that in mind, the center of a city should, ideally, portray the best the city has to offer. Visual clues, such as the type of businesses that thrive in the area, indicate something about the town.

A quick scan around downtown Easton on a winter weekday afternoon, however, makes clear that there is much to be desired in this eastern Pennsylvania town. For instance, the prominence of the Peace Candle, standing proudly in the center of the traffic circle, assumes a grandiosity that fails to actualize itself. No matter which direction one enters the circle from, the peace candle sits straight ahead. The off-white concrete representing the wax looks grungy and neglected. Some melted wax drips down the sides in light blue cascades of color encrusting each corner. The stiff flame of orange and red metal sits atop the structure, too unassuming to project the proper vibrancy. It's all supported by a series of black visible cables emphasizing the candle's behemoth existence as almost menacing. The display of fire intends to signify energy and soul, an attempt to spark downtown into a bustling hub of city commerce full of life rather than old and dull as the mostly rundown space actually is. Instead, darkened windowpanes and boarded up entrances encircle the mammoth centerpiece.

The bright white, freshly painted outside of the new Dunkin' Donuts provides a clear contrast to the lifeless grey buildings that surround it. The signature orange and pink lettering adorns both sides of this corner edifice and its large windows showcase the patrons the establishment actually is attracting. All of these attributes, dissimilar to the dreary display downtown Easton usually offers, might suggest that the area is on the rise. Indeed, the revamped Dunkin' Donuts building and the business it brings are nice.

There are a few more exceptions to the lifeless environment intermittently placed among the abandoned properties. Pearly Bakers restaurant sits inconspicuously in one corner despite its neon green sign. Easton is also home to Crayola crayons and across the street, a building complex dominates the scene, advertising all things Crayola (and a McDonald's to boot!); a giant crayon box acts as a sign to identify--if gaudily--the gift shop entrance. It is also a relatively new building with plenty of windows and one of the taller buildings in the circle.

Considering the already successful Crayola complex and built-in McDonald's, it is clear that bigger corporations are not new to downtown. Now, though, with the addition of a Dunkin' Donuts, the precedent is set for what kind of companies can be successful within the circle: anything with a brand name. Crayola and Dunkin' Donuts both have name recognition, which is a primary reason they are

Guide to Responding

the most prominent attractions to Easton's center. The chance the center circle once had to become a thriving, eclectic neighborhood now seems impossible. Even if small businesses remain for a while, it is the Dunkin' Donuts that will draw the most business from Crayola's downtown existence and vice versa. The patronage these two businesses will bring to downtown might create some spillover business for the other establishments, but these two primary attractions seem to complement each other the most. And so the problem remains: less patronage for small businesses begets fewer attractions to offer Eastonians. There won't be any compelling postcards of the hustle and bustle of the charming city to sell. An image of a humdrum town with an emerging strip mall for a downtown region, however, is easily imaginable, if less compelling.

There are bright spots within this dismal image, though. During the summertime, provided good weather, Easton's center circle plays host to a farmer's market every week. Consisting of stands selling products from produce to freshly milled soap, it is a time when there is an alternative offering--transient as it may be--to draw a crowd. And that crowd is outside and socializing, delivering a livelier image than the downtown area used to.

Should one take a picture of these two different downtown environments, position them next to each other and then draw conclusions about what type of place Easton is to live, the results would obviously be quite different. Whether one picture is more accurate, or whether the real Easton experience is somewhere in between ultimately is irrelevant. The fact remains that a city projects a certain experience through its surroundings. Is it welcoming, impressive, expansive, busy, or a combination? Usually a trip to Easton's center circle would not yield a particularly promising impression of what Easton has to offer. Maybe the recent addition of a Dunkin' Donuts will improve downtown's condition. On the other hand, maybe it will cement its deterioration.

If your rhetorical situation does not call for an evaluation like Alexis Walker's, you can consider the following other options.

ALTERNATIVE ASSIGNMENTS

1. What happens when an image gets printed in a different medium or a design appears in a different context? How does this new context affect a viewer's or a user's experience of that image or that object? For example, how does the visual effect of a painting by Vincent van Gogh differ when it's displayed in a gallery and when it's reprinted on mugs and t-shirts? Or, how does a response to a urinal differ when it appears in a bathroom and when it appears in a museum? Write a three- to four-page analysis of how the medium or the context affects a response to an image or object.

2. As you learned throughout this chapter, descriptive details are at the heart of any analysis of our visual culture. Write a three- to four-page descriptive essay in which you help readers visualize a particular image or object and try to draw out a particular emotional response to the image or object.

3. Charles and Ray Eames designed their chairs not only as a way to express their creative vision but also, and more importantly, to solve problems they saw in people's everyday lives. Identify a design problem that affects the work or play of people on your campus or in the surrounding community. Write a three- to four-page investigative report that describes the problem and helps readers better understand how it shapes their lives in negative ways and how their lives might be different if the design were improved.

10 | CAUSES AND CONSEQUENCES OF THE GLOBAL VILLAGE: RESPONDING WITH CRITICAL ANALYSES

Cell phones are ubiquitous on college campuses; students and teachers alike punch keys on their way out the classroom door. Students' text messages and phone calls keep them connected to their friends on campus or their families in their hometowns. Now that technologies such as cell phones, satellite television, and the Internet have brought communities around the world into close contact with one another, many people speak of the global village, in which news flows between communities on different continents faster than it spreads among people living in the same town.

You have probably heard the phrase *global village* many times before. It usually suggests the positive potential for people in different parts of the world to form relationships, learn from each other, and participate in cultural exchange.

The image at the right, created by students at the University of Texas for a holiday card, represents this perspective on the idea of a global village. The global village has also become a common metaphor for the Internet's effect of connecting millions of people all over the world. But you may have heard about negative effects of the increasing interconnectedness of the world's cultures. For example, the communications networks that link so many of us create inequalities worldwide because they exclude communities that lack access to the required technology.

Writers use critical analysis to understand the specific cultural, economic, political, and social forces that have given shape to the global village, as well as to explore the consequences that have occurred or might occur as a result of its existence. This type of analysis, writers hope, can help people to be more aware of how and why they use technologies in their daily lives. In some cases, writers hope to change how people use technologies to create the kinds of virtual and physical communities in which they want to live and work.

Real Situations

Students searching the Web read articles from sites hosted around the world; farmers in rural areas use computers to keep up with international food prices; and a tsunami in Southeast Asia prompts an international outpouring of sympathy and monetary support only hours later. These are just a few examples of what it means to live in a world where electronic technology connects many people instantly. You know how to use email, to access movies made in foreign countries, to find Web pages in many languages, to read news from reporters based in Iraq—in short, how to navigate the information highway. In fact, you may believe that, in many ways, communications technology has shrunk the world to the size of a global village.

With technological developments allowing messages to be sent instantaneously around the world, many more people know about the affairs of communities and countries that may have once seemed distant from them—not only physically but intellectually as well. Being concerned with the news and affairs of others, especially those far away, is at the heart of the concept of the global village. Whereas news once spread from person to person and from home

Situations for Writers

In Qatar, journalist George Stephanopoulos interviews General Tommy Franks.

to home, it now spreads via cable and satellite to distant places. People no longer face only their own daily concerns but become vicariously—and directly—invested in what happens in far-flung places.

Along with the technological developments that led to cell phones, satellite television, and the Internet have come developments in the ways in which people create and circulate information. Individuals and organizations now create blogs to draw attention to a range of cultural perspectives and voices rarely heard in the mainstream media. Global Village Voices, to cite just one example, claims that its blog "aggregates, curates, and amplifies the global conversation online—shining light on places and people other media often ignore." The diverse global village has gotten the at-

Students in China use the Internet.

People in Saudi Arabia watch American television via satellite.

tention of some mainstream media outlets, however. The BBC's Web site, for example, highlights the 2004 series "Global Village Voices," which solicited, collected, and presented the stories of migrants from all over the world.

Despite any trend toward media inclusiveness and representation, however, a significant percentage of the world's population is not part of the global village. Limited access to communications technologies means that only groups with access get to participate in and shape the global village. That is, the images and words that represent communities without access are chosen by those who *do* have access.

Many activist groups, philanthropic organizations, and academic institutions are working to remedy this digital divide. Their shared goal is to provide marginalized populations with Internet access as a platform for speaking for themselves and participating in the global village. Some of these groups are providing the technology necessary for access; others are teaching the rhetorical skills necessary for producing Web content. The hope is that more people will help to shape the global village with their contributions, rather than simply consume information from it. In "Community Computing and Citizen Productivity," Jeffrey T. Grabill claims that computer networks can only be helpful to marginalized communities if they can be used in "village building," not as "information dumps" but as "communicative and productive spaces."

Of course, many individuals and groups are marginalized and voiceless within their own cities or countries, to say nothing of the global village. Some-

John Davies displays the Classmate PC, a low-cost laptop computer created by Intel for schoolchildren in Brazil.

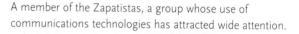
A member of the Zapatistas, a group whose use of communications technologies has attracted wide attention.

times, marginalized people find that the only way they can circulate their messages is to use the communications technologies available to them. Later in this chapter, you'll read about the Zapatistas (officially known as the Ejército Zapatista de Liberación Nacional, or the EZLN), who have gained international attention for their subversive use of fax machines, radio, satellite television, and the Internet. Because they have no access to the officially sanctioned Mexican media, the Zapatistas use other means to promote indigenous musicians and story-tellers and broadcast political speeches by EZLN leaders directly to the global village.

The concern about access to the global village, then, involves important questions about who participates, what their participation entails, how various communities are represented online and in other global media, and just what (and whose) information and ideas are available throughout this village.

DESCRIBING THE GLOBAL VILLAGE

1. Look again at the images in this section. In what ways does each one prompt you to think about what the global village is and why it's an important phenomenon to analyze more thoroughly?

2. Select the two images that resonate most strongly with you as you begin to understand more about the global village. What interests you the most about these particular images?

3. Write for five minutes about what each of the two images you chose makes you think about the causes or the consequences of living, learning, and working within the global village. Be prepared to share your answers with your classmates.

4. Look once more at all the images in this section. Which ones challenge your thinking about the global village and the positive or negative consequences that follow from it? In what specific ways do they present an opposing perspective to your own?

COMMUNITY CONNECTIONS

1. Write for five to ten minutes about your experiences using technologies such as a cell phone, satellite television, or the Internet to communicate with or learn about people in other parts of the world. What kinds of information tend to come to you without your making much effort? What kinds of information do you tend to seek out actively?

2. Write for another five minutes about your experiences communicating face to face with people from other parts of the world—either when traveling or through contacts with visitors to this country. What have you learned about these people, their cultures, and their worldviews through this type of interaction?

continued

3. Take five minutes to analyze the differences between your virtual and physical interactions with people from around the world. How and what do you learn through each type of interaction?

4. Reread your responses to questions 1–3, and then spend five to ten minutes writing about the consequences (for yourself personally, for people in your particular community or country, or for people in the world at large) of living, working, and communicating within the global village.

Real Responses to Real Situations

Tracing the causes and consequences of the global village

For a decade, from the mid-1960s to the mid-1970s, Marshall McLuhan was North America's media guru. His provocative theories and public pronouncements about media, technology, and the effects of electronic communication made him a leading pop cultural figure. He was interviewed on national television in Canada and the United States, featured on the cover of *Newsweek,* and parodied in *New Yorker* cartoons; his opinions on the social and cultural effects of media were debated internationally in newspapers, in classrooms, and on television. His best-known books, *Understanding Media: The Extensions of Man* and *The Medium Is the Massage,* sold millions of copies around the world.

Marshall McLuhan sought to understand the impact of electronic media.

McLuhan was fascinated by the explosion of mass media that occurred in the post–World War II economic boom, and he was passionately concerned with the direction in which it was taking society. He was worried that not enough people were paying attention to the role media and electronic communication played in their lives. In an interview with journalist Eric Norden, he reiterated this caution:

Today, in the electronic age of instantaneous communication, I believe that our survival, and at the very least our comfort and happiness, is predicated on understanding the nature of our new environment, because unlike previous environmental changes, the electric media constitute a total and near instantaneous transformation of culture, values, and attitudes. This upheaval generates great pain and identity loss, which can be ameliorated only through a consciousness of its dynamics. If we understand the revolutionary transformations caused by new media, we can anticipate and control them; but if we continue in our self-induced subliminal trance, we will be their slaves.

McLuhan was convinced that everyone living in developed nations needed to understand how technology was shaping their social and political life as the world moved from the industrial revolution to the information revolution.

This photo collage by Hulleah Tsinhnahjinnie, called "Mattie Looks for Steve Biko," can be seen as an interpretation of the concept of a global village.

It was McLuhan's 1964 electronic media project (in particular, *Understanding Media: The Extensions of Man*) that would make him a household name as well as a sensation on the lecture and interview circuit. In *Understanding Media*, McLuhan observed that modern society was moving into a new era of "all-at-onceness" defined by a tremendous speedup in daily life, the connection of people and economies around the world regardless of time and space, and "almost overnight cultural change." During an interview on the Canadian television show *Explorations*, McLuhan explained what he meant: "The world is now like a continually sounding tribal drum, where everybody gets the message all the time—a princess gets married in England and boom, boom, boom go the drums. We all hear about it. An earthquake in North Africa, a Hollywood star gets drunk, away go the drums again." The nature of electronic media was making the world smaller and more interconnected—what McLuhan identified as a global village.

In *Understanding Media*, McLuhan highlighted the unifying effects of this technology. We are all interconnected, McLuhan seemed to be arguing—and people should begin to consider the consequences of this new interconnectedness.

MARSHALL MCLUHAN
Excerpt from Understanding Media: The Extensions of Man

Today, the instantaneous world of electric information media involves us all, all at once. Ours is a brand-new world of all-at-onceness. Time, in a sense, has ceased and space has vanished. Like primitives, we now live in a global village of our own making, a simultaneous happening. The global village is not created by the motor car or even by the airplane. It is created by instant electronic information movement. The global village is at once as wide as the planet and as small as the little town where everybody is maliciously engaged in poking his nose into everybody else's business. The global village is a world in which you don't necessarily have harmony; you have extreme concern with everybody else's business and much involvement in everybody else's life. It's a sort of Ann Landers column written larger. And it doesn't necessarily mean harmony and peace and quiet, but it does mean huge involvement in everybody else's affairs. And so, the global village is as big as a planet and as small as the village post office. . . .

Tokyo isn't much farther away than the suburbs in point of time. So the patterns of human association vary enormously with the amount of acceleration possible. I think now of the city as the planet itself, the urban village or global village. And, in fact, you could say that with the satellite, the global village has become a global theater, with everybody on the planet simultaneously participating as actors. Students around the globe feel an entire unity among themselves; they feel a homogeneity of interest. They live in an information environment created by electricity. They share the same information or electric environment of information and they share the same outlook around the world. . . .

> "Mental breakdown . . . is the very common result of uprooting and inundation with new information . . ."

Electric speed in bringing all social and political functions together in a sudden implosion has heightened human awareness of responsibility to an intense degree. It is this implosive factor that alters the position of the Negro, the teenager, and some other groups. They can no longer be *contained,* in the political sense of limited association. They are now involved in our lives, as we in theirs, thanks to the electric media.

This is the Age of Anxiety for the reason of the electric implosion that compels commitment and participation, quite regardless of any "point of view." . . .

Electric speed . . . has revealed the lines of force . . . from Western technology in the remotest areas of bush, savannah, and desert. One example is the Bedouin with his battery radio on board the camel. Submerging natives with floods of concepts for which nothing has prepared them is the normal action of all of our technology. But with electric media Western man himself experiences exactly the same inundation as the remote native. We are no more prepared to encounter radio and TV in our literate milieu than the native of Ghana is able to cope with the literacy that takes him out of his collective tribal world and beaches him in individual isolation. We are as numb in our new electronic world as the native involved in our literature and mechanical culture. Electric speed mingles the cultures of prehistory with the dregs of industrial marketers, the nonliterate with the semiliterate and the postliterate. Mental breakdown of varying degrees is the very common result of uprooting and inundation with new information and endless new patterns of information.

Though many people enthusiastically embraced McLuhan's argument that electronic media would bring an eventual unification of people and points of view, the concept of the global village was not wholly positive. Electronic media might be making the world smaller but were not necessarily making the world a better place. According to McLuhan, the greater unification and interconnectedness of the world would be disturbing to the people involved. No village, not even the global village, could be without conflict and violence. Writing about the

Marshall McLuhan might have imagined the Newseum (the Interactive Museum of News in Washington, DC) when he said, "Ours is a brand-new world of all-at-onceness." "All-at-onceness" is embodied on the museum's video wall.

potential power of technology to make the world one small village, McLuhan admonishes his readers to think about the negative consequences of that power.

Today, we contemplate a possible link between violent video games and violent crimes. Public forums are given over to discussions of how much televised and online coverage of tragedies is enough. As yet another school-related tragedy, the massacre at Virginia Tech, prompted days of media analyses, we wondered how much personal information, how much psychological background, how much footage of the shooter's weapons display do we really need to access? In the global village of the twenty-first century, such ruminations are commonplace. But well over forty years ago—long before email, the Web, or violent computer games were in anyone's imagination—McLuhan had already recognized that the race toward electronic technology (whatever that technology might turn out to be) would not lead to unilaterally positive results and might even lead to "mental breakdown."

Not everyone thought Marshall McLuhan was a genius. A cult of "McLuhanism" grew up around his ideas, but critics called his popularity "McLuhanacy" and decried his broad generalizations and often obscure writing style. Philip Marchand, McLuhan's biographer, observed in *Medium and Messenger:* "It was possible he was a true intellectual giant, of the sort who forces subsequent generations to perceive the world in new ways. On the other hand, many serious academics and intellectuals dismissed him outright as a charlatan or a crank."

Jonathan Miller was one who disparaged McLuhan's ideas about the international effects of electronic media such as television. In his 1971 book, *Marshall McLuhan,* Miller claimed that McLuhan was carried away by his own predictions and that he downplayed the negative effects of technology on society. Where McLuhan saw unification, Miller saw division brought about by the spread of electronic media. He feared that an embrace of McLuhan's idea of the global village might lead people to ignore ways that media were being used, for example, to portray people from other countries as outsiders.

JONATHAN MILLER
Excerpt from Marshall McLuhan

. . . As usual, however, McLuhan exaggerates and distorts the details of this fickle communion. According to him the electronic network has re-tribalized modern man, overcome the fissiparous influence of print, and restored the human race to its rightful place in the "global village."

> "A stirring slogan, but is it anything more?"

A stirring slogan, but is it anything more? The so-called community called into existence by television has very little more than a metaphorical affinity with a village, whose distinctive character is significantly defined by the face-to-face collaboration of the people who form its enduring nucleus. A genuine village community exists only through the local institutions that embody the shared interests of its inhabitants. Such institutions more or less effectively exclude the participation of outsiders who do not contribute directly to their upkeep.

It is true, of course, that television allows us to share the experiences of those who live at a great distance. But the whole point about such "shared" experiences is that they are essentially vicarious, and have little or nothing in common with the experiences that define the characteristic collectivism of village life. For example, when Americans viewed the television pictures of the Vietnam war—especially the live transmissions—their concern and interest were expressed mainly for the condition of "our boys out there." That is to say, television illustrated the fate of *American* "villagers." Insofar as television excited concern on behalf of the *Vietnamese,* it did not do so because the viewers recognized them as fellow villagers, but rather because they acknowledged them as human personalities to whom certain generalized obligations were due. . . .

[It] is important to distinguish such abstract principles from the concrete scruples that control the way in which tribal villagers behave toward one another. For the essential feature of tribal or village morality is that it is not realized with reference to general principles—or at least not to principles that can be articulated independently of the contexts to which they immediately apply. The moral imperatives that shape the collective conduct of village life are insepa-rable from the immediate circumstances which they control. They are embedded in the social context that gives them meaning, and it is very doubtful whether the people who behave in accordance with them would ever recognize their existence as an independent body of moral regulations. . . .

McLuhan also underestimated the destructive features of television, and he has overlooked those which actually undermine the sense of global community.

For a start, there are now so many documentary and current-affairs programs that insofar as television *has* enlarged the family of man, it has done so beyond the point where genuine sentiment can be expressed for all its constituent members. There is after all a limit upon the number of moral obligations that any individual can feel himself capable of discharging. Confronted as he is now by the image of so many human predicaments, the spectator becomes confused, frustrated, and finally, in self-protection, isolationist. He almost deliberately exempts himself from the concern that these programs would otherwise seem to solicit.

This sense of alienation is reinforced by certain sensory features of the medium contrary to what McLuhan asserts. Television is strikingly visual and the images it presents are curiously dissociated from all the other senses. The viewer sits watching them all in the drab comfort of his own home, cut off from the pain, heat, and smell of what is actually going on. Even the sound is artificial. . . . All these effects serve to distance the viewer from the scenes he is watching, and eventually he falls into the unconscious belief that the events that happen on television are going on in some unbelievably remote theater of human activity.

The alienating effect is magnified by the fact that the television screen reduces all images to the same visual quality. Atrocity and entertainment alternate with one another on the same rectangle of bulging glass. Comedy and politics merge into one continuous ribbon of transmission. It is hard to see how ordinary village life can survive under such conditions, let alone that of a global village.

ANALYZING THE RHETORICAL SITUATION

1. Who might have been the intended audience for Marshall McLuhan's book *Understanding Media*? What textual evidence can you provide to support your answer?

2. To what exigence might McLuhan have been responding in his book *Understanding Media* (keep in mind that it was published in 1964)?

3. How does McLuhan use the rhetorical appeals of ethos, logos, and pathos in the excerpt from *Understanding Media*? Which of the appeals is most dominant? Provide textual evidence to support your answer.

4. Why do you think McLuhan says "the global village is a world in which you don't necessarily have harmony"?

5. What does Jonathan Miller think makes a community a "genuine village"? What does he think are the negative effects of the spread of television? Do you agree?

Tools for bringing the world together

Since Marshall McLuhan first discussed the global village, the world has been shaped in profound ways by the spread of communications technologies such as television, cellular phones, and the Internet. You can stay on top of political events around the globe on cable television news outlets such as CNN,

Google Earth's Crisis in Darfur project tracks the devastating effects of genocide in that country.

Fox News, and MSNBC. By downloading Google Earth, you can witness the effects of the genocide in Darfur through interactive mapping technologies enhanced with research from the United States Holocaust Museum. You can also write a blog to narrate your daily experiences, from the incredible to the mundane, and comment on the atmosphere for women on campus or the political leanings of the candidates for president of the student government; you can link readers of your blog to a hilarious video you just saw on YouTube or review the latest CD by your favorite musician. You can create friendships with students at colleges and universities all over the world through online forums such as MySpace and Facebook. All of these activities make use of emerging digital technologies in ways that seem to forge new connections between people around the globe, bringing the news and the opinions of many individuals and groups into public view.

Just as in McLuhan's time, cultural critics, political commentators, and engaged citizens have debated the consequences of the proliferation of digital technologies. They have analyzed the ways in which communities and societies have responded to the flood of images and texts detailing events in other parts of the world. They have debated the extent to which such images and texts reflect the truth of particular communities' experiences and worldviews. And they have analyzed the causes and the consequences of some communities' inability to access the technologies that would enable them to enter the global village. These critical analyses of the global effects of communications technologies show that McLuhan's vision of the information society continues to prompt inquiry and reflection.

Many news analysts and cultural commentators have looked at digital activities such as blogging and podcasting and online forums such as Wikipedia and YouTube and seen a radical reshaping of the ways knowledge is produced and distributed throughout the world. In effect, they seem to suggest, the global village is becoming more pluralistic and more democratic as more individuals have the tools for communicating their ideas and the events of their lives throughout the world via the Web. *Time* magazine was supporting the idea that average individuals increasingly shape the global village when it made its much anticipated announcement of "Person of the Year" for 2006: "You." *Time*'s editors acknowledged that the materials made available through the Internet vary in value. Nevertheless, they saw exciting political, cultural, and social consequences for the global village arising from the technologies that allow individuals to create text, audio, and video and upload their creations to the Web.

LEV GROSSMAN
Time's Person of the Year: You

The "Great Man" theory of history is usually attributed to the Scottish philosopher Thomas Carlyle, who wrote that "the history of the world is but the biography of great men." He believed that it is the few, the powerful and the famous who shape our collective destiny as a species. That theory took a serious beating this year.

To be sure, there are individuals we could blame for the many painful and disturbing things that happened in 2006. The conflict in Iraq only got bloodier and more entrenched. A vicious skirmish erupted between Israel and Lebanon. A war dragged on in Sudan. A tin-pot dictator in North Korea got the Bomb, and the President of Iran wants to go nuclear too. Meanwhile nobody fixed global warming, and Sony didn't make enough PlayStation3s.

But look at 2006 through a different lens and you'll see another story, one that isn't about conflict or great men. It's a story about community and collaboration on a scale never seen before. It's about the cosmic compendium of knowledge Wikipedia and the million-channel people's network YouTube and the online metropolis MySpace. It's about the many wresting power from the few and helping one another for nothing and how that will not only change the world, but also change the way the world changes.

The tool that makes this possible is the World Wide Web. Not the Web that Tim Berners-Lee hacked together (15 years ago, according to Wikipedia) as a way for scientists to share research. It's not even the over-hyped dotcom Web of the late 1990s. The new Web is a very different thing. It's a tool for bringing together the small contributions of millions of people and making them matter. Silicon Valley consultants call it Web 2.0, as if it were a new version of some old software. But it's really a revolution.

And we are so ready for it. We're ready to balance our diet of predigested news with raw feeds from Baghdad and Boston and Beijing. You can learn more about how Americans live just by looking at the backgrounds of YouTube videos—those rumpled bedrooms and toy-strewn basement rec rooms—than you could from 1,000 hours of network television.

And we didn't just watch, we also worked. Like crazy. We made Facebook profiles and Second Life avatars and reviewed books at Amazon and recorded podcasts. We blogged about our candidates losing and wrote songs about getting dumped. We camcordered bombing runs and built open-source software.

America loves its solitary geniuses—its Einsteins, its Edisons, its Jobses—but those lonely dreamers may have to learn to play with others. Car companies are running open design contests. Reuters is carrying blog postings alongside its regular news feed. Microsoft is working overtime to fend off user-created Linux. We're looking at an explosion of productivity and innovation, and it's just getting started, as millions of minds that would otherwise have drowned in obscurity get backhauled into the global intellectual economy.

Who are these people? Seriously, who actually sits down after a long day at work and says, I'm not going to watch *Lost* tonight? I'm going to turn on my computer and make a movie starring my pet iguana? I'm going to mash up 50 Cent's vocals with Queen's instrumentals? I'm going to blog about my state of mind or the state of the nation or the *steak-frites* at the new bistro down the street? Who has that time and that energy and that passion?

The answer is, you do. And for seizing the reins of the global media, for founding and framing the new digital democracy, for working for nothing and beating the pros at their own game, TIME's Person of the Year for 2006 is you.

Sure, it's a mistake to romanticize all this any more than is strictly necessary. Web 2.0 harnesses the stupidity of crowds as well as [the] wisdom. Some of the comments on YouTube make you weep for the future of humanity just for the spelling alone, never mind the obscenity and the naked hatred.

But that's what makes all this interesting. Web 2.0 is a massive social experiment, and like any experiment worth trying, it could fail. There's no road map for how an organism that's not a bacterium lives and works together on this planet in numbers in excess of 6 billion. But 2006 gave us some ideas. This is an opportunity to build a new kind of international understanding, not politician to politician, great man to great man, but citizen to citizen, person to person. It's a chance for people to look at a computer screen and really, genuinely wonder who's out there looking back at them. Go on. Tell us you're not just a little bit curious.

> "The new Web is a very different thing."

With the 2006 "Person of the Year" award, the editors of *Time* proclaimed a revolution in the global village, with more and more people communicating about their lives, through blogs, MySpace pages, podcasts, and YouTube videos. Many commentators, though, have drawn attention to the lack of access among marginalized groups to technologies such as computers, Internet connections, and digital and audio production equipment. They argue that getting such technologies into the hands of people living on the economic, political, and cultural margins of society will make the global village a more inclusive and potentially more revolutionary place.

Other cultural critics, though, such as Syracuse University professor Adam J. Banks, argue that we need to think more critically about what this access must look like—and what access *should* look like if the Internet is to be truly revolutionary. In his book *Race, Rhetoric, and Technology: Searching for Higher Ground*, Banks questions three common assumptions about African Americans' access to and use of technology: (1) that African Americans have not made significant, productive uses of and advances in technology; (2) that meaningful access to computer and Internet technologies merely entails ownership of a computer and a rudimentary set of skills for consuming information through it; and (3) that the Internet has created a global village in which people are free from real-world constraints created by racial and cultural differences. In the following passage, Banks points to the positive cultural and social consequences for African Americans of working within online spaces, particularly of those uses of computer and Internet technologies that have traditionally been deemed unproductive. And in his analysis of users of the Web site BlackPlanet, Banks demonstrates how important ethnic, racial, linguistic, political, cultural, and social identities are within the global village. In fact, online identities are every bit as important to individuals as are their real-world identities in cities, towns, and villages.

Race, Rhetoric, and Technology

Searching for Higher Ground

40 years later and we barely got the signs taken down

Adam J. Banks

Adam J. Banks
Excerpt from Race, Rhetoric, and Technology: Searching for Higher Ground

Real Responses

"Sometimes I wish they didn't even have these things in here. Kids just have no idea how powerful a tool they have in front of them. If we had something like this when we were in school, hell, I would have graduated at 15 or 16." This comment, from a Cleveland Public Library employee, says a great deal about how people who are charged with providing technology access understand technologies, understand access. I worked part-time for the library . . . , filling in at neighborhood branches, assisting patrons when the library system was just beginning to make computers and Internet connections available to its patrons. [Its] approach to this task was to outfit each branch with four to six computers in the hope that patrons would become more technologically literate as a result.

And the patrons responded—especially children and young adults. Librarians and other staff members at many branches became disillusioned, however, because these children and young adults weren't making what they saw as "productive" uses of computers or the Internet. The most popular activities were chatting on sites like BlackPlanet, Yahoo, BlackVoices and others, downloading music lyrics (often the uncensored versions, which really frustrated the staff), and viewing music-related Web sites. Some branches specifically prohibited chatting and downloading music lyrics, and some branches [had] policies banning these activities at certain hours.

The Cleveland Public Library employee's comment points to several issues, from cultural nostalgia to the frustration librarians and library staff feel about not being able to do more to help young people, to the potential uses students and others might put computers. I include it here to show the ways recreational uses of technologies are often seen as problematic rather than valuable. There are many people for whom a study of African Americans' recreational uses of the Internet would seem odd, or even counterproductive. There would appear to be far more important sites in which to study African American technology use and far more important kinds of online communication to study—

> "... Black people do connect with technologies in meaningful ways when they have access."

e-mail and other workplace documents, college student writing, online student-teacher interaction, political organizations' or grassroots activists' uses of digital technologies. But there is a case to be made that African Americans' recreational uses of the Web are just as important a subject of study as any other, because those uses occur in spaces that are removed from the disciplinary forces of schools, libraries, and other organizations where literacies are taught. . . .

Individual usernames begin to show this claiming of space: space for an individual identity on the Planet, a connection to African American and Afro-diasporic culture, and public space in broader online and real world discourse. It is sometimes easy to dismiss the importance of online nicknames as merely whimsical, but their importance is clear here on BlackPlanet for several reasons. One of those reasons is that they show the site's members embracing Blackness clearly and openly, and in rich complexity, in clear opposition to theories about computers and cyberspace that assumed fragmentation and "identity tourism" would be the norm, or those theories and technology practices that assumed Whiteness as a default, because after all, "it doesn't matter who you are online." These nicknames make connections to Black musical traditions (2in2Prince, MoreHouseBlues, old-schoolmusicman, kweli, methodwoman); they claim space and authority to speak on political, cultural, and technical subjects (BlackbyDesign, WebDesignTips, liberatedlady); they proclaim Black sexuality as healthy in spite of the power of stereotypes of that sexuality (SensualOne, skillz); they show members' participation in African American organizations (Blackman_06, AKATude, EasternStar); they misbehave and poke fun at assumptions about "good" behavior (legitballin, old-skoolplaya, dpimptress); they resist monolithic beauty standards and identify Black aesthetics as the standards for beauty in this space (bmorelocs, chocolate-beauty, redbonenubian). Those names and the names of other members reveal complexity and diversity in notions of exactly what constitutes a Black identity, but all of the

continued

users—many overtly through their usernames—participate in and claim a Black identity for themselves. These names also call attention to online identities that are free to claim all of these qualities and connections even as they question or revise them.

In [accounting] for the rarity of African American scientists, Lois Powell makes the claim . . . . that African American and Latino youth avoid majoring in science because their cultures have constructed negative images of scientists and believe careers in the sciences to be unrealistic goals . . . . Powell asserts that these unfavorable images include those of scientists as strange, unhappy, and iconoclastic, no matter how intelligent. Although Powell seems to be genuinely concerned with increasing the numbers of African Americans pursuing mathematics and science careers, the argument seems to follow the same old conservative diatribes launched against African Americans: namely, that the problem is cultural rather than systemic.

BlackPlanet users respond to this perception, though, and show that Black people do connect with technologies in meaningful ways when they have access. Members "talk b(l)ack" to perceptions like this by refiguring both technology and the image of the computer geek, connecting both to Black culture. Some of the forums on the site show this redefinition at work, covering topics from Linux [to] IT certification, tips for web designers, and Internet entrepreneurship. The language of the prompts of others might demonstrate the degree to which BP members have made technology connect with Black identity: a forum titled "what works what

doesn't?" offers the following question: "What makes a good personal page? When you look at other people's personal pages on BP, what stands out?" This question might not seem significant in a discussion of cultural identity and technology, but the prompt foregrounds what other members of BP have done in establishing criteria for the broader genre of the personal web page. Another forum, "you know you are hooked on the Net when . . ." begins "Ok, chat heads, techies, geeks, 'puter lovers . . . let's get real. Y'all know you spend way too much time on the Net when . . ." Black people are techies and geeks in this forum, and their use of [African American Vernacular English] suggests how comfortably [they fit] within Black culture. And while the joke in the prompt might suggest that Net use is discouraged, the tone and appropriation of the long-standing "you know you ghetto when" jokes show that they are accepted in the forum and on the Planet, even if they do suggest a line between being involved with technology and being hooked.

A final forum is called "Triflin Personal Pages," and leads with this comment: "Okay, I have about had it with some of these pages that are about the equivalent of Mr. T's gold chains. Too much mess!! Does anybody feel me on here?" This is a normalizing move, in which the user posting to the forum is attempting to get the group to set some expectations for page design, but of course this call looking for a response is also laced with echoes of an entire oral tradition: holla!!! Ya heard? Nahmeen?

ANALYZING THE RHETORICAL SITUATION

1. According to the editors of *Time*, what exactly is the "new Web"? What economic, social, and technological events have led to its creation? How does the new Web relate to the reformation of the global village? You may want to draw on your own experiences working with digital technologies as you compose your response.

2. What evidence do Adam J. Banks and the editors of *Time* include to support their evaluations of good and bad Internet use? Who is the audience for each analysis?

3. What exigence sparks Banks's analysis? What problem does Banks analyze?

4. How does Banks define "meaningful access" to computer and Internet technologies? What positive consequences follow from such access? What specific evidence does Banks provide to support his analysis?

5. How do the editors of *Time* and Banks use ethos, pathos, and logos to build the arguments they make in their critical analyses? (Provide textual evidence to support your answer.) Which of the rhetorical appeals is most evident in each analysis? Be prepared to share your answer with the rest of the class.

6. What available means do the editors of *Time* and Banks use to enter the conversation about the global village?

COMMUNITY CONNECTIONS

1. Write for ten minutes about your response to the analysis of communications technologies and the global village crafted by Marshall McLuhan or the editors of *Time*. How does that analysis align with your own experiences with such technologies?

2. Write for ten minutes responding to the arguments of Jonathan Miller and Adam Banks. How do their arguments coincide with or diverge from your experiences in working with old or new forms of media?

3. In terms of the critical analyses by McLuhan, Miller, the editors of *Time*, and Banks, how does your campus or community relate to the global village? What specific developments (technological, economic, cultural, political, or social) enable students or local citizens to contribute to or consume within the global village? Which of those developments have been planned? Unplanned?

4. How would you describe the ideal global village? What practices would shape it? What activities would take place within it? Who would contribute to and participate in these practices?

Critical Analyses: A Fitting Response

Two critical analyses of the global village

There can be little doubt that digital media and communications technologies have shaped present-day societies in significant ways. Disagreement arises, however, when people begin to debate the causes and the consequences of this technological and social transformation. Some ask whether the characteristics of certain media lead people to feel closer to or more remote from what they see and hear from communities around the globe; some question the extent to which the global village does or does not represent the perspectives of all groups, particularly the poor and the powerless, in various societies. The proliferation of digital media and the integration of communications technologies into so many people's lives—and the lack of integration into the lives of so many others—create a particularly compelling exigence for critical analysis.

Thomas L. Friedman, a columnist for the *New York Times,* responded to this exigence in a column he wrote eight months after the terrorist attacks of September 11, 2001. During his travels around the world, Friedman observed how the media, with ever increasing speed and ever fewer filters, present the perspectives of others to people in widespread cultural communities. Friedman offers a critical analysis of the consequences when instant communication is not accompanied by a heightened ability to understand and analyze the information presented.

As you read this critical analysis, notice the ways Friedman addressed each feature of his rhetorical situation: exigence, purpose, audience, and available means. Notice, too, how he meets the requirements of any critical analysis: (1) he describes the situation or phenomenon in specific detail and explains why it is worth analyzing; (2) he makes an explicit argument about the causes and/or the consequences of the situation or phenomenon he is analyzing; (3) he presents evidence and examples to support his assertion; and (4) he acknowledges and responds to alternative perspectives on the situation or phenomenon.

Thomas L. Friedman

Global Village Idiocy

During a dinner with Indonesian journalists in Jakarta [Indonesia], I was taken aback when Dini Djalal, a reporter for *The Far Eastern Economic Review,* suddenly launched into a blistering criticism of the Fox News Channel and Bill O'Reilly. "They say [on Fox], 'We report, you decide,' but it's biased—they decide before us," she said. "They say there is no spin, but I get dizzy looking at it. I also get upset when they invite on Muslims and just insult them." Why didn't she just not watch Fox when she came to America, I wondered? No, no, no, explained Ms. Djalal: The Fox Channel is now part of her Jakarta cable package. The conservative Bill O'Reilly is in her face every night. [1]

On my way to Jakarta I stopped in Dubai, where I watched the Arab News Network at 2 a.m. ANN broadcasts from Europe, outside the control of any Arab government, but is seen all over the Middle East. It was running what I'd call the "greatest hits" from the Israeli-Palestinian conflict: nonstop film of Israelis hitting, beating, dragging, clubbing and shooting Palestinians. I would like to say the footage was out of context, but there was no context. There were no words. It was just pictures and martial music designed to inflame passions. [2]

An Indonesian working for the U.S. Embassy in Jakarta, who had just visited the Islamic fundamentalist stronghold of Jogjakarta, told me this story: "For the first time I saw signs on the streets there saying things like, 'The only solution to the Arab-Israel conflict is jihad—if you are true Muslim, register yourself to be a volunteer.' I heard people saying, 'We have to do something, otherwise the Christians or Jewish will kill us.' When we talked to people to find out where [they got these ideas], they said from the Internet. They took

[1] Friedman opens his critical analysis with an anecdote that reveals his exigence.

[2] The writer provides another example to describe the situation he will analyze, including details to help readers understand why it is worth analyzing.

for granted that anything they learned from the Internet is true. They believed in a Jewish conspiracy and that 4,000 Jews were warned not to come to work at the World Trade Center [on Sept. 11]. It was on the Internet." **[3]** What's frightening him, he added, is that there is an insidious digital divide in Jogjakarta: "Internet users are only 5 percent of the population—but these 5 percent spread rumors to everyone else. They say, 'He got it from the Internet.' They think it's the Bible."

If there's one thing I learned from this trip to Israel, Jordan, Dubai and Indonesia, it's this: thanks to the Internet and satellite TV, the world is being wired together technologically, but not socially, politically or culturally. We are now seeing and hearing one another faster and better, but with no corresponding improvement in our ability to learn from, or understand, one another. So integration, at this stage, is producing more anger than anything else. **[4]** As the writer George Packer recently noted in *The Times Magazine,* "In some ways, global satellite TV and Internet access have actually made the world a less understanding, less tolerant place."

At its best, the Internet can educate more people faster than any media tool we've ever had. **[5]** At its worst, it can make people dumber faster than any media tool we've ever had. The lie that 4,000 Jews were warned not to go into the World Trade Center on Sept. 11 was spread entirely over the Internet and is now thoroughly believed in the Muslim world. Because the Internet has an aura of "technology" surrounding it, the uneducated believe information from it even more. They don't realize that the Internet, at its ugliest, is just an open sewer: an electronic conduit for untreated, unfiltered information.

Worse, just when you might have thought you were all alone with your extreme views, the Internet puts you together with a community of people from around the world who hate all the things and people you do. **[6]** And you can scrap the BBC and just get your news from those Web sites that reinforce your own stereotypes.

A couple of years ago, two Filipino college graduates spread the "I Love You" virus over the Internet, causing billions of dollars in damage to computers and software. But at least that virus was curable with the right software. **[7]** There is another virus going around today, though, that's much more serious. I call it the "I Hate You" virus. It's spread on the Internet and by satellite TV. It infects people's minds with the most vile ideas, and it can't be combated by just downloading a software program. It can be reversed only with education, exchanges, diplomacy and human interaction—stuff you have to upload the old-fashioned way, one on one. Let's hope it's not too late.

[3] Friedman includes other voices in his analysis to convince readers that he is not alone in seeing a need to analyze the causes and the consequences of this situation.

[4] Although they come in the middle of the piece rather than closer to the beginning, the first three sentences of this paragraph serve as Friedman's thesis.

[5] Friedman uses the preceding short sentence to acknowledge a counterargument. He uses the next sentence to respond to that counterargument, and he then provides an example to support his assertion.

[6] Friedman provides another example that reinforces his thesis.

[7] Friedman begins his conclusion by setting up a contrast that will reinforce his analysis of the problem.

In the following *Newsweek* article, Russell Watson (with contributors John Barry, Christopher Dickey, and Tim Padgett) examines how some communities who have traditionally lacked a political voice in their countries have appropriated communications technologies to announce their presence within and transmit their messages throughout the global village.

Russell Watson

When Words Are the Best Weapon

Situations for Writers

[1] The writer uses a dash in the preceding sentence to dramatic effect, as he upends most readers' expectations of what revolutionary fighters' "most valuable equipment" would be.

[2] Like Thomas L. Friedman, Watson presents a detailed example in the introductory paragraph as a way of engaging readers' interest and revealing his exigence.

[3] Watson uses a direct quotation from Subcomandante Marcos to offer readers the revolutionary group's perspective.

[4] The writer makes an assertion here about information technology, and he supports this claim in the sentences that follow.

[5] Watson underscores his claim about the importance of information technology for present-day revolutionary groups, noting that they accomplish "little or nothing on the battlefield." He further supports his claim with the quotation from an expert that follows.

[6] Here Watson explains how contemporary information technology differs from older forms.

Here's how to wage a revolution in the Information Age: two weeks ago Mexican government troops lunged into the rain forests of Chiapas state in renewed pursuit of the Zapatista rebels. When the federal soldiers reached an insurgent stronghold at Guadalupe Tepeyac, the guerrillas melted into the jungle, leaving behind a few trucks but taking with them their most valuable equipment— fax machines and laptop computers. **[1]** In retreat, the Zapatistas faxed out a communiqué claiming that the army was "killing children, beating and raping women . . . and bombing us." Soon the government was taking another public relations beating. It stopped the offensive and allowed reporters into the area. They found no signs of atrocities or bombing. But the government attack had been thwarted, and the rebels were free to fight on, with words as their best weapons. **[2]**

The Zapatistas' chief spokesman, Subcomandante Marcos (the government says his name is Rafael Guillén), knows that he will never obtain political power from the barrel of a gun. "What governments should really fear," he told a *Newsweek* reporter last summer, "is a communications expert." **[3]** Information technology has always been seen as a potentially revolutionary weapon. **[4]** Almost as soon as the printing press was invented, governments and churches tried to control it, and the Ottoman Empire shunned the technology for almost 300 years. The American Revolution was spurred on by Benjamin Franklin, a printer; Thomas Paine, a pamphleteer; and Samuel Adams, a propagandist. In the modern era, vulnerable governments have been challenged by proliferating means of communication. Long-distance telephone service, for example, helped to undermine the Soviet Union, connecting dissidents to each other and to supporters outside the country. Other Communist regimes have been weakened by radio and television signals: West German programs beamed into East Germany, and broadcasts from Hong Kong feeding the appetite for reform in mainland China.

Violent revolutions, especially those that resort to terrorism, often have the most success with relatively low-tech weapons. But like the Zapatistas, many of today's revolutionaries are better talkers than fighters, accomplishing little or nothing on the battlefield. **[5]** "These new insurgencies, in the end, are aimed more at high-intensity lobbying and low-intensity fighting," says William Leo-Grande of the American University in Washington, an expert on leftist movements. Now they have the tools they need. Older communications technology, such as radio and television, is centralized and subject to government control, if only through the assignment of frequencies and the jamming of unauthorized signals. The latest gear, such as satellite television receivers or computers linked to the Internet, is decentralized, diffused and—so far—almost impossible to police or control. **[6]**

The Internet is the fastest-growing communication tool, with as many as 30 million subscribers in 92 countries. Even Chinese dissidents are beginning to use e-mail. News about the fight against Chinese repression in Tibet is regularly gathered and circulated by the London-based Tibet Information Network, one of dozens of human-rights organizations using the Information Superhighway. In the Soviet Union, the Internet played a small but vital role in defeating the attempted coup by Communist hard-liners in 1991. Soviet computer scientists had hooked up to the Internet only a few months before. When Boris Yeltsin and his reformists holed up in the White House, the Russian republic's Parliament, someone inside the building started sending bulletins, including Yeltsin's edicts, on the Internet. They were picked up by the Voice of America (VOA), which broadcast them back to the Soviet Union by radio, helping to rally public support for Yeltsin. **[7]**

Since then, the VOA has made a big investment in the Internet. It now offers computer users written news reports in 47 languages and audio bulletins in 16. Access is obtained through two of the Internet's standard communications protocols: Internet Gopher and FTP (File Transfer Protocol). Those aren't the most advanced access gates, but that's precisely why the VOA chose them; more users overseas are likely to have them. The VOA currently logs about 100,000 uses of its Internet service each week. That's minuscule compared with the 92 million weekly VOA radio listeners. But Christopher Kern, the VOA's director of computer services, says the Internet has "wonderful demographics"; users are educated and influential. They also seem to have sensitive political antennae. **[8]** Recently, when Washington and Beijing got into a nasty dispute over trade, no one in China logged on to the VOA Internet for an entire week. The next week, with the trade issue under negotiation, they came back online.

On a much more modest scale, the Internet also has become a platform for the Zapatistas. One of the services offering information about the movement is run from Mexico City by Barbara Pillsbury, a 24-year-old American who works for a development organization. She transmits bulletins about the Zapatistas and communiqués from Subcomandante Marcos to subscribers around the world. (Her Internet address: pueblo@laneta.apc.org.) She says interest in the Zapatistas helped introduce many Mexicans to cyberspace. "Beyond their concerns about Chiapas," says Pillsbury, "Mexicans have realized that they need to be part of this technology."

Satellite TV is much easier to use, given the proper dish-shaped antenna and decoding equipment. **[9]** The technology has become popular in many countries where the native TV menu is limited. There are thought to be more than 150,000 dishes in Saudi Arabia, pulling in programming as varied as CNN, Italian game shows, soft pornography from Turkey, sitcoms from Israel and religious fulminations from Iran, the kingdom's archenemy. China, where dishes are institutionally owned, would seem to be at the opposite end of the scale as a market for satellite TV. But four months ago the VOA began [by aiming] a weekly hour of TV news in Mandarin Chinese from the AsiaSat, which has a good broadcast "footprint" over the mainland. Is anyone watching? The VOA doesn't know yet. "We shot an arrow in the air," says Kern.

Authoritarian governments of all political persuasions would like to shoot down satellite TV. Jamming is much more difficult than with radio, which uses a narrower and more vulnerable bandwidth. A more productive approach is to

[7] Watson provides several (recent) historical examples to support his point in the previous paragraph that the latest communications technologies are "almost impossible to police or control."

[8] The two previous sentences make another analytical point: many Internet users have "sensitive political antennae" that make them attentive to, if not necessarily in agreement with, the revolutionary messages being broadcast within the global village.

[9] Watson here makes a clear transition from analyzing use of the Internet to analyzing use of satellite TV. He follows this transitional sentence with statistics and examples that support its assertion about satellite TV being "much easier to use" as a means for communicating political and cultural messages.

Guide to Critical Analyses

outlaw the dish antennas. The conservative Saudi government banned them last year, threatening a fine of $180,000 on anyone who continues to use them. Fundamentalist Iran outlawed the dishes last month. The mullahs who rule Iran have been fighting a rear-guard action against communications technology ever since they took power in 1979. Previously they tried—and failed—to suppress videocassettes and camcorders.

The irony is that Ayatollah Ruhollah Khomeini and his followers overthrew the Shah of Iran by using even more primitive communications technology. While Khomeini was still exiled in Paris, his calls to rebel against the shah were disseminated throughout Iran on tape cassettes. Any means of communication can be an instrument of revolution, as long as it's in fairly widespread use. For years, Iraqi dictator Saddam Hussein banned private ownership of typewriters. He remembered the subversive power of the mimeograph machine when he was an ambitious young rebel plotting his own takeover.

The most tightly closed societies, such as North Korea, and the most violently repressive ones, such as Iraq or Libya, may not be susceptible to an Information Age revolution. **[10]** In North Korea, shortwave radios are unavailable, even to the few who could afford them. Fax machines, privately owned computers and satellite TV are unheard-of. Partly to constrict the flow of information, travel is severely limited, within the country as well as outside it; even bicycles were banned until about three years ago. Iraq and Libya have considerably more open societies, but their regimes remain in power through the most ruthless terror tactics, killing off opponents, real or imagined, and utterly intimidating the rest of the population, which in any case has little access to outside information.

Even in less rigid dictatorships, communications technology cannot make a revolution by itself. The Soviet Union was done in by its own economic failures and a ruinous arms race, not by long-distance phone calls or foreign radio broadcasts. **[11]** In Iran, the conditions for revolution were created by the shah's brutal repression and his breakneck modernization program, which outraged Muslim tradition. But the flow of information helps to undermine such regimes, and the faster it flows, the more trouble they're in. Few states can afford to opt out of the Information Age; they have to keep up with at least some of the latest scientific, technical and commercial developments. "We have a kind of knowledge market going on which is, in a way, impervious to the efforts of states to control it," says Paul Wilkinson, professor of international relations at the University of St. Andrews in Britain. If dictatorships want to play any part in the modern world, they have to risk exposing themselves to ideas and information that could inspire reform or spark a revolution.

The preceding critical analyses present two different perspectives on how communications technologies are shaping life within the global village. Both writers use compelling examples to focus readers' attention on specific technological causes and social, political, and cultural consequences. Both present

[10] In this paragraph, Watson examines counterexamples that may tend to weaken his claim about the potential revolutionary consequences of information age technologies.

[11] Watson builds his appeals of ethos and logos here as he qualifies his argument about the consequences that follow from revolutionary groups' use of communications technologies.

specific thesis statements that articulate an idea about those causes or consequences; both offer concrete details, logical evidence, and direct quotations from authorities to support these arguments; both acknowledge counterarguments and respond in ways that strengthen their respective thesis statements.

WHAT MAKES IT A CRITICAL ANALYSIS?

The following questions are ones you should consider when thinking critically about any critical analysis. For now, try applying them to the column by Thomas L. Friedman and the article by Russell Watson to determine how closely those writers followed the conventions for critical analyses.

1. Does the writer describe the situation or phenomenon he or she will examine in a way that helps readers understand why it needs to be analyzed? Does the writer help readers feel invested in the analysis?

2. Does the writer's description of the situation or phenomenon being analyzed seem to shape the discussion of the causes and/or the consequences?

3. Do the causes and/or the consequences the writer introduces seem logically connected to the situation or phenomenon? Does the writer present sufficient evidence and examples to convince you of the logical connection between the situation or phenomenon and its causes or consequences?

4. Does the writer acknowledge alternative perspectives on the situation or phenomenon? Has the writer responded to these alternative perspectives with logical arguments?

5. Does the writer help readers understand how the situation or phenomenon affects their lives?

Understanding the Rhetorical Situation

Identifying an exigence

In his column decrying Internet-enabled "Idiocy," Thomas L. Friedman identifies a specific challenge to any positive claims for the global village: most people do not realize how very deeply technology influences their knowledge of and attitudes toward other people and other cultures. His critical analysis, then, suggests the need for more than greater amounts of information obtained faster than ever before; we need to understand how that information is affecting us.

Consider, for example, the kinds of communications technologies you use in your everyday life: the Internet, telephone, cell phone, Blackberry, Palm Pilot, radio, broadcast or cable TV, iPod or MP3 player. Or, think about the specific kinds of content you consume or create through these technologies: virtual tourism sites, Facebook or MySpace pages, news updates from South America, YouTube videos of political demonstrations in eastern Europe, podcasts from artists in central Africa. Make a list of the various kinds of participation allowed by the communications technologies you use. How exactly are you participating in the global village—as both consumer and producer of information or entertainment? Can you identify the social interests, economic developments, or political or cultural views that underpin the information you're consuming (or producing)? What interests or perspectives might be missing from the global village? What do you gain personally from participating in the global village?

Consider your understanding of and participation in the global village in terms of the people with whom you communicate, such as students in other countries who share similar academic, cultural, or political interests. Maybe you have increased your understanding of and empathy for the experiences of students in other cultures as you read their emails or watched videos depicting their experiences, or perhaps you sense that you cannot get the whole picture about them in that way. You may even feel overwhelmed by the sheer volume of information on the Internet or at times want to unplug yourself from the Web.

1. Make a list of the communications technologies you use regularly to participate in the global village. For each technology, list the kinds of content you create or consume. Provide as many details as possible to describe each type of content and explain whether you found your experiences with that type of content to be positive or negative.

2. Make two columns—in which you list the positive and negative aspects of your global village experiences: subject matter, quality of the audio or visual components, language differences, presence or absence of instant communication with other people, and so forth. Provide specific details about each aspect.

3. Choosing one or two kinds of content, grab a screen shot that best represents some positive or negative feature you discussed in question 2. Or take photos or make sketches of yourself using a technology, paying particular attention to the physical details that best characterize the nature of your participation within the global village.

4. Choose a type of content and draft four or five brief descriptions of its positive or negative aspects. Vary your descriptions: for example, one description might focus on a group of people who are obviously profoundly affected by the content; another description could emphasize a group seemingly unaffected (especially if you think they should be affected). Or you could highlight the sensory details of the Web site, video, podcast, or news program where you encountered the content.

Locating an audience

For his analysis of the use of communications technology by the Zapatista rebels, Russell Watson had to consider an audience that would be interested in the topic but would hold a variety of opinions on the political legitimacy of revolutionary groups. The structure and language of his critical analysis, then, conformed to the demands of readers interested in learning more about the subject but not necessarily allied with the worldviews of the Zapatista movement. In theory, the members of the audience would be committed to promoting communication and the exchange of information rather than the use of violent force.

What audience should you consider for your critical analysis? First, you should consider who is directly and indirectly affected by the situation or phenomenon you're analyzing. Then, you need to consider how you can make those people feel concerned enough about the situation or phenomenon to want to read an analysis of its causes or consequences. For instance, if you think that U.S. students need to develop more politically or culturally meaningful content to contribute to the global village, you might consider your classmates as an immediately accessible and relevant audience for your analysis. You'll want to think carefully about the opinions, motivations, interests, and attitudes that your classmates have about using the Internet or other communications technologies. Once you have identified your potential audience, you'll want to consider how to analyze the causes and/or the consequences of the situation—college students could be creating more relevant content for the World Wide Web.

The following questions can help you locate your rhetorical audience as well as identify the relationship they have to the situation or phenomenon you're analyzing. Then, you'll be able to choose the best way to present your analysis.

1. List names of groups who directly contribute to or who are affected by the situation or phenomenon you're analyzing. On another list, write the names of groups who indirectly contribute to or are indirectly affected by the situation or phenomenon. You may need to do some research to compose a list that accounts for all the various groups with a stake in analyzing this situation more fully.

2. Next to the name of each potential audience, write possible reasons that audience could have for acknowledging the situation or phenomenon and understanding its causes or consequences. In other words, what would motivate these audiences to analyze how these activities or these technologies influence their lives?

3. What responses could these audiences reasonably be expected to have to your analysis? In other words, what conclusions might they be persuaded to draw, what attitudes might they be likely to create, what opinions might they be willing to reconsider? After exploring these possible responses, decide which audience you most want to or need to reach with your critical analysis.

4. With your audience's interests and capabilities in mind, look again at the descriptions of the type of content that you composed in the preceding section on identifying an exigence. Decide which description might enable these readers to feel connected to the situation or phenomenon you want to analyze—which description might help the readers become invested in understanding its causes or consequences. At this point, you may need to revise, tailoring your best description to your intended audience.

Identifying a Fitting Response

Finding a purpose and shaping a fitting response

You have explored uses of digital media and communications technologies on your campus or in your community. You have identified a situation or phenomenon concerning communication within the global village and an audience that might want to or need to think more deeply about how such communication and its content affects their lives. But what do you want to accomplish with your writing? How could your writing help to bring a deeper understanding of this situation or phenomenon to your intended audience? Answering these types of questions should provide you with your purpose, which in turn will inform the specific kind of text you create.

Identifying a situation or phenomenon and getting others to recognize it as one worth analyzing is only the beginning of your response to your rhetorical situation. You need to formulate an explicit claim about the causes or the consequences of the situation or phenomenon you are analyzing. And you need to generate and clarify reasons to support this claim. The most effective supporting reasons and evidence are those that help readers accept the logic of your claim. For example, Thomas L. Friedman provides evidence in the form of direct quotations from an Indonesian working for the U.S. Embassy in Jakarta to illustrate how inflammatory rumors have spread through the Internet and then through much of the Indonesian population.

As you know, different audiences and different purposes require different kinds of texts. For example, to analyze critically the consequences for international understanding that follow from virtual tourism Web sites, you might create your own Web page or an extended post to the message board of such a site. Your analysis of the causes that lead to the emergence of online communities for the world's youth might lead you to create a pamphlet for distribution at local public libraries. As these two examples suggest, once you identify your exigence, audience, and purpose, you need to determine what kind of text will best respond to your rhetorical situation.

Use the following questions to help you narrow your purpose and shape your response:

1. What specific assertion do you want to make about the causes or the consequences of the situation or phenomenon you're analyzing? What reasons support this particular claim? What evidence or examples can you provide to convince readers that each reason logically supports your analysis of these causes or consequences?
2. Which supporting reasons are most likely to resonate with or be convincing to your audience? What are the audience's beliefs, attitudes, or experiences that lead you to this conclusion?
3. What specific response are you hoping to draw from your audience? Do you want to affirm readers' existing beliefs about some negative or positive aspects of the global village? Do you want to draw their attention to overlooked content on the Web or have them reconsider their views on a particular type of content? Do you want readers to perform different types of activities as they participate in the global village?
4. What might be the best way to present your argument to your audience? That is, what kind of text is this audience most likely to respond to?

Your instructor (or your rhetorical situation) may prompt you to write a pamphlet, a newsletter, a Web page, or some other form of written response. Anna Seitz's experience with online learning could have been the basis for a fascinating memoir, if her purpose had been to look back on the years she spent getting her degree and recreate her experience for others. If she had been primarily interested in giving advice to a nephew who was considering getting a degree online, she might have written up a list of pros and cons in an informal email—or relayed the information in a phone call. But Anna wanted to take her experience apart and put it back together in a way that made sense to her and that clarified her conclusions for others. Her critical analysis (on pages 344–348) does just that. If, like Anna, you are prompted to write a critical analysis in response to your rhetorical situation, use the following assignment as a guide.

Writing a Critical Analysis: Working with Your Available Means

Shaping your critical analysis

You are probably familiar with the form and arrangement of critical analyses because you read many of them in your daily life: editorials and feature articles, for example, are often in this genre. The introduction of a critical analysis grabs readers' attention as it presents a detailed example or description that helps readers visualize the situation or phenomenon that needs to be analyzed. The introduction also helps readers understand why this situation or phenomenon needs to be analyzed. The introduction also states the thesis, a claim about the causes or the consequences of the situation or phenomenon. Thomas L. Friedman composed a somewhat lengthy introduction to his critical analysis, but his introduction has three concrete examples that illustrate the situation he sees as problematic and emphasize why this situation should be analyzed. After presenting these examples, he offers a three-sentence sequence that sets up and delivers his thesis, a claim about the consequences of this situation: the integration of new media into our lives "is producing more anger than anything else."

The body of a critical analysis presents and elaborates on the primary (and, depending on the depth of the analysis, the secondary) causes and consequences of the situation or phenomenon being analyzed. Here the writer clearly articulates how each cause contributes to and each consequence follows from the situation or phenomenon. The writer creates strong appeals to logos as he or she presents reasons supporting the claim about each cause or consequence. Russell Watson, for instance, describes a situation in which the rebel group the Zapatistas use communications technology as "a potentially revolutionary weapon," and he describes the specific technological and cultural changes that helped to bring about this situation. He continues throughout subsequent body paragraphs to more fully develop his argument that the primary cause of revolutionary groups' abilities to make political advances is the ability to connect to the global village.

Writers also create strong appeals to logos as they present brief anecdotes, direct quotations, and statistics to strengthen each supporting reason and to help readers see more clearly how each cause or consequence is linked to the situation or phenomenon. For example, Watson details the Zapatistas' use of the Internet as an international platform via the bulletins and communiqués that Barbara Pillsbury transmits "to subscribers around the world." And he explains that the Zapatistas' Internet use has motivated more Mexicans to try to obtain access to cyberspace. Watson reinforces this point with a short, focused quote from Pillsbury: "Beyond their concerns about Chiapas, Mexicans have realized that they need to be part of this technology." Often, direct quotations can help writers to compose persuasive appeals to ethos, as they signal to readers that the writers have sought out experts' opinions in order to deepen their knowledge about the topic.

The body paragraphs of a critical analysis also acknowledge and respond to alternative viewpoints about the situation or phenomenon being analyzed. Writers make this rhetorical move to improve both their appeals to logos, as they acknowledge and fill gaps in their arguments, and their appeals to ethos, as they present themselves to readers as rhetors who can thoughtfully consider the perspectives of other stakeholders in the issue. Watson, for example, concedes the fact that the "most tightly closed societies, such as North Korea, and the most violently repressive ones, such as Iraq or Libya, may not be susceptible to an Information Age revolution"; he continues through the rest of that paragraph to present concrete examples of specific measures governments in those countries have taken to limit revolutionary groups' ability to use communications technology. And he also explains that "[e]ven in less rigid dictatorships, communications technology cannot make a revolution by itself." Through such statements, Watson acknowledges counterarguments to his claim about the revolutionary possibilities of the Internet and satellite television.

Finally, the conclusion of a critical analysis reinforces the positive benefits that the audience can reap from analyzing this situation or phenomenon. Or, depending on the topic, the conclusion can illustrate the negative situation that may result if readers ignore the writer's critical analysis. And, as Friedman demonstrates, writers can also use the conclusion to present effective appeals to pathos. Friedman uses one final example, the "I Love You" computer virus, to dramatize the severity of the situation he has analyzed. He explains that unlike this computer virus, which had a technological solution, the "I Hate You" virus that is spread through uncritically examined communications in the global village can be cured only by genuine individual efforts to understand the truth of different cultures. He uses his final sentence—"Let's hope it's not too late"—to call for readers to start addressing this problem right now.

Many writers include visuals in their critical analyses to help them achieve their rhetorical purposes and to help their audiences better understand the causes or the consequences. As you draft your critical analysis, you may want to consider whether a visual or two will strengthen your claim. Consider capturing an image from your Internet browser window that depicts a unique destination within the global village. You might photograph people using communications technology to create content that represents their community to the rest of the global village. Or you might create a Web page with visuals that illustrate the cultural uniformity of the global village despite ethnic, national, or linguistic differences.

CHECKING OVER A CRITICAL ANALYSIS

✓ The critical analysis presents a situation or phenomenon that needs to be analyzed.

✓ This situation or phenomenon is one that concerns a significant number of people, including the audience to which the analysis is directed.

✓ The critical analysis makes an explicit claim about the causes or the consequences of the situation or phenomenon being analyzed.

✓ The claim about the causes or the consequences connects logically to the situation or phenomenon being described.

✓ The critical analysis provides evidence and examples to support the claim.

✓ The critical analysis acknowledges and responds to alternative perspectives concerning the situation or phenomenon.

Student paper

In the following essay, Anna Seitz analyzes a modern phenomenon, the online degree.

Anna Seitz

Professor James

English 275

January 31, 2008

The Real-Time Consequences of an Online Degree

I'm a mother of three small children, and I'm much more interested

in spending time with my kids than spending time in a classroom. When I

decided to pursue an advanced degree, I opted for an online program. I didn't

know exactly what it would be like, but I knew what I wanted out of it--

flexibility to complete the program on my own schedule. And while I got that, I

also found that my decision had other consequences.

The immediate consequence of taking online classes was that I did, in fact,

have even more flexibility than I'd imagined. That was good and bad. I had an

impressive selection of electives each term, especially because my advisor gave

me almost total freedom to select my courses. The more remote consequence

of this freedom is that I won't be graduating with the exact same skills and

experiences as everyone else in my class--we all have different specialties

and will be competing for different jobs. Also, none of my classes had set

meeting or chat times, and I was able to do my readings, write my papers, and

participate in discussion forums in fits and spurts (and in pajamas!). I read

at night and during nap times, in the car, and at the playground. I learned to

do most of my research online, and when I had to use local libraries, I simply packed up my gang for the children's story hour. Some of my professors provided the entire term's contents on day one, which helped me plan my work.

The flip side of this particular consequence was that planning my work was a bigger challenge than doing the work. Because my days with the children were always unpredictable, I lost a lot of sleep while learning how to pace myself in terms of taking care of my family and keeping up with my school work. There were times when my kids got stuck with a distracted mommy who cut corners on suppers and bedtime stories. I had to keep careful records of tasks and due dates, and I had to create my own deadlines as I learned how to divide big projects into manageable sections. After all, with online courses, the only regular reminders and announcements from the teachers are discussion board reminders (only useful if you log in and read them, of course). I'm nearly finished with the program, and I still haven't settled on an acceptable frequency for checking the class message board. Either I waste time checking constantly and finding nothing, or I go out for a day only to come home and find out that I've missed contributing to some major discussion or development.

Taking responsibility for my own learning at my own pace has always been comfortable for me. I've always been independent, and the idea of doing these classes "all by myself" was very appealing. Unfortunately, a secondary consequence of the online environment caught me by surprise. I was soon forced to admit that as much as I wanted to do things myself, my way, my professors and my classmates profoundly affected my learning, my grades, and my enjoyment of the classes. I had a few professors who spent as much or more time on my online classes as they would have on a face-to-face class, producing online PowerPoint lectures, enrichment activities, and discussion prompts, and making personal contact with each student. In those classes, I got to know my classmates, worked with others on projects, and learned things that I can still remember years later. The efforts of our professor inspired us to put in our own best efforts, and I would count those experiences to be on par with my best face-to-face classroom experiences.

I also had a few "teachers" who simply selected textbooks that came with lots of extras, such as a publisher's Web site with quizzes and assignments. In one of those classes, the publisher's Web site actually did the grading for the quizzes and calculated my class grade. I was really offended and kind of disgusted that my "teacher" would be so lazy. I felt that I wasn't getting what I'd paid for, and I felt neglected. Ultimately, I was embarrassed because I felt that it gave merit to all of the criticisms that I'd heard about online education. In one of those classes, I simply sat down with my textbook and did the entire term's quizzes in one night. I didn't learn a thing. I should have acted like a grown-up and made the best of it, but I just jumped through the hoops and collected my credits. I got an A in that class doing work which would have flunked me out of any face-to-face class, and that made me mad, too.

One of the remote consequences is that I began to consider my teacher's performance, and to discuss it with my classmates. When I was in college at 18, I was more focused on what I was putting into my classes than what I was getting out of them. I didn't notice what the teachers were or were not doing. In my current program, however, nearly all of the students are busy adults with careers and families who are paying their own way through school so that they can enhance their careers. My classmates and I are only there to improve our skills and we want to get our money's worth. There are a lot of complaints when we don't. I can think of dozens of examples of students voicing their complaints about the teacher, materials, or assignments as part of the class discussion, and since the communication is public, the teachers nearly always have to make improvements.

Another remote consequence is that there is surprisingly little privacy in an online class when compared to a face-to-face class, and that was very difficult to get used to. I can't just slink in, sit in the back of the class, keep my head down, and hope the teacher never learns my name. The comments I am required to post each week can be read, and in fact *must be read* by the entire class. Everyone knows what I've read, what I think about it, and how well I express myself. Everyone reads my papers, and I read theirs. For an independent person like me, this was tough to swallow. I didn't like comparing my work to others', even when it compared favorably. I dreaded the times when it compared unfavorably, and when I saw a classmate do particularly good work, I wanted to, too. It was a healthy and productive sort of peer pressure, and I did things I'd never tried to do before, and sometimes even did them well.

Ultimately, the primary consequence is that I am completing my degree, so my goal of getting a degree while managing my family responsibilities will soon be met. I did have a few complaints, but I could get bad teachers anywhere, and it's not just any program that would allow me to stay home with my kids all day while earning a degree. I missed a few of my teachers' emails, forgot people's names because I never saw their faces, and gave up hundreds of hours of sleep, but in the end, online education did work for me.

If your rhetorical situation does not call for a critical analysis like Anna Seitz's, you can consider the following other options.

ALTERNATIVE ASSIGNMENTS

1. In what ways are other students at your school or other people in your community contributing to or consuming information from the global village? What specific technologies are they using to link to other communities around the world? What specific kinds of content are they creating and reading, watching, or viewing? What do they learn from the virtual exchanges? What do they seem to be ignoring about their participation in the global village? Conduct primary research to learn more about the specific activities that classmates or fellow community members undertake in relation to the global village. Then compose a four-page investigative report on these activities, paying particular attention to the political, economic, social, and cultural realities that make such participation in the global village possible.

2. Write a four-page memoir exploring an experience you have had using technology to navigate within the global village. Describe your experience in as much specific detail as possible, using quotations and examples that help answer these questions: In what specific ways did the particular experience with technology bring you closer to the concerns and feelings of other people? In what ways did it create distance between you and other people and issues with which you are not directly concerned? What might be different about your academic, civic, or personal life if you did not have access to the online technology? If you had greater access? As you compose your memoir, consider who might be most interested in reading about what you learned through your experience.

3. Locate a Web site, television program, or some other media presentation that seems to represent some part of the global village. Consider all of the various materials (visuals, videos, audio clips, texts) that this site or program uses to depict places, cultures, and events throughout the world, as well as the implicit or explicit argument that it makes about the people and places it presents. Then compose a four-page critical review of this presentation, focusing on the message it seeks to convey as well as the means through which it seeks to do so. Be sure to create a clear set of evaluative criteria to use and to provide evidence and examples to support your evaluation.

11

EVERYDAY READING:
RESPONDING WITH LITERARY ANALYSES

Since 1996, television show host and entrepreneur Oprah Winfrey has sparked significant public discussion about literature. For Oprah's Book Club, she has selected over sixty books, including classics, contemporary fiction, and memoirs for her viewers to read. As with Toni Morrison's visit to the program in 1996, special episodes of *The Oprah Winfrey Show* have been devoted to interviewing the authors of these books and fostering audience discussion. In recent years, Winfrey has also devoted a section of her Web page to hosting message boards for discussing these books, giving viewers opportunities to join smaller online reading groups, sponsoring essay writing contests about these books, providing tips to help interested viewers host their own book discussions in their communities, answering questions that readers might have about the books, and presenting "Reader of the Week," an article that features one member of Oprah's Book Club.

Although it has stimulated interest in reading, Oprah's Book Club has not gone without criticism. Jonathan Franzen, author of the novel Winfrey planned to feature in September 2001, was unsettled by all the attention Winfrey was receiving for his book. Franzen told the *Portland Oregonian* that he was thrilled to learn that his publisher had printed 800,000 copies of *The Corrections*—but every

copy had the Oprah's Book Club logo on the front cover. "I see this as my book, my creation, and I didn't want that logo of corporate ownership on it," Franzen said. In another interview, Franzen said, "I had some hope of actually reaching a male audience" with *The Corrections,* but he suggested that many potential male readers believe the books selected for Oprah's Book Club are meant for women. Shortly after Franzen made these and other comments, Winfrey revoked her invitation to him to appear on her show, creating even more controversy.

Despite such controversy, Winfrey's ability to motivate people to read more literature cannot be denied. Journalist Edward Wyatt reported that from 1996 to 2002, books selected for Oprah's Book Club typically saw their sales increase by more than a million copies, a staggering figure, given that sales of twenty thousand copies are typically sufficient to make a book a commercial success. Little wonder then that publishers, such as Knopf Publishing Group chairman Sonny Mehta, have been forthright in acknowledging Winfrey's influence. According to Mehta, the book club has "brought the act of reading home to people in a way that publishers have not always been successful at doing."

The resurgence in widespread public projects aimed at encouraging the community to read, discuss, and write about literature has been spurred on by campaigns similar to Oprah's Book Club. In 1998, for example, the Seattle-based Washington Center for the Book initiated One Book, One Community, a series of reading promotion programs. For these programs, which have been run in towns, cities, counties, and regions in all fifty states as well as the District of Columbia, one book is selected for all residents to read. Responses to the book take

the form of community discussions, public readings, essay contests, and other activities. In some places, separate One Book, One Community programs have been created for local youth; in Evansville, Indiana, for example, the youth program for 2004 focused on Margaret McMullan's Civil War novel, *How I Found the Strong.*

Perhaps you have felt the urge to discuss one of Oprah's Book Club selections with an online book group, or maybe you lent a favorite novel to a friend with a note about why she would find it interesting or explained to your mother why a character in a play you had just seen together seemed miscast. In all of these cases, you were responding to literature. When you want to develop a more extended response about your understanding of a literary work and your interpretation of its purpose, you'll write a literary analysis. Literary analysis can sharpen your ability to pull together meaning from the various elements of a text—the plot, setting, characters, point of view, and stylistic techniques of a novel, short story, poem, or play. Understanding more about these elements and how they interact can enrich all your responses to literature.

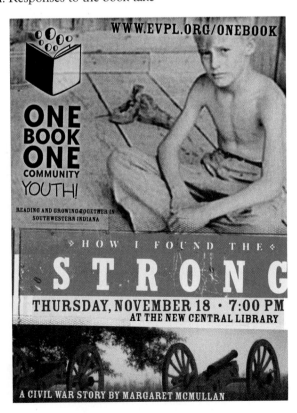

Oprah's Book Club and the One Book, One Community programs have sought to encourage people to carve out time and space to enjoy and discuss literature, but other public campaigns have aimed to bring literature to people in the midst of their daily routines. The Poetry Society of America, for example, has teamed with Barnes & Noble Booksellers and New York's Metropolitan Transit Authority to create Poetry in Motion. A major part of this campaign is the placement of Poetry in Motion posters in New York City subways and buses. The posters encourage commuters, local residents, and visitors to take a few minutes' break from their hectic schedules to contemplate some ideas and images that poets have created with language.

All of us have encountered verses on the greeting cards we send at birthdays, anniversaries, graduations, and other special occasions, but some established literary authors have circulated their poems through this form. Former U.S. poet laureate Maya Angelou has, since 2002, produced her own collection of greeting cards for Hallmark Cards, Inc. She explains, "My partnership with Hallmark creates a new way for my message to reach millions of women and families, many of whom may not be familiar with my work, but most of whom seek an expanded viewpoint on courage, spirituality, and personal expression." Angelou's comments express a view held by many that everyday encounters with literature can help people gain new perspectives on their professional, communal, and familial lives.

Angelou drew international attention to the uses of poetry when she read her poem "On the Pulse of the Morning" at the first inauguration of U.S. President William Jefferson Clinton on January 20, 1993. On that day, Angelou read her poem to encourage both reflection and meditation on where our nation had come from and on its future course.

Angelou's reading at the inauguration marked a significant national event, but many other people regularly read their poetry to audiences in clubs, bars, coffee houses, libraries, student unions, and writing centers in cities, communities, and colleges across the country. A prominent part of

Poetry in Motion poster featuring "Out Beyond Ideas of Wrongdoing and Rightdoing," by Jelaluddin Rumi.

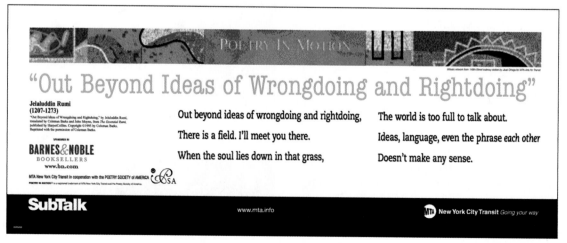

the movement to make poetry and other literary forms public has been the Poetry Slam circuit. A poetry slam involves a spoken performance of poetry in a competitive setting, where randomly selected members of the audience judge the different poets on their lyrical skills as well as their stage presence. Some literary critics have attacked Poetry Slam and warned that the popularity of the movement, in the words of Harold Bloom, signals "the death of art." But who gets to decide what is or is not "art"? The Poetry Slam competitions wrest that decision from academic and literary critics, who have long held the sole power over it. These events place this power in the hands of the audience members, who say what performances and what poems do and do not move them.

Maya Angelou reading her poem "On the Pulse of the Morning" at President Clinton's 1993 inauguration.

Beau Sia reads his poetry at the Poetry Slam Face Off at the Nuyorican Poets Cafe in New York City.

Alexis Ignatovich writes a poem in Union Square Park.

Given the broad popularity of poetry of all kinds, we're all likely to interact with poetry in public spaces—from hearing it on a daily walk to class to seeing it posted on buses or subways. Artists of all types use public spaces to craft ideas and images with language, as does 17-year-old Alexis Ignatovich, who scrawls a poem on the walkway in New York City's Union Square Park. And we needn't write in chalk on sidewalks to contribute to public engagement with literary texts. The company Magnetic Poetry, Inc., has put together magnetic poetry kits that can inspire people to put their own poems on refrigerators and filing cabinets in their homes and offices. Some groups have made such magnetic poetry available in public spaces. The University of Pennsylvania, for example, set up a magnetic poetry wall project on the College Green as part of a celebration of National Poetry Month in 1998. These sorts of public poetry projects aim to get people more engaged in and talking about literature and to experience the excitement and fun that come from composing their own literary creations.

Some people have been using their cell phones' text-messaging capabilities to send short poems to their friends. Published poet Fredrik Lloyd and producer Dahlan Lassalle have commercialized this activity by developing poemme, a service in the United Kingdom that sends a short, whimsical poem to subscribers' mobile phones each day. Lassalle suggests that Lloyd's poems can give people a moment to pause and reenergize themselves during their otherwise hectic days.

A passerby rearranges words on the magnetic poetry wall at the University of Pennsylvania.

Like poem-me, DailyLit is a service that distributes literature electronically.

These are just a few of the ways you encounter literature every day—you can probably think of many more. This chapter will give you an opportunity to sharpen your ability to read, interpret, and formulate ideas about the significance of literary texts. You will use writing throughout this chapter not just to present your polished ideas about a literary work but also to record your thoughts and perceptions before, during, and after you read it. Rereading your own developing thoughts about a text will help you to identify a critical question that you find interesting and that will sustain your writing.

DESCRIBING EVERYDAY ENCOUNTERS WITH LITERATURE

1. Working with a classmate, choose two of the images in this section and list specific details about that public presentation of creative writing. What can you tell about the contexts within which people encounter these texts? When might people see these texts? Where might they see them? How long might they spend reading these texts or talking or writing about them?

2. How do the contexts for the texts influence the ways in which people read and respond to the texts? How might these contexts affect the meaning that people take from these pieces of writing?

3. Who is the audience that the writer of each text wanted to reach? What kind of responses do you think this writer wanted to evoke in this audience? How might the context in which this text was to be read or heard have affected the way the writer created it?

4. If you wanted to respond to one of these pieces of writing, what means (or media) are available to you? In other words, what physical means do you have for developing a response? How many kinds of fitting responses can you imagine?

COMMUNITY CONNECTIONS

1. As you look again at the images in this section, which of them seems familiar to you? In other words, have you ever seen or encountered literature in an everyday context like that portrayed in any of the images?

2. Which of the images depicts a situation or a form of literary text that you'd like to encounter? Why?

3. Which of the images surprised you the most? Why did it surprise you to find this image in a discussion of reading and writing about literature?

4. Which of the images depicts a form of text that you normally would not recognize as being literary? What leads you to characterize this form of writing in that way?

5. Select the form of literary expression that you would be most interested in learning more about or analyzing in more detail. What most interests you about this form? What about this kind of text or the context in which you would normally encounter it makes it particularly compelling to you? Be as specific as you can.

Real Responses to Real Situations

Writers on reading

We read texts with a variety of purposes in mind. We read instruction sets to follow some process, such as installing a new program on a computer or preparing a package of macaroni and cheese. We read textbooks to learn more about topics in academic fields of study, such as the functions of mitochondria or the probable causes of the Civil War. We read literary works for specific purposes, too. Some of us read science fiction novels to imagine what life on Earth might be like in the distant future. Others read literature about groups whose cultures and lives differ from our own in order to learn about their experiences. Some of us read plays by William Shakespeare to gain greater insight into the depths of human motivations and passions; others read these texts merely to enjoy the poetic language of Elizabethan dramatic verse.

Whatever our motivations might be for reading literary works, the needs or desires that shape *why* we read affect *how* we read. Each of us pays particular attention to certain characters, certain scenes, or certain sentences or phrases that seem most important to us, given the interests and experiences we bring to the text. The following readings illustrate this fact. The first was written by a literary and philosophical scholar; the second and third were written by successful literary writers. The topic of each is the act of reading itself.

Throughout his career, Mortimer Adler committed himself to persuading all Americans, not just those privileged enough to formally pursue higher education, to acquire a liberal education and appreciate the insights to be gained from great writings in philosophy, science, religion, history, and literature. To further these goals, Adler co-founded the Center for the Study of the Great Ideas, the Great Books Foundation, and the University of Chicago's Basic Program of Liberal Education for Adults. Adler also developed and edited the book series Great Books of the Western World and served as editor-in-chief of the journal *Philosophy Is Everybody's Business*. His essay "How to Mark a Book," which first appeared in the *Saturday Review of Literature* in 1940, reflects his pursuit of this lifelong goal of encouraging all adults, no matter their background, to read, analyze, and discuss classical works of literature. Adler believed that a person truly possesses a book only when he or she has written in it, actively engaged with it, and made personal responses to the ideas in its pages.

MORTIMER ADLER
How to Mark a Book

You know you have to read "between the lines" to get the most out of anything. I want to persuade you to do something equally important in the course of your reading. I want to persuade you to "write between the lines." Unless you do, you are not likely to do the most efficient kind of reading. I contend, quite bluntly, that marking up a book is not an act of mutilation but of love.

You shouldn't mark up a book which isn't yours. Librarians (or your friends) who lend you books expect you to keep them clean, and you should. If you decide that I am right about the usefulness of marking books, you will have to buy them. Most of the world's great books are available today, in reprint editions, at less than a dollar.

There are two ways in which one can own a book. The first is the property right you establish by paying for it, just as you pay for clothes and furniture. But this act of purchase is only the prelude to possession. Full ownership comes only when you have made it a part of yourself, and the best way to make yourself a part of it is by writing in it. An illustration may make the point clear. You buy a beefsteak and transfer it from the butcher's icebox to your own. But you do not own the beefsteak in the most important sense until you consume it and get it into your bloodstream. I am arguing that books, too, must be absorbed in your bloodstream to do you any good.

Confusion about what it means to *own* a book leads people to a false reverence for paper, binding, and type—a respect for the physical thing—the craft of the printer rather than the genius of the author. They forget that it is possible for a man to acquire the idea, to possess the beauty, which a great book contains, without staking his claim by pasting his bookplate inside the cover. Having a fine library doesn't prove that its owner has a mind enriched by books; it proves nothing more than that he, his father, or his wife, was rich enough to buy them.

There are three kinds of book owners. The first has all the standard sets and best sellers—unread, untouched. (This deluded individual owns woodpulp and ink, not books.) The second has a great many books—a few of them read through, most of them dipped into, but all of them as clean and shiny as the day they were bought. (This person would probably like to make books his own, but is restrained by a false respect for their physical appearance.) The third has a few books or many—every one of them dog-eared and dilapidated, shaken and loosened by continual use, marked and scribbled in from front to back. (This man owns books.)

Is it false respect, you may ask, to preserve intact and unblemished a beautifully printed book, an elegantly bound edition? Of course not. I'd no more scribble all over a first edition of *Paradise Lost* than I'd give my baby a set of crayons and an original Rembrandt. I wouldn't mark up a painting or a statue. Its soul, so to speak, is inseparable from its body. And the beauty of a rare edition or of a richly manufactured volume is like that of a painting or a statue.

But the soul of a book *can* be separate from its body. A book is more like the score of a piece of music than it is like a painting. No great musician confuses a symphony with the printed sheets of music. Arturo Toscanini reveres Brahms, but Toscanini's score of the G Minor Symphony is so thoroughly marked up that no one but the maestro himself can read it. The reason why a great conductor makes notations on his musical scores—marks them up again and again each time he returns to study them—is the reason why you should mark your books. If your respect for magnificent binding or typography gets in the way, buy yourself a cheap edition and pay your respects to the author.

Why is marking up a book indispensable to reading? First, it keeps you awake. (And I don't mean merely conscious; I mean awake.) In the second place, reading, if it is active, is thinking, and thinking tends to express itself in words, spoken or written. The marked book is usually the thought-through book. Finally, writing helps you remember the thoughts you had, or the thoughts the author expressed. Let me develop these three points.

If reading is to accomplish anything more than passing time, it must be active. You can't let your eyes glide

> "... books ... must be absorbed in your bloodstream to do you any good."

across the lines of a book and come up with an understanding of what you have read. Now an ordinary piece of light fiction, like, say, *Gone With the Wind*, doesn't require the most active kind of reading. The books you read for pleasure can be read in a state of relaxation, and nothing is lost. But a great book, rich in ideas and beauty, a book that raises and tries to answer great fundamental questions, demands the most active reading of which you are capable. You don't absorb the ideas of John Dewey the way you absorb the crooning of Mr. Vallee. You have to reach for them. That you cannot do while you're asleep.

If, when you've finished reading a book, the pages are filled with your notes, you know that you read actively. The most famous active reader of great books I know is President Hutchins, of the University of Chicago. He also has the hardest schedule of business activities of any man I know. He invariably reads with a pencil, and sometimes, when he picks up a book and pencil in the evening, he finds himself, instead of making intelligent notes, drawing what he calls "caviar factories" on the margins. When that happens, he puts the book down. He knows he's too tired to read, and he's just wasting time.

But, you may ask, why is writing necessary? Well, the physical act of writing, with your own hand, brings words and sentences more sharply before your mind and preserves them better in your memory. To set down your reaction to important words and sentences you have read, and the questions they have raised in your mind, is to preserve those reactions and sharpen those questions.

Even if you wrote on a scratch pad, and threw the paper away when you had finished writing, your grasp of the book would be surer. But you don't have to throw the paper away. The margins (top and bottom, as well as side), the end-papers, the very space between the lines, are all available. They aren't sacred. And, best of all, your marks and notes become an integral part of the book and stay there forever. You can pick up the book the following week or year, and there are all your points of agreement, disagreement, doubt, and inquiry. It's like resuming an interrupted conversation with the advantage of being able to pick up where you left off.

And that is exactly what reading a book should be: a conversation between you and the author. Presumably he knows more about the subject than you do; naturally, you'll have the proper humility as you approach him. But don't let anybody tell you that a reader is supposed

to be solely on the receiving end. Understanding is a two-way operation; learning doesn't consist in being an empty receptacle. The learner has to question himself and question the teacher. He even has to argue with the teacher, once he understands what the teacher is saying. And marking a book is literally an expression of differences, or agreements of opinion, with the author.

There are all kinds of devices for marking a book intelligently and fruitfully. Here's the way I do it:

1. *Underlining (or highlighting):* of major points, of important or forceful statements.
2. *Vertical lines at the margin:* to emphasize a statement already underlined.
3. *Star, asterisk, or other doo-dad at the margin:* to be used sparingly, to emphasize the ten or twenty most important statements in the book. (You may want to fold the bottom corner of each page on which you use such marks. It won't hurt the sturdy paper on which most modern books are printed, and you will be able take the book off the shelf at any time and, by opening it at the folded-corner page, refresh your recollection of the book.)
4. *Numbers in the margin:* to indicate the sequence of points the author makes in developing a single argument.
5. *Numbers of other pages in the margin:* to indicate where else in the book the author made points relevant to the point marked; to tie up the ideas in a book, which, though they may be separated by many pages, belong together.
6. *Circling or highlighting of key words or phrases.*
7. *Writing in the margin, or at the top or bottom of the page, for the sake of:* recording questions (and perhaps answers) which a passage raised in your mind; reducing a complicated discussion to a simple statement; recording the sequence of major points right through the [books]. I use the end-papers at the back of the book to make a personal index of the author's points in the order of their appearance.

The front end-papers are to me the most important. Some people reserve them for a fancy bookplate. I reserve them for fancy thinking. After I have finished reading the book and making my personal index on the back end-papers, I turn to the front and try to outline the book, not page by page or point by point (I've already done that at the back), but as an

continued

integrated structure, with a basic unity and an order of parts. This outline is, to me, the measure of my understanding of the work.

If you're a die-hard anti-book-marker, you may object that the margins, the space between the lines, and the end-papers don't give you room enough. All right. How about using a scratch pad slightly smaller than the page-size of the book—so that the edges of the sheets won't protrude? Make your index, outlines and even your notes on the pad, and then insert these sheets permanently inside the front and back covers of the book.

Or, you may say that this business of marking books is going to slow up your reading. It probably will. That's one of the reasons for doing it. Most of us have been taken in by the notion that speed of reading is a measure of our intelligence. There is no such thing as the right speed for intelligent reading. Some things should be read quickly and effortlessly and some should be read slowly and even laboriously. The sign of intelligence in reading is the ability to read different things differently according to their worth. In the case of good books, the point is not to see how many of them you can get through, but rather how many can get through you—how many you can make your own. A few friends are better than a thousand acquaintances. If this be your aim, as it should be, you will not be impatient if it takes more time and effort to read a great book than it does a newspaper.

You may have one final objection to marking books. You can't lend them to your friends because nobody else can read them without being distracted by your notes. Furthermore, you won't want to lend them because a marked copy is kind of an intellectual diary, and lending it is almost like giving your mind away.

If your friend wishes to read your *Plutarch's Lives,* *Shakespeare,* or *The Federalist Papers,* tell him gently but firmly, to buy a copy. You will lend him your car or your coat—but your books are as much a part of you as your head or your heart.

Sherman Alexie, a Spokane/Coeur d'Alene from Wellpinit, Washington, wrote the following essay in 1998 for the *Los Angeles Times'* series "The Joy of Reading and Writing." In this essay, Alexie describes his first encounters with the material of literature—bound books and their texts—and explains how his family and community experiences have shaped his experiences of reading and writing. Alexie encourages his readers to reflect on how cultural and economic circumstances shape reading practices and on the value and use of reading and writing. He wants to encourage today's Native American students to see that writing is not "something beyond Indians" and to motivate them to save their cultures through recording, reworking, and reviving their communities' stories, experiences, and worldviews.

SHERMAN ALEXIE
Superman and Me

I learned to read with a Superman comic book. Simple enough, I suppose. I cannot recall which particular Superman comic book I read, nor can I remember which villain he fought in that issue. I cannot remember the plot, nor the means by which I obtained the comic book. What I can remember is this: I was 3 years old, a Spokane Indian boy living with his family on the Spokane Indian Reservation in eastern Washington state. We were poor by most standards, but one of my parents usually managed to find some minimum-wage job or another, which made us middle-class by reservation standards. I had a brother and three sisters. We lived on a combination of irregular paychecks, hope, fear and government surplus food.

My father, who is one of the few Indians who went to Catholic school on purpose, was an avid reader of westerns, spy thrillers, murder mysteries, gangster epics, basketball player biographies and anything else he could find. He bought his books by the pound at Dutch's Pawn Shop, Goodwill, Salvation Army and Value Village. When he had extra money, he bought new novels at supermarkets, convenience stores and hospital gift shops. Our house was filled with books. They were stacked in crazy piles in the bathroom, bedrooms and living room. In a fit of unemployment-inspired creative energy, my father built a set of bookshelves and soon filled them with a random assortment of books about the Kennedy assassination, Watergate, the Vietnam War and the entire 23-book series of the Apache westerns. My father loved books, and since I loved my father with an aching devotion, I decided to love books as well.

I can remember picking up my father's books before I could read. The words themselves were mostly foreign, but I still remember the exact moment when I first understood, with a sudden clarity, the purpose of a paragraph. I didn't have the vocabulary to say "paragraph," but I realized that a paragraph was a fence that held words. The words inside a paragraph worked together for a common purpose. They had some specific reason for being inside the same fence. This knowledge delighted me. I began to think of everything in terms of paragraphs. Our reservation was a small paragraph within the United States. My family's house was a paragraph, distinct from the other paragraphs of the LeBrets to the north, the Fords to our south and the Tribal School to the west. Inside our house, each family member existed as a separate paragraph but still had genetics and common experiences to link us. Now, using this logic, I can see my changed family as an essay of seven paragraphs: mother, father, older brother, the deceased sister, my younger twin sisters and our adopted little brother.

At the same time I was seeing the world in paragraphs, I also picked up that Superman comic book. Each panel, complete with picture, dialogue and narrative was a three-dimensional paragraph. In one panel, Superman breaks through a door. His suit is red, blue and yellow. The brown door shatters into many pieces. I look at the narrative above the picture. I cannot read the words, but I assume it tells me that "Superman is breaking down the door." Aloud, I pretend to read the words and say, "Superman is breaking down the door." Words, dialogue, also float out of Superman's mouth. Because he is breaking down the door, I assume he says, "I am breaking down the door." Once again, I pretend to read the words and say aloud, "I am breaking down the door" In this way, I learned to read.

> "I loved those books, but I also knew that love had only one purpose. I was trying to save my life."

This might be an interesting story all by itself. A little Indian boy teaches himself to read at an early age and advances quickly. He reads "Grapes of Wrath" in kindergarten when other children are struggling through "Dick and Jane." If he'd been anything but an Indian boy living on the reservation, he might have been called a prodigy. But he is an Indian boy living on the reservation and is simply an oddity. He grows into a man who often speaks of his childhood in the third-person, as if it will somehow dull the pain and make him sound more modest about his talents.

A smart Indian is a dangerous person, widely feared and ridiculed by Indians and non-Indians alike. I fought with my classmates on a daily basis. They wanted me to stay quiet when the non-Indian teacher asked for answers, for volunteers, for help. We were Indian children who were expected to be stupid. Most lived up to those expectations inside the classroom but subverted them on the outside. They struggled with basic reading in school but could remember how to sing a few dozen powwow songs. They were monosyllabic in front of their non-Indian teachers but could tell complicated stories and jokes at the dinner table. They submissively ducked their heads when confronted by a non-Indian adult but would slug it out with the Indian bully who was 10 years older. As Indian children, we were expected to fail in the non-Indian world. Those who failed were ceremonially accepted by other Indians and appropriately pitied by non-Indians.

I refused to fail. I was smart. I was arrogant. I was lucky. I read books late into the night, until I could barely keep my eyes open. I read books at recess, then during lunch, and in the few minutes left after I had finished my classroom assignments. I read books in the car when my family traveled to powwows or basketball

continued

games. In shopping malls, I ran to the bookstores and read bits and pieces of as many books as I could. I read the books my father brought home from the pawnshops and secondhand. I read the books I borrowed from the library. I read the backs of cereal boxes. I read the newspaper. I read the bulletins posted on the walls of the school, the clinic, the tribal offices, the post office. I read junk mail. I read auto-repair manuals. I read magazines. I read anything that had words and paragraphs. I read with equal parts joy and desperation. I loved those books, but I also knew that love had only one purpose. I was trying to save my life. Despite all the books I read, I am still surprised I became a writer. I was going to be a pediatrician. These days, I write novels, short stories, and poems. I visit schools and teach creative writing to Indian kids. In all my years in the reservation school system, I was never taught how to write poetry, short stories or novels. I was certainly never taught that Indi-

ans wrote poetry, short stories and novels. Writing was something beyond Indians. I cannot recall a single time that a guest teacher visited the reservation. There must have been visiting teachers. Who were they? Where are they now? Do they exist? I visit the schools as often as possible. The Indian kids crowd the classroom. Many are writing their own poems, short stories and novels. They have read my books. They have read many other books. They look at me with bright eyes and arrogant wonder. They are trying to save their lives. Then there are the sullen and already defeated Indian kids who sit in the back rows and ignore me with theatrical precision. The pages of their notebooks are empty. They carry neither pencil nor pen. They stare out the window. They refuse and resist. "Books," I say to them. "Books," I say. I throw my weight against their locked doors. The door holds. I am smart. I am arrogant. I am lucky. I am trying to save our lives.

Marianne Gingher has written four books, including the novel *Bobby Rex's Greatest Hit* and a memoir, *A Girl's Life: Horses, Boys, Weddings & Luck*. She teaches creative writing at the University of North Carolina at Chapel Hill. The following excerpt is from an essay about a book by Eudora Welty. Gingher's experience reading Eudora Welty's novel inspired her toward a career in writing, as she came to realize the miracle that fiction writers perform as they "transform the drudge and drone of prose into language as airborne as birdsong."

MARIANNE GINGHER
Excerpt from The Most Double-D-Daring Book I Read

It was gentle Eudora Welty's rowdy little romance, *The Robber Bridegroom,* that incited me to throw protocol and every good manner my mother ever taught me out the window and barge my way into a party, uninvited. I blame that book entirely with its spitfire heroine, its rollicking blend of American folklore, European fairy tale, and confection of language so luscious I wanted to eat every page. Best of all, *The Robber Bridegroom* was written in 1943, when political correctness was only a tyrannical gleam in the critic's eye. Just imagine! A writer could write about a bandit who kidnapped a plantation owner's daughter, deflowered her (the maid enjoyed

it!), and set her up cooking and cleaning for him and his band of rogues in an isolated hovel. Not only does she not complain, she whistles like a lark while she love-slaves her life away.

Welty's only thematic agenda was to weave a sly and witty entertainment, wicked with hyperbole, that portrays the profound gains and losses inherent in civilizing a behemoth Southern wilderness. This is a madcap bucking bronco of a book filled with galloping diversions that have confounded and irritated literary scholars looking to rein it in. That must be the chief reason it enthralled me.

> "My third reading
> of the book was
> a submersion in
> language. I found
> myself trying to
> memorize passages
> I admired. . . ."

I came upon it at a time in my education when I relished the refreshment of literature that reminded me of why I had loved reading as a child—for the sensation of wholehearted adventure.

I didn't read Eudora Welty until the early 1970s, when I was in graduate school. Somehow, although I had grown up in the South, I had missed all the Southern writers, except Faulkner. Not all of Welty's fiction is as fanciful as *The Robber Bridegroom*, of course, but the chief appeal to me of all her writing is its Yeats-like lyricism and imagery as concrete and well aimed as a stone expertly skipped across water. I thought of myself in those days as a failed poet. That Welty, a writer of fiction, could transform the drudge and drone of prose into language as airborne as birdsong seemed nothing short of miraculous to me—and an inspiration.

My teacher, Fred Chappel, frequently suggested books I might enjoy, recommending everything from Aristotle to Tolstoy to H. P. Lovecraft. On one occasion we were standing near a bookshelf in his den, and something I had said made him reach for *The Robber Bridegroom*. . . .

I took *The Robber Bridegroom* home and gulped it down in one sitting, admiring its mix of beauty and rambunctiousness. On a second reading I paid close attention to the many liberties Welty takes with the conventions of the tale. Her heroine, Rosamond, is no passive fairy tale princess waiting for some prince to rouse her from her stupor with a kiss. Rosamond is spirited, industrious, and loyal; but she is also habituated to lying and takes a few pratfalls normally reserved for the buffoon. The book's hero, Jamie Lockhart, thief and lover, is no paragon of family values. He is however, a hero "with the power to look both ways and see a thing from all sides." Sometimes his hesitation and thoughtfulness waylay his success. It's the couple's lack of perfection, their rascally virtue that defines Jamie and Rosamond as recognizably modern.

My third reading of the book was a submersion in language. I found myself trying to memorize passages I admired so that when I returned the book—which was then out of print—the afterglow of its imagery would permanently flicker across my brain. I read of one character so festooned with jewelry "that she gave out spangles the way a porcupine gives out quills." A bucket of fresh milk had "the sound of foam in it." Daylight was so tentative "that the green was first there, then not there in the treetops, but green seemed to beat on the air like a pulse." Six ugly girls were "as weighted down with freckles as a fig tree is with figs."

Several months passed before I felt ready to part with the book. To tell the truth, my brain felt feverish from reading it so many times, a little wild and woolly. When Fred opened the door, I'm sure I looked like somebody who needed to have her temperature taken. I apologized for the late return. "How'd you like it?" he asked.

"It's one of the most unruly books I ever read," I declared. Fred laughed. As he took the book, I imagined he could feel its palpitations in sync with my own.

"Romance, murder, sorrow, comedy, violence, charm, and poetry—it has everything. I loved it so much I've been trying to memorize it."

Marianne Moore was one of the leading poets of the modernist movement in the United States, which spanned the first four decades of the twentieth century. She published her poems in the leading literary journals of her time (*Others, Poetry: A Magazine of Verse,* and the *Dial*), and the poems were then reprinted in small books, including *Poems* (1921), *Observations* (1924), *What Are Years?* (1941), and *Nevertheless* (1944). Her *Collected Poems* (1951) won the Pulitzer Prize and the National Book Award in 1952. As she accepted the National Book Award, Moore suggested that critics called her work "poetry" because there simply weren't any other categories to put it in. Moore often spoke of enjoying her biology courses while earning her BA at

Bryn Mawr College from 1905 to 1909; literary scholars Elaine Oswald and Robert L. Gale suggest that this enjoyment of scientific study probably resulted in Moore's "love of intricately shaped animals" and her "life respect for precision in description." Moore makes a call for precise writing in the following poem. All types of writing are important, Moore suggests, but poetry, with its precise descriptions of both the physical world and the ideas conjured up by the human imagination, helps us better understand ourselves and the world around us.

While serving as the judge for Mount Holyoke College's 1955 Glascock Poetry Competition, Marianne Moore spoke with student Sylvia Plath.

MARIANNE MOORE
Poetry

I, too, dislike it: there are things that are important beyond all this fiddle.
    Reading it, however, with a perfect contempt for it, one discovers that there is
        in
it after all, a place for the genuine.
    Hands that can grasp, eyes
        that can dilate, hair that can rise
            if it must, these things are important not because a
high-sounding interpretation can be put upon them but because they are
    useful. When they become so derivative as to become unintelligible,
      the same thing may be said for all of us, that we
        do not admire what
        we cannot understand: the bat
           holding on upside down or in quest of something to
eat, elephants pushing, a wild horse taking a roll, a tireless wolf under
    a tree, the immovable critic twitching his skin like a horse that feels a flea, the
        base
    ball fan, the statistician--
        nor is it valid
        to discriminate against "business documents and
school-books"; all these phenomena are important. One must make a distinction
      however: when dragged into prominence by half poets, the result is not poetry,
      nor till the poets among us can be
      "literalists of
        "the imagination"--above
          insolence and triviality and can present

for inspection, "imaginary gardens with real toads in them," shall we have
   it. In the meantime, if you demand on the one hand,
      the raw material of poetry in
         all its rawness and
         that which is on the other hand
            genuine, you are interested in poetry.

ANALYZING THE RHETORICAL SITUATION

1. Spend several minutes describing your own strategies for reading a literary work. Do you read with a pen or pencil or highlighter in your hand? Do you use any of the marking techniques Mortimer Adler recommends? How do these reading strategies affect how you respond to a literary work and what you later remember about that text?

2. Why did Sherman Alexie read when he was a student at the reservation school? What evidence for your answer does his essay provide? For Alexie, what is the purpose of reading for children on the reservation?

3. Given what you have learned about Alexie from his essay, how would you describe his reading process? What textual features would he be most likely to notice and remember? On what features would he be least likely to focus? How might Alexie's personal experiences have shaped his reading preferences and practices?

4. How did Marianne Gingher read *The Robber Bridegroom*? How did her ways of interpreting, analyzing, or appreciating the novel change during subsequent readings?

5. Why might Marianne Moore have begun "Poetry" with the line "I, too, dislike it"? With whom might she be agreeing? What exigence does Moore want to address with her poem?

6. What is poetry, according to Moore? How does Moore use comparison and contrast to clarify her definition? What purpose does she see in writing poetry, and what does she believe people can gain from reading it? Be sure to cite passages from "Poetry" to support your answers.

7. Spend several minutes writing in as much detail as you can about a memorable reading experience you have had. What were you reading, and why were you reading it? To what features of the text were you paying the most attention? What were your initial reactions while reading the text? Describe how your reactions to or thoughts about the text have changed since you initially read it.

COMMUNITY CONNECTIONS

1. Write for ten minutes about your response to one of the four texts in this section. How do the writer's arguments or opinions about reading coincide with or diverge from your own perspective on reading? *continued*

2. Write for ten minutes in response to another of the four texts. How do this writer's arguments or opinions about reading coincide with or diverge from your perspective?

3. Write for ten minutes about how any of the four texts in this section caused you to think differently about literature, reading, and the importance of interpretation or confirmed your own perspective.

Literary Analyses: A Fitting Response

Genres of literature

As you've seen in earlier chapters of this book, genres such as reports, memoirs, and proposals can be identified by their particular features and conventions. Literary genres are no different. Some genres are timeless and culturally universal (drama and poetry, for instance); others have developed within a specific period and culture (detective fiction is a recent Western cultural phenomenon). Just as you can recognize film genres—action, suspense, horror, comedy, animated, Western, and science fiction—you can identify various literary genres: from poetry and drama to essays and narratives. Just as film genres sometimes overlap (for example, when an action film is partially animated), so do literary genres. Some poems are referred to as prose poems, some plays are written in verse. But even when genres overlap, the identifiable features of each genre remain evident.

Some of the most widely studied literary genres are fiction, drama, and poetry, though many forms of nonfiction (including personal essays and memoirs, literacy narratives, and manifestos) are being studied in college courses on literature. All imaginative literature can be characterized as fictional, but the term **fiction** applies specifically to novels and short stories.

Drama differs from all other imaginative literature in one specific way: it is meant to be performed—whether on stage, on film, or on television—with the director and actors imprinting the lines with their own interpretations. In fact, the method of presentation distinguishes drama from fiction, even though the two genres share many of the same elements (setting, character, plot, and dialogue). In a novel, you often find extensive descriptions of characters and setting, as well as passages revealing what characters are thinking. In a play, you learn what a character is thinking when he or she shares thoughts with another character in dialogue or presents a **dramatic soliloquy** (a speech delivered to the audience by an actor alone on the stage). And like fiction, nonfiction, and poetry, drama can be read; in which case, you bring your interpretative abilities to what is on the printed page rather than to a performance of the work.

Poetry shares many of the components of fiction and drama. It, too, may have a narrator with a point of view. Dramatic monologues and narrative poems sometimes have a plot, a setting, and characters. But poetry is primarily characterized by its extensive use of concentrated language, or language that relies on imagery, allusions, figures of speech, symbols, sound and rhythm, and precise word choice, all of which allow poets to make a point in one or two words rather than spelling it out explicitly.

Elements of literary texts

Characters The characters are the humans or humanlike personalities (aliens, creatures, robots, animals, and so on) who carry along the action. The main character is called the **protagonist,** who is in external conflict with another character or an institution or in internal conflict with himself or herself. This conflict usually reveals the theme, or the central idea of the work.

Because writing about literature often requires character analysis, you need to understand the characters in any work you read. You can do so by paying close attention to their appearance, their language, and their actions. You also need to pay attention to what the narrator or other characters are saying about any character in terms of physical, mental, or social attributes. Whether you are writing about characters in a novel, a play, or a poem, you will want to concentrate on what those characters do and say—and why.

Point of view Each literary work is told by a **narrator,** and this speaking voice can be that of a specific character (or those of characters taking turns), can seem to be that of the work's author (referred to as the **persona** or **speaker** and not to be confused with the actual author himself or herself), or can be that of an all-knowing presence (referred to as an **omniscient narrator**) that transcends both characters and author. Whatever the type of voice, the narrator's tone reveals his or her attitude toward events and characters and even, in some circumstances, toward readers.

In some literary texts, the narrator tells the story using the first-person pronoun *I*. As a reader, you are able to understand this narrator not only from his or her actions and speech but also from his or her thoughts, which are revealed. First-person narration can reveal a reliable narrator—one who seems to convey the story fairly accurately—but a first-person narrator can also be unreliable, meaning that he or she reveals thoughts that suggest he or she is not telling the reader the whole, unvarnished truth. An unreliable narrator is sometimes a child or mentally distressed person who for one reason or another is incapable of describing events and other characters accurately.

In other texts, the point of view is third person, and all characters are referred to by name or third-person pronoun (*he* or *she*). If the narrator appears to follow one character around and reveal just that character's thoughts, the point of view is **third person, limited.** If the narrator knows and tells readers about the thoughts, motivations, and attitudes of all the characters, the point of view is **third person, omniscient.**

Once you are able to identify the perspective from which the story is being told, you'll want to consider what this perspective allows you and other readers to know about different characters and events, as well as what this perspective does not allow you to know.

Plot The **plot** is what happens, the sequence of significant events (the narrative)—and more. Narrative answers "What comes next?" and plot answers "Why?" Plot usually begins with a conflict, an unstable situation that sets events in motion. In what is called the **exposition,** the author introduces the characters, setting, and background—the elements that not only constitute the unstable situation but also relate to the events that follow. The subsequent series of events leads to the climax, the most intense **turning point** because what follows is **falling action** (or **dénouement**) that leads to a resolution of the conflict and a stable situation. Thus, the plot establishes how events are patterned or related in terms of conflict and resolution.

Setting **Setting** involves place—not just the physical setting, but also the social setting (the morals, manners, and customs of the characters). Setting also involves time—not only historical time, but also the length of time covered by the narrative. Setting includes **atmosphere,** or the emotional response to the situation, often shared by the reader with the characters. Elements of the setting can often help you understand the motivations of characters or the reasons for certain events in the plot. Ask yourself this question as you consider how, if at all, the setting may shape the story you are reading: would the story be significantly different if it took place somewhere else?

Figurative language Writers often use metaphors and similes as a means of communicating complex ideas and meanings to readers. **Metaphors** are statements in which the writer says that an object or idea is something else, as when Hisaye Yamamoto compares a character's money to a pair of scissors: "his money was a sharp pair of scissors that snipped rapidly through tangles of red tape." Such a statement encourages readers to see how the first object or idea takes on specific qualities or characteristics of the second. **Similes** are statements in which the writer says that an object, idea, or person is *like* something else, as in Alice Walker's comparison of a man to a piece of china: "He was like a piece of rare and delicate china which was always being saved from breaking and finally fell." Despite the slight difference in language, the purpose of a simile is the same as that of a metaphor—to help readers understand something complicated or unfamiliar by comparing it to something readers might be more familiar with.

Symbol and imagery Frequently used by writers of literature, a **symbol** is an object, usually concrete, that stands for something else, usually abstract. For example, the kitchen table in Joy Harjo's poem "Perhaps the World Ends Here" (which appears later in this chapter) has meaning beyond its simple composition of a flat surface and four legs, meaning that Harjo attempts to convey through her careful, vivid description of the significant and everyday experiences that take place on and around the table.

When you write about a particular symbol, first note where it appears in the literary work. To determine what the symbol might mean, consider why it appears where it does and to what effect. Once you have an idea about the meaning, trace the incidents in the literary work that reinforce your interpretation.

Imagery refers to words and phrases that appeal to readers' senses. Most imagery is visual and helps readers "see" a particular image in their mind's eye (think, for instance, of how Marianne Moore called on poets to help readers visualize "real toads" in "imaginary gardens"). However, writers also use imagery to appeal to readers' senses of hearing, smell, taste, and touch. Vivid imagery involves the use of precise nouns and verbs and concrete descriptive details.

Rhythm and rhyme Most writers give considerable thought to the sound of the language they use in their literary works. Poets, in particular, pay utmost attention to rhythm and rhyme. A poet creates the rhythm of a poem through careful arrangement of syllables, words, and line breaks. Some poems have a regular rhythm, with each line containing a particular pattern of short and long syllables; other poems have a less structured, even patternless (yet no less significant) rhythm of words and syllables. Rhyming of words, either within the same line or between different lines, can also help poets create or stress a particular rhythm. Whether regular or irregular, a poem's rhythm can evoke emotions in readers or emphasize specific words and ideas, either by speeding readers through one or more lines and then slowing them down in subsequent lines or by forcing them to consider an image or idea more carefully.

Theme The **theme** of a literary work is the particular message the text delivers about a character, a relationship, an event, or a place. Depending on how they interpret a work, readers may identify different themes. To test whether the theme you have identified is central to the work in question, check to see if it is supported by the setting, plot, characters, point of view, and symbols. If you can relate these components to the idea you are considering, then that idea can be considered the work's theme. The most prominent literary themes arise out of conflict: person versus person, person versus self, person versus nature or technology, or person versus society.

A literary analysis

People write literary analyses in order to make arguments about how other readers should interpret the elements of a text and make meaning from them. Rhetorical situations compel writers to compose a literary analysis when they sense that readers are ignoring, misreading, or failing to understand significant features of a text. In other instances, writers compose literary analyses in order to discover answers to interesting questions, questions about the text itself or about its potential influence on people and their interactions.

This latter exigence motivated Ralph Rees to write the following literary analysis about the poetry of Marianne Moore. As his introduction suggests, Rees wrote this article partly in order to contribute to a conversation about a question that many literary critics have long tried to answer: What do authors of literary works help us to understand about the relationship between reality and imagination? Rees writes about Marianne Moore's work because he thinks that Moore offers a compelling perspective on how imagination and reality interact with one another. In his literary analysis, he presents evidence from her poem "Poetry."

Literary analyses like Rees's can be challenging to read—until you get used to the specialized vocabulary and dense language. If you take the time to work through them, though, they can be very rewarding. As you read the following analysis, take your time, pausing at the end of each sentence to be sure you've understood and looking up unfamiliar words as you go. You might even try out some of Mortimer Adler's techniques for marking a text.

Situations for Writers

[1] Rees uses a conventional strategy to open his essay. After telling readers the general topic—different perspectives on reality—in his first sentence, he presents several examples of different perspectives. Then he explains which perspective is Marianne Moore's.

[2] Although he doesn't signal it explicitly, Rees presents his thesis in the second half of this paragraph. Note, too, that he begins to build his argument, one that tries to persuade others that his interpretation of Moore's ideas is the appropriate way to read her work.

[3] Rees presents a passage from Moore's "Poetry" as a means of beginning to build evidence to support his argument.

[4] Rees follows the quoted passage with his own analysis because he wants readers to understand it in a specific way.

[5] Rees uses attributive tags such as this one before each direct quotation so that readers know the source.

Ralph Rees

The Reality of Imagination in the Poetry of Marianne Moore

Reality means different things to different people. To most, fact and the stimuli of the senses define reality; to some, the products of the intellect may be added to the above; to a few, the offspring of the imagination must also be considered. **[1]** Marianne Moore belongs to the last group, for she finds imagination as much a part of reality as fact. Many realists ignore the figments of the mind because they do not feel that such things have actuality; they deal only with the apparent, the sensed. Moore finds a more immediate reality in thoughts than in facts and the things that arouse the senses. The imagined, because it is more individual and more personal than the other phenomena, seems to her the very essence of reality. The way a thing *seems* is truth; its definitions and its composition are not realities but stimuli to the imagination, which creates actuality. The experience of the fact and the sensed is reality. **[2]**

In speaking of poetry, Moore says,

> nor till the poets among us can be
>   "literalists of
>   the imagination"—above
>   insolence and triviality and can present
>
> for inspection, "imaginary gardens with real toads in them," shall we have
>   it. In the meantime, if you demand on the one hand,
>   the raw material of poetry in
>   all its rawness and
>   that which is on the other hand
>   genuine, you are interested in poetry.[1] **[3]**

It can be seen that she wants poets to accept the products of their imaginations as realities that can be put down in their poems as actualities. She sees no need for the poet to separate his imaginings from that which is sensed or founded in fact. A truer actuality exists in mental experiences than in sensuality. **[4]** "A single shawl—Imagination's—is wrapped tightly round us since we are poor."[2] Morton Zabel says, **[5]**

> In her poem on [poetry] Miss Moore improves [William Butler] Yeats' characterization of [William] Blake by insisting that poets must be "literalists of the imagination"; they must see the visible at that focus of

intelligence where sight and concept coincide, and where it becomes transformed into the pure and total idealism of ideas. By this realism, the imagination permits ideas to claim energy from what is usually denied them—the vital nature that exists and suffers, and which alone can give poetic validity to the abstract or permit the abstract intelligence to enhance experience.[3] [6]

[6] Rees quotes other literary scholars' interpretations of Moore's work as a means of supporting his own argument.

In finding "the visible at that focus of intelligence where sight and concept coincide" Moore discovers the matter and the method of her poetry. With such an approach a poet can find material in everything; no limits restrict a poetic concept. "The idealism of ideas" accepts everything and rejects nothing in establishing material suitable to poetry. As R. P. Blackmur has said,

> The whole flux of experience and interpretation is appropriate subject matter to an imagination *literal* enough to see poetry in it; an imagination, that is, as intent on the dramatic texture (on what is involved, is tacit, is immanent) of the quotidian, as the imagination of the painter is intent, in Velasquez, on the visual texture of lace.[4]

Imagination, then, must be looked upon as the force which blends the other qualities together; through imagination the experienced, the observed, the studied are brought into a single heightened experience, which enhances the singularity of the idea of a thing while discarding much that has adhered to it through constant usage and casual observance. [7]

   . . . This emphasis on imagination gives the cohesive quality to many of her poems. At first, the reader may have difficulty in finding the connections between the various subjects brought into a single poem; the search for traditional logical development deludes him. When he is willing to accept the imaginative connections between the various matters of the poem, he will readily see that the common qualities are brought about by the ideal states of the many things mentioned. For this reason, most ideas can be compared with objects, with other ideas, with animals, and with man. Within the world of the imagination no barriers limit the poet or the reader to believe that only obvious likes may be compared with each other or that comparisons may be made only between members of a single class.

[7] Just as he did with the passage from "Poetry," Rees follows quotations from other scholars with his own analysis of their arguments.

   Moore has said that "the artist biased by imagination is a poet."[5] By this definition many of our so-called poets may be placed in the artist class, which she seems to place below that of poet. [8] The true poet, the person with aesthetic possibilities, permits his imagination to be the guide to his artistic capabilities. Such a person does not draw close distinctions between that which is dreamed of and that which is sensed. He accepts as the world of poetry all things that he can experience, whether physically or mentally. Imagination not only allows the poet to invoke comparisons that are fresh, interesting and constructive but to achieve a level of thought that is all-encompassing. The poet is the artist without bias, barriers, or prejudices of any kind; he permits his imagination to have full control of his creative processes and, by so doing, creates a world which seems new and startling to the unimaginative reader although the poet would say that this is the world that has always had existence, that has always remained the same while the factual was constantly changing through new concepts and ideas.

[8] Rees explains how his topic (Moore's concept of reality) connects to questions that concern many of his readers: who is and is not a poet, and how we can best evaluate a poet's creative work.

The power of imagination in its stimulation and growth from the factual and the sensed has the utmost importance to the poet. **[9]** It demonstrates the mind at its most original and refreshing. The rest of experience is important only as stimuli; experience that does not stimulate the imagination is of little value. It is for this reason that Moore says, "The power of the visible / is the invisible."[6] The "visible" gains importance only as it affects the imagination. In other words, Moore finds that the factual and the sensed, those things which most people accept as the "all" of reality, are important only as the stimuli of the imagination. Such an idea turns the world of the realist upside down; actuality becomes that which is not concrete and which can never be "proved." . . .

It has been shown that Marianne Moore is a realist, by her own definition and by her own actions. The standard conception of realist would exclude her and her poetic creations; but, by showing that only that which she herself has experienced has actuality for her, she has designated herself a realist of the imagination. **[10]** In his essay "Jubal, Jabal and Moore," M. L. Rosenthal says,

> Miss Moore's vivid emphasis on the details of subhuman organic life—she is the botanist's and the zoologist's poet, as well as the poet's poet—makes her poetry swarm with symbolic observation. The pretense is that all this occurs in a hothouse or a zoo, where one watches the flora or the curious beasts with amused and sympathetic detachment, making polite conversation all the while. But how intense the interest really is, how uncompromising the preciseness of detail, how persistent the drive toward universalizing ethical import; how irritated the poet is with soft-headedness of any kind! The ostrich "digesteth harde yron" and is therefore superior to all the absurdities of his appearance and, more important, to his ridiculous common mortality. Sometimes her famous "imaginary gardens with real toads in them"—Miss Moore's image for genuine poetic creations—are really not so far from [William] Blake's tiger-haunted forests.[7]

Rosenthal is not the only critic to point out Moore's battle against soft thinking; others have commented on her constant struggle for thought that is as direct as it is stimulating. Wallace Stevens says that she has "the faculty of digesting the 'harde yron' of appearance."[8] It is important to emphasize Stevens' use of the word "digesting," because Moore accomplishes such a process through her imagination; she "digests" fact by using her imagination. Without such a function to act upon it, the fact itself would be of little or no importance to the individual. Imagination, then, has become the only criterion by which reality and actuality can be measured. **[11]**

NOTES

1. Marianne Moore, "Poetry," *Collected Poems* (New York: Macmillan, 1951), p. 41. (All subsequent quotations from her poetry are from this work.)

2. Marianne Moore, "A Bold Virtuoso," *Predilections* (New York: Viking, 1955), p. 43.

3. Morton Zabel, "A Literalist of the Imagination," *Poetry*, 47 (March, 1936), 329–30.

4. R. P. Blackmur, "The Method of Marianne Moore," *Language As Gesture* (New York: Harcourt, Brace, 1952), p. 267.
5. Marianne Moore, "Paul Rosenfeld," *Nation*, 163 (Aug. 17, 1946), 192.
6. *Collected Poems*, "He 'Digesteth Harde Yron,'" p. 104.
7. M. L. Rosenthal, "Jubal, Jabal and Moore," *New Republic*, 126 (April 7, 1952), 21.
8. Wallace Stevens, "About One of Marianne Moore's Poems," *Quarterly Review of Literature*, 4 (1948), 149.

WHAT MAKES IT A LITERARY ANALYSIS?

The following questions are ones you should consider when thinking critically about any literary analysis. For now, try applying them to the article by Ralph Rees to determine how closely he followed the conventions for literary analysis.

1. Does the writer introduce other interpretations of the literary work under investigation and explain what these perspectives might be missing? Or does the writer present a specific question about the literary work that he or she believes needs to be answered?

2. Does the writer present a clear argument, or thesis, about the literary work and explain how this thesis addresses some concern that other readers of this literary work have ignored or misrepresented?

3. Does the writer quote specific passages from the text to provide evidence supporting the thesis?

4. Does the writer explicate the quoted passages, directing readers' attention to particular aspects of the literary work that support his or her thesis?

Three Literary Works for Analysis

This section presents a short story, a poem, and a play on which you can practice and hone your skills in analytical reading and writing. Freewriting prompts will help you focus your readings of these texts and begin to identify the aspect of one text to which you'll respond in your essay. Your freewriting can also serve you well as you begin to compose the first draft of your essay.

Reading actively

Through this section, you'll construct your own reading of a text. Reading actively when you read a literary work is a first step toward making an argument about that work and its significance. There is no one specific way to make sense of any literary work; what's important is that you support your argument with evidence from the text. Moreover, you want to demonstrate to other readers, including your classmates, why your particular reading of the text is an important one for them to consider. That is, you want to convince readers that your interpretation helps them to understand the literary work in a new way.

To construct an interpretation that provides readers with significant insight, you first need to choose a feature of the literary work that genuinely interests you. Second, you formulate an interpretive question that you'll answer, with supporting evidence, throughout your essay. Actively reading the text—recording your reactions in the margins, highlighting passages that confuse you, noting sections that seem to be central to the events or the characters—will help you identify and begin to answer such a question.

Keeping a reading journal

To help you craft your interpretive question, you'll keep a reading journal in which you'll freewrite in response to the following series of prompts. Read these prompts *before* you read the literary text so that you can focus your thinking as you read; then write responses to the prompts after you have read the text once or twice. Later, your journal freewrites will help you identify and clarify the interpretive question on which you'll center your essay and focus your analysis of the literary work.

FREEWRITING PROMPTS FOR COMPOSING A LITERARY ANALYSIS

1. Freewrite for ten minutes in response to these questions about the characters in the literary work: Who do you think the most important character in the piece is? How does that character change or not change through the course of the piece? What is the significance of this change or lack of change? How do the other characters in the piece contribute to or prevent this change?

2. Freewrite for ten minutes on the importance of the setting in the literary work: Where does the piece take place? Do you notice anything significant about the setting that affects how you read the piece?

3. Freewrite for ten minutes about the point of view of the literary work: What is the point of view? What role does the narrator (or speaker) play? What does the narrator (or speaker) know and not know? How does the narrator's (or speaker's) knowledge about events and the ideas and attitudes of other characters shape how you read and understand the piece?

4. Freewrite for ten minutes about the plot of the literary work: What do you think is the single most important event or moment? Why do think this moment is so important or crucial?

5. Freewrite for ten minutes about the theme, what the author is trying to say through the literary work: What does the piece make you think about? What does it make you see about the people or events?

A short story

Alice Walker was born in 1944 in Eaton, Georgia, the eighth child of sharecroppers Minnie Lou Grant and Willie Lee Walker. During Walker's teenage years, the Civil Rights Movement of the 1960s opened up opportunities for more African American children to attend college. Walker attended both Spelman College in Atlanta and Sarah Lawrence College near New York City, earning her undergraduate degree from the latter school. Two years later, in 1967, she published her first literary work, the short story "To Hell with Dying." In 1983, she became the first black woman to receive the Pulitzer Prize for fiction, for *The Color Purple,* her third novel.

Walker is credited with first using the term *womanist* to refer to a theoretical stance toward understanding, illuminating, and building on the lived experiences of African American women. Her literary works engage the dominant stereotypes and limiting conceptions about who African American women (particularly Southern black women) are and who they could be as well as provide spaces wherein these women have their own voices with which to articulate the significance of their lives. According to Barbara T. Christian, Walker's short story "Everyday Use" "is especially significant in that perhaps for the first time in contemporary United States literary history, a writer features a variety of *Southern* black women's perspectives."

Alice Walker.

Alice Walker

Everyday Use

I will wait for her in the yard that Maggie and I made so clean and wavy yesterday afternoon. A yard like this is more comfortable than most people know. It is not just a yard. It is like an extended living room. When the hard clay is swept clean as a floor and the fine sand around the edges lined with tiny, irregular grooves, anyone can come and sit and look up into the elm tree and wait for the breezes that never come inside the house.

    Maggie will be nervous until after her sister goes: she will stand hopelessly in corners, homely and ashamed of the burn scars down her arms and legs, eying her sister with a mixture of envy and awe. She thinks her sister has held life always in the palm of one hand, that "no" is a word the world never learned to say to her.

You've no doubt seen those TV shows where the child who has "made it" is confronted, as a surprise, by her own mother and father, tottering in weakly from backstage. (A pleasant surprise, of course: What would they do if parent and child came on the show only to curse out and insult each other?) On TV mother and child embrace and smile into each other's faces. Sometimes the mother and father weep, the child wraps them in her arms and leans across the table to tell how she would not have made it without their help. I have seen these programs.

Sometimes I dream a dream in which Dee and I are suddenly brought together on a TV program of this sort. Out of a dark and soft-seated limousine I am ushered into a bright room filled with many people. There I meet a smiling, gray, sporty man like Johnny Carson who shakes my hand and tells me what a fine girl I have. Then we are on the stage and Dee is embracing me with tears in her eyes. She pins on my dress a large orchid, even though she has told me once that she thinks orchids are tacky flowers.

In real life I am a large, big-boned woman with rough, man-working hands. In the winter I wear flannel nightgowns to bed and overalls during the day. I can kill and clean a hog as mercilessly as a man. My fat keeps me hot in zero weather. I can work outside all day, breaking ice to get water for washing; I can eat pork liver cooked over the open fire minutes after it comes steaming from the hog. One winter I knocked a bull calf straight in the brain between the eyes with a sledge hammer and had the meat hung up to chill before nightfall. But of course all this does not show on television. I am the way my daughter would want me to be: a hundred pounds lighter, my skin like an uncooked barley pancake. My hair glistens in the hot bright lights. Johnny Carson has much to do to keep up with my quick and witty tongue.

But that is a mistake. I know even before I wake up. Who ever knew a Johnson with a quick tongue? Who can even imagine me looking a strange white man in the eye? It seems to me I have talked to them always with one foot raised in flight, with my head turned in whichever way is farthest from them. Dee, though. She would always look anyone in the eye. Hesitation was no part of her nature.

"How do I look, Mama?" Maggie says, showing just enough of her thin body enveloped in pink skirt and red blouse for me to know she's there, almost hidden by the door.

"Come out into the yard," I say.

Have you ever seen a lame animal, perhaps a dog run over by some careless person rich enough to own a car, sidle up to someone who is ignorant enough to be kind to him? That is the way my Maggie walks. She has been like this, chin on chest, eyes on ground, feet in shuffle, ever since the fire that burned the other house to the ground.

Dee is lighter than Maggie, with nicer hair and a fuller figure. She's a woman now, though sometimes I forget. How long ago was it that the other house burned? Ten, twelve years? Sometimes I can still hear the flames and feel Maggie's arms sticking to me, her hair smoking and her dress falling off her in little black papery flakes. Her eyes seemed stretched open, blazed open by the flames reflected in them. And Dee. I see her standing off under the sweet gum tree she used to dig gum out of; a look of concentration on her face as she watched the last dingy gray board of the house fall in toward the red-hot brick chimney. Why don't you do a dance around the ashes? I'd wanted to ask her. She had hated the house that much.

I used to think she hated Maggie, too. But that was before we raised money, the church and me, to send her to Augusta to school. She used to read to us without pity; forcing words, lies, other folks' habits, whole lives upon us two, sitting trapped and ignorant underneath her voice. She washed us in a river of make-believe, burned us with a lot of knowledge we didn't necessarily need to know. Pressed us to her with the serious way she read, to shove us away at just the moment, like dimwits, we seemed about to understand.

Dee wanted nice things. A yellow organdy dress to wear to her graduation from high school; black pumps to match a green suit she'd made from an old suit somebody gave me. She was determined to stare down any disaster in her efforts. Her eyelids would not flicker for minutes at a time. Often I fought off the temptation to shake her. At sixteen she had a style of her own: and knew what style was.

I never had an education myself. After second grade the school was closed down. Don't ask me why: in 1927 colored asked fewer questions than they do now. Sometimes Maggie reads to me. She stumbles along good-naturedly but can't see well. She knows she is not bright. Like good looks and money, quickness passes her by. She will marry John Thomas (who has mossy teeth in an earnest face) and then I'll be free to sit here and I guess just sing church songs to myself. Although I never was a good singer. Never could carry a tune. I was always better at a man's job. I used to love to milk till I was hooked in the side in '49. Cows are soothing and slow and don't bother you, unless you try to milk them the wrong way.

I have deliberately turned my back on the house. It is three rooms, just like the one that burned, except the roof is tin; they don't make shingle roofs any more. There are no real windows, just some holes cut in the sides, like the portholes in a ship, but not round and not square, with rawhide holding the shutters up on the outside. This house is in a pasture, too, like the other one. No doubt when Dee sees it she will want to tear it down. She wrote me once that no matter where we "choose" to live, she will manage to come see us. But she will never bring her friends. Maggie and I thought about this and Maggie asked me, "Mama, when did Dee ever have any friends?"

She had a few. Furtive boys in pink shirts hanging about on washday after school. Nervous girls who never laughed. Impressed with her they worshiped the well-turned phrase, the cute shape, the scalding humor that erupted like bubbles in lye. She read to them.

When she was courting Jimmy T she didn't have much time to pay to us, but turned all her faultfinding power on him. He flew to marry a cheap city girl from a family of ignorant flashy people. She hardly had time to recompose herself.

When she comes I will meet—but there they are!

Maggie attempts to make a dash for the house, in her shuffling way, but I stay her with my hand. "Come back here," I say. And she stops and tries to dig a well in the sand with her toe.

It is hard to see them clearly through the strong sun. But even the first glimpse of leg out of the car tells me it is Dee. Her feet were always neat-looking, as if God himself had shaped them with a certain style. From the other side of the car comes a short, stocky man. Hair is all over his head a foot long and hanging from his chin like a kinky mule tail. I hear Maggie suck in her breath. "Uhnnnh," is what it sounds like. Like when you see the wriggling end of a snake just in front of your foot on the road. "Uhnnnh."

Dee next. A dress down to the ground, in this hot weather. A dress so loud it hurts my eyes. There are yellows and oranges enough to throw back the light of the sun. I feel my whole face warming from the heat waves it throws out. Earrings gold, too, and hanging down to her shoulders. Bracelets dangling and making noises when she moves her arm up to shake the folds of the dress out of her armpits. The dress is loose and flows, and as she walks closer, I like it. I hear Maggie go "Uhnnnh" again. It is her sister's hair. It stands straight up like the wool on a sheep. It is black as night and around the edges are two long pigtails that rope about like small lizards disappearing behind her ears.

"Wasuzo-Teano!" she says, coming on in that gliding way the dress makes her move. The short stocky fellow with the hair to his navel is all grinning and he follows up with "Asalamalakim, my mother and sister!" He moves to hug Maggie but she falls back, right up against the back of my chair. I feel her trembling there and when I look up I see the perspiration falling off her chin.

"Don't get up," says Dee. Since I am stout it takes something of a push. You can see me trying to move a second or two before I make it. She turns, showing white heels through her sandals, and goes back to the car. Out she peeks next with a Polaroid. She stoops down quickly and lines up picture after picture of me sitting there in front of the house with Maggie cowering behind me. She never takes a shot without making sure the house is included. When a cow comes nibbling around the edge of the yard she snaps it and me and Maggie and the house. Then she puts the Polaroid in the back seat of the car, and comes up and kisses me on the forehead.

Meanwhile Asalamalakim is going through motions with Maggie's hand. Maggie's hand is as limp as a fish, and probably as cold, despite the sweat, and she keeps trying to pull it back. It looks like Asalamalakim wants to shake hands but wants to do it fancy. Or maybe he don't know how people shake hands. Anyhow, he soon gives up on Maggie.

"Well," I say. "Dee."

"No, Mama," she says. "Not 'Dee,' Wangero Leewanika Kemanjo!"

"What happened to 'Dee'?" I wanted to know.

"She's dead," Wangero said. "I couldn't bear it any longer, being named after the people who oppress me."

"You know as well as me you was named after your aunt Dicie," I said. Dicie is my sister. She named Dee. We called her "Big Dee" after Dee was born.

"But who was she named after?" asked Wangero.

"I guess after Grandma Dee," I said.

"And who was she named after?" asked Wangero.

"Her mother," I said, and saw Wangero was getting tired. "That's about as far back as I can trace it," I said. Though, in fact, I probably could have carried it back beyond the Civil War through the branches.

"Well," said Asalamalakim, "there you are."

"Uhnnnh," I heard Maggie say.

"There I was not," I said, "before 'Dicie' cropped up in our family, so why should I try to trace it that far back?"

He just stood there grinning, looking down on me like somebody inspecting a Model A car. Every once in a while he and Wangero sent eye signals over my head.

"How do you pronounce this name?" I asked.

"You don't have to call me by it if you don't want to," said Wangero.

"Why shouldn't 1?" I asked. "If that's what you want us to call you, we'll call you."

"I know it might sound awkward at first," said Wangero.

"I'll get used to it," I said. "Ream it out again."

Well, soon we got the name out of the way. Asalamalakim had a name twice as long and three times as hard. After I tripped over it two or three times he told me to just call him Hakim-a-barber. I wanted to ask him was he a barber, but I didn't really think he was, so I didn't ask.

"You must belong to those beef-cattle peoples down the road," I said. They said "Asalamalakim" when they met you, too, but they didn't shake hands. Always too busy: feeding the cattle, fixing the fences, putting up salt-lick shelters, throwing down hay. When the white folks poisoned some of the herd the men stayed up all night with rifles in their hands. I walked a mile and a half just to see the sight.

Hakim-a-barber said, "I accept some of their doctrines, but farming and raising cattle is not my style." (They didn't tell me, and I didn't ask, whether Wangero (Dee) had really gone and married him.)

We sat down to eat and right away he said he didn't eat collards and pork was unclean. Wangero, though, went on through the chitlins and corn bread, the greens and everything else. She talked a blue streak over the sweet potatoes. Everything delighted her. Even the fact that we still used the benches her daddy made for the table when we couldn't effort to buy chairs.

"Oh, Mama!" she cried. Then turned to Hakim-a-barber. "I never knew how lovely these benches are. You can feel the rump prints," she said, running her hands underneath her and along the bench. Then she gave a sigh and her hand closed over Grandma Dee's butter dish. "That's it!" she said. "I knew there was something I wanted to ask you if I could have." She jumped up from the table and went over in the corner where the churn stood, the milk in it clabber by now. She looked at the churn and looked at it.

"This churn top is what I need," she said. "Didn't Uncle Buddy whittle it out of a tree you all used to have?"

"Yes," I said.

"Un huh," she said happily. "And I want the dasher, too."

"Uncle Buddy whittle that, too?" asked the barber.

Dee (Wangero) looked up at me.

"Aunt Dee's first husband whittled the dash," said Maggie so low you almost couldn't hear her. "His name was Henry, but they called him Stash."

"Maggie's brain is like an elephant's," Wangero said, laughing. "I can use the chute top as a centerpiece for the alcove table," she said, sliding a plate over the chute, "and I'll think of something artistic to do with the dasher."

When she finished wrapping the dasher the handle stuck out. I took it for a moment in my hands. You didn't even have to look close to see where hands pushing the dasher up and down to make butter had left a kind of sink in the wood. In fact, there were a lot of small sinks; you could see where thumbs and fingers had sunk into the wood. It was beautiful light yellow wood, from a tree that grew in the yard where Big Dee and Stash had lived.

After dinner Dee (Wangero) went to the trunk at the foot of my bed and started rifling through it. Maggie hung back in the kitchen over the dishpan. Out came Wangero with two quilts. They had been pieced by Grandma Dee and then Big Dee and me had hung them on the quilt frames on the front porch and quilted them. One was in the Lone Star pattern. The other was Walk Around the Mountain. In both of them were scraps of dresses Grandma Dee had worn fifty and more years ago. Bits and pieces of Grandpa Jattell's Paisley shirts. And one teeny faded blue piece, about the size of a penny matchbox, that was from Great Grandpa Ezra's uniform that he wore in the Civil War.

"Mama," Wangero said sweet as a bird. "Can I have these old quilts?"

I heard something fall in the kitchen, and a minute later the kitchen door slammed.

"Why don't you take one or two of the others?" I asked. "These old things was just done by me and Big Dee from some tops your grandma pieced before she died."

"No," said Wangero. "I don't want those. They are stitched around the borders by machine."

"That'll make them last better," I said.

"That's not the point," said Wangero. "These are all pieces of dresses Grandma used to wear. She did all this stitching by hand. Imagine!" She held the quilts securely in her arms, stroking them.

"Some of the pieces, like those lavender ones, come from old clothes her mother handed down to her," I said, moving up to touch the quilts. Dee (Wangero) moved back just enough so that I couldn't reach the quilts. They already belonged to her.

"Imagine!" she breathed again, clutching them closely to her bosom.

"The truth is," I said, "I promised to give them quilts to Maggie, for when she marries John Thomas."

She gasped like a bee had stung her.

"Maggie can't appreciate these quilts!" she said. "She'd probably be backward enough to put them to everyday use."

"I reckon she would," I said. "God knows I been saving 'em for long enough with nobody using 'em. I hope she will!" I didn't want to bring up how I had offered Dee (Wangero) a quilt when she went away to college. Then she had told they were old-fashioned, out of style.

"But they're priceless!" she was saying now, furiously; for she has a temper.

"Maggie would put them on the bed and in five years they'd be in rags. Less than that!"

"She can always make some more," I said. "Maggie knows how to quilt."

Dee (Wangero) looked at me with hatred. "You just will not understand. The point is these quilts, these quilts!"

"Well," I said, stumped. "What would you do with them?"

"Hang them," she said. As if that was the only thing you could do with quilts.

Maggie by now was standing in the door. I could almost hear the sound her feet made as they scraped over each other.

"She can have them, Mama," she said, like somebody used to never winning anything, or having anything reserved for her. "I can 'member Grandma Dee without the quilts."

I looked at her hard. She had filled her bottom lip with checkerberry snuff and gave her face a kind of dopey, hangdog look. It was Grandma Dee and Big Dee who taught her how to quilt herself. She stood there with her scarred hands hidden in the folds of her skirt. She looked at her sister with something like fear but she wasn't mad at her. This was Maggie's portion. This was the way she knew God to work.

When I looked at her like that something hit me in the top of my head and ran down to the soles of my feet. Just like when I'm in church and the spirit of God touches me and I get happy and shout. I did something I never done before: hugged Maggie to me, then dragged her on into the room, snatched the quilts out of Miss Wangero's hands and dumped them into Maggie's lap. Maggie just sat there on my bed with her mouth open.

"Take one or two of the others," I said to Dee.

But she turned without a word and went out to Hakim-a-barber.

"You just don't understand," she said, as Maggie and I came out to the car.

"What don't I understand?" I wanted to know.

"Your heritage," she said, and then she turned to Maggie, kissed her, and said, "You ought to try to make something of yourself, too, Maggie. It's really a new day for us. But from the way you and Mama still live you'd never know it."

She put on some sunglasses that hid everything above the tip of her nose and chin.

Maggie smiled; maybe at the sunglasses. But a real smile, not scared. After we watched the car dust settle I asked Maggie to bring me a dip of snuff. And then the two of us sat there just enjoying, until it was time to go in the house and go to bed.

A poem

Joy Harjo was born in Tulsa, Oklahoma, in 1951 and is enrolled as a member of both the Creek and Muscogee Tribes. At the age of sixteen, she moved to the Southwest to attend the Institute of American Indian Arts in Santa Fe, New Mexico. Harjo eventually switched her major from the visual arts to poetry and moved to Albuquerque to attend the University of New Mexico, where she

Joy Harjo.

earned her BA in English. She went on to earn an MFA in creative writing from the University of Iowa. On her Web site (www.joyharjo.com), Harjo says that she "began writing poetry when the national Indian political climate demanded singers and speakers" and that she was quickly "taken by the intensity and beauty possible in the craft."

Harjo has published a number of books of poetry, one of which, *In Mad Love and War,* received an American Book Award from the Before Columbus Foundation in 1990. In the 1990s, Harjo also learned to play the saxophone and has combined her poetic and musical talents as the lead member of the group Joy Harjo and Poetic Justice. The group has released two albums, *Letter from the End of the 20th Century* (1997) and *Native Joy for Real* (2005). In addition to her writing and performing, Harjo teaches as the Joseph M. Russo Professor of Creating Writing at the University of New Mexico. The following poem appears in the poetry collection *Sweeping Beauty: Contemporary Women Poets Do Housework.*

Joy Harjo

Perhaps the World Ends Here

The world begins at a kitchen table. No matter what, we must eat to live.

The gifts of earth are brought and prepared, set on the table. So it has been since creation, and it will go on.

We chase chickens or dogs away from it. Babies teethe at the corners. They scrape their knees under it.

It is here that children are given instructions on what it means to be human. We make men at it, we make women.

At this table we gossip, recall enemies and the ghosts of lovers.

Our dreams drink coffee with us as they put their arms around our children. They laugh with us at our poor falling-down selves and as we put ourselves back together once again at the table.

The table has been a house in the rain, an umbrella in the sun.

Wars have begun and ended at this table. It is a place to hide in the shadow of terror. A place to celebrate the terrible victory.

We have given birth on this table, and have prepared our parents for burial here.

At this table we sing with joy, with sorrow. We pray of suffering and remorse. We give thanks.

Perhaps the world will end at the kitchen table, while we are laughing and crying, eating of the last sweet bite.

A play

According to the Web site for Kingston, Ontario's Fishbowl Theatre, Jane Martin "has been referred to as 'America's best known, unknown playwright.'" Although Martin has been nominated for the Pulitzer Prize and twice won the American Theatre Critics Association's New Play Award, she has never been photographed for publication or made public appearances. Indeed, many critics believe that "Jane Martin" is a pseudonym for a playwright who first garnered national attention for *Talking With . . .*, a collection of monologues produced by Actors' Theatre of Louisville for the 1981 Humana Festival of New American Plays.

Jon Jory, the former artistic director of Actors' Theatre, has accepted these awards on Martin's behalf, and he has also served as Martin's spokesperson. Many critics believe that Jory *is*, in fact, Jane Martin, since almost all of Martin's plays have premiered at the Actors' Theatre and have been directed by Jory. Jory has often refuted this, however, explaining that whoever writes the plays clearly feels that she would be unable to do so if her identity became public knowledge. Martin has written ten full-length plays, six one-act plays, and numerous short plays, of which the following, *Beauty*, is one.

Jane Martin

Beauty

CHARACTERS

Carla

Bethany

An apartment. Minimalist set. A young woman, Carla, on the phone.

CARLA: In love with me? You're in love with me? Could you describe yourself again? Uh-huh. Uh-huh. And you spoke to me? (*A knock at the door.*) Listen, I always hate to interrupt a marriage proposal, but . . . could you possibly hold that thought? (*Puts phone down and goes to the door. Bethany, the same age as Carla and a friend, is there. She carries the sort of Mideastern lamp we know of from Aladdin.*)

BETHANY: Thank God you were home. I mean, you're not going to believe this!

CARLA: Somebody on the phone. (*Goes back to it.*)

BETHANY: I mean, I just had a beach urge, so I told them at work my uncle was dying . . .

CARLA: (*motions to Bethany for quiet*) And you were the one in the leather jacket with the tattoo? What was the tattoo? (*Carla again asks Bethany, who is gesturing wildly that she should hang up, to cool it.*) Look, a screaming eagle from shoulder to shoulder, maybe. There were a lot of people in the bar.

BETHANY: (*gesturing and mouthing*) I have to get back to work.

CARLA: (*on phone*) See, the thing is, I'm probably not going to marry someone I can't remember . . . particularly when I don't drink. Sorry. Sorry. Sorry. (*She hangs up.*) Madness.

BETHANY: So I ran out to the beach . . .

CARLA: This was some guy I never met who apparently offered me a beer . . .

BETHANY: . . . low tide and this . . . (*The lamp.*) . . . was just sitting there, lying there . . .

CARLA: . . . and he tracks me down . . .

BETHANY: . . . on the beach, and I lift this lid thing . . .

CARLA: . . . and seriously proposes marriage.

BETHANY: . . . and a genie comes out.

CARLA: I mean, that's twice in a . . . what?

BETHANY: A genie comes out of this thing.

CARLA: A genie?

BETHANY: I'm not kidding, the whole Disney kind of thing, swirling smoke, and then this twenty-foot-high, see-through guy in like an Arabian outfit.

CARLA: Very funny.

BETHANY: Yes, funny, but twenty feet high! I look up and down the beach, I'm alone. I don't have my pepper spray or my hand alarm. You know me, when I'm petrified I joke. I say his voice is too high for Robin Williams, and he says he's a castrati. Naturally. Who else would I meet?

CARLA: What's a castrati?

BETHANY: You know . . .

The appropriate gesture.

CARLA: Bethany, dear one, I have three modeling calls. I am meeting Ralph Lauren!

BETHANY: Okay, good. Ralph Lauren. Look, I am not kidding!

CARLA: You're not kidding what?!

BETHANY: There is a genie in this thingamajig.

CARLA: Uh-huh. I'll be back around eight.

BETHANY: And he offered me *wishes!*

CARLA: Is this some elaborate practical joke because it's my birthday?

BETHANY: No, happy birthday, but I'm like crazed because I'm on this deserted beach with a twenty-foot-high, see-through genie, so like sarcastically . . . you know how I need a new car . . . I said fine, gimme 25,000 dollars. . .

CARLA: On the beach with the genie?

BETHANY: Yeah, right, exactly, and it rains down out of the sky.

CARLA: Oh sure.

BETHANY: (*pulls a wad out of her purse*) Count it, those are thousands. I lost one in the surf.

Carla sees the top bill. Looks at Bethany, who nods encouragement. Carla thumbs through them.

CARLA: These look real.

BETHANY: Yeah.

CARLA: And they rained down out of the sky?

BETHANY: Yeah.

CARLA: You've been really strange lately, are you dealing?

BETHANY: Dealing what, I've even given up chocolate.

CARLA: Let me see the genie.

BETHANY: Wait, wait.

CARLA: Bethany, I don't have time to screw around. Let me see the genie or let me go on my appointments.

BETHANY: Wait! So I pick up the money . . . see, there's sand on the money . . . and I'm like nuts so I say, you know, "Okay, look, ummm, big guy, my uncle is in the hospital" . . . because as you know when I said to the people at work my uncle was dying, I was on one level telling the truth although it had nothing to do with the beach, but he was in Intensive Care after the accident, and that's on my mind, so I say, okay, Genie, heal my uncle . . . which is like impossible given he was hit by two trucks, and the genie says, "Yes, Master" . . . like they're supposed to say, and he goes into this like kind of whirlwind, kicking up sand and stuff, and I'm like, "Oh my God!" and the air clears, and he bows, you know, and says, "It is done, Master," and I say, "Okay, whatever-you-are, I'm calling on my cell phone," and I get it out and I get this doctor who is like dumbstruck who says my uncle came to, walked out of Intensive Care and left the hospital! I'm not kidding, Carla.

CARLA: On your mother's grave?

BETHANY: On my mother's grave.

They look at each other.

CARLA: Let me see the genie.

BETHANY: No, no, look, that's the whole thing . . . I was just, like, reacting, you know, responding, and that's already two wishes . . . although I'm really pleased about my uncle, the $25,000 thing, I could have asked for $10 million, and there is only one wish left.

CARLA: So ask for $10 million.

BETHANY: I don't think so. I don't think so. I mean, I gotta focus in here. Do you have a sparkling water?

CARLA: No. Bethany, I'm missing Ralph Lauren now. Very possibly my one chance to go from catalogue model to the very, very big time, so, if you are joking, stop joking.

BETHANY: Not joking. See, see, the thing is, I know what I want. In my guts. Yes. Underneath my entire bitch of a life is this unspoken, ferocious, all-consuming urge . . .

CARLA: (*trying to get her to move this along*) Ferocious, all-consuming urge . . .

BETHANY: I want to be like you.

CARLA: Me?

BETHANY: Yes.

CARLA: Half the time you don't even like me.

BETHANY: Jealous. The ogre of jealousy.

CARLA: You're the one with the $40,000 job straight out of school. You're the one who has published short stories. I'm the one hanging on by her fingernails in modeling. The one who has creeps calling her on the phone. The one who had to have a nose job.

BETHANY: I want to be beautiful.

CARLA: You are beautiful.

BETHANY: Carla, I'm not beautiful.

CARLA: You have charm. You have personality. You know perfectly well you're pretty.

BETHANY: "Pretty," see, that's it. Pretty is the minor leagues of beautiful. Pretty is what people discover about you after they know you. Beautiful is what knocks them out across the room. Pretty, you get called a couple of times a year; *beautiful* is twenty-four hours a day.

CARLA: Yeah? So?

BETHANY: So?! We're talking *beauty* here. Don't say "So?" Beauty is the real deal. You are the center of any moment of your life. People stare. Men flock. I've seen you get offered discounts on makeup for no reason. Parents treat beautiful children better. Studies show your income goes up. You can have sex anytime you want it. Men have to know me. That takes up to a year. I'm continually horny.

CARLA: Bethany, I don't even like sex. I can't have a conversation without men coming on to me. I have no privacy. I get hassled on the street. They start pressuring me from the beginning. Half the time, it never occurs to them to start with a conversation. Smart guys like you. You've had three long-term relationships, and you're only twenty-three. I haven't had one. The good guys, the smart guys are scared to death of me. I'm surrounded by male bimbos who think a preposition is when you go to school away from home. I have no woman friends except you. I don't even want to talk about this!

BETHANY: I knew you'd say something like this. See, you're "in the club" so you can say this. It's the way beauty functions as an elite. You're trying to keep it all for yourself.

CARLA: I'm trying to tell you it's no picnic.

BETHANY: But it's what everybody wants. It's the nasty secret at large in the world. It's the unspoken tidal desire in every room and on every street. It's the unspoken, the soundless whisper . . . millions upon millions of people longing hopelessly and forever to stop being whatever they are and be beautiful, but the difference between those ardent multitudes and me is that I have a goddamn genie and one more wish!

CARLA: Well, it's not what I want. This is me, Carla. I have never read a whole book. Page six, I can't remember page four. The last thing I read was *The Complete Idiot's Guide to WordPerfect*. I leave dinner parties right after the dessert because I'm out of conversation. You know the dumb blonde joke about the application where it says, "Sign here," she put Sagittarius? I've done that. Only beautiful guys approach me, and that's because they want to borrow my eye shadow. I barely exist outside a mirror! You don't want to be me.

BETHANY: None of you tell the truth. That's why you have no friends. We can all see you're just trying to make us feel better because we aren't in your league. This only proves to me it should be my third wish. Money can only buy things. Beauty makes you the center of the universe.

Bethany picks up the lamp.

CARLA: Don't do it. Bethany, don't wish it! I am telling you you'll regret it.

Bethany lifts the lid. There is a tremendous crash, and the lights go out. Then they flicker and come back up, revealing Bethany and Carla on the floor where they have been thrown by the explosion. We don't realize it at first, but they have exchanged places.

CARLA/BETHANY: Oh God.

BETHANY/CARLA: Oh God.

CARLA/BETHANY: Am I bleeding? Am I dying?

BETHANY/CARLA: I'm so dizzy. You're not bleeding.

CARLA/BETHANY: Neither are you.

BETHANY/CARLA: I feel so weird.

CARLA/BETHANY: Me too. I feel . . . (*Looking at her hands.*) Oh, my God, I'm wearing your jewelry. I'm wearing your nail polish.

BETHANY/CARLA: I know I'm over here, but I can see myself over there.

CARLA/BETHANY: I'm wearing your dress. I have your legs!

BETHANY/CARLA: These aren't my shoes. I can't meet Ralph Lauren wearing these shoes!

CARLA/BETHANY: I wanted to be beautiful, but I didn't want to be you.

BETHANY/CARLA: Thanks a lot!!

CARLA/BETHANY: I've got to go. I want to pick someone out and get laid.

BETHANY/CARLA: You can't just walk out of here in my body!

CARLA/BETHANY: Wait a minute. Wait a minute. What's eleven eighteenths of 1,726?

BETHANY/CARLA: Why?

CARLA/BETHANY: I'm a public accountant. I want to know if you have my brain.

BETHANY/CARLA: One hundred thirty-two and a half.

CARLA/BETHANY: You have my brain.

BETHANY/CARLA: What shade of Rubinstein lipstick does Cindy Crawford wear with teal blue?

CARLA/BETHANY: Raging storm.

BETHANY/CARLA: You have my brain. You poor bastard.

CARLA/BETHANY: I don't care. Don't you see?

BETHANY/CARLA: See what?

CARLA/BETHANY: We both have the one thing, the one and only thing everybody wants.

BETHANY/CARLA: What's that?

CARLA/BETHANY: It's better than beauty for me; it's better than brains for you.

BETHANY/CARLA: What? What?!

CARLA/BETHANY: Different problems.

Blackout.

Understanding the Rhetorical Situation

Identifying an exigence

In his literary analysis of Alice Walker's "Everyday Use" (which appears at the end of this section), student Matthew Marusak articulates a clear objection to the way many readers have interpreted the story: they vilify Dee without considering the ways in which the mother/narrator may not be reliable. The exigence for Marusak's essay is his desire to have people reread "Everyday Use" and consider more carefully how they come to their conclusions about the characters as well as the story's theme. His essay, then, presents evidence and analysis to support such a rereading of Walker's classic short story.

To identify an exigence for your essay, reread the journal freewrites that you composed earlier. Reflect on those journal entries as you respond to these questions:

1. What features of the literary work interested you the most?
2. What features of the story, poem, or play seemed most problematic or most significant in terms of helping you to interpret the text?
3. What features of the story, poem, or play do you disagree with your classmates about?
4. What were your initial reactions to the literary work when you read it for the first time, and how did those reactions change as you reflected on and wrote about different features of the literary work?

There is a good chance that as you respond to these questions, you'll begin to hone an interpretive question on which you can base your essay. If you still need some help identifying a question, take time to think about important points where *change* occurs in the text. Novelist Raymond Carver has said on this point, "In the best fiction, the central character, the hero or heroine, is also the 'moved' character, the one to whom something happens in the story that *makes a difference*. Something happens that changes the way that character looks at himself and hence the world." So, in order to arrive at a question on which to focus your essay, respond to the following questions:

1. At what places within the text does some element—a character, the plot, the setting, the point of view—undergo a significant change?
2. What are the specific details of that change?
3. What might be the significance of the change in relation to the entire text?
4. What were your reactions to the change?
5. What might have been the writer's point in incorporating the change into the text?

Now, articulate a question about the text. This question should be one readers could answer in different ways and are genuinely interested in.

Once you have articulated this question, spend several minutes freewriting an answer. Try to mention specific parts of the text that are informing your answer as you do this freewriting. Write about whatever ideas come into your head. Don't worry about punctuation, grammar, or organization. You want to begin to direct your reading, interpreting, and writing in the direction of identifying your exigence and answering that one critical question.

Locating an audience

For his article on Marianne Moore's poetry, Ralph Rees identified a group of literary critics who were engaged in a conversation about a topic that he felt Moore's writing could help them better understand. Rees wrote his analysis, then, in a way that helps readers see how Moore's poems and her ideas on the imagination can contribute to an answer to a question of that audience: how do we come to know reality?

What audience should you consider for your literary analysis? First, you have to determine what groups have already been discussing the particular text or the question your analysis will explore. For instance, if you think that Joy Harjo's "Perhaps the World Ends Here" asks readers to reconsider how ordinary objects shape day-to-day experiences, you'll want to identify a group of people who tend to overlook the significance of such objects in their everyday lives. You'll want to consider how you can present your analysis of Harjo's poem to this audience in a way that helps them understand why it's important to take time to reflect on the ordinary things in our lives.

The following questions can help you locate your rhetorical audience as well as identify the relationship they have to the question you have identified. Then, you'll be able to choose the best way to present and support your answer.

1. List the names of the persons or groups who are talking about the literary work you're analyzing or who have questions about its meaning or importance.
2. Next to the name of each potential audience, write reasons that audience might have for acknowledging your analysis of the literary work. In other words, what would persuade them to read the story, poem, or play and interpret it in a different way?
3. What responses could these audiences reasonably be persuaded to have to your essay and to the text you're analyzing?
4. With your audience's interests and capabilities in mind, look again at the question and initial answer you composed in the preceding section on identifying an exigence.

Decide how you can enable your audience to feel engaged by your question and invested in hearing how you interpret the text in ways that answer it. At this point, you may find it necessary to revise your question so that it speaks more directly to the concerns of your audience.

Identifying a Fitting Response

Finding a purpose and shaping a fitting response

You have examined your initial and subsequent responses to a literary work, and you have also explored how specific features of the text contributed to your responses. You have identified an interpretive question about the text that you want to answer through your literary analysis, and you have considered your audience and how those readers might be expected to respond. But what, specifically, do you want to accomplish with your writing? How could your analysis help bring about the change in perspective on the literary work that you want? Answering these types of questions should help you clarify your purpose for writing, which in turn will inform the specific kind of text you create.

Identifying an interpretive question and getting others to recognize it as interesting or important is only the beginning of your efforts to begin translating your freewriting and planning into an analytical essay. You need to identify an appropriate form in which to respond to this rhetorical situation, as well. Your response should consider the information you have already generated about your exigence and your audience, such as the interpretations they have already formed about the text. Your analysis should also be a fitting response in the sense that it addresses the context within which your audience is likely to consider it. For example, to analyze how Joy Harjo's "Perhaps the World Ends Here" demonstrates that everyday objects such as the kitchen table shape our personal interactions with others, you might consider writing an "Arts & Entertainment" column for the local newspaper. To reinterpret the significance of the quilts in Alice Walker's "Everyday Use," you might want to create a newsletter that you could distribute at a local crafts store. Or, to explore how Jane Martin's *Beauty* speaks to the pressures of growing up in an image-obsessed culture, you might consider shaping your analysis into the form of a Web page or a blog entry that could appear within an Internet site devoted to activist efforts on the part of the world's young adults. The point here is that once you identify your exigence, audience, and purpose, you need to consider what kind of text will best respond to the rhetorical situation.

Use the following two questions to help you narrow your purpose and shape your response:

1. Are you asking the audience to simply reread the literary work in a new light or to perform some particular action in response to this new way of interpreting the text?
2. What is the best way to contact this audience? That is, what kind of text is this audience most likely to respond to?

Your instructor (or your rhetorical situation) may prompt you to write a letter, a brochure, a literacy narrative, or some other form of written response. As you'll see when you read his essay on pages 394–399, Matthew Marusak's reading of "Everyday Use" could easily have prompted him to write in one of several genres, including a literary review to submit to the student newspaper (if he wanted to recommend summer reading, for example) or an entry on a blog devoted to the work of Alice Walker (if he wanted to join an online conversation about the story). Knowing that his primary audience—his English instructor—would expect him to pose and respond to a specific question about the story and would be most receptive to an essay organized around a clear thesis statement, Matthew decided that the most appropriate genre would be a literary analysis. If, like Matthew, you are prompted to write a literary analysis, use the following assignment as a guide.

Writing a Literary Analysis: Working with Your Available Means

Shaping your literary analysis

You'll have done a good deal of thinking, writing, and planning by the time you begin to draft your essay. As you start to draft it, your primary focus will be on establishing the significance of your interpretive question, providing sufficient evidence from the text to support your answer to this question, and explaining the larger implications of your answer for understanding the text.

Your introduction should explain which literary work you're going to analyze and why. Ralph Rees, for example, states that he will examine how Marianne Moore's poetry addresses the relationship between imagination and reality. The introduction also presents your interpretive question about the literary work as well as your initial attempt to persuade readers that this question is an interesting and important one to answer. At some point in the introduction, you need to pose this question explicitly for your readers. You can briefly summarize the different answers that other readers, including your classmates, have posed or might be likely to pose to this question. Rees, for example, reviews the three different perspectives that literary critics tend to have about reality. Keep in mind, too, that you might need to quickly summarize a main point or describe a main element of the text in order to help your readers understand the precise nature of the question that you're asking.

Finally, before you conclude your introduction, you should provide your readers with your thesis statement—in this case, a one- or two-sentence answer to the interpretive question you have posed. You can often present this answer in the form of a statement that begins "In this essay, I argue that . . . ." Some writers, like Rees, for example, prefer to phrase their thesis statement in a way that makes it sound as if the author of the work is arguing the particular point. In either case, the thesis statement advances a particular interpretation of the meaning of the text.

As you turn your attention to drafting the body of your essay, focus on the main reasons that support your specific answer to the interpretive question. Use paragraph divisions to distinguish each supporting reason. Strengthen your appeals to logos by arranging these paragraphs in a pattern that moves readers progressively toward the most interesting or most persuasive of your supporting reasons.

The body paragraphs should provide readers with direct references to the literary work. These direct quotations are your primary means of providing evidence for your reasons; consequently, the more compelling or appropriate the passages you choose to quote, the stronger appeals to logos you can make. Early in his analysis, Rees cites a long passage from the end of Moore's "Poetry." With this quotation, Rees introduces several key terms, such as *literal, imagination, real,* and *genuine,* that he will explore in more depth as he presents his interpretation of Moore's work. Rees wants readers to understand explicitly what meaning he takes away from this work.

Another way to support your thesis in the body paragraphs is to directly address other readers' interpretations of the text. Here you can strengthen your appeals to ethos by drawing support from other literary critics who share your perspective. Rees does this several times in his analysis, as when he cites Morton Zabel's reference to Moore's definition of the poet as a "literalist of the imagination." Conversely, you can also work to support your thesis by conceding or refuting alternative interpretations.

After providing sufficient evidence to support your major reasons, conclude your essay by situating it within a larger conversation about the literary work you're analyzing. In other words, explain to readers how your answer to your interpretive question helps deepen their understanding of the entire work. In his conclusion, Matthew Marusak explains how thinking carefully about what the narrator reveals makes us, as readers, "continually reevaluate our own perceptions of Alice Walker's story." You can also use the conclusion to point to other questions that, while related to the one you have answered in your essay, remain unanswered and could help to unlock additional meanings of the text.

You should consider whether visuals could strengthen your analysis. Consider sketching the scene for Jane Martin's *Beauty* if such a sketch would help readers to better understand a specific point you're making about how the two main characters interact. Photograph an object from your everyday life that has significance similar to that of the kitchen table in Joy Harjo's "Perhaps the World Ends Here." Or you might compile a slide presentation that incorporates digital photos and videos of Alice Walker speaking about "Everyday Use."

CHECKING OVER A LITERARY ANALYSIS

✓ The literary analysis poses a specific question about a literary work.

✓ This question is one that addresses a concern that a significant number of readers have about the text (or should have, if they have been overlooking critical features of it).

✓ The literary analysis presents a clear, identifiable thesis that answers this question.

✓ The literary analysis focuses on specific features or passages of the text.

✓ The literary analysis explains these key features or passages of the text and tries to persuade readers to interpret them in a particular way.

✓ The literary analysis directly engages other interpretations of the text, conceding points where appropriate and presenting evidence to counter these interpretations where necessary.

Student paper

In the following analysis of "Everyday Use," Matthew Marusak zeroes in on the character of the mother, whose point of view colors most interpretations of the story. Matthew argues for reading beyond the mother's point of view.

Matthew Marusak

Professor Glenn

English 496

March 2, 2007

Backward Enough: Alice Walker's Unreliable Narrator

Alice Walker's "Everyday Use" is a poignant short story about a dysfunctional family, whose members disagree over the meaning and importance of heritage--a disagreement stemming from the overarching tension already deeply seated among the family. Specifically, Walker presents an apparent contrast between heritage that is merely put on for show and that which is used on a daily basis. When the more sophisticated Dee returns home to visit her sister and mother, who live in the country, the characters inevitably grapple with one another in a clash of personalities, ideals, and belief systems. "Everyday Use" encompasses a wide range of human emotions and complex themes that we, as readers, have a responsibility to unravel throughout the course of the story. And while Walker's message about heritage is an undeniably important one, I see something more vital taking place concerning the nature of familial relationships. I will argue that we must effectively look beyond our fairly obvious interpretations of the text and focus instead on *how* the story brings us to those interpretations, a problem that lies entirely with the narrative voice.

Alice Walker crafts complex characters that truly encompass the themes of the story, yet this complexity relies heavily on the audience's own interpretation. If we read the story flat, it becomes impossible for the complexity and nuances of character to shine through. We must keep in mind that the only point of view expressed in "Everyday Use" is, in fact, the mother's. Therefore, I argue that the mother, as the speaking voice of the story, is not necessarily a reliable narrator, allowing us to see only what she sees in an entirely subjective manner. The narrator introduces herself and her daughters, immediately setting up the main theme (and conflict) in the story: familial relations. She explains: "Maggie will be nervous until after her sister [Dee] goes: she will stand hopelessly in corners, homely and ashamed of the burn scars down her arms and legs, eying her sister with a mixture of envy and awe" (23). But we never really know what Maggie is thinking. The only depiction we get of her is that, according to the mother, of a painfully reserved young woman left physically and emotionally scarred by tragedy; nothing more is learned about Maggie's past or her motivations except for what the mother tells us. "She thinks her sister has held life always in the palm of one hand," the mother continues, "that 'no' is a word the world never learned to say to her" (23). Her depiction of Maggie is certainly not a favorable one, and she seems to view her daughter with a mere observer's pity rather than a mother's empathy. The cause of Maggie's discomfort with her sister becomes clearer when we actually meet Dee. Yet even before Dee enters the scene, the mother gives us the sense that Dee is a force to be reckoned with.

The mother, too, seems to be in conflict with Dee, who, we are told, is embarrassed about her home and her family: "This house is in a pasture, too, like the other one. No doubt when Dee sees it she will want to tear it down. She wrote me once that no matter where we 'choose' to live, she will manage to come see us. But she will never bring her friends" (27). Yet herein lies another contradiction in the mother's narration: Dee does, in fact, bring her boyfriend home to meet her family. This is not the act of a woman as deeply ashamed of her family as we are meant to believe. Obviously, Dee wants her boyfriend to meet her family, or she would not have made the effort. Not only is the mother's claim disproved, she never even acknowledges her own mistaken assumption. The mother paints an ugly and unfair portrait of Dee before she even arrives--a picture that only gets darker as the story progresses.

When Dee finally arrives with Hakim-a-barber, we meet a beautiful, poised, and sophisticated woman, yet the mother is quick to judge Dee's attire as "so loud it hurts my eyes" (28). (Perhaps worth mentioning here is that the film version of "Everyday Use" presents Dee as very chic and not nearly as garishly dressed as her mother would have us believe. This may have been a deliberate choice on the filmmaker's behalf to set up this contradiction between the mother's misguided opinion of Dee and how Dee is in reality.) Evidently, the mother does not and seemingly cannot understand Dee's personality, as Dee has undertaken a new way of life. Clearly, the tension when Dee arrives is the result of a clash of cultures, marked by Dee's embracing of all things trendy and metropolitan, having left behind a life of simplicity and stillness--in other words, everything her family has come to represent.

The mother views Dee as more or less going through the motions of being a good daughter but never fully understanding what that role truly entails. Then again, we only know as much as the mother tells us; in this context, getting into Dee's head is not likely in the least. In Dee's defense, leaving her family was tantamount to survival. She could never have thrived in such an environment, nor could she have been happy. And though we never get Dee's side of the story, this seems like a fairly reasonable conclusion to draw. Of course, the mother would never admit this. She is too stuck in her ironclad determination to resent her daughter, never once attempting to understand *why* Dee left, but only that she did.

When heritage comes into the picture, then, the tension within the family naturally grows even greater. When the mother calls her daughter "Dee," Dee is quick to correct her, saying that her name is "Wangero Leewanika Kemanjo," and that she could no longer bear "being named after the people who oppress me" (29). Even after her mother says she was named after her aunt, Wangero argues that the name "Dee" is a symbol of oppression, traceable back to slavery. Again, here we cannot fully understand Wangero's motives, yet our narrator in her tone is not hesitant to let us know that she thinks this name change is baloney. A skeptic might get the impression that Wangero seems less concerned about oppression than the novelty of having a recognizably and fashionably Afrocentric name. Yet if we take her character only at face value--only as the mother sees her--we, like the mother, end up making quick and harsh judgments that would be better reserved for a character we truly get to know.

The episode with the quilts addresses the theme of lived heritage versus heritage for show only. When Wangero suggests Maggie is "backward enough to put [the quilts] to everyday use" (33), we find Wangero seemingly arguing that heritage is only worth something when it is put on display. Her opinion of heritage is different from that of her mother and sister, but it's a valid opinion all the same, an idea that the mother never addresses. In these final scenes, Wangero comes across as selfish and ignorant upon first, even second, reading; but it bears reiterating that we only see her through the mother's eyes. Wangero seems far more in tune with her heritage than the mother would care to admit. And just because Wangero has a different way of expressing her affection for her heritage does not make her any less worthy of that heritage than the others.

"Everyday Use" demands meticulous reading of its audience, revealing themes that are universal but not always considered on a daily basis. My interpretation necessarily requires a closer reading of the story, one that focuses on the narrative voice as an essential element in our understanding of a text. In this case, we are faced with an unreliable narrator and thus are forced to continually reevaluate our own perceptions of Alice Walker's story--an ambiguity that adds further richness to a text we can revisit over and over again.

Work Cited

Walker, Alice. "Everyday Use." *Everyday Use*. Ed. Barbara T. Christian. New Brunswick: Rutgers UP, 1994. 23–35. Print.

Guide to Responding

Consider the following assignments as alternatives to writing a literary analysis of the type Matthew Marusak produced.

ALTERNATIVE ASSIGNMENTS

1. Tell the story of a literary work from the point of view of a minor character. Account for this character's different interpretation of events in the narrative.

2. Deliver an analysis of a literary work in a form other than an essay: a review in a newspaper or magazine, an entry for a blog about the work or its author, or some other form. Once you choose another means of delivery, you'll need to make adjustments to the focus and elements of your analysis.

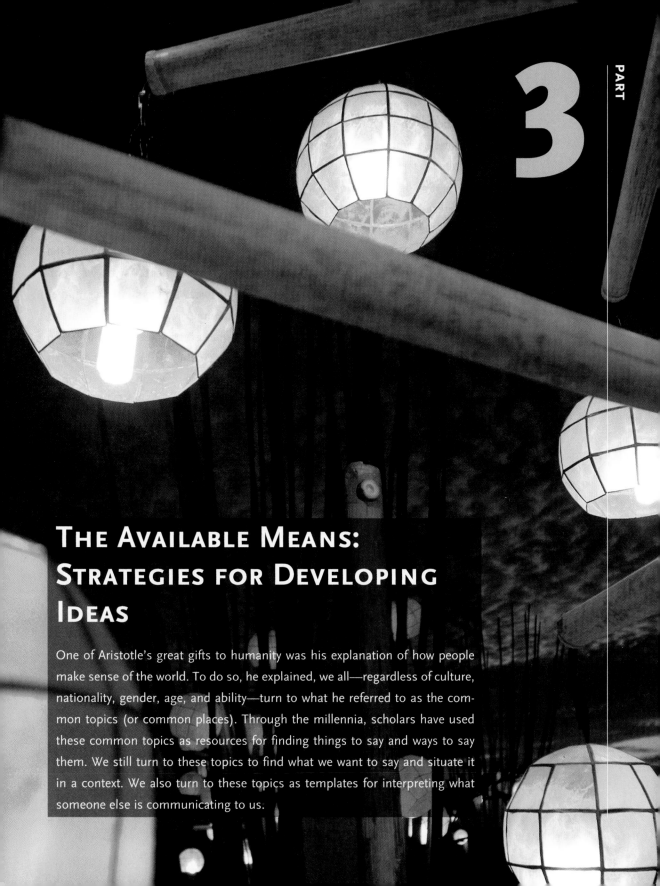

THE AVAILABLE MEANS: STRATEGIES FOR DEVELOPING IDEAS

One of Aristotle's great gifts to humanity was his explanation of how people make sense of the world. To do so, he explained, we all—regardless of culture, nationality, gender, age, and ability—turn to what he referred to as the common topics (or common places). Through the millennia, scholars have used these common topics as resources for finding things to say and ways to say them. We still turn to these topics to find what we want to say and situate it in a context. We also turn to these topics as templates for interpreting what someone else is communicating to us.

Aristotle's list was complex, including both common topics, which can be used to make sense of any kind of knowledge or information, and special topics, which (as their name implies) are used for specialized knowledge, as in legal arguments. In this book, however, we will consider only four common topics: definition, comparison, relationship, and circumstance. Although Aristotle also included testimony as one of his common topics, this book treats testimony (which includes such support as authority, witnesses, laws, statistics, proverbs, and precedents) as an important element of the other four common topics. After all, no matter what you're asserting or arguing, you'll need to support it.

These four common topics are the organizing principles for this part of the book, which presents the rhetorical methods of development. As you will soon see if you don't already suspect, the common topics complement one another and are sometimes used in support of one another. When we compare two things, for instance, we often need to define what exactly these two things are. In this way, definition supports and complements comparison. So that you can clearly see each rhetorical method as a means available to you, however, this part of the book presents them in separate chapters. You can use any of the common topics to develop fitting responses for the assignments in Chapters 4–11.

Definition (Chapter 12) explicates what something is as a whole and as an assembly of constituent parts. Both the whole and the parts can be defined. You probably will not be surprised, then, to discover that the rhetorical methods of development we refer to as definition, classification and division, description, and exemplification are all found in this chapter.

Comparison (Chapter 13), which is closely related to definition, examines more than one thing—usually two—to determine how and to what degree the things are similar and how and to what degree they are different. Little wonder, then, that the rhetorical method of development comparison and contrast is the focus here.

As for relationship (Chapter 14), this common topic allows us to consider the causes or effects of something, what comes before or after something, or how something unfolded. Cause-and-effect analysis, process analysis, and narration are the rhetorical methods of development found in Chapter 14.

Circumstance (Chapter 15) serves as the basis for argument and persuasion. After all, arguments always arise out of particular circumstances; only in terms of a circumstance can we argue what is possible or impossible, what course of action to take (or not take), or what happened, is likely to happen, or should happen. The rhetorical method of argument is covered in this chapter.

DEFINITION 12

What word or phrase best defines the sculpture in the photograph? Write for five minutes about that word or phrase, extending your definition to describe the specific details and overall effect of the sculpture. Your definition should not only encompass the essence of the sculpture but also differentiate this sculpture from others similar to it. Be prepared to share your definition with the rest of the class. As definitions are read aloud, keep track of which ones are similar and which ones are markedly different.

Definition as an Available Means

As you and your classmates examined the photograph of the sculpture, you probably concentrated on the characteristics that distinguish that piece of art as a sculpture, then on the features of the particular sculpture that distinguish it from other sculptures as well as from other pieces of art. Whenever your mind works to classify something by describing it (in this case, as a sculpture) and then distinguishing it (in this case, from other sculptures or pieces of art), you're tapping into a common topic and using the rhetorical method of development called **definition.** As you can see, definition makes use of strategies such as description, exemplification, and classification and division, all of which we discuss in this chapter. And all of these strategies, as you'll find out, are means of clarification and thus can be considered under the broad concept of definition.

What Is Definition?

When we think of definition, we usually think of dictionaries, with their succinct explanations of things in the world around us. Sometimes, we turn to a dictionary to make sure we have the correct word for the meaning we want (for example, *it's* or *its*), or to see that we need to spell *embarrass* with two *r*'s and two *s*'s. But more often than not, we look in dictionaries for definitions, for learning exactly what a word means (often conveyed through classification and description), how it is used (through exemplification), and how it is different from words close to it in meaning (through division).

Whenever we're introduced to something new—a new word, an academic subject, a sport, an activity, another language—we need to develop a new vocabulary. Whether we're learning the vocabulary of cooking (*chop, slice, mince, stir, fold, whip, fry, sauté*), golf (*ace, birdie, bogey, chip, drive, duff*), or human evolution (*prosimians, hominoids, paleoanthropology, australopithecines, isotopes*), we're expanding our world with new concepts and ideas. Definition is essential to our learning and our understanding.

No matter what we're learning or learning about, we use definition. And whether or not we're conscious of it, we always employ the three steps of definition:

1. First, we name the specific concept, action, person, or thing; in other words, we provide a term for it.
2. Then, we classify that term, or place it in a more general category. (See pages 407–408.)
3. Finally, we differentiate the specific term from all the other concepts, actions, persons, or things in that general category, often using examples. (See pages 408–409.)

For instance, if you're studying human evolution, you'll no doubt need to learn what distinguishes primates from other mammals.

Term	Class	Differentiation
Primates are	mammals	that have "a lack of strong specialization in structure; prehensile hands and feet, usually with opposable thumbs and great toes; flattened nails instead of claws on the digits; acute vision with some degree of binocular vision; relatively large brain exhibiting a degree of cortical folding; and prolonged postnatal dependency. No primate exhibits all these features, and indeed the diversity of primate forms has produced disagreement as to their proper classification" (*Encyclopedia Britannica*).

The preceding definition is a **formal, or sentence, definition,** the kind you'll find in a dictionary. A formal definition is a good start toward understanding a complex concept, and an **extended definition** can help you become even more familiar with such a concept. For instance, if you look at the Web site www.primate.org, you'll find an extended definition of primates:

> Primates are the mammals that are humankind's closest biological relatives. We share 98.4% of [our] DNA with chimpanzees. Apes, monkeys, and prosimians such as lorises, bush babies, and lemurs make up the 234 species of the family tree. About 90% of the primates live in tropical forests. They play an integral role in the ecology of their habitat. They help the forest by being pollinators, seed predators, and seed dispersers.

You can see how the extended definition introduces additional differentiating features that include names for the various primates, where they live, and how they live.

But extended definitions are not the only way we receive additional information; a **historical definition** can provide a longitudinal overview of how the term has been used or what the term has described through time. If you read the history of primates on the Web page www.chimpanzoo.org/history_of_primates, you'll find this overview:

> **65 mya** [million years ago]: Tertiary period and Paleocene epoch begin. . . . The earliest primates evolve. These primates were small insectivores who were most likely terrestrial. During this epoch, primates began to include food items such as seeds, fruits, nuts and leaves in their diet.

> **53.5 mya:** Eocene epoch begins. Primates diversify and some become arboreal. Primates have developed prehensile hands and feet with opposable thumbs and toes and their claws

have evolved into nails. Arboreal primates evolve relatively longer lower limbs for vertical clinging and leaping. Their eye sockets are oriented more frontally resulting in stereoscopic vision. Primates of this epoch belong to the prosimian family.

The historical overview continues to the twenty-first century. This historical definition introduces you to a number of additional concepts and terms related to primates, all of which you'll need to understand. One of the best things about learning a new subject is that the initial vocabulary introduces more vocabulary, so the learning never ends.

A historical definition may also show when and where the term was established and how it has been pronounced and used over time. The *Oxford English Dictionary* (or OED) is the most popular and reliable resource for information about the history of words. Here's how the OED defines *primates:*

> **Primates** (prAI´meItiz), sb [substantive, or noun]. *pl. Zool.* Sing. **Primas** (prAI´mæs), also anglicized **primate.** [L. *primātēs,* pl. of *prīmās* PRIMATE *sb.,* in mod. L. (linn.) name of an order.] The highest order of the *Mammalia,* including man, monkeys, and lemurs, and in the Linnæan order, bats
>
> **1774** GOLDSM. *Nat. Hist.* IV. V. 138 This was sufficient motive for Linnæus to give it the title of a Primas, to rank it in the same order as mankind. **1826** GOOD *Bk. Nat.* (1834) II. 47 The 1ˢᵗ order, Primates or chieftains, is distinguished by the possession of four cutting teeth in each jaw. **1863** LYELL *Antiq. Man* xxiv. 474 All modern naturalists, who retain the order under Primates, agree to exclude from it the bats or cheiroptera. **1871** DARWIN *Desc. Man* I.i.24 Man differs conspicuously from all the other Primates in being almost naked. **1899** J. FISKE *Through Nat. to God* II. V. 83 Forthwith . . . she [natural selection] invested all her capital in the psychical variations of this favoured primate.
>
> *attrib.* **1898** *Westm. Gaz.* 26 Aug. 8/2. It was a fixed fact that man is a member of the primate order.

You can see that this historical definition opens with the word's part of speech, sb, or substantive, also known as a noun, and then denotes the singular and plural forms. After connecting the word with the specialized terminology of zoology, it identifies the language of origin, which is Latin. Along a historical timeline, the OED lists the first mention of *primates* in print by year and author: the word first appeared in Oliver Goldsmith's 1774 *Natural History.* The definition then notes later mentions in 1826, 1863, 1871, and 1899, the last being in John Fiske's *Through Nature to God.* Historical definitions are often fun to read, and just as fun to research and write.

Sometimes, you'll need to write a **negative definition** to clarify for your readers not only what a term means but also what it does not mean. In conversation, you often say something like this: "When I talk about success, I'm not talking about making money," or "You cannot define a college education only in terms of a career." In these definitions, *success* and *education* encompass far more than money and preparing for a career. Success could involve money, of course, but also personal integrity, fulfillment in interpersonal relationships, and exciting professional challenges. Education means being introduced to all kinds of people from all over the world and exploring a wide variety of subjects (from music appreciation and art history to political science and social psychology). A college education can, indeed, lead to a career, but the road to that career should be filled with rich intellectual and social experiences of all kinds. Even primates can be defined negatively, as W. E. Le Gros Clark wrote in his classic book *The Antecedents of Man:* "The Primates as a whole have preserved rather a generalized anatomy and, if anything, are to be mainly distinguished from other [mammalian] orders by a negative feature—their lack of specialization."

Finally, in some situations, you may come across or write a **stipulative definition,** one that limits—or stipulates—the range of the term's meaning or application. A stipulative definition announces to the reader exactly how the writer will be using the term in the specific rhetorical situation. Sometimes, the writer includes reasons for the stipulation, sometimes not. For instance, if you want to write about *families,* you might include this stipulative definition: "For the purposes of this paper, a *family* will be defined as a group of people who live together, some of whom are children." If you write about *success,* you might define it like this: "In this paper, *success* will be defined in terms of how quickly college graduates entered the job market."

Look again at the photograph that opens this chapter. However you and your classmates defined that sculpture, you no doubt used a variety of words and phrases. The artist himself defined it as *Silence.* You can see why. Women have traditionally been expected to keep silent, especially in public. We know the woman is entering the public sphere because she's covered her head, as many women around the globe do when they leave their homes. She's also carrying a basket, in which to put her gatherings or purchases. Finally, she has her hand over her mouth; no words can come out. By defining his work as *Silence,* the artist gives this female figure a reason to look the way she looks. Her silence can be appreciated and respected. The piece is not called *Shyness* or *Aloofness* or *Sadness*—but *Silence.*

Classification and Division

Classification (placing something in a more general category) and **division** (distinguishing among things within a category) are common methods for helping us make sense of the world around us. A department store, a hospital, a telephone book, a university directory, a university library, or a book store—all of these are classified and divided in order to enhance accessibility to their information or contents. When you go to a hospital, for instance, you look at the directory by the entrance to find out information about the classification of areas within the building (reception area, visitor information, emergency room, outpatient clinic, waiting room, obstetrics, patient rooms, gift shop, snack bar, and cafeteria). When you arrive at any one of those areas (patient rooms, for instance), you look to see how that general area has been divided up (into floors and then individual rooms). In important ways, the categorizing of the areas in the hospital and further dividing of those same areas serves to define those places. The hospital room you want to find is defined by belonging to the category of *patient rooms* and then differentiated from (or divided from) other patient rooms by being on the fifth floor, end of the hallway, to the left.

In fact, every time you define, you provide a term and then place that term in its general category of origin. Primates belong in the larger class of mammals, and *Silence* belongs in the more general class of sculptures. Once the term is linked to a category or class, it must be differentiated or divided from all the other members of that category or class. All successful definitions work this way, by classifying and then dividing. For example, Jon Katz classifies and differentiates two types of dogs:

> The Perfect Dog is an enticing fantasy pooch. It's the dog that instantly learns to pee outdoors, never menaces or frightens children, plays gently with other dogs, won't jump on the UPS guy, never rolls in gross things, eats only the appropriate food at the right time, and never chews anything not meant for him. This dog does not exist. . . . [The Disney Dog is] the one who loves you alone, who will sacrifice his life to pull your toddler back from the busy street, who will cross 1,000 miles of towering snowdrifts to find you if you accidentally leave him behind in the Arctic.
>
> —**Jon Katz**, "Finding the Perfect Dog"

Both of these types of dogs are, of course, in the general category *dogs,* but they are differentiated from all other beings in that class by being perfectly behaved or infinitely faithful.

Exemplification

The rhetorical strategy of **exemplification** makes a generalization and uses an example or series of examples in support of that generalization. If you want to clarify why Veronica is the best sales clerk in your favorite store, you can provide a series of examples that define *best sales clerk:* Veronica dresses well herself, she has positive energy, she provides dressing-room truth, she never pushes a sale, and she helps you look like the very best version of yourself. Or, if you want to add interest to a generalization about your terrific Santa Fe vacation, you might talk about the clear blue skies, warm days, and cool nights; you could include anecdotes about being upgraded to a suite when you checked into the hotel, about visiting your cousin who lives out on a pueblo and meeting more cousins, about attending an art gallery opening and meeting the artists; you could describe shopping for turquoise jewelry and Acoma pottery and the Indian-made Christmas presents you found as you shopped on the plaza. You could also include tantalizing, sensory descriptions of the delicious food—Frito pie, chocolate-covered chile creams, carne adovada, and natillas. All these examples add interest to your generalization that you enjoyed a terrific vacation—and define what you mean by that phrase.

In the following passage, Pulitzer Prize–winner William Styron defines *suicidal* through his examples of suicidal thoughts.

> He asked me if I was suicidal, and I reluctantly told him yes. I did not particularize—since there seemed no need to—did not tell him that in truth many of the artifacts of my house had become potential devices for my own destruction: the attic rafters (and an outside maple or two) a means to hang myself, the garage a place to inhale carbon monoxide, the bathtub a vessel to receive the flow from my opened arteries. The kitchen knives in their drawers had but one purpose for me. Death by heart

attack seemed particularly inviting, absolving me as it would of active responsibility, and I had toyed with the idea of self-induced pneumonia—a long, frigid, shirt-sleeved hike through the rainy woods. Nor had I overlooked an ostensible accident . . . by walking in front of a truck on the highway nearby. These thoughts may seem outlandishly macabre—a strained joke—but they are genuine.

—William Styron, Darkness Visible

Styron admits to his physician that he is, indeed, depressed to the point of being suicidal, but he reserves the persuasive examples of his mental state for readers of his memoir.

Description

As you and your classmates "read" the sculpture called *Silence,* you no doubt relied on specific visual details in order to obtain an overall impression. Specific details can converge in a **description,** a verbal accounting of what we have experienced through any or all of our five senses, through what we see, hear, smell, touch, or taste.

Description helps us make sense of the world in a number of ways—for ourselves and for the people with whom we're communicating. Our descriptions always carry with them **sensory details** that have to do with our physical sensations or **sensibility details** that have to do with our intellectual, emotional, or physical state (alertness, gullibility, grief, fear, loathing, exuberance, coordination, clumsiness, relaxation, agitation, and so on).

José Antonio Burciaga's definition of *tortilla* is an extended definition that relies heavily on sensory details:

> For Mexicans over the centuries, the *tortilla* has served as the spoon and the fork, the plate and the napkin. . . . When I was growing up in El Paso, *tortillas* were part of my daily life. I used to visit a *tortilla* factory in an ancient adobe building near the open *mercado* in Ciudad Juárez. As I approached, I could hear the rhythmic slapping of the *masa* as the skilled vendors outside the factory formed it into balls and patted them into perfectly round corn cakes between the palms of their hands. The wonderful aroma and the speed with which the women counted so many dozens of *tortillas* out of warm wicker baskets still linger in my mind. Watching them at work convinced me that the most handsome and *deliciosas tortillas* are handmade. Although machines are faster, they can never adequately replace generation-to-generation experience. There's no place in the factory assembly line for the tender slaps that give each *tortilla* character. The best thing that can be said about mass-producing *tortillas* is that it makes it possible for many people to enjoy them.
>
> —José Antonio Burciaga, "I Remember Masa"

The sensory details that infuse Burciaga's definition of *tortilla* make his definition entertaining and memorable. Because description makes such use of details, it serves to define what is being described in particular ways. Just as Burciaga's details clarify what he means by *tortilla,* your description of your car as "a four-year-old Ford Focus with a forest green exterior and an interior that smells like stale, cherry air freshener from the last time it went in for repairs" defines your car by classifying the make and differentiating it from other green Focuses that do not smell of stale, cherry air freshener.

Definition and the Rhetorical Situation

Although definition can be employed in many ways—as part of a description, a cause-and-consequence analysis, a narrative, and so on—it is always used to fulfill its primary purpose of explaining features of the world around us. Such an explanation is often used to inform; it is sometimes used to argue a point. The understanding that comes through classification, division, exemplification, and description helps us learn, understand, weigh decisions, and make up our minds.

At its most basic level, though, definition is about meaning. It's about understanding the meanings of the words we encounter and about infusing the words we use with our intended meaning. Every time we read a sentence, we define one word after another in order to understand what message that sentence is sending. When we listen to someone else talking, we define what is said. When we speak, we define every word we produce. We've been selecting words according to their definitions ever since we spoke our first word. We choose one word instead of another because it carries with it the meaning we want to deliver. And whenever we're at a loss for words or struggling to come up with just the right word, we're frustrated, maybe even embarrassed. We may be experiencing some emotion (frustration, grief, happiness, fright, anger, or excitement) that interferes with our ability to select the word we want.

Definition helps us fulfill two basic rhetorical purposes, then: to explain or inform and to argue a point. If you're sitting around with your friends, wondering what a word means, you'll probably turn to a dictionary or some other reference work and fulfill both purposes at once. For instance, although many people use the words *imply* and *infer* interchangeably, according to many language-watchers, such usage is incorrect. Consider the following definitions and distinctions:

§174. **infer / imply**

People sometimes confuse *infer* with *imply*, but the distinction is a useful one. When we say that a speaker or sentence implies something, we mean that information is conveyed or suggested without being stated outright: *When the mayor said that she would not rule out a business tax increase, she implied* (not *inferred*) *that some taxes might be raised.* Inference, on the other hand, is the activity performed by a reader or interpreter in drawing conclusions that are not explicit in what is said: *When the mayor said that she would not rule out a tax increase, we inferred that she had been consulting with some new financial advisers, since her old advisers were in favor of tax reductions.* —*The American Heritage® Book of English Usage*

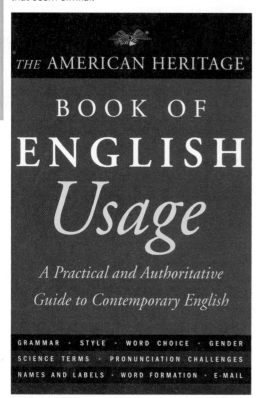

The *American Heritage® Book of English Usage* can help you choose between two words that seem similar.

The definitions presented and discussed in this usage guide are readily available to anyone who takes the time to look them up. As such, they meet the needs of the rhetorical situation: they address an exigence ("Is it *imply* or *infer*?"); they address an audience (the person who looks them up, wanting to know more); they fulfill a purpose (to explain a distinction in meaning); they provide a fitting response (brief and to the point); and they take advantage of the available means (by being accessible in print and online).

Using definition to address an exigence

All definitions and all effective writing that includes any definition address an exigence. The writer or speaker must determine what the problem is as well as how that problem can be resolved with a definition. The U.S. judicial system has been resolving exigencies like this for years, working to define contested terms such as *freedom of speech, disability, integration,* and *pornography.* Definitions of these terms have earned serious and steady attention—but not all definitions carry such gravity. Every day, we face smaller-scale exigencies that can be resolved by definitions. If you're baking a cake, you might need to know how the recipe defines *done.* Will the cake pull away from the pan, spring back when you press it in the center, or jiggle just a bit so it's not overdone? If you're working on an essay for a teacher who has announced "no late work," you'll want to know how she defines *late.* Does it mean after the beginning of class on the due date, or will slipping it under her office door any time that day be acceptable? If you're planning a special vacation, you'll want to know what the resort's Web site means by *all-inclusive.* At

"I never said 'I love you.' I said 'I love ya.' Big difference!"

A cartoon defining *affection.*

many resorts, that term means that all meals and accommodations are included; at some resorts, it means that unlimited rounds of golf and scuba diving excursions as well as tips, taxes, and airport transfers are also covered. Knowing how exactly the term is being defined resolves your exigence.

Using definition to address an audience

Whenever we compose a definition, we do so with an intended audience in mind. For instance, if the man in the cartoon were in love with his date, he'd say "I love you," not "I love ya." We all use the term *love* in various ways, depending on our intended audience. Rarely do we mean the same thing when we say "I love you" to a partner, a parent, a child, or a pet. When we sign off with "love" at the end of a thank-you note to an aunt and uncle, our intended meaning differs from signing off the same way to a fiancé. We know the difference; the aunt and uncle know the difference, and so does the fiancé. We use the word *love* with many people, but it has a different meaning in each rhetorical situation, depending on our audience.

In the following excerpt, Dottie Indyke defines *retablos* and *bultos* for readers who are familiar with but might confuse the two closely related terms. Note how she uses the rhetorical method of division to differentiate the terms:

> In honor of Mother's Day, Gallery A, in Taos, will host a benefit show of *retablos* and *bultos,* featuring likenesses of such historically significant women as the Virgin Mary and Our Lady of Guadalupe.
>
> An age-old Spanish Colonial folk-art form, *retablos* are painted depictions of saints traditionally created on pine panels that are varnished with sap from piñon trees, although today's artists use a variety of mediums and techniques. *Bultos* are their three-dimensional counterparts, carved from the roots of indigenous trees, often cottonwood and junipers. Since the 17th century, New Mexicans have prayed to these saintly stand-ins for everything from a bountiful harvest to help in finding missing objects. —**Dottie Indyke,** "Mother's Day Exhibition of *Retablos* and *Bultos*"

With Mother's Day as the exigence for the show, both the art gallery and the writer gauged their message to their respective audiences. The art gallery takes an audience of viewers and potential buyers into consideration, linking the celebration of Mother's Day with its show (and perhaps subsequent sales) of holy mothers in the New Mexican tradition. The writer takes her audience into consideration as well, defining the essential terms at the same time as she reminds her readers how familiar the terms—and the art itself—already are.

The enduring qualities of racism provided an exigence for Gloria Yamato, a teacher with the San Francisco Writerscorps, a group that works to strengthen communities. Yamato's students usually include youths aged six to twenty-one who are in need. Her extended definition of *racism* appeared in an essay intended for an audience of college students and teachers. Yamato's opening paragraph includes exemplification, a list of various definitions of *racism,* all of which contribute to the difficulties alluded to in the title of her essay:

> Racism is pervasive to the point that we take many of its manifestations for granted, believing "that's life." Many believe that racism can be dealt with effectively in one hellifying workshop, or one hour-long heated discussion. Many actually believe this

monster, racism, that has had at least a few hundred years to take root, grow, invade our space and develop subtle variations . . . this mind-funk that distorts thought and action, can be merely wished away. I've run into folks who really think that we can beat this devil, kick this habit, be healed of this disease in a snap. In a sincere blink of a well-intentioned eye, presto—poof—racism disappears. "I've dealt with my racism . . . (envision a laying on of hands) . . . Hallelujah! Now I can go to the beach." Well, fine. Go to the beach. In fact, why don't we all go to the beach and continue to work on the sucker over there? Cuz you can't even shave a little piece off this thing called racism in a day, or a weekend, or a workshop.

—**Gloria Yamato,** "Something about the Subject Makes It Hard to Name"

Only later in her essay does Yamato present a formal definition: "Racism is the systematic, institutionalized mistreatment of one group of people by another based on racial heritage." Given her intended audience (college students and teachers), Yamato uses her introductory definitions to engage their interest and her formal definition to anchor their understanding.

When East Harlem resident Robert Carmona began the program POPS (Paternity Optimizes Potential Success) to help men reconnect emotionally and financially with their children, he understood the importance of defining *manhood* in ways that his intended audience would understand. As a participant in POPS admitted, "I thought manhood was, 'I'm better than you, I'm smackin' my girl around.' But since I've been coming here, I've found out that a man is responsible. A real man knows what love is." What it means to be a man might be debatable, but not for the men in Carmona's program. His success in redefining *manhood* for his audience demonstrates how important it is to gauge each definition according to your audience.

In fact, the words you use, the definitions you provide, are dependent on your audience. You want to convey your intended meaning and fulfill your rhetorical purpose by carefully calibrating your definitions according to your audience.

Using definition with a rhetorical purpose

By now, you've no doubt realized that definitions can be used in a wide variety of situations, not only in reference books but in advertisements, essays, text-books, and Web sites, to name only a few. Whether they are used alone or as part of another rhetorical method of development, definitions can help you fulfill one of two basic rhetorical purposes: to inform or explain or to argue a point.

Using definition to inform or explain Explanatory definitions are especially useful when a writer wants to emphasize the significance of a specific meaning. How a word is being used often has broad ramifications. Consider writer Rose Del Castillo Guilbault's explanation of how the definition of *macho* changes according to whether the term is being used by Hispanics or most non-Hispanic Americans.

What is *macho*? That depends which side of the border you come from.

Although it's not unusual for words and expressions to lose their subtlety in translation, the negative connotations of *macho* in this country are troublesome to Hispanics.

Take the newspaper description of alleged mass murderer Ramon Salcido. That an insensitive, insanely jealous, hard-drinking, violent Latin male is referred to as *macho* makes Hispanics cringe.

"*Es muy macho,*" the women in my family nod approvingly, describing a man they respect. But in the United States, when women say, "He's so macho," it's with disdain.

The Hispanic *macho* is manly, responsible, hardworking, a man in charge, a patriarch. A man who expresses strength through silence. What the Yiddish language would call a *mensch.*

The American *macho* is a chauvinist, a brute, uncouth, selfish, loud, abrasive, capable of inflicting pain, and sexually promiscuous.

Quintessential *macho* models in this country are Sylvester Stallone, Arnold Schwarzenegger, and Charles Bronson. In their movies, they exude toughness, independence, masculinity. But a closer look reveals their machismo is really violence masquerading as courage, sullenness disguised as silence, and irresponsibility camouflaged as independence.

If the Hispanic idea of *macho* were translated to American screen roles, they might be Jimmy Stewart, Sean Connery, and Laurence Olivier.

In Spanish, *macho* ennobles Latin males. In English it devalues them. This pattern seems consistent with the conflicts ethnic minority males experience in this country. Typically the cultural traits other societies value don't translate as desirable characteristics in America.

—**Rose Del Castillo Guilbault,** "Americanization Is Tough on 'Macho'"

Guilbault uses classification and description (describing the characteristics that fall into the category of *macho*), division (distinguishing between the Hispanic *macho* and Americanized *macho*), and exemplification (citing Jimmy Stewart, Sean Connery, and Laurence Olivier as examples) to define *macho* and develop her article.

Explanatory definitions like Guilbault's can constitute part of a piece of writing that uses comparison and contrast, description, narration, or any form. In fact, a definition can energize any piece of writing by infusing it with vivid, informative detail.

Using definition to argue a point Definitions can also be used effectively in arguing a point. Car advertisements that use a single word (*luxury* or *security*) to define the product usually underlay the term with photos of the car's interior and exterior and of passengers who are dressed elegantly or seat-belted securely. Cosmetic companies define their products with *quick fix, lasting,* or *fresh* and then attempt to describe those distinguishing qualities in more detail. Candy companies define their products as *small, dark, and handsome* and *curiously strong.* Any advertisement that uses definition is doing so in order to argue a point: buy this product.

But definitions that argue are not always pushing a product. They push ideas and opinions as well. Presidential candidates argue over the definition of *good American.* Your parents might argue over the definition of *mealtime, vacation,* or *financial planning;* you might argue with your parents over the meaning of *curfew, responsibility,* or *good grades.* And you and your classmates might have argued about the meanings of various technical terms used by your professors as well as about such everyday academic terms as *class participation, plagiarism,* and *collaboration.* Every time you want to make sure you understand someone else's intended meaning or clarify the meaning you're trying to convey, you argue for a particular definition.

In the following passage, Paul Theroux questions a traditional definition of *manhood,* arguing that, rather than inspiring men, that definition is often debilitating:

> I have always disliked being a man. The whole idea of manhood in America is pitiful, in my opinion. This version of masculinity is a little like having to wear an ill-fitting coat for one's entire life (by contrast, I imagine femininity to be an oppressive sense of nakedness). Even the expression "Be a man!" strikes me as insulting and abusive. It means: Be stupid, be unfeeling, obedient, soldierly and stop thinking. Man means "manly"—how can one think about men without considering the terrible ambition of manliness? And yet it is part of every man's life. It is a hideous and crippling lie; it not only insists on difference and connives at superiority, it is also by its very nature destructive—emotionally damaging and socially harmful.
>
> —**Paul Theroux,** "Being a Man"

Whether you agree with Theroux's argument might be a topic for further discussion. The point here is that he is using definition to argue a point, that the American "idea of manhood" is "a hideous and crippling lie."

Using definition as a fitting response

Recognizing an exigence, deciding to respond, locating an audience, aiming to fulfill a rhetorical purpose—those are initial steps in using definition as a fitting response. As you know by now, if the exigence (or problem) is certain to be resolved, there's no need for a fitting response. And if it can never be resolved, there's no need for one, either. But if the exigence is contingent—that is, it must and can be resolved—then you're ready to begin shaping a fitting response. As you work toward a fitting response, you'll need to keep the following three criteria in mind: a fitting response must be (1) appropriate for the problem, (2) delivered in a suitable medium that reaches the intended audience, and (3) satisfying to that audience.

Advertisement from the Office of National Drug Control Policy/ Partnership for a Drug-Free America.

So you smoked pot.

And now your kid's trying it and you feel you can't say anything. Get over it. Smoking pot can affect the brain and lead to other risky behaviors. So you have to set the rules and expect your kid to live drug free, no matter how hypocritical it makes you feel. Because to help them with their problem, first you have to get over yours. To find out more, call 800.788.2800 or visit theantidrug.com.

The antidrug is A C T I O N.

The Partnership ● for a Drug-Free America®

For example, an advertisement that appeared in magazines such as *Newsweek* is aimed at the parents of current pot smokers and sponsored by the Office of National Drug Control Policy/Partnership for a Drug-Free America. It represents what that organization believes is a fitting response to the exigence of young people's drug use. As you can see, the coffee mug, instead of reading "#1 Mom" or "#1 Golfer," reads "#1 Hypocrite." The text below the image of the coffee mug opens with, "So you smoked pot." That opening, printed in bold, hooks the magazine reader, an adult interested in current events. One pressing current event, according to the ad, is this: "And now your kid's trying it and you feel you can't say anything." The ad continues by suggesting a fitting response to the exigence of that feeling:

> Get over it. Smoking pot can affect the brain and lead to other risky behaviors. So you have to set the rules and expect your kid to live drug free, no matter how hypocritical it makes you feel. Because to help them with their problem, first you have to get over yours. To find out more, call 800.788.2800 or visit theantidrug.com.

At the bottom of the ad, the antidrug is defined as "A C T I O N." Both *#1 Hypocrite* and *action* are defined in such a way as to persuade parents to intervene in their children's experimentation with drugs. What does this ad sell? No product, just action.

READING A TEXT FOR DEFINITION

1. Take a moment to look over the examples of definitions in this section. Label each definition (that isn't already labeled) as formal, extended, negative, stipulative, or historical. What rhetorical purpose does each of the definitions strive to fulfill? Be prepared to share your findings with the rest of the class.

2. What exigence might Paul Theroux have been facing when he wrote his criticism of a traditional definition of *manhood*? Who might comprise his intended audience?

3. Compare and contrast the three definitions of *manhood* in this section, accounting for the exigence and audience for each definition. After considering these definitions, do you see an exigence for developing your own definition? If so, what is it? How do you define *manhood*? And for whom? Be prepared to share your response with the rest of the class.

Using definition as an available means

Every rhetorical situation includes the available means of persuasion—the physical means of delivering the message (verbally, visually, in print, online), the place from which the rhetor creates and sends the message (from a computer, a drawing board, a jail cell), and the rhetorical elements of the message itself (the use of rhetorical appeals, evidence, method of development, and so on). If you consciously think about all of these rhetorical concerns every time you speak or write, you may feel overwhelmed. But if you keep in mind that you've been employing the available means of rhetorical situations since you were a little child (crying to get your diaper changed, saying "please" to get a cookie, writing a thank-you note to get approval or another gift next year), you'll understand that you've been unconsciously juggling these concerns for many years, doing so as automatically and quickly as you keyboard. You're already pretty good, and you're getting even better.

You're undoubtedly familiar with Martin Luther King, Jr.'s "Letter from Birmingham Jail," which he composed after being arrested for public demonstrations to end racial segregation and discriminatory hiring practices. On the day of his arrest, he read in a newspaper a letter from eight white clergymen, all of whom supported his politics and political vision but rejected his method of publicly demonstrating. They urged him to stop protesting and launch a lawsuit instead. Although these men were addressed as the recipients of King's reply, a much larger body of readers was his intended audience, for he knew his letter would be widely distributed. His available means before this time had included sermons, public speeches, demonstrations and marches, private conversations and correspondence, and the words and actions of his followers. But once he was in custody, in solitary confinement, the means available to him were a pen and paper. One prominent issue for King was the definition of a *just law* versus an *unjust law*:

> You express a great deal of anxiety over our willingness to break laws. This is certainly a legitimate concern. Since we so diligently urge people to obey the Supreme Court's decision of 1954 outlawing segregation in the public schools, at first glance it may seem rather paradoxical for us consciously to break laws. One may well ask: "How can you advocate breaking some laws and obeying others?" The answer lies in the fact that there are two types of laws: just and unjust. I would be the first to advocate obeying just laws. One has not only a legal but a moral responsibility to disobey unjust laws. I would agree with St. Augustine that "an unjust law is no law at all."
>
> Now, what is the difference between the two? How does one determine whether a law is just or unjust? A just law is a man-made code that squares with the moral law or the law of God. An unjust law is a code that is out of harmony with the moral law. To put it in the terms of St. Thomas Aquinas: An unjust law is a human law that is not rooted in eternal law and natural law. Any law that uplifts human personality is just. Any law that degrades human personality is unjust. All segregation statutes are unjust because segregation distorts the soul and damages the personality. It gives the segregator a false sense of superiority and the segregated a false sense of inferiority. Segregation, to use the terminology of the Jewish philosopher Martin Buber, substitutes an "I-it" relationship for an "I-thou" relationship and ends up relegating persons to the status of things. Hence segregation is not only politically, economically, and sociologically unsound, it is morally wrong and sinful. Paul Tillich has said that sin is separation. Is not segregation an existential expression of man's tragic separation, his awful estrangement, his terrible sinfulness? Thus it is that I can urge men to obey the 1954 decision of the Supreme Court, for it is morally right; and I can urge them to disobey segregation ordinances, for they are morally wrong.
>
> —**Martin Luther King, Jr.**, "Letter from Birmingham Jail"

King successfully establishes his ethos by appealing to his readers as a morally committed, thoughtful, well-educated man, who weighs the issues before acting or directing the action of others. His reasoning, or logos, is careful and thoughtful. And his emotional appeal (pathos) to the moral sense of his readers

Development Strategies

brings home his point: segregation ordinances are morally wrong and, therefore, must be disobeyed. He draws on the authority of St. Augustine, St. Thomas Aquinas, Martin Buber, Paul Tillich, and the U.S. Supreme Court to support his definitions of just and unjust laws. And throughout the passage, he uses the definitions to argue a point. A letter written from jail, after he'd been arrested for disobeying segregation ordinances, was the best use of the means available to him.

USING DEFINITION IN YOUR WRITING

1. In what assignments (for chemistry, biology, engineering, math, and so on) are you asked to include a definition as part of your response? What kinds of definitions (formal, extended, historical, stipulative, or negative) are you most often asked to provide?

2. Bring to class an example of a definition, perhaps one you've come across in your pleasure reading or one that you've noticed in a textbook (but not one from a dictionary). As you choose your example, think about the ways the definition is used as support or explanation within a larger piece of writing.

CHECKING OVER A DEFINITION

Answering the following questions will help you review your own definitions as well as those of your classmates.

✓ What exigence needs to be resolved?
✓ What specific audience can resolve or influence the resolution of that exigence?
✓ What kind of definition (formal, extended, historical, negative, or stipulative) might best resolve this exigence? Why? What formal definition could anchor any of the other types?
✓ What is the overall purpose of this definition: to inform, to explain, or to argue a point? How exactly does the purpose relate to the audience, and vice versa?
✓ What examples might best develop this definition? How might division be used to develop the definition?
✓ Where is description used in the definition? Would some kind of visual complement or clarify the description?

Development Strategies

COMPARISON | 13

WRITE FOR FIVE

Like many Americans, you may eat cold cereal for breakfast. Pick out two cereals, either by looking at the photo or by thinking about ones you've eaten recently. Write for five minutes about these breakfast choices, noting similarities and differences between the names of the cereals and the colors and graphics on the boxes. As you write, consider the audience (or consumer) for each of the cereals, the exigence to which its producers might be responding, and the reasons you might have for choosing one of the cereals over the other. Be prepared to share your comparison with the rest of the class.

Comparison as an Available Means

Two cereal boxes you might recognize are those for Lucky Charms and Cheerios. The Lucky Charms box is red, the most eye-catching color on a grocer's shelves. (And if you have any experience grocery shopping with young children, you'll know that cereals like Lucky Charms are always shelved low, where the children can more readily spot them.) The character on the front of the box is a cheerful Irish leprechaun, wearing a green suit and hat, adorned with a shamrock. The frosted oat cereal and colored marshmallows swirl around the leprechaun, forming a rainbow. There's no mention on the box's front of the nutritional value or the sugar content of this cereal.

Cheerios, on the other hand, comes in a yellow box with a big red heart on the front, and the print touts the cereal's nutritional value. The banner across the heart reads, "As part of a heart-healthy diet, the soluble fiber in Cheerios can reduce your cholesterol!" And in the lower-left corner of the box's front is another assertion: "Three grams of soluble fiber daily from whole-grain oat foods, like Cheerios, in a diet low in saturated fat and cholesterol, may reduce the risk of heart disease. Cheerios has 1 gram per cup." As you probably know, Cheerios is shelved at adults' eye level; it's aimed at adults.

Side by side, these two cereal boxes promote different eating experiences—one fun, the other healthful. The information you can glean from the boxes themselves—the ways the two cereals are alike and different—helps you evaluate which breakfast cereal to choose.

When your exigence prompts you to consider similarities and differences or to determine what is superior and what is inferior, you can respond with the two-part method of rhetorical development known as **comparison and contrast.**

What Is Comparison and Contrast?

We use comparison and contrast from the moment we wake up (often comparing the advantages to getting up with those of staying in bed) until we go to bed at night (comparing that option with staying up later). We use **comparison** to consider how two or more things are alike, and we use **contrast** to show how related things are different. The method of comparison and contrast helps us make sense of the world around us and clarify the issues we need to understand, whether we're explaining, making a decision, shaping an argument, opening a discussion, or crafting an entertaining narrative.

If you're deciding which cereal to have for breakfast, you can initiate comparison and contrast by establishing a **basis for comparison,** the feature shared by the things being compared. Lucky Charms and Cheerios are both cold breakfast cereals, indeed, but that doesn't make them the same. By setting up **points of comparison,** you can clarify the ways in which the two cereals are the same or comparable as well as different. You may already know the answers to the questions of which cereal tastes better, which one is better for you, and which one will sustain you until lunch. But you may not be familiar with the information that supports those answers. So, you might examine both cereal boxes more closely.

The nutrition information panels on the boxes indicate that both cold cereals have been approved by the American Heart Association because both are low in saturated fats and cholesterol, with 0 grams of saturated fat and 0 milligrams of cholesterol. Both are also pretty low in sodium (200 milligrams and 210 milligrams), carbohydrates (25 grams and 22 grams), and protein (2 grams and 3 grams)—but what do these figures mean? If you want to follow the recommended daily allowances (RDAs), you'll want 30 percent of your daily calories to come from fat, 55 percent from carbohydrates, and 15 percent from protein. Neither of the cereals comes close to fulfilling the RDAs, as the charts on the boxes show. But what about the recommended daily requirements (RDRs) for necessary vitamins and minerals? The nutrition charts show that these cereals provide the same amounts of vitamins A, C, D, B_6, and B_{12}. In terms of other nutrients—calcium, thiamin, riboflavin, niacin, folic acid, and zinc—they are also the same. Cheerios, however, offers more iron (nearly half the RDR), phosphorus, magnesium, and copper. But will those differences affect your choice? What difference will be decisive for you? It might be the amount of sugar. Lucky Charms has 13 grams, whereas Cheerios has only 1 gram. The extra sugar might make Lucky Charms taste better; if you want to make it to lunch, however, you might choose Cheerios, so you don't go to work on a sugar high and then crash midmorning.

All the information you can glean from the side of a cereal box helps you understand the ingredients of the cereal and make a choice. If you wanted to discuss the choice of cereal with children and persuade them to make the "right" choice, you could use much of that information. Whether you could ultimately persuade them to choose Cheerios over Lucky Charms is, of course, another story.

Suppose you wanted to open a discussion with your children about moving from the city to the suburbs. You might rely on comparison and contrast to present ways in which a move to the suburbs would improve their daily lives as well as their future chances. They might resist, and one of them might produce the following article:

> . . . People who flee urban schools in pursuit of more wholesome settings may be surprised by this report card: Suburban students engage in just as much sex, drugs, and fighting as city kids do.
>
> Among the results of the study released Wednesday by The Manhattan Institute, a New York–based conservative think tank:

- Two-thirds of suburban and urban 12th-graders have had sex; 43 percent of suburban 12th-graders and 39 percent of urban 12th-graders have had sex outside of a "romantic relationship."
- 74 percent of suburban 12th-graders and 71 percent of urban 12th-graders have tried alcohol more than two or three times.
- 22 percent of suburban 12th-graders and 16 percent of urban 12th-graders say they have driven while drunk.

—**Wire Reports,** "City, Suburban Student Behavior Similar"

The basis for comparison is student behavior, and the points of comparison are sexual activity, alcohol consumption, and drinking and driving. The comparisons are striking and perhaps surprising: two-thirds of all twelfth-graders have had sex, and nearly three-fourths of both suburban and urban twelfth-graders have tried alcohol more than two times. The percentage gap between the number of suburban and urban twelfth-graders who have driven while drunk reflects the fact that many urban youths have easy access to public transportation and thus no need to drive. An urban twelfth-grader could ride a bus when drunk. This comparison and contrast indicates that the problems urban teens face are not a result of living in the city but of being an American teenager today.

The Elements of Comparison and Contrast

The basis of comparison

We compare and contrast on a regular basis, always starting with a basis of comparison, whether we're deciding which college to attend, which route to drive into work, which place to board our dog, or which assignment to do first. Every time we write, we compare and contrast sentences, paragraphs, and examples, revising and making choices according to which passage is more effective. The basis of comparison is what two things have in common: college reputation, a route to work, kennel facilities, or an academic obligation.

Most writers open a comparison-and-contrast essay by establishing a quickly understandable basis of comparison. In an often reprinted essay, Bruce Catton sets up the basis of comparison for the two Civil War generals, Ulysses S. Grant and Robert E. Lee:

> They were two strong men, these oddly different generals, and they represented the strengths of two conflicting currents that, through them, had come into final collision.   —**Bruce Catton,** "Grant and Lee: A Study in Contrasts"

Other than being generals, Grant and Lee had little in common, hence the basis for Catton's essay. Catton didn't intend to demonstrate that one man was better than the other, but rather that each man authentically reflected the society he represented.

Bharati Mukherjee uses comparison and contrast to evaluate the choices she and her sister (also Indian-born) have made with regard to whether to become U.S. citizens:

> This is a tale of two sisters from Calcutta, Mira and Bharati, who have lived in the United States for some 35 years, but who find themselves on different sides in the current debate over the status of immigrants. I am an American citizen and she is not. I am moved that thousands of long-term residents are finally taking the oath of citizenship. She is not.   —**Bharati Mukherjee**, "Two Ways of Belonging in America"

Even though these sisters have much in common, sharing a place of birth, place of education, and place of employment, their opinions of U.S. citizenship differ, with one wanting her expertise and social contributions to outweigh her immigrant status and the other seeing her U.S. citizenship as of utmost value to herself and the nation. The national controversy over the status of immigrants served as the exigence for Mukherjee's op-ed piece.

You don't spend time comparing and contrasting kennel facilities with homework assignments or your sister with Robert E. Lee—these pairs have nothing in common, no basis of comparison, unless, of course, you're using a special form of comparison called analogy.

Analogy

An **analogy** equates two unlike things, explaining one in terms of another, such as comparing the human brain with a computer or the human eye with a camera. David Sedaris even likens his grandmother to an ATM machine in the following passage:

> My brother and I came to view our Ya Ya as a primitive version of an ATM machine. She was always good for a dollar or two, and because we were boys, all we had to do was open her car door or inform her the incense had just set fire to one of her embroidered cushions. I'd learned never to accompany her in public, but aside from that, Ya Ya and I had no problem. I saw her as a benign ghost, silent and invisible until you needed a little spending money.   —**David Sedaris**, "Get Your Ya-Ya's Out!"

Of course, Sedaris's grandmother isn't really an ATM machine, but she is "silent and invisible until you needed a little spending money." Whenever you can use analogy, whenever you can explain one thing in terms of another, you should try it; an analogy often breathes new life into an otherwise ordinary comparison-and-contrast passage or essay.

The points of comparison

After establishing a basis of comparison, you need to clarify the points of comparison, the ways in which the two (or more) things or people are alike or different, the features you want to emphasize. Whether you wrote or thought about it, or discussed it with your family over the course of several months, your choice of college no doubt involved comparison and contrast. The points of comparison you used probably involved such features as distance from home, yearly tuition, costs of room and board, reputation, and range of available majors. Or maybe your comparison and contrast was between attending college or working full-time, with the points of comparison being your interest, financial status, and financial obligations. Whether you're choosing a college or choosing to attend college, you're making your decision based on points of comparison.

One of the most familiar sources of information for comparison and contrast is *Consumer Reports,* where readers look for help in choosing the best used car, washing machine, interior paint, and so on. Sometimes, the magazine features advice on how to consume rather than what to consume. In a feature titled "Dollars & Sense, A Tale of Two Shoppers," the spending patterns of two women are compared and contrasted. Both women bought groceries at the same store, but one woman "was armed with coupons, the store's shopper card, a store circular, and a smart shopper's savvy." The image shows the points of comparison: peanut butter, carrots, ice cream, instant breakfast mix, nacho chips, and preserves. The visuals accompanying the essay complement the text: although the food purchases appear to be the same (same Alpo, same Breyers, same Cap'n Crunch), the purchases by "The Savvy Shopper" total nearly eighty dollars less.

Comparison of costs for "The Big Spender" and "The Savvy Shopper" from *Consumer Reports.*

THE BIG SPENDER

- Buy a jar of national-brand peanut butter: $3.79.
- Buy 2 pounds of precut carrot sticks: $7.16.
- Buy Rocky Road ice cream, without using coupon or store card: $3.99.
- Buy 14 single-serving cans of ready-to-drink instant breakfast: $18.06.
- Buy four small bags of nacho chips from near the checkout lane: $3.96.
- Buy a jar of fancy black-currant preserves, without coupon: $4.79.

THE SAVVY SHOPPER

- Buy a jar of store-brand peanut butter: $2.50. **Saving: $1.29.**
- Buy a 2-pound bag of carrots: $1.29. **Saving: $5.87.**
- Buy Rocky Road, with a coupon and store card: $0.99. **Saving: $3.00.**
- Buy a 14-serving canister of powdered mix, plus milk: $8.13. **Saving: $9.93.**
- Buy one big bag of nacho chips from the aisle: $1.49. **Saving: $2.47.**
- Buy garden-variety blueberry preserves, with coupon: $1.29. **Saving: $3.50.**

Total cost: $135

Total cost: $56

Comparison and Contrast and the Rhetorical Situation

Whether we're shopping for groceries, deciding what to wear to an interview, or answering exam questions, we're drawing on our capacity to compare and contrast. Examiners tend to have a special fondness for comparison and contrast questions, as you'll quickly discover, if you haven't already. Your history professor may want you to compare and contrast the public's attitudes toward the war in Vietnam and the war in Iraq for several reasons, some of which may well have to do with your understanding of the causes and consequences of such conflicts. Your English professor might ask you to compare and contrast the treatment of female characters in two of Shakespeare's comedies, perhaps so you can explore the dramatic purpose behind each of the female roles. And your education professor might ask you to compare literacies learned at school with those learned outside of school, so that you can begin to appreciate all the learning that happens when young students are not in school. Physicians, too, ask you to think in terms of comparison and contrast: Is your headache worse than the last time you were here? How is this cold different from the ones that do not bring you to the doctor's office? What's the difference between putting weight on your right ankle and putting it on your left ankle?

These are the kinds of comparisons and contrasts that we use on a regular basis, the kinds we've been using since we were children and knew that we preferred creamy peanut butter over crunchy, our sandwiches cut on the diagonal rather than straight across, Levi's rather than Wranglers, and so on. Some of the preferences that arise from our comparisons and contrasts may not make much sense to others; partners think that if crunchy peanut butter's on sale, it's the kind you ought to eat; babysitters don't appreciate being able to eat the points off a sandwich half; and parents cannot see one bit of difference between two pairs of jeans except on the price tag. But when we compare and contrast (even if we do it in a split second), the results make a difference to us: creamy peanut butter doesn't scratch the roof of your mouth; diagonally cut sandwiches can also be dipped in soup; and one kind of jeans fits better through the thighs and has flared legs. They simply look better on, and the price difference is worth it.

Whether you use comparison and contrast to frame an entire essay, to organize a supporting passage in another kind of essay, or to make a point in a conversation or an argument, this rhetorical method of development is used to fulfill four general purposes: to explain, to evaluate choices, to argue a point, and to entertain. In every case, the use of comparison and contrast is meeting the needs of a rhetorical situation, addressing an exigence and an audience with a specific rhetorical purpose.

Using comparison and contrast to address an exigence

The minute you read that first essay exam question asking for a response that uses comparison and contrast, you'll recognize an exigence. Not all exigencies, however, present themselves in such a clear way. Sometimes, it's up to you to shape a rhetorical exigence that you can address, out of any of a multitude of details that comprise your life.

Let's say that you and your family begin noticing a change in your mail delivery service. Over supper, someone might ask when the mail finally came, because it hadn't arrived at lunchtime, as it usually does. A week or so later, another family member may complain about the torn cover of his latest *Rolling Stone*. And a few days after that, you might notice that a package is lying at the end of the driveway; the postal carrier hadn't bothered to bring it up to the door. If you get angry and want to complain, you may have just shaped an exigence to resolve: your mail delivery is bad, and you want an immediate improvement. If you decide to complain, you can get on the U.S. Postal Service Web site and follow the links "Contact Us" and "email Us." Complaining at the supper table, trading tales with the neighbors, seething—none of these actions will resolve the exigence. Someone at the postal service is the only one who can resolve your problem, either by speaking to your current carrier or putting your former carrier back on your route. In an email, you can describe—by comparing and contrasting—the good service you used to have (timely, careful, to the door) with the bad service (late, careless, lazy) you're currently enduring. A short comparison-and-contrast essay will serve as a fitting response within the resources and constraints of this rhetorical situation.

Rhetors use comparison and contrast to address an exigence when they are complaining about a product or service (comparing their expectations of it to the reality), evaluating a choice ("Should I work this summer or take classes and try to graduate early?"), arguing a point (buying a used car is always a better financial decision than driving a new one off the lot), or entertaining a friend ("You think your childhood was bad, let me tell you about mine!"). Whether the exigence is a problem to be solved or an opportunity to enliven an otherwise flat conversation, comparison and contrast can be the basis for the most fitting response.

Using comparison and contrast to address an audience

Who cares about your use of comparison and contrast? In other words, who can resolve or influence the resolution of the exigence that your words are addressing? Who is your audience? In the case of poor mail service, the U.S. Postal Service is really the only place for you to send your words. Only a supervisor can help make your mail delivery better. If you're trying to weigh the advantages of getting a job over taking summer classes, you and your parents might be the joint audience. You'll need to decide what choice is better for you—but you'll probably also need the financial support of your parents if you decide to take classes. And if you're telling a story, comparing your childhood with that of a friend's, you might find yourself with an even larger audience—all the people attending a party, for instance.

Your audience, of course, determines the information you'll include in your comparison and contrast. The phrasing in your complaint to the U.S. Postal Service will probably be more moderate than the ranting you do at the supper table, with your family. The reasons you give your parents for wanting to take summer classes rather than going home to work might be markedly different from the reasons you provide to an on-campus love interest. And how you describe your childhood experiences, in a kind of competition with your friends, could hurt your parents' feelings, so you'd likely provide a softer set of comparisons if they were around. Like all the other methods of development, comparison and contrast is flexible. It can be used in many ways to reach any audience in any rhetorical situation.

Using comparison and contrast with a rhetorical purpose

As you know, comparison and contrast is used to fulfill one of four rhetorical purposes: to explain, evaluate choices, argue a point, or entertain. When a comparison-and-contrast essay addresses an exigence and an audience at the same time that it fulfills its rhetorical purpose, it's a fitting response.

Using comparison and contrast to explain When paleoanthropologists Karen R. Rosenberg and Wenda R. Trevathan found themselves trying to explain why humans require assistance with childbirth, they called on comparison and contrast, comparing human anatomy with that of our closest primate relatives:

> Despite the monkey infant's tight squeeze, its entrance into the world is less challenging than that of a human baby. In contrast to the twisted birth canal of modern humans, monkeys' birth canals maintain the same cross-sectional shape from entrance to exit. . . . A monkey infant enters the birth canal headfirst, with the broad back of its skull against the roomy back of the mother's pelvis and tailbone. That means that the baby monkey emerges from the birth canal face forward—in other words, facing the same direction as its mother.
>
> Firsthand observations of monkey deliveries have revealed a great advantage in babies' being born facing forward. . . . As the infant is born, the mother reaches down to guide it out of the birth canal and toward her nipples. In many cases, she also wipes mucus from the baby's mouth and nose to aid its breathing. Infants are strong enough at birth to take part in their own deliveries. Once their hands are free, they can grab their mother's body and pull themselves out.
>
> If human babies were also born face forward, their mothers would have a much easier time. Instead the evolutionary modifications of the human pelvis that enabled hominids to walk upright necessitate that most infants exit the birth canal with the back of their heads against the pubic bones, facing in the opposite direction as the mother. . . . For this reason, it is difficult for the laboring human mother . . . to reach down and guide the baby as it emerges. This configuration also greatly inhibits the mother's ability to clear a breathing passage for the infant, to remove the umbilical cord from around its neck or even to lift the baby up to her breast. If she tries to accelerate the delivery by grabbing the baby and guiding it from the birth canal, she risks bending its back awkwardly against the natural curve of its spine. Pulling on a newborn at this angle risks injury to its spinal cord, nerves and muscles.
>
> —**Karen R. Rosenberg and Wenda R. Trevathan,** "The Evolution of Human Birth"

Rosenberg and Trevathan devote their entire essay to comparison and contrast, elucidating how evolution has deprived human females of the ability to give birth alone, while primates and most other mammals have managed to hold onto that ability.

American golfer from the 1930s.

Using comparison and contrast to evaluate choices Often the explaining we do or the understanding we establish through the use of comparison and contrast helps us evaluate choices, whether those choices are as seemingly straightforward as deciding which breakfast cereal to eat and which cell phone contract is best or as harrowing as deciding which set of cancer treatments to endure and which surgeon to trust. Sometimes, however, comparison and contrast is used to evaluate choices that are more subtle, choices that are neither mundane nor life-threatening. For instance, during World War II, anthropologist Margaret Mead was commissioned by the United States and Great Britain to figure out why the two English-speaking countries were unable to communicate smoothly. She used comparison and contrast to evaluate some of their language choices, for example, when naming their favorite color: "American servicemen quickly came up with a color, but the British asked, 'Favorite color for what? A flower? A necktie?'" So Mead set out to discover how the citizens of the two English-speaking nations evaluated their choice of "favorite color." According to Patrick Cooke, she concluded that

. . . Americans, raised in a melting pot, learned to seek a simple common denominator. To the British, this came across as unsophisticated. Conversely, the class-conscious British insisted on complex categories, each with its own set of values. . . . "The British show an unwillingness to make comparisons," Mead wrote. "Each object is thought of as having a most complex set of qualities, and color is merely a quality of an object."

The allies eventually overcame their differences and rallied to defeat Hitler, but for decades afterward you could see Mead's revelations reflected in the men's fashions of Britain and America. For Yanks what mattered was an overall "look." An American boy learned from his father, his schoolmates and ads for Hickey Freeman suits that the goal was to combine elements that complemented one another: *the tie goes with the jacket, the shoes go with the belt.* To the British, on the other hand, what mattered more than the whole was its parts. Where a post-war American male might have been neatly described as "the man in the gray flannel suit," an Englishman of the same era was "the man in the gray flannel suit—also wearing plaid socks, a striped shirt, paisley tie and checked jacket with a floral handkerchief in the pocket."

—**Patrick Cooke**, "Coalition of the Differing"

The Duke of Windsor, circa 1930.

When you look at the Duke of Windsor (former King Edward VIII of England) in his busily patterned golfing clothes, you can see they differ markedly from the outfits worn by American golfers at the same time.

Using comparison and contrast to argue a point We can often employ comparison and contrast to persuade others. Many languages that are used by small populations, and thus not for international communication or trade, are facing extinction. The threat looms especially large in the American West, where only 20 of the 110 native languages are still spoken by mothers to their children. The problem of how to save, maybe even rejuvenate, these threatened languages is one that language specialists have been pondering for decades. Robert Struckman argues for the superiority of immersion programs:

> Native language immersion schools are one of the best ways to breathe life into a dying language, according to Native language experts. In contrast, adult classes at tribal colleges, summer language camps, and bilingual programs in public schools rarely, if ever, produce fluent speakers. But few efforts are more difficult to start and run than an immersion school. "Every tribe wants an immersion school, but the hurdles are just tremendous," says Inee Yang Slaughter, of the Indigenous Languages Institute in New Mexico. "Most fail."
>
> —**Robert Struckman**, "Pass It On"

Preschool students in an Arapaho language immersion program.

Development Strategies

Despite the challenges of getting an immersion program up and running, ranging from obtaining financial support to finding fluent, certified teachers, immersion provides the only hope that the elderly speakers will be able to pass on their mother tongue, which is the core carrier of cultural tradition, to the youngest generation, the speakers of the future.

Using comparison and contrast to entertain Whenever we can, we use comparison and contrast to entertain. In fact, it's our creative use of analogy and metaphor that help us bring home our points, whether we're comparing campus-area rents to criminal extortion or cafeteria food to hog slop. David Sedaris uses comparison and contrast to lament the deterioration of his friendship with a fellow actor-in-training:

> Lois and I had been friends for six months when our relationship suddenly assumed a competitive edge. I'd never cared who made better grades or had more spending money. We each had our strengths; the important thing was to honor each other for the thing that person did best. Lois held her Chablis better than I, and I respected her for that. Her frightening excess of self-confidence allowed to her march into school wearing a rust-colored Afro wig, and I stood behind her one hundred percent. She owned more records than I did, and because she was nine months older,

also knew how to drive a car and did so as if she were rushing to put out a fire. *Fine,* I thought, *good for her.* My superior wisdom and innate generosity allowed me to be truly happy for Lois up until the day she questioned my ability to understand the visiting actor. The first few times he visited, she'd been just like the rest of them, laughing at his neck brace and rolling her eyes at the tangerine-sized lump in his tights. *I* was the one who first identified his brilliance, and now she was saying I couldn't understand him? Methinks not.   —**David Sedaris**, "The Drama Bug"

Sedaris compares himself to his friend Lois. The basis of comparison is their friendship; the points of comparison are their potential as actors and "the thing that person did best." Lois's strengths include being able to hold her wine, drive fearlessly fast, confidently wear wigs to school, and collect record albums. But Sedaris's strengths, fewer though they are, are impressive: "superior wisdom and innate generosity."

Using comparison and contrast as a fitting response

Once you've identified the exigence to which you'll respond, your next consideration is deciding which of the rhetorical methods of development will lead to the most fitting response. In making this decision, you'll need to consider your rhetorical audience—those who can be changed or can influence change—as well as the constraints and resources of the rhetorical situation you've identified.

Whether you're reading or writing, you can appreciate comparison and contrast as part of any fitting response that considers the attributes and shortcomings of or the connections and disconnections between two or more things. When the attacks of September 11, 2001 displaced the Oklahoma City bombing as the worst act of terrorism ever committed on American soil, those two actions offered an exigence that could best be explained with comparison and contrast. Since that day, analysts have continued to compare and contrast those two attacks in terms of who was involved, why the acts were committed, and what the consequences have been.

Michael Kimmel writes that gender issues, particularly threats to masculine identity, may be the underlying cause of the two attacks. And he goes on to compare and contrast the gender anxiety of white supremacists such as Timothy McVeigh with that of members of al Qaeda:

These white supremacists are mostly younger . . . lower-middle-class men, educated at least through high school and often beyond. They are the sons of skilled workers in industries like textiles and tobacco, the sons of the owners of small farms, shops, and grocery stores. Buffeted by global political and economic forces, the sons have inherited little of their fathers' legacies. The family farms have been lost to foreclosure, the small shops squeezed out by Wal-Marts and malls. These young men face a spiral of downward mobility and economic uncertainty. They complain that they are squeezed between the omnivorous jaws of global capital concentration and a federal bureaucracy that is at best indifferent to their plight and at worst complicit in their demise.

Development Strategies

   . . . For the most part, the terrorists of September 11 come from the same class, and recite the same complaints, as American white supremacists.

   Virtually all were under 25, educated, lower middle class or middle class, downwardly mobile. . . . Central to their political ideology is the recovery of manhood from the emasculating politics of globalization.

                                           —Michael Kimmel, "Gender, Class, and Terrorism"

Kimmel continues to compare the two subcultures in terms of threats to their economic status and notions of masculine privilege. He claims that the two attacks "resulted from an increasingly common combination of factors—the massive male displacement that accompanies globalization, the spread of American consumerism, and the perceived corruption of local [national] political elites—fused with a masculine sense of entitlement." Comparison and contrast helped him clarify the issues and, thereby, provide a fitting response to grave concern about such attacks.

Comparison and contrast can also frame a fitting response to the most mundane of situations, such as choosing the best dictionary. When YiLing Chen-Josephson set out to find the best dictionary, she soon discovered that comparison and contrast offered her the most appropriate way to respond to her exigence. In an online post, Chen-Josephson sets out the points of comparison to use in such a search:

> Before I tell you the results of my tests, there are some hard questions you should ask yourself about what it is that you want from a dictionary. For starters, what type of usage advice do you favor? Would you prefer your dictionary to be prescriptive (espousing and promoting the idea of a "correct" way to use language) or descriptive (reflecting in a neutral manner the way language actually gets used)? One of the primary differences among dictionaries is the extent to which they try to steer you away from disputed uses (*Oxford American*'s "Frequency of misuse has not changed the fact that the spelling sherbert and the pronunciation /sher´bert/ are wrong and should not be considered acceptable variants" is at one end of the spectrum, and the laissez-faire attitude of *Merriam-Webster's* "**sherbet**/sher´bet/ *also* **sherbert**/-bert/" is at the other.) Another question is: In what order do you want to find the various meanings of a word? Most dictionaries list the most commonly sought definition first, but *Merriam-Webster's* and *Webster's New World* give them in historical order. This means that if you're looking up, say "rehearse" in *Merriam-Webster's,* it won't be until Definition 4a that you'll find the familiar meaning "to practice for a performance." Finally: To what extent do you want your dictionary to serve as an encyclopedia? Some dictionaries offer everything from photos, maps, and relatively detailed biographical information to lists of presidents, populations, world currencies, and notable deserts. Depending on your tastes, these could be a strong selling point or mere bells and whistles. **—YiLing Chen-Josephson,** "Word Up"

Like description, narration, cause-and-consequence analysis, and process analysis, comparison and contrast can either provide the framework for an entire essay or serve as an integral passage in an essay shaped by another rhetorical method.

1. Take a few minutes to reread the excerpt from "Word Up," about searching for the best dictionary. What are the elements of the writer's rhetorical situation? How does the writer's search for the best dictionary align with or diverge from your choice of a dictionary? Does your dictionary meet your needs? Be prepared to share your response with the rest of the class.

2. Looking again at the same excerpt, account for the ways the writer uses comparison and contrast to make various points.

Using comparison and contrast as an available means

Whatever rhetorical method you choose, you'll also have to choose among the various means of delivery available to you. You may want to use a visual and enhance it with a verbal explanation. You may decide to deliver your comparison-and-contrast piece online or via a poster. Your choice of means of delivery is always dependent on the facilities to which you and your audience have access. Your choice also depends on the familiarity you and your audience have with various forms of technology (hypertext, tape recorder, video conferencing, or some other means). And, finally, your choice of means of delivery should always take into consideration the constraints and resources of your rhetorical situation.

If you're working for a health service organization on an Indian reservation or in an Amish community, you might be worried about the high incidence of diabetes in the community. If your goal is to teach people how to improve their eating habits and thus their health, you'll probably need to use comparison and contrast to make your point. You might use posters, recipe cards, before-and-after photographs, and diet plans to help fulfill your rhetorical purpose, to argue in favor of necessary dietary changes. You might decide that a diabetic who has used diet to improve her health would be an effective speaker. If you're working in a suburban setting, maybe in a physician's office, you are likely to have a broad choice of means of delivery. You may be able to direct some patients to Web sites, online chat rooms, or support groups—in addition to choosing from means of delivery such as posters, brochures, and recipe sheets. If you're a parent of a small child with diabetes, you can educate the child daily as you prepare meals, thereby controlling the child's diet.

There are clearly many ways available to deliver your message; the right one depends on your audience and the constraints and resources of each rhetorical situation. Therefore, you'll want to evaluate all the means to choose the right one for your purpose and your audience.

USING COMPARISON AND CONTRAST IN YOUR WRITING

1. With a classmate, draft a short comparison-and-contrast essay about your experiences growing up: where you each grew up, in what kind of home, your most vivid school-related experiences (school trips, for instance), your most memorable family vacations, and so on. Be sure to establish a basis for comparison and a set of points of comparison. If you can imagine using any kind of visual to help make your points, describe (or supply) it. Take into account the constraints of the rhetorical situation (your classroom, other classmates) as you prepare a response to share with the rest of the class.

2. Consider the writing you do in other courses or on the job. In what situations do you use comparison and contrast to explain, demonstrate, or justify? Be prepared to share your response with the rest of the class.

3. Bring to class an example of the use of comparison and contrast that you found in something you read for another course or for pleasure. Be prepared to explain to the class why the writer used this rhetorical method of development—and to what effect.

CHECKING OVER A COMPARISON AND CONTRAST

You can refer to the following checklist as you review your own draft, a comparison-and-contrast essay written by one of your peers, or a professional piece of writing.

✓ What is the specific exigence to which the writer is responding? Did the writer identify or create that exigence? Does that exigence specifically call for the use of comparison and contrast?

✓ What basis of comparison does the writer establish? Does it seem appropriate to you?

✓ What specific audience can resolve or influence the resolution of the exigence?

✓ What is the overall purpose for using comparison and contrast: to explain, evaluate a choice, argue a point, or entertain? Or some combination of these? How does the writer's purpose relate to the audience?

✓ What points of comparison does the writer set out? Are they all applied to both (or all) of the things being compared and contrasted? Why or why not? Are they all of interest to the rhetorical audience? How could the writer improve the number or selection of points of comparison?

✓ What means are used to deliver this piece of writing? How do those means accommodate the resources and constraints of the rhetorical situation?

✓ If a visual is included, how does it enhance or otherwise complement the use of comparison and contrast? How does it help the writer fulfill the rhetorical purpose? If a visual is not included, what kind of visual might enhance this piece?

14 RELATIONSHIP

Write for five minutes about the possible relationship between the two images shown here, using whatever information you can glean from them. Pay close attention to the details in the two photographs.

Relationship as an Available Means

As you compared the photographs on the chapter-opening page, you undoubtedly wondered why the second photograph differed so markedly from the first one. You might have asked yourself what the two photographs had in common: what is their relationship? You can see that the photographs feature the same pathway and large trees, which might lead you to think about what happened after the first and before the second photograph was taken. What is the *cause* of the devastation shown in the second photograph? What *process* caused that apparent devastation? What are the *effects* of what happened? How would the story of what happened be *narrated*? When an exigence prompts you to respond to questions such as these, you can make use of the common strategies for development known as cause-and-effect analysis, process analysis, and narration.

What Is Cause-and-Effect Analysis?

Whenever you find yourself concentrating on either causes or effects, explaining why certain events have occurred, or predicting that particular events or situations will lead to specific effects, you're conducting a **cause-and-effect analysis.** We spend a good deal of time trying to figure out why some things happen or trying to predict the consequences that might follow from a particular event or situation. For instance, if one of our bookshelves collapses, we check whether the shelf braces have been screwed into studs, the books are too heavy, or additional braces are needed as support. When we have a fender-bender on the way to work or school, we try to figure out the reasons that led to the accident: low visibility, snowy or icy roads, poorly marked roads, brake failure, missing taillights on the car in front, speeding, inattention (eating or putting a CD back into its case), or some combination of causes. If we're gaining weight, we try to figure out if the reason is a lifestyle that's too sedentary, overeating, or a medical problem. Once the United States invaded Iraq, ordinary citizens wondered if Iraq and al Qaeda were working together, if Iraq was stockpiling biological and chemical weapons, or if the Iraqi people welcomed the invading forces. Whether a situation or event is personal or political, important or relatively inconsequential, we often spend a good deal of time and energy trying to trace out the causes that have contributed to it.

We spend just as much time—maybe more—evaluating the effects of situations and events. You're enrolled in college and thus already considering the effects of having a college degree, most of them positive (you'll have to work hard, but you'll be well employed when you're finished). If you're thinking about getting married, you're analyzing the effects of that choice (you'll have to move to Boston to work in the family business, but you'll be with the love of your life). If you're following current events, you know that the effects of the war in Iraq include the deaths of nearly 4,000 Americans and 80,000 Iraqis and a good deal of public discontent.

Your school, work, and personal life offer endless opportunities to conduct cause-and-effect analysis, some of it superficial to the point of being practically mindless (what are the effects of overfilling my coffee mug?) and some in-depth and critical (why did my sister develop leukemia; what are the effects of her medical treatment?). Cause-and-effect analysis helps us make sense of the world around us and plan accordingly.

Look again at the two photographs that open this chapter. The first photograph shows a beautiful old church surrounded by big trees. It's the Trinity Episcopal Church in Pass Christian, Mississippi, which was built in 1849. Set among live oaks and lush lawns, Trinity served as a landmark for over a century. In the second photo, some—but not all—of the big trees are still standing, but there's no church, just the stairs and pathway leading up to the church. This photograph of the church site was taken on August 18, 1969, the day after Hurricane Camille smashed into the Mississippi Gulf Coast, with wind speeds in excess of two hundred miles per hour and water levels twenty-four feet above normal high tide, making it the strongest storm in U.S. history. By the time Camille dissipated on August 22, it had run a course along the Gulf Coast and then moved inland, toward the northeast into the Appalachians of southern Virginia. At final count, the death toll from Camille was 143 along the Gulf Coast and 113 inland. Another effect was $1.4 billion in damages (which is equivalent to $6.9 billion in 2000).

It's likely that no one in your class recognized one of the most famous photos from Hurricane Camille. Nevertheless, the cause-and-effect analyses that you and your classmates produced might accurately reflect the situation in Mis-

Development Strategies

Path of Hurricane Camille in August 1969.

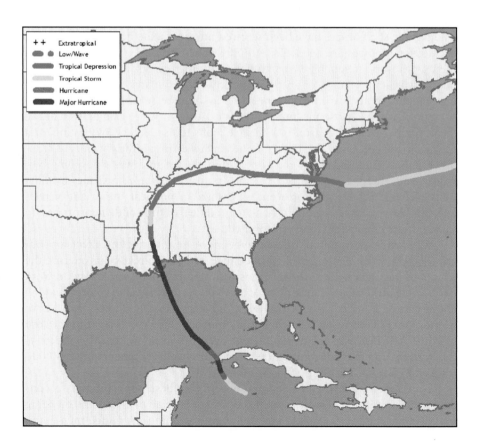

sissippi in August 1969 or perhaps be informed by your knowledge of the destruction caused by the more recent Hurricane Katrina. On the other hand, some of your analyses might be completely off the wall. What's important is to develop your ability to look for causes and effects and tease out an analysis. Doing so will help you better understand the world.

The Elements of Cause-and-Effect Analysis

As you well know, several causes may contribute to an event or situation, and several effects may result from an event or situation; however, those causes and those consequences don't necessarily carry equal importance. To conduct a thorough analysis of the causes or the effects for any situation or event, you'll need to distinguish among them.

Primary cause and contributory causes

The most important cause is the **primary cause.** Causes that advance a situation or event but do not directly cause it are referred to as **contributory causes.**

Let's say you've just discovered that you've gained ten pounds since school began a few months ago. It's true that you're not eating the same as you did at home, in neither content nor amount. After all, at home your parents prepared balanced meals and filled the pantry with healthful snacks; at school, you're getting most of your meals at the cafeteria's buffet line, and you're spending your weekend nights out on the town—eating and drinking—with your friends. It's also true that you're not exercising as much as you did at home, especially when you were playing high school sports. In addition, you're not sleeping well, which experts have identified as yet another contributing factor to weight gain. On the nights you're not staying up (too) late studying and snacking, you're lying awake hoping that the guy down the hall will turn down that music. Coming to college has brought many changes, not only in terms of your studies but also in terms of your daily life. You're feeling stressed as you cope with being away from your family, your friends, your routine, and your own kitchen.

The primary cause of your weight gain is stress, the stress of being in a new environment. And moving from the familiar (home) to the unfamiliar (college) can trigger all sorts of stress-related behaviors, overeating (especially of high-calorie comfort foods) being just one of those behaviors. But there are contributory causes as well—the changes in your social life and daily habits. You're snacking late into the night with your roommate, skipping breakfast and grabbing vending-machine snacks, and spending so much time studying (and socializing) that you've ditched your former exercise routine.

Immediate cause and remote causes

The **immediate cause** directly produces the event or situation, whereas the **remote causes** are not as close in time to the event or situation.

In the weight gain example, the immediate cause of your weight gain is that you're taking in more calories than you're burning. The remote causes include your late-night snacking, your weekend partying, and your lack of exercise. Lack of sleep is yet another remote cause of your weight gain.

Primary effect and secondary effects

The most important effect of an event or situation is the **primary effect.** Other effects that follow an event or situation but are not as important as the primary effect are called **secondary effects.**

The primary cause of your weight gain is the stress of being in a new environment, but what might the effects of that weight gain be? The primary effect is your loss of energy. The secondary effects, although not as important as the primary effect, do have their own negative consequences in this case. Your clothes don't fit any more, so you don't feel good about the way you look when you go out. Your weight gain has also affected your ability to concentrate on your studies and work efficiently to meet various deadlines. And the constellation of these effects seems to have derailed the sense of purpose that brought you to college in the first place. That primary effect, then, could lead eventually to your taking a temporary (even a permanent) break from college. Although few freshmen enter college anticipating such an effect from weight gain, many freshmen, in fact, don't return for sophomore year.

Immediate effect and remote effects

Although the **immediate effect** always appears first, the **remote effects,** which appear later, might be just as or more important than the immediate one.

In the weight gain example, if you're stressed out by your new environment (and most people have to work to find ways to cope with and settle into a new environment), the immediate effect might be that you overeat. Remote effects might include losing sleep, getting sick, missing classes, and losing your sense of academic direction. You might become so behind in your academic obligations that you receive poor grades and are placed on academic probation. The most remote effect of all might be that you drop out of school at the end of your first year.

Causal chain

A timeline that shows how one cause or effect precedes another and, therefore, perhaps leads to it and that identifies the various causes and effects in a hierarchy of significance is called a **causal chain.** To create a causal chain, you first need to analyze carefully whether each situation or event might be a cause or an effect. Then you'll need to analyze its relationship with the event or situation that precedes or follows it. But you'll need to keep in mind that chronological position does not equate with cause or effect. As you consider the causal chain shown here, you can see that events happened in a particular order and some led to others. But no one would think that there's a direct, uncomplicated link from starting college to dropping out.

Move to college ⟶

   New living quarters and social events ⟶

     New friends and courses ⟶

      STRESS ⟶

     More/less studying and less exercise ⟶

      More/less socializing ⟶

     Change in eating habits ⟶

     Change in sleeping habits ⟶

    Some depression ⟶

   Confusion ⟶

    Dropping out

Cause-and-Effect Analysis and the Rhetorical Situation

Cause-and-effect analyses provide informative insights into how things work and why things happen. Such analyses help us understand reasons for causes and help us predict effects or formulate results. Whether we're trying to understand the causes and effects of Hurricane Camille, weight gain by first-year college students, Ray Charles's death, a high school dance class, gun-related murders in the United States, or data loss on computers, we're engaging in a cause-and-effect analysis.

Whenever we experience a situation or event and wonder how it happened or what might come of it, we're posing the questions that launch a cause-and-effect analysis. How did Hurricane Camille develop? What ecological and material damages were caused by the hurricane? What are the possible effects of gaining fifteen pounds in one year? How will Ray Charles's death affect the music world?

Cause-and-effect analyses, just like the other rhetorical methods of development, can best be explained within the framework of the rhetorical situation. When writing or reading such an analysis, you'll want to pay special attention to all of the elements of the rhetorical situation—how you're addressing them or how the other writer did. You'll learn a great deal by simply being conscious of what you're doing and how others do it.

Using cause-and-effect analysis to address an exigence

When you embark on a cause-and-effect analysis, you're often doing so because you're experiencing an event or situation that is troublesome to you. Of course, you don't always write in response to something troubling—you might speak, draw, work, or throw a glance. If your car won't start in the morning, you immediately speculate about the effects of having no car. You also want to know why it won't start. You'll use causal analysis to get to the bottom of that problem—perhaps by calling a mechanic and describing the situation.

Or perhaps you and your friends were among those who watched college football's national championship in 2007. Some of you were shocked at previously undefeated Ohio State's loss; others were thrilled by Florida's win. Perhaps you stayed up half the night analyzing the causes of the outcome. Various morning papers, as well as weekly news and sports magazines, offered analyses of the result. The exigence of the Gators' win over the Buckeyes was not a problem to be solved so much as a question to be answered. Franz Beard, a sportswriter for GatorCounty.com, saw defense as the primary cause of Florida's big win. Beard describes a tackle of Ohio State tailback Antonio Pittman:

> When Pittman hit the ground, the air you heard escaping from his lungs was matched by the gasp emitted by some 55,000 Buckeye fans, groaning in unison. They were dead in the water and they knew it. The Buckeye myth was exposed and [the] Florida defensive line was the reason.
>
> —**Franz Beard,** "Myth Dispelled: It Started in the Trenches"

Beard's conclusion may not be agreeable to everyone, especially Buckeye fans, who would not call their team's superiority a "myth." But he addresses the exigence with a causal analysis: a great defense is what held Ohio State to 14 points, versus Florida's 41.

Using cause-and-effect analysis to address an audience

Every weekend, Click and Clack the Tappet Brothers (Tom and Ray Magliozzi) appear on *Car Talk,* a radio program syndicated by National Public Radio. The program has a call-in format: car owners phone in to describe events or situations having to do with cars. These callers want to know the causes of the situation or the effects—and because the brothers are first-rate car mechanics, they are the perfect audience for such an inquiry. In addition to calls, they also accept email queries. In the following transcript, a writer wants to know what has caused the stink in his car:

> I have a problem. I recently bought a 1992 Subaru Loyale. I hope it will be the best $400 car I ever bought, but there is one small problem. The heat stinks! I started taking out the dash in the car, searching for the mouse and squirrel keg party gone wrong. After getting the dash about halfway out, the pile of screws and panels was higher than the dash itself. I got scared and put it back together. What do I do?
>
> —Gabe

> TOM: There are several possibilities, Gabe. The one you should pray for is a plugged-up evaporator drain. When the air conditioner removes moisture from the passenger compartment, that moisture is supposed to drip out under the car through the evaporator drain.

RAY: That drain can easily get plugged up with debris. So, start by asking someone to blow out the evaporator drain with compressed air and treat the ducts with some mold-killing spray, and hope that solves your problem.

TOM: When it doesn't, you're going to be forced to conclude that what's causing your smell is a decomposing mouse.

RAY: I'll even tell you where it is. It's in the box that surrounds the heater core. So you were right to start taking apart the dashboard to get to it.

TOM: But, having looked at the repair manual for the '92 Loyale, you were right to stop, too. I don't blame you for leaving that as a last resort.

RAY: What's your first resort? Although it can take months, the mouse will eventually decompose completely. You can hasten the process, and make it more bearable, by emptying a can of Lysol in there. To do it, turn on the engine, put the heat and fan on high, open all of the windows and spray the deodorizer into the fresh-air intake at the cowl, outside the car where the hood meets the windshield. Then let it work its way through the vents for a while. It should help.

TOM: You'll probably need to do it several more times during the next few months.

RAY: But just as important, you need to prevent future mice from following in this little rodent's tragic footsteps and seeking warmth in your heating ducts. You need to either park in a garage, use a secure car cover or put some sort of screening inside the cowl to prevent mice from climbing into your heating system.   —**Tom and Ray Magliozzi,** *Car Talk*

Not only do Tom and Ray offer two possible causes for the stink (a plugged-up drain or a dead rodent), they also provide directions for resolving each of the problems now and for preventing them in the future.

Using cause-and-effect analysis with a rhetorical purpose

It's easy to think that cause-and-effect analysis always provides information or explanation, but that is not the case. In addition, cause-and-effect analysis can entertain, speculate, or argue a point. As soon as you determine your intended audience, you can gauge which of these purposes will best help you reach and influence that audience.

Using cause-and-effect analysis to explain Explanatory cause-and-effect analyses often include information. Sometimes, the analysis provides specific instructions for producing effects or eliminating causes; other times, it's merely informational. If you were to read a causal analysis of hurricanes, for instance, you'd know what weather conditions lead to their formation, but you wouldn't be able to duplicate the process. When you read Franz Beard's analysis of why the Gators won the college football championship, you understand the causes, but you probably cannot duplicate the outcome.

When a writer elucidates causes or effects, readers readily understand why things happen or what might follow. Not all writers rank causes and effects as primary and contributory or immediate and remote, but when they do, readers can understand which ones are more important than others. In the following excerpt from Jason Silverman's review of *Super Size Me,* documentary film-maker Morgan Spurlock discusses (but doesn't rank) the effects of his month-long Big Mac binge:

> "There are three things that happen to me in the film that we heavily medicate for in this country," Spurlock said. "I was incredibly depressed—and how many people are on Prozac? I started to get impotence, which we prescribe massive amounts of Viagra for. I was having periods of not being able to focus or think or remember things—the symptoms of ADHD—which one out of every four or five kids are medicated for in America today."
>
> —**Jason Silverman**, "Billions Unnerved: Super Size Diet Crisis"

The informative documentary discusses the causes of junk-food culture as well as the effects, none of which are positive.

Using cause-and-effect analysis to entertain Entertainment brings enjoyment, to be sure. Our enjoyment in a cause-and-effect analysis might come from a satisfying understanding of the causes contributing to an event or the effects arising from that event. We derive this kind of satisfaction from nonfiction of all kinds, from histories and biographies to natural histories and travelogues. Such satisfaction can be found in reading Melissa Nelson's essay about the challenges of integrating her *métis,* or mixed-blood ancestry. Nelson analyzes the effects of the pressure on her parents to "become American":

> Not having grown up on the land my indigenous ancestors called home and being the most recent offspring from a long line of "half-breeds" on my mother's side, I was not raised within my Anishinabe tradition. My mother remembered some of her Anishinabemowin, her native tongue, but even that was mixed with Cree and Canadian French. When she was sent away to Catholic boarding school she was forbidden to speak this strange "Michef" [or métis] language. My father remembered some Norwegian, but his parents were swayed by the dominant culture to "become American—drop that past nonsense." For my mom this "choice" was reinforced by the implementation of federal relocation and assimilation policies. After she returned to her reservation and completed high school, she was selected to be a part of the relocation program that sent reservation Indians into major urban centers around the country. My mother was given a one-way train ticket to California and ended up in downtown Oakland, close to where I was later born.
>
> —**Melissa Nelson**, "Becoming Métis"

Nelson's intended audience, readers interested in culture and identity, will be informed by her essay while being entertained by her skill in relating a family history.

Using cause-and-effect analysis to speculate In his provocative study of bio-technology, bioethicist Francis Fukuyama writes about the possible effects of scientific advances on human life. Of course, he cannot chart those effects with certainty. He speculates reasonably and believably, however, asking his readers to consider several scenarios, which are distinct possibilities for the future:

> The first has to do with new drugs. As a result of advances in neuropharmacology, psychologists discover that human personality is much more plastic than formerly

believed. It is already the case that psychotropic drugs such as Prozac and Ritalin can affect traits like self-esteem and the ability to concentrate, but they tend to produce a host of unwanted side effects and hence are shunned except in cases of clear therapeutic need. But in the future, knowledge of genomics permits pharmaceutical companies to tailor drugs very specifically to the genetic profiles of individual patients and greatly minimize unintended side effects. Stolid people can become vivacious; introspective ones extroverted; you can adopt one personality on Wednesday and another for the weekend. There is no longer any excuse for anyone to be depressed or unhappy; even "normally" happy people can make themselves happier without worries of addiction, hangovers, or long-term brain damage.

—Francis Fukuyama, Our Posthuman Future

Fukuyama's exigence is biotechnological advances; his audience is people who are interested in the possible effects of biotechnology; and his purpose is to speculate responsibly about these effects. His book, *Our Posthuman Future,* seems to be a fitting response to the rhetorical situation.

Using cause-and-effect analysis to argue a point In the final paragraphs of his book-length study, Fukuyama argues for only the most thoughtful biotechnological advances and regulations; otherwise, he argues, we'll lose major parts of what makes us human and end up living in a "posthuman world":

> Many assume that the posthuman world will look pretty much like our own—free, equal, prosperous, caring, compassionate—only with better health care, longer lives, and perhaps more intelligence than today.
>
> But the posthuman world could be one that is far more hierarchical and competitive than the one that currently exists, and full of social conflict as a result. It could be one in which any notion of "shared humanity" is lost, because we have mixed human genes with those of so many other species that we no longer have a clear idea of what a human being is. It could be one in which the median person is living well into his or her second century, sitting in a nursing home hoping for an unattainable death. Or it could be the kind of soft tyranny envisioned in *Brave New World*, in which everyone is healthy and happy but has forgotten the meaning of hope, fear, or struggle.
>
> We do not have to accept any of these future worlds under a false banner of liberty, be it that of unlimited reproductive rights or of unfettered scientific inquiry. We do not have to regard ourselves as slaves to inevitable technological progress when that progress does not serve human ends. True freedom means the freedom of political communities to protect the values they hold most dear, and it is that freedom that we need to exercise with regard to the biotechnology revolution today.

—Francis Fukuyama, Our Posthuman Future

In his conclusion, Fukuyama forcefully argues a point, offering several speculations, any or all of which could come to fruition.

Using cause-and-effect analysis as a fitting response

When we respond to an exigence, whether it's a wedding celebration or a death in the family, we wonder if our response is fitting. That's why we often revise and rehearse the wedding toast we're planning to make or spend so much thought and effort on writing a sympathy note. That's also why so many people are reluctant to make a public toast and send preprinted sentiments rather than composing their own—it's often not laziness but rather concern about their ability to offer a fitting response.

Just like all the other methods of rhetorical development, cause-and-effect analysis can shape a fitting response. It's often the best form for a response that addresses the problem, reaches the intended audience through an appropriate medium, and successfully satisfies that audience. For example, when Republican party fundraiser Georgette Mosbacher was asked in an interview published in *Harper's Bazaar* about how she became "privy to the epicenter of power" in Washington, DC, she replied fittingly, as only a confident, well-established businesswoman might do. She set her interviewer (and that interviewer's reading audience) at ease by saying, "Every time I went to the White House, I thought, *How did a girl from Highland, Indiana, who ironed shirts to get through college, end up here?* The truth was, I got lucky and fell in love with a man who took me there." Had Mosbacher been interviewed by a writer for *Newsweek,* she might have answered differently. But maybe not. Her answer seems to be honest and engaging. Rather than claiming unparalleled beauty or intellect, she credits her powerful husband, former Secretary of Commerce Robert Mosbacher, Sr., for her White House invitations.

Former NFL player Terry Bradshaw composed a fitting response to the exigence of men's depression. With one in fourteen American men suffering but avoiding treatment for depression, perhaps a very masculine role model like a professional football player is the best person to reach those who need help. In a Sunday feature magazine, Bradshaw speaks frankly to interviewers and to readers interested in this condition:

> "I'd bawl all day long," says Terry Bradshaw, 55, the Hall of Fame quarterback who snagged four Super Bowl wins and later won two Emmys for sports broadcasting. "I started having breakdowns in my 20s. I kept trying to make myself happy by winning more games, accumulating more stuff, going through one wife, two wives, three wives. The only thing I could do was work, and I worked myself to death so I could escape."   **—Dianne Hales and Dr. Robert E. Hales,** "Too Tough to Seek Help?"

Readers, especially those who see themselves as "too tough to seek help," might be moved by Bradshaw's testimonial. His is a fitting response, one that reaches the intended audience in an appropriate way and through an easily accessible available means, the Sunday paper.

READING A TEXT FOR CAUSE-AND-EFFECT ANALYSIS

1. Read through the passages by Francis Fukuyama presented in this section. What are the causes of the biotechnological advances he's concerned about? He speculates on the possible effects of these advances; can you speculate on the possible causes for them? What might be the primary and contributory causes? Be prepared to share your analysis with the rest of the class.

2. What exigence might Georgette Mosbacher's interviewer have wanted to resolve? What audience holds the power to resolve or effect the resolution of that exigence?

3. If Terry Bradshaw investigated the causes of his depression, what do you think they might be? Be prepared to share your response with the rest of the class.

Using cause-and-effect analysis as an available means

By now, you have come to understand the wide range of available means at your disposal: Web pages or blogs, word-processed documents, handwritten letters, posters, slide presentations, and so forth. Your choice of available means will affect the form of your fitting response, for these two features of the rhetorical situation are closely interrelated.

If you were a survivor of the shootings at Columbine high school in 1999, you might have set up a Web site to explain either the causes or the effects of that tragedy. If you were one of the parents of the students, you might have gone on a speaking tour to protest the easy availability of guns and live ammunition. If you were a specialist in secondary education or adolescent psychology, you might have researched and written a book on bullying. But if you were documentary filmmaker Michael Moore, you would have raised money for the production of *Bowling for Columbine*. Responding to the same exigence, each of these rhetors would have to choose a different physical means by which to deliver the message. In doing so, each of the rhetors would adapt the message to

Michael Moore in *Bowling for Columbine*.

the means of delivery, to the particular audiences, and to the contextual constraints and resources of the rhetorical situation.

Moore took advantage of the funding he obtained to travel all over the United States to conduct research and interview a wide variety of people. That funding also permitted him to hire the staff necessary to film, edit, and distribute a documentary, to support all of those involved in the filmmaking and distribution, and to provide the infrastructure for his business (from Web page to business accounting). In addition, Moore already had an established reputation as a successful, controversial filmmaker, as attested by his many awards and prizes. The means available to him were and are, no doubt, markedly different from the means available to you as you put together your cause-and-effect analysis.

It's important that you determine the resources and constraints of the rhetorical situation you've decided to enter and then consciously take advantage of every resource you can. Doing so takes practice and experience, but seeing how other writers have succeeded can also help you. Consider, for example, the following excerpt, which created a good deal of controversy when it first appeared:

> I have been tested for HIV three times. I've gone to clinics and stuck my arm out for those disposable needles, each time forgetting the fear and nausea that descend upon me before the results come back, those minutes spent in a publicly financed waiting room staring at a video loop about "living with" this thing that kills you. These tests have taken place over five years, and the results have always been negative—not surprisingly in retrospect, since I am not a member of a "high-risk group," don't sleep around and don't take pity on heroin-addicted bass players by going to bed with them in the hopes of being thanked in the liner notes of their first major independent release. Still, getting tested always seemed like the thing to do. Despite my demographic profile, despite the fact that I grew up middle class, attended an elite college and do not personally know any women or straight men within that demographic profile who have the AIDS virus, I am terrified of this disease. I went to a college where condoms and dental dams lay in baskets in dormitory lobbies, where it seemed incumbent on health service counselors to give us the straight talk, to tell us never, ever to have sex without condoms unless we wanted to die; that's right, *die*, shrivel overnight, vomit up our futures, pose a threat to others. (And they'd seen it happen, oh, yes, they had.) They gave us pamphlets, didn't quite explain how to use dental dams, told us where we could get tested, threw us more fistfuls of condoms (even some glow-in-the-dark brands, just for variety). This can actually be fun, they said, if only we'd adopt a better attitude.
>
> We're told we can get this disease and we believe it and vow to protect ourselves, and intend (really, truly) to stick by this rule, until we don't because we just can't because it's just not fair, because our sense of entitlement exceeds our sense of vulnerability. So we blow off precaution again and again, and then we get scared and get tested, and when it comes out OK, we run out of the clinic, pamphlets in hand, eyes cast upward, promising ourselves we'll never be stupid again. But of course we are stupid, again and again. And the testing is always for the same reasons and with the same results, and soon it becomes more like fibbing about SAT scores ten years after the fact than lying about whether we practice unsafe sex, a lie that sounds like such a breach of contract with ourselves that we might as well be talking about putting a loaded gun under our pillow every night. —**Meghan Daum**, "Safe-Sex Lies"

An already established writer, Daum's essays have appeared in many publications with national circulation, so she has many resources available to her: she can expect a wide readership. The constraints of her situation include the fact that she is best known for her writing, not for public speaking, production of visuals, or blogging, so she must once again reach an audience through writing. She takes advantage of the rhetorical appeals, establishing her ethos of a middle-class woman who attended an elite college and regularly gets tested for HIV. But after she establishes her ethos, she analyzes the causes for unsafe sex within such a well-educated, thoughtful, drug-free group.

When you choose to use cause-and-effect analysis to develop an entire essay or part of an essay, you'll want to also consider your rhetorical purpose: whether you want to inform, entertain, speculate, or argue a point. As you consider your intended audience in relation to your purpose, you'll begin to narrow down the means of delivery available to you. Finally, you'll choose the available means that allows you to best shape a fitting response.

USING CAUSE-AND-EFFECT ANALYSIS IN YOUR WRITING

1. In what course assignments (chemistry, biology, engineering, math, and so on) are you asked to include an analysis of causes or effects? Be prepared to share your response with the rest of the class.

2. Bring to class an example of an analysis of causes or effects, perhaps one you've created as part of an assignment in another course or come across in your reading. As you choose your example, think about how the analysis is used as support or explanation.

CHECKING OVER A CAUSE-AND-EFFECT ANALYSIS

Answering the following questions will help you review your own cause-and-effect analyses as well as those of your classmates.

✓ What exigence needs to be resolved?
✓ What specific audience can resolve or influence the resolution of that exigence? What expectations might they be bringing to this situation?
✓ What is the purpose of this cause-and-effect analysis: to inform, entertain, speculate, or argue a point? Does the analysis focus on causes or effects, or does it consider both?
✓ How exactly does the purpose relate to the intended audience?
✓ What is the relationship of each of the causes or effects to the exigence?
✓ Can you identify which of the causes and effects are primary or contributory (secondary) and which are immediate or remote?
✓ How is the cause-and-effect analysis arranged, in chronological or emphatic order? (Emphatic order is order of importance.)

A process analysis at www.scunci.com tells readers how to recreate the hairstyle worn by Nicole Kidman at the 75th Annual Academy Awards.

What Is Process Analysis?

Any time you think about or try to explain how something is done, you are engaging in **process analysis.** As a development strategy, process analysis involves dividing up an entire process into a series of ordered steps so that the audience will be able to see the relationship among those steps and understand or replicate the process. A process analysis always includes a series of separate, chronological steps that provide details about a process. Such an analysis often reads like a narrative, whether it's an explanation of how volcanoes erupt, how a diamond is formed, or how leukemia is treated. Many process analyses, however, take the form of a list, with distinct and often numbered steps, as in recipes, instruction manuals (for using small appliances), and installation guides (for shower heads, computer software, and garage door openers).

Television programs and DVDs present processes we can duplicate: we can learn how to dress to enhance our body shape by watching *What Not to Wear* or how to prepare a certain dish by watching Alton Brown's show on the Food Network; we can view DVDs such as *How to Be a Ballet Dancer* and *How to Play Rippin' Lead Guitar,* although these presentations probably wouldn't provide enough training for us to duplicate the processes they describe. Whether the processes are conveyed visually or verbally, whether we're reading cookbooks, car-repair manuals, or how-to instructions for installing software, we're using process analysis.

Process analyses come in two basic forms: **directive process analysis** is used to teach the reader how to do something, how to duplicate a process; **informative process analysis** is used to explain a process, so the reader can understand it or be persuaded by it. An example of a directive process analysis can be found on the Web site of the hair products manufacturer scünci. Featured under "celebrity style" are steps for recreating the hairstyle of several celebrities, including one worn by Nicole Kidman at the Academy Awards:

1. Create a 2 inch × 2 inch square section in the front part of your hair and secure it with a bobby pin or mini jaw clip.
2. Brush the rest of your hair back smoothly (be careful not to include the sectioned hair) and hold it with your hand at the center of the back of your head.
3. Roll your hair upward and tightly to your head, then tuck the ends under for a classic French twist look and secure with bobby pins.
4. Remove the pin (or clip) from the front section and brush that section of hair back smoothly.

5. Wrap the end of the hair around the top of the French twist and secure it with a bobby pin.

NOTE: You may use hairpins to secure this classic style, or you can accessorize your French twist using the new Sophisticomb®. **—www.scunci.com**

This kind of directive process analysis might have you or one of your female friends sporting a celebrity's hairstyle in just a couple of minutes. For most of us, however, the process is informative, an entertainment of sorts.

The following passage, taken from a popular suspense novel, includes an informative process analysis on how to use fingerprints for identifying perpetrators or victims:

> Detective Matt Chacon knew that unlike the TV cop shows—where actors sit in front of a computer monitor and instantaneously pull up a digital fingerprint record that matches a perp or a victim—trying to ID someone using prints in the real world can be mind-numbing work. There are thousands of prints that have never been entered into the computer data banks, and thousands more on file that, because of poor quality, are virtually unusable for comparison purposes. On top of that, figure in the small cop shops who haven't got the money, manpower, and equipment to transfer print records to computers, and the unknown number of print cards that were left in closed felony cases and sit forgotten in basement archives at police departments all over the country, and you've got a data-bank system that is woefully inadequate and incomplete. Finally, while each fingerprint is unique, the difference between prints can be so slight that a very careful analysis must be made to confirm a perfect match. Even then, different experts can debate the results endlessly, since it isn't an exact science.
>
> Chacon had started his career in law enforcement as a crime scene technician with a speciality in fingerprint and tool-mark identification, so of course Lieutenant Molina had sent him off to the state police headquarters to work the state and federal data banks to see if he could get a match.
>
> He'd been at it all night long and his coffee was starting to taste like sludge, his eyes were itchy, and his butt was numb. Using an automated identification system, Chacon had digitally stored the victim's prints in the computer and then started scanning for a match against those already on file.
>
> The computer system could identify possible matches quickly, but then it became a process of carefully analyzing each one and scoring them according to a detailed classification system. So far, Chacon had examined six dozen sets of prints that looked like possible equivalents and had struck out. But there was another baker's dozen to review.
>
> He clicked on the next record, adjusted the monitor to enhance the resolution of the smudged prints, and began scoring them in sequence. Whoever had printed the subject had done a piss-poor job. He glanced at the agency identifier. It was a Department of Corrections submission.
>
> Chacon finished the sequence and used a split screen to compare his scoring to the victim's print. It showed a match. He rechecked the scoring and verified his findings.
>
> For the first time, he looked at the subject's name. The victim was Victoria Drake, a probation and parole officer with the Department of Corrections, assigned to a regional office in the southern part of the state.

He printed out a hard copy. Moved his chair to another monitor, accessed the motor vehicle computer system, typed in the woman's personal information from the record, and a driver's license photograph of Drake appeared on the screen. The dead woman in the van was most definitely Victoria Drake, although she'd looked much better in life than in death.   —**Michael McGarrity**, *Everyone Dies*

This process analysis informs and entertains at the same time as it argues a point—that fingerprint matching is a complicated and often time-consuming procedure, not the quick fix often depicted on television. Process analysis provides the overall structure of the passage, but the passage also uses several other rhetorical strategies for development.

This passenger safety card for a Boeing 737 shows important procedures for takeoffs, landings, and emergencies.

Process analyses, whether directive or informative, address an exigence ("How did Nicole Kidman fix her hair?" or "How will the good guys identify the victim?"), for a specific audience, with a rhetorical purpose (to inform or teach, to entertain, or to explain), all within the resources and constraints of the rhetorical situation. Note, too, that a process analysis can constitute an entire message or be just part of the full message (within a novel, proposal, or report, for example).

If you've ever taken an airplane trip, you're familiar with the passenger safety card found in the pocket of the seat in front of yours. As you follow along, the flight attendant goes over the step-by-step directions for various safety procedures during takeoffs, landings, and emergencies: how to buckle and unbuckle your seat belt, how to use an oxygen mask, where the life preserver is stored and how to inflate it, and so on. Many passengers can understand the language in which the flight attendant is giving these instructions, but, for those who cannot, the visuals on the card provide the necessary details for full understanding. Whether the information is taken in aurally or visually, it represents a directive process analysis, meant to teach passengers how to be safe.

The Elements of Process Analysis

Because process analysis is so common in everyday life, you may not have realized that it has distinctive elements: whether it's a directive or informative process analysis, it has a thesis statement, it's broken into steps (with details divided up accordingly), it's chronological, and it has a definite point of view. Try to identify these elements in etiquette expert Peggy Post's process analysis about how to quit a job:

> There are five things you should know about quitting your job.
> 1. Tell your immediate boss first. It's a professional courtesy, plus she may want to ask you to reconsider.
> 2. Establish a last day. Two weeks is usually about right—enough time to complete projects but not enough for lame-duck syndrome to set in.
> 3. Finish all your work so the transition will be easy for your successor. (Good karma for your new job!)
> 4. Don't burn bridges by sounding off about everything that's wrong with the company. You never know where your former employers will turn up next.
> 5. Avoid acting too happy to be "free"—after all, your colleagues still have to stick it out at the company.
>
> —**Peggy Post**, *Good Housekeeping*

Thesis statement

The thesis statement for any process analysis provides an overview of the process and usually alludes to the significance of that process. In other words, the thesis statement is a promise to the reader about the terms of the analysis, whether it's directive or informative, what its rhetorical purpose is, and what point of view the writer is taking on the subject under analysis. Peggy Post opens her process analysis with a thesis statement: "There are five things you should know about quitting your job." Her thesis statement prepares you for a directive process analysis, a series of five steps, and the point of view of an expert. She's not suggesting that you might want to consider her ideas. Post is telling you what you need to know. Period.

Series of steps

Often, process analysis involves a series of steps that are mutually exclusive, with each step including its own set of specific details ("professional courtesy," "lame-duck syndrome," and so on). Occasionally, however, some of the steps overlap (as steps 4 and 5 of Post's directive analysis do).

Chronological organization

Most of the time, process analyses are organized chronologically. Because of this arrangement, process analysis often reads like a narrative, a sequence of events that tell a story, most often the story of how something is done.

Point of view

Process analyses can be composed in the first person (*I* or *we*), second person (*you*), or third person (*he, she,* or *they*). When the process analysis is directive, it is most often told from the second-person point of view: "First you do this, and then you do that." Post's advice uses the second-person point of view. Even when she's not using the pronouns *you* and *your,* it's clear that she's writing to "you," the reader. Recipes, knitting directions, car-repair manuals, and the like are often written in the second person, with the second-person pronoun (*you*) rarely stated because it's understood.

Process Analysis and the Rhetorical Situation

We use and compose process analyses every day, whether we're studying a bus schedule so that we take the right bus to work, reading an IRS pamphlet so that we fill out our tax return correctly, or writing directions so that our friends can get to our house for a party. Process analyses are used for many reasons, but their basic rhetorical purposes are three: to inform or teach, to entertain, and/or to argue a point. These purposes may overlap in a single analysis. Every process analysis—whether directive or informative—aims to address each of the elements of the rhetorical situation at the same time that it fulfills a rhetorical purpose.

A process analysis, then, is responsive to an exigence that the rhetor has either created or identified. Once the rhetor determines exactly what the exigence is (and it must be resolvable in some way), the rhetor identifies a specific audience that has the capability to directly or indirectly resolve that exigence. After focusing on exigence and audience, the rhetor can determine a purpose for the process analysis. For instance, if my niece is reluctant to work in the summer in order to help pay for her college education, I might identify her resistance as an exigence that I could address by informing her how I put myself through college. But given the constraints and resources of the rhetorical situation (does any young person really care how hard an aunt, even a well-loved one, worked to put herself through college?), providing an informative process analysis of my success may not be the best way to resolve that exigence. A more fitting response might be to work out a proposed budget with her, based on how much money she needed during her first year of college, and then try to project the amount she might need for the second year. From those figures, we could develop a process by which she could come up with enough money to return to college, a process that includes applying for fellowships, grants, and loans, as well as working. Developing the process by means of a dialogue in which she's included would probably be more effective than giving her a step-by-step account of her aunt's past efforts and success. Keeping in mind all of the elements of the rhetorical situation—exigence, audience, purpose, fitting response, and available means—will help you better develop and deliver your process analysis as well as appreciate the analyses of others.

Using process analysis to address an exigence

Every process analysis is composed in response to an exigence: someone needs to know how to do something or wants to know how something is done. When Julia Alvarez discusses her process for writing, she does so in response to "one of the questions that always comes up during question-and-answer periods after readings . . . about the writing life."

The more sophisticated, practiced, questioners usually ask me, "Can you tell us something about your process as a writer?" Younger, less self-conscious questioners tend to be more straightforward, "What do you write with? Is it a special kind of pen? What time do you start? How many hours do you spend at the computer? Do you keep a journal?"   —**Julia Alvarez**, "Writing Matters"

Alvarez goes on to explain that the questioners are not so much curious about how she writes but rather eager to know how to write better:

[It] has to do with a sense we all have that if we can only get a hold of the secret ingredients of the writing process, we will become better writers. We will have an easier time of it if we only find that magic pencil or know at which hour to start and at which hour to quit and what to sip that might help us come up with the next word in a sentence.   —**Julia Alvarez**, "Writing Matters"

The key to responding to any exigence, then, is to identify what the exigence actually is and what the most fitting response might be.

Using process analysis to address an audience

Some of you will never pick up a cookbook; others couldn't care less how to get a better putting stroke. No matter how clearly the processes of cooking or golfing are described, they won't do you any good because you're not part of the

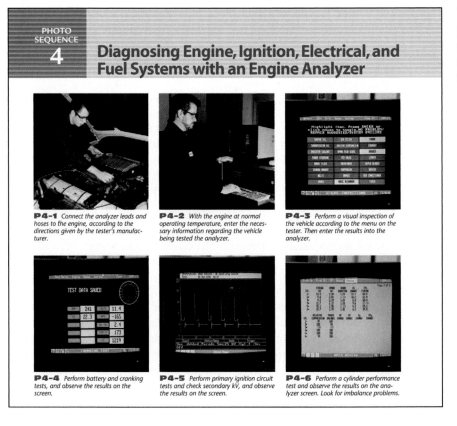

PHOTO SEQUENCE 4

Diagnosing Engine, Ignition, Electrical, and Fuel Systems with an Engine Analyzer

P4-1 *Connect the analyzer leads and hoses to the engine, according to the directions given by the tester's manufacturer.*

P4-2 *With the engine at normal operating temperature, enter the necessary information regarding the vehicle being tested the analyzer.*

P4-3 *Perform a visual inspection of the vehicle according to the menu on the tester. Then enter the results into the analyzer.*

P4-4 *Perform battery and cranking tests, and observe the results on the screen.*

P4-5 *Perform primary ignition circuit tests and check secondary kV, and observe the results on the screen.*

P4-6 *Perform a cylinder performance test and observe the results on the analyzer screen. Look for imbalance problems.*

This highly visual process analysis was created for a specific audience—automotive technology students.

Development Strategies

intended audience. People who repair their own cars constitute a specific audience that car-repair manual writers are addressing. If you're into car racing and feel that the only thing preventing your Honda from winning a race is lack of four-wheel disc brakes, then you've identified an exigence that can be addressed with a process analysis. The magazine *Honda Tuning* has a fitting response, a 42-step process analysis on how to upsize the front rotors, relocate the calipers, and then convert the rear stock drums to discs. With visuals accompanying each written step, the process analysis begins with step 1:

> . . . the car is raised, placed on jackstands, and the wheels are removed. Then Inline Four technician Phong Nguyen gets to the nitty gritty by tackling the forward passenger-side brakes first (the process is identical on the driver-side front brakes). He unbolts the caliper to start, fastened to the steering knuckle with twin 17 mm bolts.
>
> —**Editor Bob**, "Disc Doctorin"

This analysis ends with visual proof of the success of the installation, in which the new brakes are described as being able to "deliver some killer stopping power." If you're the intended audience for this process analysis, you're already familiar with the constraints and resources of this particular rhetorical situation: you'll know the vocabulary of car parts (for instance, *caliper, steering knuckle*) and installation equipment (*jackstands*), and you'll be aware that the process will require at least six hours.

When Julia Alvarez responded to the question of how she writes, she, too, aimed her response to a specific audience: those question posers who hoped for a directive process analysis:

> I always tell my questioners the truth: listen, there are no magic solutions to the hard work of writing. There is no place to put the writing desk that will draw more words out of you. . . .
>
> But even as I say so, I know I am talking out both sides of my mouth. . . . Even as recently as this very day, I walk into my study first thing in the morning, and I fill up my bowl of clear water and place it on my desk. And though no one told me to do this, I somehow feel this is the right way to start a writing day.
>
> Of course, that fresh bowl of water sits on my desk on good *and* bad writing days. I know these little ceremonies will not change the kind of day before me any more than a funeral service will bring back the dead or a meditation retreat will keep trouble out of my life. The function of ritual is not to control this baffling universe but to render homage to it, to bow to the mystery. Similarly, my daily writing rituals are small ways in which I contain my dread and affirm my joy and celebrate the mystery and excitement of the calling to be a writer.
>
> — Julia Alvarez, "Writing Matters"

Alvarez actually addresses two audiences: the people who ask questions of her after she's given a reading and the readers of her collection of essays. Both audiences need to know that she doesn't have a magic formula for bringing words to the page or screen, but she does have a ritual or two, which work to honor the magic of the creative process. Thus, Alvarez addresses her intended audience in an informative (and entertaining) passage on how she writes.

Using process analysis with a rhetorical purpose

You've now read a number of process analyses, and you're no doubt able to distinguish those that direct from those that inform, even when the categories blur a bit. You're also aware that various process analyses fill one of three rhetorical purposes: to inform, to entertain, or to argue a point. However, those categories sometimes blur as well. Once you've established the exigence you want to address and the audience you want to reach, you can decide which of the three purposes will best fulfill your rhetorical goal.

Using process analysis to inform In his best-selling *How to Read a Book*, Mortimer Adler informs his readers on how to get the most out of reading: by writing back to the words in the book. According to Adler, "there are all kinds of devices for marking a book intelligently and fruitfully," including *underlining* the major points, *drawing vertical lines* at the margin for emphasis, *starring* or *asterisking* the author's ten or twenty most important statements, *numbering* the sequence of steps in an argument, *placing page numbers* in the margin to indicate other places the author has made relevant points, *circling key words* or phrases, and *writing in the margins* to ask questions, make connections, or condense an argument. Adler also encourages taking chronological notes and writing outlines on blank pages in the fronts and backs of books. Adler provides a careful, step-by-step explanation of how, exactly, to mark up a book you're reading. He makes it all sound easy—as though anyone who took the time could read as successfully as he does.

Using process analysis to entertain To some degree, Adler's process analysis of how to read a book is entertaining, especially his variety of marks and the specific way he uses each one. Still, Adler wants his readers to be able to duplicate his process: his purpose is directive as well as informative. David Sedaris, on the other hand, doesn't want readers to duplicate the process of making hot chocolate he explains; he wants them to be entertained by his rendition of how a young boy makes hot chocolate at a hotel beverage stand:

> It was a complicated business, mixing a cup of hot chocolate. You had to spread the powdered cocoa from one end of the table to the other and use as many stirrers as possible, making sure to thoroughly chew the wetted ends before tossing them upon the stack of unused napkins. This is what I like about children: complete attention to one detail and complete disregard of another. When finally finished, he scooted over to the coffee urn, filling two cups, black, and fitting them with lids. The drinks were stacked into a tower, then tentatively lifted off the table. "Whoa," he whispered. Hot chocolate seeped from beneath the lid of the bottom cup and ran down his hand.   —**David Sedaris**, "Chicken in the Henhouse"

By inserting his own opinions ("This is what I like about children") along with vivid descriptive details of the boy's actions and the seeping cup of chocolate, Sedaris manages to tap other methods of rhetorical development at the same time as he builds his informative process analysis. He takes an everyday event, a young boy making hot chocolate, and transforms it into a funny little story, bringing readers a good measure of pleasure.

Using process analysis to argue a point You've probably already considered the possibilities of using process analysis to argue a point. After all, why would anyone want to tell anyone else how to do something unless there was a good reason for doing it that way, whether it's how to install disc brakes, quit a job, or pay homage to the magic of writing.

For example, before he lays out the steps for marking up a book and thereby reading it successfully, Mortimer Adler offers the reasons readers should follow his method. In other words, he uses process analysis to argue a point:

> You may ask, why is writing necessary? Well, the physical act of writing, with your own hand, brings words and sentences more sharply before your mind and preserves them better in your memory. To set down your reaction to important words and sentences you have read, and the questions they have raised in your mind, is to preserve those reactions and sharpen those questions. . . .
> . . . Reading a book should be . . . a conversation between you and the author. . . . And marking a book is literally an expression of your differences, or agreements of opinion, with the author.   **—Mortimer Adler,** *How to Read a Book*

Although his process analysis doesn't consist of a lock-step method, it includes a series of steps that should be approached in a general order: preparing yourself to mark a book, knowing where you might mark, and marking in order to hold a conversation with the author.

Weight-loss books, self-help guides, money-making plans, study guides—all of these process analyses argue a point (or two) about the benefits, advantages, or downsides to a given process. In fact, David Sedaris's entertaining process analysis of hot chocolate making also argues a point: children can give their complete attention to one detail while completely ignoring another.

Using process analysis as a fitting response

On June 5, 2002, Elizabeth Smart was abducted from her bedroom in the early hours of the morning. There was an intense regional and national search, but no one came up with any useful clues for locating her or her kidnapper until October, when Mary Katherine, her younger sister, who had witnessed the kidnapping, walked into her parents' bedroom and told them what she had finally remembered about the man who had taken Elizabeth. Mary Katherine, the only eyewitness to the incident, had never been interviewed by unskilled detectives or sketch artists; therefore, her traumatized memory of the suspect remained uninfluenced by suggestions or photos, floating intact to the surface nearly five months later. During those five months, however, she, her family, and the police were objects of a great deal of criticism; not working with a sketch artist was thought by some to be negligent or even blameworthy.

The kidnapping and eventual recovery, thanks to Mary Katherine's description and naming of the suspect, provided an exigence: how best to solve a crime. One fitting response to the exigence was an in-depth, informative article analyzing the ultimately successful process that brought Elizabeth home. Included in that fitting response is a directive process analysis, a step-by-step procedure for helping to solve a crime if you're a victim or an eyewitness:

1. DURING THE CRIME, if at all possible, observe characteristics that are least subject to change. A suspect can discard clothing and cut hair. Try to look closely at features such as the lips, eyes, nose, teeth, and gait.
2. WRITE DOWN A DESCRIPTION of the suspect before you're interviewed by police to help solidify your thoughts and make yourself less vulnerable to suggestion. This can help prevent memory distortion during the investigation.
3. INSIST ON OPEN-ENDED QUESTIONS from police interviewers. Don't allow the use of visual aids like photographs or software catalogs of facial components if you're questioned for a composite sketch.
4. CONSIDER TAPE-RECORDING YOUR INTERVIEWS with police personnel. You want to ensure that your thoughts are not inadvertently misconstrued, misparaphrased, or overly abbreviated. Compare the tape to the written police reports, which you have the right to obtain.

— "The Memory Artist," *O, The Oprah Magazine*

An article on the subject of eyewitnesses, their fragile memories of traumatic events, and how those memories can be preserved in order to solve crimes is obviously a fitting response to the exigence of Elizabeth Smart's kidnapping in that it respects the constraints (the pressure to interview the eyewitness, form a composite likeness of the suspect, and circulate the sketch no matter how accurate or inaccurate) and resources (that fragile memory, readers' interest) of the rhetorical situation. But rather than leaving the story at that—at a recounting of the events—the article includes a four-step list that directs interested readers in what to do and why. This fitting response is delivered in an appropriate medium—*O, The Oprah Magazine,* a popular national periodical read by millions.

READING A TEXT FOR PROCESS ANALYSIS

1. Read the excerpt about using fingerprints by Michael McGarrity. What is the thesis statement of the passage? What steps does detective Mike Chacon follow? What resources and constraints must he work within? What additional information is necessary to make this a directive process analysis?

2. What is the exigence for the process described by Peggy Post? Who is her audience?

3. If you were in conversation with Julia Alvarez, how might you explain the process of your own writing?

Using process analysis as an available means

Process analyses lend themselves to many means of delivery, especially in the United States, a nation of how-to buffs. Browsing through any bookstore will give you an idea of the wide range and great popularity of how-to books, videos, audios, and DVDs. You can listen to audios and learn how to relax or make money; you can watch videos that will teach you how to meditate or exercise. In fact, amazon.com lists over 100,000 books with "how to" in the title, the most popular include *Flip: How to Find, Fix, and Sell Houses for Profit* by Rick Villani, Clay Davis, and Gary Keller; *How to Win Friends and Influence People* by Dale

Carnegie; and *How to Talk So Kids Will Listen and How to Listen So Kids Will Talk* by Adele Faber and Elaine Mazlish.

As you know, the available means for any rhetorical situation include the physical means of delivering and receiving information. In our culture, getting and giving directions and information no longer occur only through a printed page or face-to-face contact. Instead of reading a cookbook, we turn on The Food Channel; instead of hiring a painter, we visit homedepot.com. So, whether you send someone a process analysis in English or Spanish, over the telephone or via email, in complete detail or in shorthand depends on that person's home language, access to various means of communication, and understanding of the subject matter. You also need to consider whether a visual will enhance or detract from your verbal analysis. For example, someone installing disc brakes for the first time will no doubt appreciate the forty-two photos that accompany the forty-two explanatory steps in the *Honda Tuning* article.

USING PROCESS ANALYSIS IN YOUR WRITING

1. In what assignments (chemistry, biology, engineering, math, and so on) are you often asked to include a process analysis as part of your response? Are these analyses informative or directive?

2. Bring to class an example of a process analysis, one you've come across in your reading for courses or you've composed for an assignment. Be prepared to explain how the process analysis supports a larger piece of writing.

CHECKING OVER A PROCESS ANALYSIS

Answering these questions will help review your own process analyses as well as those of your classmates.

✓ What exigence needs to be resolved?

✓ What specific audience can resolve or influence the resolution of that exigence?

✓ Is the process analysis directive or informative?

✓ What is the purpose of this process analysis: to inform, to entertain, or to argue a point?

✓ How does the purpose relate to the intended audience? What does the audience know about the process being considered? How much background information do readers need? What terms need to be defined for them?

✓ Given the audience and purpose, how many steps are necessary to clarify the process? Can any of them be combined? Should any of them be explained further? What specific details accompany each of the steps?

✓ Is the process analysis ordered chronologically? Does it need to be? What transitional words or phrases help move the reader along?

✓ Would a visual or visuals enhance the effectiveness of this process analysis? How, exactly?

✓ What is the thesis statement of this process analysis?

✓ If the process analysis has a conclusion, what is the purpose of it? Will readers feel confident that they can duplicate the process if they wish?

What Is Narration?

In the photograph, you see three people dressed up to look like ZZ Top, a band inducted a few years ago into the Rock and Roll Hall of Fame. The bearded characters in the black hats and long black coats represent guitarists Billy Gibbons and Dusty Hill; the guy without a beard and in a short black coat is meant to be drummer Frank Beard. The bearded guys are holding up fake guitars covered in fake fur, like the band's real fur-covered guitars currently on display at the Hall of Fame. All three of the people are giving a thumbs-up, ZZ Top's trademark gesture, which was displayed on many of the band's MTV videos,

What narrative can be constructed from this photo?

perhaps most prominently on "Sharp-Dressed Man." The three characters seem to be standing in front of a spotlight, as though they were just finishing a performance. The obviously fake guitars, beards, and moustache, together with the Halloween decorations, signal a Halloween costume party, perhaps one that included a talent show. One possible narration could be that after receiving their invitation, these three friends got together, dreamed up the costumes that would allow them to portray ZZ Top, and put together a lip-sync performance for their neighborhood Halloween party. After their performance, all the rest of the guests gave them a thumbs-up.

WRITE FOR FIVE

Write for five minutes, constructing a short narration based on the details in the photograph. As you write, pay special attention to the characters and the setting. Be prepared to share your narration with the rest of the class and note the differences and similarities among your stories.

As you composed a story about the photograph, you no doubt focused on its prominent elements: three people in costumes, a setting, props, and what looks to be a performance of some kind. Such demands converge in a **narration,** a rhetorical method of development that tells a story. We use narration every day as we make sense of the world for ourselves and for others. Whether we're retelling a fairy tale, a religious story, a family legend, or the final minutes of the Super Bowl, we're using narration, telling a story. Narration may frame an entire story (such as "Cinderella" or the exodus from Egypt), or it may briefly provide an example (of why your ancestors immigrated to the United States) or support an argument (those final plays that prove the Giants deserved to win the Super Bowl).

Usually our narrations are verbal; after all, we want to tell "what happened." Verbal narrations appear in newspaper accounts of child snatchings, historical accounts of battles, psychological studies, police reports, situation comedies, television dramas and most movies, and radio and television reports. Such verbal narrations might consist of one particular sequence of events (those in a novel or made-for-television movie, for example) or include a series of separate incidents that shape an overall narrative (a series of short stories that, together, comprise a novel, or a series of news stories that comprise a television news magazine).

The Elements of Narration

The need to tell stories seems to be embedded in human DNA. The relationship among the basic narrative elements of **characters** (people in the story), **dialogue** (direct speech among the characters), **setting** (the time and place), **description** (the selected details about the characters, dialogue, and setting), and **plot** (the sequence of events) stimulates our understanding of people, places, and especially of events.

It's impossible to write a narration without using several of these elements, especially characters, setting, and a sequence of events. Sometimes the characters don't use dialogue or speak at all, but they always do something. In the following passage, Sherman Alexie relies on all of the narrative elements defined above—characters, dialogue, setting, description, and a plot—to tell a story.

> Betty Towle, missionary teacher, redheaded and so ugly that no one ever had a puppy crush on her, made me stay in for recess fourteen days straight.
> "Tell me you're sorry," she said.
> "Sorry for what?" I asked.
> "Everything," she said and made me stand straight for fifteen minutes, eagle-armed with books in each hand. One was a math book; the other was English. But all I learned was that gravity can be painful.
> For Halloween I drew a picture of her riding a broom with a scrawny cat on the back. She said that her God would never forgive me for that.
> Once, she gave the class a spelling test but set me aside and gave me a test designed for junior high students. When I spelled all the words right, she crumpled up the paper and made me eat it.
> "You'll never learn respect," she said.
> She sent a letter home with me that told my parents to either cut my braids or keep me home from class. My parents came in the next day and dragged their braids across Betty Towle's desk.
> "Indians, Indians, Indians." She said it without capitalization. She called me "Indian, Indian, Indian."
> And I said, *Yes, I am. I am Indian. Indian, I am.*
>
> —**Sherman Alexie**, "Indian Education"

Anecdotes

In the previous excerpt, Sherman Alexie successfully uses all the narrative elements, but it's his use of **anecdotes**—brief, illustrative stories—that propels his narrative forward. Barbara Huttman uses an anecdote in much the same way to launch her narrative:

> "Murderer," a man shouted. "God help patients who get *you* for a nurse."
>
> "What gives you the right to play God?" another one asked.
>
> It was the Phil Donahue show where the guest is a fatted calf and the audience a two-hundred-strong flock of vultures hungering to pick at the bones. I had told them about Mac, one of my favorite cancer patients. "We resuscitated him fifty-two times in just one month. I refused to resuscitate him again. I simply sat there and held his hand while he died."   —**Barbara Huttman**, "A Crime of Compassion"

Point of view

Besides its story-telling elements, a narration also has a **point of view,** the viewpoint from which the story is told. In both the Alexie and the Huttman excerpts, the story is told in the first person, which means that the **narrator** (the voice telling the story) uses *I* and/or *we*. When the narrator uses *he, she, it,* and *they,* the story is being told in third person, as in the following passage:

> Angels never refer to the past, only to the future.
>
> When the angel Gabriel dropped in on Mary, he told her of an impossible future, the strange child she was going to have. It was as if her whole life had been preparation, though she couldn't have known that at the time. In one familiar Renaissance illustration, as Gabriel comes in through the window, Mary puts her finger on the page of the book she's reading, as if to mark her place. It is the calmest gesture. No sense of alarm or awe. She has been interrupted by this man with wings flying through her window, and she wants to mark her place so she can return to it when the interruption is over. She holds her other hand up to Gabriel, her eyes on the book, as if to say, "Please wait a second. Let me finish this paragraph."
>
> —**Ed Madden**, "Entertaining Angels"

Like all narrations, this one has characters (Gabriel and Mary), a setting (a room in which Mary is reading), dialogue ("Please wait a second"), description ("calmest gesture," "man with wings"), and plot (Gabriel comes through the window to tell Mary she'll be giving birth to Jesus). It also has a point of view: it's told in third person (". . . Mary puts her finger on the page of the book she's reading").

Climax

The turning point of the narration, which is usually organized in chronological order, is the **climax.** In "Cinderella," for instance, all of the events lead up to the moment when the glass slipper fits Cinderella's tiny foot. It's only then that the prince knows her real identity. After the climax, events turn toward a resolution. In this case, Cinderella and the prince marry and live happily ever after.

Flashback and flashforward

When narrations are not organized chronologically, they often use **flashback** and **flashforward,** which take the reader to past and future events, respectively. Though interruptive, these techniques can add interest to a story, for they provide glimpses of other times, which illuminate the present as it is being recounted in an otherwise straightforward, chronological organization.

Transitions

In order to move narrations forward (or backward), narrators depend on **transitions,** words or expressions that link ideas or events within a paragraph, an essay, even a novel. Transitions can support chronological organization (with words such as *first*, *then*, and *finally*), comparison and contrast (*likewise, in comparison*, and *instead*), causes or effects (*as a result* or *consequently*), and so on.

Narration and the Rhetorical Situation

We rely on narration so often that we tend to think it's useful for most situations—and it is. For instance, you might use narration with a few anecdotes to establish a contrast between you and your irresponsible siblings, thereby gaining permission to travel to Europe alone this summer. Or you might include the story of your young cousin who died of jaw cancer in an essay for a health and human development course, arguing against underage smoking. In your history class, however, you might use narration as an end in itself, demonstrating to your instructor that you understand the series of events leading up to the bombing of Hiroshima.

Using narration to address an exigence

Every narration is composed in response to an exigence: someone needs to know what happened. The exigence can involve something small in scope (the desire to know what happened on last night's episode of *Grey's Anatomy*) or large (the desire to know someone's life story). For example, when someone dies, that event creates an exigence to which many people respond: friends and family write notes of condolence; a religious leader prepares funeral remarks; the monument designer plans the gravestone; and a newspaper writer composes an obituary. Many of these messages include narrative features. The obituary on the following page includes characters (Robert M. Hettema, his parents, wife, and children), implied dialogue (among all the characters and among the people who will attend the memorial service), settings (the Mount Nittany Medical Center, Purdue University, Pearl Harbor, and State College), descriptive details about his life in each of those settings, and the sequence of events that constituted his life span.

Using narration to address an audience

If you've ever read a bedtime story to a small child, you used narration to address a specific audience, a rhetorical audience capable of changing his or her

Robert M. Hettema
September 21, 1917—February 6, 2004

Robert M. Hettema, 86, of State College, died Friday, Feb. 6, 2004, at Mount Nittany Medical Center. Born Sept. 21, 1917, in Passaic, N. J., he was a son of the late Guy and Nellie Hettema.

On Feb. 15, 1947, he married Ursula Virginia Lee, who survives. Bob and Ursula had six children, Lee, Virginia, Arthur, Mark, James and Terry. They also had 12 grandchildren. All survive Bob except Arthur, who died in 2002.

Bob received his civil engineering degree from Purdue University in 1939 and began work at Turner Construction Co. where he worked for 32 years. He was working for Turner in Oahu, Hawaii, when Pearl Harbor was attacked in 1941. He joined the Navy in 1944 and served in the South Pacific during World War II as a Seabee.

He became a vice president at Turner and he managed several large construction projects, including Madison Square Garden and the McGraw-Hill Building in New York City.

He moved to State College in 1973 and worked at Penn State for the last 10 years of his career where he was a professor in the College of Architectural Engineering, teaching construction management. He was a member of the American Society for Engineering Education and authored a textbook titled, "Mechanical and Elecrical Construction Management." He helped organize youth hockey in State College in 1973. Bob coached the Penn State Hockey Team and was inducted into the Penn State Hockey Hall of Fame.

Throughout his life, Bob had a keen interest and involvement in politics, gardening, dancing, the arts and sports.

A memorial service will be held at 11 a.m. Friday at Eisenhower Chapel on the Penn State campus, with the Reverend Thomazine Shanahan officiating.

opinion or action. In this case, your narration served to change the audience from being awake to drowsing off. You knew to choose a narration appropriate for a small child—a fairy tale or *Good Night, Moon*. When songwriters compose for country-western singers, they're also composing for a country-western audience; they write of broken hearts, faithless lovers, faithful dogs, good horses, fast trucks, and the glories of these United States of America. They know their audience, and they design a message suitable for influencing that audience.

The best rhetors gauge their message to their intended audience, often adjusting the basic message to influence the opinions or actions of the particular audience. For example, when Bobby Hatfield died, his hometown newspaper no doubt ran an obituary about him, his music, and his family. But *Rolling Stone* magazine ran an obituary different from the daily newspaper kind. The basic message remained: music great Bobby Hatfield of the Righteous Brothers was dead. But the *Rolling Stone* obituary was recast to suit its readers, who would be able to appreciate Hatfield's contribution to popular music. Opening with dialogue from legend Billy Joel, this obituary features a photograph of Hatfield performing with the other half of the duo, Bill Medley. Another well-known character in the narration is music producer Phil Spector. The obituary includes a setting—Kalamazoo, Michigan—as well as a sequence of events; in this case, a series of Righteous Brothers' hits, such as "You've Lost That Lovin'

An obituary for Bobby Hatfield in *Rolling Stone* focuses on his life in music.

Hatfield (left), with Medley, 1965

1940–2003

BOBBY HATFIELD

One half of the Righteous Brothers, 63

SOMETIMES WHITE PEOPLE can actually be soulful," Billy Joel said when he inducted the Righteous Brothers into the Rock & Roll Hall of Fame earlier this year. For Robert Lee "Bobby" Hatfield and Bill Medley—the pair behind legendary "blue-eyed soul" hits such as "You've Lost That Lovin' Feelin'" and "Unchained Melody"—that honor was both important and, as it turned out, timely. Hatfield died of a heart attack on November 5th at a hotel in Kalamazoo, Michigan, shortly before a show. He was sixty-three.

The Righteous Brothers' biggest hit, "You've Lost That Lovin' Feelin'"—produced by Phil Spector—is often credited as the most frequently played song in American radio history. But the duo had hits both before and after their records with Spector. Following a six-year separation, Hatfield and Medley reunited in 1974 and returned to the top of the charts with "Rock & Roll Heaven." In 1990, their exquisite performance on "Unchained Melody" became a smash hit once more when the song was featured in the movie *Ghost*.

Hatfield is survived by his wife and four children. DAVID WILD

Feelin'," "Unchained Melody," and "Rock & Roll Heaven." Hatfield's wife and children aren't mentioned until the last sentence. Given the *Rolling Stone* audience, the focus on Hatfield's music and his musical associates was more important than a focus on his family.

Using narration with a rhetorical purpose

Whenever narration is the rhetorical method chosen for addressing an exigence and an audience, it is used with a purpose. The basic purposes of narration are to supply information (or explanation), to support an argument (or thesis), to provide an example, and to set a mood. Both of the obituaries for Bobby Hatfield supply information; your cousin's death from cancer provides an example or, written differently, can support an argument. A musical tribute, shaped as a

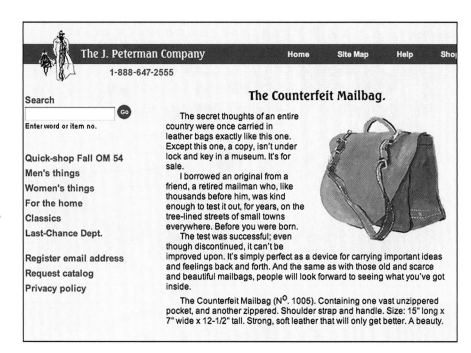

The J. Peterman catalogue uses narration to inform customers.

narration, can set a mood. Successful narrations serve as fitting responses for many rhetorical situations.

Using narration to supply information If you ever watched *Seinfeld*, you know that Elaine wrote catalogue copy for J. Peterman. She was always coming up with an exotic story—an informative narration—to accompany the product, such as the "urban sombrero." Her marketing goal, of course, was to sell the item, but her rhetorical purpose was to inform.

We use narrations all the time to inform others. Newscasters use stories of accidents to inform listeners of icy road conditions. Physicians tell stories of successful recuperations to inform patients as to what to expect. And professors tell stories of their own job searches in order to inform graduate students of the steps they'll need to take and the emotions they'll go through as they look for a job.

Using narration to explain After writer and illustrator Marjane Satrapi moved from Iran to Austria and then France, she discovered that many of her new friends had no knowledge of the Iranian revolution of 1979 and little understanding of life under the Ayatollah Khomeini. She found herself telling stories about her childhood to provide examples that counterbalanced the more familiar narratives put forth by the news media—narratives that focused on radical fundamentalists who seemed quite alien to many Westerners. When Satrapi decided to try to explain recent Iranian history to a larger audience, she determined that one means available to her as an illustrator and a writer was the graphic novel, a medium popularized by works such as Art Spiegelman's *Maus*. In the excerpt from her novel *Persepolis* shown on the following page, the last of the three frames in the chronological sequence supports the explanation that

In *Persepolis,* Marjane Satrapi presents a narrative of Iranian life.

Satrapi and her peers were not very different from children raised in other countries, rejecting what they considered to be strict and arbitrary rules. For an audience of non-Iranians, the visual and written narrative provides a clear explanation of Satrapi's experience.

Using narration to provide an example Often, as you're devising a larger argument, you'll use an example to help prove one of your points. Susan Orlean includes one of owner Leo Herschman's narrations to exemplify what she means when she says his store "has the look of a Swiss village all but obliterated by an Alpine slide":

"We're jammed to hell in here," Mr. Herschman was complaining the other day as he extracted an order form from a pile of boxes, flyers, fan catalogs, newspapers, and stationery on his desk. "I keep planning to get this place organized. When my late wife and I opened Modern Supply, in 1932, we had a beautiful store on Fulton Street. We sold all manner of appliances—refrigerators, ovens, everything. But the Fulton Street building was torn down for the World Trade Center, and we moved to this lousy place. We brought what I would call the minimum from Fulton Street—fans and motors. Now all I sell is ceiling fans. It's still too crowded in here. A designer was here once buying a fan, and he said to me, 'Sir would you care to retain me to redesign your store?' I said, 'What are you planning to do, set fire to it?'"

—**Susan Orlean,** "Fans"

Using narration to set a mood Telling ghost stories is a great way to set a mood around a campfire—for kids, part of the thrill of camping out is scaring themselves. Adults still use narration to set a mood: We go to the movies to see *28 Days Later, Halloween,* or some other thriller. We read romance novels that portray struggle followed by unmitigated happiness. We read war novels and watch old John Wayne movies to experience a patriotic mood. We tell jokes to create a happy mood, and we deliver eulogies to set a mood of acceptance.

By all accounts, award-winning writer Dorothy Allison had a rough childhood in South Carolina. But she and her sisters remained steadfastly close throughout it—as well as devoted to their mother. In the following passage, Allison sets a mood of loving tenderness, as she describes the sisters preparing their mother for burial:

> We had gone through Mama's things together, talked about buying something special, but finally chosen clothes for Mama that she had worn and loved—her lucky shirt, loose-fitting cotton trousers, and her most comfortable shoes. "Only woman ever buried in her bingo outfit," I would tell friends later. But choosing those clothes, we had not laughed; we had felt guided by what Mama would have wanted. It was when I watched Wanda fasten Mama's lucky necklace—the little silver racehorse positioned in the hollow of Mama's throat—that I saw.
>
> Wanda was being Mama, doing what Mama would have done, comforting us the way only Mama had known to do. I looked around and saw Anne holding my stepfather's shoulder as he sobbed, looked down and saw my own hands locked on the little bag of Mama's jewelry we had found in her dresser. For a moment I wanted to cry, and then I didn't. Of all the things I had imagined, this was the one I had not foreseen. We had become Mama.
>
> —**Dorothy Allison,** *One or Two Things I Know for Sure*

Narration is one of the best ways to set a mood, as most narratives are replete with descriptive details ("her lucky shirt, loose-fitting cotton trousers, and her most comfortable shoes," "her bingo outfit," "the little silver racehorse," "in the hollow of Mama's throat"). The actions of characters also enhance a mood—in this case, the three sisters attending to the details that would have pleased their mother.

Using narration as a fitting response

As you know by now, the first step in orchestrating a fitting response is recognizing—or creating—an exigence within a rhetorical situation. If you decide you want to respond to this exigence, you need to consider which rhetorical method

TEARS FOR A LEGEND

Nashville pays tribute to Johnny Cash

By Jason Fine

BONO CALLED HIM "ST. JOHN." Ray Charles described him as a "crazy old soldier." And Hank Williams, Jr. said simply, "He was my buddy," adding, "We used to like to shoot cannons off on Franklin Road and knock the books off people's shelves."

Friends, family members and musicians paid tribute to Johnny Cash on November 10th at Nashville's Ryman Auditorium—where Cash was permanently banned from playing in 1965 after he kicked out all the stage lights in a drugged-out rage. (Bono and Charles appeared via video because they could not attend in person. The concert aired November 15th on CMT.)

From Cash's original bass player, Marshall Grant, to former Vice President Al Gore, friends painted Cash, who died September 12th, as a complex, generous, sometimes self-destructive and always deeply spiritual man. He was "a hell-raiser," said the show's host, actor Tim Robbins, but also "a seeker of truth." The musical highlights were many: Steve Earle's hard-edged "Folsom Prison Blues"; John Mellencamp's spare arrangement of "Hey Porter"; Kris Kristofferson, Willie Nelson and George Jones trading verses on "Big River"; and Williams' "Ring of Fire," in which he nearly perfectly replicated Cash's booming baritone.

With the exception of Kid Rock, who admitted, "I probably knew Johnny less than any of you," each of the performers seemed to have been affected in some profound way by Cash. Ronnie Dunn of the duo Brooks and Dunn wore a long black coat that he said Cash had given him one night after he'd arrived in Nashville with no money. Rodney Crowell, the ex-husband of Cash's daughter Rosanne, recalled trying to persuade Cash to let the couple share a bedroom on a visit to the family's Jamaica retreat shortly after the two started dating. "Son," Cash told him, "I don't know you well enough to miss you if you're gone."

And Rosanne, who performed a beautiful version of his 1958 song "I Still Miss Someone," later recalled that when she and her sisters fought as kids, Cash repeated a lesson: "You can choose love or you can choose hate. I choose love."

Cash's five children prepared a montage of family photos set to a heartbreaking new Rosanne Cash song, "September When It Comes," which features some of her dad's last vocals. Then, two dozen family members, including Cash's brother Tommy, Cash's first wife, Vivian Liberto, and June's daughter Carlene, packed the stage to sing one of Cash's own final songs, "We'll Meet Again."

"Tears for a Legend" describes the Nashville tribute to Johnny Cash.

might best suit your intended audience (those who can be changed or influenced to effect change) and the constraints and resources of the rhetorical situation.

Given its flexibility, narration serves as a fitting response in many situations, for it can be easily delivered verbally or visually. When you're confronting an exigence that seems to call for describing an experience, narration can be the most fitting response. When an exigence calls for an example, narration works well. And when you need a story or anecdote, to create a mood—whether it's a joke to open a speech or a parable that teaches a sobering lesson—narration can do the trick.

As you consider narration as a purposeful response to a rhetorical situation, you'll begin to notice that you're experiencing narrations throughout the day, whether you're gossiping with friends, watching television, or reading your homework assignments. You'll see how pervasive narrations are as fitting responses to various exigencies. For instance, when Johnny Cash died, the people at Country Music Television (CMT) strived to prepare a fitting response to the exigence of his death. Although television viewers constituted one audience, they were not the only one: Cash's admirers, collaborators, and fellow musicians comprised another audience, and his family comprised yet another. So, to prepare a fitting response to the exigence, one that reached all the members of this tripartite audience, as well as worked within the constraints and resources of television production, Nashville's Ryman Auditorium (where it was taped), and various performers' professional schedules, CMT developed a two-hour memorial tribute to Cash. Kris Kristofferson, Larry Gatlin, Willie Nelson, Cheryl Crow, Rodney Crowell, Steve Earle, George Jones, John Mellencamp, Hank Williams, Jr., and many others told stories about their musical debt to Cash as a prelude to their performances. The tribute seemed to be as fitting a response as a group of colleagues could put together, especially given the means available to them.

READING A TEXT FOR NARRATION

1. Read through "Tears for a Legend" again, this time trying to identify the elements of the rhetorical situation. Be prepared to share your response with the rest of the class.

2. What are the narrative elements in "Tears for a Legend"?

3. What is the setting for this narration? How is this specific setting essential to this narration?

Using narration as an available means

"The Nashville Memorial Tribute to Johnny Cash," taped before a standing-room only audience at Ryman Auditorium, was telecast two months after Cash's death. With the financial backing of CMT and the professional expertise of the various performers, the planners of the memorial tribute made productive use of the available means: money, talent, star power, availability, and willingness converged into an appropriate narration.

James McConnon's
stone memorial.

The available means, however, do not always translate into a televised event. For the story of James McConnon, the available means appear to be smaller in magnitude. Instead of a televised memorial, his is a modest stone one, providing minimal information about his life: he died in 1930 and had a wife, Mary, who died 19 years later. The newspaper account of his death was another means of conveying this and other information about McConnon. And when his friends and family gathered to mourn his passing, they, no doubt, used conversation as the means to tell stories that honored his life—and death. Each of these narrations would have been replete with characters, settings, dialogue, description, and a sequence of events.

Using Narration in Your Writing

1. Although it might not seem obvious at first, many of your college assignments (from lab reports to explanations of how you solved math problems) ask you to use narration. Many of your assigned readings are narrative in nature. Think for a few minutes about the reading and writing you do for your other classes; then prepare a list of examples of narration to share with the rest of the class.

2. If you can, bring to class one of the examples from your list. Be prepared to explain how the narration supports either a larger piece of writing or a class assignment.

CHECKING OVER A NARRATION

Answering these questions will help you review your own narratives as well as those of your classmates.

✓ What is the specific exigence to which the writer is responding? Did the writer identify or create that exigence?

✓ What specific audience can resolve, be influenced by, or influence the resolution of that exigence?

✓ What is the overall purpose of the narration: to supply information (or explanation), to support an argument (or thesis), to provide an example, or to set a mood? How does that purpose relate to the intended audience?

✓ What is the (explicit or implied) thesis statement of the narration? How do the exigence, audience, and purpose converge in that thesis statement?

✓ Is the setting included in the narration?

✓ How do the characters demonstrate their importance to the narration?

✓ How does the dialogue enrich this narration? In what specific ways could the dialogue be improved?

✓ Is the length of this narration appropriate to its overall purpose? As a fitting response to the exigence?

✓ What means are used to deliver this narration? How do those means accommodate the resources and constraints of the rhetorical situation?

✓ How is the sequence of events ordered? Would flashback or flashforward enhance the narration?

Development Strategies

15 | CIRCUMSTANCE

Circumstance as an Available Means

You're exposed to thousands of visual arguments each day—delivered via television, movies, print advertisements, billboards, swooshes, and golden arches. These arguments can be resisted or ignored or go entirely unnoticed. The number of verbal arguments that barrage you each day is even higher because many visual arguments are accompanied by verbal ones. Almost everything you read is, on some level, an argument that strives to change your attitude, your opinion, or your behavior.

The advertisement on the chapter-opening page, like promotional materials for many colleges, makes an argument about what is possible (you as a Northampton Community College student), about particular circumstances that gave rise to past actions (the individuals shown made the decision to attend that college and are now working in their chosen careers), and about probable future outcomes (you will have access to any of the careers represented by the uniforms worn under graduation gowns). When your exigence prompts you to consider what is possible or impossible or how circumstances led to past actions and all likely future outcomes, you can respond with the common rhetorical strategies for development known as argument and persuasion.

What Is Argument?

Argument and *persuasion* are often used interchangeably, despite the technical distinctions between the two terms. **Argument** refers to the verbal or visual delivery of a point of view and the use of logical reasoning to help an audience understand that point of view as true or valid. **Persuasion,** on the other hand, refers to the use of emotions as well as logical reasoning to move the audience a step or two beyond the understanding that accompanies successful argument. The goal of persuasion is to change the attitude, opinion, or behavior of that audience. Because any visual or verbal argument can include emotional appeals as well as logical reasoning and because any argument holds the potential for changing the collective mind or action of an audience, the broader term *argument* is used throughout this book and chapter.

We employ and respond to arguments all day long, as we work to understand and explain to others the world around or within us. Some of our arguments focus on defending our opinions or questioning the opinions of others, opinions about whether the university's junior running back should turn pro, where to get the best pizza, which gym is the best bargain, or whether a low-carb diet is truly healthful, after all. Sometimes, an argument involves exploring and clarifying our own opinions, as we weigh all sides of an issue and various possible consequences of our preferences or choices. Often, we employ that kind of analytical argument when we're considering some of life's big issues: surgery, divorce, marriage, a new job, racism, sexism, and so on. For instance, if your brother announces that he wants to marry a woman from another country whom no one else in the family knows, chances are the entire family will be talking about and weighing the consequences of your brother's decision as well as the consequences of their own positions. Before you decide where you stand, you may listen to all these opinions. At other times, however, an argument is invitational: it invites the audience to understand your position (even if they're not convinced to change) and to take the opportunity to explain their position to you (even if you're not convinced to change). Invitational argument works especially well when the speaker and the audience need to work together to solve a problem (what to do about school violence, the spread of the AIDS virus, or unemployment), to construct a position that represents diverse interests (arguing for or against universal health coverage, the professionalization of college athletics, or affirmative action), or implement a policy that requires broad support (implementing a draft system or allowing gay marriage).

The Elements of Argument and Rhetorical Fallacies

Identifiable issue

An **identifiable issue** is the topic under discussion, one that the writer chooses from a multitude of issues confronted daily, from poor service at a restaurant to poverty, homelessness, poor-quality schooling, and so on. Often, we don't take the time to address such problems in any productive way, perhaps because we cannot pinpoint the specific issue within the problem that we want to argue for or against.

But suppose you experienced both bad service and bad food at a restaurant. That experience might not be a real problem unless you became violently ill and you thought it was from the chile relleno, which didn't taste quite right. In that case, you would have identified a specific issue you can argue about, as you express your opinion that the preparation of the food, the quality of the ingredients, or the sanitary conditions of the restaurant are in need of improvement. Or suppose you've identified one specific issue that contributes to the poor quality of your neighborhood school, the fact that most children don't eat breakfast before they come to school. The need for free school breakfasts might be the position you want to take in making an argument to the school board.

Teresa Heinz Kerry speaking at the Democratic National Convention.

When political figures speak, they often need to focus on one issue while touching on a number of others. When Teresa Heinz Kerry spoke before the 2004 Democratic National Convention, her speech forecasted an enduring political climate, one full of anxieties about candidates who have experiences foreign to many Americans and about women as real political contenders. Kerry addressed many issues, including the importance of equality, opportunity, democracy, freedom of speech, and her husband's election. But the most identifiable issue in her

Development Strategies

remarks is freedom of speech, especially for someone like her, foreign-born and female:

> I have a very personal feeling about how special America is, and I know how precious freedom is. It is a sacred gift, sanctified by those who have lived it and those who have died defending it. My right to speak my mind, to have a voice, to be what some have called "opinionated," is a right I deeply and profoundly cherish. And my only hope is that, one day soon, women—who have all earned their right to their opinions—instead of being called opinionated, will be called smart and well-informed, just like men.
>
> —**Teresa Heinz Kerry**, speech at 2004 Democratic National Convention

Once a rhetor has identified an issue, the rhetor can make a claim about it.

Claim

A **claim** is the arguable position taken (of several possible ones) concerning an issue. As you think about the issue, you'll want to make sure that your claim is one that can be argued and responded to. For instance, when Teresa Heinz Kerry identified the issue of women who speak their minds being characterized as merely "opinionated," she struck a chord with Americans still undecided on how to respond to such women as public figures. If you think back to the controversy created by First Lady Hillary Rodham Clinton when she tried to put a national health care program in place, as well as more recent criticisms of House

Senator Hillary Clinton, speaking out.

Speaker Nancy Pelosi when she traveled to Syria and met with the Syrian president and of 2004 presidential campaigner Kerry when she verbally pushed back at an overly aggressive journalist with "Shove it," you'll remember the public discomfort with these opinionated women.

Realizing that the American public has been talking about her outspokenness, Kerry addresses the issue head on:

> This evening, I want to acknowledge and honor the women of this world, whose wise voices for much too long have been excluded and discounted. It is time—it is time for the world to hear women's voices, in full and at last.
>
> —**Teresa Heinz Kerry**, speech at 2004 Democratic National Convention

Among all the possible views of opinionated public women—from Madonna and Courtney Love to Barbara Walters and Rosie O'Donnell—Kerry selects her claim: "It is time for the world to hear women's voices, in full and at last." Kerry's claim serves as the basis of her thesis statement, just as, in most cases, your claim will ground your thesis statement.

Common ground

The **common ground** of an argument consists of the goals, beliefs, values, and/ or assumptions that the rhetor shares with the audience. Once you've established common ground, you've assured your audience that, despite any misunderstandings or disagreements, you and they actually share a good deal, which provides a starting point for you to speak or write. For instance, if you and your parents agree that your getting a college degree is paramount, then you can come together on many other issues, from financial support to study time. And when Kerry prepared to face the delegates and the television audience of the Democratic National Convention, she knew she had to establish common ground with them if she was going to be successful in getting them to listen to what she had to say. So, she began by saying, "By now I hope it will come as no surprise that I have something to say. Tonight, as I have done throughout this campaign, I would like to speak to you from the heart." This opening clearly acknowledged that she and her multiple audiences already agreed on one thing: Teresa Heinz Kerry always seems to have something to say. But she also justifies her outspokenness with the idea that she speaks "from the heart." The common ground Kerry initially establishes is appropriate and rhetorically useful. Sometimes, common ground is confirmed or extended in the use of each of the rhetorical appeals.

Rhetorical appeals

Rhetorical appeals are strategies employed to emphasize **ethos** (trustworthiness as a rhetor), **logos** (the reasoning within the argument itself), and **pathos** (an emotional connection with the audience).

Ethos Throughout her speech, Kerry uses the three rhetorical appeals, opening with an ethical appeal that not only establishes common ground with her live and viewing audiences but also establishes her as a woman of good will, good sense, and good moral character, the three qualities of an ethical rhetor. To her credit, Kerry greets a wide spectrum of Americans in their own languages, establishing herself as a well-educated, well-traveled American woman, who understands that not all Americans use English as their home language:

> Y a todos los Hispanos, y los Latinos; a tous les Franco Americains, a tutti Italiani; a toda a familia Portugesa e Brazileria; and to all the continental Africans living in this country, and to all the new Americans in our country: I invite you to join in our conversation, and together with us work towards the noblest purpose of all: a free, good and democratic society.
>
> —**Teresa Heinz Kerry**, speech at 2004 Democratic National Convention

The foreign-born Kerry moves quickly from inclusive, multilingual greetings to stressing the importance of democracy. Like every good rhetor, she wants to establish her ethos by establishing her credibility as a knowledgeable person who can and should be believed and trusted. Thus, she provides examples of her good will toward all Americans, her good sense in valuing democracy and opportunity, and, especially, her good moral character in terms of equality and justice:

Like many other Americans, like many of you, and like even more of your parents and grandparents, I was not born in this country. And as you have seen [on a video preceding her remarks], I grew up in East Africa, in Mozambique, in a land that was then under a dictatorship. . . .

As a young woman, I attended Witwatersrand University in Johannesburg, South Africa, which was then not segregated. But I witnessed the weight of apartheid everywhere around me. And so, with my fellow students we marched in the streets of Johannesburg against its extension into higher education. This was the late 1950s, at the dawn of the civil rights marches in America. . . .

I learned something then, and I believe it still. There is a value in taking a stand whether or not anybody may be noticing it and whether or not it is a risky thing to do. And if even those who are in danger can raise their lonely voices, isn't it more that is required of all of us, where liberty had her birth?

—**Teresa Heinz Kerry**, speech at 2004 Democratic National Convention

Kerry's established ethos sustains the body of her argument, even as she emphasizes a logical appeal. She outlines several forward-looking and logical reasons why Americans should vote for her husband. Like the best of rhetors, Kerry wants to be understood, to use rhetoric purposefully and ethically. If she's persuasive, so much the better, but persuasion cannot come at the cost of her ethos.

Logos   Kerry uses logos compellingly, walking her audience through the logical (yet also emotional) reasons that Americans should vote for John Kerry:

I have been privileged to meet with Americans all across this land. They voiced many different concerns, but one they all share was about America's role in the world—what we want this great country of ours to stand for.

To me, one of the best faces America has ever projected is the face of a Peace Corps volunteer. That face symbolizes this country: young, curious, brimming with idealism and hope—and a real, honest compassion. Those young people convey an idea of America that is all about heart and creativity, generosity and confidence, a practical, can-do sense and a big, big smile.

. . . And that for me is the spirit of America—the America you and I are working for in this election. It is the America that people all across this nation want to restore. . . . It is the America the world wants to see, shining, hopeful and bright once again. And that is the America that my husband John Kerry wants to lead. John believes in a bright future. He believes that alternative fuels will guarantee that not only will no American boy or girl go to war because of our dependence on foreign oil, but also that our economy will forever become independent of this need.

We can, and we will, create good, competitive and sustainable jobs while still protecting the air we breathe, the water we drink and the health of our children, because good environmental policy is good economics. John believes that we can, and we will, give every family and every child access to affordable health care, a good education, and the tools to become self-reliant.

And John believes we must, and we should, recognize the immense value of the caregivers in our country—those women and men who nurture and care for children, for elderly parents, for family members in need. These are the people who build and support our most valuable assets—our families. Isn't it time—isn't it time that we began working to give parents more opportunity with their children, and wouldn't it be wonderful for parents to be able to afford a full and good family life?   —**Teresa Heinz Kerry**, speech at 2004 Democratic National Convention

By equating good jobs with environmental protection (a key position of her husband) and a good environmental policy with good economics, Kerry lays out a system of logical reasoning. Although she must compress her argument because of constraints on her time, she attempts to present a reasonable argument, one her audience will understand.

One interesting feature of logos, or the logical appeal, is how many different ways it can be constructed. Reasons and evidence provide the form for logos, but they can appear in various guises. Kerry uses personal experiences, knowledge of domestic policies, and personal observations to build her argument. But other arguments might call for facts, statistics, comparisons, anecdotes, and/or expert opinions or testimony, as well. In fact, it's through the logical appeal that many arguments tap the other rhetorical methods of development: definition, description, narration, exemplification, classification and division, comparison and contrast, process analysis, and cause-and-effect analysis.

Pathos In her concluding remarks, Teresa Heinz Kerry employs pathos, an emotional connection with her audience. As she winds down, she invokes the importance of her husband's Vietnam service, thereby connecting with Americans who are worried about national security and terrorism and those who have served in the armed services:

> John is a fighter. He earned his medals the old-fashioned way, by putting his life on the line for his country. And no one will defend this nation more vigorously than he will—and he will always, always be first in the line of fire.
>
> But he also knows the importance of getting it right. For him, the names of many friends inscribed in the Vietnam Memorial, that cold stone, testify to the awful toll exacted by leaders who mistake stubbornness for strength.
>
> And that is why, as president, my husband will not fear disagreement or dissent. He believes that our voices—yours and mine—must be the voices of freedom. And if we do not speak, neither does she.
>
> In America, the true patriots are those who dare speak truth to power. And the truth that we must speak now is that America has responsibilities that it is time for us to accept again.
>
> —**Teresa Heinz Kerry**, speech at 2004 Democratic National Convention

Kerry moves from one emotionally laden topic to the next, from war to freedom of speech, working to connect with her audience on the issue of American patriotism. She speaks about the importance and relevance of her husband's Vietnam service. And she speaks to the connections among free speech, truth, and freedom.

Truth and *freedom* are, of course, words that strike an emotional chord in the hearts of most Americans. But not all terms carry such dependably positive connotations—neither do all examples, observations, or reasons. The success of the pathetic appeal always depends on the rhetorical situation. The trick, then, is to strike just the right chord. Too little emotional connection with your audience can make you appear to be cold and calculating, thereby damaging your ethos. Too many emotion-packed examples or anecdotes can make your argument appear to be specious or manipulative. Your audience may think that you've resorted to emotion because the logic of your argument is weak. When you use pathos, you'll want it to enhance both your ethos and your logos, not detract from them.

Rhetorical fallacies

Rhetorical fallacies are errors in reasoning or logic. Sloppy reasoning, snap judgments, quickly drawn conclusions, missing data, one-sided opinions—all of these errors signal that a rhetor's thinking is not trustworthy and that the argument is not well reasoned. When we encounter problems in someone else's argument, we respond, "That's simply not so" or "That's an unfair tactic" or "Just because X happened doesn't mean Y will" or "What does that have to do with anything?" Because it's often easier to detect flaws in someone else's argument than in our own, even the most experienced rhetors inadvertently make the following kinds of errors.

Non sequitur The phrase *non sequitur* is Latin for "it does not follow." This rhetorical fallacy serves as the basis for many other fallacies, for it is an error in cause-and-consequence analysis, a faulty conclusion about consequences: "Helen loves the stars; she'll major in astronomy"; "My client is not guilty of speeding because he did not see the posted speed limit"; "I need a raise because of my child support payments"; "The war in Vietnam was a disaster for the United States; U.S. troops should not be in Iraq." Each of these statements is based on the faulty claim that there's a logical connection between its parts.

Ad hominem *Ad hominem* is Latin for "toward the man himself." This fallacy is an attack on the person, which draws attention away from the issue under consideration. Such errors in reasoning involve personal attacks on another person rather than on the opinion that person holds: "I don't want golfing tips from my neighbor; she may be a professional golfer, but she believes in . . . ." Whether the neighbor believes in a woman's right to abortion, the value of plastic surgery, the importance of a war in Iraq, gay marriage, a comprehensive health plan, or lower taxes, the golf tips are being refused for the wrong reason.

Appeal to tradition Many people resist change—it unsettles their routines and comforts. An appeal to tradition is thus often invoked by rhetors: "That's how we've always done it, so you should, too" or, to put it another way, "That's how it's always been done, so it should continue." This appeal is often used in political campaigns ("Four more years"), social organizations ("We've never invited X and Y to our group; let's not start now"), and personal situations ("My father never got on the highway without at least a half a tank of gas, so you should fill up now"; "My mother always cut the end off the ham before she put it in the oven, so you should, too").

Bandwagon The bandwagon fallacy is "Everyone's doing or thinking it, so you should, too." Highway patrolmen often hear this plea: "Everyone else was speeding, so I was merely keeping up with the traffic." And parents hear pleas from their children like these: "Everyone else gets to go to that concert" and "Everyone else is wearing that brand of jeans."

Begging the question Often referred to as a circular argument and similar to equivocation, begging the question is the fallacy of simply restating the initial arguable claim as though it's a conclusion or a good reason. In other words, that arguable claim has not been supported in any way: "O. J. Simpson did not kill his wife because he is a world-class football player, not a murderer"; "I can talk to my parents any way I choose because of freedom of speech"; "We must fire the worst teachers in order to improve the students' test scores." In each of these examples, the initial claim needs to be established and argued, whether it's Simpson's innocence, your right to speak to your parents however you choose, or the blameworthiness of certain teachers for students' low scores.

False analogy Effective rhetors often use analogies to equate two unlike things, explaining one in terms of another (see p. 423), for example, comparing a Mercedes Benz car to a security blanket or a diamond ring to eternal love. False analogies, however, stretch beyond a valid resemblance to a false or invalid comparison: "Vietnam war veterans returned to the animosity of an antiwar U.S. populace; therefore, Iraqi war veterans will also return to the same antipathy"; "Often compared to the beautiful and talented Elizabeth Taylor, Jennifer Lopez will be married at least eight times, too."

False authority One of the most prevalent rhetorical fallacies, false authority assumes that an expert in one field can be credible in another field. Just think of all the professional athletes or celebrities who argue that a particular brand of car, coffee, undershorts, soft drink, vacation, charge card, or political candidate is the best one, and you'll understand immediately how false authority works—and why it's often undetected. When producer Kevin Wall brought together Al Gore, the Red Hot Chili Peppers, and Kanye West for "Live Earth," a seven-city, twenty-four-hour concert to be telecast across all seven continents, he said, "Our success, I hope, is to act like a tipping point for a lot of movements that are already happening. This is not a political show, but this is a show that asks for action and deserves results" ("Live from Planet Rock"). Wall's words may have encouraged a good number of people to tune in to the concert, but do his words actually carry any authority in scientific circles? After all, he's an expert in music, not in the environment.

False cause Also referred to by the Latin phrase *post hoc, ergo propter hoc,* a false cause is the assumption that because A occurs before B, A is, therefore, the cause of B. We all know that events that follow in time do not necessarily have a causal relationship; for example, if I sneeze right before the lights go out, my sneeze did not cause an electrical outage. The fallacy of false cause, however, often appears when there might actually be some relationship between two events but not a direct causal one: "Jim got fired from his job, and his wife divorced him; therefore, his job loss caused his divorce." Jim's job loss might be the last of several job losses he's suffered in the past three years, and his wife, tired of depending on him to hold a job, filed for divorce.

False dilemma Also referred to as the either/or fallacy, the false dilemma sets up only two choices for resolving a complex situation, when there are in fact more than two. In addition, the false dilemma offers the rhetor's choice as the only good option, implying that the only other choice is unthinkable: "If we don't spank our children, they will run wild"; "If you don't get straight A's, you won't be able to get a job."

Guilt by association An unfair attempt to make someone responsible for the beliefs or actions of others is the fallacy of guilt by association. This false reasoning is why so many Arabs living in the United States were brutally beaten after the attacks of September 11, 2001. Many innocent people suffered for the deeds of the Arab terrorists.

Hasty generalization A conclusion based on too little evidence or on exceptional or biased evidence is a hasty generalization, apparent in statements such as these: "Fred failed his political science exam; he'll never get into law school"; "All Mexican food is fattening." The otherwise very intelligent Fred may have a good reason for failing one exam, and although beef-and-cheese burritos may be high in calories, many Mexican dishes rely on the healthy staples of black beans and rice.

Oversimplification Closely related to the hasty generalization, the oversimplification also represents a jump to a conclusion, in this case by omitting relevant considerations and implying that there is only one cause or solution to a complex issue. "Just say 'no'" was the antidrug battle cry of the 1980s, but avoiding drug use can be much more complicated than just saying no. The "virginity pledge" is an oversimplified solution to the problem of unwanted teenage pregnancy, given how many teenagers need to become educated about safe sex practices, sexually transmitted diseases, and aspects of sexual behavior.

Red herring A diversion intended to distract attention from the real issue under consideration, the red herring is intended to mislead, whether it appears as a false clue in a mystery novel or in an argument: "I cannot go to the doctor for my mammogram until I lose weight"; "I cannot stop smoking until I get through my finals"; "We cannot defeat terrorism while we're involved in the Israeli-Palestinian conflict." The real issue of each of the preceding statements (the importance of getting a mammogram, stopping smoking, or defeating terrorism) is blurred by another issue that, while important, is not the primary one under consideration.

Slippery slope In order to show that an initial claim is unacceptable, the fallacy of the slippery slope states that an unacceptable situation or event is sure to follow from that initial claim: "Confidential personnel meetings will lead to a fascist English department"; "If I make an exception for you, I'll have to make an exception for everyone else"; "People who try marijuana end up using crack cocaine"; "Living wills will lead to putting people down like dogs and cats." We all hear these kinds of slippery slope arguments every day.

Argument and the Rhetorical Situation

Argument is a common part of everyday life. Whether we're explaining why we're ordering a salad and not a cheeseburger for lunch, negotiating to change an airline ticket, or asking our boss to reconsider the company's vacation policy, we're using argument. When we watch Marlo Thomas providing a tour of St. Jude's Children's Hospital and decide to donate money to that charity, when we read a newspaper account of Don Imus's firing and take a stand on whether or not the dismissal was warranted, or when we see those golden arches just off the freeway and decide to stop for a burger, we've responded to an argument. In some way, then, everything's an argument. Every time you transfer meaning or understanding from yourself to another person, you've made a successful argument. And every time you've understood what someone else is saying to you, you've responded to a successful argument. But whether you are the sender or the recipient of an argument, you'll need to be attentive to each element of the rhetorical situation.

Using argument to address an exigence

Whenever you put together an argument, whether on the spur of the moment or after some deliberation, you always start by identifying the exigence that can be resolved in some way. As you know by now, the exigence doesn't have to be a negative problem; it can be as positive as choosing the theme for a winter dance or as banal as picking the toppings for a pizza. During World War II, however, an exigence arose that threatened the lives and livelihoods of many U.S. residents of foreign descent, especially those with German or Japanese ancestry. By Executive Order 9066, signed by President Roosevelt, over 120,000 Japanese-Americans (two-thirds of whom were U.S. citizens) were relocated to internment camps in the western states; they were removed from their homes, businesses, schools, and sometimes their families. It took several months to move all of the people to such camps, and many of them rightfully resisted. The photograph on the following page illustrates an argument that responds to the exigence of this relocation. The argument "I am an American" is especially poignant and, though not ultimately persuasive to the powers that be, effectively addressed the exigence of Mr. Wanto's rhetorical situation.

Thomas Jefferson's response to a political exigence was ultimately successful, as it eventually resulted in the United States of America. In the Declaration of Independence, Jefferson challenges the received belief that

High school at a Japanese internment camp.

monarchs ruled by divine right at the same time as he addresses the exigence of taxation without representation:

> When in the course of human events, it becomes necessary for one people to dissolve the political bands which have connected them with another, and to assume among the powers of the earth, the separate and equal station to which the laws of Nature and of Nature's God entitle them, a decent respect to the opinions of mankind requires that they should declare the causes which impel them to the separation.
>
> We hold these truths to be self-evident, that all men are created equal, that they are endowed by their Creator with certain unalienable rights, that among these are life, liberty and the pursuit of happiness. That to secure these rights, governments are instituted among men, deriving their just powers from the consent of the governed. That whenever any form of government becomes destructive of these ends, it is the right of the people to alter or to abolish it, and to institute new government, laying its foundation on such principles and organizing its powers in such form, as to them shall seem most likely to effect their safety and happiness. Prudence, indeed, will dictate that governments long established should not be changed for light and transient causes; and accordingly all experience hath shewn, that mankind are more disposed to suffer, while evils are sufferable, than to right themselves by abolishing the forms to which they are accustomed. But when a long train of abuses and usurpations, pursuing invariably the same object, evinces a design to reduce them under absolute despotism, it is their right, it is their duty, to throw off such government, and to provide new guards for their future security.
>
> Such has been the patient sufferance of these Colonies; and such is now the necessity which constrains them to alter their former systems of government. The history of the present King of Great Britain is a history of repeated injuries and usurpations, all having in direct object the establishment of an absolute tyranny over these States. To prove this, let facts be submitted to a candid world.
>
> —**Thomas Jefferson,** Declaration of Independence

Closed store of Mr. Wanto, who was relocated to an internment camp.

Jefferson goes on to list abuses of the colonists by the king, protracting the logical appeal of what would become one of the most important political documents in history.

Using argument to address an audience

Whether they transfer understanding or induce a change, successful arguments address the right audience, a rhetorical audience capable of being influenced or of bringing about the desired change. Even though Mr. Wanto's sign didn't prevent his relocation, it did transfer meaning to everyone who saw it, including those who were under orders to take him away. The Declaration of Independence might have failed at inducing a positive change in British governance of the colonies, yet it did influence American colonists to rebel.

Many arguments miss their mark, not because they haven't been aimed toward an appropriate audience (think of weight-loss commercials ignored by the obese, admonitions to stop smoking dismissed by people with lung cancer, and flyers for academic support services tossed in the trash by students who are flunking out of school), but because of constraints of the rhetorical situation that the rhetor cannot predict or adjust (obese people who aren't yet ready to diet, smokers who want to die "happy," and students who have given up). Successful arguments, however, hit their mark, and the savviest rhetors locate the audience that is willing to listen, maybe even to change.

Although his "Letter from Birmingham Jail" circulated broadly, Dr. Martin Luther King, Jr., was responding directly to the eight Birmingham clergymen who had criticized some of the specific activities of the nationwide nonviolent protest movement that King was leading:

> While confined here in the Birmingham city jail, I came across your recent statement calling my present activities "unwise and untimely." Seldom do I pause and answer criticism of my work and ideas. If I sought to answer all of the criticisms that cross my desk, my secretaries would have little time for anything other than such correspondence in the course of the day, and I would have no time for constructive work. But since I feel that you are men of genuine good will and that your criticisms are sincerely set forth, I want to try to answer your statement in what I hope will be patient and reasonable terms.
>
> —**Martin Luther King, Jr.,** "Letter from Birmingham Jail"

King wanted to maintain the support of these eight clergymen as well as the rest of the Southern Christian Leadership Conference, but he wanted them all to understand what he was doing—and why. So he wrote to them, explaining at length his reasons for leading the civil rights movement in the way he was as well as the reasons he would not be taking their advice.

Using argument with a rhetorical purpose

Throughout this chapter, you've seen some of the ways arguments are used to fulfill a rhetorical purpose. In general, arguments can be used to fulfill one of three purposes, though these sometimes overlap: (1) to express or defend a position or an opinion; (2) to question or argue against an established belief or a course of action, or (3) to invite or convince an audience to change an opinion or practice.

Using argument to express or defend a position or an opinion In the following excerpt, controversial feminist Camille Paglia uses argument to express her opinion that feminists (or, rather, feminists not like her) have exaggerated the occurrence of rape:

> Rape is an outrage that cannot be tolerated in civilized society. Yet feminism, which has waged a crusade for rape to be taken more seriously, has put young women in danger by hiding the truth about sex from them.

In dramatizing the pervasiveness of rape, feminists have told young women that before they have sex with a man, they must give consent as explicit as a legal contract's. In this way, young women have been convinced that they have been the victims of rape. On elite campuses in the Northeast and on the West Coast, they have held consciousness-raising sessions, petitioned administrations, demanded inquests. At Brown University, outraged, panicky "victims" have scrawled the names of alleged attackers on the walls of women's rest rooms. What marital rape was to the '70s, "date rape" is to the '90s.

The incidence and seriousness of rape do not require this kind of exaggeration. Real acquaintance rape is nothing new. It has been a horrible problem for women for all of recorded history. Once fathers and brothers protected women from rape. Once the penalty for rape was death. I come from a fierce Italian tradition where, not so long ago, in the motherland, a rapist would end up knifed, castrated, and hung out to dry.

But the old clans and small rural communities have broken down. In our cities, on our campuses far from home, young women are vulnerable and defenseless. Feminism has not prepared them for this. Feminism keeps saying the sexes are the same. It keeps telling women they can do anything, go anywhere, say anything, wear anything. No, they can't. Women will always be in sexual danger.

—**Camille Paglia,** "It's a Jungle Out There"

Paglia is responding to an exigence, one created by feminists "in dramatizing the pervasiveness of rape." Her audience isn't clear—perhaps it is feminists other than herself. But her opinion is clear, and she spends the rest of her essay defending her position that the term *rape* is often wrongly applied to sexual encounters.

Using argument to question or argue against an established belief or a course of action Current events always offer a wide array of arguments against established beliefs or courses of action. Conservative Christians arguing against the consequences of contemporary feminism for traditional family structures, peace activists protesting the escalation of warfare in Afghanistan and Iraq, and vegans questioning the slaughter of farm animals represent just a few of the groups launching verbal and visual arguments against established beliefs or courses of action. PETA (People for the Ethical Treatment of Animals) is one such group. The basis for this activist group's many activities and interests is this argument:

PETA believes that animals deserve the most basic rights—consideration of their own best interests regardless of whether they are useful to humans. Like you, they are capable of suffering and have interests in leading their own lives; therefore, they are not ours to use—for food, clothing, entertainment, or experimentation, or for any other reason.   —**www.peta.org**

As the ads on the following page demonstrate, PETA's ad campaigns are influential, arguing against such practices as the enjoyment of meat or leather clothing and the use of animals for medical or commercial research.

In the following excerpt, prolific writer William F. Buckley, Jr., argues against the established U.S. practice of not complaining, a course of nonaction that he finds irritating if not downright maddening:

A few weeks ago at a large movie theater I turned to my wife and said, "The picture is out of focus." "Be quiet," she answered. I obeyed. But a few minutes

The activist group PETA routinely creates arguments against established beliefs or practices.

later I raised the point again, with mounting impatience. "It will be all right in a minute," she said apprehensively. . . . I waited. It was *just* out of focus—not glaringly out, but out. My vision is 20-20, and I assume that is the vision, adjusted, for most people in the movie house. So, after hectoring my wife throughout the first reel, I finally prevailed upon her to admit that it *was* off, and very annoying. We then settled down, coming to rest on the presumption that: a) someone connected with the management of the theater must soon notice the blur and make the correction; or b) that someone seated near to the rear of the house would

make the complaint in behalf of those of us up front; or c) that—any minute now—the entire house would explode into catcalls and foot stamping, calling dramatic attention to the irksome distortion.

What happened was nothing. The movie ended, as it had begun, *just* out of focus, and as we trooped out, we stretched our faces in a variety of contortions to accustom the eye to the shock of normal focus.

I think it is safe to say that everybody suffered on that occasion. And I think it is safe to assume that everyone was expecting someone else to take the initiative in going back to speak to the manager. And it is probably true even that if we had supposed the movie would run right through the blurred image, someone surely would have summoned up the purposeful indignation to get up out of his seat and file his complaint.

But notice that no one did. And the reason no one did is because we are all increasingly anxious in America to be unobtrusive, we are reluctant to make our voices heard, hesitant about claiming our rights; we are afraid that our cause is unjust, or that if it is not unjust, that it is ambiguous; or if not even that, that it is too trivial to justify the horrors of a confrontation with Authority; we will . . . endure a racking headache before undertaking a head-on, I'm-here-to-tell-you complaint. That tendency to passive compliance, to a heedless endurance, is something to keep one's eyes on—in sharp focus.

—**William F. Buckley, Jr.,** "Why Don't We Complain?"

Many arguments against established beliefs and practices require a monumental effort to marshal, which is why they can be so intimidating to compose. But if you consider the everyday kinds of beliefs and practices that cause your discomfort—whether it is the spyware in the department store dressing rooms or the mechanical "Did you find everything?" as you check out with groceries—you can locate an exigence to which you'd like to respond and about which you have an opinion that can be argued.

Using argument to invite or convince an audience to change an opinion or practice Because your goal is to use rhetoric well and ethically, you won't always be able to convince your audience to change an opinion or practice. Thus, you'll want to learn to be satisfied when they agree to consider your argument and when they understand your position.

Lettuce Lady Kim Hefner might not convince any of us to change our eating practices, but her visual argument gets our attention and maybe even our consideration. Too often, vegetarians have been thought to be old hippies, strict followers of certain religions, or members of health-conscious organizations. But with vegetarianism becoming more common in college communities, celebrity circles, and fine restaurants, its advantages are becoming better understood. Playing on the enlistment poster "Uncle Sam Wants YOU," the advertisement features Hefner in a scant Uncle Sam–like costume, point-

I WANT **YOU** TO GO VEGETARIAN

ing at readers, whom she wants to convert to vegetarianism. She might be able to change their course of action.

When Peter Gomes, Plummer Professor of Christian Morals at Harvard Divinity School, read a report that over 400 incarcerated gay bashers felt that their religious leaders and traditions sanctioned their behavior, he knew he needed to respond. Gomes went straight to the Bible for guidance, and an article in the *New York Times* was the result. Stunned by the *Boston Globe*'s finding that "Christians opposed to political and social equality for homosexuals nearly always appeal to the moral injunctions of the Bible, claiming that Scripture is very clear on the matter and citing verses that support their opinion," Gomes attempted to convince the homophobic Christians to change their opinion:

> Three references from St. Paul are frequently cited (Romans 1:26–2:1, I Corinthians 6:9–11, and I Timothy 1:10). But St. Paul was concerned with homosexuality only because in Greco-Roman culture it represented a secular sensuality that was contrary to his Jewish-Christian spiritual idealism. He was against lust and sensuality in anyone, including heterosexuals. To say that homosexuality is bad because homosexuals are tempted to do morally doubtful things is to say that heterosexuality is bad because heterosexuals are likewise tempted. For St. Paul, anyone who puts his or her interest ahead of God's is condemned, a verdict that falls equally upon everyone.
>
> And lest we forget Sodom and Gomorrah, recall that the story is not about sexual perversion and homosexual practice. It is about inhospitality, according to Luke 10:10–13, and failure to care for the poor, according to Ezekiel 16:49–50: "Behold, this was the iniquity of thy sister Sodom, pride, fullness of bread, and abundance of idleness was in her and in her daughters, neither did she strengthen the hand of the poor and needy." To suggest that Sodom and Gomorrah is about homosexual sex is an analysis of about as much worth as suggesting that the story of Jonah and the whale is a treatise on fishing.
>
> . . . Fortunately, those that speak for the religious right do not speak for all American Christians, and the Bible is not theirs alone to interpret. The same Bible that the advocates of slavery used to protect their wicked self-interests is the Bible that inspired slaves to revolt and their liberators to action.
>
> The same Bible that the predecessors of Mr. Falwell and Mr. Robertson used to keep white churches white is the source of the inspiration of the Rev. Martin Luther King, Jr., and the social reformation of the 1960s.
>
> The same Bible that antifeminists use to keep women silent in the churches is the Bible that preaches liberation to captives and says that in Christ there is neither male nor female, slave nor free.
>
> And the same Bible that on the basis of an archaic social code of ancient Israel and a tortured reading of Paul is used to condemn all homosexuals and homosexual behavior includes metaphors of redemption, renewal, inclusion, and love—principles that invite homosexuals to accept their freedom and responsibility in Christ and demands that their fellow Christians accept them as well.
>
> —**Peter Gomes**, "Homophobic? Re-read Your Bible"

The preceding excerpt may not change a heterosexist's mind; in fact, the *New York Times* in which it appeared might never have made it inside the prisons where the gay bashers are housed. Nevertheless, Gomes makes his case that the Bible does not and never did endorse gay bashing, what he calls our nation's "last acceptable prejudice."

Using argument as a fitting response

When Walker Evans and James Agee put together their book, *Let Us Now Praise Famous Men,* their rhetorical purpose was to call attention to the life of the average tenant farmer as a means for questioning established beliefs about social responsibility and human dignity in the United States during the 1930s. But rather than attacking one federal policy after another, criticizing one rich landowner after another, or exaggerating the physical, emotional, and spiritual suffering of the sharecroppers, the two men used description, narration, and cause-and-effect analysis to carry forward their reasoned and successful argument, an argument rendered visually as well as verbally. Their argument culminated in a book, which would reach many more people than would a government report, a single newspaper column, or a photography exhibition. In over four hundred pages of prose—poems, confessional reveries, imagined and real dialogues, and catalogues and descriptions of possessions, objects, sights, sounds, feelings, smells, and tastes—accompanied by sixty-four pages of stark portraits and photographs, the two talented men devised a fitting response to their exigence.

For example, Agee's disquisition into the significance of overalls (which the sharecroppers pronounce "overhauls") beautifully complements Evans's masterful photograph of the freshly washed, dignified man who wears the garment every day:

> Try . . . to imagine and to know, as against other garments, the difference of their feeling against your body; drawn-on, and bibbed on the whole belly and chest, naked from the kidneys up behind, save for broad crossed straps, and slung by these straps from the shoulders; the slanted pockets on each thigh, the deep square pockets on each buttock; the complex and slanted structures, on the chest, . . . the coldness of sweat when they are young, and their stiffness; their sweetness to the skin and pleasure of sweating when they are old; the thin metal buttons of the fly; the lifting aside of the straps and the deep slipping downward in defecation . . . the swift, simple, and inevitably supine gestures of dressing and of undressing, which, as is less true of any other garment, are those of harnessing and of unharnessing the shoulders of a tired and hard-used animal.
>
> —**James Agee,** *Let Us Now Praise Famous Men*

Agee and Evans's inventive response to the exigence of human suffering—their book—was fitting. And like Roosevelt's New Deal (an innovation in policy), their book was an artistic innovation, a groundbreaking experiment in form that transcended usual photographic and journalistic practices. In fact, Agee wouldn't even use the word *art* to

Let Us Now Praise Famous Men, by Walker Evans and James Agee.

An image from *Let Us Now Praise Famous Men.*

From *Let Us Now Praise Famous Men.*

refer to his contribution to the project; instead he called it a "disease, perhaps a fury" and directed readers to turn Beethoven's Seventh "up loud" and "get down on the floor" if they wanted to understand what it was he had done:

> Jam your ear as close into the loudspeakers as you can get it and stay there, breathing as lightly as possible, and not moving, and neither eating nor smoking nor drinking. . . . You won't hear it nicely. If it hurts you, be glad of it. As near as you will ever get, you are inside the music; not only inside it, you are it; your body is no longer your shape and substance, it is the shape and substance of the music.
>
> —**James Agee,** *Let Us Now Praise Famous Men*

With words and photographs, Agee and Evans meet every expectation of their rhetorical situation.

You are not likely to have to respond to such a monumental problem as the one Agee and Evans tackled. Nevertheless, you'll need to compose fitting responses to a variety of exigencies that call for argument. If you keep in mind the rhetorical purposes of argument and consider the means available to you, you'll expand your options of what you might say, how you might say it, and how best to deliver it in an appropriate medium. In fact, the best feature of argument is its flexibility: it can draw on all the other rhetorical methods of development to achieve its purpose at the same time as it provides a fitting response.

READING A TEXT FOR ARGUMENT

1. Make a list of all the words and phrases in the passages from *Let Us Now Praise Famous Men* that work to fulfill a specific rhetorical purpose. What rhetorical purpose have you identified? Be prepared to share your findings with the rest of the class.

2. What other exigencies might Peter Gomes address if he's using the Bible for his source of support? What controversies arise from various interpretations and readings of the Bible? Where is there common ground in each of these controversies? On your own or with a classmate, prepare a list to share with the rest of the class.

3. Choose one of the visuals in this chapter. How does the image employ the three rhetorical appeals? To what effect? How could it be improved? Be prepared to share your response with the rest of the class.

Using argument as an available means

The means available for delivering an argument are practically limitless, particularly given the ease with which a rhetor can use the other rhetorical methods of development. Visual, verbal, architectural, electronic, musical arguments—all of these can incorporate the features of a successful argument. The means available to you are limited only by your imagination, creativity, and willingness to learn how to deliver your arguments in new ways and from new starting places, employing the rhetorical appeals within the constraints and the resources of your rhetorical situation.

Walker Evans and James Agee understood clearly how best to take advantage of available means. They delivered their argument in book form, visually and verbally. They effectively employed the rhetorical appeals, beginning with ethos. Their professional reputations preceded them into the project, and their commitment to the project, evidenced by their spending four weeks with a poor white tenant farmer's family, established their good will, good moral character, and good sense. The logos of their argument is demonstrated in the detailed manner in which they describe and narrate the lives of these hard-working people and analyze the causes and consequences of human suffering. The emotional appeal hits home in the respectful photographic and verbal portraits of the people and their surroundings:

> The bureau was at some time a definitely middle-class piece of furniture. It is quite wide and very heavy, veneered in gloomy red rich-grained woods, with intricately pierced metal plaques at the handles of the three drawers, and the mirror is at least three feet tall and is framed in machine-carved wood.
>
> The veneer has now split and leafed loose in many places from the yellow soft-wood base; the handles of the three drawers are nearly all deranged and two are gone; the drawers do not pull in and out at all easily.
>
> The mirror is so far corrupted that it is rashed with gray, iridescent in parts, and in all its reflections a deeply sad thin zinc-to-platinum, giving to its framings an almost incalculably ancient, sweet, frail, and piteous beauty, such as may be seen in tintypes of family groups among studio furnishings or heard in nearly exhausted jazz records made by very young, insane, devout men who were to destroy themselves, in New Orleans, in the early nineteen twenties.
>
> —**James Agee**, *Let Us Now Praise Famous Men*

Reflecting the exhausted, devout sharecroppers, the mirror figures as an emotional link among the audience, the authors, and the subjects.

Every rhetor chooses among the available means at his or her disposal. For Agee and Evans the written word and the visual image provided their respective rhetorical resources, which they used to counterbalance the contextual constraints of governmental policies, the Depression, and tenant farmers' living conditions.

USING ARGUMENT IN YOUR WRITING

1. Throughout your schooling, you've read hundreds of arguments—and probably even written some. What was the last writing assignment you completed? Can you identify any argumentative strategies you used in that piece of writing, such as employing rhetorical appeals or establishing common ground? You may find that you were using argument as a means of development without even being aware of doing so.

2. The most important element of a successful argument is the author's interest in the topic. What belief do you hold strongly? Write that belief in one sentence. Next, make a list of the reasons for your belief. What support can you supply for your belief? Finally, write a paragraph about the origin of your belief. Who or what influenced you to believe the way you do?

3. What belief do you hold about the importance of education? Write one sentence stating that belief. What information supports your belief? What information could be used to argue against your belief?

CHECKING OVER AN ARGUMENT

Answering these questions will help you review your own arguments as well as those of your classmates.

✓ What is the topic or issue under examination? How is it arguable? In other words, what exigence does it provide that calls for resolution?

✓ What specific audience can resolve or influence the resolution of that exigence?

✓ What is the purpose of this argument: to express or defend a position or an opinion, to question or argue against an established belief or a course of action, or to invite or convince an audience to change an opinion or practice? How does the purpose relate to the intended audience?

✓ How does the rhetor establish good will, good sense, and good moral character? How does the rhetor establish common ground with the audience?

✓ What claim is the rhetor making? What specific support is provided for that claim? Is the support relevant and accurate?

✓ Can you identify any rhetorical fallacies in the argument? How might you repair those fallacies?

✓ Where and how does the rhetor acknowledge and respond to opposing viewpoints?

✓ How, where, and how well does the rhetor employ pathos in this argument?

✓ What does the rhetor achieve in the conclusion?

✓ Would a visual enhance this argument in any way? How?

Development Strategies

A Guide to Research

Throughout this part of the book, you'll use your knowledge of the rhetorical situation to understand the research process. Chapter 16 will help you use the elements of the rhetorical situation to get started on your research projects. Chapters 17 and 18 contain information on the many different types of sources available to you and where to find them. Chapter 19 provides strategies for managing the research process. Chapter 20 explains how to evaluate and use sources. Chapter 21 provides detailed guidelines on acknowledging sources and formatting research papers, as well as sample student papers.

Clues to Compulsive Collecting

SEPARATING USELESS JUNK FROM OBJECTS OF VALUE

AN INTRIGUING NEW STUDY MAY help researchers understand why some people are compelled to hoard useless objects. Steven W. Anderson, a neurologist, and his colleagues at the University of Iowa examined 63 people with brain damage from stroke, surgery or encephalitis. Before their brains were damaged, none had problems with hoarding, but afterward, nine began filling their houses with such things as old newspapers, broken appliances or boxes of junk mail, despite the intervention of family members.

WHY DO SOME PEOPLE COLLECT USELESS OBJECTS LIKE OLD NEWSPAPERS, BROKEN APPLIANCES AND JUNK MAIL?

These compulsive collectors had all suffered damage to the prefrontal cortex, a brain region involved in decision making, information processing and behavioral organization. The people whose collecting behavior remained normal also had brain damage, but it was instead distributed throughout the right and left hemispheres of the brain.

Anderson posits that the urge to collect derives from the need to store supplies such as food—a drive so basic it originates in the subcortical and limbic portions of the brain. Humans need the prefrontal cortex, he says, to determine what "supplies" are worth hoarding. His study was presented at the annual conference of the Society for Neuroscience.

—*Richard A. Lovett*

---

1. In "Clues to Compulsive Collecting," Richard Lovett describes research first presented by Steven Anderson and his colleagues at a neuroscience conference. After reading this article, write a paragraph or two in which you discuss the article in terms of Lovett's and the original researchers' rhetorical situations. How are they similar? How are they different?

2. In answering question 1, you likely noted significant differences in the rhetorical situations of the article writer and the original researchers, even though their subject matter was the same. In order to prepare for the research you may have to do for college classes, describe a rhetorical situation you might encounter in one of your classes. Explain how research would help you prepare a fitting response.

An Overview of Research

Research is part of our lives. As students, professionals, and citizens, we read about research, we talk about research, and we conduct research. You have read the article by Richard Lovett, talked about it in class, and thought about ways to conduct your own research. When people hear the word *research,* they often think of laboratory experiments, archaeological digs, or hours spent in the library or at the library's Web site. They overlook the ordinary research they do every day as they decide what to buy, how to fix something, how to perform a function on their computer, what books to read, or where to spend their vacation. Research is common to everyone's experience.

When people move to a new place, they must find information about schools, clinics, stores, and other locations of importance or interest. They must also find out about dentists, doctors, veterinarians, and accountants. They obtain the information they need by doing research—that is, by talking with other people, visiting Web sites, and reading brochures and other materials.

Many people do research at work. Business owners must keep abreast of new technology, marketing trends, and changes in the tax code. Doctors must have current information on diagnostic procedures and effective treatments, therapies, and pharmaceuticals. Some types of research that professionals do may be surprising. Librarians, for example, have to know about the latest print materials and information technology, but in order to prepare their operating budgets, they also have to know the costs of items and numbers of library users. The type of research people do in the workplace depends on their jobs, but most professionals consult other people they consider knowledgeable, read materials on specific topics, and visit useful Web sites.

Students, of course, conduct many types of research, starting in elementary school and continuing through college. Their research enables them to prepare lab reports, posters, term papers, oral presentations, and other types of assignments. Some of their research entails laboratory experimentation. Other research takes place in the field, as students conduct surveys, make observations, and attend performances. Much research focuses on written records such as articles and books, government documents, old letters, and personal journals.

Regardless of the form of the research or the context in which it takes place, all research is done in response to an *exigence:* a call or need for more information. Depending on the nature of the exigence, you may or may not have to record the results of your research. Once you obtain the information on which store has the best prices on electronics, you simply go to that store. In contrast, research projects prepared in response to an assignment usually require writing—at all stages of the process. Researchers often freewrite to come up with ideas, create project designs and work plans, take notes, and eventually draft a paper. It is hard to imagine a researcher in an academic setting without a pen, pencil, or keyboard.

For the results of research to be valuable, the process must be taken seriously. Researchers who chase down facts to attach to opinions they already have are doing only superficial research. These researchers are not interested in finding information that may cause them to question their beliefs or that may make their thinking more complicated. Genuine research, on the other hand, involves crafting a good research question and pursuing an answer to it, both of which require patience and care.

Exigence and the Research Question

As you know from reading chapter 3, the starting point for any writing project is determining your exigence—what has prompted you to write. For research assignments, the exigence also includes what has prompted you to look for more information. Once you are sure of your exigence, you can craft a question to guide your research.

To make the most of your time, choose a specific question early in your research process. Having such a question helps you avoid collecting more sources than you can possibly use or finding sources that are only tangentially related. A student who chooses a general topic—say, the separation of church and state—will waste time if he or she neglects to narrow the topic into a question, such as one of the following: What did the framers of the Constitution have in mind when they discussed the separation of church and state? How should the separation of church and state be interpreted in law? Should the Ten Commandments be posted in government buildings? Should the phrase *under God* be removed from the Pledge of Allegiance?

Good questions often arise when you try to relate what you are studying in a course to your own experience. For instance, you may start wondering about the separation of church and state when, after reading about this topic in a history class, you notice the number of times politicians refer to God in their speeches, you remember reciting the phrase *under God* in the Pledge of Allegiance, or you read in the newspaper that a plaque inscribed with the Ten Commandments has been removed from the State House in Alabama. These observations may prompt you to look for more information on the topic. Each observation, however, may give rise to a different question. You will choose the question that interests you the most and that will best help you fulfill the assignment.

To generate research questions, you may find it helpful to return to chapter 3, where you read about two sets of questions: journalists' questions (Who? What? Where? When? Why? How?) and the pentad (questions based on understanding the relationships among act, actor, scene, agency, and purpose). Here are some other kinds of questions that commonly require research:

QUESTIONS ABOUT CAUSES

Why doesn't my college offer athletic scholarships?

What causes power outages in large areas of the country?

Questions about Consequences

What are the consequences of taking antidepressants for a long period of time?

How would the atmosphere in a school change if a dress code were established?

Questions about Processes

How can music lovers prevent corporations from controlling

the development of music?

How does my hometown draw boundaries for school districts?

Questions about Definitions or Categories

How do you know if you are addicted to something?

What kind of test is "the test of time"?

Questions about Values

Should the Makah tribe be allowed to hunt gray whales?

Would the construction of wind farms be detrimental to the environment?

TRICKS OF THE TRADE

If the assignment doesn't specify a topic and you are not sure what you want to write about, you may need some prompting. Consider these questions:

▮ Can you remember an experience that you did not understand fully or that made you feel uncertain? What was it that you didn't understand? What were you unsure of?

▮ What have you observed lately (on television, in the newspaper, on your way to school, or in the student union) that piqued your curiosity? What were you curious about?

▮ What local or national problem have you recently heard or read about and would like to help solve?

▮ Is there anything you find unusual that you would like to explore? Lifestyles? Political views? Religious views?

As you consider which question will most appropriately guide your research, you may find it helpful to discuss your ideas with other people. Research and writing both require a great deal of time and effort, and you will find the tasks more pleasant—and maybe even easier—if you are sincerely interested in your question. Moreover, enthusiasm about your work will motivate you to do the best you can; indifference breeds mediocrity. By talking with other people, you may find out that the question you have chosen is a good one.

On the other hand, you may discover that you need to narrow the question or change it in some other way. You may even realize that the question you initially chose really does not interest you very much. To get a conversation about your ideas started, have someone you are familiar with ask you some of the following questions. You may also use these questions for a focused freewriting exercise.

- Why is it important for you to answer the question? What is the answer's significance for you? How will answering the question help you? How is the question related to your exigence?
- Will the answer to your question require serious research? (A genuine research question does not have a simple or obvious answer.)
- What types of research might help you answer your question? (You may already have some ideas; for other ideas, see chapter 17.) Will you be able to carry out these types of research in the amount of time you have been given?

Research and Audience

In part 1, you learned that a fitting response successfully satisfies your audience. In order to meet the expectations of your readers, you must know something about them. First, you must find out who your audience is. If you are writing in response to a course assignment, your instructor may define your audience for you (usually, it is the instructor and your classmates). However, sometimes your instructor may ask you to imagine a different audience so that you have experience writing for a wider range of people. For example, your instructor might ask you to write a letter to the editor of your local paper. In this case, your audience is much broader. It still comprises your instructor and classmates, but it also includes the editor of the newspaper as well as all the newspaper's readers.

As your writing career progresses, the number of audiences you write for will increase. You may easily name your audience—college students, science teachers, mechanical engineers, pediatricians, or the general public—but to make sure that you satisfy any audience you choose to address, you need to go beyond labels. When you do research, you must take into account what types of sources your audience will expect you to use and which sources they will find engaging, convincing, or entertaining.

Keep in mind that when you write for an audience you are joining an ongoing conversation. To enter that conversation, you need to pay attention to what's being said and who the participants are. You can begin by reading the sources the participants in the conversation use. By reading what they read, you'll learn what information is familiar to them and what information may need to be explained in detail.

Both the brief article from *Bostonia,* Boston University's alumni magazine, and the Web page for the Pucker Gallery (on page 500) contain information about the artist Joseph Ablow. In the *Bostonia* article, the abbreviation CFA is not explained, because the intended audience, alumni of Boston University, will know that it refers to the College of Fine Arts. If you were writing an article for an alumni magazine, you too would be able to use abbreviations and acronyms

Ablow's Objets d'Art

Large Still Life Frieze, *oil on canvas, 32"x 66", 1986.* Photograph by S. Petegorsky

IN A LECTURE this fall at Amherst College, Joseph Ablow described a major change in his artistic direction in the late 1950s. He had been working on large, classically inspired themes for a decade and "something did not feel right."

"My subjects no longer held much meaning for me," said Ablow, a CFA professor emeritus of art, "and I began to realize that painting and inventing from memory had left me visually parched. It was obvious to me that I had to start over."

The reevaluation pulled him back to the studio, where, he says, "simply as exercises, I returned to the subject of still life," something he had avoided since art school. "But it was not long before the motley collection of objects I had assembled began quietly to organize themselves into configurations that suggested unexpected pictorial possibilities to me.

"I soon discovered that these objects may be quiet, but that did not mean that they remained still. What was to have been a subject that suggested ways of studying the look of things within a manageable and concentrated situation became an increasingly involved world that could

be surprisingly disquieting and provocative. I may have been the one responsible for arranging my cups and bowls on the tabletops, but that did not ensure that I was in control of them.

"The ginger jars and the compote dishes were real, particular, and palpable and yet had no inherent significance. Their interest or importance would be revealed only in the context of a painting."

Born in 1928, Ablow studied with Oskar Kokoschka, Ben Shahn, and Karl Zerbe. He earned degrees from Bennington and Harvard and taught at Boston University from 1963 until 1995. He is currently a visiting artist at Amherst College, which hosted the exhibition of his paintings that is coming to BU.

Still lifes painted over some thirty-five years highlight Joseph Ablow: A Retrospective, *from January 13 through March 5 at the Sherman Gallery, 775 Commonwealth Avenue. Hours are Tuesday through Friday, 11 a.m. to 5 p.m., Saturday and Sunday, 1 to 5 p.m. There will be an opening reception on Thursday, January 15, from 6 to 8 p.m.* ◆

Pucker Gallery

HOME

EXHIBITIONS

ARTISTS

DIRECTOR'S
CHOICE

SHOP AT
THE GALLERY

PUBLICATIONS

ABOUT US

JOSEPH ABLOW

Represented by Pucker Gallery since 1979

BORN: 1928 in Salem, Massachusetts
RESIDES: Brookline, Massachusetts

Most Recent Exhibition:
Familiar Objects 21 April 2001 - 23 May 2001

Joe Ablow was born in Salem, Massachusetts and has lived, worked and taught in the Boston area his entire life. After studying painting at the School of the Museum of Fine Arts, Boston, receiving his Bachelors from Bennington College and his Masters from Harvard University, Ablow continued his instruction in painting with names such as Oskar Kokoschka and Ben Shahn. In addition to his own exhibitions, Ablow has been a professor at Boston University for thirty-five years and written countless academic articles on Art in the Twentieth Century.

Joseph Ablow
In the Balance, 2001
Oil on Canvas
34 x 36"
JA194

Joseph Ablow
Gathering Place, 2001
Oil on Canvas
40 x 50"
JA172

familiar to those who attended that college or university. However, if your audience were broader, such abbreviations and acronyms would have to be explained the first time you used them. The same criteria can be used to make decisions about content. If you were researching one of Joseph Ablow's still life paintings, you would find that sources on Ablow's work do not define what a still life painting is; the authors of these sources assume that their readers are familiar with the term. However, if you were writing for readers who knew next to nothing about painting, you would provide a definition for the term.

TRICKS OF THE TRADE

To determine which sources your audience will find authoritative, study any bibliographies that you encounter in your research. If a source is mentioned on several bibliographic lists, the source is likely considered authoritative. Also, the bibliographies of sources you find useful can direct you to other relevant sources.

Readers of an academic research paper expect the author to be knowledgeable. You can demonstrate your knowledge through the types of sources you use and the ways you handle them. Because you aren't likely to have established credibility as an expert on the topic you are researching, you'll usually have to depend on the credibility of the sources you use. Once you have done enough research to understand your audience, you'll be better able to select sources that will give you credibility. For example, to persuade your readers of the value of a vegetarian diet, you could choose among sources written by nutritionists, ethicists, religious leaders, and animal rights proponents. Your decision would be based on which kinds of sources your audience would find most credible.

Readers of an academic research paper also expect the author to be critical. They want to be assured that an author can tell whether the source information is accurate or deceptive, whether its logic is strong or weak, and whether its conclusions are justifiable. Your readers may accept your use of a questionable source as long as you show why it is problematic. You will learn ways of establishing your credibility and demonstrating your critical abilities in chapter 20.

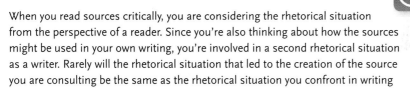

Wait a Minute . . .

When you read sources critically, you are considering the rhetorical situation from the perspective of a reader. Since you're also thinking about how the sources might be used in your own writing, you're involved in a second rhetorical situation as a writer. Rarely will the rhetorical situation that led to the creation of the source you are consulting be the same as the rhetorical situation you confront in writing for a class. Of course, there may be overlap, particularly in audience, but the exigence and purpose of the two pieces of writing are likely to be different.

Research and Purpose

In chapter 1, you saw how your rhetorical audience and your rhetorical purpose are interconnected. They cannot be separated. In general, your rhetorical purpose is to have an impact on your audience; more specifically, your aim may be to entertain them, to inform them, to explain something to them, or to influence them to do something. Research can help you achieve any of these purposes. For example, if you are writing a research paper on the roots of humor for a psychology class, your primary purpose is to inform. You may want to analyze a few jokes, in order to show how their construction can incite laughter, but you'll need research to support your claim. Your audience will be more inclined to believe you if you show them, say, experimental results indicating that people routinely find certain incidents funny.

Writers of research papers commonly define their rhetorical purposes in the following ways:

■ *To inform an audience.* The researcher reports current thinking on a specific topic, including opposing views but not siding with any particular one.

Example: To inform the audience of current guidelines for developing a city park

To analyze and synthesize information and then offer tentative solutions to a problem. The researcher analyzes and synthesizes information on a subject (for example, an argument, a text, an event, a technique, or a statistic), looking for points of agreement and disagreement and for gaps in coverage. Part of the research process consists of finding out what other researchers have already written about the subject. After presenting the analysis and synthesis, the researcher offers possible ways to address the problem.

Example: To analyze and synthesize various national health-care proposals

To persuade an audience or to issue an invitation to an audience. The researcher states a position and backs it up with data, statistics, texts illustrating a point, or supporting arguments found through research. The researcher's purpose is to persuade or invite readers to take the same position.

Example: To persuade people to vote for a congressional candidate

Often, these purposes co-exist in the same piece of writing. A researcher presenting results from an original experiment or study, for instance, must often achieve all of these purposes. In the introduction to a lab report, the researcher might describe previous work done in the area and identify a research niche—an area needing research. The researcher then explains how his or her current study will help fill the gap in existing research. The body of the text is informative, describing the materials used, explaining the procedures followed, and presenting the results. In the conclusion, the researcher may choose, given the results of the experiment or study, to persuade the audience to take some action (for example, give up smoking, eat fewer carbohydrates, or fund future research).

The sources you find through research can help you achieve your purpose. If your purpose is to inform, you can use the work of established scholars to enhance your credibility. If your purpose is to analyze and synthesize information, sources you find can provide not only data for you to work on but also a backdrop against which to highlight your own originality or your special research niche. If your purpose is to persuade, you can use sources to support your assertions and to counter the assertions of others.

ANALYZING THE RHETORICAL SITUATION

Read the following introductory paragraphs to a research article by Timothy Quinn. Then try to determine the author's exigence, audience, and purpose(s).

Coyotes (*Canis latrans*) are becoming increasingly common in human modified habitats throughout North America (Atkinson and Shackleton 1991, MacCracken 1982). One possible explanation for this trend is that human-dominated areas produce abundant food sources for coyotes. Coyotes living in urban habitats have relatively small home ranges (Atkinson and Shackleton 1991, Shargo 1988), which may indicate abundant food sources. However, little is known about the diet of coyotes in these areas. MacCracken's (1982) description of the annual diet of coyotes in residential

Research

habitats was based on a small number of scats ($n = 97$) collected during a single month. Atkinson and Shackleton (1991) described the diet of coyotes in an area that was mostly agricultural (>50% of the study area) and Shargo's (1988) description of urban coyote diet was based on 22 scats. Additionally, none of these studies looked at diet as a function of human density.

Coyotes may play an important role in human modified landscapes. Soulé et al. (1988) suggested that coyotes may reduce the abundance of house cats (*Felis catus*) and other small mammalian carnivores that prey on songbirds and thus indirectly contribute to the maintenance of native avifauna. My objectives were to document the annual diet of coyotes in three types of urban habitat of western Washington and to qualitatively assess how coyote diets changed as a function of land use patterns and human density.

—**Timothy Quinn,** "Coyote (*Canis latrans*) Food Habits
in Three Urban Habitat Types of Western Washington"

Research and a Fitting Response

Like any kind of writing you do, your research report needs to address the rhetorical situation. There are many different kinds of research, just as there are many different ways to present research findings. Shaping a fitting response means considering the following kinds of questions:

- *Is your researched response appropriate to the problem?* The focus and thus the kind of research called for (library, Internet, naturalistic, laboratory, or some combination of these), depend on the nature of the problem. Engineers studying the question of how to prevent future natural disasters from causing the kind of damage wrought in New Orleans by Hurricane Katrina in 2005 would need to be sure their research focused on environmental and geographical conditions specific to that area. Research on the success of levees built along the Danube in Europe might not be applicable. The researchers would also likely need to combine many different kinds of research in order to determine the best method of prevention.

- *Is your researched response delivered in a medium that will reach its intended audience?* Writers presenting research findings want to be sure their work finds its way into the right hands. Engineers researching the issue of how best to rebuild the levees in New Orleans could certainly summarize their findings in a letter to the editor of the New Orleans *Times Picayune*. However, if they wanted approval from a government agency for future work, they would likely need to present the research in a document addressed directly to that agency, such as a written application for funding or a proposal.

- *Will your researched response successfully satisfy the intended audience?* Research papers in different academic disciplines have different content and formats. To help make sure their audience will be satisfied, researchers take care to notice the research methods used in the discipline and deliver writing that is presented and documented according to the accepted style of the discipline. (For information on different kinds of documentation styles, see chapter 21.)

As always, a fitting response must also be considered in terms of the available means.

Research and Constraints and Resources

In chapter 2, you learned how the means available to you for responding are shaped by both the *constraints* (obstacles or limits) and the *resources* (positive influences) of the rhetorical situation. In reviewing the brief *Psychology Today* article that opened this chapter, you saw how one writer, Richard Lovett, worked within specific constraints and resources. You may have identified the primary elements of the rhetorical situation, noting constraints such as the need to deliver complex and specialized information from the field of neurology to readers of a popular magazine. In addressing this constraint, Lovett made allowances for his readers' knowledge of how the brain works by defining unfamiliar terms (*prefrontal cortex,* for example). You may also have noted some of the resources available to Lovett in writing for this kind of publication. The image that accompanies his text is a resource that allows readers to absorb the topic at a glance, while the pull-quote (the quotation in large type in the middle of the article) makes the scientists' research question explicit.

As a researcher in an academic setting, you are no doubt aware that many of your rhetorical situations share various constraints. For instance, an academic research assignment usually involves some kind of specifications from an instructor. Following are some common constraints for such writing assignments:

- *Expertise.* As a student, you rely to some degree on documenting what others have said in order to build credibility.
- *Geography.* Although the Internet gives researchers unprecedented access to materials not available locally, most students are still somewhat constrained by what's close at hand. A student at the University of Kansas researching protest materials used during the civil rights movement would have much easier access to primary documents (such as posters, flyers, and newsletters) housed in that university's special collections than would a student at Eastern Connecticut University.
- *Time.* In most cases, your research will be subject to a time limit. Your readers—whether they are instructors, colleagues, or other decision makers—need to see your research before it goes out of date and before the deadline to make a decision (about what action to take or what grade to assign) has passed.

Constraints such as these can, however, suggest resources. What primary documents might you have access to in your geographical location? What unique opportunities do you have for reaching your audience that a recognized expert in the field might not have? Can working within a particular time frame provide motivation?

Of course, each rhetorical situation is different. Every time you begin research, you'll face a new set of constraints and resources. To participate effectively in an ongoing conversation, you'll need to identify specific resources to help you manage your particular set of constraints.

ANALYZING THE RHETORICAL SITUATION

Recall a possible research question mentioned earlier in this chapter: should the Ten Commandments be posted in government buildings? Suppose you were going to undertake research on this question as preparation for writing a letter to the editor of your local newspaper. What constraints and resources would this rhetorical situation present?

British Cool on Hot Tea

But Turkish steeps climb

There's less time for teatime in the U.K. these days. Historically the British ranked as the world's leading tea drinkers, but rushed lifestyles—along with a new thirst for alternative beverages—have caused their consumption of tea to plummet in recent years.

According to Datamonitor, a London-based business information firm, the British consumed 4.94 pounds of tea per person in 2002. That amounts to about 1,100 cups—down from 1,300 in 1997. Datamonitor analyst John Band points to several reasons for the trend. Younger British consumers are drinking more iced tea and trendy specialty coffees. They tend to dismiss hot steeped tea as old-fashioned, slow to prepare, and inconvenient to drink on the run. And although they are buying more herbal, fruit, and green teas, consumption of these teas is minuscule compared to black tea, the mainstay of the traditional "cuppa."

Now the world champion tea drinkers are the Turks, whose tea consumption in 2002 came to 5.05 pounds per person. Turkish custom calls for endless small servings (above). A tea-loving Turk can knock back more than 20 tiny glasses of the hot brew daily. Turkish coffee may be world famous, but inside Turkey tea is more popular. "There's a saying in my country," says Turkish tea authority Pelin Aylangan. "Conversations without tea are like a night sky without the moon."

—*Margaret G. Zackowitz*

2002 Tea Totals
(All types of tea, per person)

Turkey	5.05 pounds
U.K.	4.94 pounds
Ireland	3.33 pounds
Hong Kong	3.24 pounds
Poland	2.67 pounds
Morocco	2.60 pounds
Russia	2.60 pounds
Egypt	2.47 pounds
Israel	2.38 pounds

1. Why do you think Margaret G. Zackowitz (and the editors at *National Geographic*) decided to use a photograph and a list of statistics with the article "British Cool on Hot Tea"? What kind of research do you think she and her editors did to prepare this article and the accompanying graphics? In other words, what might they have read or observed, whom might they have questioned, and so on? If you wanted to check their facts, what would you do?

2. Think back to a research paper you wrote. What kind of research did you conduct for that project? Where did you go to find your sources? Given more time and more resources, what additional kinds of research might you have done?

Sources for Research

Although the library will probably play an important role in your research, it often will not be the only location in which you conduct research. During the research process, you might find yourself at home using the Internet, in your instructor's office getting suggestions for new sources, or even at the student union taking notes on what you observe about some aspect of student behavior. More than likely, the authors of the sources you gather did not confine themselves to one particular kind of research either—or do it all in one particular location. Responding to their own rhetorical situations, the authors of your sources specified a goal for their research, a group of readers who might be interested in their findings, and the type of document that would best express their thoughts. Based on their purpose, audience, and genre, the authors determined what kinds of research would be most suitable. Like the authors of your sources, you need to consider your rhetorical situation when determining which kinds of research to conduct. In order to make effective decisions, you need to know what kinds of research you will be able to do at the library and on the Internet. (Research in the field, another option, is covered in the next chapter.)

Library and Internet research continue to evolve, as librarians find new ways to make emerging research technologies more accessible and scholars and other authors find new ways to use the Internet to deliver information. In general, though, the types of sources available through the library and the Internet can be broken down into three main categories: books, periodicals, and online and audiovisual sources.

Books

Three types of books are often consulted in the research process. **Scholarly books** are written by scholars for other scholars in order to advance knowledge of a certain subject. Most include original research. Before being published, these books are reviewed by experts in the field (in a process referred to as a peer review). **Trade books** may also be written by scholars, though they may be authored by journalists or freelance writers as well. But the audience and purpose of trade books differ from those of scholarly books. Rather than addressing other scholars, authors of trade books write to inform a popular audience, often about research that has been done by others; thus, trade books are usually **secondary sources**—as opposed to **primary sources,** which contain original research. **Reference books** such as encyclopedias and dictionaries provide factual information. Reference books often contain short articles written and reviewed by experts in the field. The audience for these secondary sources includes both veteran scholars and those new to a field of study.

Periodicals

Periodicals include scholarly journals, magazines, and newspapers. Because these materials are published more frequently than books, the information they contain is more recent. Like scholarly books, **scholarly journals** contain original research (they are primary sources) and address a narrow, specialized audience. Many scholarly journals have the word *journal* in their names: examples are *Journal of Business Communication* and *Consulting Psychology Journal*. **Magazines** and **newspapers** are generally written by staff writers for the general public. These secondary sources carry a combination of news stories, which are intended to be objective, and essays, which reflect the opinions of editors or guest contributors. Both national newspapers (such as the *New York Times* and the *Washington Post*) and regional or local newspapers may have articles, letters, and editorials of interest to researchers.

Online and audiovisual sources

Books, journals, magazine articles, and newspaper articles can all be found online. But when you read documents on Web sites, created specifically for access by computer, you need to determine who is responsible for the site, why the site was established, and who the target audience is. To find answers to these questions, you can first check the domain name, which is at the end of the main part of the Internet address. This name will give you clues about the site. An Internet address with the domain name **.com** (for commerce) tells you that the Web site is associated with a profit-making business. The domain name **.edu** indicates that a site is connected to an educational institution. Web sites maintained by the branches or agencies of a government have the domain name **.gov**. Nonprofit organizations such as Habitat for Humanity and National Public Radio have **.org** as their domain name.

You can also find out about the nature of a Web site by clicking on navigational buttons such as "About Us" or "Vision." Here is an excerpt from a page titled "About NPR" on the National Public Radio Web site:

WHAT IS NPR?

NPR is an internationally acclaimed producer and distributor of noncommercial news, talk, and entertainment programming. A privately supported, not-for-profit, membership organization, NPR serves more than 770 independently operated, noncommercial public radio stations. Each member station serves local listeners with a distinctive combination of national and local programming.

WAIT A MINUTE . . .

Although it was once the case (and not so long ago!) that most sources accessed online were less reliable than those found in print, the difference is becoming less pronounced. Reputable scholarly (peer-reviewed) journals are found online, and personal Web log entries (blogs) are being collected and published in books. It's generally still the case, however, that you'll locate the scholarly journals you need at your library or through your library's subscription service (such as LexisNexis). Likewise, standards for print publication are still higher than those for the Internet—after all, anyone can put up a Web site on any topic whatsoever, whereas most print materials have met a minimum set of standards.

The most common audiovisual sources are documentaries, lectures, and radio and television interviews. **Documentary films and television programs** are much like trade books and magazines. They are created for a popular audience, with the purpose of providing factual information, usually of a political, social, or historical nature. **Lectures** generally take place at universities or in public auditoriums. Lectures given in a university setting are usually more technical or scholarly than those given in a public auditorium. Lecturers, who are usually experts in their field of study, deliver prepared speeches on a variety of topics. Sometimes lectures are like editorials in that the creator's perspective is presented in high profile. **Interviews** are a special type of conversation in which a reporter elicits responses from someone recognized for his or her status or accomplishments. Interviews are aired for a general audience, with the purpose of providing information about the interviewee's achievements or about his or her views on a specific issue.

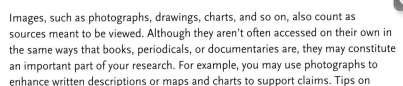

WAIT A MINUTE . . .

Images, such as photographs, drawings, charts, and so on, also count as sources meant to be viewed. Although they aren't often accessed on their own in the same ways that books, periodicals, or documentaries are, they may constitute an important part of your research. For example, you may use photographs to enhance written descriptions or maps and charts to support claims. Tips on locating still images will be provided later in this chapter.

Finding Sources in Print and Online

In the first part of this chapter, you learned about the different types of sources available to you. Once you have a basic understanding of the genre, audience, and purpose of potential sources, you'll find it easier to select your sources. For example, for an advanced course in your discipline, you'll want to consult primary sources, such as online or printed journal articles that present original research. However, if you have chosen a topic that is brand new to you, it may be more productive to consult secondary sources along with primary sources, as the primary sources may contain so much technical terminology that you might misunderstand the content. In this section, you'll learn how to find different types of sources in your library and online.

Finding books

The easiest way to find books on a topic is to consult your library's online catalog. Once you are logged on, navigate your way to the Web page with search boxes similar to those shown on the following page. An author search or title search is useful when you already have a particular author or title in mind. When a research area

Keyword Search

Subject headings:		Find it
Author (last name first):		Find it
Title:		Find it
Journal or serial title:		Find it

Search boxes from a library online catalog.

is new to you, you can find many sources by doing either a keyword search or a subject search. For a keyword search, choose a word or phrase that you think is likely to be found in titles or notes in the catalog's records.

An advanced search page such as the one on the facing page allows the user to specify a language, a location in the library, a type of book (or a type of material other than a book), how the results should be organized, a publisher, and a date of publication. A keyword search page also provides some recommendations for entering words. By using a word or part of a word followed by asterisks, you can find all sources that have that word or word part, even when suffixes have been added. For example, if you entered *environment*, the search would return not only sources with *environment* in the title but also sources whose titles included *environments, environmental,* or *environmentalist.* This shortening technique is called **truncation.** You can enter multiple words by using operators such as *and* or *or.* You can exclude words by using *and not.* When you enter multiple words, you can require that they be close to each other by using *near*; if you want to specify their proximity, you can use *within,* followed by a number indicating the greatest number of words that may separate them.

Subject searches in most libraries are based on categories published by the Library of Congress. You may be able to find sources by entering words familiar to you. However, if your search does not yield any results, ask a reference librarian for a subject-heading guide or note the subject categories that accompany the search results for sources you have already found.

Once you locate a source, write down its call number. The call number corresponds to a specific location in the library's shelving system, usually based on the classification system of the Library of Congress. Keys to the shelving system are usually posted on the walls of the library, but staff members will also be able to help you find sources.

In addition to using your library's online catalog, you can also search books online. Over 20,000 free books are listed on the University of Pennsylvania's Online Books Page (onlinebooks.library.upenn.edu). To find a book, though, you'll need to know the author's name or the book's title. Several commercial Web sites offer subject searches for books, but you have to pay to download or order the books you find at these sites.

TRICKS OF THE TRADE

Amazon.com has a feature called Search Inside!, which allows a reader to search for keywords inside a virtual text. If the search locates the keywords, the reader can then preview the relevant pages of the text. Researchers can use such a search-and-preview feature to locate books unavailable locally, which they may want either to purchase or to order from an interlibrary loan service.

Type the WORD(S) you want, then click Submit Search

Language: ANY

Material Type: ANY

Book/Serial: ANY

Location: ANY

Search and Sort: Date

Publisher:

Year: After _____ and Before _____

Search

SIMPLE SEARCH   START OVER

	Type in Words to search:	EXAMPLES
ADJACENCY	Multiple words are searched together as one phrase.	United States supreme court
TRUNCATION	Words may be right-hand truncated using an asterisk. Use a single asterisk * to truncate from 1-5 characters. Use a double asterisk ** for open-ended truncat ion.	environment* polic* fyodor dost**
OPERATORS	Use "and" or "or" to specify multiple words in any field, any order. Use "and not" to exclude words. Parentheses group words together when using Boolean operators.	(annotated bibliography) and child* (alaska or canada) and (adventure and not vacation)
PROXIMITY	Use "near" to specify words close to each other, in any order. Use "within #" to specify terms which occur within # words of each other in the record.	California near university america within 3 econom*

Finding articles

Your library's online catalog lists the titles of periodicals (journals, magazines, and newspapers); however, it does not provide the titles of individual articles within these periodicals. The best strategy for finding print articles is to use an electronic database. Similar to an online catalog, a database allows you to search for sources by author, title, subject, keyword, and other features. Because so much information is available, databases focus on specific subject areas.

You can access your library's databases from a computer in the library or, if you have a password, via an Internet link from a computer located elsewhere. Libraries subscribe to various database services, but these are some of the most common:

OCLC FirstSearch or EBSCOhost: Contains articles and other types of records (for example, electronic books and DVDs) on a wide range of subjects.

ProQuest: Provides access to major newspapers such as the *New York Times* and the *Wall Street Journal* and to consumer and scholarly periodicals in areas including business, humanities, literature, and science.

Lexis Academic Universe: Includes articles on business, legal, and medical topics and on current events.

To find sources through a database, you can use some of the same strategies you learned for navigating an online catalog. However, search pages often differ, so there is no substitute for hands-on experimentation. Your library may use a general database, such as OCLC FirstSearch or EBSCOhost. The first box on the EBSCOhost search page asks you to specify a subject area. Just underneath that box is a drop-down menu that lets you choose among several databases: including ERIC (Educational Resources Information Center), MLA (Modern Language Association), and PsycINFO (Psychology Information). After you choose the particular database you would like to search, you can search by keyword, author, title, source, year, or a combination of these attributes. You click on the question-

The EBSCOhost database allows you to search various smaller databases, such as ERIC.

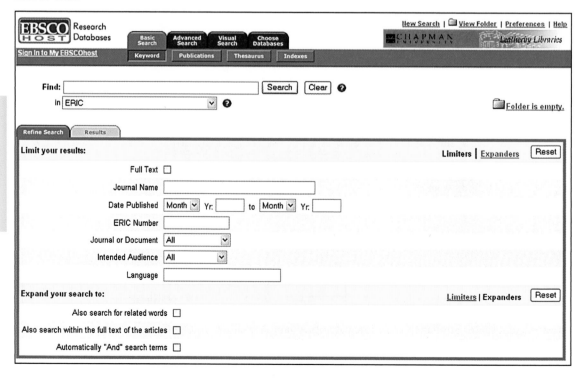

mark icon to the right of the search entry box to get directions for searching according to that attribute. In the Refine Search menu, you can click on a checkbox to limit a search to full texts only. In this case, your search will bring back only sources that include the complete text of an article, which can be downloaded and printed. Otherwise, the database search generally yields the source's bibliographic information and an **abstract,** which is a short summary of an article's content. To find the full text, you note the basic bibliographic information and then look up that book or periodical in the library's online catalog, as described earlier.

TRICKS OF THE TRADE

Although most researchers use databases to find current articles, databases contain other types of information. LexisNexis, for example, provides the following kinds of reference material:

- Biographical information on politicians and other public figures
- Facts and statistics about countries and states
- Polls and surveys conducted by the Roper Center for Public Opinion Research
- Quotations on a range of topics
- A world almanac

Finally, some periodicals are available online. Highwire is a service that lists many science journals that offer free issues; you can find this list by going to highwire.stanford.edu/lists/freeart.dtl. Global Development Network lists journals from a wide range of academic disciplines at www.gdnet.org. Online articles are not always free, however. Be sure to check for subscription services that are available through your library's Web site before paying for an archived article on a newspaper's home page. You might save yourself a good deal of money!

Finding images

Internet and database searches yield all kinds of images for writers to choose from. You can search for images on the Web by using a search engine such as Google, Ditto, or Yahoo. Because other types of searches are also available, be sure to specify that you are looking for images—usually by clicking on a button. Also consider visiting the Web sites of specific libraries, museums, and government agencies such as the Library of Congress, the Smithsonian Institute, and the U.S. Census Bureau; they often have databases of special collections.

Once you find an image that suits your purpose, download it from the Web site onto your desktop by right-clicking on the image and selecting Save Image As (or Save This Image As). To insert the image from your desktop into your paper, use the Insert command from your word processor's pull-down menu. (Some programs may allow you to drag the image into your text.) If you need to resize the image you have chosen, click on its corners and drag your mouse to enlarge it or reduce it.

The last step in using an image is to give credit to its creator and, if necessary, acquire permission to use it. If you are not publishing your paper in print or online, fair-use laws governing reproduction for educational purposes might allow you to use the image without permission. If you are uploading your paper to a Web site or publishing it in any other way, determine whether the image is copyrighted; if so, you'll have to contact its creator for permission to use it and then include a credit line underneath the image, after the caption.

Keep in mind that before you decide to include an image in your paper, you should be sure to identify your purpose for doing so. Avoid using images as mere decoration.

Finding online and audiovisual sources

On the Internet, you'll find not only text and image files but also audio and video files. To find information relevant to your project, you can use search engines. The following are commonly used search engines:

Ask.com	www.ask.com
Google	www.google.com
WebCrawler	webcrawler.com
Yahoo!	www.yahoo.com

When using a search engine for research, you'll probably want to check the Help links to learn about advanced search options. Using these options will allow you to weed out results that are not of interest to you. Advanced searches are performed in much the same way with search engines as they are with online catalogs and databases. You can specify words or phrases, how close words should be to each other, which words should be excluded, and whether the search should return longer versions of truncated words.

Meta-search engines are also available. *Meta* means "transcending" or "more comprehensive." Meta-search engines check numerous search engines, including those listed above. Try these for starters:

Dogpile	www.dogpile.com
Mamma metasearch	www.mamma.com
MetaCrawler	www.metacrawler.com

Although searching the Internet is a popular research technique, it is not always the most appropriate technique. Search engines cover only the portion of the Internet that allows free access. You will not find library books or database materials using a search engine because library and database services are available only to paid subscribers (students fall into this category). If you do decide to use the Internet, remember that no one search engine covers all of it, and surprisingly little overlap occurs when different search engines are used to find

Research

information on the same topic. Thus, using more than one search engine is a good idea. (See chapter 20 for help in evaluating Web sites.)

Sometimes when you click on a link, you end up at a totally different Web site. You can keep track of your location by looking at the Internet address, or URL, at the top of your screen. URLs generally include the following information: server name, domain name, directory and perhaps subdirectory, file name, and file type.

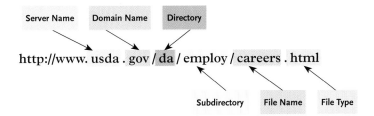

Be sure to check the server and domain names whenever you are unsure of your location.

USING RESEARCH IN YOUR WRITING

Using the same keywords, perform a database search and then a Web search. For each type of search, print the first screen of results you get. Compare the two printouts, explaining how the results of the two searches differ.

Finding government documents

You can find government documents by using library databases such as Marcive and Lexis Academic Universe. In addition, the following Web sites are helpful:

FedWorld Information Network	www.fedworld.gov
Government Printing Office	www.gpoaccess.gov
U.S. Courts	www.uscourts.gov

Finding other sources

You have learned how to find books, articles, images, Web sources, and government documents. You may be interested in still other sources. General encyclopedias and dictionaries such as the *Encyclopedia Britannica* and the *American Heritage Dictionary* provide basic information on many topics. Specialized encyclopedias and dictionaries cover topics in greater depth. In addition to overviews of topics, they also include definitions of technical terminology, discussions of major issues, and bibliographies of related works. Specialized encyclopedias and dictionaries exist for all major disciplines. Here is just a small sampling:

Art	*Grove Dictionary of Art, Encyclopedia of Visual Art*
Biology	*Concise Encyclopedia of Biology*
Chemistry	*Concise Macmillan Encyclopedia of Chemistry, Encyclopedia of Inorganic Chemistry*
Computers	*Encyclopedia of Computer Science and Technology*
Economics	*Fortune Encyclopedia of Economics*
Education	*Encyclopedia of Higher Education, Encyclopedia of Educational Research*
Environment	*Encyclopedia of the Environment*
History	*Dictionary of American History, New Cambridge Modern History*
Literature	*Encyclopedia of World Literature in the 20th Century*
Music	*New Grove Dictionary of Music and Musicians*
Philosophy	*Routledge Encyclopedia of Philosophy, Encyclopedia of Applied Ethics*
Psychology	*Encyclopedia of Psychology, Encyclopedia of Human Behavior*
Religion	*Encyclopedia of Religion*
Social sciences	*International Encyclopedia of the Social Sciences*
Women's studies	*Women's Studies Encyclopedia, Encyclopedia of Women and Gender*

You can find these kinds of sources by doing a title search of your library's online catalog. For other specialized encyclopedias, contact a reference librarian or consult *Kister's Best Encyclopedias*.

Most libraries have special collections that you might also find useful, such as art collections, including drawings and paintings; audio and video collections, including records, audiotapes, CDs, videotapes, and DVDs; and computer resources, usually consisting of programs that combine text, audio, and video. You can find these resources by navigating through your library's Web site or by asking a reference librarian for help.

1. You may have used a U-Scan machine at the supermarket. Even if your local store doesn't have a machine that allows customers to check out their groceries by themselves, you're no doubt familiar with various technologies designed to make our hectic lives a little easier by making routine tasks more efficient. Take a moment to list several such technologies that you've encountered recently.

2. Choose one item on your list and consider its effect(s): What or whom does it replace? How is it changing human behavior? To take this activity further, go to a place where the technology is in use. Observe the scene for twenty minutes or so, noting effects of the technology on human behavior. Do your observations differ from your assumptions? If so, what is unexpected or surprising?

Basic Principles of Naturalistic Study

By now, you are familiar with the rhetorical situation and how it supports reading, writing, speaking—and research. In this chapter, you'll apply your knowledge of the rhetorical situation to develop an understanding of a local situation, an understanding that usually cannot be easily reached through traditional library, online, or laboratory research. Although these methods are effective, they cannot address all research questions.

Some research questions can be answered only by **fieldwork,** research carried out in the field, rather than in a library, laboratory, or some other controlled environment. Following are some research questions calling for the collection of data in a real-world, or naturalistic, environment:

What nights of the week are busiest at the student union?

How popular is the foreign film series shown on campus, in terms of both

attendance and satisfaction? How do the responses of students, faculty,

and staff differ?

What do hair stylists do at work?

What is the effect of self check-out machines in local grocery stores?

How do mothers and adult daughters communicate?

How useful is the library's help desk? Who uses it? How often? When? Why?

All of these questions call for careful observation in the field (even though the field is actually the library in the case of the final question) and some means of data collection.

Observation in a real-world environment

A **naturalistic study** is based on observation in a real-world environment. The researcher observes and records some human behavior or phenomenon in its natural setting. Whether the goal is to establish the learning patterns of museum visitors, the daily driving habits of commuters, or the benefits of home schooling, the researcher conducting a naturalistic study observes, employing any or all of the following research methods:

- Watching the behavior or phenomenon and recording what he or she sees
- Using audiovisual equipment, such as tape recorders or video cameras
- Listening in on conversations or comments and taking notes
- Distributing questionnaires or administering pretests and posttests about a situation, phenomenon, or behavior
- Conducting interviews with individuals or focus groups

Whichever of these methods is employed, the researcher himself or herself is the most significant instrument for the collection and analysis of data.

Testing assumptions

Researchers often undertake a naturalistic study because they want to investigate an **assumption,** an idea taken for granted or accepted as true without proof. Whether expressed as a problem ("English majors dominate class discussion"), a question ("How much do hair stylists think as they do their job?"), or a belief ("The student union is always busy"), the assumption may be the researcher's alone or be commonly held. By collecting and analyzing data, the researcher compares the assumption with possible conclusions. The researcher tests the assumption with two goals in mind: (1) to interfere as little as possible with the subject or phenomenon under observation and (2) to minimize systematically the ways in which mere participation in the study influences patterns and outcomes. In other words, the fact that the researcher is observing, listening, or conducting interviews should not affect the behavior or beliefs of the participants. The researcher's goals overlap with the researcher's ethics.

Triangulation

To minimize inaccuracies and distortions, a researcher usually sets up a three-way process for gathering information, referred to as **triangulation.** When the process depends on using different sets of information from a variety of sources, it is called **data triangulation.** For instance, to triangulate responses to the question of how useful the library's help desk is, you might gather opinions from several different groups of people, looking for commonalities in their responses. When two or more researchers work together in order to compare their observations and findings, the approach is known as **investigator triangulation.** And, finally, **methodological triangulation** involves using multiple methods (observation, questionnaires, and so on) to study a single problem, person, or phenomenon.

Deborah Tannen, author of *You're Wearing That?*

Research

Basic principles at work: Deborah Tannen's naturalistic study

After publishing a book about adult family relationships, *I Only Say This Because I Love You,* Deborah Tannen discovered that her readers were most interested in the chapter on communication between mothers and adult daughters. With that knowledge, she launched the naturalistic study that became the book *You're Wearing That?* Tannen's preresearch assumption was that mothers and their adult daughters have a uniquely intense relationship; she felt sure this was true, given her own relationship with her mother. Tannen observed, recorded, and then transcribed many conversations; she also conducted interviews (or what she refers to as "focused conversations"), asked people she knew for examples from their own lives, and drew on her own ongoing communication with her mother. This process of observing, talking, asking questions, recording, and listening to the opinions of others was an example of methodological triangulation.

As Tannen observed and recorded, she also began to analyze what she was witnessing, an analysis based on her expertise in sociolinguistics (and on her status as an adult daughter). Toward the end of her research process, she compared her preresearch assumption (the mother–adult daughter relationship is uniquely intense) with the emerging conclusion that mother–adult daughter communication "continues to evoke powerful emotions long after it has ceased."

Like all experienced researchers, Tannen knows that naturalistic studies may be generalizable—but only to a point. Naturalistic studies are like the rhetorical situation itself: time-bound and context-bound, with all the entities of the study (observer or recorder, analysis, and subject or behavior under observation) shaping one another simultaneously.

USING NATURALISTIC STUDY IN YOUR WRITING

Before you embark on a naturalistic study, take a minute to write a one-sentence preresearch assumption about each of these three phenomena:

1. Consider a class you are currently taking. What are the talking, interrupting, and listening practices in that class?

2. What are the mealtime communication patterns of your family or a group you regularly eat with?

3. What activity attracts the most attention in your student union?

Now choose one of your assumptions and test it with observation and analysis.

1. Conduct a naturalistic study of a class discussion. Your goal is to observe and describe who speaks and who remains silent, who interrupts and who waits his or her turn, and whose topics get attention and whose topics get ignored. If you work with a classmate, you can compare your observations, preresearch assumptions, and conclusions, thereby providing a richer description of class discussions. Be prepared to report your findings to the rest of the class.

2. Conduct a naturalistic study of mealtime communication patterns within a group you know fairly well. You might observe and record what topics are discussed, whose opinion carries the most weight, and how people respond to one another. Be prepared to report your findings to the rest of the class.

3. Try conducting a naturalistic study at your school's student union, focusing on the various ways students, faculty, and staff use it. You might concentrate on traffic and ordering patterns at the coffee stand, the food stations, the

convenience store, or some other location in the student union. During your observation, notice what feature is used the most and the least and by whom. If you work in pairs, you can compare your preresearch assumptions with your observations and conclusions. Be prepared to report your findings to the rest of the class.

After listening to classmates' reports on their naturalistic studies, answer the following questions:

1. How well did the preresearch assumptions align with the findings of you and your classmates? Be prepared to share your answer with the rest of the class.

2. Of all the information in all the studies, including the one that you conducted, what information or tentative finding did you find most interesting? In other words, what information were you naturally attracted to? (Your answer to this question might help you discover what kinds of information you "naturally" record or neglect and begin to be aware of your own biases and blind spots.)

3. Did any information or finding disturb you? By answering this question you can reveal to yourself your biases, stereotypes, and comfort zone.

Methods for a Naturalistic Research Study

Observing, taking notes, and asking questions are the three activities at the heart of a naturalistic study, as you have probably gathered from reading about Deborah Tannen's research and trying your hand at a brief study of your own. In his study of the intellectual processes necessary for conducting ordinary kinds of work, Mike Rose describes these three elements at work together:

> When at a job site or in a classroom, I observed people at work, writing notes on their activity and, when permissible, taking photographs of the task at hand. Once I got a sense of the rhythms of the work—its moments of less intense focus and its pauses—I would begin asking questions about what people were doing and why, trying to gain an understanding of their behavior and the thinking that directed it. As they got more familiar with me and I with them and their work, I was able to ask increasingly specific questions, probing the reasons for using one implement rather than another, for a particular positioning of the body, for the benefits of this procedure over that one. I wondered aloud how they knew what to do, given the materials and constraints of the present task, what they had in mind to do next, how they knew something was wrong. . . . Over time, the exchanges became more conversational, and frequently people on their own began explaining what they were doing and what their thinking was for doing it, a kind of modified think-aloud procedure, long used in studies of problem solving.   —**Mike Rose**, *The Mind at Work*

Notice how Rose talks about the material conditions of his observation: he watches, takes notes, sometimes takes photographs, and asks ever-more-sophisticated questions as he begins to understand the procedures more and more. Each activity occurs in coordination with the others, but we'll look at them one at a time.

Using observation

Observation—watching closely what is happening and trying to figure out why—plays a central role in naturalistic studies of all kinds. After all, a naturalistic study depends most heavily on the researcher himself or herself, which is its advantage. The researcher is right there on the scene, conducting the research, with direct access to the person or phenomenon.

By the time Rose was ready to write up his observation, he was able to describe the results of his naturalistic study with style, grace, and a good deal of detail. In the following passage, he writes about the thinking that goes into the hair styling that Vanessa does.

Mike Rose

Excerpt from The Mind at Work

Vanessa works in a trendy salon but also cuts hair in her apartment—for a few friends and friends of friends. [1] Her client Lynn sits in a small barber's chair by the window, the place where you'd imagine a breakfast table, a mirror leaning against the wall in front of her. On the floor by the mirror there is a small bowl for Vanessa's dog and a vase with three yellow flowers. Vanessa stands behind Lynn, asking her questions about her hair, chitchatting a little. She keeps her eyes on Lynn's hair as she moves her fingers through it, lifting up, then pulling down one section, then another, then gesturing with her hands around the hair, indicating shape and movement. "How did you like the last haircut?" she asks. How did it handle? Was it easy to manage? What's bugging you now? Does it feel heavy up front? Lynn answers these questions, describing what she wants, relying on adjectives that have more to do with feeling than shape. She wants the cut "freshened," wants it "sassy." [2]

A pair of scissors, a comb, and a round hand mirror sit on the stove, to Vanessa's side. She reaches for the scissors and begins. She starts at the crown and moves around Lynn's head, picking a strand of hair, pulling it down gently along Lynn's face, eyeballing it, then elevating it, cutting into it, "point cutting," she calls it, not a "blunt" cut, [3] her scissors angling into the hair, layering it, "giving it a softer look."

Vanessa likes to cut dry hair—at least hair like Lynn's, baby fine, short—because she "can see what it's doing immediately . . . where it's heavy, where it needs to be cut into." [4] ("You can comb hair and cut it," she explains, "only to have it move into a different shape than the one you just cut.") [5] When she does cut hair wet, because a particular style demands it, she "can't wait to dry it and then go in and do *my* work. . . . The initial shape might be there, but the whole interior can change. Eighty percent of the haircut is after you dry it."

As Vanessa continues, cutting, comparing one length of hair to another, her gaze circling her client's head, she tells me more about her work. Though she can do "technical, precise" cuts, like a graduated bob (a bob tapered at the nape of the neck), she most likes to cut "freehand," as she is doing now, a more "flowing" cut, and flowing process. "I don't like authority," she laughs, "so I love cutting this way." Even with that graduated bob, she adds, after it's dry, she'll "go in and add my own touch, a signature."

[1] Already readers can see how much information Rose has gleaned by talking with Vanessa as he observes her.

[2] It is clear how much of Rose's report depends on careful note taking or tape recording. He includes details that could be retained only with note taking or tape recording.

[3] Rose has taken the time to learn the vocabulary of the people he's observing.

[4] This information could have been obtained only by asking interview questions, not by observation.

[5] You can almost hear Rose asking the questions that elicited these specific answers.

Vanessa certainly has an idea of how a haircut should look, an idea based on the characteristics of the hair she's cutting and the client's desires, discerned from those opening questions, and, if the client's a regular, from their history together. And she is methodical. But she does not plan her cut in advance to the degree that some stylists do; cognitive psychologists would characterize her planning style as incremental or opportunistic. **[6]** As the cut progresses, she observes what the hair is doing, how it's falling and moving, and reacts to that. "I do a lot of visual when I cut." And, in fact, about two-thirds of the way through Lynn's haircut, Vanessa exclaims, "Oh, this is starting to look really cute!" Moments like this are pivotal to Vanessa, aesthetically and motivationally. **[7]** It excites her, is the art of it all, to use her skill in a way that is responsive to, interactive with, the medium of hair, watching the cut emerge, shaping it incrementally, guided by her aesthetic sense and enabled by her repertoire of techniques. **[8]** Lynn is pleased with the outcome. It *is* a "sassy" cut. "Vanessa understands hair like mine."

[6] Rose invokes the library research he has done, which underpins the assumption he is exploring with his naturalistic study.

[7] Notice how Rose is weaving in his results, conclusions, and inferences.

[8] Because readers do not know whether Vanessa actually told Rose these things, they can only infer that he is making inferences based on his naturalistic study.

ANALYZING THE RHETORICAL SITUATION

With a classmate or two, reread Rose's description of Vanessa's work and then answer the following questions:

1. What assumption, problem, or question is Rose exploring?
2. Why is observation a necessary component of his research?
3. Whom is Rose observing? Why?
4. What behaviors or actions is Rose observing? Why?
5. Where is he conducting his observations? Why?
6. How does he use observation to advance his exploration of the assumption?
7. Why does Rose need to use more than observation to conduct his study?

Be prepared to share your answers with the rest of the class.

USING OBSERVATION IN YOUR WRITING

Now apply the questions in the preceding Analyzing the Rhetorical Situation to a naturalistic study that you would like to conduct. Provide written answers and be prepared to share them with the class.

Taking notes

The second part of the naturalistic research process is **note taking,** writing down what you observe or hear. You can tell by reading Rose's account of his observations that he took copious notes as he watched Vanessa work. Otherwise, he would not have been able to compose such a realistic and compelling narrative about his observations. An important feature of note taking, however, is what Krista Ratcliffe refers to in her book *Rhetorical Listening: Identification, Gender, Whiteness* as "rhetorical listening": "a stance of openness that a person may choose to assume in relation to any person, text, or culture." We all have a tendency to allow our expectations and experiences to influence how we process what we encounter. The openness that we adopt when listening rhetorically keeps us aware of difference and newness. Rhetorical listening also helps researchers translate what they observe and hear into spoken and written language (questions and research drafts). If we listen with the intent to understand (rather than waiting for a spot to insert our own voice), we'll have an easier time writing and speaking about unfamiliar topics from a standpoint of authentic knowledge and goodwill. Thus, careful observing, listening, and note taking all support the researcher's perceptions—and improve the results.

Researchers like Rose take notes during observations for two reasons: to record very specific detail and to record their own reactions to what they observe. Without notes, few people can remember all the details of what they have observed. While observing, researchers can experience a range of reactions: they might find what they've observed to be in line with what they expected, or they might find it comforting, puzzling, or even infuriating or distressing. By jotting down their reactions as they occur, researchers can minimize the degree to which their preconceptions influence those reactions. Some naturalistic researchers simply (or not so simply) take notes about what they observe, trying to jot down snatches of conversation and specialized terms or insider phrases that they will need to ask about later. They might also record specific actions or sequences of movements.

Whether you keep your notes in a notebook, on separate note cards or pieces of paper, or on your laptop, you can choose among various ways of recording what you observe and your responses.

You might write notes that combine narration, description, and evaluation. In the following passage, student Bethanie Orban uses a combination of narration, description, and evaluation to focus on the question "Who talks the most, and what are the different ways of communicating?"

Cody, Andrea, and Tom are friends who eat lunch together. Andrea comes to the table first followed by Tom. Both wait for Cody to join them before they start to eat. Cody comes to the table humming. As soon as he sits down, he immediately begins talking about his history exam. "I don't know where the professor got the questions!" Cody says. Andrea assures Cody he did fine, trying to comfort him. Tom makes a joke that Cody probably didn't study. Cody begins gesturing with his hands that he did study a lot. Tom laughs and holds up his hand. He tells Cody it was a joke. Cody begins to eat his soup and Tom takes a drink of his milk. Andrea begins telling them about her weekend in New York with her friend. She describes the Broadway show she saw. Andrea keeps describing how great it was. Cody begins a story about going to a movie over the weekend. Tom says he saw the movie a while back. Cody thinks it was the best movie he ever saw. "It was awesome." Cody looks around at the other tables to see if anyone is listening to what he's saying, which makes him look like he likes to be the center of attention. Andrea excuses herself to go get a cookie. She asks if anyone else wants anything, but both Tom and Cody say they are full.

You might begin by describing what you observe and then go back later to add your evaluation of what you saw, as Bethanie Orban did in the following passage from her double-entry notebook. A **double-entry notebook** is a journal that has two distinct parts: observational details and response to those details. The double-entry notebook thus allows researchers to keep their observations separate from their responses to what they observe. In addition, it encourages researchers to push their observations further, with responses to and questions about what they see or think they see. Some researchers draw a heavy line down the middle of each page of the notebook, putting "Observations" at the top of the left-hand side of the page and "Response" at the top of the right-hand side. Others lay the notebook flat and use the right-hand page for recording their observations and the left-hand page for responding to those observations. If you're using a computer, you can format your entries the way Bethanie did:

Observations	Response
Andrea, Cody, and Tom meet up for lunch. Andrea thinks they need to find a table first before they get food. Cody thinks it would be nice to sit by the window, so they put their stuff down. Andrea is the first back to the table and	I found that Cody seems to talk the most. However, a lot of this is based on my own opinions. Cody is shorter and has glasses. He likes to be the center of attention, possibly because he wants to make up for something. He tends

continued

waits for everyone else before eating. Cody tells the other two about his exam. He doesn't think he did well. Andrea thinks he probably did fine, but Tom makes a joke about it. Eventually Andrea begins talking about her weekend in New York. Cody tells about the movie he saw. When he's done, Andrea goes to get a cookie. Tom and Cody continue to talk about their weekends. The dining commons smells like fried food and cookies. Everyone thinks the food tastes good. The tables feel a little sticky. There is the constant noise of students talking. Andrea returns with her cookie while Tom and Cody continue their conversation about the weekend.

to be loud and look around at other tables to see if anyone else heard. Andrea waits her turn to speak, but gets really passionate when she talks about Broadway. I feel like maybe she feels out of place with two guys, but wants to engage others in conversation. Tom seems the most laid back and likes to joke around. He has really curly hair so he doesn't mind teasing, perhaps to take it off himself. I believe many of my observations were colored by my own take on each student: Cody wanting attention, Andrea feeling uncomfortable, and Tom's use of humor.

In the following passage, Mike Rose discusses his observations of a high school shop class, focusing on the "talk" necessary for Mr. Devries to teach and for Felipe and his peers to learn about cabinetmaking:

I want to consider a seemingly unrelated element of the vocabulary of work operating in Mr. Devries's classroom, one so familiar and ever-present that it frequently escapes mention: talk. Traditional discussions of technology tend, in various ways, to separate the technical and the social—and with the social, the play of language. What is so clear in this workshop setting, though, is the intimate interconnection of tool use, wood construction, and speech. Electrician and poet Susan Eisenberg captures the mix: "work and talk flowing like / wire through a well-laid pipe."

Here is Jerry Devries showing Felipe and his peers how to make a "layout stick," a long, thick piece of wood that has the measurements of the main components of their cabinet marked and labeled on it. As Mr. Devries demonstrates, he repeats for his students the names of the new components (the *mullion* is the center support of the front, or "face," frame of the cabinet); queries them on the functional justification for these components ("You're not gonna make a sixty-eight-inch cabinet without a mullion, why?"); informs them of pertinent codes ("Anything over thirty-six inches requires support"); asks them to think through the mathematical consequences of the interrelation of the cabinet's components ("How will you adjust for the presence of the two-inch mullion?"); voices functional or aesthetic biases ("Some cabinetmakers like a lot of face frame; I don't like as much face frame"); and has Felipe and company think about the physical context of their cabinet ("Is it going up to the height of the ceiling?"). The fashioning of the layout stick is surrounded by statements of fact, questions, opinions. All of Mr. Devries's instruction—before the whole class, in small groups, or individually—involves speech and gesture, and, as we've seen, peer-to-peer instruction is oral and gestural as well.

If we were able to record a day's worth of the more informal talk in Mr. Devries's classroom—or, for that fact, at a typical construction site—we'd get a wide range of types and topics: gossip, banter, commentary on the events of the day, declarations of things hoped for, plans and goals, chronicles of life on the home front. A lot of it would be crude and combative. What interests me, though, is the way this informal talk—as we saw with the hairstylists—functions as an open channel, rich in cognitive possibility; the way information, procedures, and tricks of the trade flow in and out of the banter, fantasy, and dirty jokes.   —**Mike Rose**, *The Mind at Work*

Like all human beings, Rose brings his personal experience and disposition to every research situation. For Rose, some talk is positive, and other talk is negative. After labeling some verbal communication as "crude and combative," he deems other talk as "rich in cognitive possibility." Chances are most observers would agree with him, but few would come to the same conclusion that he does about the very same snippets of conversation.

Our biases and preferences sometimes prevent us from seeing what is going on right in front of our eyes. Besides bringing our personal preferences to what we observe, we also bring our personal understanding—or lack thereof. Our level of expertise with procedures, history, and terminology can enhance our understanding or prevent us from understanding what we are seeing. For these reasons, most of us need to train ourselves to become better observers of our surroundings, better at seeing and hearing, more attuned to all of our senses. As award-winning writer Diane Ackerman reminds us in *A Natural History of the Senses,* "There is no way in which to understand the world without first detecting it through the radar-net of our senses."

Researchers conducting naturalistic studies have to push themselves to see more clearly, and questioning often helps. The best researchers ask many questions before, during, and after their observations. You can tell by rereading the second excerpt from Rose's book that he asked a lot of questions. Successful researchers also rely on other means to triangulate what they think they are seeing and hearing: interviews, questionnaires, tape recordings, or the work of another researcher.

Asking questions

The third part of the naturalistic research process consists of asking questions. Researchers may ask their questions all at once or over an extended period of time during their observations and afterward. They may ask questions face to face, over the phone, online, or in a distributed questionnaire. We'll first consider face-to-face interviews and then explore methods for preparing and distributing questionnaires. Understanding how to prepare for and conduct interviews will advance your ability to carry on conversations all through your research study and beyond. This understanding will also help you think through the design of a questionnaire, if you decide to compose one.

Interviews An interview conducted as part of a naturalistic study can be formal, based on a set of predetermined questions, or more casual, almost like a conversation. But the friendly nature of good conversational interviews belies the serious planning that goes into them. After all, asking questions (interviewing) is an important component of data collection, often just as valuable as observing and note taking.

Whatever method you decide to use for your interview, you must obtain permission to conduct the interview, schedule the interview, and obtain permission to tape record or take notes during the interview. After the interview (or series of conversations) is complete, you'll want to send a thank-you note to the person and include a complimentary copy of your study.

Perhaps the most important element of interviewing is choosing **interview subjects,** the specific people who can provide useful information for your naturalistic study. In other words, whom do you want to interview and why? Your interview subjects might be **key participants** in the phenomenon you are studying, or they might be experts on the subject you are studying. Whatever rationale you use for choosing interview subjects, the most important criterion should be that each person can provide you with information you need to proceed with your research.

All successful questioning involves **background research**—in other words, doing your homework before you begin asking questions. Many television programs, from shows on MTV and BET to *The Today Show* and *Oprah,* feature interviews. When you watch an interview (especially one in the guise of a casual conversation), you can see how well or badly the interviewer prepared. The burden is on the researcher or interviewer to know enough about the person or phenomenon to ask intelligent questions, just as Rose did when studying the hairstylist and the shop teacher. Good interview questions will help guide your research.

Your **interview questions** should serve your research in two ways. First, they should put your subjects at ease so that they willingly talk, amplify their answers, and provide rich examples. Second, your interview questions should advance your research study by progressing purposefully from one subject to another. Successful researchers write out a series of questions to which they want answers, arranging them so that one question leads logically to the next. In addition, your interview questions should indicate that you have done your homework about the interviewee and the process or phenomenon you are studying—and that you have been paying close attention during your observations. They should also demonstrate that you appreciate the time and information the interviewee is giving you.

Interview questions that can be answered with yes or no will not yield much information unless they are followed with a related question. For example, if you follow a question like "Do you like your job?" with a journalist's question ("Why?" "When?" or "How?"), you give your interviewee a chance to elaborate. Effective interviews usually contain a blend of open, or broad, questions and focused, or narrow, questions. Here are a few examples:

OPEN QUESTIONS

What do you think about _____?

What are your views on _____?

Why do you believe _____?

FOCUSED QUESTIONS

How long have you worked as a _____?

When did you start _____?

What does _____ mean?

Why did you _____?

TRICKS OF THE TRADE

Experienced researchers realize that they must balance the need to move the interview in a purposeful direction with the need to make their interview subjects feel relaxed enough to speak freely. Preparing a list of questions before an interview is essential, but do not just read them off the list during the encounter. An interview is a special kind of conversation. Although you will be guiding it, you may find that your interviewee says something you had not expected but would like to know more about. Do not be afraid to veer from your list to ask other questions that come to mind during the interview.

Whatever kind of interview you conduct—face-to-face, telephone, email, or online—you should not rely on your memory alone, no matter how good it is. You need to take notes or record the conversation in order to keep track of the questions you pose and the responses you receive. Many researchers use a tape recorder during face-to-face interviews so that they can focus their attention on the interviewee, establishing the personal rapport that invigorates any interview. During telephone interviews, you may want to use the speakerphone function so that you can tape the interview or take notes. Because taking notes and transcribing recordings are both time-consuming (and sometimes tedious) tasks, some researchers conduct email or online interviews. These electronic techniques have the advantage of providing a written record of your questions and the answers. They also allow you a convenient way to "meet" the person. Perhaps the biggest disadvantage of electronic interviews is the burden they place on the interviewee, who has to take the time and energy to think through and then compose cogent answers. Talking is often much easier for the interviewee.

After the interview, you need to read through your notes and listen to any recordings. Many researchers find this to be the best point in the process for transcribing recordings. As you read your materials, consider a number of questions:

▌ What information surprised you? Why?
▌ How does that reaction affect your study?
▌ What do you now understand better than you did? What was said that illuminated your understanding?
▌ What specific passages best forward the purpose of your research? How does that information help answer or address your research assumption?
▌ What exactly would you like to know more about?

When you have answered these questions, you'll know what else needs to be done. You may find that you need to make further observations, go to the library, or conduct more interviews.

After you have read through your notes and listened to any recordings, you can begin writing up results, based on what you have observed, listened to, asked about, and perhaps researched in other ways. Writing up results launches the analysis that will shape your final report.

Questionnaires Whereas an interview elicits information from one person whose name you know, questionnaires provide information from a number of anonymous people. To be effective, questionnaires need to be short and focused. If they are too long, people may not be willing to take the time to fill them out. If they are not focused on your research, you'll find it difficult to integrate the results into your paper.

The questions on questionnaires take a variety of forms:

▌ Questions that require a simple yes-or-no answer
Do you commute to work in a car? (Circle one.)
Yes   No

▌ Multiple-choice questions
How many people do you commute with? (Circle one.)
0   1   2   3   4

▌ Questions with answers on a checklist
How long does it take you to commute to work? (Check one.)
___ 0–30 minutes   ___ 30–60 minutes   ___ 60–90 minutes   ___ 90–120 minutes

- **▌** Questions with a ranking scale

  If the car you drive or ride in is not working, which of the following types of transportation do you rely on? (Rank the choices from 1 for most frequently used to 4 for least frequently used.)

  ___ bus ___ shuttle van ___ subway ___ taxi

- **▌** Open questions

  What aspect of commuting do you find most irritating?

The types of questions you decide to use will depend on the purpose of your project. The first four types of questions are the easiest for respondents to answer and the least complicated for you to process. Open questions should be asked only when other types of questions cannot elicit the information you want.

Be sure to begin your questionnaire with an introduction stating what the purpose of the questionnaire is, how the results will be used, and how long it will take to complete the questionnaire. In the introduction, you should also assure participants that their answers will be kept confidential. To protect participants' privacy, colleges and universities have committees set up to review questionnaires. These committees are often referred to as **institutional review boards.** Before you distribute your questionnaire, check with the institutional review board on your campus to make certain you are following its guidelines.

Administering a questionnaire can sometimes be problematic. Many questionnaires sent through the mail are never returned. If you do decide to mail out your questionnaire, provide a self-addressed envelope and directions for returning the questionnaire. It is always a good idea to send out twice as many questionnaires as you think you need, because the response rate for such mailings is generally low. If you are on campus, questionnaires can sometimes be distributed in dormitories or in classes, but such a procedure must be approved by campus officials.

Once your questionnaires have been completed and returned, tally the results for all but the open questions on a single unused questionnaire. To assess responses to the open questions, first read through them all. You might find that you can create categories for the responses. Answers to the open question "What aspect of commuting do you find most irritating?" might fall into such categories as "length of time," "amount of traffic," or "bad weather conditions." By first creating categories, you'll be able to tally the answers to the open questions.

To put the results of a questionnaire to work in your research, ask yourself questions similar to the ones you reflect on after an interview:

- **▌** What information surprised you? Why?
- **▌** How does that reaction affect your study?
- **▌** What do you now understand better than you did? Which particular results illuminated your understanding?
- **▌** What exactly would you like to know more about?

Research

These reflective questions will guide you in determining what else needs to be done, such as make further observations, go to the library, or conduct interviews. The questions will also help with your analysis. Analysis is part of a naturalistic study from the beginning, when you conceive an assumption you want to explore. But analysis becomes particularly important as you bring together all three parts of your methodology (observing, note taking, and asking questions) and begin the final step of writing up your research.

Organizing a Naturalistic Research Study

Like other kinds of research papers, a report on a naturalistic study is arranged into distinct sections. Many effective writers use headings to differentiate among the sections of a long piece of writing. Besides making reading easier, headings make writing easier. You can end one section and start another one, rather than spending time on building transitions between sections.

- The **introduction** conveys the assumption under investigation, expressed as a problem, a question, or a belief. You might also use the introduction to explain the significance of your assumption.
- A **literature review** can be part of the introduction or can form a separate section. In the literature review, you demonstrate that you have conducted some library or online research about the assumption under examination. In fact, your assumption might even have grown out of that prior work.
- A **methodology** section explains the process you used to study the assumption you set out in your introduction. In the case of a naturalistic study, you explain how you gathered information. Whatever method of triangulation you used is also explained in this section.
- In the **results** section, you report your findings. Your findings might be a solution to a problem, an explanation for or answer to a question, or an evaluation of an assumption. In this section, you might include graphs, photographs, or other kinds of visuals that help support your verbal explanation of your results.
- A **discussion** section provides a place to interpret your findings, compare them with what others have discovered or believe, and relate them to the assumption with which you started.
- Finally, a **conclusion** closes a research report. One way to shape a conclusion is to break it into three subsections: (1) the clearcut, obvious conclusions you can draw from your study; (2) the inferences you can draw, given your current knowledge of the subject under study; and (3) the implications of your research in terms of further research or practical application.

Many research studies also merit a references or a works-cited list (see chapter 21).

Research Log

Page____

Ancestor's name: _____

First _____ Middle _____ Last (Maiden) _____

Born: _____ Married: _____ Died: _____

☐ Male
☐ Female

This person is on pedigree chart number ____, line number ____, and/or is child number ____ on the family group record of (Husband's name):

Research objective: Question about an event, relationship, place, or subject	Name and Location of source. Include name and address of the source person, object or record repository. When it applies, include title, author, publisher of book, document, writing, electronic database, web site, etc.	Search Date	Notes about source. May include a: reason for its selection, description of its condition, summary and analysis of information found, etc.	File number you assigned to notes/copy made of information from source

1. Genealogists use various tools to help them keep track of discoveries they have made and the evidence backing up their discoveries. One such tool is a genealogy research log. Examine the example you see here. Based on what genealogists record in their logs, what kinds of information do you think are valued in this kind of research?

2. If you were going to modify this log to make it useful to your own academic research, what changes would you make? What categories would you keep?

Now that you've considered what kinds of sources might be useful to you and where to find them, you need a plan for proceeding with the research process. Without a clear plan and a method of tracking your progress, it's easy to lose track of your ideas and goals. Not even experienced researchers attempt to remember which sources they've consulted, how those sources fit into their research, and what their next steps will be. To keep their research moving ahead, researchers take advantage of tools such as research logs and use ordered methods similar to the ones outlined in the following pages.

Keeping a Research Log

Research logs come in different forms, but whatever their form—electronic or printed, detailed or brief—they help researchers stay focused. The items included on a log depend on the particular kind of research. For instance, a sociologist's log of field observations might include spaces for recording descriptions of the location, the time, and even the weather conditions—in addition to comments about what he observed and notes about what steps should be taken next. (See chapter 18 for more on conducting observations.) An architect working on a proposal for renovating an old courthouse might use a log to document her findings on the history of the building, noting locations and details of the photographs, sketches, and correspondence she comes across. A psychology student beginning his research with the library's PsycINFO database may save himself time in the long run by recording keyword combinations he uses in his searches, circling the keywords he wants to plug into similar databases. (See page 510 for help in choosing keywords.)

Researchers make decisions about what to include in their logs by anticipating what kind of information will be most important in helping them answer their research question and document their results. Generally, entries in a research log relate to one of the following activities:

- Establishing the exigence, purpose, and research question
- Identifying the sources
- Taking notes
- Responding to notes
- Establishing the audience

Your research log may also be where you keep track of progress on the following activities, which are important to the writing process:

- Preparing a working bibliography
- Annotating a bibliography
- Crafting a working thesis
- Dealing with areas of tension in the research

Depending on your assignment, you may want to include entries related to all of these types of activities or just a few of them. We'll discuss each kind of entry in this chapter.

Establishing the exigence, purpose, and research question

In the introductory entry in your research log, identify your research question and your reasons for choosing it. You might include some preliminary, tentative answers to your question if you have any, given what you already know. Next, state your overall research purpose. What is your purpose in presenting your research to others: to inform, to analyze, or to persuade? Rereading this initial entry every so often may help you stay focused. Here is the first entry in a research log kept by Matthew Marusak, an English major at The Pennsylvania State University, in connection with a project he did with fellow student Bethanie Orban.

Exigence, Purpose, and My Research Question

I want to enter into the debate about Penn State's decision to relocate the Creamery, one of its landmarks. I know that other landmarks and traditions have changed in the past (like those involving the Nittany Lion), and Bethanie pointed out that the library is not the same as it always was. I wonder what we can learn from newspaper or journal articles--or other historical texts--about the nature of the changes to the landmarks. Maybe the changes to the Creamery will seem more positive if we look at them in relation to the other landmarks. We'll probably need to look at some Web resources, too, and possibly interview other students.

I think we'll have more than one purpose in the end: to inform our audience about the evolution of many Penn State landmarks, as well as to persuade readers that the move of the Creamery will be a positive step toward forming new traditions.

Identifying the sources

Before you start to take notes from any source, jot down important identifying features of the source, in case you need to return to it or cite it. If you expect to have only a few sources, you may want to include complete bibliographic information with your notes. If you will be consulting a number of sources, create an entry in your working bibliography (see page 539) and then include with your content notes only basic information, such as the author's name and the page number.

Taking notes

Most of your entries, whether in a research log or on note cards, will consist of detailed notes about the research you have done. Often these notes will be based on your reading, but they may also cover observations, interviews, and other types of research. As you take notes, you may choose to quote, paraphrase, or summarize your sources. These ways of recording research findings are discussed in more detail in chapter 20.

As you write, keep in mind the purposes of your notes. Ask yourself how you might use each source in your paper; how you intend to use a source generally determines the nature of the notes you take. You might use a source to provide context for your readers or deeper understanding for yourself. If you were researching a problem, for instance, you would look for information on what's already been done to try to address the problem. You might refer to sources that explain why previous attempts failed—or why they succeeded to some degree but not completely. A pithy quotation from an expert may encourage your readers to consider your proposed solution. If you find a quotation or statistic that you might want to use in your introduction, write it down word for word, and then double-check your notes to make sure you have recorded it and identified the source accurately.

TRICKS OF THE TRADE

Instead of keeping a research log, some researchers jot down information on note cards. Most people use four-by-six-inch cards, recording one note per card. If a note is particularly long, they staple a second card to it. Keeping separate cards allows a researcher to test different arrangements of information during the drafting stage. If you decide to use note cards, be sure to indicate the source of each note at the bottom of the card so that you will have the information you need to cite or document the source in your paper. See pages 539–540 for a list of source information to write down.

Responding to notes

With your notes, you'll want to include your responses to what you have recorded from the sources. You may wish to comment on what you agree or disagree with, what you question, why you find some item of information particularly interesting, and what connections you draw between one source and another. Like your notes, your responses should be purposeful. When you find a source with which you agree or disagree, you'll probably copy down or paraphrase excerpts you wish to emphasize or dispute; if you do not also note *why* you agree or disagree, however, you may not be able to reconstruct your initial response later when you are composing your essay. If you take the time to carefully record your responses to sources, you will be able to make a smooth transition from taking notes to composing your essay.

Especially when you are recording source notes and your responses to those notes in the same place, it's crucial to have a system for making clear which ideas come from the source and which are your own. Even professional authors have damaged their research—and their credibility—by assuming they would remember which ideas came from their sources and which were their responses to those sources. Guard against this danger by writing your responses in a different color ink or in a different font, enclosing your responses in brackets, or using some other technique to make the distinction. You might want to use a double-entry notebook, as described in chapter 18.

Here is another excerpt from Matt Marusak's research log. It contains bibliographic information about a source, a bulleted list of notes, and his reflection on these notes.

Source 1:

Miller, Chris, and Matt Ritsko, eds. *Save the Creamery!* N.p., n.d. Web.

12 Nov. 2006.

According to the Web site, the petition to keep the Creamery open in its current location has over 3,600 signatures. The primary reasons for not closing the old Creamery seem to be these:

- "The Creamery is an intrinsic part of Penn State. . . . Moving it is a change of tradition, and these days there are less and less traditions in the Penn State community."

- There is another option: keep the old Creamery as a branch location of the new one.

- The informal data survey reveals that students will visit the Creamery less in its new location.

This Web site makes clear some of the main arguments against moving the Creamery. A primary objection we'll have to examine is the idea that a great tradition will die along with the expansion and relocation of the Creamery. Since our audience includes Penn State students, this site is an important source. But I should also look for other points of view from students in other sources.

An audience for a research paper on the Segway might want to see a photo like this one.

A research log helps you keep track of your investigation. It also serves as a testing ground for information and thoughts you may include in your paper. Matt and Bethanie, for instance, found a place in their essay for the quotation Matt jotted down and for an excerpt from Matt's response. When you are writing in your log, then, remember that composing your entries carefully may save you time when you write your paper. Notice that Matt wrote down some ideas for further research. Like most students, Matt has many other obligations besides writing this research paper, so he took these notes to remind himself of the follow-up research he and Bethanie intended to do.

Establishing the audience

A research log is a good place to jot notes about your audience so that you can keep your readers in mind as you compose. Let's say you're interested in finding out about the benefits of using a Segway. If you are aware that your audience knows nothing about this means of transport, you will have to be sure to provide a detailed description of the device. You might even include a photograph. However, if you are writing for an audience that has already been introduced to this type of transportation, a detailed description is unnecessary.

USING A RESEARCH LOG IN YOUR WRITING

1. In your research log, write two or three paragraphs in which you introduce your research question and articulate your purpose. Be sure to discuss why you are asking the question in the first place, what the benefits of answering the question will be, and what types of research are likely to be helpful.

2. After you've written notes about a source in your log, take a moment to write out a response, making sure to clearly distinguish your response from the notes you took. Here are some questions to ask yourself as you respond: What do I agree and disagree with? What do I not understand fully? What do I want to know more about? How does what this source says relate to (agree or disagree with) what other sources have said? What purpose might this source serve in my paper? What other research should I do?

3. In your research log, create an entry that describes your prospective readers and explains what you need to keep in mind to ensure that you are addressing them. In addition, make a list of the types of sources that you think this audience will find credible and explain why.

Preparing a Working Bibliography

Whenever you plan to consult a number of sources in a research project, dedicate a section of your research log to your working bibliography. A **working bibliography** is a preliminary record of the sources you find as you conduct your research. The working bibliography will serve as a draft for your final list of references or works cited.

The following sample templates indicate what bibliographic information you should record for books, articles, and Web sites. To save yourself work later as you prepare the bibliography for your paper, you may find it useful to take a few moments to look at how bibliographic information is conventionally recorded in your field. If you have been asked to follow the conventions of the Modern Language Association (MLA) or the American Psychological Association (APA), see chapter 21.

BOOKS

Author(s) and/or Editor(s): _____

Title: _____

Publisher: _____

Place of Publication: _____

Date of Publication: _____

Page Numbers of Particular Interest: _____

For online books, also provide as much of the following information as possible:

Title of the Internet Site: _____

Editor of the Site: _____

Version Number: _____

Date of Electronic Publication: _____

Name of Sponsoring Institution or Organization: _____

Date of Access: _____

URL for Book: _____

ARTICLES

Author(s): _____

Title of Article: _____

Title of Journal or Magazine: _____

Volume and Issue Numbers: _____

Date of Publication: _____

Page Numbers of Entire Article: _____

Page Numbers of Particular Interest: _____

For articles from a database, also provide as much of the following information as possible:

Name of Database: _____

Name of Service: _____

Name of Library: _____

Location (City and State) of Library: _____

Date of Access: _____

URL for the Service's Home Page: _____

Research

Name of Site:_____

Name of Sponsoring Entity: _____

Author(s) or Editor(s) (if any): _____

URL: _____

Date of Publication: _____

Date of Last Update: _____

Date of Access: _____

TRICKS OF THE TRADE

If you are keeping your notes on cards, you can put all the relevant bibliographic information for a source on one card—the bibliography card—and then just write the author's name or the title of the source and the page number(s) on the cards where you record content. Some researchers use colored cards or smaller (three-by-five-inch) cards as bibliography cards.

USING A WORKING BIBLIOGRAPHY IN YOUR WRITING

Find three sources related to your research question and list them in your working bibliography with all relevant information.

Annotating a Bibliography

An **annotated bibliography** is a list of works cited, or sometimes works consulted, that includes descriptive or critical commentary with each entry. By preparing an annotated bibliography, you show that you have understood your sources and have thought about how to incorporate them into your paper. Some instructors require students to include annotated bibliographies with their papers. However, even if an annotated bibliography is not required, you might want to create one if you are working on a research project that will take several weeks to complete, as it can help you keep track of sources. To prepare entries that will help you solidify your knowledge of sources and your plans for using them, follow these guidelines:

- Begin each entry with bibliographic information. Follow the guidelines on pages 565–581 for MLA documentation style or those on pages 599–611 for APA documentation style if your instructor requires you to use one of these styles.
- Below the bibliographic information, write two or three sentences that summarize the source.
- After summarizing the source, write two or three sentences explaining the usefulness of the source for your specific research project.

Here is an example of an entry for an annotated bibliography:

"About Us." *University Creamery.* 29 June 2006. Web. 5 Nov. 2006.

This page and its linked pages provide information on the Creamery's history, present operations, and future plans. A virtual tour and information on "short courses" are also provided for those who are interested in visiting. The history link offers detailed information on the Creamery's three previous locations, as well as photos of each location.

I can use some of the material in this source to support my point that the Creamery has not always been at its current location. The explanation of how the move will improve the Creamery--from the University's perspective--gives me another point of view to consider besides that of the students who want to keep the Creamery open in its current location.

USING AN ANNOTATED BIBLIOGRAPHY IN YOUR WRITING

If you have already constructed a working bibliography, add annotations for the sources you think will be most useful. Be sure to include both a summary of the source and an explanation of how the source will be useful to you.

Planning a Research Paper

Strategies for planning a research paper are not that different from the general strategies you learned in chapter 3: listing, keeping a journal, freewriting, questioning, clustering, and outlining. If you have been keeping a research log, you have already used many of these methods. When writing the first draft of your paper, you may want to use some of these methods to generate or organize ideas.

Crafting a working thesis

The most important step to take as you begin to prepare your first draft is to write your thesis. If you started the research process with a question, now is the time to answer that question. A **working thesis** is a tentative answer to a research question. By forming such a thesis, you can test a possible framework for your fitting response. For example, Matt and Bethanie started with the question "How will the move of the University Creamery affect Penn State and its beloved traditions?" They transformed their question into this thesis: "Change has been an integral element to Penn State's success, and the move of the Creamery will be a positive step toward forming new traditions." Because Matt and Bethanie had done some research, they knew that their supporting paragraphs could address specific ways in which change has been beneficial to their school and encourage their readers to agree that the proposed changes to the Creamery would be in line with a tradition of positive change. Even though they knew they would have to do more research, Bethanie and Matt felt confident and focused because they had a good question to guide them through their research.

Keep in mind that once you have written a working thesis, you may find that you need to adjust it. You can test your thesis as you try to support it in the body of your paper. Do not be concerned if you change your mind; writers often do. Writing a thesis is just a starting point in the drafting process.

Dealing with areas of tension in the research findings

As you sifted through all your information in an attempt to find an answer to your research question, you probably encountered information that was at odds with other information. Perhaps two authors disagreed, perhaps one study contradicted another, or perhaps your own experience provided evidence counter to another author's thesis. You may also have found flaws in the reasoning or gaps in the evidence. Look closely at these areas of tension, because they can provide an exigence and a purpose for your writing. You may even find ways to introduce them into your thesis. Kendra Fry's experience provides an illustration.

Kendra had been studying how mathematics is taught in elementary schools and observing students in a fifth-grade classroom. Her research question was "What are the most effective methods for teaching mathematics to students in elementary school?" Both in the articles Kendra read and in the classes she observed, she found a great deal of emphasis placed on writing. Students were often asked to write down explanations for their answers to math problems. The initial working thesis she drafted was "Although language arts and mathematics are often kept separate in coursework, writing may be key to teaching mathematics in elementary school." When observing students, though, Kendra found that some students who were able to solve math equations easily still had difficulty explaining the process. She thought this difficulty made a few of them dislike their math lessons. As Kendra started to draft her paper, she changed her thesis to take into account the tension between the type of mathematics teaching that was prescribed and the effect on learning that she was witnessing: "Although students in elementary schools are encouraged to explain their mathematical reasoning, this practice may have an adverse effect on some students' motivation to study math." In the process of trying to answer a broader question, Kendra found an exigence and a purpose for a research paper she was really interested in writing.

Like Kendra, you can find a genuine research agenda when you pay attention to what doesn't fit neatly into an early outline you have or into your initial plans for what you will say.

The following is an excerpt from an interview conducted by Sharifa Rhodes-Pitts with Debra Dickerson, author of *The End of Blackness: Returning the Souls of Black Folks to Their Rightful Owners.*

RHODES-PITTS: You've spoken about how *The End of Blackness* grew out of your frustration with the way racial politics get played out in what you call "black liberal" sectors. Can you elaborate a bit on what you mean?

DICKERSON: Part of what brought about the book in the first place was a lifetime spent having to bite my tongue because of the way black liberals wage the battle on race. It doesn't need to be a battle. It ought to be a dialogue—it ought to be a family discussion. Instead you're either with them or you're against them. If you don't think exactly like them you're the enemy or you're insane.

I think that comes from a couple of things. The moral urgency that there once was—when people were being lynched or were sitting in the back of the bus or being defrauded of their citizenship—is no more. But even though it's 2004 and we don't confront the same problems, people go at it as if it's still 1950 and nothing has changed. A lot of people read about what Fannie Lou Hamer and Martin Luther King went through and slip into an us-against-the-world kind of mode and pretend that things are more dire than they are. There's a temptation to want to feel like you're waging a crusade and the forces of evil are arrayed against you. But I think there's a real sloppiness of thought there.

1. In one paragraph, summarize the interview excerpt as objectively as you can.
2. Look over your paragraph and reflect in writing on the following questions: (a) What strategies did you use to put the source's ideas into your own words? (b) How did you indicate the source of any direct quotes you included? (c) How did you respond to the ideas expressed in the interview? If you were expanding your written response, which parts of your summary paragraph would you include? How would you alter those parts, if at all?

Reading with Your Audience and Purpose in Mind

Keeping purposeful notes as you read your sources can save you from needless scrambling the night before your paper is due. In chapter 19, you learned that your notes will be more useful to you in the later stages of the writing process if you keep your purpose and audience in mind as you write them. In the first part of this chapter, you'll learn to summarize, paraphrase, and quote from your sources. Each of these techniques for recording information can help you achieve your purpose and satisfy your audience. In the second part of this chapter, you'll learn strategies for evaluating and responding to your sources.

Summarizing

Researchers regularly use summaries in their writing to indicate that they have done their homework—that is, that they are familiar with other work done on a topic. In summarizing other sources, researchers restate the information they have read as concisely and objectively as they can, thereby demonstrating their understanding of it and conveying their own credibility. Researchers may have additional reasons for using summaries. For instance, they may use the information to support their own view, to deepen an explanation, or to contest other information they have found. In academic research papers, summaries appear most frequently as introductory material.

Using function statements

Depending on your purpose, you may decide to summarize an entire source or just part of it. Summarizing an entire source can help you understand it. To compose such a summary, you may find it useful to first write a **function statement** for each paragraph. A function statement goes beyond restating the content of the paragraph; it captures the intention of the author. For example, an author may introduce a topic, provide background information, present alternative views, refute other writers' positions, or draw conclusions based on evidence provided.

The words you use to indicate who the author is and what he or she is doing are called **attributive tags** because they attribute information to a source. Attributive tags help you assign credit where credit is due. Most tags consist of the author's name and a verb. These verbs are often used in attributive tags:

acknowledge	concede	emphasize	note
advise	conclude	endorse	object
agree	consider	explain	offer
analyze	criticize	find	oppose
argue	declare	illustrate	reject
assert	deny	imply	report
believe	describe	insist	state
claim	disagree	list	suggest
compare	discuss	maintain	think

Other attributive tags are phrases, such as *according to the researcher, from the author's perspective,* and *in the author's mind.*

Jacob Thomas used function statements to develop a summary of the following article. Jacob chose the article as a possible source for a research project addressing the question "How do the media use language to deceive the public?" His function statements follow the essay.

WILLIAM LUTZ
Doubts about Doublespeak

During the past year, we learned that we can shop at a "unique retail biosphere" instead of a farmers' market, where we can buy items made of "synthetic glass" instead of plastic, or purchase a "high-velocity, multipurpose air circulator," or electric fan. A "wastewater conveyance facility" may "exceed the odor threshold" from time to time due to the presence of "regulated human nutrients," but that is not to be confused with a sewage plant that stinks up the neighborhood with sewage sludge. Nor should we confuse a "resource development park" with a dump. Thus does doublespeak continue to spread.

Doublespeak is language which pretends to communicate but doesn't. It is language which makes the bad seem good, the negative seem positive, the unpleasant seem attractive, or at least tolerable. It is language which avoids, shifts or denies responsibility; language which is at variance with its real or purported meaning. It is language which conceals or prevents thought.

Doublespeak is all around us. We are asked to check our packages at the desk "for our convenience" when it's not for our convenience at all but for someone else's convenience. We see advertisements for "preowned," "experienced" or "previously distinguished" cars, not used cars and for "genuine imitation leather," "virgin vinyl" or "real counterfeit diamonds." Television offers not reruns but "encore telecasts." There are no slums or ghettos just the "inner city" or "substandard housing" where the "disadvantaged" or "economically nonaffluent" live and where there might be a problem with "substance abuse." Nonprofit organizations don't make a profit, they have "negative deficits" or experience "revenue excesses." With doublespeak it's not dying but "terminal living" or "negative patient care outcome."

There are four kinds of doublespeak. The first kind is the euphemism, a word or phrase designed to avoid a harsh or distasteful reality. Used to mislead or deceive, the euphemism becomes doublespeak. In 1984 the U.S. State Department's annual reports on the status of human rights around the world ceased using the word "killing." Instead the State Department used the phrase "unlawful or arbitrary deprivation of life," thus avoiding the embarrassing situation of government-sanctioned killing in countries supported by the United States.

A second kind of doublespeak is jargon, the specialized language of a trade, profession or similar group, such as doctors, lawyers, plumbers or car mechanics. Legitimately used, jargon allows members of a group to communicate with each other clearly, efficiently and quickly. Lawyers and tax accountants speak to each other of an "involuntary conversion" of property, a legal term that means the loss or destruction of property through theft, accident or condemnation. But when lawyers or tax accountants use unfamiliar terms to speak to others, then the jargon becomes doublespeak.

In 1978 a commercial 727 crashed on takeoff, killing three passengers, injuring 21 others and destroying the airplane. The insured value of the airplane was greater than its book value, so the airline made a profit of $1.7 million, creating two problems: the airline didn't want to talk about one of its airplanes crashing, yet it had to account for that $1.7 million profit in its annual report to its stockholders. The airline solved both problems by inserting a footnote in its annual report which explained that the $1.7 million was due to "the involuntary conversion of a 727."

A third kind of doublespeak is gobbledygook or bureaucratese. Such doublespeak is simply a matter of overwhelming the audience with words—the more the better. Alan Greenspan, a polished practitioner of bureaucratese, once testified before a Senate committee that "it is a tricky problem to find the particular calibration in timing that would be appropriate to stem the acceleration in risk premiums created by falling in-

continued

comes without prematurely aborting the decline in the inflation-generated risk premiums."

The fourth kind of doublespeak is inflated language, which is designed to make the ordinary seem extraordinary, to make everyday things seem impressive, to give an air of importance to people or situations, to make the simple seem complex. Thus do car mechanics become "automotive internists," elevator operators become "members of the vertical transportation corps," grocery store checkout clerks become "career associate scanning professionals," and smelling something becomes "organoleptic analysis."

Doublespeak is not the product of careless language or sloppy thinking. Quite the opposite. Doublespeak is language carefully designed and constructed to appear to communicate when in fact it doesn't. It is language designed not to lead but mislead. Thus, it's not a tax increase but "revenue enhancement" or "tax-base broadening." So how can you complain about higher taxes? Those aren't useless, billion dollar pork barrel projects; they're really "congressional projects of national significance," so don't complain about wasteful government spending. That isn't the Mafia in Atlantic City; those are just "members of a career-offender cartel," so don't worry about the influence of organized crime in the city.

New doublespeak is created every day. The Environmental Protection Agency once called acid rain "poorly buffered precipitation" then dropped that term in favor of "atmospheric deposition of anthropogenically-derived acidic substances," but recently decided that acid rain should be called "wet deposition." The Pentagon, which has in the past given us such classic doublespeak as "hexiform rotatable surface compression unit" for steel nut, just published a pamphlet warning soldiers that exposure to nerve gas will lead to "immediate permanent incapacitation." That's almost as good as the Pentagon's official term "servicing the target," meaning to kill the enemy. Meanwhile, the Department of Energy wants to establish a "monitored retrievable storage site," a place once known as a dump for spent nuclear fuel.

Bad economic times give rise to lots of new doublespeak designed to avoid some very unpleasant economic realities. As the "contained depression" continues so does the corporate policy of making up even more new terms to avoid the simple, and easily understandable, term "layoff." So it is that corporations "reposition," "restructure," "reshape" or "realign" the company and "reduce duplication" through "release of resources" that involves a "permanent downsizing" or a "payroll adjustment" that results in a number of employees being "involuntarily terminated."

Other countries regularly contribute to doublespeak. In Japan, where baldness is called "hair disadvantaged," the economy is undergoing a "severe adjustment process," while in Canada there is an "involuntary downward development" of the work force. For some government agencies in Canada, wastepaper baskets have become "user friendly, space effective, flexible, deskside sortation units." Politicians in Canada may engage in "reality augmentation," but they never lie. As part of their new freedom, the people of Moscow can visit "intimacy salons," or sex shops as they're known in other countries. When dealing with the bureaucracy in Russia, people know that they should show officials "normal gratitude," or give them a bribe.

The worst doublespeak is the doublespeak of death. It is the language, wrote George Orwell in 1945, that is "largely the defense of the indefensible . . . designed to make lies sound truthful and murder respectable, and to give an appearance of solidity to pure wind." In the doublespeak of death, Orwell continued, "defenseless villages are bombarded from the air, the inhabitants driven out into the countryside, the cattle machine-gunned, the huts set on fire with incendiary bullets. This is called pacification. Millions of peasants are robbed of their farms and sent trudging along the roads with no more than they can carry. This is called transfer of population or rectification of frontiers." Today, in a country once called Yugoslavia, this is called "ethnic cleansing."

It's easy to laugh off doublespeak. After all, we all know what's going on, so what's the harm? But we don't always know what's going on, and when that happens, doublespeak accomplishes its ends. It alters our perception of reality. It deprives us of the tools we need to develop, advance and preserve our society, our culture, our civilization. It breeds suspicion, cynicism, distrust and, ultimately, hostility. It delivers us into the hands of those who do not have our interests at heart. As Samuel Johnson noted in 18th century England, even the devils in hell do not lie to one another, since the society of hell could not subsist without the truth, any more than any other society.

Sample Function Statements

Paragraph 1: Lutz begins his article on doublespeak by providing some examples: a "unique retail biosphere" is really a farmers' market; "synthetic glass" is really plastic.

Paragraph 2: Lutz defines *doublespeak* as devious language—"language which pretends to communicate but doesn't" (22).

Paragraph 3: Lutz describes the wide use of doublespeak. It is used in all media.

Paragraph 4: Lutz defines the first of four types of doublespeak—euphemism, which is a word or phrase that sugarcoats a harsher meaning. He provides an example from the U.S. State Department.

Paragraph 5: Lutz identifies jargon as the second type of doublespeak. It is the specialized language used by trades or professions such as car mechanics or doctors. But Lutz believes the use of jargon is legitimate when it enables efficient communication among group members. Jargon is considered doublespeak when in-group members use it to communicate with nonmembers who cannot understand it.

Paragraph 6: Lutz shows how an airline's annual report includes devious use of jargon to camouflage a disaster.

Paragraph 7: According to Lutz, the third type of doublespeak has two alternative labels: *gobbledygook* or *bureaucratese*. The distinguishing feature of this type of doublespeak is the large number of words used.

Paragraph 8: Lutz states that the final type of doublespeak is inflated language.

Paragraph 9: Lutz is careful to note that doublespeak is not the product of carelessness or "sloppy thinking" (23) but rather an attempt to deceive.

Paragraph 10: Lutz emphasizes that instances of doublespeak are created on a daily basis and provides examples.

Paragraph 11: Lutz attributes increases in the use of doublespeak to a bad economy. Doublespeak serves to gloss over the hardships people experience.

Paragraph 12: Lutz notes that doublespeak is also used in other countries.

Paragraph 13: Lutz singles out the doublespeak surrounding the topic of death as the worst type of doublespeak.

Paragraph 14: Lutz concludes his article by establishing the harmfulness of doublespeak, which can leave us without "the tools we need to develop, advance and preserve our society, our culture, our civilization" (24).

Clustering and ordering

After you have written a function statement for each paragraph of an essay, you may find that statements cluster together. For example, the statements Jacob Thomas wrote for paragraphs 4 through 8 of William Lutz's article all deal with the different categories of doublespeak. If an essay includes subheadings, you can use them to understand how the original author grouped ideas. By finding clusters of ideas, you take a major step toward condensing information. Instead of using a sentence or two to summarize each paragraph, you can use a sentence or two to summarize three paragraphs. For example, Jacob might condense his function statements for paragraphs 4 through 8 into one sentence: "Lutz believes that euphemism, jargon, gobbledygook (or bureaucratese), and inflated language are four types of doublespeak."

Summaries often present the main points in the same order as in the original source, usually with the thesis statement of the original source first, followed by supporting information. Even if the thesis statement appears at the end of the original source, you should still state it at the beginning of your summary. If there is no explicit thesis statement in the original source, you should state at the beginning of your summary the thesis (or main idea) that you have inferred from reading that source. Including a thesis statement, which captures the essence of the original source, in the first or second sentence of a summary provides a reference point for other information reported in the summary. The introductory sentences of a summary should also include the source author's name and the title of the source.

After you finish your summary, ask yourself the following questions to ensure that it is effective:

- Have I included the author's name and the title of the source?
- Have I mentioned the thesis (or main idea) of the original source?
- Have I used attributive tags to show that I am referring to someone else's ideas?
- Have I remained objective, not evaluating or judging the material I am summarizing?
- Have I remained faithful to the source by accurately representing the material?

Direct quotations can be used in summaries, but they should be used sparingly. Guidelines for quotations are discussed in more detail on pages 553–555. All quotations and references to source material require accurate citation and documentation. In-text citation and documentation formats are presented in chapter 21.

Sample student summary

Jacob Thomas used the MLA citation and documentation guidelines in producing the following summary. Notice that Jacob chose to include only those details he found most important. The notes he took on paragraphs 9, 11, and 13 were not included.

Thomas 1

Jacob Thomas

Professor Brown

English 101, Section 13

January 22, 2008

Summary of "Doubts about Doublespeak"

In "Doubts about Doublespeak," William Lutz describes the deviousness

of doublespeak, which he defines as "language which pretends to communicate

but doesn't" (22). It is language meant to deceive. "Unique retail biosphere" for

the phrase *farmers' market* and "revenue enhancement" for the word *taxes* are

just a few of the examples Lutz provides. Such use of deceptive language is

widespread. According to Lutz, it can be found around the world, and it is

created anew on a daily basis. Lutz defines four types of doublespeak.

Euphemisms are words or phrases that sugarcoat harsher meanings. The U.S.

State Department's use of "unlawful or arbitrary deprivation of life" for *killing*

is an example (22). Jargon is the second type of doublespeak Lutz discusses. It

is the specialized language used by trades or professions such as car mechanics

or doctors. Although Lutz believes the use of jargon is legitimate when it

enables efficient communication among group members, he considers it

doublespeak when in-group members use it to communicate with

nonmembers who cannot understand it. Lutz distinguishes the third type of

doublespeak, gobbledygook (or bureaucratese), by noting the large number

of words used; these, he says, serve to overwhelm readers. The final type

Research

of doublespeak, according to Lutz, is inflated language, which is the use of
elaborate or impressive terms to describe something quite ordinary. Lutz
concludes his article by establishing the harmfulness of doublespeak. He
believes that doublespeak can alter our perception and thus leave us without
"the tools we need to develop, advance and preserve our society, our culture,
our civilization" (24).

Work Cited

Lutz, William. "Doubts about Doublespeak." *State Government News* July 1993:
22-24. Print.

Partial summaries

Jacob Thomas summarized almost an entire article. Depending on his purpose and the expectations of his audience, he might have chosen to write a partial summary instead. Partial summaries of varying size are frequently found in research papers. A one-sentence summary may be appropriate when the researcher wants to focus on a specific piece of information. If Jacob had been interested in noting what various writers have said about doublespeak, he could have represented William Lutz's ideas as follows:

> In "Doubts about Doublespeak," William Lutz describes abuses of language and explains why they are harmful.

Partial summaries of the same source may vary depending on the researcher's purpose. How does the following partial summary of Lutz's article differ from Jacob's more comprehensive summary provided earlier?

SAMPLE PARTIAL SUMMARY

> Authors frequently cite the work of George Orwell when discussing the abuses of language. In "Doubts about Doublespeak," William Lutz describes different types of doublespeak—language used to deceive—and explains why they are harmful. He quotes a passage from Orwell's "Politics and the English Language" in order to emphasize his own belief that the doublespeak surrounding the topic of death is the worst form of language abuse: "defenseless villages are bombarded from the air, the inhabitants driven out into the countryside, the cattle machine-gunned, the huts set on fire with incendiary bullets. This is called pacification. Millions of peasants are robbed of their farms and sent trudging along the roads with no more than they can carry. This is called transfer of population or rectification of frontiers" (qtd. in Lutz 24).

This partial summary focuses on George Orwell's work, rather than on the uses of doublespeak.

Paraphrasing

A **paraphrase** is like a summary in that it is a restatement of someone else's ideas, but a paraphrase differs from a summary in coverage. A summary condenses information to a greater extent than a paraphrase does. When you paraphrase, you translate the original source into your own words; thus, your paraphrase will be approximately the same length as the original. Researchers usually paraphrase material when they want to clarify it or integrate its content smoothly into their own work.

A paraphrase, then, should be written in your own words and should cite the original author. A restatement of an author's ideas that maintains the original sentence structure but substitutes a few synonyms is not an adequate paraphrase. In fact, such a restatement is plagiarism—even when the author's name is cited. Your paraphrase should contain different words and a new word order; however, the content of the original source should not be altered. In short, a paraphrase must be accurate. Any intentional misrepresentation of another person's work is unethical.

Below are some examples of problematic and successful paraphrases. The source citations in the examples are formatted according to MLA guidelines.

SOURCE

Wardhaugh, Ronald. *How Conversation Works*. Oxford: Basil Blackwell, 1985. Print.

ORIGINAL

Conversation, like daily living, requires you to exhibit a considerable trust in others.

PROBLEMATIC PARAPHRASE

Conversation, like everyday life, requires you to show your trust in others

(Wardhaugh 5).

SUCCESSFUL PARAPHRASE

Ronald Wardhaugh compares conversation to everyday life because it requires people to trust one another (5).

ORIGINAL

Without routine ways of doing things and in the absence of norms of behaviour, life would be too difficult, too uncertain for most of us. The routines, patterns, rituals, stereotypes even of everyday existence provide us with many of the means for coping with that existence, for reducing uncertainty and anxiety, and for providing us with the appearance of stability and continuity in the outside world. They let us get on with the actual business of living. However, many are beneath our conscious awareness; what, therefore, is of particular interest is bringing to awareness just those aspects of our lives that make living endurable (and even enjoyable) just because they are so commonly taken for granted.

Problematic Paraphrase

Without habitual ways of acting and without behavioral norms, life would be too uncertain for us and thus too difficult. Our routines and rituals of everyday life provide us with many of the ways for coping with our lives, for decreasing the amount of uncertainty and anxiety we feel, and for giving us a sense of stability and continuity. They let us live our lives. But many are beneath our awareness, so what is of interest is bringing to consciousness just those parts of our lives that make life livable (and even fun) just because we generally take them for granted (Wardhaugh 21-22).

Successful Paraphrase

Ronald Wardhaugh believes that without routines and other types of conventional behavior we would find life hard because it would be too unstable and unpredictable. Our habitual ways of going about our everyday lives enable us to cope with the lack of certainty we would experience otherwise. Many of our daily routines and rituals, however, are not in our conscious awareness. Wardhaugh maintains that becoming aware of the ways we make life seem certain and continuous can be quite interesting (21-22).

Notice how the attributive tags in the successful paraphrases help the writer vary sentence structure.

Quoting Sources in Your Paper

Whenever you find a quotation that you would like to use in your paper, you should think about your reasons for including it. Quotations should be used only sparingly; therefore, make sure that when you quote a source, you do so because the language in the quotation is striking and not easily paraphrased. A pithy quotation in just the right place can help you emphasize a point you have mentioned or, alternatively, set up a point of view you wish to refute. If you overuse quotations, though, readers may decide that laziness prevented you from making sufficient effort to express your own thoughts.

Using attributive tags

The direct quotations in your paper should be exact replicas of the originals. This means replicating not only the words but also punctuation and capitalization. Full sentences require quotation marks and usually commas to set them off from attributive tags. Such a tag can be placed at the beginning, middle, or end of your own sentence.

ATTRIBUTIVE TAG AT THE BEGINNING OF A SENTENCE

> André Aciman reminisces, "Life begins somewhere with the scent of lavender" (1).

ATTRIBUTIVE TAG IN THE MIDDLE OF A SENTENCE

> "Life," according to André Aciman, "begins somewhere with the scent of
>
> lavender" (1).

ATTRIBUTIVE TAG AT THE END OF A SENTENCE

> "Life begins somewhere with the scent of lavender," writes André Aciman (1).

Including question marks or exclamation points

If you choose to quote a sentence that ends with a question mark or an exclamation point, the punctuation should be maintained; no comma is necessary.

> "Why are New Yorkers always bumping into Charlie Ravioli and grabbing
>
> lunch, instead of sitting down with him and exchanging intimacies, as friends
>
> should, as people do in Paris and Rome?" asks Adam Gopnik (106).

> "Incompatibility is unacceptable in mathematics! It must be resolved!" claims
>
> William Byers (29).

Quoting memorable words or phrases

You may want to quote just a memorable word or phrase. Only the part of the sentence you are quoting appears within quotation marks, and generally no comma is necessary.

> Part of what Ken Wilber calls "boomeritis" is attributable to excessive emotional
>
> preoccupation with the self (27).

Modifying quotations with square brackets or ellipsis points

In order to make a quotation fit your sentence, you may need to modify the capitalization of a word. To indicate such a modification, use square brackets:

Pollan believes that "[t]hough animals are still very much 'things' in the eyes of American law, change is in the air" (191).

You can also use square brackets to insert words needed for clarification:

> Ben Metcalf reports, "She [Sacajawea] seems to have dug up a good deal of the topsoil along the route in an effort to find edible roots with which to impress Lewis and Clark . . ." (164).

For partial quotations, as in the example above, use three ellipsis points to indicate that some of the original sentence was omitted.

Using block quotations

If you want to quote an extremely long sentence or more than one sentence, you may need to use a block quotation. MLA guidelines call for a block quotation to be set off by being indented one inch (or ten spaces) from the left margin. You should use a block quotation only if the quoted material takes up more than four lines on your paper's page. No quotation marks are used around a block quotation.

> Francis Spufford describes her experience reading *The Hobbit* as a young child:
>
> > By the time I reached *The Hobbit*'s last page, though, writing
> > had softened, and lost the outlines of the printed alphabet, and
> > become a transparent liquid, first viscous and sluggish, like a jelly
> > of meaning, then ever thinner and more mobile, flowing faster and
> > faster, until it reached me at the speed of thinking and I could not
> > entirely distinguish the suggestions it was making from my own
> > thoughts. (279)

APA guidelines call for using a block format when quoting forty or more words. The page number for the in-text citation follows *p.* for "page." More information about in-text citations can be found in chapter 21.

Evaluating and Responding to Your Sources

To incorporate sources effectively, you should not only summarize, paraphrase, quote, and document them but also respond to them. Your research log is a good place to record your initial responses. You can then craft more complete responses to your sources during the process of writing your paper.

Your response to a source will be based on your evaluation of it. Readers of academic research papers expect the authors to be critical. They want to know whether facts are accurate or erroneous, whether logic is apt or weak, whether plans are comprehensive or ill-conceived, and whether conclusions are valid or invalid. Thus, researchers evaluate their sources to ensure that their readers' concerns are being addressed; however, they also critique sources to set up their own research niche. They try to show that previous research is lacking in some way in order to establish an exigence for their study.

Questions that can help you evaluate your sources fall into five categories: currency, coverage, reliability, reasoning, and author stance. In the following sections, you'll learn more about these categories and read brief sample responses to research.

Currency

Depending on the nature of your research, the currency of sources or of the data they present may be important to consider. Using up-to-date sources is crucial when you are writing about events that have taken place recently or issues that have arisen recently. However, if you are doing historical research, you may want to use primary sources from the period you are focusing on.

QUESTIONS ABOUT CURRENCY

- Do your sources and the data presented in them need to be up to date? If so, are they?
- If you are doing historical research, are your sources from the relevant period?
- Since you began your project, have events occurred that you should take into account? Do you need to find new sources?

SAMPLE RESPONSE TO RESEARCH

According to the author, only 50 percent of all public schools have Web pages (23); however, this statistic is taken from a report published in 1997. A more recent count would likely yield a much higher percentage.

Coverage

Coverage refers to the comprehensiveness of research. The more comprehensive a study is, the more convincing are its findings. Similarly, the more examples a writer provides, the more compelling are the writer's conclusions. Claims that are based on only one instance are likely to be criticized for being merely anecdotal.

QUESTIONS ABOUT COVERAGE

▪ How many examples is the claim based on?
▪ Is this number of examples convincing or are more examples needed?
▪ Are the conclusions based on a sufficient amount of data?

SAMPLE RESPONSE TO RESEARCH

Johnson concludes that middle-school students are expected to complete an

inordinate amount of homework given their age, but he bases his conclusion on

research conducted in only three schools (90). To be more convincing, Johnson

would need to conduct research in more schools, preferably located in different

parts of the country.

Reliability

Research, especially research based on experiments or surveys, must be reliable. Experimental results are reliable if they can be replicated in other studies—that is, if other researchers who perform the same experiment or survey get the same results. Any claims based on results supported by only one experiment are extremely tentative.

Reliability also refers to the accuracy of data reported as factual. Researchers are expected to report their findings honestly, not distorting them to support their own beliefs and not claiming ideas of others as their own. Researchers must resist the temptation to exclude information that might weaken their conclusions.

Sometimes, evaluating the publisher can provide a gauge of the reliability of the material. As a rule, reliable source material is published by reputable companies, institutions, and organizations. If you are using a book, check to see whether it was published by a university press or a commercial press. Books published by university presses are normally reviewed by experts before publication to ensure the accuracy of facts. Books published by commercial presses may or may not have received the same scrutiny, so you will have to depend on the reputation of the author and/or postpublication reviews to determine reliability. If you are using an article, remember that articles published in journals, like books published by academic presses, have been reviewed in draft form by two or three experts. Journal articles also include extensive bibliographies so that readers can examine the sources

Research

used in the research. Magazine articles, in contrast, seldom undergo expert review and rarely include documentation of sources. If you decide to use an online source, be sure to consider the nature of its sponsor. Is it a college or university (identified by the suffix *.edu*), a government agency (*.gov*), a non-profit organization (*.org*), a network site (*.net*), or a commercial business (*.com*)? There is no easy way to ascertain the reliability of online sources. If you are unsure about an online source, try to find out as much as you can about it. First click on links that tell you about the mission of the site sponsor and then perform an online search of the sponsor's name to see what other researchers have written about the company, institution, or organization.

QUESTIONS ABOUT RELIABILITY

- Could the experiment or survey that yielded these data be replicated?
- Are the facts reported indeed facts?
- Is the coverage balanced and the information relevant?
- Are the sources used acknowledged properly?
- Are there any disputes regarding the data? If so, are these disputes discussed sufficiently?
- Was the material published by a reputable company, institution, or organization?

SAMPLE RESPONSE TO RESEARCH

The author blames business for practically all of our nation's woes without

providing details to bolster her argument. It is not clear how business has the

impact on health care and education that she says it does.

Soundness of reasoning

When writing is logical, the reasoning is sound. Lapses in logic may be the result of using evidence that does not directly support a claim, appealing primarily (or exclusively) to the reader's emotions, or encouraging belief in false authority. Faulty logic is often due to the presence of rhetorical fallacies. These fallacies occur often enough that each one has its own name. Some of the most common rhetorical fallacies are listed below; after each is a question for you to ask yourself as you consider an author's reasoning. (See chapter 15 for a more detailed discussion of rhetorical fallacies.)

- *Ad hominem* (Latin for "toward the man himself"). Has the author criticized or attacked the author of another source based solely on his or her character, not taking into account the reasoning or evidence provided in the source?

  Faulty: The arguments against abortion are weak because they are written by a Catholic priest.

  The reasoning is faulty because it does not take into account the arguments given by the priest to support his opposition to abortion.

Appeal to tradition. Does the author support or encourage some action merely by referring to what has traditionally been done?

Faulty: Democracy is the best type of government because it was the government of our forefathers.

Although there may be a number of reasons for promoting democracy, the fact that it was the type of government chosen by previous generations does not mean it is the best.

Bandwagon. Does the author claim that an action is appropriate because many other people do it?

Faulty: The speed limit should be raised to 80 mph on the freeway because everyone drives that fast anyway.

Driving over the speed limit may be common, but this is not a sufficient reason for raising the speed limit. Speed limits are created to ensure safety. Higher speed limits would make it more difficult to achieve that goal.

False authority. When reporting the opinions of experts in one field, does the author incorrectly assume that they have expertise in other fields?

Faulty: As the Dixie Chicks argued, the United States should not have gone to war against Iraq.

Musical skill or popularity does not qualify someone to be an expert in foreign policy.

False cause (sometimes referred to as the Latin *post hoc, ergo propter hoc,* which translates as "after this, so because of this"). When reporting two events, does the author incorrectly believe (or suggest) that the first event caused the second event?

Faulty: Students protested against the tuition hike, so the administration decided not to increase tuition this year.

Although the students' protest may have influenced the administration, it was probably not the sole reason for the decision.

False dilemma (also called the *either/or fallacy*). Does the author provide only two options when more than two exist?

Faulty: Either the United States uses military force to achieve its goals, or it will not be considered a world power.

The reasoning is faulty because use of military force is not the only way to secure a reputation as a world power.

Hasty generalization. Are the author's conclusions based on too little evidence?

Faulty: The students in that high school are not prepared for college because their SAT scores are low.

This statement fails to take into account other measures that predict success in college, such as course grades and community service.

Oversimplification. Does the author provide unreasonably simple solutions?

Faulty: If parents spent more time with their children, there would be less crime.

This statement ignores the many difficulties of raising a family as well as the many causes of crime.

Research

■ *Slippery slope.* Does the author predict an unreasonable sequence of events?

Faulty: Establishing strict laws regarding the possession of weapons will be the first step toward becoming a police state.

This statement is an exaggeration; countries such as Canada and England have gun-control laws but are not police states.

TRICKS OF THE TRADE

Enter "rhetorical fallacies" in the Google search box. You will find even more ways reasoning can go awry. One student found over ten thousand sites devoted to the topic.

Stance of the author

All authors have beliefs and values that influence their work. As you read a work as part of your research, it is your job to decide whether the author is expressing strong views because of deep commitment or because of a desire to deceive. As long as authors represent information truthfully and respectfully, they are acting ethically. If they twist facts or otherwise intentionally misrepresent ideas, they are being dishonest.

QUESTIONS ABOUT THE STANCE OF THE AUTHOR

■ Has the author adequately conveyed information, or has the author oversimplified information or ignored relevant information?

■ Has the author been faithful to source material, or has the author distorted information and quoted out of context?

■ Has the author adequately supported claims, or has the author used unsupported generalizations?

SAMPLE RESPONSE TO RESEARCH

The author believes that artificial environments are detrimental to the natural environment because they draw people away from the outdoors. In his mind, one must spend time outside in order to be an environmentalist (78). The author, though, owns a rafting service and thus is promoting his own business, which occurs in a natural environment. He fails to account for the many benefits of artificial environments, such as providing exercise opportunities to people who do not live near natural areas.

ACKNOWLEDGING SOURCES | 21

1. The coffee cups pictured here may be a familiar sight, but you may not have thought of them as demonstrating the use of sources. How does Starbucks credit the sources of the quotations? What information is given? What does that information tell you? What information about the sources is left out?

2. Even if you're not used to seeing quotations on coffee cups, you've likely seen them elsewhere; they appear on everything from teabags to t-shirts, bumper stickers to baseball caps. If you wanted to place a quotation on something you own, what item and what quotation would you choose? What source information, if any, would you provide to accompany it?

Why Acknowledge Sources?

Just as you decide whether authors of sources are credible, your readers will decide whether your work is trustworthy. One of the most important ways to demonstrate credibility as an author is to acknowledge the sources from which you have drawn. Writers who do not provide adequate acknowledgment are accused of **plagiarism**, the unethical and illegal use of others' words and ideas. By acknowledging your sources, you also give your readers the information they need to find those sources in case they would like to consult them on their own. Such acknowledgment should occur in the body of your paper (in-text citations) and in the bibliography at the end of your paper (documentation). The Modern Language Association (MLA) and the American Psychological Association (APA) provide guidelines for both formatting papers and acknowledging sources. These guidelines are summarized in the following sections and illustrated with annotated sample papers.

Which Sources to Cite

If the information you use is considered common knowledge, you do not have to include an in-text citation. Common knowledge is information that most educated people know and many reference books report. For example, you would not have to include an in-text citation if you mentioned that New Orleans was devastated by Hurricane Katrina. However, if you quoted or paraphrased what various politicians said about relief efforts following Katrina, you would need to include such citations.

You should include citations for all facts that are not common knowledge, statistics (whether from a text, table, graph, or chart), visuals, research findings, and quotations and paraphrases of statements made by other people. Be sure that when you acknowledge sources you include the following:

- The name(s) of the author(s); if unknown, include the title of the text
- Page number(s)
- A bibliographic entry that corresponds to the in-text citation
- Quotation marks around material quoted exactly

Common Citation Errors

To avoid being accused of plagiarism, be on the lookout for the following errors:

- No author (or title) mentioned
- No page numbers listed
- No quotation marks used
- Paraphrase worded too similarly to the source
- Inaccurate paraphrase
- Images used with no indication of the source
- No bibliographic entry corresponding to the in-text citation

MLA Guidelines for In-Text Citations

If you are following the style recommended by the Modern Language Association, you will acknowledge your sources within the text of your paper by referring just to authors and page numbers. If the author's name is unknown, you use the title of the source in the in-text citation. By providing in-text citations and a works-cited list at the end of your paper, you offer your readers the opportunity to consult the sources you used.

You will likely consult a variety of sources for any research paper. The following examples are representative of the types of in-text citations you might use.

1.   Work by one to three authors

Although New York State publishes a booklet of driving rules, **Katha Pollit** has found no books on "the art of driving" (**217**).

No books exist on "the art of driving" (**Pollit 217**).

Other researchers, such as **Steven Reiss and James Wiltz** (**734-36**), rely on tools like surveys to explain why we watch reality television.

Survey results can help us understand why we watch reality television (**Reiss and Wiltz 734-36**).

Citizens passed the bond issue in 2004, even though they originally voted it down in 2001 (**Jacobs, Manzow, and Holst 120**).

The authors' last names can be placed in the text or within parentheses with the page number. The parenthetical citation should appear as close as possible to the information documented—usually at the end of the sentence or after any quotation marks. When citing a range of page numbers of three digits, leave out the hundreds' digit for the higher number: 201-97.

2. Work by four or more authors

When citing parenthetically a source by more than three authors, you can either include all the authors' last names or provide just the first author's last name followed by the abbreviation *et al.* (Latin for "and others"): (Stafford, Suzuki, Li, and Brown 67) or (Stafford et al. 67). The abbreviation *et al.* should not be underlined or italicized in citations.

3. Work by an unknown author

The Tehuelche people left their handprints on the walls of a cave, now called Cave of the Hands (**"Hands of Time"** 124).

If the author is unknown, use the title of the work in place of the author's name. If the title is long, shorten it, beginning with the first word used in the corresponding works-cited entry ("Wandering" for "Wandering with Cameras in the Himalaya"). If you use the title in the text, however, you do not have to place it in the parenthetical reference.

4. An entire work

Using literary examples, **Alain de Botton** explores the reasons people decide to travel.

Notice that no page numbers are necessary when an entire work is cited.

5. A multivolume work

President Truman asked that all soldiers be treated equally (**Merrill 11: 741**).

The volume number and page number(s) are separated by a colon.

6. Two or more works by the same author(s)

Kress refers to the kinds of interpretive skills required of children who play video games to argue that we should recognize multiple forms of reading, not just those already encouraged in our school systems (***Literacy*** 174).

Marianne Celce-Murcia and Diane Larsen-Freeman claim that grammar involves three dimensions (***Grammar Book*** 4).

To distinguish one work from another, include a title. If the title is long (such as *Literacy in the New Media Age*), shorten it, beginning with the first word used in the corresponding works-cited entry.

7. Two or more works by different authors with the same last name

If the military were to use solely conventional weapons, the draft would likely be reinstated (**E. Scarry** 241).

To distinguish one author from another, use their initials. If the initials are the same, spell out their first names.

8. Work by a corporate or government author

Strawbale constructions are now popular across the nation (**Natl. Ecobuilders Group** 2).

Provide the name of the corporate or government author and a page reference. If the author's name is extremely long, you may use common abbreviations—for example, *assn.* for "association" and *natl.* for "national."

9. Indirect source

According to **Sir George Dasent**, a reader "must be satisfied with the soup that is set before him, and not desire to see the bones of the ox out of which it has been boiled" **(qtd. in Shippey 289).**

Use the abbreviation *qtd.* to indicate that you found the quotation in another source.

10. Work in an anthology

"Good cooking," claims **Jane Kramer**, "is much easier to master than good writing" **(153).**

Either in the text or within parentheses with the page number, use the name of the author of the particular section (chapter, essay, or article) you are citing, not the editor of the entire book, unless they are the same.

11. Poem

The final sentence in **Philip Levine's** "Homecoming" is framed by conditional clauses: "If we're quiet / if the place had a spirit" **(38-43).**

Instead of page numbers, provide line numbers, preceded by *line(s)* for the first citation; use numbers only for subsequent citations.

12. Drama

After some hesitation, the messenger tells Macbeth what he saw: "As I did stand my watch upon the hill / I looked toward Birnam and anon methought / The wood began to move" **(5.5.35-37).**

Instead of page numbers, indicate act, scene, and line numbers.

13. Bible

The image of seeds covering the sidewalk reminded her of the parable in which a seed falls on stony ground **(Matt. 13.18-23).**

Instead of page numbers, mention the book of the Bible (using the conventional abbreviation), chapter, and verse.

14. Two or more works in one parenthetical citation

Usage issues are discussed in both academic and popular periodicals **(Bex and Watts 5; Lippi-Green 53).**

Use a semicolon to separate citations.

15. Material from the Internet

Alston describes three types of rubrics that teachers can use to evaluate student writing **(pars. 2-15).**

If page numbers are not available, provide paragraph or screen numbers. Precede paragraph numbers with *par.* or *pars.* and screen numbers with *screen* or *screens.*

MLA Guidelines for Documenting Works Cited

To provide readers with the information they need to find all the sources you have used in your paper, you must prepare a bibliography. According to MLA guidelines, your bibliography should be titled *Works Cited* (not in italics). It should contain an entry for every source you cite in your text, and, conversely, every bibliographic entry you list should have a corresponding in-text citation. Do not include entries for works that you consulted but did not cite in your paper.

Alphabetize the entries in your works-cited list according to the author's (or the first author's) last name. When the author is unknown, alphabetize according to title. Use the first major word of the title; in other words, ignore any initial article (*a, an,* or *the*). If a source was written by four or more authors, you have two options: either list all the authors' names or provide just the first author's name followed by the abbreviation *et al.* (not italicized). Many people prefer to list all the authors so that their contributions are recognized equally.

Double-space the entire works-cited list. The first line of each entry begins flush with the left margin, and subsequent lines are indented one-half inch or five character spaces. (Your word processor may refer to the indented line as a *hanging indent.*) If you have used more than one work by the same author (or team of authors), alphabetize the entries according to title. For the first entry, provide the author's name; for any subsequent entries, substitute three hyphens (---).

The current guidelines from the *MLA Handbook for Writers of Research Papers,* 7e, recommend italicizing in place of underlining. MLA also recommends that the consulted medium of publication be stated in the documentation. In the following examples, note the use of italics for the book titles. The medium of publication, *Print* (not italicized), appears at the end of these entries. Other medium designations include *CD-ROM, LP, Television, Radio,* and *Web* (not italicized).

Rodriguez, Richard. *Brown: The Last Discovery of America.* New York: Viking, 2002. Print.

---. *Hunger of Memory: The Education of Richard Rodriguez.* New York: Bantam, 1982. Print.

If two or more entries have the same first author, alphabetize the entries according to the second author's last name.

Bailey, Guy, and Natalie Maynor. "The Divergence Controversy." *American Speech* 64.1 (1989):
12-39. Print.

Bailey, Guy, and Jan Tillery. "Southern American English." *American Language Review* 4.4 (2000):
27-29. Print.

For more details on various types of sources, use the following directory to find relevant sections. For an example of a works-cited list, see page 595. If you would like to use a checklist to help ensure that you have followed MLA guidelines, see page 581.

DIRECTORY OF WORKS-CITED ENTRIES ACCORDING TO MLA GUIDELINES

Books

Books

| Author(s) | Title | Subtitle |

Lightman, Alan. *A Sense of the Mysterious: Science and the Human Spirit.* New York: Pantheon, 2005. Print.

| City of Publication | Name of Publisher | Year of Publication | Medium of Publication |

Title page of *A Sense of the Mysterious.*

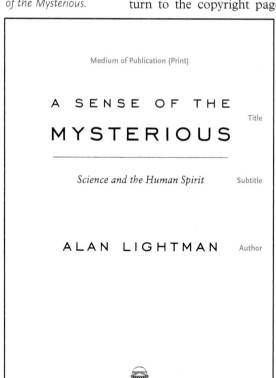

Medium of Publication (Print)

A SENSE OF THE

MYSTERIOUS   Title

Science and the Human Spirit   Subtitle

ALAN LIGHTMAN   Author

Name of publisher   *Pantheon Books, New York*   City of publication

You can find most of the information you need for a works-cited entry on a book's title page. If you cannot find the date of publication on the title page, turn to the copyright page. Works-cited entries for books generally include three units of information: author, title, and publication data.

Author The author's last name is given first. Use a comma to separate the last name from the first, and place a period at the end of this unit of information. When two or more authors are listed, only the first author's name is inverted. For a source by more than three authors, either list all the authors' names or provide just the first author's name followed by the abbreviation *et al.* (not italicized).

Atherton, Lewis.

Blyth, Carl, Sigrid Becktenwald, and Jenny Wang.

Rand, George, Peter Mathis, Sali Hudson, and Victor Singler.

OR

Rand, George, et al.

Title Include the title and, if there is one, the subtitle of the book. Use a colon to separate the subtitle from the title. Italicize every part of the title and subtitle, including any colon; however,

Year of
publication   Copyright © 2005 by Einstein Dreams, Inc.

All rights reserved under International and Pan-American Copyright
Conventions. Published in the United States by Pantheon Books,
a division of Random House, Inc., New York, and simultaneously
in Canada by Random House of Canada Limited, Toronto.

Pantheon Books and colophon are registered trademarks
of Random House, Inc.

Owing to limitations of space, all acknowledgments
for permission to reprint previously published material
may be found preceding the author's biography.

Library of Congress Cataloging-in-Publication Data

Lightman, Alan P., [date]
A sense of the mysterious : science and the human spirit /
Alan Lightman.
     p.   cm.
ISBN 0-375-42320-6 (hardback)
1. Creative ability in science—United States. 2. Science—Philosophy.
3. Lightman, Alan P., [date] 4. Scientists—United States—20th
century—Biography. I. Title.
Q172.5.C74L54 2005 501—dc22 2004052052

www.pantheonbooks.com

Book design by M. Kristen Bearse

Printed in the United States of America
First Edition
2 4 6 8 9 7 5 3 1

Copyright page
of *A Sense of the
Mysterious.*

do not italicize the final period, which marks the end of the second unit of information.

Visual Explanations: Images and Quantities, Evidence and Narrative.

Publication data For the third unit of information, list the city of publication, the publisher's name, the copyright date, and the medium of publication you consulted (in this case, *Print*). Place a colon between the city of publication and the publisher's name, a comma between the publisher's name and the copyright date, a period between the date and medium of publication, and a period at the end of this unit of information. When more than one city appears on the title page, use only the first one listed. You can usually shorten a publisher's name by using the principal name (*Random* for Random House or *Knopf* for Alfred A. Knopf) or by using the abbreviation *UP* for University Press (*Yale UP* for Yale University Press).

1. Book by one author

Pinker, Steven. *The Language Instinct: How the Mind Creates Language.* New York: Harper, 2000. Print.

2. Book by two or three authors

Gies, Joseph, and Frances Gies. *Life in a Medieval City.* New York: Harper, 1981. Print.

List the authors' names in the order in which they appear on the title page, not in alphabetical order. Include full names for all of the authors, even if they have the same last name. Invert the name of only the first author.

Research

3. Book by four or more authors

Biber, Douglas, Stig Johansson, Geoffrey Leech, Susan Conrad, and Edward Finegan. *Longman*

   Grammar of Spoken and Written English. New York: Longman, 1999. Print.

Biber, Douglas, et al. *Longman Grammar of Spoken and Written English*. New York: Longman, 1999.

   Print.

Provide the names of all the authors in the order in which they appear on the title page, with the first author's name inverted, or list only the first author's name, followed by a comma and *et al.*

4. Book by a corporate author

American Heart Association. *The New American Heart Association Cookbook*. 6th ed. New York:

   Clarkson Potter, 2001. Print.

Omit any article (*a, an,* or *the*) that begins the name of a corporate author, and alphabetize the entry in the works-cited list according to the first major word of the corporate author's name.

5. Book by an anonymous author

Primary Colors: A Novel of Politics. New York: Warner, 1996. Print.

Alphabetize the entry according to the first major word in the title of the work.

6. Book with an author and an editor

Dickens, Charles. *Pickwick Papers*. Ed. Malcolm Andrews. Boston: Tuttle, 1997. Print.

Begin the entry with the author's name. Place the editor's name after the title of the book, preceded by *Ed.* for "edited by."

7. Book with an editor instead of an author

Hudson, Susan, and Lynne Gilberg, eds. *Roofing and Siding*. Menlo Park: Sunset, 1994. Print.

Begin the entry with the name(s) of the editor(s), using the abbreviation *ed.* for "editor" or *eds.* for "editors."

8. Second or subsequent edition

Cameron, Rondo, and Larry Neal. *A Concise Economic History of the World: From Paleolithic Times*

   to the Present. 4th ed. New York: Oxford UP, 2003. Print.

After the title, place the number of the edition in its ordinal form, followed by *ed.* for "edition." Note that the letters *th* following the number appear in regular type, not as a superscript.

9. Introduction, preface, foreword, or afterword to a book

Peri, Yoram. Afterword. *The Rabin Memoirs*. By Yitzhak Rabin. Berkeley: U of California P, 1996.

   422-32. Print.

Begin the entry with the name of the author of the introduction, preface, foreword, or afterword, followed by the name of the part being cited (e.g., *Afterword*). If the part being cited has a title, include the title in quotation marks between the author's name and the name of the part being cited. Provide the name of the author of the book, preceded by *By,* after the title of the book. Provide the page number(s) of the part being cited after the publication information and complete the entry with the medium of publication.

10. Anthology

Ramazani, Jahan, Robert O'Clair, and Richard Ellman, eds. *The Norton Anthology of Modern*
    and Contemporary Poetry. 3rd ed. New York: Norton, 2003. Print.

The entry begins with the anthology's editor(s), with the first (or only) editor's
name inverted. Use the abbreviation *ed.* for "editor" or *eds.* for "editors."

11. Single work from an anthology

Savignon, Sandra J. "Communicative Language Teaching for the Twenty-First Century."
    Teaching English as a Second or Foreign Language. 3rd ed. Ed. Marianne Celce-Murcia.
    Boston: Heinle, 2001. 13-28. Print.

Begin the entry with the name of the author of the work you are citing, not the
name of the anthology's editor. The title of the work appears in quotation marks
between the author's name and the title of the anthology. The editor's name
is preceded by *Ed.* for "edited by." (Note that because *Ed.* stands for "edited
by," not "editor," there is no need to make the abbreviation plural for multiple
editors, as you do when listing editors before the title.) After the publication
information, include the numbers of the pages on which the work appears and
conclude with the medium of publication.

12. Two or more works from the same anthology

Jarratt, Susan C. "Feminist Pedagogy." Tate, Rupiper, and Schick 113-31.

Mutnick, Deborah. "On the Academic Margins: Basic Writing Pedagogy." Tate, Rupiper, and
    Schick 183-202.

Tate, Gary, Amy Rupiper, and Kurt Schick, eds. *A Guide to Composition Pedagogies*. New York:
    Oxford UP, 2001. Print.

When citing more than one work from the same anthology, include an entry
for the entire anthology as well as entries for the individual works. In entries for
individual works, list the names of the author(s) and the editor(s) and the title
of the work, but not the title of the anthology. Then specify the page or range of
pages on which the work appears. Note that only the third, complete entry ends
with the medium of publication.

13. Book with a title within the title

Koon, Helene Wickham. *Twentieth Century Interpretations of* Death of a Salesman: *A Collection of*
    Critical Essays. Englewood Cliffs: Prentice Hall, 1983. Print.

When an italicized title includes the title of another work that would normally be
italicized, do not italicize the embedded title. If the embedded title normally requires
quotation marks, it should be italicized as well as enclosed in quotation marks.

14. Translated book

Rilke, Rainer Maria. *Duino Elegies*. Trans. David Young. New York: Norton, 1978. Print.

The translator's name appears after the book title, preceded by *Trans.* However,
if the material cited in your paper refers primarily to the translator's comments
rather than to the translated text, the entry should appear as follows:

Young, David, trans. *Duino Elegies*. By Rainer Maria Rilke. New York: Norton, 1978. Print.

15. Republished book

Alcott, Louisa May. *Work: A Story of Experience.* 1873. Harmondsworth, Eng.: Penguin, 1995. Print.

Provide the publication date of the original work after the title.

16. Multivolume work

Banks, Lynne Reid. *The Indian in the Cupboard.* Vol. 3. New York: Morrow, 1994. Print.

Feynman, Richard Phillips, Robert B. Leighton, and Matthew L. Sands. *The Feynman Lectures on Physics.* 3 vols. Boston: Addison, 1989. Print.

Provide only the specific volume number (e.g., *Vol. 3*) after the title if you cite material from one volume. Provide the total number of volumes if you cite material from more than one volume.

17. Book in a series

Restle, David, and Dietmar Zaefferer, eds. *Sounds and Systems.* Berlin: Walter de Gruyter, 2002. Print. Trends in Linguistics. 141.

After the medium of publication at the end of the entry, provide the name of the series and the series number, separated by a period.

Articles

ARTICLE IN A JOURNAL

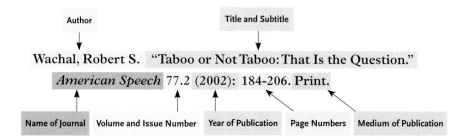

You can generally find the name of the journal, the volume number, and the year of publication on the cover of the journal. Sometimes this information is also included in the journal's page headers or footers. To find the title of the article, the author's name, and the page numbers, you'll need to locate the article within the journal.

ARTICLE IN A MAGAZINE

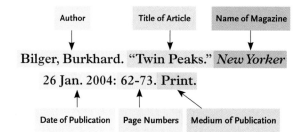

Research

To find the name of the magazine and the date of publication (ignore volume and issue numbers), look on the cover of the magazine. Sometimes this information is also included in the magazine's page headers or footers. To find the title of the article, the author's name, and the page numbers, you'll have to look at the article itself.

Works-cited entries for articles generally include three units of information: author, title of article, and publication data.

Author List the author, last name first. Use a comma to separate the last name from the first, and place a period at the end of this unit of information. If there is more than one author, see the information given for book entries on pages 569–570.

Title of article Include the title and, if there is one, the subtitle of the article. Use a colon to separate the subtitle from the title. Place the entire title within quotation marks, including the period that marks the end of the unit of information.

"Sounding Cajun: The Rhetorical Use of Dialect in Speech and Writing."

Publication data The publication data that you provide depends on the type of periodical in which the article appeared. However,

Name of journal

AMERICAN SPEECH

A Quarterly of Linguistic Usage

Volume number   Volume 82, Number 4

WINTER 2007   Year of publication

*Published by Duke University Press
for the American Dialect Society*

Cover of an academic journal.

for all entries, include the title of the periodical (italicized), the date of publication, the page numbers of the article, and the medium of publication. When citing a range of three-digit page numbers, omit the hundreds' digit on the higher number (154-59). If you are using a journal, include the volume and issue numbers as well. Next, provide the date of publication. For journals, put the year of publication within parentheses. For magazines, give the day, month (all months except May, June, and July are abbreviated to three letters), and year. No punctuation separates the title and the date of publication. After the date of publication, place a colon and then the page numbers for the article. Conclude with the medium of publication. Note that current MLA guidelines no longer make a distinction between journals that are numbered continuously (e.g., Vol. 1 ends on page 208, Vol. 2 starts on page 209) or numbered separately; that is, each volume starts on page 1. No matter how the journal is paginated, all of them must contain volume *and* issue numbers. One exception are journals with issue numbers only; simply cite the issue numbers alone as though they are volume numbers.

18. Article in a journal

Burt, Susan Meredith. "Solicitudes in American English." *International Journal of Applied Linguistics* 13.1 (2003): 78-95. Print.

Place the title of the article in quotation marks between the author's name and the name of the journal. Provide the volume and issue numbers (separated by a period), the year of publication (in parentheses and followed by a colon), the range of pages on which the article appears, and the medium of publication.

19. Article in a monthly magazine

Moran, Thomas E. "Just for Kicks Soccer Program." *Exceptional Parent* Feb. 2004: 36-37. Print.

Provide the publication month and year after the title of the magazine. Abbreviate the names of all months except May, June, and July.

20. Article in a weekly magazine or newspaper

Ratnesar, Romesh. "Al-Qaeda's New Proving Ground." *Time* 28 Oct. 2002: 35-36. Print.

Provide the day, month, and year of publication after the title of the publication.

21. Article in a daily newspaper

Knickerbocker, Brad. "US Ponders Overhauling Beef Rules." *Christian Science Monitor* 30
    Dec. 2003: 1+. Print.

Provide the day, month, and year of publication. If the article does not appear on consecutive pages, add a plus sign after the first page number.

22. Unsigned article

"Beware the Herd." *Newsweek* 8 Mar. 2004: 61. Print.

Alphabetize the entry according to the first major word in the title, ignoring any article (*a, an,* or *the*).

23. Editorial in a newspaper or magazine

Goodman, Ellen. "Get Old Quick, Kids." Editorial. *Seattle Times* 5 Dec. 2003: B6. Print.

Place the word *Editorial,* followed by a period, between the title of the editorial and the name of the newspaper or magazine.

24. Book or film review

Morgenstern, Joe. "See Spot Sing and Dance: Dog Cartoon 'Teacher's Pet' Has Enough Bite for
    Adults." Rev. of *Teacher's Pet*, dir. Timothy Björklund. *Wall Street Journal* 16 Jan. 2004: W1+.
    Print.

Place the reviewer's name first, followed by the title of the review (if any) in quotation marks. Next, provide the title of the work reviewed, preceded by *Rev. of* for "review of," and then mention the name of the author, translator, editor, or director of the original work. The word *by* precedes an author's name, *trans.* precedes a translator's name, *ed.* precedes an editor's name, and *dir.* precedes a director's name.

Other print sources

25. Letter to the editor

Azar, Zarin. Letter. *Los Angeles Times* 2 Apr. 2006: M4. Print.

Following the author's name, use *Letter.* Then provide the name of the periodical, the date of publication, the page number, and the medium of publication.

26. Encyclopedia entry

"Heckelphone." *The Encyclopedia Americana*. 2001. Print.

Begin with the title of the entry, unless an author's name is provided. Provide the edition number (if any) and the year of publication after the title of the encyclopedia. Conclude with the medium of publication. Other publication information is unnecessary for familiar reference books.

27. Dictionary entry

"Foolscap." Def. 3. *Merriam-Webster's Collegiate Dictionary*. 10th ed. 2001. Print.

A dictionary entry is documented similarly to an encyclopedia entry. If the definition is one of several listed for the word, provide the definition number or letter, preceded by *Def.* for "definition."

28. Government publication

United States. Executive Office of the President and Council of Economic Advisors. *Economic Report of the President*. Washington: GPO, 2004. Print.

If no author is provided, list the name of the government (e.g., *United States, Montana,* or *New York City*), followed by the name of the agency issuing the publication.

29. Pamphlet or bulletin

Ten Ways to Be a Better Dad. Gaithersburg: National Fatherhood Institute, 2000. Print.

An entry for a pamphlet is similar to one for a book. List the author's name first, if an author is identified.

30. Dissertation

Dittmer, Timothy. *A Property Rights Approach to Antitrust Analysis*. Diss. U of Washington, 1998. Ann Arbor: UMI, 1998. Print.

If the dissertation has been published, proceed as for a book, but add *Diss.* for "dissertation" after the title, followed by the name of the institution that issued the degree and the year the degree was granted. In this example, *UMI* stands for "University Microfilms International," which publishes many dissertations. If the dissertation has not been published, enclose the title of the dissertation in quotation marks rather than italicizing it.

Live performances and recordings

31. Play performance

Roulette. By Paul Weitz. Dir. Tripp Cullmann. John Houseman Theater, New York. 9 Feb. 2004. Performance.

Begin with the title of the play (underlined) followed by the names of key contributors such as author, director, performers, and/or translator. The location of the performance (the theater and the city), the date of the performance, and the word *Performance* complete the entry.

32. Lecture or presentation

Childs, David. "Tower Evolutions." Paul Rudolph Lecture. Hastings Hall, Yale U, New Haven. 12 Jan. 2004. Lecture.

Ryken, Leland. Class lecture. English 216. Breyer 103, Wheaton College, Wheaton. 4 Feb. 2004.
Lecture.

Provide the name of the speaker, the title of the lecture (if any) in quotation marks, the sponsoring organization (if applicable), the location and date of the lecture or presentation, and the form of delivery. If the lecture or presentation is untitled, provide a description after the name of the speaker.

33. Interview

Blauwkamp, Joan. Telephone interview. 14 Mar. 2004.

Kotapish, Dawn. Personal interview. 3 Jan. 2004.

Provide the name of the interviewee, a description of the type of interview conducted (e.g., *Telephone interview* or *Personal interview*), and the date on which the interview occurred.

34. Film

Bus Stop. Dir. Joshua Logan. Twentieth Century Fox, 1956. Film.

Monroe, Marilyn, perf. *Bus Stop*. Screenplay by George Axelrod. Dir. Joshua Logan. Twentieth
Century Fox, 1956. Film.

Give the title of the film, the name of the director (preceded by *Dir.* for "directed by"), the distributor, the year of release, and the medium consulted. To highlight the contribution of a particular individual, start with the individual's name, followed by an indication of the nature of the contribution, abbreviated if possible. For example, *perf.* means "performer."

35. Radio or television program

"Blue Blood and Beans." Narr. Garrison Keillor. *A Prairie Home Companion*. Natl. Public Radio.
KJZZ, Phoenix. 21 Feb. 2004. Radio.

Simon, Scott, narr. *Affluenza*. Prod. John de Graaf and Vivia Boe. PBS. KCTS, Seattle. 2
July 1998. Television.

Provide the title of the segment (in quotation marks), the title of the program (italicized), the name of the network, the call letters and city of the broadcasting station, the date of the broadcast, and the medium of reception. Information such as the name of an author, performer, director, or narrator may appear after the title of the segment. When referring especially to the contribution of a specific individual, however, place the individual's name and an abbreviated identification of the contribution before the title.

36. Sound recording or compact disc

Indigo Girls. *All That We Let In*. Sony, 2004. CD.

Begin with the name of the performer, composer, or conductor, depending on which you prefer to emphasize. Then provide the title of the recording, the manufacturer's name, the date of the recording, and the medium (in this case, *CD*). Other types of medium to indicate may be *LP, Audiocassette, DVD*, etc. When referring to an individual song, provide its name in quotation marks after the name of the performer, composer, or conductor.

Images

37. Work of art

Vermeer, Johannes. *Woman Holding a Balance*. 1664. Oil on canvas. Natl. Gallery of Art,

Washington.

Begin with the artist's name and the title of the work (italicized). Then provide the date the work was created (if not available, use the abbreviation *n.d.* for *no date*) and the medium of composition. End your citation with the location where the artwork is housed (that is, the name of the museum or institution that owns the piece) and the city in which it is located.

38. Photograph

Lange, Dorothea. *Migrant Mother*. 1936. Photograph. Prints and Photographs Division, Lib. of

Congress, Washington.

Provide the photographer's name, the title of the work (italicized), the medium of composition, and the name and location of the institution that houses the work. If the photograph has no title, briefly describe its subject.

39. Cartoon or comic strip

Cheney, Tom. "Back Page by Tom Cheney." Cartoon. *New Yorker* 12 Jan. 2004: 88. Print.

The description *Cartoon* appears before the title of the publication.

40. Advertisement

McCormick Pure Vanilla Extract. Advertisement. *Cooking Light* Mar. 2004: 177. Print.

Identify the item being advertised, and then include the description *Advertisement* before the usual publication information.

41. Map or chart

Scottsdale and Vicinity. Map. Chicago: Rand, 2000. Print.

Treat the map or chart as you would an anonymous book, including the description *Map* or *Chart* before the usual publication information.

Online sources and databases

Current MLA guidelines do not require you to include a Web address (URL) if your readers can easily locate the online source by searching for the author's name and the title of the work. For cases in which your readers cannot easily locate a source, provide the complete URL (between angle brackets) following the date of access and period. The closing angle bracket should also be followed by a period.

Journal Article from a Library Subscription Service

You can usually find much of the information you will need for your works-cited entry on the first page of the article. Works-cited entries for online periodicals generally include six units of information: author, title (and subtitle, if any) of article, print publication data, electronic publication data, date of access (URL if needed), and medium of publication.

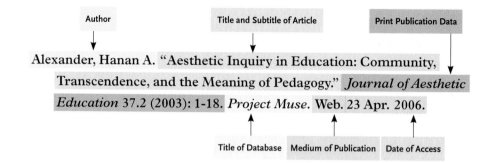

Alexander, Hanan A. "Aesthetic Inquiry in Education: Community, Transcendence, and the Meaning of Pedagogy." *Journal of Aesthetic Education* 37.2 (2003): 1-18. *Project Muse.* Web. 23 Apr. 2006.

Author The author's name is given, last name first. Use a comma to separate the last name from the first, and place a period at the end of this unit of information. If there is more than one author, see the information given for book entries on pages 569–570.

Title of article Include the title and, if there is one, the subtitle of the article. Use a colon to separate the subtitle from the title. Place the entire title within quotation marks, including the period that marks the end of the unit of information.

Print publication data The publication data that you provide depends on the type of periodical in which the article appeared. For detailed information, see the discussion of publication data for periodicals on pages 573–574.

Electronic publication data If possible, include the name of the database in which the periodical can be found.

Medium of publication The medium of publication identifies the medium consulted, in this case *Web*.

Date of access (with URL if needed) The date of access is the date on which you consulted a source. It can be found on any printout of the material you used. For cases in which your readers cannot easily locate a source, place the URL— the Internet address at which the source is located—between angle brackets (<>). Be sure to include its access-mode identifier (*http, ftp, telnet*) and all punctuation. If the address must continue onto a second line, break it after a slash. If the URL is excessively long or complicated (more than one full line), provide just the search page you used to find the article. If there is no search page, use the site's home page.

Electronic sources vary significantly; thus, as you prepare your works-cited list, you'll need to

First page of article in online journal.

follow the models shown here closely. On occasion, you may not be able to find all the information mentioned. In such cases, provide as much of the information as you can. When no publication date is available, use the abbreviation *n.d.* for *no date.* When no publisher or sponsor is available, use *N.p.* for *No publisher.*

42. Online book

Austen, Jane. *Emma.* London: Murray, 1815. *Gutenburg.net.* 1994. Web 20 Nov. 2006.

Begin with the information you always provide for an entry for a book (author, title, and publication information, if available). Then provide as much of the following electronic publication information as possible: title of the Internet site (italicized), version number (if provided), date of electronic publication, and name of any sponsoring organization. Conclude with the medium of publication and the date of access.

43. Article in an online journal

Ballard, Karen. "Patient Safety: A Shared Responsibility." *NursingWorld* 8.3 (2003). Web. 15 Jan. 2007.

Begin with the information you provide for an entry for an article in a print journal, and conclude with the medium of publication and the date of access.

44. Article in an online magazine

Cloud, John. "The Gurus of YouTube." *Time.* Time, 16 Dec. 2006. Web. 18 Dec. 2006.

Begin with the information you provide for an entry for an article in a print magazine, adding the name of any sponsor. Conclude with the medium of publication and the date of access.

45. Article in an online newspaper

"Haitian Rebels Occupy Police Headquarters." *Seattle Times.* The Seattle Times Company,
     1 Mar. 2004. Web. 19 Oct. 2006.

Begin with the information you provide for an entry for an article in a print newspaper, adding the name of any sponsor. Conclude with the medium of publication and the date of access.

46. Review in an online newspaper

Safire, William. "Not Peace, but a Sword." Rev. of *The Passion of the Christ,* dir. Mel Gibson.
     New York Times. New York Times, 1 Mar. 2004. Web. 6 Sept. 2006.

Begin with the information you provide for an entry for a review in a print newspaper, adding the name of any sponsor. Conclude with the medium of publication and the date of access.

47. Article from a library subscription service

Fenn, Donna. "Can the Boss Make the Grade?" *Inc.* May 1996: n. pag. *ABI/INFORM.* Web.
     11 Mar. 2007.

After providing the usual information for the article, include the italicized name of the database, the medium consulted, and the date of access. If a complete range of pages is not known for the original publication, indicate "n. page."

48. Online work of art

Picasso, Pablo. *Guitar.* 1912. Museum of Modern Art, New York. Web. 17 Dec. 2006.

Begin with the information you always provide in an entry for a work of art and conclude with the medium of publication and the date of access. Note that the medium of composition is omitted.

49. Online government publication

United States. Dept. of Health and Human Services. *Dietary Guidelines for Americans 2005.*
      12 Jan. 2005. Web. 2 Dec. 2006.

Begin with the information you provide for an entry for a print government publication and conclude with the publication medium and the date of access.

50. Web site

BrainConnection. 2006. Scientific Learning, 2006. Web. 25 Oct. 2006.

Provide the title of the site (italicized), the version number (if provided), the name of any sponsoring organization, and the date of publication or latest update. Conclude with the medium of publication and the date of access.

51. Section of a Web site

Pycha, Anne. "Jean Piaget: Father of Developmental Psychology." *BrainConnection.* Scientific
      Learning, 2006. Web. 25 Mar. 2006.

Provide the information you include in an entry for an entire Web site, but place the title of the section you are citing in quotation marks before the title of the Web site. If the section has an author, list his or her name (inverted) first.

52. Course home page

Owens, Kalyn. General Chemistry. Course home page. Jan. 2004-Mar. 2004. Chemistry Dept.,
      Central Washington U. Web. 18 Jan. 2004.

List the instructor's name (inverted), the course title, the description *Course home page,* the course dates, the name of the department offering the course, and the name of the institution. Conclude with the medium consulted and the date of access.

53. E-mail message

Kivett, George. "Hydrogen Fuel Cell Technology." Message to Theodore Ellis. 28 Jan. 2004. E-mail.

Give the name of the author of the message, the title (taken from the subject line of the message and enclosed in quotation marks), a description of the communication (including the recipient's name), the date the message was sent, and the medium of transmission.

54. Posting to discussion group or forum

Sykes, Randy. "Social Security." Online posting. 2 Mar. 2004. Talk of the Nation. Web. 8 Mar. 2007.

Provide the name of the author (inverted) and the title of the posting (in quotation marks), followed by the description *Online posting.* Include the date the material was posted, the name of the forum, the medium consulted, and the date of your access.

55. Synchronous communication

Bruckman, Amy. 8th Birthday Symposium "Educational MOOs: State of the Art." 17 Jan. 2001.

    MediaMOO. Web. 10 Mar. 2005.

Provide the name of the writer (inverted) and a description of the discussion. Indicate any discussion title in quotation marks. The name of the forum appears between the date of the communication and the medium. The entry concludes with your date of access.

56. CD-ROM

Ultimate Human Body. Camberwell, Austral.: DK, 2002. CD-ROM.

Provide all the information you include for a print book. Add a description of the medium (e.g., *CD-ROM*, *Diskette*, *Magnetic tape*), followed by a period, after the publication information.

CHECKING OVER A WORKS-CITED LIST

✓ Is the title, *Works Cited* (not italicized), centered one inch from the top of the page? Is the first letter of each word capitalized?

✓ Is the entire list double-spaced?

✓ Are initial lines of entries flush with the left margin and subsequent lines indented one-half inch?

✓ Is there a works-cited entry for each in-text citation? Is there an in-text citation for each works-cited entry?

✓ Are the entries alphabetized according to the first author's last name? If the author of an entry is unknown, is the entry alphabetized according to title (ignoring any initial *a, an,* or *the*)?

✓ If the list contains two or more entries by the same author, are the entries alphabetized according to title? After the author's full name is used for the first entry, are three hyphens substituted for the name in subsequent entries?

✓ Are book and periodical titles italicized? Are names of databases italicized?

✓ Are quotation marks used to indicate article titles?

✓ Are URLs (when needed) enclosed in angle brackets?

Sample MLA Research Paper

The MLA recommends omitting a title page (unless your instructor requires one) and instead providing the identification on the first page of the paper. One inch from the top, on the left-hand side of the page, list your name, the name of the instructor, the name of the course, and the date—all double-spaced. Below these lines, center the title of the paper, which is in plain type (no italics, underlining, or boldface). On the right-hand side of each page, one-half inch from the top, use your last name and the page number as a header. Double-space the text throughout the paper, and use one-inch margins on the sides and bottom. Indent every paragraph (including the first one) one-half inch (or five spaces).

[1] The running head includes the authors' last names and the page number.

[2] The heading and the rest of the paper are double-spaced.

[3] The title of the paper is centered.

[4] Each paragraph, including the first, begins with an indent of one-half inch or five spaces.

[5] The parenthetical citation gives only a page number as the author of the source is mentioned earlier in the sentence.

Research

Matthew Marusak [2]

Bethanie Orban

Professor Glenn

English 495

December 5, 2006

Now Serving New Traditions: The Move of the Penn State Creamery [3]

[4] The Pennsylvania State University recently celebrated its 150th birthday, and now more people than ever want to participate in its grand legacy. In fact, Penn State had a record number of acceptants for the 2006-2007 school year, which means that more students than ever before decided to come to Penn State after having been accepted. Not just another large school, Penn State offers us as students what most do not: a chance to be a part of an extraordinary tradition. For all students, past and present, Penn State is a large family and its own great community, made great by its traditions. In a recent issue of the *Penn Stater*, alumnus Mike Toth reflects upon his return to his alma mater: "At first it seemed that very little had changed in 25 years. . . . This place was a giant time capsule!" (9). [5] For Toth and so many others, Penn State's age-old traditions have remained unchanged and unchangeable. And with such a deep connection in the past, it is understandable why the prospect of changing these traditions could be upsetting.

In 2003, officials at Penn State announced a decision to relocate the campus Creamery, our favorite place to enjoy ice cream. Since then, we have watched the construction of Penn State's new Food Sciences Building, which will house the new Creamery. Despite the assertion by Creamery manager Thomas Palchak that the establishment will be a vast improvement over the present one, some students are not pleased with the university's course of action. For both students and visitors, according to the Creamery's Web site, "getting ice cream at the Creamery has been a tradition since 1896" ("Tradition"). **[6]** The current location at Borland Laboratory has been a special place for decades. Memories are often sparked by simply being in a familiar setting; thus, those students opposing the move might feel that the connection between locale and tradition will be compromised. But these dissenters fail to realize that growth and transformation can only enhance and encourage these traditions, while resistance to positive change only weakens a progressive community. The Creamery has expanded and moved a few times over its history, as have other beloved emblems, buildings, and landmarks. These include the Nittany Lion (including the Nittany Lion Shrine), the Nittany Lion Inn, and the library, all of which have been improved and updated over the years. These modifications ultimately strengthen tradition by allowing more people to become involved, providing more space and opportunities to enjoy the benefits of the Penn State community, now and into the future.

The Nittany Lion is easily the most familiar icon of Penn State, but even this symbol has evolved. The tradition of the Nittany Lion extends across generations, "treasured by Penn State students throughout the years, dat[ing] from 1906," when the school mascot first appeared (Dunaway 440). **[7]** Later, in the 1920s, two stuffed mountain lions were situated in the Recreation Building; also around this time, the first student donned a "furry lion outfit" for athletic events (Bezilla 30). The symbol of the Lion became so immensely popular over the next few years that students began to push for a shrine for their school mascot--"a place where they could gather to hold pep rallies and celebrate sports victories (and have their picture

[6] This parenthetical citation gives the title of a source that had no author.

[7] The square brackets in "dat[ing]" in this sentence indicate that the authors of the essay modified the spelling in the original source, to incorporate the quotation smoothly.

Research

Fig. 1. The Nittany Lion Shrine. Photograph by Bethanie Orban. **[8]**

taken with Mom and Dad)" (Bezilla 30). The dedication of the Nittany Lion Shrine, sculpted by Heinze Warnecke, took place during Homecoming Weekend on Saturday, October 24, 1942 (Dunaway 441) (see fig. 1).

The Nittany Lion has since become an empowering symbol of what it means to be a Penn Stater, according to Joe Paterno, Penn State's head football coach for more than forty years:

> The Shrine is more than just another location on campus dedicated to some tradition or another: it is the embodiment of what we believe Penn State represents. . . . The Nittany Lion symbolizes Penn State's past accomplishments while reflecting its hopeful future, which is the key to Penn State's success in all its academic and athletic endeavors. A great university must simultaneously represent what it has been and promise what it will be. No school symbol does that better than Penn State's Nittany Lion. (Paterno and Paterno x) **[9]**

In the last twenty-five years, students have proven their dedication to the Shrine by enacting the yearly ritual of "Guard the Lion Shrine." To protect the shrine from would-be vandals (such as the Syracuse fans who defaced the Lion with permanent orange paint in the 1960s), students gather each year with the Army ROTC during Homecoming Weekend (Gabsewics). The Nittany Lion is such a powerful symbol that people are willing to go to great lengths to preserve and protect its sanctity.

As a result of the natural expansion of the University Park campus and branch campuses, the Nittany Lion's presence increased significantly. For example, in 1969, other shrines to the Lion were placed on branch campuses throughout the state (Bezilla 30). These additional shrines, therefore, did not detract from tradition in any way; rather, they contributed to the legacy of the Nittany Lion.

Though it started out as simply a mascot, the Nittany Lion quickly became associated not only with sports but with important campus buildings, permeating every part of the Penn State life. One of Penn State's most popular and frequently updated attractions is the Nittany Lion Inn (see fig. 2). Because of large-scale improvements over the past eight decades, the Nittany Lion Inn has become a well-known and reputable place for visitors to eat, sleep, and celebrate. Dubbed "Penn State's Living Room" by former Penn State President Eric Walker, the Inn celebrated its 75th birthday in May 2006 ("Penn State's Living Room" 34). However, the Inn was not always the majestic place it is today. The Nittany Lion Inn opened in 1931 as "a [first-class] dining and hotel facility . . . to accommodate visitors attending conferences, athletic events, graduations, and other campus events," something the community of State

Fig. 2. The Nittany Lion Inn. Photograph by Bethanie Orban.

College was in dire need of (Bezilla 143). The Inn originally had seventy-five rooms, each including a bed, a private bath, a blanket chest, a writing table, and an upholstered armchair. In 1954, a second wing was added, which included seventy-five more rooms and a coffee shop. And in 1992, a third wing was added, featuring 112 additional rooms and various other amenities.

The Nittany Lion Inn is practically a monument in its own right: people associate holidays and other special occasions with Penn State, school pride, and innumerable fond memories. A member of the National Trust Historic Hotels of America, the Inn has hosted over 1,400 wedding receptions, as well as class reunions since 1933 and a Thanksgiving banquet every year. Martin Luther King, Jr., was the guest of honor at a January 1965 banquet, while the Executive Suite has housed several U.S. presidents, including Dwight Eisenhower, Richard Nixon, Ronald Reagan, and Bill Clinton ("Penn State's Living Room"

Research

35-37). The benefits of the Nittany Lion Inn also extend beyond the public sphere and into the classroom, giving Hotel Management students practical hands-on experience. Without the necessary accommodations and expansions, the Nittany Lion Inn would not be the fine and well-respected establishment it is today. These expansions have allowed alumni to once again feel the closeness to their university and the Nittany Lion.

Without the necessary expansion to secure the Nittany Lion's position in the Penn State community, the various traditions surrounding it would not have grown to the epic proportions they have today. "The image of the Nittany Lion has been etched not only in stone, but in the memories of tens of thousands of Penn Staters" (Bezilla 30). The sense of togetherness evoked by the symbol of the Nittany Lion has undeniably contributed to its beneficial evolution.

Because Penn State is often associated exclusively with the Nittany Lion, football, and various other sports, people sometimes forget that the school is also known as a prestigious academic institution. The Pattee and Paterno Libraries are symbols of educational excellence on campus, featuring a staggering collection of books, periodicals, and electronic resources (see fig. 3). But if not for various technological and architectural improvements, we would be limited in the amount and the depth of the research materials available. When the university opened in 1859, the library was small and poorly organized, with no head librarian and limited use to the public. Its first expansion was in 1887, and by 1930, the new Carnegie Library contained over 120,000 volumes (Dunaway 356-62). From 1937 to 1940, construction took place for the new Pattee Library, which would eventually require three major additions itself, including what is now the Paterno Library ("Paterno Library").

Research

Fig. 3. Pattee Library. Photograph by Bethanie Orban.

Clearly, all these changes have been for the best, giving Penn Staters more resources and a more efficient system of locating the resources we need. Without these changes, Penn State would not be able to maintain its reputation as a major research and education facility.

Now, like other buildings before it, the Creamery is slated for improvement, spurring on a debate over its impending relocation. While both the Nittany Lion Inn and the library have had the luxury of continual development as well as architectural resources and physical space to expand at their current locations, the Creamery has not had the same advantages. Perhaps because the Inn and library have not changed physical location, there seemed to be little (if any) distress over the changes that were gradually made. Some students are upset that the Creamery is moving to a completely different building, but they are neglecting the fact that the Creamery has been moved and changed before--even if not in recent memory.

The Creamery has not always been situated at Borland Laboratory, but generations of Penn Staters have come to regard this current location as an imperative part of the Creamery tradition and the Penn State experience. When the original Creamery opened in 1865, it shared a building, the "College Barns," with a blacksmith shop and a hayloft ("History"); it was nearly twenty-five years until the Creamery became its own building. It would then move one more time before settling into its current home at Borland Lab in 1932 ("History").

Today, the Creamery is still very much a part of Penn State life (see fig. 4). With such carefully and skillfully made ice cream, it's rare not to see someone excited to visit the Creamery. In fact, Penn State recommends stopping at the Creamery as one of the best things to do while on campus: "The Creamery has long been a must-see stop for visitors, and the ice cream is so popular that some

Fig. 4. The Creamery, in its current location. Photograph by Bethanie Orban.

students take home half-gallons packed in dry ice. Ice cream and cheese also are sold online" (Chute B2). Creamery ice cream is such a favorite that it's now offered to students in the various dining commons around campus. Upon returning to Penn State, many alumni now see visiting the Creamery as essential as attending a football game or taking a walk around their alma mater. Even during festivals and other local events, the Creamery sets up a tent closer to downtown State College so that more people can enjoy the ice cream without having to walk as far. Creamery ice cream is only sold and served on campus and in select restaurants downtown, so it truly is a special treat when in State College, which naturally promotes a sense of community. In a sense, the Creamery is tied to the very roots of the university itself, given that Penn State used to be an entirely agricultural college--proof that building on the past really can and does lead to some tremendous traditions.

Because of strong ties with the university, many students are afraid that such a drastic move might negatively affect the way the Creamery functions in the community as a reminder of a long-honored tradition. Penn State student Robert Teisher says there is "too much nostalgia" wrapped up in the Creamery (Raffaele), while fellow student Matt Ritsko argues "The Creamery is an intrinsic part of Penn State. . . . Moving it is a change of tradition, and these days there are less and less traditions in the Penn State community" (Miller and Ritsko). Furthermore, he says he would be disappointed to bring his kids and grandkids to visit the campus and not have the Creamery in the same location. Ritsko and Chris Miller, another Penn State student, are adamantly against the relocation of the Creamery and have organized a group known as "Save the Creamery." Ritsko and Miller are concerned that "an important piece of history will be lost when the University Creamery closes," and they hope to collect ten thousand signatures from current students and alumni via an Internet petition (Raffaele). As of July 2006, the petition had received more than 3,600 signatures (Miller and Ritsko). As Martha Raffaele reports, the group has proposed other options besides saving the physical location of the Creamery building, including allowing both Creamery locations to remain open for business, as well as nominating Borland Lab as an historic site with the National Register of Historic Places. The dissenters' intentions are certainly noble, but they do nothing to rectify the many problems that plague the current location.

The Creamery occupies a very problematic space, despite its familiarity. While the lab offers a larger space for the actual production of the ice cream, the store occupies a very small area. Creamery employee Caitlin Dietrich remarks that the smallness of the space is definitely a negative aspect of the Creamery, especially the problem of overcrowding and very little room for "growth and improvement" (Dietrich). **[10]** With the Creamery being one of the few places to purchase the ice cream, more people are going to be crowding the tiny shop.

[10] The authors of the essay cite a personal interview.

Long lines often form, sometimes even wrapping around the outside of the building on busy days (as most of us have surely experienced). There is only one line and one register, certainly not an efficient way to run a store as busy as the Creamery. With so many orders in succession, it's often difficult to keep everyone's order straight. Another major problem is the limited parking available for customers. The lot across the street is small and features meter parking only, causing most customers to have to park elsewhere and often walk farther than is necessary. Finally, unless visitors have some degree of familiarity

Research

with the campus, the Creamery is not an easily recognizable building, and its small sign out front is outdated and sometimes hard to see from a distance. As for the building, it has not been updated in quite some time and would benefit from closer attention to its architecture. Because of the university's increasing enrollment and its continually expanding landscape, it does not seem that all these problems can be rectified to meet the recent demands on the current Creamery.

But with the move of the Creamery down the street and into a bigger complex, officials have ensured that the majority of these issues will be resolved. The Creamery will move about two hundred yards but still remain in the same vicinity (Chute). Specifically, the new building will have "new and better facilities and energy efficiencies," as Jessica Annas reports (par. 29, screen 6). Paul Ruskin, Office of Physical Plant spokesman, said the move will allow for more efficiency in heating, cooling, and lighting (Annas). Not only will the new building be safer and more efficient, but it will also be a great deal larger to accommodate all the fans eager to partake in one of their favorite pastimes (see fig. 5). Student reporter Josh Pontrelli notes the following additional advantages: a more spacious Creamery will allow for multiple customers to be helped simultaneously; there will be increased indoor and outdoor space, and hints have been made at better parking; football fans will have an easier walk to the Creamery from Beaver Stadium; and it will also be easier to find for newcomers to campus.

While all of these changes will add to the experience, those who are working on the new building are sensitive to the opposing stance. According to Creamery manager Thomas Palchak, "steps [will] be taken to ensure the

Research

Fig. 5. The Creamery's future location. Photograph by Bethanie Orban.

tradition of the Creamery is not lost, including displays of Creamery memorabilia and a time capsule" (Lash). These changes are certainly necessary and beneficial, offering more space and less frustration with long lines and inefficient service. More of us can stop and get a cone--even between classes-- without having to worry about a long wait time. The location will be different, but the tradition will remain intact. The ice cream and the experience will always be the same, regardless of the Creamery's location. "I think the move is a good thing," says Caitlin Dietrich, "because of what it means for the business, and because I know that in the future it will have the homey feeling of the old place. . . . You have to accept the move as a positive factor." And though some are upset with these changes, ultimately they will strengthen tradition by giving a better experience to all those who choose to create new memories at a new facility, building on the past and contributing to the future of the Penn State community.

Research

The location of a building will not determine a tradition if people hold true to it. Penn State has been built on its traditions, and a few necessary improvements will not affect that. Those who are against the Creamery's move are often those closest and most connected to the Penn State community. These students who want to "save the Creamery" exemplify how important Penn State experiences are. The Nittany Lion symbol, Shrine, and Inn, and the library have all experienced updates and changes throughout their history, but the traditions associated with them are still some of the oldest at Penn State. It is no different for the Creamery. A great deal of attention is needed for the Creamery to do all that it needs to do. Like many other landmarks, it has moved and grown several times. As Eleanor Chute wrote in her *Pittsburgh Post-Gazette* article, "without these moves through history, the Creamery would not be the celebrated Penn State tradition that it is today, and this new facility should only build and enhance that tradition over time." In the end, the Creamery's expansion will provide an even better way to enjoy the long-standing tradition to more people. Penn State has been about community experiences since its beginning. The move of the Creamery is preparing the way to the future for all of us and for those students who will some day call themselves "Penn Staters."

Research

Works Cited [11]

Annas, Jessica. "Changing Old for New: PSU Buildings." *Digital Collegian.*

Collegian, 25 Aug. 2005. Web. 5 Nov. 2006. [12]

Bezilla, Michael. *Penn State: An Illustrated History.* University Park:

Pennsylvania State UP, 1985. Print.

Chute, Eleanor. "Some Are Cold to Ice Cream Scheme at PSU; Students Push to

Keep Creamery Site." *Pittsburgh Post-Gazette* 3 Mar. 2005, sooner ed.: B1.

LexisNexis. Web. 5 Nov. 2006. [13]

Dietrich, Caitlin. Personal interview. 4 Nov. 2006. [14]

Dunaway, Wayland Fuller. *History of the Pennsylvania State College.* Lancaster:

Lancaster, 1946. Print. [15]

Gabsewics, Caroline. "PSU Traditions Show Real Blue and White." *Digital

Collegian.* Collegian, 28 Aug. 2003. Web. 12 Nov. 2006. [16]

"History." *University Creamery.* Pennsylvania State U, 29 June 2006. Web.

5 Nov. 2006.

"History of the Libraries." *Library Information Access System.* Pennsylvania

State U, 16 Aug. 2005. Web. 12 Nov. 2006.

Lash, Devon. "Students Petition to Keep Creamery Scooping at Historic Borland

Locale." *Digital Collegian.* Collegian, 23 Mar. 2005. Web. 4 Nov. 2006.

Miller, Chris, and Matt Ritsko, eds. *Save the Creamery!* N.p., n.d. Web.

12 Nov. 2006 [17]

Paterno, Joe, and Sue Paterno. Foreword. *The Nittany Lion: An Illustrated Tale.*

By Jacqueline R. Esposito and Steven L. Herb. University Park:

Pennsylvania State UP, 1997. ix-x. Print.

"Paterno Library." *Centre Daily Times.* Centre Daily Times, 22 Feb. 2005. Web.

9 Nov. 2006.

[11] The works-cited list begins on a new page, with the heading centered.

[12] Every entry in the list starts flush with the left margin and has subsequent lines indented one-half inch. Entries are listed in alphabetical order.

[13] This entry documents a source from a library subscription service.

[14] This is an entry for a personal interview.

[15] The publisher's name, Lancaster Press, is shortened to Lancaster in this entry.

[16] This entry documents an online newspaper article.

[17] This entry documents a Web site.

Research

[18] This is an entry for an article from a journal.

"Penn State's Living Room." *Penn Stater* 93.5 (2006): 34-37. Print. [18]

Pontrelli, Josh. "New, Larger Creamery Location Offers Same Taste." *Digital*

    Collegian. Collegian, 22 Oct. 2003. Web. 4 Nov. 2006.

Raffaele, Martha. "Penn State Students Campaign to Preserve University

    Creamery." *Associated Press State & Local Wire* 1 Apr. 2005: n. page.

    LexisNexis. Web. 12 Nov. 2006.

Toth, Mike. "Gathering Memories." *Penn Stater* 92.6 (2006): 9. Print.

"Tradition." *University Creamery*. Pennsylvania State U, 29 June 2006. Web.

    5 Nov. 2006.

APA Guidelines for In-Text Citations

If you are following the style recommended by the American Psychological Association, your in-text citations will refer to the author(s) of the text you consulted and the year of its publication. In addition, you must specify the page number(s) for any quotations you include; the abbreviation *p.* (for "page") or *pp.* (for "pages") should precede the number. For electronic sources that do not include page numbers, specify the paragraph number and precede it with the abbreviation *para.* or the symbol ¶. When no author's name is listed, you provide a shortened version of the title of the source. If your readers want to find more information about your source, they will look for the author's name or the title of the material in the bibliography at the end of your paper.

You will likely consult a variety of sources for your research paper. The following examples are representative of the types of in-text citations you might use.

1. Work by one or two authors

Wachal (2002) discusses dictionary labels for words considered taboo.

Dictionary labels for taboo words include *offensive* and *derogatory* **(Wachal, 2002).**

Lance and Pulliam (2002) believe that an introductory linguistics text should have "persuasive power" **(p. 223).**

On learning of dialect bias, some students expressed outrage, often making "a 180-degree turn-around" from their original attitudes toward a standard language **(Lance & Pulliam, 2002, p. 223).**

Authors' names may be placed either in the text, followed by the date of publication in parentheses, or in parentheses along with the date. When you mention an author in the text, place the date of publication directly after the author's name. If you include a quotation, provide the page number(s) at the end of the quotation, after the quotation marks but before the period. When citing a work by two authors, use the word *and* between their names; when citing two authors in parentheses, use an ampersand (&) between their names. Always use a comma to separate the last author's name from the date.

Research

2. Work by three, four, or five authors

FIRST MENTION

Johnstone, Bhasin, and Wittkofski (2002) describe the speech of Pittsburgh, Pennsylvania, as *Pittsburghese.*

The speech of Pittsburgh, Pennsylvania, is called *Pittsburghese* **(Johnstone, Bhasin, & Wittkofski, 2002).**

SUBSEQUENT MENTION

Johnstone, Bhasin, and Wittkofski (2002) cite *gumband* and *nebby* as words used in *Pittsburghese.*

The words *gumband* and *nebby* are used by speakers of *Pittsburghese* **(Johnstone et al., 2002).**

When first citing a source by three, four, or five authors, list all the authors' last names. In subsequent parenthetical citations, use just the first author's last name along with the abbreviation *et al.* (Latin for "and others"). The abbreviation *et al.* should not be italicized in citations.

3. Work by six or more authors

Taylor et al. (2001) have stressed the importance of prohibiting the dumping of plastic garbage into the oceans.

In both the first and subsequent mentions of the source, use only the first author's last name and the abbreviation *et al.*

4. Work by an unknown author

A recent survey indicated increased willingness of college students to vote in national elections **("Ending Apathy," 2004).**

The documents leaked to the press could damage the governor's reputation **(Anonymous, 2001).**

When no author is mentioned, use a shortened version of the title instead. If the word *Anonymous* is used in the source to designate the author, use that word in place of the author's name.

5. Two or more works by the same author

Smith (2001, 2003, 2005) has consistently argued in support of language immersion.

Bayard (1995a, 1995b) discusses the acquisition of English in New Zealand.

In most cases, the year of publication will distinguish the works. However, if the works were published in the same year, distinguish them with lowercase letters, assigned based on the order of the titles in the bibliography.

6. Two or more works by different authors with the same last name

J. P. Hill and Giles (2001) and **G. S. Hill and Kellner (2002)** confirmed these findings.

When two or more authors have the same last name, always include first initials with that last name.

7. Work by a group

Style refers to publishing guidelines that encourage the clear and coherent presentation of written text (**American Psychological Association [APA], 2001**).

Spell out the name of the group when you first mention it. If the group has a widely recognizable abbreviation, place that abbreviation in square brackets after the first mention. You can then use the abbreviation in subsequent citations: (APA, 2001).

8. Work by a government author

Taxpayers encounter significant problems with two different taxes: the sole proprietor tax and the alternative minimum tax (**Internal Revenue Service [IRS], 2004**).

Spell out the name of the government entity when you first mention it. If the entity has a widely recognizable abbreviation, place that abbreviation in square brackets after the first mention. You can then use the abbreviation in subsequent citations: (IRS, 2004).

9. Indirect source

According to Ronald Butters, the word *go* is frequently used by speakers born after 1955 to introduce a quotation (**as cited in Cukor-Avila, 2002**).

Use *as cited in* to indicate that you found the information in another source.

10. Two or more works in one parenthetical citation

A speaker may use the word *like* to focus the listener's attention (**Eriksson, 1995; Ferrar & Bell 1995**).

When you include two or more works within the same parentheses, order them alphabetically. Arrange two or more works by the same author by year of publication, mentioning the author's name only once: (Kamil, 2002, 2004).

11. Personal communication

Revisions will be made to the agreement this month (**K. M. Liebenow, personal communication, February 11, 2004**).

Letters, email messages, and interviews are all considered personal communications, which you should cite in the text of a paper. Because personal communications do not represent recoverable data, you should not include entries for them in the references list.

APA Guidelines for Documenting References

To provide readers with the information they need to find all the sources you have used in your paper, you must prepare a bibliography. According to APA guidelines, your bibliography should be titled *References* (not italicized). It should contain all the information your readers would need to retrieve the sources if they wished to consult them on their own. Except for personal communications, each source you cite in your text should appear in the references list.

Alphabetize your references according to the author's (or the first author's) last name. If the author is unknown, alphabetize according to title (ignoring any initial article—*a, an,* or *the*). When you have more than one source by the same author(s), order them according to the year of publication, with the earliest first.

Frazer, B. (2000).

Frazer, B. (2004).

If two or more works by the same author(s) have the same year of publication, the entries are ordered alphabetically according to the works' titles, and lower-case letters are added to the date to distinguish the entries.

Fairclough, N. (1992a). The appropriacy of "appropriateness."

Fairclough, N. (1992b). *Critical language awareness.*

Fairclough, N. (1992c). *Discourse and social change.*

When an author you have cited is also the first of two or more authors of another entry, list the source with a single author first.

Allen, J. P. (1982).

Allen, J. P., & Turner, E. J. (1988).

When two or more entries have the same first author, alphabetize the list according to the names of subsequent authors.

Fallows, M. R., & Andrews, R. J. (1999).

Fallows, M. R., & Laver, J. T. (2002).

Double-space all of your entries, leaving the first line flush with the left margin and indenting subsequent lines one-half inch or five character spaces. (Your word processor may refer to the indented line as a *hanging indent.*)

For more details on various types of sources, use the following directory to find relevant sections. For an example of a references list, see page 619. If you would like to use a checklist to help ensure that you have followed APA guidelines, see page 611.

DIRECTORY OF REFERENCES ENTRIES ACCORDING TO APA GUIDELINES

Books

Books

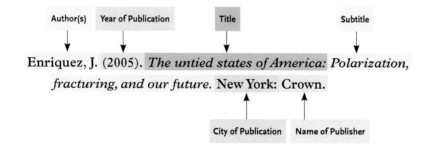

You can find most of the information you need to write a reference entry on a book's title page. If you cannot find the date of publication on the title page, turn to the copyright page. Reference entries for books generally include four units of information: author, year of publication, title, and publication data.

The UNTIED
States of America

...

Title

POLARIZATION, FRACTURING,

and OUR FUTURE

Juan Enriquez

Title page of *The Untied States of America*.

Year of publication Copyright © 2005 by Juan Enriquez

All rights reserved.
Published in the United States by Crown Publishers, Name of publisher
an imprint of the Crown Publishing Group,
a division of Random house, Inc., New York. City of publication
www.crownpublishing.com

CROWN is a trademark and the Crown colophon
is a registered trademark of Random House, Inc.

LIBRARY OF CONGRESS CATALOGING - IN- PUBLICATION DATA

Enriquez, Juan, 1959–
The untied states of America : polarization, fracturing, and our future /
Juan Enriquez — 1st ed.
p. cm.
Includes bibliographical references.
1. Polarization (Social sciences). 2. Regionalism—United States.
3. Alienation (Social psychology)—United States. 4. Secession—United States.
5. Sovereignty. 6. Nationalism. I. Title.
HN90.P57E67 2005
306'.0973 – dc22
2005013651
ISBN-13: 978-0-307-23752-1
ISBN-10: 0-307-23752-4
Printed in the United States of America

Design by Barbara M. Bachman

10 9 8 7 6 5 4 3 2 1

FIRST EDITION

Copyright page of *The Untied States of America*.

Author The author's last name appears first, followed by the first and (if given) the second initial. Use a comma to separate the last name from the initials, and place a period at the end of this unit of information. If there is more than one author, invert all the authors' names, following the pattern described for a single author. Separate the names with commas, adding an ampersand (&) before the name of the last author.

Hooker, R.

Montgomery, M., & Morgan, E.

McCrum, D., Kurath, H., & Middleton, S.

Year of publication Place the year of publication in parentheses after the author's name. Mark the end of this unit of information with a period.

Title Include the title and, if there is one, the subtitle of the book. Capitalize *only* the first word of the title and the subtitle, plus any proper nouns. Use a colon to separate the subtitle from the title. Italicize the title and subtitle.

Social cognition: Key readings.

Research

Publication data For the fourth unit of information, start with the city of publication, adding the common two-letter state abbreviation unless the city is Baltimore, Boston, Chicago, Los Angeles, New York, Philadelphia, or San Francisco. For works published abroad, add the name of the country unless the city is Amsterdam, Jerusalem, London, Milan, Moscow, Paris, Rome, Stockholm, Tokyo, or Vienna. Place a colon between the city of publication and the publisher's name. Use a shortened version of the publisher's name if possible. Although the word *Press* or *Books* should be retained, *Publishers, Company* (or *Co.*), and *Incorporated* (or *Inc.*) can be omitted.

1. Book by one author

Gladwell, M. (2002). *The tipping point: How little things can make a big difference*. New York: Little,

    Brown.

2. Book by two or more authors

Alberts, B., Lewis, J., & Johnson, A. (2002). *Molecular biology of the cell*. Philadelphia: Taylor &

    Francis.

If there are more than six authors, provide the names of the first six authors, inverted, and then use *et al.* to indicate that there are additional authors.

3. Book with editor(s)

Good, T. L., & Warshauer, L. B. (Eds.). (2002). *In our own voice: Graduate students teach writing*.

    Needham Heights, MA: Allyn & Bacon.

Provide the abbreviation *Ed.* or *Eds.* in parentheses after the name(s) of the editor(s).

4. Book with an author and an editor

Lewis, C. S. (2003). *A year with C. S. Lewis: Daily readings from his classic works* (P. S. Klein, Ed.).

    Grand Rapids, MI: Zondervan.

Provide the editor's name and the abbreviation *Ed.* in parentheses after the title of the book.

5. Book by a corporate author

Modern Language Association of America. (1978). *International bibliography of books and articles*

    on the modern languages and literatures, 1976. New York: Author.

Alphabetize by the first major word in the corporate author's name. List the publisher as *Author* when the author and the publisher are the same.

6. Book by an anonymous author

Primary colors: A novel of politics. (1996). New York: Warner.

List the title of the book in place of an author. Alphabetize the entry by the first major word of the title.

7. Second or subsequent edition

Cember, H. (1996). *Introduction to health physics* (3rd ed.). New York: McGraw-Hill.

Maples, W. (2002). *Opportunities in aerospace careers* (Rev. ed.). New York: McGraw-Hill.

Provide the edition number in parentheses after the title of the book. If the revision is not numbered, place *Rev. ed.* for "revised edition" in parentheses after the title.

8. Translated book

De Beauvoir, S. (1987). *The woman destroyed* (P. O'Brien, Trans.). New York: Pantheon. (Original work published 1969)

Insert the translator(s) name(s) in parentheses after the title, and conclude with the original publication date. Note the absence of a period at the end of the entry. In the text, provide both publication dates as follows: (De Beauvoir, 1969/1987).

9. Republished book

Freire, P. (1982). *Pedagogy of the oppressed* (2nd ed.). London: Penguin. (Original work published 1972)

Conclude the entry with the original publication date. In the text provide both dates: (Freire, 1972/1982).

10. Multivolume work

Doyle, A. C. (2003). *The complete Sherlock Holmes* (Vols. 1–2). New York: Barnes & Noble.

Maugham, S. W. (1977–1978). *Collected short stories* (Vols. 1–4). New York: Penguin.

Include the number of volumes after the title of the work. If the volumes were published over a period of time, provide the date range after the author's name.

11. Government report

Executive Office of the President. (2003). *Economic report of the President, 2003* (GPO Publication No. 040-000-0760-1). Washington, DC: U.S. Government Printing Office.

Provide the publication number in parentheses after the name of the report. If the report is available from the Government Printing Office (GPO), that entity is the publisher. If the report is not available from the GPO, use *Author* as the publisher.

12. Selection from an edited book

Nunan, D. (2001). Syllabus design. In M. Celce-Murcia (Ed.), *Teaching English as a second or foreign language* (3rd ed., pp. 55–65). Boston: Heinle & Heinle.

The title of the selection is not italicized. The editor's name appears before the title of the book. Provide the page or range of pages on which the selection appears.

13. Selection from a reference book

Mammals. (1998). In P. Alden (Ed.), *National Audubon Society field guide to the Pacific Northwest* (pp. 330–367). New York: Knopf.

Provide the page number or range of pages after the title of the book. If the selection has an author, give that author's name first.

Bruce, F. F. (1991). Hermeneutics. In *New Bible Dictionary* (p. 476). Wheaton, IL: Tyndale.

Articles in print

ARTICLE IN A JOURNAL

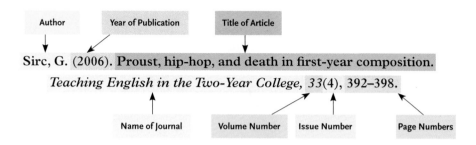

Sirc, G. (2006). Proust, hip-hop, and death in first-year composition.
Teaching English in the Two-Year College, 33(4), 392–398.

You can generally find the journal title, the volume and issue numbers, and the year of publication on the cover of the journal. Sometimes this information is also included in the journal's page headers or footers. To find the title of the article, the author's name, and the page numbers, you'll have to locate the article within the journal.

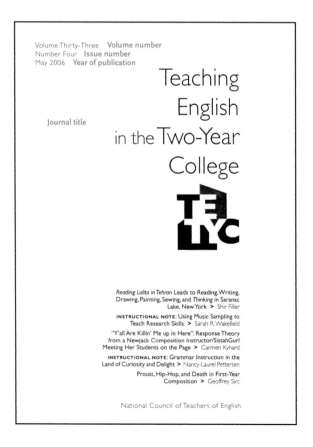

Cover of an academic journal.

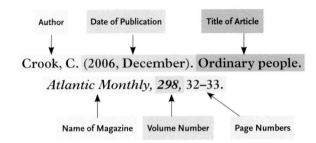

To find the name of the magazine, the volume number, and the date of publication, look on the cover of the magazine. Sometimes this information is also included in the magazine's page headers or footers. For the title of the article, the author's name, and the page numbers, look at the article itself. Reference entries for articles generally include four units of information: author, date of publication, title of article, and publication data.

Author The author's last name appears first, followed by the first and (if given) the second initial. Use a comma to separate the last name from the initial(s), and place a period at the end of this unit of information. For articles with more than one author, see the information given for book entries on pages 597–598.

Date of publication For journals, place just the year of publication in parentheses after the author's name. For magazines, also specify the month and the day (if given). Mark the end of this unit of information with a period.

Title of article Include the title and, if there is one, the subtitle of the article. Capitalize *only* the first word of the title and the subtitle, plus any proper nouns. Use a colon to separate the subtitle from the title. Place a period at the end of this unit of information.

Publication data The publication data that you provide depends on the type of periodical in which the article appeared. However, for all entries, include the title of the periodical (italicized), the volume number (also italicized), and the page numbers of the article. If you are using a journal that paginates each issue separately, include the issue number as well. Place the issue number (not italicized) in parentheses following the volume number. After the issue number, place a comma and then the article's page numbers.

14. Article in a journal with continuous pagination

McCarthy, M., & Carter, R. (2001). Size isn't everything: Spoken English, corpus, and the

    classroom. *TESOL Quarterly, 35,* 337–340.

Provide the volume number in italics after the title of the journal. Conclude with the page number or page range.

15. Article in a journal with each issue paginated separately

Conrad, S. (1999). The importance of corpus-based research for language teachers. *System, 27*(1), 1–18.

Provide the issue number in parentheses after the volume number. Italicize the volume number, but not the issue number.

16. Article with three to six authors

Biber, D., Conrad, S., & Reppen, R. (1996). Corpus-based investigations of language use. *Annual Review of Applied Linguistics, 16,* 115–136.

If there are six or fewer authors, list all of the authors' names.

17. Article with more than six authors

Stone, G. W., Ellis, S. G., Cox, D. A., Hermiller, J., O'Shaughnessy, C., Mann, J. T., et al. (2004). A polymer-based, paclitaxel-eluting stent in patients with coronary artery disease. *The New England Journal of Medicine, 350,* 221–231.

Provide the names of the first six authors, and then use *et al.* to indicate that there are additional authors.

18. Article in a monthly or weekly magazine

Alter, J. (2004, March 15). The fight for the high ground. *Newsweek, 143,* 42.

Warne, K. (2004, March). Harp seals. *National Geographic, 205,* 50–67.

Provide the month and year of publication for monthly magazines or the day, month, and year for weekly magazines. Names of months are not abbreviated. Include the volume number (italicized) and the page number or page range (not italicized) after the name of the magazine.

19. Anonymous article

Ohio police hunt for highway sniper suspect. (2004, March 16). *New York Times,* p. A4.

Begin the entry with the title of the article, followed by the date of publication.

20. Article in a newspaper

Ross, E. (2004, February 25). Adaptability of bird virus studied. *The Seattle Post-Intelligencer,* p. A8.

Use *p.* or *pp.* before the page number(s) of newspaper articles. If the article appears on discontinuous pages, provide all of the page numbers, separated by commas: pp. A8, A10–11, A13.

21. Letter to the editor

Richard, J. (2004, March 8). Diabetic children: Every day a challenge [Letter to the editor]. *The Wall Street Journal,* p. A17.

Include the description *Letter to the editor* in square brackets after the title of the letter.

22. Editorial in a newspaper

Sadat, L. (2003, December 16). UN tribunal is best option [Editorial]. *USA Today,* p. 16A.

Include the description *Editorial* in square brackets after the title.

23. Book review

Kakutani, M. (2004, February 13). All aflutter, existentially [Review of the book *Dot in the universe*]. *New York Times,* p. E31.

In square brackets after the title of the review, indicate that the work cited is a review, provide a description of the medium of the work (e.g., book, film, or play), and include the title of the work.

Sources produced for access by computer

JOURNAL ARTICLE FROM A DATABASE

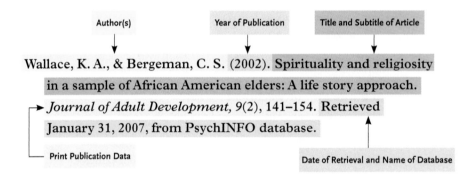

You can usually find much of the information you will need for your reference entry on the first page of the article. Each entry generally includes five units of information: author, year of publication, title and subtitle of article, print publication data, and date of retrieval and name of database.

Author The author's last name appears first, followed by the first and (if given) the second initial. Use a comma to separate the last name from the initials, and place a period at the end of this unit of information. For articles with more than one author, see the information given for book entries on pages 597–598.

Date of publication For journals, place just the year of publication in parentheses after the author's name. Mark the end of this unit of information with a period.

Title of article Include the title and, if there is one, the subtitle of the article. Capitalize *only* the first word of the title and subtitle, plus any proper nouns. Use a colon to separate the subtitle from the main title. Place a period at the end of this unit of information.

Print publication data The publication data that you provide depends on the type of periodical in which the article appeared. See the information on publication data for periodicals on page 606.

Date of retrieval and name of database Include both the date on which you accessed the database and the name of the database. Place the date after the word *Retrieved;* follow it with the word *from* and the name of the database.

Electronic sources vary significantly; therefore, as you prepare your list of references, follow the models below closely. On occasion, you may not be able to find all the information presented in a particular model. In such cases, just provide as much of the information as you can.

24. Online article based on a print source

McNamara, R. (2000). Britain, Nasser, and the outbreak of the six day war [Electronic version].
Journal of Contemporary History, 35(4), 619–639.

Place the words *Electronic version* in square brackets after the title to indicate that the article is also available in print.

25. Article in a journal published only online

Park, N., & Peterson, C. (2003, December 18). Early intervention from the perspective of positive
psychology. *Prevention & Treatment, 6,* Article 35. Retrieved April 3, 2006, from http://
journals.apa.org/prevention/volume6/pre0060035c.html

Provide the issue number and the article number (if any) after the title of the journal. Conclude with the retrieval date and the URL. Note that no period follows the URL.

26. Article in an online newspaper

Eisner, P. (2004, March 16). Back in the Caribbean heat. *The Washington Post.* Retrieved May 11,
2006, from http://www.washingtonpost.com

Provide the full date of the article after the author's name. Conclude with the retrieval date and the URL.

27. Message posted to a newsgroup

Skrecky, D. (2004, February 27). Free radical theory of aging falsified. Message posted to news://
ageing/bionet.molbio.ageing

If the author's name is unavailable, the author's screen name may be used. The protocol preceding the newsgroup address is *news.*

28. Message posted to a forum or discussion group

Vellenzer, G. (2004, January 24). Synonyms of entreaty [Msg. 2]. Message posted to http://
groups.google.com/groups?selm=MPG.1a7cacccd54e9c27989b95%40news.CIS.DFN
.DE&output=gplain

Any additional identifying information (e.g., *Msg 2*) should be provided in square brackets after the subject line of the message.

29. Article from a database

Yeh, S. (2003). An evaluation of two approaches for teaching phonemic awareness to children in
Head Start. *Early Childhood Research Quarterly, 18,* 513–529. Retrieved January 15, 2007,
from PsycINFO database.

Conclude with the date of retrieval and the name of the database.

30. Article from an information service

Dixon, L. Q. (2003). *The bilingual education policy in Singapore: Implications for second language acquisition.* Chicago: Spencer Foundation. (ERIC Document Reproduction Service No. ED478019)

Provide the ERIC document number in parentheses at the end of the entry.

31. Authored document from a Web site

Harvey, S. (1994, September). *Dynamic play therapy: An integrated expressive arts approach to the family treatment of infants and toddlers.* Retrieved December 28, 2006, from http://www.zerotothree.org/aboutus/dialogue.html

When the document apears on a large Web site such as a university or government Web site, provide the name of the host organization before the URL:

Darling, C. (2002). *Guide to grammar and writing.* Retrieved September 12, 2006, from Capital Community College Web site: http://cctc2.commnet.edu/grammar/modfiers.htm

32. Document from a Web site with no identified author

Wine Institute. (2004, February 10). *California wine grape crush down five percent to 2.94 million tons in 2003.* Retrieved April 5, 2006, from http://www.wineinstitute.org/communications/statistics/crush_2003.htm

Use the name of the organization hosting the Web site as the author of the document.

33. Online government publication

Administration on Aging. (2003). *A profile of older Americans: 2003.* Retrieved January 3, 2007, from http://www.aoa.gov/prof/Statistics/profile/2003/profiles2003.asp

Use *(n.d.)* in place of a publication date if the date is unknown.

34. Email message

Personal communications such as email messages, letters, telephone conversations, and personal interviews do not appear in the references list, but should be cited in the text as follows: (S. L. Johnson, personal communication, September 3, 2003).

Other sources

35. Motion picture

Jurow, M. (Producer), & Edwards, B. (Writer/Director). (1963). *The pink panther* [Motion picture]. United States: United Artists.

Begin with the name of the producer or the director, or both. Include the description *Motion picture* in square brackets after the title of the film. Conclude with the country of origin and the name of the movie studio.

36. Television program

Godeanu, R. (Producer). (2004, March 17). *In search of ancient Ireland* [Television broadcast]. Alexandria, VA: Public Broadcasting Service.

Begin with the name of the producer. Italicize the title of the program, and follow the title with the description *Television broadcast* in square brackets.

37. Music recording

Connor, S. (2004). Bounce. On *Sarah Connor* [CD]. New York: Sony.

Porter, C. (1936). Easy to love [Recorded by H. Connick, Jr.]. On *Come by me* [CD]. New York: Columbia. (1999)

Start with the name of the songwriter and the date the song was written. If someone other than the songwriter recorded the song, add *Recorded by* and the singer's name in square brackets after the song title. Indicate the medium on which the recording was made in square brackets after the album title. Conclude the entry with the year the song was recorded, in parentheses, if that date is not the same as the date the song was written.

38. Interview

Brock, A. C. (2006). Rediscovering the history of psychology: Interview with Kurt Danziger. *History of Psychology, 9*(1), 1–16.

For a published interview, follow the format for an entry for an article. If you conducted the interview yourself, cite the name of the person you interviewed in the body of your paper and include in parentheses the words *personal communication*, followed by a comma and the interview date. Do not include an entry for a personal interview in the list of references.

CHECKING OVER A REFERENCES LIST

✓ Is the title, *References* (not italicized), centered one inch from the top of the page? Is the first letter capitalized?

✓ Is the entire list double-spaced?

✓ Are initial lines flush with the left margin and subsequent lines indented one-half inch?

✓ Is there an entry in the references list for each in-text citation (except for personal communications)? Is there an in-text citation for each entry in the references list?

✓ Are the entries alphabetized according to the first author's last name? If the author of an entry is unknown, is the entry alphabetized according to title (ignoring any initial *a, an,* or *the*)?

✓ If the list contains two or more entries by the same author, are the entries arranged according to year of publication (earliest one first)?

✓ Are book and periodical titles italicized?

✓ Is capitalization used for only the first words of book and article titles and subtitles and any proper nouns they contain?

Sample APA Research Paper

The APA provides the following general guidelines for formatting a research paper. The title page is page 1 of your paper. In the upper right-hand corner, place a manuscript page header consisting of a shortened version of your title (two or three words) and the page number, separated by five character spaces. The page number should be one-half inch from the top of the page and one inch from the right edge. This manuscript page header should appear on every page. On the left-hand side of the title page, below the manuscript page header, place the running head. The running head is also a shortened version of the title, but it need not be as short as the title in the page header; it should be no longer than fifty characters (including punctuation and spaces). Capitalize each letter in the running head. Place the full title in the center of the page, using both uppercase and lowercase letters. Below it, put your name and affiliation (double-spaced)—unless your instructor asks you to include such information as the date and the course name and number instead of your affiliation.

If your instructor requires one, include an abstract—a short summary of your research—as the second page of your paper. The abstract should be no longer than 120 words. The word *Abstract* should be centered at the top of the page.

The first page of text is usually page 3 of the paper (following the title page and the abstract). The full title of the paper should be centered one inch from the top of the page. Double-space between the title and the first line of text. Use a one-inch margin on all sides of your paper (left, right, top, and bottom). Do not justify the text; that is, leave the right margin uneven. Indent paragraphs and block quotations one-half inch. Double-space your entire paper, including block quotations.

[1] Perceptions of Peers' 1

Running head: PERCEPTIONS OF PEERS' DRINKING BEHAVIOR [2]

[1] The manuscript page header contains the first two or three words of the title and the page number. The header is typed in uppercase and lowercase letters.

[2] The running head includes no more than fifty characters, with all letters capitalized.

Perceptions of Peers' Drinking Behavior [3]

Catherine L. Davis

Central Washington University [4]

[3] The title is typed in uppercase and lowercase letters.

[4] An instructor may require such information as the date and the course name and number instead of an affiliation.

Research

[5] The heading is cen-
tered on the page width.

Abstract [5]

This study is an examination of how students' perceptions of their peers'

drinking behavior are related to alcohol consumption and alcohol-related

problems on campus. Four hundred nine randomly selected college students

were interviewed using a modified version of the Core Survey (Presley,

Meilman, & Lyeria, 1995) to assess alcohol consumption and its related

[6] The abstract should
not exceed 120 words.

problems. [6]

Research

Perceptions of Peers' Drinking Behavior   **[7]**

Studies typically report the dangers associated with college students' use of alcohol (Wechsler, Davenport, Dowdall, Moeykens, & Castillo, 1994; Wechsler, Dowdall, Davenport, & DeJong, 1995). **[8]** Nonetheless, drinking is still highly prevalent on American campuses. Johnston, O'Malley, and Bachman (1998) found that 87% of the college students they surveyed reported drinking during their lifetime. Most of the students are 21 or 22 years old and report frequent episodes of heavy drinking (i.e., binge drinking).

Heavy episodic drinking is particularly problematic. Johnston et al. (1998) found that 41% of college students engage in heavy episodic drinking, which they defined as having at least five or more drinks in a row at least once in the 2 weeks prior to being surveyed. Heavy episodic drinking is related to impaired academic performance, interpersonal problems, unsafe sexual activity, and sexual assault and other criminal violations (Moore, Smith, & Catford, 1994). The magnitude of such problems has led Wechsler et al. (1995) **[9]** to conclude that heavy episodic drinking is the most serious drug problem on college campuses.

Massad and Rauhe (1997) **[10]** report that college students engage in heavy episodic drinking in response to social pressure or physical discomfort. Often students simply drink to get drunk (Wechsler et al., 1995). Recent research suggests that students' misperceptions of their peers' drinking behavior contribute to increased alcohol consumption (Perkins, 2002).

College students commonly perceive their social peers as drinking more often and in greater quantities than they actually do (Baer, Stacy, & Larimer, 1991). When these students see their peers as heavy drinkers, they are more

[7] The full title of the paper is centered on the page width.

[8] Authors of sources are named in parenthetical citations, including the year of publication of each source.

[9] This is a subsequent mention of a work by four authors.

[10] Authors are named in the text; the year of publication is placed in parentheses after the names.

Research

[11] This is a citation of
a work by two authors.

likely to engage in heavy drinking (Perkins & Wechsler, 1996). [11] The goal of

this study was to determine whether students' perceptions of their peers' use of

alcohol are related to alcohol consumption and alcohol-related problems on

campus.

Method

Participants

For the purposes of this study, a randomly selected sample ($N = 409$) of

undergraduate students from a university in the Pacific Northwest was drawn.

The mean age of participants, 55.8% of whom were female, was 24 years; 54.5%

of participants were White, 19% were Hispanic, 14.8% were Asian/Pacific

Islander, 5% were African American, 0.5% were American Indian, and 6.3%

indicated "Other" as their ethnicity.

Instrument

The study used a modified version of the short form of the Core Survey

(Presley, Meilman, & Lyeria, 1995). The Core Survey measures alcohol and other

drug (AOD) use as well as related problems experienced by college students.

For the purposes of this study, the Core was modified from a self-administered

format to an interview format.

Procedure

Interviews were conducted by telephone. Each interview took an average of

16 minutes to complete. The refusal rate for this survey was 12%, and those

refusing to participate were replaced randomly.

Alcohol use was defined as the number of days (during the past 30 days)

that respondents drank alcohol. *Heavy episodic drinking* was defined as five or more drinks in a single setting, with a drink consisting of one beer, one glass of wine, one shot of hard liquor, or one mixed drink (Presley et al., 1995). **[12]** Respondents indicated the number of occasions in the past 2 weeks that they engaged in heavy episodic drinking. *Alcohol-related problems* were defined as the number of times in the past 30 days respondents experienced any of 20 specific incidents.

To determine alcohol-related problems, the interviewer asked students how many times they (a) had a hangover, (b) damaged property, (c) got into a physical fight, (d) got into a verbal fight, (e) got nauseous or vomited, (f) drove a vehicle while under the influence, (g) were criticized by someone they knew, (h) had memory loss, or (i) did something they later regretted. To determine their perceptions of the amount of alcohol normally consumed by their peers, students were asked to respond on a 7-point ordinal scale that ranged from 0 = never to 6 = almost daily.

[The data analysis and statistical report of results have been omitted.]

Discussion

The relationship found here concerning the normative perception of alcohol use is somewhat consistent with past research (Baer & Carney, 1993; Perkins, 2002) **[13]** that suggested drinking norms are related to alcohol use. Readers should note, however, that respondents' perceptions of the drinking norm were consistent with the actual norm for 30-day use. This indicates that students are fairly accurate in assessing their peers' drinking frequencies. Unfortunately, the current study did not include a perception question for heavy episodic drinking, making it unclear whether respondents accurately perceive

[12] This is a subsequent mention of a work by three authors.

[13] A semicolon separates sources in the same parenthetical citation.

Research

their peers' drinking quantity. Conceptually, misperceptions of drinking quantity might be better predictors of heavy episodic drinking. That is, students might falsely believe that their peers drink heavily when they drink. Such a misperception would be compounded by the fact that most students accurately estimate frequency of their peers' drinking. The combination of an accurate perception of frequency coupled with an inaccurate perception of quantity might result in an overall perception of most students being heavy, frequent drinkers. As expected, this study also revealed a positive and moderately strong pathway from alcohol use, both heavy episodic drinking and 30-day drinking, to alcohol-related problems.

This study represents an effort to add to the literature concerning college students' alcohol consumption and its related problems. The results of the study suggest that students' perceptions of their peers' drinking habits are important predictors of drinking or drinking-related problems. Future studies along similar lines might help prevention specialists better design media campaigns related to drinking norms and high-risk behaviors.

Research

References [14]

Baer, J. S., & Carney, M. M. (1993). Biases in the perceptions of the consequences of alcohol use among college students. *Journal of Studies on Alcohol, 54,* 54–60. [15]

Baer, J. S., Stacy, A., & Larimer, M. (1991). Biases in the perception of drinking norms among college students. *Journal of Studies on Alcohol, 52,* 580–586. [16]

Johnston, L. D., O'Malley, P. M., & Bachman, J. G. (1998). *National survey results on drug use from the Monitoring the Future Study. 1975–1997: Vol. 11* (NIH Publication No. 98-4346). Washington, DC: U.S. Government Printing Office.

Massad, S. J., & Rauhe, B. J. (1997). Alcohol consumption patterns in college students: A comparison by various socioeconomic indicators. *Journal for the International Council of Health, Physical Education, Recreation, Sport, and Dance, 23*(4), 60–64.

Moore, L., Smith, C., & Catford, J. (1994). Binge drinking: Prevalence, patterns and policy. *Health Education Research, 9,* 497–505.

Perkins, H. W. (2002). Social norms and the prevention of alcohol misuse in collegiate contexts. *Journal of Studies on Alcohol, 14,* 164–172. [17]

Perkins, H. W., & Wechsler, H. (1996). Variation in perceived college drinking norms and its impact on alcohol abuse: A nationwide study. *Journal of Drug Issues, 26,* 961–974.

Presley, C. A., Meilman, P. W., & Lyeria, R. (1995). Development of the Core Alcohol and Drug Survey: Initial findings and future directions. *Journal of American College Health, 42,* 248–255.

[14] The heading is centered on the page width.

[15] All entries have a hanging indent of 5 spaces or one-half inch and are double-spaced.

[16] The entries are alphabetized according to the first author's last name. If two or more entries have the same first author, the second author's last name determines the order of the entries.

[17] Entries with a single author come before entries with two or more authors and the same first author.

Research

Wechsler, H., Davenport, A., Dowdall, G., Moeykens, B., & Castillo, S. (1994). Health and behavioral consequences of binge drinking in college. *Journal of the American Medical Association, 272*, 1672–1677.

Wechsler, H., Dowdall, G., Davenport, A., & DeJong, W. (1995). Binge drinking on campus: Results of a national study. *Bulletin series: Alcohol and other drug prevention.* Bethesda, MD: The Higher Education Center for Alcohol and Other Drug Prevention.

A Rhetorical Guide to Grammar and Sentence Style

When you think of the word *grammar*, you probably also think of the word *rules*—lawlike statements that you can't ignore if you want to stay out of trouble. But *rule* has another meaning: "a description of what is true in most cases." You might think of grammar rules as statements about how language is commonly used. However, language, as you know, is used differently by different people and in different situations. You can probably list a number of people whose language, perhaps in just small ways, differs from your own. You also adjust what you say or write to suit more formal and less formal occasions. Like all writers and speakers, you have a wide variety of options for language use, and your choices depend on your rhetorical situation. (Linguists refer to this variety that language users employ as *register*.) When you express your thoughts, you have any number of words and word arrangements at your disposal.

Jack Finney began his book *Invasion of the Body Snatchers* with this sentence:

> I warn you that what you're about to read is full of loose ends and unanswered questions.

But he could have written other sentences to express a similar idea:

> Warning: what you are about to read is full of loose ends and unanswered questions.

> I warn you that you are about to read something that has many loose ends and questions that have not been answered yet.

> What you are about to read, I warn you, is full of unanswered questions and loose ends.

Can you add other versions to this list? We do not know whether Finney tried any of these or similar sentences before he settled on his first line, but we do know that the sentence he chose has lured many readers into his dystopian fantasy.

Ultimately, the decisions a writer makes form what is commonly referred to as *style*. You might be wondering, though, what style has to do with grammar. *Grammar* refers to the structure of words and sentences. When you add an *-s* to a noun to make it plural or when you put the article *the* before a noun, you are dealing with grammatical structure. *Style* refers to the way ideas are expressed in sentences. Although style depends on grammar, grammar and style are so closely related that they could be called two different sides of the language coin.

Because of the numerous grammatical (and stylistic) options available to writers, characterizing effective writing is difficult. A sentence considered succinct in one circumstance might be considered overly simplistic in another. A long passage may seem wordy under some conditions but comprehensive under others. Nonetheless, readers and writers do agree on some ways of speaking about style. The following stylistic features may or may not be relevant, depending on the rhetorical situation.

Descriptors Used to Discuss Style

1. *Precise*. Sentences are precise when they include fitting and very specific words and word combinations. Precision is important in rhetorical situations calling for exactness. If you were writing an instruction manual, you would be expected to state exactly what is supposed to be done, when, and how. However, there are rhetorical situations in which you may have to be vague. For example, if you are writing a news report of a recent crime but do not know who is responsible for the action, you may have to use a sentence that does not specify the person responsible:

   Several of the campaign signs were defaced.

2. *Conventional*. Sentences are conventional when they conform to the expectations of a particular writing community. For most of your academic assignments, you will be expected to use Standardized English, the language most often used in governmental, educational, and professional set-

tings. But on occasion—say, if you are writing dialogue for a play, essay, or story—you might use a regional variation or a home dialect instead.

3. *Complete and consistent.* A piece of writing is complete and consistent when the writer has omitted none of the words often dropped in speech and has maintained the same tone and style throughout, even when varying the sentence structure. A piece that is not consistent seems to have been written by more than one person. Writing that is incomplete has words left out, often in a way that is conversational:

We discussed a couple [of] issues at the meeting.

It is hard to think of a rhetorical situation that would not call for complete, consistent prose, but imagine that you are writing a narrative essay, short story, or poem in which you want to capture a variety of voices in dialogue. In this case, to be effective, you would not employ one consistent style.

4. *Concise.* Concise prose has been weeded—that is, all redundant or otherwise useless words have been thrown out. If you are writing a science report, your readers will expect you to report your findings as succinctly as possible:

The results of the current study suggest that students' perceptions of their peers' drinking habits are important predictors of drinking or drinking-related problems.
—**Catherine Davis**, "Perceptions of Peers' Drinking Behavior"

If you are describing an unusual event or experience, however, your readers will appreciate sentences that are long and luxurious, such as this one:

One night about eleven o'clock in Las Vegas I watched a bride in an orange mini-dress and masses of flame-colored hair stumble from a Strip chapel on the arm of her bridegroom, who looked the part of the expendable nephew in movies like *Miami Syndicate.*　—**Joan Didion**, *"Marrying Absurd"*

5. *Coherent.* Coherent writing has adjacent sentences that are clearly connected to each other. Words such as pronouns and synonyms often provide strong links that make the progression from one idea to the next easy for readers to follow. In a letter to the editor, for example, a writer might use restatement to link a sentence to the one that came before:

Members of the community planning board failed to consider affordable living alternatives for tenants of the old apartment building before approving the high-cost condominiums. This unfortunate oversight has put an additional burden on social services that were already strained.

The great majority of the writing you do in college should be coherent, but the degree of coherence may vary. A student in a creative writing class may choose to write a poem that reflects the senseless nature of an experience; that poem would not have to be coherent according to the standards applicable to a business report.

6. *Varied.* Variation is the spice of paragraph structure. In order to write appealing paragraphs, a writer uses both short sentences and longer ones.

When sentences vary in length, they usually also vary in rhythm and emphasis. The optimal degree of variation can change from one writing situation to another. Whereas a reader of a friendly letter will quickly become bored with a lack of variety, someone reading a lab report isn't likely to notice such a lack.

7. *Parallel.* Parallelism refers to the expression of related ideas in similar structures. For example, if you want to say that you enjoy three activities, you could write

I like skiing, golfing, and swimming.

Notice that each of the activities ends in *-ing.* These parallel words express the meaning clearly and rhythmically. But there may be a situation in which you break from the expectation in order to emphasize a point. To describe a friend, you could start with two adjectives and then switch to a noun phrase:

My friend Alison is pretty, kind, and the smartest mathematician at this school.

As you read this part, "A Rhetorical Guide to Grammar and Sentence Style," you will learn to identify rhetorical options at the word and sentence levels. Understanding your options will help you craft a fitting response to any rhetorical situation. Chapter 22 focuses on word classes, and chapter 23 on sentence structure. Both of these chapters will introduce you to ways to connect your study of grammar to your study of sentence style. Chapter 24 goes into more detail on sentence style. Chapter 25 presents punctuation and mechanics options. Common spelling and usage troublespots are covered in the Glossary of Usage.

WORD CLASSES AND RHETORICAL EFFECTS | 22

When you look up a word in the dictionary, you will usually find it followed by one of these labels: *adj., adv., conj., det., interj., n., prep., pron.,* or *v.* (or *vb.*) These are the abbreviations for the traditional word classes, or parts of speech: adjectives, adverbs, conjunctions, determiners, interjections, nouns, prepositions, pronouns, and verbs. The definition of a word depends on which of these labels applies to the word. For example, when labeled as a noun, the word *turn* has several meanings, one of which is "curve":

> We were surprised by the turn in the road.

When *turn* is labeled as a verb, one of its possible meanings is "to change color":

> The leaves have turned.

By learning the word classes, not only will you be able to use a dictionary effectively, you will also better understand the feedback your teacher, supervisor, or peers give you and provide fellow writers with more specific recommendations. Someone reading your work, for example, may suggest that you use more action verbs. And you may note, as you read another's work, that it would be improved by balancing abstract nouns such as *nutrition* with concrete nouns such as *spinach*.

Nouns

Most nouns are labels for people, places, things, events, or ideas. A **common noun** refers to a member of a class or category: *student, university, document, protest, education.* In contrast, a **proper noun** is a specific name: *Jean Fadiman, Western Washington University,* the *Constitution,* the *Boston Tea Party.* Proper nouns are capitalized.

A common noun that has both singular and plural forms is called a **count noun**: *book, books.* A **noncount noun** has only one form because it refers to something that is not normally counted: *democracy, architecture.* A **collective noun** refers to a group of people or things: *clergy, committee, herd, bunch.*

EXERCISE 22.1

Decide whether each noun is common or proper. If it is common, decide whether it is a count, noncount, or collective noun.

1. the Sun Belt
2. university
3. team
4. senator
5. Senator John Glenn

Thinking rhetorically about nouns

The best time to think about whether you've chosen appropriate nouns and other words is usually during the revision process. If you worry too much about word choices during planning or drafting, you may not be able to generate all the ideas you need for a comprehensive response. So write a rough draft first. Then, when you feel that your ideas are in place, look at your nouns and decide whether they are abstract or concrete. An **abstract noun** like *entertainment* refers to a concept. A **concrete noun** refers to someone or something perceivable by the senses: *guitar, vocalist.*

Choose nouns that express precisely what you want your readers to sense or to understand. Some rhetorical situations call for the use of abstract terms. For example, you may be asked to write an art history paper using words like *impressionism* and *cubism.* Nonetheless, many writers forget to include the tangible details conveyed through concrete terms, which enable readers to see in their minds the colors and brushstrokes of Claude Monet, Pablo Picasso, or any of a number of other painters.

EXERCISE 22.2

Fill in the topic sentence with your favorite type of music (an abstract noun). Then write several supporting sentences that include concrete nouns.

If I could listen to only one type of music, it would be _____.

Determiners

A **determiner** narrows the reference of a common noun. Either of the determiners *a* and *the* can combine with *building,* but the scope of their reference differs. *A building* refers to one nonspecific member of a category consisting of buildings; *the building* refers to a specific building. The determiners *this* and *that* also affect the reference to a noun. *This* indicates physical or mental proximity: *this book, this idea. That* indicates physical or psychological distance: *that book, that idea.* The following are the five main types of determiners:

- Articles: *a, an, the*
- Demonstrative determiners: *this, that, these, those*
- Possessive determiners: *my, your, his, her, its, our, their* (sometimes called *possessive pronouns*)
- Quantifiers: *some, many, both, few, little*
- Numerals: *one, two, fourteen, three hundred,* and so on

EXERCISE 22.3

Underline each determiner in the following paragraph and identify its type.

> The rivalry between the Boston Red Sox and the New York Yankees is legendary. These two teams have faced each other in many dramatic playoff games. According to tradition, the rivalry began in 1918, when a financially strapped Red Sox owner sold his star player, Babe Ruth, to the Yankees. Up until 2004, the Yankees had won every decisive match the two teams had played. In 2004, what Red Sox fans call "the curse of the Bambino" was broken.

Thinking rhetorically about determiners

Sometimes sentences in a rough draft are only loosely related. You can make the connection between two sentences tighter by using a combination of determiner plus noun. Articles, demonstrative determiners, or possessive determiners can combine with nouns to refer to information in the previous sentence, creating coherence.

> My chemistry professor invented a new material. The/This/His invention was patented in 2003.

> The researchers published an article on avalanche control in a well-known journal. The/This/Their report described several new methods for controlling avalanches in recreational areas.

EXERCISE 22.4

For each sentence, provide a determiner plus noun combination that could begin a subsequent sentence.

1. The journalist investigated the politician's fund-raising record.
2. My friend explained string theory to me.
3. Alan Lee illustrated Tolkien's trilogy.

Verbs

Verbs refer to actions, sensations, events, or states of being. **Action verbs** are verbs that convey activity or change, such as *eat, happen, write,* and *study.* **Linking verbs** can be divided into two types. The linking verbs *be, seem,* and *become* refer to states of being. The linking verbs *look, taste, smell, feel,* and *sound,* also called **sensory verbs,** refer to perceptions.

Sometimes the verb in a sentence is just one word, such as the action verb *attend* in this sentence:

We <u>attended</u> the caucus.

However, at other times, a main verb may be accompanied by one or more **auxiliary verbs,** such as the following:

Be (am, is, are, was, were, been):

aux main verb
The students <u>are registering</u> for classes today.

Have (has, had):

aux main verb
My friend <u>has studied</u> in Japan.

Do (does, did):

aux   main verb
They <u>do</u> not <u>support</u> the proposal.

Modal verbs (can, may, should, will, and others):

aux main verb
We <u>should finish</u> by 5:00.

Some words can be a main verb or an auxiliary verb. In fact, sometimes the same word is used twice in a sentence—once as a main verb and once as an auxiliary.

Jamie <u>did</u> not help prepare lunch, but he <u>did</u> the dishes.

EXERCISE 22.5

Underline the verbs, including auxiliary verbs, in the following sentences.

1. The chair of the committee explained the proposal.
2. Everyone was talking at the same time.
3. No one could understand the logic of the proposal.
4. A similar proposal had been introduced a week ago.
5. The motion did not pass.

Thinking rhetorically about verbs

Decide which of the following sentences evokes a clearer image.

The team captain <u>was</u> happy. In fact, she <u>was</u> absolutely ecstatic.

Grinning broadly, the team captain <u>shot</u> both her arms into the air.

Although *be* in its many forms is the most frequently used verb, it is often avoided by writers whose rhetorical situation calls for vibrant imagery and stylistic variety. Instead, these writers favor strong action verbs.

EXERCISE 22.6

Revise the following sentences so that the verbs help to evoke vivid images. You'll likely need to include sensory details.

1. We were tired.
2. My friend was surprised.
3. The road was extremely treacherous.

Phrasal Verbs

A **phrasal verb** has two parts: a verb and an adverbial particle (see page 636), such as *down, in,* or *up.* The two parts of a phrasal verb work together to create meaning. When not forming the phrasal verb, the two parts have their own distinct meanings. For instance, the two individual words *run* and *up* might make you think of an action and a direction: *running up a hill* or *running up the road.* When the two words work together in the phrasal verb *run up,* though, the meaning changes. If someone runs up a bill or a debt, that person is buying items on credit that he or she will have to pay for later.

Occasionally, the meaning of a phrasal verb can be derived from the meanings of its parts, especially when the particle *up* or *down* adds a sense of completion, as in *eat up* or *gobble down.* If you are unsure of the meaning of a phrasal verb, you can look for its verb in a comprehensive dictionary. Phrasal verbs are usually listed at the end of a verb's entry.

There are two types of phrasal verbs: separable and inseparable. As their name suggests, **separable phrasal verbs** can be separated. Notice how the parts of a separable phrasal verb can be separated by a pronoun or a short noun phrase (see page 636) but not by a long noun phrase:

I turned <u>it</u> in.

I turned <u>the test</u> in early.

I turned in <u>my paper on the harmful effects of secondhand smoke.</u>

The verb and the adverbial particle of an **inseparable phrasal verb** must always occur together:

    into
I ran some friends into yesterday.
   ^

Grammar and Style

EXERCISE 22.7

Only one sentence in each of the following pairs contains a phrasal verb. Decide which sentence it is and explain how you know.

1. They looked up the road.
   They looked up the word.
2. I put the book on the shelf.
   I put the costume on.
3. He carried out the plan.
   He carried the specimens out the door.

Thinking rhetorically about phrasal verbs

As you know, informal language is appropriate for some rhetorical situations, but not for all. Because many phrasal verbs are considered conversational, you should find one-word synonyms for those that may sound too informal to your audience.

> *understood*
> They ˅caught on to the idea immediately.

EXERCISE 22.8

Replace the phrasal verbs with more formal one-word verbs.

1. You and your lab partner left out one step.
2. The stock prices went down rapidly.
3. The firefighters put out the wildfire.
4. The assistants put away the new shipment of paper.
5. The news editor blew up the old photograph.
6. Her explanation mixed me up even more.
7. The sponge did not take up much water.
8. The builders threw up that house in a month.
9. She turned down the job offer.
10. The young actress tried out for the play.

| Adjectives |

Adjectives modify nouns. *Modify* means to "qualify or limit the meaning of." If you use the noun *car* but want to limit the many different cars that may come to mind for your readers, you can add a modifier such as *black, rusty,* or *used.* **Attributive adjectives** usually precede, but occasionally follow, nouns or pronouns, as in *something special*. **Predicative adjectives** follow linking verbs such as *be, seem,* and *look* (when its meaning is "seem or appear"):

My schedule is <u>full</u>.　　She seems <u>nervous</u>.　　His face looks <u>familiar</u>.

EXERCISE 22.9

Use both attributive and predicative adjectives to modify the following nouns.

1. building
2. book
3. song
4. idea
5. dinner

Thinking rhetorically about adjectives

You have already learned that using concrete nouns and action verbs can make your writing vivid. Not all rhetorical situations call for such writing, but if yours does, you should also choose precise adjectives that help you convey sensation or intensity. So instead of describing a movie you did not like with the overused adjective *bad* or *boring*, you could call it *tedious* or *predictable*. When you sense that you might be using a lackluster adjective, search for an alternative in a thesaurus. If you come across unfamiliar words, be sure to look them up in a dictionary so that you do not misuse them.

EXERCISE 22.10

Find a movie review in a newspaper or online. Identify the adjectives used to describe the film and its actors, and note whether they are as precise as they can be.

Adverbs

Like adjectives, **adverbs** are modifiers. Instead of modifying nouns, however, they modify verbs, adjectives, and other adverbs. As modifiers of verbs, they provide information about time, manner, place, and frequency.

Time:　　　The festival begins <u>today</u>.

Manner:　　She stated her position <u>forcefully</u>.

Place:　　　We will meet you <u>there</u> after lunch.

Frequency:　They <u>usually</u> close at five.

Depending on which words in a sentence you want to stress, you can move an adverb modifying a verb to other positions within the sentence:

Today the festival begins.

She forcefully stated her position.

Adverbs that modify adjectives or other adverbs intensify or otherwise qualify the meanings of these words.

Adverb modifying adjective: The child was mysteriously clever.

Adverb modifying another adverb: He ran astonishingly fast.

Thinking rhetorically about adverbs

Adverbs of manner can enliven your prose in a number of ways. Adding such an adverb can help you create a sharp portrayal of an action.

After he entered the end zone, the fullback delicately set the ball down beneath the goalposts.

When you are writing dialogue, you can use an adverb of manner to depict how somebody is speaking.

"You're late," he whispered vehemently.

Adverbs of manner modify not only action verbs but adjectives as well. Adverbs can add detail to a description:

He was curiously intelligent.

Adverb-adjective combinations are common in book, movie, and theater reviews. Here are a few from *The New Yorker: blazingly apt, fastidiously elegant, enchantingly quaint, fascinatingly indecipherable, cautiously hopeful, mesmerizingly persuasive.*

EXERCISE 22.11

Write a short paragraph in which you describe a movie or someone performing a task. Include at least three adverbs.

Pronouns

As its name suggests, a **pronoun** is similar to a noun. Like nouns, pronouns refer to people, places, things, events, or ideas. However, without context, determining which person, place, thing, event, or idea is the referent for a pronoun is impossible. If you read just the sentence *They are visiting campus today,* you would not know who the visitors were. In contrast, if that sentence were preceded by *Ten students from Japan arrived yesterday,* you would know immediately that *they* refers to the ten students from Japan. Pronouns fall into several categories: personal, demonstrative, interrogative, reflexive or intensive, and indefinite.

Personal pronouns

To understand the usage of personal pronouns, you must first learn about person, number, and case. The **person** of a pronoun distinguishes between the writer (first person), the reader (second person), and the person or thing discussed (third person). The **number** of a pronoun indicates whether there is just one or more than one referent. That is, pronouns can be either singular or plural. **Case** refers to the form a pronoun takes depending on its function in the sentence. Pronouns can be subjects, objects, or possessives. (You will learn more about subjects and objects in chapter 23.) When they function as subjects, personal pronouns are in the subjective case; when they function as objects, they are in the objective case; and when they are possessives, they are in the possessive case.

	SUBJECTIVE		OBJECTIVE		POSSESSIVE	
NUMBER	*Singular*	*Plural*	*Singular*	*Plural*	*Singular*	*Plural*
PERSON						
First person	I	we	me	us	mine	ours
Second person	you	you	you	you	yours	yours
Third person	he, she, it	they	him, her, it	them	his, hers, its	theirs

Demonstrative pronouns

The **demonstrative pronouns** are *this, that, these,* and *those.*

That was the year when more people voted than ever before.

Demonstrative pronouns indicate physical or psychological proximity in either space or time.

Interrogative pronouns

Interrogative pronouns are question words that appear in the same positions in sentences as nouns do. *What* and *which* can be subjects or objects. *Who* is used as a subject, while its counterpart, *whom,* is used as an object. *Whose* is a possessive interrogative pronoun.

Subjective interrogative pronoun: Who won the award?

Objective interrogative pronoun: Whom did you consult?

Possessive interrogative pronoun: Whose is it?

Who, which, whom, and *whose* can also be found in relative clauses, which are discussed on pages 658–660.

Grammar and Style

Reflexive or intensive pronouns

Myself, yourself, himself, herself, itself, ourselves, yourselves, and *themselves* are used as either **reflexive pronouns** or **intensive pronouns.** Both types of pronouns are objects and must be accompanied by subjects. Reflexive pronouns are used when the performer and recipient of an action are the same. Intensive pronouns are used to provide emphasis.

> *Reflexive pronoun:*   He was always talking to himself.

> *Intensive pronoun:*   I, myself, delivered the letter.

Indefinite pronouns

Indefinite pronouns do not have specific referents. Here are some of the most common indefinite pronouns:

everybody	everything	everyone
somebody	something	someone
nobody	nothing	none
one	each	any
few	some	many

EXERCISE 22.12

Circle each pronoun in the paragraph below. Then, indicate what kind of pronoun each is (personal, demonstrative, interrogative, reflexive, intensive, indefinite).

I ran across a dim photograph of him the other day, going through some old things. He's been dead about forty years. His name was Rex (my two brothers and I named him when we were in our early teens) and he was a bull terrier. "An American bull terrier," we used to say, proudly; none of your English bulls. He had one brindle eye that sometimes made him look like a clown and sometimes reminded you of a politician with derby hat and cigar. The rest of him was white except for a brindle saddle that always seemed to be slipping off and a brindle stocking on a hind leg.

— **James Thurber,** "A Snapshot of Rex"

Thinking rhetorically about pronouns

Because pronouns must have context to make their referents clear, be sure that you provide your readers with enough information to understand who or what each pronoun represents. Vague uses of *it, they, this,* and *that* can make your writing hard to follow. Notice the difficulty of identifying what *this* is in the following sentence:

The study found that students succeed when they have clear directions, consistent and focused feedback, and access to help. This has led to the development of a tutoring center at our university.

This could refer to the study, the information provided by the study, or perhaps just to the finding that students need access to help. If you find that you have used a vague pronoun, add enough text to make the referent easily identifiable:

> The finding that successful students have access to help has led to the development of a tutoring center at our university.

EXERCISE 22.13

Underline vague uses of pronouns in the following sentences. Then revise the sentences so that the pronouns have clear referents.

1. Has anyone proposed removing the tax on textbooks, or is this unlikely?

2. The young and innovative research team used unconventional procedures to produce provocative results. They will be described in today's newspaper.

3. When employees suggested that management might be guilty of some wrongdoing, it attracted the attention of journalists.

Prepositions and Adverbial Particles

Prepositions combine with pronouns, nouns, or noun phrases (see page 641) to form prepositional phrases: *at us, toward midnight, in an argument.* A prepositional phrase functions as either an adjective or an adverb.

> My parents immediately noticed the stain on the carpet. [modifying *the stain*]

> She put the check on the table. [modifying *put*]

Prepositions usually consist of only one word. Prepositions containing more than one word are called **phrasal prepositions.**

COMMON PREPOSITIONS

about	beneath	in	regarding
above	beside	inside	round
across	between	into	since
after	beyond	like	through
against	by	near	to
among	concerning	of	toward
around	despite	off	under
as	down	on	unlike
at	during	out	until
before	except	outside	up
behind	for	over	upon
below	from	past	with

according to	by way of	in spite of
along with	due to	instead of
apart from	except for	on account of
as for	in addition to	out of
as regards	in case of	with reference to
as to	in front of	in/with regard to
because of	in lieu of	with respect to
by means of	in place of	

An **adverbial particle** may look like a preposition, but its function is different. Whereas a preposition combines with a noun or noun substitute, an adverbial particle combines with a verb. The resulting verb plus particle unit is a **phrasal verb** (see page 629). The adverbial particle may sometimes be separated from the verb by pronouns or short noun phrases:

I <u>turned</u> my paper <u>in</u> yesterday.   I <u>blew</u> it <u>out</u>.

COMMON ADVERBIAL PARTICLES

about	back	on
across	down	out
ahead	forward	over
along	in	out
apart	off	through

EXERCISE 22.14

Identify the prepositions and adverbial particles in the following paragraph.

As a Columbia College freshman, in 1960, I took the Humanities (Great Books) course with a gruff, crewcut philosophy instructor named Robert G. Olson, who was genially contemptuous of us and the institution. He used to stub his cigarettes out on the floor and mumble a wish that one day the place would burn down. I liked his irreverent, sardonic manner—even when he dressed me down for stealing others' ideas—and at last it dawned on me, after he chose me as the best student in his section (an honor that came with a $20 certificate at the university bookstore) that he liked me.

—**Philip Lopate,** Untitled, in *For the Love of Books* by Ronald B. Shwartz

Thinking rhetorically about prepositions and adverbial particles

Prepositions and adverbial particles are often found in idioms. An **idiom** is a word combination that has a meaning independent of the meanings of its individual words. For example, when we *come across* some money, we find it by chance. When we *come into* some money, we inherit it. Knowing the typical meanings of *come, across,* and *into* does not lead you to these definitions. There is no simple explanation as to why we use *across* with *come* in one idiom and *into* in the other.

Using idioms accurately will help ensure that you are expressing your thoughts clearly. Because many idioms are not included in conventional dictionaries, it is important to study how writers use them and to consult a specialized reference book such as *The BBI Dictionary of Word Combinations.*

EXERCISE 22.15

Use each of the following idioms correctly in a sentence.

1. give back, give in, give out, give up
2. show regard for, in regard to, to regard someone as, to regard someone with
3. to chance upon, to leave something to chance, by chance, on the off chance

Conjunctions

The English word *conjunction* has its roots in the Greek word *sundesmos,* which means "binding together." And that is exactly what a conjunction does. A **coordinating conjunction** joins words or groups of words of the same grammatical category; for example, it links noun to noun, verb phrase to verb phrase, or independent clause to independent clause (see page 658).

Gabon <u>and</u> Cameroon share a border. [connecting proper nouns]

They were successful entrepreneurs, <u>but</u> they never boasted of their achievements. [connecting independent clauses]

There are seven coordinating conjunctions: *for, and, nor, but, or, yet, so.* Combining the first letters of these words gives *fanboys.* This made-up word can help you remember the coordinating conjunctions.

A **correlative conjunction** is a two-part conjunction. The four most common correlative conjunctions are *both . . . and, either . . . or, neither . . . nor,* and *not only . . . but also.* Like coordinating conjunctions, correlative conjunctions link words or groups of words of the same category.

She has a degree <u>not only</u> in medicine <u>but also</u> in law. [connecting prepositional phrases]

Subordinating conjunctions introduce dependent clauses—clauses that must be linked to a main clause, or independent clause.

COMMON SUBORDINATING CONJUNCTIONS

after	in case	though
although	in that	till
as if	inasmuch as	unless
as though	insofar as	until
because	lest	when, whenever
before	now that	where, wherever
even if	once	whether
even though	since	while
how	so that	why
if	than	

EXERCISE 22.16

The paragraph below is from Stacy Simkanin's first draft of the essay that is featured in chapter 3. Identify the underlined words as coordinating or subordinating conjunctions. Be prepared to explain your answers.

But at the same time that technology brings these advantages, it also inhibits learning and writing. I know that when I'm conducting online research I may be missing out on information or on the quality of information because I'm limiting my searching to electronic sources. Nowadays, students don't really have to learn to use the library, where often more information can be found than what appears in an online search. I fear that students are placing convenience over quality. I know I do sometimes. The information online isn't always reliable, either. Students don't often take the time to investigate sources.

Thinking rhetorically about conjunctions

Your use of conjunctions conveys how you think ideas are related, so you must choose conjunctions carefully. Determining whether ideas are being compared, contrasted, or just presented sequentially is the first step in choosing an appropriate conjunction. Conjunctions convey a variety of meanings—addition, comparison, contrast, and purpose, to mention just a few. Some conjunctions are more specific than others, however. The conjunction *and,* for instance, can often be replaced by a more exact conjunction.

My grandparents moved away when I was little, ∧ and I seldom saw them.
                                                so

Also be sure that the meaning of the conjunction you use is not ambiguous. In the following sentence, *since* could mean either "after" or "because of."

Since he arrived, we decided to leave.

The subordinating conjunction *after* or *because* would clarify the meaning in this sentence.

Revise the following sentences so that the connections are more precise.

1. As we were discussing my performance, the coach mentioned my slow times in the freestyle.

2. The clock struck one, and we were not finished.

3. Since she was elected to office, the deficit has decreased.

Expletives

The word *expletive* has its origin in a Latin word meaning "to fill out." The expletives *there* and *it* take the subject position in sentences either because there is no clear subject, as in *It's raining,* or because the information usually placed in the subject position has been moved to a position after the verb, as in *There's a fly in my soup.* Note that the expletive *there* is different from the adverb *there,* and the expletive *it* is different from the personal pronoun *it:*

I live over <u>there</u>. [adverb]

<u>There</u> is a full moon tonight. [expletive]

We liked the apartment, but <u>it</u> was too expensive. [pronoun]

<u>It</u> was surprising to see so many people at the rally. [expletive]

Find examples of the expletives *it* and *there* in the excerpt by Adina Levin on page 261.

Thinking rhetorically about expletives

The expletives *it* and *there* allow information to be presented later in a sentence and thus stressed.

A storm will be moving in tonight.

There will be a storm moving in tonight.

When *there* opens the sentence, *storm* receives more emphasis than when it is in the subject position. Similarly, the placement of *it* at the beginning of the second sentence in the following pair allows the underlined information to be emphasized:

That <u>we survived the ordeal</u> was amazing.

It is amazing that <u>we survived the ordeal</u>.

Grammar and Style

Revise the following sentences so that the information in the subject position comes later in each sentence. Identify which words are stressed in the original and which are stressed in your revision.

1. A pod of orcas is floating in Puget Sound.
2. That we have actually finished the project is hard to believe.
3. A quartet is singing in the alleyway.
4. A crowd is waiting outside the courthouse.
5. That no one noticed the problem earlier was odd.

Interjections

Some types of writing call for expressions of emotion. Such expressions are called **interjections,** which usually appear at the beginning of a sentence but may also occur in the middle or at the end of a sentence.

> Phew! That test burned up my synapses.
>
> My brothers, alas, were left to fend for themselves.

Thinking rhetorically about interjections

Most likely you will use interjections only in writing that is meant to mimic speech, as in this excerpt:

> Rosemary unlatches their tool kit, a tackle box. From it, Peter extracts a pair of jeweler's spectacles, a plastic mask with bulging lenses, which make him look like Robinson Crusoe from Mars. "Okay, Famous Bird," Peter says. "Ow! Famous Bird has decided to bite the hand that feeds him." He grasps the finch with one hand and its head sticks out observantly from his fist. The bird is about the size of a sparrow, and jet-black, with a black beak and shiny dark eyes.
>
> —**Jonathan Weiner,** *The Beak of the Finch*

EXERCISE 22.20

Write a short paragraph in which you use one or two of the following interjections, or choose your own.

oh	yow	phew
hey	sheesh	wow
yay	hooray	ouch
well	no way	no

Sentence Structure and Rhetorical Effects

In chapter 22, you studied the smaller parts of sentences—word classes such as nouns, pronouns, verbs, and so on. In this chapter, you'll see how these parts combine to form phrases and sentences and how they can be manipulated to help you achieve rhetorical effect. Studying elements of sentence structure in this chapter will help you write clear, concise, and complete sentences.

Phrases

If you were asked to define *phrase,* the first definition to pop into your head might be "a group of words." Though this definition is accurate, its vagueness becomes apparent when you try to apply it. Try locating all the groups of words in the following sentence:

> Just as we painstakingly fit photos into albums or, in the new age, organize them into computer folders and make digital copies for safekeeping, so I hang on to the impression of a stainless-steel wristwatch that once applied a familiar force of weight to my left wrist.   —**Marshall Jon Fisher,** "Memoria ex Machina"

Is *applied a familiar* a phrase? Is *weight to my left* a phrase? Clearly, these are groups of words, but the words in them are not related in a way that seems as natural to us as the groupings *a familiar force* and *my left wrist.*

Groupings occur at various levels in English. At the level of the word, a group consists of a root word and its prefix and/or suffix: <u>reexamining</u>. At the level of the phrase, most groups form around a **head word**. For example, *force* is the head word of *a familiar force,* and *wrist* is the head word of *my left wrist.* Types of phrases are named for their head words: in noun phrases, the head word is a noun; in verb phrases, the head word is a verb; and so on.

Noun phrases

A **noun phrase** is a group of words with a noun as the head word. The other words in the group modify the head word. In *the new age,* the determiner *the* indicates a specific referent, and the adjective *new* provides information to distinguish the age being referred to from other ages. See if you can pick out the head words in these noun phrases: *computer folders, a stainless-steel wristwatch, digital copies.* If you chose *folders, wristwatch,* and *copies,* you are right.

Thinking rhetorically about noun phrases

When you studied word classes, you learned the importance of being precise. A corollary of being precise is being concise. To write concisely, though, does not mean using only short sentences; rather, it means that you make each word count. During the editing stages of writing, look for words that can be deleted. Here are some likely candidates that you may find in noun phrases:

Nouns that are close in meaning:	The significance and importance of this new law was not immediately apparent.
Adjectives that are close in meaning:	She was given an award for her new and innovative design.
Unnecessary determiners:	Each and every student in the program received a progress report.
Unnecessary adjective:	You will receive a complimentary gift.

Prepositional phrases

A **prepositional phrase** is a combination of a preposition and a noun phrase. Such a phrase normally modifies another element in a sentence, providing information about time, location, direction, cause, accompaniment, and so on.

> They moved to a small town near Boise. [*To a small town* modifies *moved*, providing information about direction. *Near Boise* modifies *town*, providing information about location.]

Because prepositions are generally followed by noun phrases, they do not usually appear at the ends of sentences. In fact, you may have heard the rule "Never end a sentence with a preposition." However, most style manuals, including *The Chicago Manual of Style* (probably the most widely used style guide), consider this rule outmoded, especially regarding prepositional phrases found in adjectival clauses (see page 658). Notice how much more natural this sentence sounds with a final preposition:

Those are the principles <u>on</u> which we relied.

Those are the principles we relied <u>on</u>.

Thinking rhetorically about prepositional phrases

When you are writing descriptive passages, you can use prepositional phrases beginning with *like* or *as* to make comparisons.

He had always been so strange and had lived, <u>like a prophet</u>, in such unimaginably close communion with the Lord that his long silences which were punctuated by moans and hallelujahs and snatches of old songs while he sat at the living-room window never seemed odd to us. —**James Baldwin,** "Notes of a Native Son"

Fog, melancholy <u>as a rain-soaked dog</u>, drifts through the highlands, beading my hair with moisture. On the path ahead a vermilion flycatcher, burning scarlet against the muted greens of the cloud forest, bursts up in flight. He flies to a space just over my head and flutters there furiously, an acrobatic stall, a tiny wild commotion that hounds me down the muddy trail, until I pass beyond the small arena of his life.

—**Barry Lopez,** "Wide-eyed in Galápagos"

These prepositional phrases are called **similes.** By including a simile, you can add details to a sentence or paragraph that needs further development.

EXERCISE 23.3

Add similes to the following sentences.
1. Fireworks drifted down from the black heavens.
2. His diagram confused us all.
3. The crowd surged from the subway doors.

Verb phrases

Like a noun phrase, a **verb phrase** has a head word, which, in this type of phrase, is the main verb. Although a sentence may contain just a main verb, it also often includes **auxiliary verbs,** sometimes called **helping verbs.** In the following sentences, *work* is the main verb; *is, has, does,* and *might* are auxiliary verbs.

She <u>works</u> for IBM.

She <u>is working</u> this Saturday.

She <u>has worked</u> there since 1995.

<u>Does</u> she <u>work</u> near her home?

She <u>might work</u> late tonight.

Notice that the main verb *work* has four different forms:

work, works, working, worked

All **regular verbs** have four forms: (1) a base form, which is the form you find in the dictionary (*play, carry*); (2) an *-s* form, which consists of the base form and the suffix *-s* or, in some cases, *-es* (*plays, carries*); (3) an *-ing* form, also called the *present participle,* which is a combination of the base form and the suffix *-ing* (*playing, carrying*); and (4) an *-ed* form, which consists of the base form and the suffix *-ed* (*played, carried*). The *-ed* form has two alternative labels. When used without any auxiliary verb, it is called the *past form:*

They *played* soccer together.

When used with an auxiliary verb, it is called the *past participle:*

She *has carried* a heavy load.

VERB FORMS OF REGULAR VERBS

Base Form	-s Form (Present Tense, Third Person, Singular)	-ing Form (Present Participle)	-ed Form (Past Form or Past Participle)
talk	talks	talking	talked
match	matches	matching	matched
reply	replies	replying	replied
shop	shops	shopping	shopped

Irregular verbs have as few as three forms (*put, puts, putting*) up to as many as eight forms (*be, am, is, are, was, were, being, been*). The base form, the *-s* form, and the *-ing* form of an irregular verb (*drive, drives, driving*) are often similar to those forms of a regular verb. However, the past form (*drove*) and the past participle (*driven*) are not the regular *-ed* form. Some irregular verbs even have two acceptable past forms (*dived, dove*) or past participles (*beat, beaten*). For irregular verbs with only three forms, the base form, the past form, and the past participle are all the same (*let*). If you are unsure about verb forms, consult the following chart or a dictionary.

VERB FORMS OF IRREGULAR VERBS

Base Form	-s Form (Present Tense, Third Person, Singular)	-ing Form (Present Participle)	Past Form	Past Participle
beat	beats	beating	beat	beaten, beat
begin	begins	beginning	began	begun
forget	forgets	forgetting	forgot	forgotten
give	gives	giving	gave	given
lay	lays	laying	laid	laid

Base Form	-s *Form* (Present Tense, Third Person, Singular)	-ing *Form* (Present Participle)	Past Form	Past Participle
lie	lies	lying	lay	lain
put	puts	putting	put	put
rise	rises	rising	rose	risen
set	sets	setting	set	set
steal	steals	stealing	stole	stolen
swim	swims	swimming	swam	swum
write	writes	writing	wrote	written

There are four types of auxiliary verbs: (1) *do, does, did;* (2) modal auxiliary verbs; (3) *will, be, have;* and (4) auxiliary verbs used in the passive voice (see page 654).

The auxiliary verb *do* is used to form yes/no questions, negations, and emphatic sentences.

Do you like your classes?

He does not spend much money.

I did return his phone call.

A **modal auxiliary verb,** the second type, adds information about such conditions as possibility and obligation to the main verb.

COMMON MEANINGS OF MODAL AUXILIARY VERBS

Meaning	Modal Auxiliary	Main Verb	Example
ability	can	solve	He *can* solve the problem.
advice	should	wear	You *should* wear sunscreen.
certainty	will	finish	They *will* finish before the deadline.
obligation	must	pay	She *must* pay the fine by Friday.
permission	may	use	They *may* use our equipment.
possibility	might	go	I *might* go to China this summer.

The auxiliary verbs *will, be,* and *have* are used to indicate verb tense and verb aspect. To fully understand how these auxiliary verbs work in verb phrases, you'll need to recognize the difference between tense and aspect.

Grammar and Style

English has three tenses: present, past, and future. Verbs are marked for aspect as well as for tense. **Aspect** provides information about the completion of an action, event, or state and about the relation of one verb to other verbs in a time sequence. The sentences *The wind blows in the spring* and *The wind is blowing hard* both use the present tense, but they differ in aspect. *Blows,* in the first sentence, refers to a habitual action; *is blowing,* in the second sentence, refers to an incomplete action. To indicate the difference in aspect, *blows* is labeled as the **simple present** and *is blowing* is labeled as the **present progressive**. There are four aspect labels: simple, progressive, perfect, and perfect progressive. Sometimes two different aspects are used in one sentence to show a sequence of actions:

I had been talking on the telephone when the storm hit.

The past perfect progressive *had been talking* indicates that the action was ongoing and occurred prior to the action indicated by the simple past *hit*.

The following chart provides labels for and examples of verb tense–aspect combinations.

TENSE–ASPECT COMBINATIONS AND THEIR USES

	TENSE		
ASPECT	*Present*	*Past*	*Future*
Simple	Simple present **study, studies** Use to refer to current states, habitual actions, and general truths: *Judith studies every night she's not working.*	Simple past **studied** Use to refer to completed past events or actions: *We studied together last night.*	Simple future **will study** Use to refer to future states or actions: *I will study for my French exam over the weekend.*
Progressive	Present progressive **am, is, are studying** Use to refer to activities in progress or situations considered temporary: *Carlos is studying until he has to leave for class.*	Past progressive **was, were studying** Use to signal a repeated or ongoing action or event in the past: *Reese and Krissi were studying architecture while in Italy.*	Future progressive **will be studying** Use to refer to actions that will be ongoing in the future: *You will be studying while I am at the gym.*

	TENSE		
ASPECT	*Present*	*Past*	*Future*
Perfect	*Present perfect*	*Past perfect*	*Future perfect*
	has, have studied	**had studied**	**will have studied**
	Use to refer to a situation originating in the past but continuing into the present or to a past action or state with current relevance: *I have studied Japanese for five years now.*	Use to indicate that a completed action occurred prior to another action in the past: *Marie thought that she had studied long enough.*	Use to refer to a future action that will be completed by a specified time: *By the time I have to leave for work, I will have studied my biology notes.*
Perfect progressive	*Present perfect progressive*	*Past perfect progressive*	*Future perfect progressive*
	has been, have been studying	**had been studying**	**will have been studying**
	Use to show that an action or state originating in the past is ongoing or incomplete: *Ryan has been studying for less than ten minutes.*	Use to show that an ongoing past action occurred prior to another completed action: *Lori had been studying so hard that she overslept the next morning.*	Use to refer to an ongoing action that will continue for a specific amount of time: *In 30 minutes, we will have been studying for five straight hours.*

EXERCISE 23.4

Identify the tense and aspect of the verb phrases in the following sentences; explain why they have been used, inventing context as necessary.

1. He will deliver your package tomorrow.
2. She has taught kindergarten for twenty years.
3. The team has been practicing since October.
4. I have read that book already.
5. My neighbor usually goes to the park on Sundays.
6. It had snowed two feet that day.

continued

7. Earlier that afternoon, they had been playing chess.
8. They are experts in their field.
9. He is planning a party.
10. By the end of 2009, we will have visited all the states.
11. My friend and I are working in a national park this summer.
12. We paid for our own tickets.
13. Everyone will be celebrating this weekend.
14. In ten minutes, I will have been dancing for twenty-four hours.
15. My son was laughing through the entire movie.

Thinking rhetorically about verb tense

A fiction writer may use the present tense to tell a story because it makes the events seem immediate.

> We <u>drive</u> past Half Moon Bay and Pacifica and Seaside, the condos on the left and the surfers on the right, the ocean exploding pink. We <u>pass</u> through cheering euca-lyptus and waving pines, cars <u>reflect</u> wildly as they <u>come</u> at us, they <u>seem</u> to come right for us, and I <u>look</u> through their windshields for the faces of those coming at us, for a sign, for their understanding, for their trust, and I <u>find</u> their trust and they <u>go</u> by. Our car <u>thrums</u> loudly and I <u>turn</u> up the radio because I <u>can</u>. I <u>drum</u> the steering wheel with open palms, then fists, because I <u>can</u>. Toph <u>looks</u> at me. I <u>nod</u> gravely.
>
> —**Dave Eggers**, *A Heartbreaking Work of Staggering Genius*

EXERCISE 23.5

To get a sense of the difference between the uses of the present and past tenses, change all of the underlined verbs in the excerpt by Dave Eggers to the past tense.

Verbal phrases

Verbal phrases are phrases with verb forms that are not marked for tense: the present participle (*asking*), the past participle (*asked*), and the infinitive (*to ask*). Depending on which form is used and what its role is in the sentence, a verbal phrase may be a gerund phrase, a participial phrase, or an infinitive phrase.

A **gerund phrase** has the present participle (*-ing* form) at its core. Even though a gerund is a verb form, it plays the role of a noun. Notice how the gerund phrase in the following sentences can be replaced by a pronoun—just as a noun phrase can:

It
Wrapping presents is easy for some people.
ʌ

A **participial phrase** is formed with either the present participle (the *-ing* form) or the past participle (the *-ed* form for regular verbs or a special form for irregular verbs). (Consult the chart on pages 644–645 for some irregular past participles.) A participial phrase differs from a gerund phrase in that it takes the role of a modifier, not a noun phrase.

Hoping to graduate in May, the students worked diligently on their final projects.

A participial phrase often begins a sentence, but it can appear in the middle or at the end of a sentence.

Encouraged by job prospects, the students worked diligently to graduate.

The students, hoping to graduate in May, worked diligently on their final projects.

The students worked diligently on their final projects, hoping to graduate in May.

An **infinitive phrase** comprises the infinitive marker *to* and the base form of a verb. An infinitive phrase takes the role of either a noun phrase or a modifier.

He continued to play the trumpet after he graduated from high school.

To solve the traffic problem, the city manager has proposed a subway system.

Notice that the infinitive phrase in the first sentence cannot be moved because it is taking the role of a noun phrase; the infinitive phrase in the second sentence could be moved to the middle or end of the sentence because it is a nonessential modifier, simply providing additional information.

The city manager, to solve the traffic problem, has proposed a subway system.

The city manager has proposed a subway system to solve the traffic problem.

EXERCISE 23.6

Identify the verbal phrases in the following paragraph.

> I see four kinds of pressure working on college students today: economic pressure, parental pressure, peer pressure, and self-induced pressure. It is easy to look around for villains—to blame the colleges for charging too much money, the professors for assigning too much work, the parents for pushing their children too far, the students for driving themselves too hard. But there are no villains, only victims.   **—William Zinsser,** "College Pressures"

Thinking rhetorically about verbal phrases

By using verbal phrases, you can make your writing both concise and varied. If some sentences sound monotonous or choppy, try combining them with a verbal phrase.

Choppy: The ecstatic fans crowded the city streets. They were celebrating their team's first state championship.

Revised: Crowding the city streets, the ecstatic fans celebrated their team's first state championship.

OR

Celebrating their team's first state championship, the ecstatic fans crowded the city streets.

Using a verbal phrase also allows you to focus on action, rather than on the agents of action.

> They bundle products together, which often results in higher consumer costs.

> <u>Bundling products together</u> often results in higher consumer costs.

It is the bundling that is the focus, not the bundlers.

EXERCISE 23.7

Combine the following pairs of sentences, using a participial phrase for the first pair, a gerund phrase for the second, and an infinitive phrase for the third.

1. He wrote frantically throughout the night.
   He completed his portfolio by class time.
2. Some drivers try to beat red lights.
   This behavior often causes accidents.
3. You could argue about this point.
   But such argument is useless in the end.

Subjects and Predicates

Every complete sentence has a subject and a predicate. The **subject** has a noun or noun substitute at its core; the **predicate** has a verb at its core. If only the core words are used, a sentence consists of two words: *Everyone laughed.* Most sentences, though, include modifiers: *Everyone in the audience laughed uproariously.* Even with modifiers, this sentence still has just two parts. *Everyone in the audience* is the subject, and *laughed uproariously* is the predicate.

The subject of a sentence generally corresponds to the topic of the sentence, and the predicate provides a comment about the topic. Most native speakers of English can easily separate the subject and the predicate. Try to do so with the following sentences:

> Many people in the United States study karate.

> Japanese forms of karate focus on simple movement.

If you separated the first sentence between *States* and *study* and the second between *karate* and *focus,* you have a head start in understanding sentence composition.

EXERCISE 23.8

Identify the subjects and the predicates in the following proverbs.

1. Practice makes perfect.
2. A rolling stone gathers no moss.
3. A stitch in time saves nine.

Thinking rhetorically about subjects and predicates

If you would like to add some variety to your sentence patterns, try moving the predicate to the front of a sentence.

> A small dog with large brown eyes <u>was peering through the window</u>.

> <u>Peering through the window</u> was a small dog with large brown eyes.

Sentences in which a verb phrase includes the present participle (*-ing* form) are good candidates for this type of inversion. When you move the *-ing* form of the verb to the beginning of the sentence and place the subject at the end of the sentence, you not only vary the sentence structure but also create some suspense. The reader must wait to find out who or what is peering through the window—that is, who or what is the agent of the action.

EXERCISE 23.9

Rewrite each sentence so that the predicate occurs before the subject.

1. A group of protestors were standing by the door.
2. Two of my friends were vying for first place.
3. A distant cloud of smoke was attracting everyone's attention.

Sentence Patterns

Sentence patterns are determined by the type of verb found in the predicate—a linking verb or an action verb (see pages 627–628). There are six common patterns. The first pattern includes a linking verb, such as *be, seem,* or *look,* followed by a **subject complement**, usually a noun phrase or an adjectival phrase (a phrase in which the head word is an adjective).

1. SUBJECT + LINKING VERB + SUBJECT COMPLEMENT

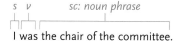
I was the chair of the committee.

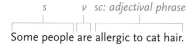
Some people are allergic to cat hair.

Related to this pattern is another in which the linking verb is followed by an adverbial phrase, usually signaling time or place.

2. SUBJECT + LINKING VERB + ADVERBIAL PHRASE

They are in the library.

The remaining patterns all have action verbs as their predicate cores. Action verbs can be divided into two types: transitive and intransitive. These labels come from the stem *trans*, meaning "over or across." The action of a **transitive verb** carries over to an object—most frequently a noun phrase. The action of an **intransitive verb** does not carry over; the verb occurs by itself or with an adverb or adverb substitute.

3. SUBJECT + INTRANSITIVE VERB

The situation improved.

The situation improved dramatically.

In contrast, a transitive verb is followed by at least one noun phrase (or sometimes just a noun or pronoun) called the **direct object**. The direct object generally receives the action of the verb.

4. SUBJECT + TRANSITIVE VERB + DIRECT OBJECT

He wrote detective stories.

In some sentences, the direct object is followed by a noun phrase or adjectival phrase that identifies or describes it. This type of phrase is called an **object complement.** Object complements help complete the meaning of such verbs as *consider, call,* and *elect.*

5. SUBJECT + TRANSITIVE VERB + DIRECT OBJECT + OBJECT COMPLEMENT

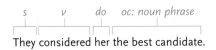

They considered her the best candidate.

The judges called my project somewhat unconventional.

In addition to a direct object, an **indirect object** may follow a transitive verb. Like a direct object, an indirect object may be a noun, a pronoun, or a noun phrase. It is most commonly used to indicate the recipient of the direct object and thus follows verbs such as *buy, give,* and *send.*

6. SUBJECT + TRANSITIVE VERB + INDIRECT OBJECT + DIRECT OBJECT

My father sent me a care package.

Identify the pattern (by number) of each of the following sentences.

1. The volcano erupted.
2. The electrician clipped the wires.
3. Your license expires tomorrow.
4. His followers considered him a guru.
5. His argument seems persuasive.
6. They are in Indonesia right now.
7. She is a member of the marketing team.
8. The judge declared him the winner.
9. The photographer showed me her recent work.
10. I found the lecture provocative.

Thinking rhetorically about sentence patterns

If you want to emphasize a contrast or intensify a feeling, use a sentence with a transitive verb and a direct object and place the direct object at the start of the sentence.

> They loved the queen. They despised the king.

> They loved the queen. The king they despised.

> I acquired English in the crib. I learned Japanese on the street.

> I acquired English in the crib. Japanese I learned on the street.

Read these sentences aloud and put a mark by the words receiving major stress. In a sentence with conventional word order (subject-verb-object), the main stress usually occurs near the end of the sentence. When you move the object to the front of the sentence, you also move the stress forward.

Move the direct object to the beginning of the second sentence of each pair to make it more emphatic. Note the differences in sentence stress.

1. Leah considers her medical studies her priority. She calls her rock band a hobby.
2. He learned to play the clarinet when he was eight. He mastered the saxophone later on.
3. They renovated the state house. They condemned the old hotel.

Passive Voice

The voice of a sentence is either active or passive. (Do not confuse these labels with aggression or submission. They simply designate the way the subject is related to the verb.) In a sentence written in the active voice, the focus is on a subject (an agent) that usually initiates an action. Conversely, in a sentence written in the passive voice, the focus is on a subject that receives or undergoes the action of the verb.

> *Active voice:* Robert Goddard launched the first liquid-fuel rocket in 1926.
>
> *Passive voice:* The first liquid-fuel rocket was launched by Robert Goddard in 1926.

Notice that the verbs in these two example sentences differ. In the passive voice, the verb phrase consists of a form of the auxiliary verb *be* and the past participle of the main verb. Depending on the tense and aspect, the auxiliary verbs *have* (or *has* or *had*), *will,* and/or a second form of *be* are also necessary parts of the verb phrase.

ASPECT AND TENSE WITH PASSIVE VOICE

	TENSE		
ASPECT	*Present*	*Past*	*Future*
Simple	*Simple present* **am, is, are asked**	*Simple past* **was, were asked**	*Simple future* **will be asked**
Progressive	*Present progressive* **am, is, are being asked**	*Past progressive* **was, were being asked**	*Future progressive* **uncommon**
Perfect	*Present perfect* **has, have been asked**	*Past perfect* **had been asked**	*Future perfect* **will have been asked**

In a sentence written in the passive voice, an agent may appear as the object of the preposition *by.* If a passive sentence does not have an agent, it is called a **short passive.**

> *Full passive:* The East Building of the National Gallery was designed by I. M. Pei.
>
> *Short passive:* The East Building of the National Gallery was completed in 1978.

EXERCISE 23.12

Identify each sentence as active or passive.

1. Alexander Graham Bell invented the telephone.
2. Radium and polonium were discovered by Marie Curie.
3. More than a thousand devices, including the phonograph, were patented by Thomas Edison.

Thinking rhetorically about the passive voice

Although the passive voice is often used in academic writing, it is not the best choice for all writing. The following tips will help you determine when to use the passive voice and when to avoid using it.

USING THE PASSIVE VOICE

▎ Use the passive voice to provide cohesion. The noun phrase at the end of one sentence and the noun phrase at the beginning of the next sentence will be closely linked.

She wrote most of her **stories** between 1936 and 1954. Her first **story** <u>was published</u> when she was just sixteen.

▎ Use the passive voice to focus on someone or something receiving or undergoing the action of the verb.

As early as 1000 BC, a writing system <u>had been devised</u> by the Phoenicians. Its twenty-two consonants <u>were written</u> horizontally, from right to left.

▎ Use a short passive when the identity of the agent is unknown, unimportant, or obvious from the larger context.

John F. Kennedy <u>was elected</u> president in 1962.

▎ Use a short passive when it is tactful to leave the agent unmentioned.

Some members of the staff <u>were excluded</u>.

▎ Use a full passive when the agent is new information that should be emphasized.

They were surrounded by people cheering and throwing confetti.

AVOIDING THE PASSIVE VOICE

▎ Avoid the passive voice if your goal is to be concise. A sentence in the passive voice will be longer than its active counterpart.

The new route <u>was discovered</u> by Lewis and Clark

Lewis and Clark <u>discovered</u> the new route.

▎ Avoid using a short passive if your readers should know who is responsible for an action.

The documents were not released until May.

The corporation did not release the documents until May.

▎ Avoid shifting to the passive voice if it would cause a distracting change in focus.

The travel agent printed the itinerary, which was then sent to the client.

The travel agent printed the itinerary and sent it to the client.

OR

The travel agent printed the itinerary; her assistant sent it to the client.

Sentence Types

Think of all the ways you use sentences every day. You probably ask questions, give directions, make suggestions, report news, give compliments, tell jokes—to mention just a few. To accomplish your purposes when writing, you'll use four common sentence types: declarative, imperative, interrogative, and exclamatory.

Declarative sentences

A **declarative sentence,** the most common type, is often used to report facts, express opinions, or share information. Declarative sentences follow the sentence patterns presented on pages 651–652.

We camped out at Crater Lake.

Imperative sentences

An **imperative sentence** differs from a declarative sentence in that its subject is rarely stated. In fact, the subject of such a sentence is often referred to as the *understood you.* You use imperative sentences when you are giving directions.

Turn left at the corner of Elm and Fairview.

Interrogative sentences

An **interrogative sentence** is a question. **Yes/no questions** are those that can be answered with *yes, no,* or a word indicating possibility such as *maybe* or *perhaps.* In contrast, **wh- questions** are used to elicit specific information. They begin with *wh-* words: *what, who, whom, where, when, why,* and *how.* Interrogative sentences are punctuated with question marks.

Yes/no question: Can we improve the design?

Wh- question: Why did the expedition succeed?

Exclamatory sentences

Any of the types of sentences just described can be written as an **exclamatory sentence** by placing an exclamation point at the end. This punctuation mark indicates emphasis, either positive or negative.

They won all three games!

Report accidents immediately!

How could they have believed such a lie!

EXERCISE 23.14

Identify the type of each sentence.

1. Who is going to the concert?
2. Go early to get good seats.
3. The concert was six hours long.
4. What an amazing night that was!

Thinking rhetorically about sentence types

One type of interrogative sentence, the rhetorical question, is not a true question because an answer is not expected. Instead, like a declarative sentence, a rhetorical question is used to state an opinion. However, a comparison between declarative sentences and rhetorical questions reveals a surprising difference. A positive question often corresponds to a negative assertion, and vice versa.

Should we allow our rights to be taken away?

We shouldn't allow our rights to be taken away.

Isn't it time to make a difference?

It's time to make a difference.

Because they are more emphatic than declarative sentences, rhetorical questions are used to focus the reader's attention on major points.

EXERCISE 23.15

Find the rhetorical question in the following excerpt. State the author's claim.

I also take a dim, or perhaps a buffaloed, view of electronic slang. Perhaps I should view it as a linguistic milestone, as historic as the evolution of Cockney rhyming slang in the 1840s. But will the future generations who reopen our hard drives be stirred by the eloquence of the e-acronyms recommended by a Web site on "netiquette"? —**Anne Fadiman,** "Mail"

Clauses

If you have not studied grammar before, you may not have realized that you have already studied clauses in this book. You have learned the essential parts of a sentence and the different types of sentences. A sentence, basically, is a clause—an **independent clause**. Sentences can include other clauses as well. Specifically, **dependent clauses** can be embedded within sentences. The following independent clause consists of a subject, transitive verb, and a direct object:

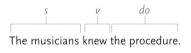

The musicians knew the procedure.

Notice how this sentence becomes more precise with the addition of embedded dependent clauses:

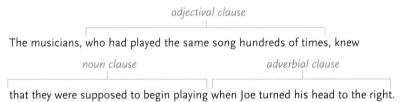

The musicians, who had played the same song hundreds of times, knew that they were supposed to begin playing when Joe turned his head to the right.

The adjectival clause provides information about the musicians, the noun clause elaborates on the procedure, and the adverbial clause adds information about time.

Relative (adjectival) clauses

A **relative clause**, also called an **adjectival clause**, modifies a pronoun, a noun, or a noun phrase. Like an adjective, then, it provides descriptive or qualifying information that helps the reader identify or recognize a referent. Compare *the architect* and *the architect who designs schools.* The latter noun phrase is more precise because it has a modifying clause.

A relative clause ordinarily begins with one of these relative pronouns: *who, whom, which,* or *that.* To provide a link to the independent clause, the relative pronoun corresponds to a word or words in the independent clause, called the **antecedent**.

The students talked to a reporter who had just returned from overseas.

Notice that the dependent clause can become an independent clause if you replace the relative pronoun with its antecedent:

A reporter had just returned from overseas.

Who* versus *whom Although a relative pronoun always begins a dependent clause, it is not always the subject.

Who as subject: They will hire someone who is trustworthy.

Whom as direct object: They will hire someone whom they can trust.

You can determine whether to use *who* or *whom* by rewriting the dependent clause as an independent clause using *someone* in place of the relative pronoun.

Someone is trustworthy.

They can trust someone.

By noting the relationship of the relative pronoun to the verb, you will be able to identify whether it is subject or direct object. (See the Glossary of Usage for more on *who* versus *whom.*)

Essential (restrictive) versus nonessential (nonrestrictive) relative clauses Knowing the difference between an essential clause and a nonessential clause will help you decide how to punctuate sentences containing such clauses. A clause that a reader needs in order to correctly identify the referent is an **essential clause.**

The person who presented the award was last year's winner.

A **nonessential clause** is *not* needed for correct identification of the referent and thus is set off by commas. A nonessential clause often follows a proper noun (a specific name).

Andrea Bowen, who presented the award, was last year's winner.

That versus which According to the traditional rule, *that* is used in essential relative clauses, and *which* is used in nonessential relative clauses.

I need a job that pays well.

I took a job, which pays well enough.

However, some professional writers do not follow both parts of this rule. Although they will not use *that* in nonessential relative clauses, they will use *which* in essential relative clauses.

According to Trask, *pragmatics* is "the branch of linguistics which studies how utterances communicate meaning in context."

EXERCISE 23.16

Punctuate the following sentences as needed. Be prepared to state whether a sentence has an essential or a nonessential relative clause.

1. Hippocrates who is credited with writing many books on the medical aspects of animal science lived in the fourth and fifth centuries BC.
2. Zoology which is the study of animals has its origin in the works of Aristotle.
3. There are four areas of study that form the cornerstones of biology: taxonomy, anatomy, physiology, and genetics.
4. What is the name of the scientist whose contributions shaped the cornerstones of biology?
5. Binomial nomenclature which was introduced by Linnaeus assigns a two-word Latin name to each species.

EXERCISE 23.17

Complete each sentence with *who* or *whom*.

1. Charles Darwin, _____ was born on February 12, 1809, was the son of a physician.
2. A professor _____ was also a good friend recommended him for a position on a scientific expedition.
3. Emma Wedgewood, _____ Darwin married in 1839, was the scientist's cousin.

Thinking rhetorically about relative clauses

If some of your sentences sound monotonous or choppy, try to combine them by using a relative clause.

Dub is a car magazine. It appeals to drivers with a hip-hop attitude.

Dub is a car magazine that appeals to drivers with a hip-hop attitude.

A Hovercraft can go where many vehicles cannot. It is practically amphibious.

A Hovercraft, which can go where many vehicles cannot, is practically amphibious.

EXERCISE 23.18

Combine the following pairs of sentences, using relative clauses.

1. Charles Darwin showed no early academic promise.
   He was interested in natural history as a boy.
2. Evolution was also studied by earlier thinkers.
   Evolution was first called "descent with modification" by Darwin.
3. Earthworms are not guided by instinct alone.
   Darwin studied earthworms for forty years.

Adverbial clauses

An **adverbial clause** provides information about time, manner, place, condition, concession, or reason. The type of information contained in such a clause is signaled by the word that begins it—a subordinating conjunction (see page 637).

Time:	You must pay a fee <u>when you register</u>.
Manner:	It looked <u>as though it were written a long time ago</u>.
Place:	<u>Wherever you find balsam root</u>, you will find lupine.
Condition:	I will be surprised <u>if my proposal is accepted</u>.
Concession:	<u>Although they were far away</u>, I could still hear their voices.
Reason:	My friends, <u>because they arrived late</u>, were asked to sit in the back row.

Another function of the adverbial clause is to add meaning to an adjective or an adjectival phrase.

After an adjective: She was pleased <u>that so many people attended the seminar</u>.

An adverbial clause may also be used in a comparison.

Comparison: The schools in this district received more funding <u>than the schools in the adjacent district did</u>.

Adverbial clauses appear at various places in sentences—at the beginning, middle, or end. Notice that when an adverbial clause begins or interrupts a sentence, it is separated from the rest of the sentence by a comma or commas. An adverbial clause that appears at the end of a sentence is not set off by a comma unless it is nonessential.

She must have been in her office, because the lights were on.

EXERCISE 23.19

Identify the adverbial clause in each sentence.

1. I went for a walk because the weather was nice.
2. I was glad that the weather was nice.
3. The weather was nicer than it usually is.
4. The wind blew less gustily than it usually does.
5. I walked until I could walk no further.
6. I had walked further than I had intended to.

Thinking rhetorically about adverbial clauses

To make your writing concise, you can condense adverbial clauses beginning with *while, when,* or *though.* You can often omit the subject and auxiliary verb *be* as long as the subject of the dependent clause is the same as the subject of the independent clause.

While we were rafting, we saw a rare owl.

While rafting, we saw a rare owl.

If the subjects of the dependent and independent clauses are not the same, the independent clause may have to be revised to ensure clarity and coherence.

I thought of
While reading the statistics, ∧ a few questions occurred to me.

EXERCISE 23.20

Write three sentences with condensed adverbial clauses. Use a different subordinating conjunction (*while, when,* or *though*) in each sentence.

Noun clauses

As its name suggests, a **noun clause** is similar to a noun or a noun phrase. Although a noun clause differs from a noun or a noun phrase because it contains a verb, it too can be a subject, a direct object, or a subject complement. To test whether a clause is a noun clause, try replacing it with a pronoun. If such a substitution is possible, then the clause is a noun clause.

It [subject]
⌐‾‾‾‾‾⌐
Whether we win or lose is not important.

this [direct object]
⌐‾‾‾‾‾⌐
The pollsters asked many students whether they would vote this year.

this [subject complement]
⌐‾‾‾‾‾⌐
The question is whether we have sufficient funding.

Noun clauses usually begin with *if, that,* or a *wh-* word such as *what* or *why*. You can omit *that* from the beginning of a noun clause as long as the sentence retains it meaning.

The author said <u>he traveled to India to do research for his book</u>.

Be sure to retain the introductory *that* when you have more than one noun clause in a sentence.

The author said <u>that</u> he traveled to India to do research for his book but <u>that</u> the story was not autobiographical.

EXERCISE 23.21

Identify the noun clauses in these sentences.

1. Some researchers believe that tests can verify the existence of intelligence.
2. Some parents ask if the tests are reliable.
3. Researchers must explain how the scores are calculated.

Thinking rhetorically about noun clauses

You may sometimes use an adjective to express your attitude toward a piece of information expressed in a noun clause.

That she will run for office again is doubtful.

When the noun clause is extremely long or when you want to emphasize it, you can start your sentence with the expletive *it* and place the noun clause after the adjective.

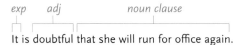

It is doubtful that she will run for office again.

If you read these two example sentences aloud, you'll be able to hear the difference in stress. The following adjectives frequently occur with the expletive *it* and a noun clause: *possible, clear, amazing, funny, nice, odd, sad, understandable, crucial, essential, important, necessary.*

EXERCISE 23.22

Rewrite each sentence, using the expletive *it*, an adjective, and a noun clause.

1. The defendant was not guilty.
2. Many citizens volunteered to help the flood victims.
3. The nighttime temperatures have dropped dramatically.

Sentence Classification

Sentences are often classified according to the number and type of clauses they contain.

Simple sentences

A **simple sentence** has one independent clause.

They solved the problem easily.

Even when a prepositional phrase or a verbal phrase is added, the sentence is still considered simple.

Having studied hard the night before, they solved the problem easily.

Compound sentences

A **compound sentence** consists of at least two independent clauses, joined by a coordinating conjunction or a semicolon.

Books were expensive, but magazines were affordable.

Books were expensive; magazines were affordable.

Complex sentences

A **complex sentence** includes at least one independent clause and at least one dependent clause. Noun clauses, adjectival clauses, and adverbial clauses are dependent clauses.

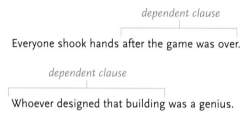

dependent clause

Everyone shook hands after the game was over.

dependent clause

Whoever designed that building was a genius.

Compound-complex sentences

A **compound-complex sentence** has the features of a compound sentence (at least two independent clauses) and a complex sentence (at least one dependent clause).

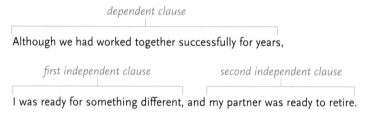

dependent clause

Although we had worked together successfully for years,

first independent clause   second independent clause

I was ready for something different, and my partner was ready to retire.

EXERCISE 23.23

Identify each sentence as simple, compound, complex, or compound-complex.

1. Designed by Frank Gehry, the Walt Disney Concert Hall is unusual yet appealing.
2. The Disney Concert Hall is the home of the Los Angeles Philharmonic.
3. Not only is the concert hall an awe-inspiring piece of architecture, it is also the perfect place to hear music.
4. Because the hall's acoustical design is excellent, many musicians hope to play there.
5. Although audiences for concert music are not as large as they used to be, the novelty of this concert hall may bring old concert-goers back, and it may lure new concert-goers in.

Thinking rhetorically about sentence structure

If you find that one of your paragraphs consists of simple sentences only, try combining some of your ideas into compound, complex, or compound-complex sentences. Here is an example of a paragraph that could use some help:

> I rode the school bus every day. I didn't like to, though. The bus smelled bad. And it was always packed. The worst part was the bumpy ride. Riding the bus was like riding in a worn-out sneaker.

Once you try combining some of your ideas, you might find that you need to add information as well.

> As a kid, I rode the school bus every day, but I didn't like to. I hated the smell, the crowd, and the ride itself. Every seat was filled with a kid, and many of the kids took their shoes off for the long ride home down a road so bumpy you couldn't even read a comic book. Riding that bus was like riding inside a worn-out sneaker.

EXERCISE 23.24

Vary the sentence structure in the following paragraph. Add details as needed.

> We arrived at the afternoon jazz concert late. We couldn't find any seats. It was hot, so we stood in the shade. We finally found seats under an umbrella. The shade didn't help, though. We could feel our brains melting. The music was cool, but we sure weren't.

24 EDITING FOR CLARITY AND STYLE

Often, just getting your thoughts down in writing provides you the distance necessary for considering possible changes in individual words and complete sentences that could clarify your meaning. For most rhetorical situations, a clear style means that the writing possesses these characteristics (described in more detail on pages 622–624):

- Precise
- Conventional
- Complete and consistent
- Concise
- Coherent
- Varied
- Parallel

As you already know, the *common* features listed here may not apply to *uncommon* rhetorical situations. For instance, poets, short story writers, and novelists often use language in unusual ways to create an atmosphere that is out of the ordinary—that may make readers slow down, weigh each word, and see connections between words they might not otherwise notice. But even when writers are playing *with* the rules, instead of *by* the rules, they benefit by knowing the difference between what is commonly expected and what may not be.

The revision process requires you to move back and forth between large-scale revision (often called **global revision**) and small-scale revision (often called **sentence-level revision**)—between making sure that you have provided enough information for your readers to understand your message and ensuring that the information is presented in a way that is easy for them to read. Many students believe that all they need to do is check for spelling and punctuation before submitting their first draft to their instructor. However, if you read your own writing carefully, especially if you let your writing "cool off" for a while, you will probably discover that you need to rethink some of your original ideas, connections, and examples. One revision can quickly lead to another. Your rewrite of a sentence, for example, might reveal the need to add more information or to rethink some of your ideas entirely. Novelist Robert Boswell describes such a possibility:

> If the first sentence of a story is the classic cliché "It was a dark and stormy night," then the writer will likely begin revising by trying to rescue the idea from the expression. Perhaps, he will first try to eradicate "was," as it is the most generic of verbs. "Dark, the stormy night blew." If he has the good sense to recognize the comedy of this sentence, he will revise again. "The air was filled with lightning." Again he sees

"was" and wishes to get rid of it. Finally, he writes, "Lightning struck the fence-post." This sentence is not only much better than the original, he now has a charred fencepost in the story, and that image may well become important to the reader's understanding of the events. It may even alter the events in future drafts of the story.   —**Robert Boswell**, *The Place of Grammar in Writing Instruction*

Boswell's hypothetical writer starts the revision process by trying to eliminate the verb *was*. This change eventually leads him to a completely different opening line. In the following pages, you will learn form-based revision, but do not be surprised if your revisions of form lead to revisions of meaning—to your own "charred fencepost."

Precision

Accurate words

Accurate words convey precise meanings. Although you may use words such as *thing* and *nice* in a rough draft, you'll want to choose words with denotations and connotations that help you accurately portray your ideas. **Denotations** refer to dictionary definitions; **connotations** refer to associated meanings. A good dictionary includes entries that help you understand how one word is related to words with similar meanings, explaining connotations as well as denotations. For example, the following entry from *Heinle's Newbury House Dictionary* could help you choose the best word for describing an event that was extremely loud. Listed first are the definitions, followed by some synonyms.

> **loud** /laud/ *adj.* **-er, -est 1** having an intense sound, noisy: *The sound of city traffic is loud.* **2** unpleasantly bright in color: *He wears bright reds and other loud colors.* *n.* **loudness.**
>
> **loud 1** deafening, earsplitting | shrill, strident *frml.* **2** flashy, garish, gaudy.

Also be sure to consider your choice of verb when revising for accuracy: writers too often depend on a form of the verb *to be* (*am, is, are, was, were*). As Boswell points out in the excerpt above, *was* is "the most generic of verbs." (See page 672 for help with revising *to be* verbs.)

Fresh expressions

As you explain a concept, you may want to use an image to make your point. Fresh images can help your readers "see" what you mean, what you're talking about. For instance, Susan Gubar wanted to explain how her mind was working as she listened to various arguments:

> While others, judging by their ardent notetaking, found enlightenment, or, at least, points for debate, I precariously moved along a spider web of speculation.
> —**Susan Gubar**, *Rooms of Our Own*

Spider web of speculation is a fresh phrase that expresses the jumbled mental state the author experienced.

You'll often find that what were once fresh expressions or examples of vivid language have become so common that they've lost their impact: *white as snow, sick as a dog,* and *strong as an ox* are just a few examples of the cobwebbed expressions called **clichés.** If you find yourself resorting to clichés in your writing, or if a peer reviewer identifies a phrase as a cliché, you will want to revise your prose in one of the following ways: you can use language that does not call forth an image or make a comparison, try to invent a new expression, or tweak the original expression to make it fresh.

Cliché: *at the drop of a hat*

Literal synonym: *immediately*

New expression: *at the click of the Send button*

Original expression with a slight change:

> We know by now that whenever politics and art collide, art loses—at least, in these United States, where anything cultural can become politicized *at the drop of a grievance.* —**Peter Schjeldahl,** "Those Nasty Brits"

Clear metaphors

When you use language that evokes images, make sure that the images are clearly related. **Mixed metaphors** include parts of two or more unrelated metaphors. The following sentence has the image of a spiral and the image of drowning, but is it possible to drown in a downward spiral?

Despite this downward spiral that we seem to be ~~drowning in~~ *sliding down*, there is hope.

Changing one of the images makes them better related.

Clear definitions

When you use a specialized term, one specific to your topic, ask yourself whether your audience will know its definition. When writing her essay on technology and learning that appears in chapter 3, Stacy Simkanin had to ask herself if her audience needed a definition of terms such as *interlibrary loan.* Since her audience (her instructor) was in the field of college education, Stacy knew that *interlibrary loan* wouldn't need a definition, but that she should provide a description of her school's ANGEL site so that her instructor would understand which features of this online class management system students actually use.

If there is any chance that readers could confuse a term's intended meaning with another of its meanings (for example, the word *reservoir* has both a general and a technical meaning) or that readers may be unfamiliar with the term, provide a definition to help them choose the meaning you have in mind.

A definition can be a formal definition, a dictionary definition, a synonym, a stipulative definition, or a negative definition (see chapter 12 for an explanation of stipulative and negative definitions). A **formal definition** places the term in a class and then differentiates it from other members of the class.

> A *reservoir* [term] is an artificial body of water [class] that is retained by a dam [differentiation].

A definition from a general or specialized dictionary may also be used.

> *Reservoir* can refer to an "underground accumulation of petroleum or natural gas" ("Reservoir," def. 3).

If you choose to quote from a dictionary, be sure to cite the number of the definition you used and include an entry for it in your bibliography (see page 575). Another way to define a word is to use a synonymous word or phrase set off by commas or dashes (see pages 705 and 708).

> They searched for a reservoir, a rock formation that retains natural gas underground, in an uninhabited area.

When you use a definition, especially a formal definition, be sure that your subject and predicate (see page 650) fit together grammatically. The term being defined should be followed by a noun or a noun phrase, not an adverbial clause. In particular, avoid using any construction that includes *is when* or *is where*.

> *the designing of systems*
> *Resource development* is ~~when systems are~~ designed for using natural resources.
> ^

> *the contest between*   *vying*
> *Exploitative competition* is ~~where~~ two or more organisms ~~vie~~ for a limited resource such as food.
>   ^   ^

Clear pronoun use

When you use pronouns, you may know whom or what the pronoun refers to, but if your reference is not clear to your readers, they will be confused. As you revise your writing, be on the lookout for any pronoun that does not have a clear **antecedent** (the word, phrase, or clause that makes the pronoun's referent clear).

> Many wildfires ignite when someone leaves a fire unattended or fails to ensure that it is extinguished. <u>This</u> has led to a stricter burn ban.

The antecedent for *this* is unclear. Is the cause for the new burn ban the unattended fire, the unextinguished fire, or something related to both? One way to clear up the murkiness of such a sentence is to add a noun.

> <u>This carelessness</u> has led to stricter burn bans.

The pronouns *this, that, it,* and *which* often lack clear antecedents. Take a second look when you come across one of these pronouns in your writing to be sure the antecedent is clear.

> *These changes*
> The team has a new coach and a new stadium. ~~That~~ will certainly improve team morale.
>   ^

> The researcher used innovative procedures to produce provocative
> *. These innovations*
> results, which will be reported in the next edition of *Science Journal*.
> ^

When you use pronouns such as *we, you,* and *they* to refer to people, be sure that the referents are clear and consistent. In written texts, *we* and *us* always refer to the writer or writers; however, other people may also be included: readers of the text, associates, or the general public.

> We [co-authors] advocate the development of writing-intensive courses.

> Let us [writer and readers] look at another example.

> As a profession, we [writer and others in the profession] need to address some difficult issues.

> Let us endeavor so to live that when we [general public] come to die even the undertaker will be sorry.

> —**Mark Twain,** *The Tragedy of Pudd'nhead Wilson and the Comedy of Those Extraordinary Twins*

Most writers avoid using the word *we* for self-reference because readers will want to know just who the word *we* includes. Rather than using what has long been called the "royal" *we* (used by royalty to include God), writers should refer to themselves as *I.* Despite the acceptability of using *I* in writing, though, many teachers and professions continue to frown on the usage.

If you decide to address readers directly, you'll undoubtedly use the pronoun *you* (as in this sentence). In this case, you'll want to be sure to clarify whether *you* refers to just one person or to people in general. Be sure to check with your teacher as to whether using *you* is acceptable. If you are told to avoid using the indefinite *you,* recast your sentences. For example, use *one* instead of *you.*

> Even in huge, anonymous cities, you find community spirit.

> Even in huge, anonymous cities, one finds community spirit.

However, owing to the formality of *one,* it might not always be the best choice. Changing the word order is another possibility.

> Community spirit can even be found in huge, anonymous cities.

If you are unsatisfied with either of these strategies, use different words.

> Community spirit arises even in huge, anonymous cities.

The pronoun *they* is used to refer to an outside group. When you revise, make sure that the outside group is specific.

> *the reporter from Cairo*
> On the news, they said the situation had improved.

If you are unsure of who comprises the outside group, try using a short passive sentence (see page 654).

> They revised the original forecast.

> The original forecast was revised.

Revise the following paragraph for precision. Be sure words are accurate, expressions are fresh, imagery is consistent, definitions are aptly worded, and pronouns have clear antecedents.

¹Roller-skating is when you use shoes fitted with small wheels for movement that is smooth as silk on rinks and paved surfaces. ²Although they introduced roller skates in the eighteenth century, the design that made them all the rage was created in 1863. ³The four-wheel skate originally had wooden and later metal wheels. ⁴In the twentieth century, these wheels were replaced by polyurethane plastic wheels that could grab various surfaces better. ⁵Another innovation that greatly affected the sport was the development of in-line skates, where there is a single row of wheels in place of the standard four-wheel configuration. ⁶In-line skating rolled to a quick take-off in popularity. ⁷In-line skaters now speed down most parkways, sidewalks, and even some store aisles.

Conciseness

Making every word count

After writing your first draft, review it to make sure that your sentences are not empty or repetitive. If you draft quickly or are worried about making the length requirement for your assignment, you may be writing rambling sentences that obscure your message rather than clarify it.

As you revise, check to be sure that you are not using three or four words when one or two will suffice. Sometimes you can just delete extra words; other times you may be able to think of a more concise alternative. (See also pages 642 and 661.)

WORDS THAT CAN BE DELETED

square ~~in shape~~
large ~~in size~~
orange ~~in color~~
at 8:00 p.m. ~~in the evening~~
~~basic~~ fundamentals
sweet~~-tasting~~ dessert
medium~~-size~~ onions
poor ~~and impoverished~~ country
~~really and truly~~ funny
return ~~back~~
connect ~~up~~
secondly, he ~~also~~

Grammar and Style

at this moment (*or* point) in time	now, today
due to the fact that	because
in view of the fact that	because
for the purpose of	for
it is clear (*or* obvious) that	clearly (obviously)
there is no question that	unquestionably, certainly
without a doubt	undoubtedly
beyond the shadow of a doubt	certainly, surely
it is my opinion that	I think (believe)
in this day and age	today
in the final analysis	finally

With some adjustment, the frequently overused constructions *there are* and *it is* (called *expletives*) can be deleted.

Nobody
There was nobody home.
ˆ

The   was dark
It was dark in the house.
            ˆ   ˆ

Eliminating wordiness from clauses

Nonessential (nonrestrictive) adjectival clauses can often be made less wordy. Sometimes just the relative pronoun (*who, which,* or *that*) can be dropped. Other times both the relative pronoun and a form of *be* (*am, is, are, was, were*) can be deleted.

The research that he did on endangered species was published last year.

The Endangered Species Act, which was passed in 1973, protects the habitat of endangered plants and animals.

When deleting a relative pronoun and a verb, you may have to make other changes to your sentence as well.

infected us with laughter.
His boisterous guffaw, which was infectious, made us all laugh.
                    ˆ

Using elliptical constructions

The term *ellipsis* comes from the Greek word meaning "to leave out." You might recognize ellipsis points (. . .), which tell you that words have been omitted (see page 709). Similarly, **elliptical constructions** leave out words readily understood from the context. By occasionally using elliptical constructions, you make your writing concise. In this sentence, the repetition of *was* is unnecessary:

In their successful collaboration, Louise was the courageous innovator, Jerome the methodical critic, and Scott the relentless editor.

Commas may be used also to indicate omissions.

In 2005, the winner was Jacqui; in 2006, Ben; and in 2007, Alison.

EXERCISE 24.2

Revise the following paragraph so that it is more concise.

[1]Louis Leakey was born in the country of Kenya in 1903 but earned a doctorate in the country of England. [2]When people hear his name in this day and age, they think of the search for the beginnings and origins of humankind. [3]But in the 1920s he caused surprise, disapproval, and dismay when he insisted that humans evolved on the continent of Africa, which was a contradiction of the common belief at the time that they originated in Asia or Europe. [4]He proved his hypothesis by returning back to Africa and finding in 1960 *Homo habilis,* which was considered the earliest known human ancestor at that time. [5]Louis was not the only Leakey curious about and interested in archaeology. [6]Other Leakeys interested in digging have made important and significant discoveries. [7]His wife, Mary, found fossil footprints that were 3.5 million years old. [8]His son, Richard, found the most complete early-human skeleton. [9]His daughter-in-law, Meave, found important new fossils. [10]His granddaughter Louise currently runs expeditions in Kenya.

Conventions

Usage

Usage refers to the types of words appropriate for a particular rhetorical situation, especially the types of words your audience expects within a specific context. Sometimes it's perfectly acceptable and expected to use slang, regionalisms, or conversational (or colloquial) words. A truck driver who hears "What's your twenty?" on the CB radio knows the other driver is asking for a location. In Philadelphia, many cheesesteak aficionados order a "wiz without" if they have a hankering for a cheesesteak with Cheez Wiz and without onions. Among friends, you might gripe that you have "tons" of research to do. Other times your rhetorical situation calls for technical language and Standardized English. However, be aware that the concept of *standard* is often accompanied by the assumption that grammatical structures or words not considered standard are incorrect and therefore inferior, even though they may be used frequently by a specific group of people. For example, if you are from the northeastern part of the United States, you might know the word *youse* as a conversational term meaning "all of you," but that usage is not favored in all parts of the country.

Instead of judging words as "correct" or "incorrect," you'll find it more productive to think of them as conventional or unconventional in relation to a specific language community. Many of the words listed in the Glossary of Usage are those that cause difficulties in rhetorical situations calling for conventional language used in academic writing.

Idioms

Idioms are fixed expressions whose meaning cannot be entirely determined by knowing the meanings of their parts—examples are *bear in mind, cut to the chase, in a nutshell,* and *a pushover.* Idioms can be particularly difficult to make sense of when English is not your native language—or when you're an outsider to any language community, since every one of these has its own idiomatic expressions. Even small variations of familiar idioms can be distracting or confusing to your audience.

> *low*
> She tried to keep a small profile.

> *a vested*
> They had an invested interest in the project.

As you edit your writing, keep an eye out for idioms you think might not be worded correctly. Then check a general dictionary or a dictionary of idioms to make sure that your usage is appropriate.

Spelling

When drafting, you may be writing so fast or concentrating so deeply that you do not pay attention to spelling. Proofreading for spelling mistakes is essential—though only after you have a solid draft. As a starting point, use a spell checker to catch your errors. However, keep in mind that the spell checker will not detect misspellings of specialized vocabulary and foreign words, keyboarding errors (*as* for *is*), or misuses of words that sound alike (*here* for *hear*). The spell checker also cannot detect words that are spelled correctly but used incorrectly.

> *by*
> We must abide with his decision.

A spell checker will also overlook a single word that should be spelled as two words or two words that should be spelled as a single word.

> *may be*
> The researchers maybe able to answer that question.

> *Someday maybe*
> Some day may be these conditions will no longer pose a problem.

TRICKS OF THE TRADE

The following strategies can help you check your spelling effectively.

- Create a special file for words you frequently misspell. Then use the Find command to locate possible misspellings in your draft.
- Add new technical or foreign words to your spell checker's dictionary by clicking on the Add button. The spell checker will then be able to check for these words.
- Reject the offer from the spell checker to correct all instances of a particular error. You are better off examining each instance yourself.
- Check suggested alternative spellings in a dictionary if you doubt their accuracy.
- After using the spell checker, be sure to proofread your draft yourself.

In addition to spell checking, learning a few basic spelling rules will help you find mistakes during the proofreading process. Spelling errors often occur when suffixes, but not prefixes, are added to base words. When a prefix is added to a base word (or root), no letters are added or dropped.

di**s**satisfy   mi**s**spell   u**n**necessary   i**m**material

When you add a suffix, however, the spelling is often affected.

mercy, merci**ful**   subscribe, subscrip**tion**   BUT electric, electrici**ty**

The spellings of words with suffixes are not totally irregular, though. Note the following patterns.

BASE WORD ENDING IN THE LETTER *E*

▌ When adding a suffix that begins with a vowel to a word that ends in *e*, drop the *e*.

behave, behav**ing**   love, lov**able**   combine, combin**ation**

A few exceptions to this rule have to be memorized: *dyeing* (changing a color), *canoeing*, and *snowshoeing*.

▌ The letters *c* and *g* each have two different sounds. To signal the *s* sound of *ce* or the *j* sound of *ge*, keep the final *e* before -*able* or -*ous*:

outrage**ous**   change**able**   notice**able**

▌ If the suffix begins with a consonant sound, the final *e* is retained.

polite, polite**ness**   sincere, sincere**ly**   hope, hope**ful**

This rule also has some exceptions: *argument, judgment, awful, ninth, truly,* and *wholly.*

DOUBLING CONSONANTS BEFORE SUFFIXES BEGINNING WITH VOWELS (-*ED*, -*ING*, -*ANCE*, -*ENCE*)

▌ If a consonant is preceded by a vowel in either a one-syllable word or a two-syllable word with a stressed second syllable, double the final consonant.

   vc   *vcc*   *vcc*   *vc*   *vcc*   *vcc*
stop, sto**pped**, stop**ping**   omit, omi**tted**, omi**tting**

▌ If there are two vowels before the consonant, the consonant is not doubled.

   vvc   *vvc*   *vvc*   *vvc*   *vvc*   *vvc*
group, group**ed**, group**ing**   review, review**ed**, review**ing**

▌ If the second syllable is not stressed, the consonant is not doubled.

edit, edit**ed**, edit**ing**   cover, cover**ed**, cover**ing**

CHANGING *Y* TO *I* BEFORE SUFFIXES

▌ Change the *y* following a consonant to *i* before adding a suffix (except -*ing*).

   c   *c*   *c*   *c*   *c*   *c*   *c*   *c*
rely, rel**ies**, rel**ied**, rel**iance**   certify, certif**ies**, certif**ied**, certif**ication**
BUT rel**ying**   BUT certif**ying**

> If *y* is preceded by a vowel, retain the *y*.

stay, stay**s**, stay**ed**   convey, convey**s**, convey**ed**, convey**ance**

> Some verb forms are irregular and thus can cause difficulties: *says, said; pays, paid.* For a list of irregular verbs, see pages 644–645.

ADDING -LY

> When adding *-ly* to a word ending in *l*, retain both *l*'s.

normal, normal**ly**   real, real**ly**   usual, usual**ly**

PLURALS

> For most nouns ending in *s, z, ch, sh,* or *x*, add *-es*.

pass, pass**es**   beach, beach**es**

> For nouns ending in a consonant and *y*, add *-es* after changing the *y* to *i*.

army, arm**ies**   company, compan**ies**   twenty, twent**ies**

> For some nouns ending in a consonant and *o*, add *-es*.

hero, hero**es**   potato, potato**es**

For others, *-s* will suffice.

video, video**s**   memo, memo**s**

Sometimes either an *-s* or *-es* suffix is correct.

tornado**s**, tornado**es**   volcano**s**, volcano**es**

> For nouns ending in *f* or *fe*, change the ending to *ve* before adding *-s* if the sound of the plural changes from *f* to *v*.

sel**f**, sel**ves**   li**fe**, li**ves**   BUT belief, belie**fs**

> Certain nouns have irregular plural forms.

woman, wo**men**   child, child**ren**   foot, f**ee**t   tooth, t**ee**th

> For the plural of most proper nouns, add *-s:* the Lee**s**; the Kennedy**s**. Add *-es* when the plural ending is pronounced as a separate syllable: the Rodriguez**es**, the Jones**es**.
> Some words borrowed from Greek or Latin form their plurals as in the original language: *alumnus, alumni; alumna, alumnae; analysis, analyses.* (For *criteria, data,* and *media,* see the Glossary of Usage.)

One other rule that may improve your proofreading is often taught as a rhyme. This rule can help you remember which words include *ie* and which include *ei*.

Put i before *e*
Except after *c*

Or when sounded like *a*
As in *neighbor* and *weigh*.

Words with *i* before *e:* bel**ie**ve, br**ie**f, f**ie**ld
Words with *e* before *i*, after *c*, **ce**iling, per**cei**ve, re**cei**pt
Words with *ei* sounding like *a* in *cake:* fr**ei**ght, th**ei**r, h**ei**r

Exceptions to this rule include *caffeine, either, neither, friend, species, foreign, leisure,* and *weird.*

Inclusive language

When you respond to a rhetorical situation, you are asking an audience to read or listen to what you have to say. Using respectful, inclusive language is essential to this endeavor. Otherwise, your readers or listeners may not bother to consider your ideas. It is important not to assume that all of your readers are part of the majority in terms of religion, race, ethnicity, sexual preference, or physical ability. A letter to the editor of your local newspaper that proposes a busy city park be off limits to all cars may be disrespectful if it does not take into account park users who must use handicapped parking to access the park.

Language used to identify groups of people in terms of their religion, race, education, politics, or other characteristic presents a distinctive challenge. In fact, try to avoid categorizing a person or persons unless such a reference is absolutely necessary for your discussion. Most people feel that their individuality transcends their membership in any one specific group. If you must mention others as belonging to a group, the best way to show them respect is to use the name they themselves have chosen (whether that's *American Indians, Native Americans, Indigenous People, First Americans,* or *Indians; Latino/Latina* or *Chicano/Chicana;* or some other name). Although there are countless groups, only a few frequently found in print are discussed in the following sections.

Referring to gender Sentences that needlessly single out a person as being male or female can be revised fairly easily.

▌ Make a pronoun or determiner and its antecedent plural.

   Reporters   *they describe*
  A reporter should be sure that he describes events accurately.

Some authors choose to use *they* or *she* as an alternative to the generic *he.* However, sentences such as *A reporter should be sure that they describe events accurately* and *A reporter should be sure that she describes events accurately* are not considered standard.

▌ Rephrase to avoid using a pronoun.

  A reporter should be sure to describe events accurately.

▌ Use a noun phrase instead of a pronoun.

                          that person
  If someone questions the procedures, he should consult the supervisor.

▌ Use both *he* and *she*.

or she
If an individual questions the procedures, he should consult the supervisor.

This option should be avoided when possible because of its awkwardness.

▌ Use an article instead of a possessive determiner

a
Every employee has his own locker.

▌ Drop the possessive determiner.

A student should submit his papers on time.

▌ Choose gender-neutral terms.

working people
Labor unions benefit the working man.

Other gender-neutral terms include the following:

anchorman, anchorwoman	anchor, news anchor
businessman	business executive, businessperson
chairman, chairwoman	chair, chairperson
clergyman	member of the clergy
congressman	member of Congress, representative, senator
man, mankind	human, human beings, humanity, humankind
repairman	technician, repair technician
salesman	salesperson, sales representative, sales clerk
workman	worker

Referring to race and ethnicity Determining which terms a particular group prefers can be difficult because preferences sometimes vary within a group and change over time. One conventional way to refer to Americans of a specific descent is to include an adjective before the term *American: African American, Asian American, European American, Latin American, Mexican American, Native American.* These words are widely used, especially by people who are not members of a given group. However, members of a particular group may identify themselves in more than one way. In addition to *African American* and *European American, black* and *white* have long been used. People of Spanish-speaking descent may prefer *Chicano/Chicana, Hispanic, Latino/Latina, Puerto Rican, Mexican,* or another term. Descendants of peoples who were indigenous to North America before European settlers arrived may prefer a specific name such as *Diné* or *Haida,* though some also accept *American Indian.* An up-to-date dictionary that includes notes on usage can help you choose appropriate terms.

Referring to age Although some people object to the term *senior citizen,* a better alternative has not yet been suggested. When used respectfully, the term refers to a person who has reached the age of retirement (but may not have decided to retire) and is eligible for certain privileges granted by society. However, if you know your audience would object to this word, find out what term is preferred.

Referring to disability or illness A current recommendation for referring to disabilities and illnesses is "to put the person first"; in this way, it is believed, the focus will be on the individual rather than on the limitation. Thus, *persons with disabilities* is preferred over *disabled persons.* When you are writing, you can find out whether such person-first expressions are preferred by noting whether they are used in the articles and books (or by the people) you consult. Be aware, though, that some writers and readers find this type of expression unnatural sounding, and others think that it does not serve its purpose because the last word in a phrase can carry the greater weight, especially at the end of a sentence.

Referring to sexual orientation Terms for sexual orientation such as *gay*, *lesbian*, and *bisexual* are used most often as adjectives rather than as nouns. In fact, using a noun to refer to specific people may be considered offensive. Noting professions or participation is thought to be more respectful: two gay lawyers, three lesbian participants. But again, note sexual orientation only when it is relevant to the discourse.

Referring to geographical areas Certain geographical terms need to be used with special care. Though most frequently used to refer to people from the United States, the term *American* may also refer to people from Canada, Mexico, and Central or South America. If your audience may be offended by this term, use *people from the United States* or *U.S. citizens* instead.

The term *Arab* refers to people of Arabic-speaking descent. Use this term only when you cannot use more specific terms, such as *Iraqi* or *Saudi Arabian,* and only when you are sure that a country's people speak Arabic and not another language. Iranians, for example, are not Arabs because they speak Farsi.

It is often helpful to distinguish between the terms *British* and *English. British* is the preferred term for referring to people from the island of Great Britain or from the United Kingdom. *English* refers to people from England (a part of the United Kingdom).

Negation

You may be unaware of the number of ways negation is used. Negative words can be formed by the addition of prefixes: *patient, impatient; logical, illogical.* Phrases, too, can be negated: *time, no time; to be, not to be.* Sentences are most frequently negated by the word *not: We do not have sufficient funding.* In some dialects of English, multiple negation signals emphasis: *They don't understand nothing.* However, when the rhetorical situation calls for the use of Standardized English, refrain from using this type of negation. Although a word with a negative prefix or a negated infinitive phrase may be used in a negative sentence (*He is not impatient* or *It would not be right not to intervene*), other types of multiple negation should be revised.

any
I don't have ∧no time.   OR   I don't have no time.

The words *barely, hardly,* and *scarcely* carry with them the sense of negative conditions, so they should not be used with *not* or *nothing.*

He couldn't hardly see.   OR   He couldn't hardly see.

anything
She could hear hardly ∧nothing.

EXERCISE 24.3

Revise the following sentences so that they follow the conventions of Standardized English.

[1]According to Cheryl Dolven, a registered deitician, a kid in the United States will consume 1,500 peanut butter sandwiches before he leaves high school in the dust. [2]Although some parents think that peanut butter is unhealthy for their children because it contains alot of fat, Dolven explains that this popular sandwich spread consists in protien, folate, niacin, and other important vitamins and minerals. [3]She does not say that peanut butter does not have no fat; she admits that there is fat but it is good fat (the unsaturated stuff). [4]Dolven recommends picking up natural peanut butter because other types of peanut butter contain sugar and partialy hydrogenated fats.

Completeness and Consistency

Talking versus writing

Conversation differs from academic writing in the number of shortcuts we use. We might say to someone, "You ready? Time to go." This snippet of conversation becomes "Are you ready?" and "It's time to go" when the two utterances are written as full sentences. Because you might be using your conversational voice when you write your first draft, be sure to revise so that all words are included, especially the small ones that are easily overlooked.

a
Missing article: Starting ∧new job does not have to be stressful.

of
Missing preposition: He mentioned a couple ∧reasons for the success.

it
Missing pronoun: The clear directions made ∧easy for us to understand the process.

has
Missing verb: She ∧spoken to the director about a raise.

It is also a good idea to look at parts of the sentence where *and* is used.

in
Missing preposition: He was interested ∧and thus focused on cellular biology.

ignored

Missing verb: We have never ˄ and will never ignore our responsibilities.

Complete and consistent comparisons

A comparison has two parts: something is compared to something else. As you edit your writing, make sure your audience knows what is being compared. A comparison can frequently be completed by adding a phrase or clause to the sentence.

from those built in the early 1990s
Printers today are quite different ˄.

than the one just published
His first novel was better ˄.

If you include both parts of a comparison in the same sentence, be sure the comparison is logical.

those of
Her test scores are higher than ˄ the other students.

In the original sentence, *scores* were being compared to *students*. You could also rewrite the sentence as follows:

Her test scores are higher than the other students'.

Because *test scores* have already been mentioned, it is clear that *students'* (with an apostrophe) is short for *students' test scores*.

Verb tense consistency

Verbs in English are described according to both tense and aspect (see pages 645–647). Consistency in the use of tense, though not necessarily in the use of aspect, ensures that your sentences link together logically. In the following paragraph, notice that the tense remains in the past, but the aspect varies among simple, perfect, and progressive.

past perfect
In the summer of 1983, I had just finished my third year of architecture school

simple past   *past perfect (compound verb phrase)*
and had to find a six-month internship. I had grown up and gone through my

past perfect
entire education in the Midwest, but I had been to New York City once on a class

simple past   *simple past*
field trip and I thought it seemed like a pretty good place to live. So, armed with

simple past
little more than an inflated ego and my school portfolio, I was off to Manhattan,

past progressive
oblivious to the bad economy and the fact that the city was overflowing with

young architects.   —**Paul K. Humiston**, *"Small World"*

If you do need to shift to another tense, you can use time markers such as these to indicate a different time period:

now, then, today, yesterday
in two years, during the 1920s
after you finish, before we left

The verb tense shifts back and forth between present and past in the following comparison of different time periods—today, when Edward O. Wilson is studying ants in the woods around Walden Pond, and the nineteenth century, when Thoreau lived there. The time markers used to cue readers are blue.

> *simple present*   *simple past*
> These woods are not wild; indeed, they were not wild in Thoreau's day. Today, the
>
>   *simple present*
> beach and trails of Walden Pond State Reservation draw about 500,000 visitors a
>
>   *simple present*   *simple present*
> year. Few of them hunt ants, however. Underfoot and under the leaf litter there is
>
>   *simple past*   *simple past*
> a world as wild as it was before human beings came to this part of North America.

> —**James Gorman,** "Finding a Wild, Fearsome World Beneath Every Fallen Leaf"

A shift in time is sometimes indicated implicitly—that is, without an explicit time marker. A writer may change tenses without including time markers for any of several reasons: (1) to explain or support a general statement with information about the past, (2) to compare and contrast two different time periods, or (3) to comment on a topic. Why do you think the author of the following paragraph used different tenses?

> Thomas Jefferson, author of the Declaration of Independence, is considered one of our country's most brilliant citizens. His achievements were many, as were his interests. Some historians describe his work as a naturalist, scientist, and inventor; others focus on his accomplishments as an educator and politician. Yet Jefferson is best known as a spokesman for democracy.

Except for the two uses of *were* in the second sentence, all verb phrases are in the present tense. The author uses the past tense in the second sentence to provide evidence from the past that supports the thesis sentence.

Consistency of pronoun usage through agreement

If you were writing about a woman named Martha, you would use the pronouns *she* and *her* to refer to that person, not *it, he, they,* or *him*. This principle of pronoun usage is called **pronoun-antecedent agreement.** Pronouns must reflect the number, the person, and sometimes the gender of the nouns they refer to.

> *third person,*   *third person,*
> *singular, feminine*   *singular, feminine*
>
> Martha went to Argentina to visit her grandparents.

When indefinite pronouns, instead of nouns, are antecedents for personal pronouns, confusion often ensues. Although we often say or write a sentence such as *Everyone has the right to their own opinion,* this usage is not acceptable in most academic writing. *Everyone* and *they* agree in number; that is, they both indicate more than one person. However, they do not agree grammatically. The indefinite pronouns *everybody, everyone, somebody, someone, anybody,* and *anyone* are grammatically singular. Note that the verb following these words is in the same form as the verb following the singular pronoun *he* or *she.*

Everybody/Everyone <u>is</u> welcome.

Somebody/Someone <u>is</u> coming.

Anybody/Anyone <u>is</u> welcome.

He <u>is</u> here.

She <u>is</u> here.

The pronouns *they* and *them,* as well as the determiner *their,* however, are plural.

They <u>are</u> here.

The problem with the sentence *Everyone has the right to their own opinion* is that *everyone* is grammatically singular but *their* is grammatically plural. You could revise this sentence in a number of ways. You could replace *their* with singular determiners: *Everyone has the right to <u>his or her</u> own opinion.* This option should rarely be used because the phrasing *his or her* is cumbersome. However, using just one pronoun (*Everyone has the right to his opinion*) is also frowned on because of sexist overtones (see pages 677–678). Another possible revision of the sentence is to use a noun instead of an indefinite pronoun: *All citizens have the right to their own opinions.* You could also use an article instead of a possessive determiner: *Everyone has the right to an opinion.*

EXERCISE 24.4

Revise the following paragraph so that it is complete and consistent.

¹When I am so hungry that my stomach starts barking orders, I skip over to the closest Chinese restaurant and order dim sum. ²*Dim sum* referred to variety of small sweet and savory dishes such as fried dumplings or pastries filled with pork, shrimp, or vegetables. ³Everyone I know says they like *dim sum,* but I'm sure I snack on dim sum more than them. ⁴For me, these little dishes really "dot the heart," which is what *dim sum* literally meant. ⁵As an English idiom, it means "hit the spot."

Coherence

Placement of old and new information

Good writers forge strong links between their sentences. One way they do this is by presenting old, or given, information at the beginning of a sentence, saving the new information for the end of the sentence. The given information is familiar and expected; the new information is unknown or unanticipated until the sentence has been read. Think of it this way: if you are at an awards ceremony, you expect the announcer to say, "The winner is Carlos Rico," not "Carlos Rico is the winner." *The winner* is old information (you are at an awards ceremony and so you assume a winner will be chosen); the name of the winner is the new, highly anticipated information.

By ordering information in this way, you create a chain: old new old new old new. What was new becomes old. After declaring the winner at the awards ceremony, the announcer may continue by describing the person's accomplishments: "Mr. Rico has starred in five Broadway plays in just eight years." Notice that in this sentence the winner's name is now old information placed at the beginning of the sentence, with the new information following it. Although there are other ways to ensure text coherence, if you want to provide this type of linking, alter the order of some of your sentences so that new and old information are tightly connected.

> *On top of one of the snow banks sat three teenagers.*

The snow plow left ample evidence of its work. ~~Three teenagers sat on top of one of the snow banks.~~

> *Her first poem was published when she was only sixteen.*

She wrote most of her poems between 1936 and 1954. ~~She was only sixteen when her first poem was published.~~

Linking through words

Words with associated meanings By choosing specific nouns, determiners, and pronouns, you can tightly connect one sentence to the next. Here is a brief overview of strategies for making your writing coherent through word choice:

- Use nouns with related meanings.

    We found most of the <u>directions</u> easy to follow, especially those in the first three chapters. Several of us, though, had difficulty understanding the <u>instructions</u> in chapter 4.

- Use determiners to indicate old information.

    The students had to write a paper comparing American and Japanese management styles. <u>The assignment</u> was due Thursday.

- Use pronouns to refer to old information.

    Susan started playing the piano at the age of six. <u>She</u> was eighteen when she began strumming the guitar.

Repetition of words and phrases Repeating words or phrases will provide coherence in a paragraph, especially when your focus is a specific item or concept.

In the following paragraph, the author focuses on taboos and thus, of course, repeats this word.

> **Taboos** come in all sizes. Big **taboos**: when I was a kid in the Italian neighborhoods of Brooklyn, to insult someone's mother meant a brutal fight—the kind of fight no one interferes with until one of the combatants goes down and stays down. Little **taboos**: until the sixties, it was an insult to use someone's first name without asking or being offered permission. Personal **taboos**: Cyrano de Bergerac would not tolerate the mention of his enormous nose. **Taboos** peculiar to one city: in Brooklyn (again), when the Dodgers were still at Ebbets Field, if you rooted for the Yankees you kept it to yourself unless you wanted a brawl. **Taboos**, big or small, are always about having to respect somebody's (often irrational) boundary—or else.
> —**Michael Ventura**, "Taboo: Don't Even Think About It!"

Be careful, though, not to overdo repetition. Repetition in the following sentences is ineffective because the word being repeated is not significant:

spend endless time browsing without buying anything.
Some shoppers ~~shop around but do not buy anything. They have time to shop, so they spend it looking through all the shops in the mall.~~

EXERCISE 24.5

Discuss the repetition in the following paragraph.

> [1] The cowboy icon has two basic incarnations: the cowboy hero and the cowboy villain. [2] Cowboy heroes often appear in roles such as sheriff, leader of a cattle drive, or what I'll call a "wandering hero," such as the Lone Ranger, who appears much like a frontier Superman wherever and whenever help is needed. [3] Writers and producers most commonly place cowboy heroes in conflict either with "Indians" or with the cowboy villain. [4] In contrast to the other classic bad guys of the Western genre, cowboy villains pose a special challenge because they are essentially the alter ego of the cowboy hero; the cowboy villain shares the hero's skill with a gun, his horse-riding maneuvers, and his knowledge of the land. [5] What distinguishes the two, of course, is character: the cowboy hero is essentially good, while the cowboy villain is essentially evil. —**Jody M. Roy,** "The Case of the Cowboy"

Parallelism—linking through structure

Parallelism refers to the repetition of a grammatical structure. Like repeated words and phrases, this type of repetition makes your writing more cohesive, but it is also considered aesthetically pleasing, just like the repeated patterns in waves, leaves, or textiles. In the following excerpt from John F. Kennedy's inauguration speech, you will find examples of parallel words, phrases, and clauses. Note that some of these elements are embedded within others.

> We dare not forget today that we are the heirs of that first revolution. Let the word go forth from this <u>time</u> and <u>place</u>, to <u>friend</u> and <u>foe</u> alike, that the torch has been passed to a new generation of Americans, <u>born in this century</u>, <u>tempered by war</u>, <u>disciplined by a hard and bitter peace</u>, <u>proud of our ancient heritage</u>, and <u>unwilling to witness or permit the slow undoing of these human rights</u> <u>to which this nation has always been committed</u>, and <u>to which we are committed today at home</u> and <u>around the world</u>.

You can use correlative conjunctions to link parallel elements, and in doing so, emphasize the connection between them.

> He won gold medals in the 100-meter dash and the 400-meter relay.

> He won gold medals in <u>both</u> the 100-meter dash <u>and</u> the 400-meter relay.

As you revise, make sure that elements joined by *both . . . and, either . . . or, neither . . . nor,* and *not only . . . but also* are parallel in structure.

>   *either*
> They will either meet with the supervisor today or tomorrow.

> They not only give money to charities but they also do charitable work.

Effective nominalizations

Look at the following pairs of words:

discuss/discussion	*occur/occurrence*	*apply/application*
describe/description	*depend/dependence*	*recommend/recommendation*
allude/allusion	*prescribe/prescription*	*present/presentation*

The first word in each pair is a verb; the second word, derived from the verb, is a noun. You can use this feature of English, called **nominalizing,** to link sentences together (the root of *nominalize* means "noun" or "name"). After using the verb in the first sentence, you can use the noun in the second. The noun becomes the old information that is linked to the new information of the previous sentence. Here is an example:

> The grammar of the written language <u>differs</u> profoundly from that of the spoken language. This <u>difference</u> is attributable to the constant innovations of spoken language.

Most verbs take endings when they are nominalized, but some do not—for example, *request, address,* and *excerpt.*

Adjectives can also be nominalized (*sad/sadness, scarce/scarcity*). Note, though, that nominalizations, whether derived from verbs or adjectives, are abstractions. A sentence with too many nominalizations seems static, because verbs showing movement have crystallized and forms of *be* have replaced them as the main verbs. A sentence with too many nominalizations may also frustrate readers because it demands that they mentally record a number of nominalized actions or states. In the following sentence, the reader has to determine how four nominalized actions are related.

> The firm is now engaged in an <u>assessment</u> of its <u>procedures</u> for the <u>development</u> of new <u>products</u>.

To revise a sentence like this one, locate the most important action and recast the sentence with this action as the main verb. The revised sentence is more concise—and quite likely clearer to your readers.

> The firm is now <u>assessing</u> its procedures for <u>developing</u> new products.

You may also decide that some actions or ideas are less important and thus can be discarded. For the preceding example sentence, the action of engaging was not important enough to be included.

Subject-verb agreement

A subject (see page 650) and a verb are linked and thus need to match in person and number. This is called *subject-verb agreement*. Notice in the chart below how the verb *be* changes according to whether the subject is singular or plural and whether the subject refers to the person(s) writing, the person(s) addressed, or the person(s) or item(s) discussed.

	NUMBER	
PERSON	*Singular*	*Plural*
First	I *am*	Joe and I *are*
Second	You *are*	All of you *are*
Third	Joe *is*	The papers *are*

Because subjects can be more than one word long (*assignment* versus *tough assignment* versus *tough assignment due tomorrow*), choosing the correct verb can sometimes be a challenge. The following chart gives examples of various types of subjects and an explanation of the agreement principle that applies in each case.

Examples	*Explanation*
The ideal workshop **has** good ventilation. [singular subject, singular verb] Safe workshops **have** good ventilation. [plural subject, plural verb]	A verb agrees in person and number with the noun that is the head of the subject. The head noun is the noun that will affect the form the verb takes. It is underlined twice in the examples.
Workshops without good ventilation **are** dangerous. [plural head noun, plural verb]	A verb agrees in person and number with the noun that is the head of the subject, regardless of an intervening phrase (here, *without good ventilation*).
Garages and basements **are** sometimes used as workshops. [compound subject, plural verb]	A compound subject—two nouns usually connected by *and*—takes a plural verb.
The designer and owner **is** responsible for employee safety. [In this case, *designer* and *owner* refer to a single person.]	If a compound subject refers to one person, the verb is singular.

continued

Grammar and Style

Examples	Explanation
Neither smoke alarms nor <u>a fire extinguisher</u> **was** installed properly. [The noun closer to the verb is singular.] Neither a fire extinguisher nor <u>smoke alarms</u> **were** installed properly. [The noun closer to verb is plural.]	In formal English, when subjects are joined by *or, either . . . or,* or *neither . . . nor,* the verb agrees in person and number with the closer noun. If a sentence with both a singular and a plural noun seems awkward, reword it so that the plural noun is closer to the verb.
There **is** <u>a workbench</u> at the center of any good shop. [singular subject, singular verb] There **are** <u>shelves</u> for small tools. [plural subject, plural verb] There **are** <u>a first aid kit and a list of emergency numbers</u> by the door. [compound subject, plural verb]	The verb following the expletive *there* agrees in person and number with the noun phrase or coordinated noun phrases that follow it. The expletive *there* is sometimes called the dummy subject; the actual subject then follows the verb.
The whole <u>family</u> **uses** the shop. [Here the family is unified: It uses the shop.]	A collective noun refers to a group of people, animals, or objects as a single unit. When the unity of the group is the focus, a collective noun takes a singular verb. The pronoun *it* can substitute for the noun.
The <u>family</u> **disagree** on the use of the shop. [The individual family members are involved: They disagree on the use of the shop.]	When the individuality of the members is the focus, a collective noun takes a plural verb.

Placing modifiers

Modifiers (words or word groups that describe, limit, or qualify) enliven writing with details, but if they are not placed correctly, they can disrupt coherence. As you revise, be sure that you place your modifiers as close as you can to the words they modify.

Limiting modifiers **Limiting modifiers** such as *almost, even, hardly, just,* and *only* are clearest when they are placed right before the words they modify. Altering the placement of any of these modifiers can alter meaning.

The committee can <u>only</u> nominate two members for the position.

[The committee cannot appoint or elect the members.]

The committee can nominate <u>only</u> two members for the position.

[The committee cannot nominate more than two members.]

<u>Only</u> the committee can nominate two members for the position.

[No person or group other than the committee can nominate members.]

Squinting modifiers A **squinting modifier** is confusing because it is not clear whether it is modifying what is before it or what comes after it. To avoid such lack of clarity, reposition the modifier or provide appropriate punctuation.

Even though Erikson lists some advantages <u>overall</u> his vision of a successful business is faulty.

Reposition: Even though Erikson lists some <u>overall</u> advantages, his vision of a successful business is faulty.

Punctuate: Even though Erikson lists some advantages, overall his vision of a successful business is faulty.

Dangling modifiers **Dangling modifiers** are words, phrases, or elliptical clauses without an appropriate noun to modify. The dangling modifier may contain a verb form that has no clear agent, or it may consist of adjectives with no noun modify. You can revise such sentences in one of the following ways:

▌ Provide a noun or pronoun.

    I didn't know the difference between
Flubbing chemistry, ^*silicon* and *silicone* were the same to me.

[According to the original sentence, *silicon* and *silicone* flubbed chemistry.]

▌ Move the modifier.

        candy-colored and versatile
Candy-colored and versatile, I use my ^silicone spatulas every day.

[According to the original sentence, the writer is candy-colored and versatile.]

▌ Reword the modifier.

Feeding my addiction to kitchen gadgets,
 ^A kitchen-gadget junkie, silicone baking pans thrill me.

[In the original sentence, an illogical connection is made between "a kitchen-gadget junkie" and "silicone baking pans."]

Connecting words, phrases, or clauses

Using conjunctions or conjunctive adverbs **Coordinating conjunctions** join words, phrases, or even clauses. Coordinating conjunctions do more than link, however; they specify a type of link.

▌ *For* signals cause.

They won the court case, <u>for</u> their argument was strong and their evidence unassailable.

▌ *And* signals addition.

They made strong claims <u>and</u> supported them with convincing evidence.

■ *Nor* signals negative alternatives.

They didn't have a strong argument, <u>nor</u> did they have convincing evidence.

■ *But* signals contrast.

They made strong claims, <u>but</u> they were unable to support them with convincing evidence.

■ *Or* signals positive alternatives.

They will win the case <u>or</u> appeal it.

■ *Yet* signals contrast.

They made strong claims, <u>yet</u> they were unable to support them with convincing evidence.

■ *So* signals consequence.

Their evidence was unassailable, <u>so</u> they won the case.

Writers sometimes use more than one coordinating conjunction to slow down the rhythm of a sentence: *The lecture was long and far-reaching and tedious.* In this sentence, each adjective receives emphasis. Note also that the sentence stretches out just as the lecture it refers to does. (The rhetorical term for this stretching strategy is **polysyndeton**.) In contrast, writers may also choose to omit an expected coordinating conjunction in order to take advantage of the resulting change in rhythm. In *His response was quick, pointed, painful,* three adjectives end the sentence in three strong beats. This type of sentence rhythm can produce the sense that a longer list could have been presented: *They served the usual—soup, salad, sandwiches, pasta.* (The strategy of omitting coordinating conjunctions is called **asyndeton**.)

Conjunctive adverbs form links between sentences. Like coordinating conjunctions, these adverbs provide *meaningful* links. Writers use them to indicate their logic—for example, to show how two sentences contrast or how one sentence builds on another. Here are some of the more common types of logical links:

■ Contrast: *however, conversely*

Many patients fear that generic drugs are not safe. <u>However</u>, the Food and Drug Administration has reported that these drugs pose no risks for patients.

■ Result: *thus, therefore, consequently, then*

The patents for several drugs will expire this year. <u>Therefore</u>, patients will be able to buy cheaper generic versions of these drugs.

■ Concession: *nevertheless, nonetheless, still*

A recent study reported differing results for generic and brand-name drugs. <u>Nonetheless</u>, no adverse effects were reported.

■ Enumeration: *first, second, next*

<u>First</u>, consult a physician.

- Addition: *furthermore, moreover, also*

  The FDA requires the generic drug to contain the same active ingredient as the brand-name drug. The agency <u>also</u> expects manufacturers of generic drugs to perform laboratory tests.

- Comparison: *similarly, likewise*

  Research studies of the brand-name drug reported no adverse side effects. <u>Similarly</u>, studies of the generic drug listed no serious health issues associated with taking the drug.

When a conjunctive adverb comes at the beginning of a clause, you can indicate the separation between the two independent clauses in two ways: (1) use a semicolon, or (2) use a period and begin a new sentence.

Many patients fear that generic drugs are not safe; <u>however</u>, the Food and Drug Administration has reported that generic medicines pose no risks for patients.

Many patients fear that generic drugs are not safe. <u>However</u>, the Food and Drug Administration has reported that generic medicines pose no risks for patients.

Although conjunctive adverbs usually appear at the beginning of a sentence or clause, some, such as *however* and *nevertheless,* can appear in the middle or at the end. In either case, use comma(s) to set off the adverb.

<u>However</u>, the generic drug did not sell well.

The generic drug, <u>however</u>, did not sell well.

The generic drug did not sell well, <u>however</u>.

Using prepositional phrases Prepositional phrases (see pages 642–643) are often used as transitions between sentences or paragraphs. They signal various logical relationships.

- Time and sequence: *at first, in addition*

  <u>At first</u>, musicals were labeled *musical comedies.*

- Contrast: *in contrast, on the one hand/on the other hand*

  For musicals, you need actors who can sing. <u>In contrast</u>, for operettas, you need singers who can act.

- Example: *for example, for instance*

  There are several differences between operettas and musicals. <u>For example</u>, operettas often include aristocratic characters, while musicals involve more ordinary people.

- Emphasis: *in fact, above all*

  Because of the seriousness of its plot, *Porgy and Bess* should not be placed in the same category as *My Fair Lady*. <u>In fact</u>, it should be labeled an *opera* rather than a *musical.*

- Restatement: *in other words, in sum*

  <u>In sum</u>, what matters is the audience's appreciation of the piece.

Using participial phrases Participial phrases (see pages 648–649) express a variety of meanings that can affect the coherence of your writing.

▌ Cause:

Noting our confusion, the lecturer provided additional examples.

▌ Purpose:

He came to the lecture looking for a debate.

▌ Result:

She concluded by presenting several provocative perspectives—effectively opening the door for further discussion.

Using subordinating conjunctions with dependent clauses Like the other connectors presented in this chapter, subordinating conjunctions signal several different types of connections, including the following:

▌ Cause: *because, since, as*

The election results were unknown because the polls were still open.

▌ Time: *after, before, since, while, until*

After the polls closed, the votes were quickly counted.

▌ Concession: *although, even though, though, while*

Although the polls were still open, news programs predicted the winner.

▌ Condition: *if, unless*

If the polls are still open, there is no winner.

Three subordinating conjunctions sometimes cause problems because they can be used in two different ways. *While* can refer to both time and concession, so *While we had disagreements, we never threw bottles* could mean either that bottles were not thrown during disagreements or that bottles were not thrown even though there were disagreements. *Since* and *as* are also potentially ambiguous; they both can refer to time or cause. When you edit your sentences, make sure that the meanings of these words are clear.

EXERCISE 24.6

Choose an essay in this book and identify ten different ways the author makes the work coherent.

Variety and Emphasis

Sentence length

Both short and long sentences have their uses. Short sentences sound direct and emphatic, so they can highlight your feelings and impressions. Long sentences allow you to develop your ideas fully. However, if you use too many short sentences, no one sentence will stand out. Instead, your writing will sound choppy. Similarly, if you overuse long sentences, you send a signal to your readers that you have not thought through your ideas enough to present them succinctly. Your sentences will seem rambling.

Using a variety of sentence lengths, Louise Rafkin recounts a sixth-grade memory in all its horror.

> In sixth grade I was shown a filmstrip on hygiene. My teacher, good-hearted but simple, screened this gem of an educational tool directly before lunch. It was a "follow the fly" documentary. We witnessed the fly in its full furry glory, magnified to horror-film proportions. We followed it to a raw-sewage treatment plant, and watched it set down and gulp a huge dollop of crud through its hydraulic pump of a mouth, the surface of the sewage swamp roiling about its hairy legs. Then the little monster up and flew right over to a nearby playground and landed on an unsuspecting kid's baloney sandwich. There, it threw up.
>
> —**Louise Rafkin**, *Other People's Dirt*

You can see the varying lengths more clearly in this list of the sentences from her paragraph:

1. In sixth grade I was shown a filmstrip on hygiene.
2. My teacher, good-hearted but simple, screened this gem of an educational tool directly before lunch.
3. It was a "follow the fly" documentary.
4. We witnessed the fly in its full furry glory, magnified to horror-film proportions.
5. We followed it to a raw-sewage treatment plant, and watched it set down and gulp a huge dollop of crud through its hydraulic pump of a mouth, the surface of the sewage swamp roiling about its hairy legs.
6. Then the little monster up and flew right over to a nearby playground and landed on an unsuspecting kid's baloney sandwich.
7. There, it threw up.

Notice how Rafkin's longer sentences carry evocative details, while her shorter ones highlight a significant event or action.

Unusual sentence patterns

A sentence usually consists of a subject followed by a predicate. However, other sentence patterns are available (see pages 651–653). When used judiciously, the unusual sentence patterns in the following chart can add variety and emphasis to your writing. Sensing a change in the expected order of words, readers will shift their attention to the stressed word that is out of place.

Pattern	Original Sentence	Revised Sentence
Begin the sentence with the complement.	He expected <u>an insult</u>. He could not accept <u>a compliment</u>.	<u>An insult</u>, he expected. <u>A compliment</u>, he could not accept.
Begin the sentence with the verb or part of the verb.	Then the brass band <u>came</u>, marching to a military cadence.	Then <u>came</u> the brass band, marching to a military cadence.
Begin the sentence with a negative word.	She did <u>not</u> understand the consequences of her action until she lost her job.	<u>Not</u> until she lost her job did she understand the consequences of her action.
Begin the sentence with an expression of location or direction.	Stacks of old magazines were <u>inside the garage</u>.	<u>Inside the garage</u> were stacks of old magazines.

Combining sentences

If you find during the revision stage that your sentences lack variety, try joining two or three short sentences into one longer one. The following chart presents several sentence-combining strategies.

Strategy	Original Sentences	Combined Sentences
Join sentences or parts of sentences with a coordinating conjunction.	My parents live in Maryland. My brother lives in Iowa. I live in Arizona.	My parents live in Maryland, my brother lives in Iowa, **and** I live in Arizona.
	The Bradleys have <u>contributed money</u>. They have also <u>volunteered to work</u>.	The Bradleys <u>have contributed money</u> **and** <u>volunteered to work</u>.
Join sentences with a semicolon.	Johnson won the gold medal. His best friend won the silver medal.	Johnson won the gold medal**;** his best friend won the silver medal.
Reduce the information in one sentence to a prepositional phrase.	<u>They worried about their mounting debt and their tense relationship.</u> As a result, they consulted a financial advisor.	**Because of** <u>their mounting debt and tense relationship</u>, they consulted a financial advisor.

Strategy	Original Sentences	Combined Sentences
Reduce the information in one sentence to a verbal phrase.	<u>I walked into the kitchen.</u> I saw something on the counter that was not supposed to be there.	**Walking** into the kitchen, I saw something on the counter that was not supposed to be there.
Reduce the information in one sentence to an appositive.	David is the head of the department. He will be leading the discussion.	David, <u>the head of the department</u>, will be leading the discussion.
Place the information in one sentence in a dependent clause.	The guide recommended staying away from the cave. The couple entered anyway.	**Although** <u>the guide recommended staying away from the cave</u>, the couple entered anyway.

If you end up with too many long sentences in an essay, you can separate some into two sentences.

Visitors to Olympic National Park, located on Washington's Olympic Peninsula,

. Many glimpse

often want to see a glacier, ~~especially~~ Blue Glacier, which cascades down Mount
⌄

Olympus, but only those willing to carry a heavy pack and walk seventeen miles can

get a close-up view.

Questions, exclamations, and imperative sentences

If your rhetorical situation allows you to take on a conversational voice—one in which you are able to ask questions, emphasize impressions, or give instructions—you can use interrogative, exclamatory, and imperative sentences.

Interrogative sentences Some questions introduce a new topic. These questions are answered within the text.

> <u>So, how does a coach motivate?</u> Well, any number of ways. Coaches, in many ways, are like child psychologists, dealing with a variety of maturity and intelligence levels. The truth is, no one method works for every player. Some players need to be kicked in the butt. Some need to be stroked and coddled. Each method could backfire if used on the wrong player.   —**Joe Theismann,** *The Complete Idiot's Guide to Football*

Other questions used by writers are **rhetorical questions**—questions that are used as statements rather than as sincere questions (see page 657).

Exclamatory sentences To express emotional responses, some writers use exclamatory sentences.

> But at other moments, the classroom is so lifeless or painful or confused—and I so powerless to do anything about it—that my claim to be a teacher seems a transparent sham. Then the enemy is everywhere: in those students from some alien planet, in the subject I thought I knew, and in the personal pathology that keeps me earning my living this way. <u>What a fool I was to imagine that I had mastered this occult art—harder to divine than tea leaves and impossible for mortals to do even passably well!</u>   —**Parker Palmer,** *The Courage to Teach*

Beware of overusing exclamation points. Your readers might decide you are being cute or melodramatic. If you are emphasizing something humorous, you don't need to signal it with your punctuation. In fact, understatement can enhance the humor of a scene.

Imperative sentences If you want to direct your readers to do something, consider using an imperative sentence.

> Now I stare and stare at people shamelessly. <u>Stare</u>. It's the way to educate your eye.
> —**Walker Evans**

EXERCISE 24.7

Choose an essay in this book and find ten different ways the author includes variety in the work.

PUNCTUATION, MECHANICS, AND RHETORICAL EFFECTS

25

Take a few minutes to thumb through this book, looking at just the punctuation marks. Stop to compare the different uses of punctuation in the excerpts from various authors. More than likely, you'll notice some personal preferences in punctuation. Now consider this description of a large Christian nightclub:

> Enter her three-level, 18,000-square-foot club—a new space inaugurated in October—and you won't find any overtly religious symbols. In the lounge below, patrons can shoot pool and order pizzas and smoothies from the bar (the closest you'll get to a stimulant is Red Bull). Upstairs, they can experience acts with a state-of-the-art sound and light system. The price tag for all the renovations: $3 million, raised through donations and loans guaranteed by the club's founder, the Living Word Christian Center.   —**Arian Camp-Flores,** "Get Your Praise On"

First, notice the variety of punctuation marks: commas, hyphens, dashes, periods, apostrophes, parentheses, and a colon. The writer's choice of punctuation marks becomes part of her message, as they are meant to serve as beacons to help readers navigate her prose. Some help us understand where one idea starts and ends. Without seeing a period after the first sentence and a capital letter at the beginning of the next, a reader could experience a few moments of confusion while trying to figure out whether religious symbols are not present in the entire club or whether they are just not visible in the lounge. Other punctuation marks help us understand which parts of the paragraph the author deems most important and which parts she considers significant but only tangentially related to her main idea. By enclosing a clause in parentheses, Camp-Flores is signaling that the remark should be understood as an aside—the equivalent of saying, "Just in case you're interested in stimulants, Red Bull is the only one available."

Now let's look at another description—an excerpt from an article in *Scientific American*.

> To understand the birth process from the mother's point of view, imagine you are about to give birth. The baby is most likely upside down, facing your side, when its head enters the birth canal. Midway through the canal, however, it must turn to face your back, and the back of its head is pressed against your pubic bones. At that time, its shoulders are oriented side to side. When the baby exits your body, it is still facing backward, but it will turn its head slightly to the side. This rotation helps to turn the baby's shoulders so that they can also fit between your pubic bones and tailbone.
>
> —**Karen R. Rosenberg and Wenda R. Trevathan,** "The Evolution of Human Birth"

In this paragraph, you can quickly pick out commas, periods, and apostrophes—conventional punctuation found in almost any piece of nonfiction writing. However, there are no dashes, colons, or parentheses. The punctuation style in this paragraph differs from that in the paragraph by Camp-Flores because the authors' rhetorical situation differs. Rosenberg and Trevathan's primary purpose is to describe the human birthing process as concisely and as straightforwardly as possible. Their readers expect to be informed, and the authors meet this expectation by using a limited number of punctuation marks so that the information is easy to read. In contrast, Camp-Flores's purpose is to be entertaining and conversational as well as informative; thus, she uses punctuation as the owner of a nightclub uses stage lights, directing bright lights toward some parts of the stage but providing subdued lighting elsewhere.

In this chapter, you will learn the punctuation options that are available to you for crafting a fitting response to each particular rhetorical situation. The Guide to Punctuation provides detailed information about each punctuation mark. This section is followed by a discussion of punctuation trouble spots and the Guide to Mechanics, which provides style guidelines for writing in an academic setting. **Mechanics** refers to the use of abbreviations, acronyms, initialisms, capital letters, italics, and numbers.

| Guide to Punctuation |

As you have seen by examining some of the excerpts in this book, writers punctuate purposefully—to indicate boundaries, to control sentence rhythm, and to modify or clarify meaning. The following guide, arranged alphabetically, provides details on uses of the individual punctuation marks.

The punctuation conventions listed here are based on those provided in *The Chicago Manual of Style* (CMS), fifteenth edition. The great majority of these conventions are also included in *The MLA Handbook for Writers of Research Papers* (MLA) and in the *Publication Manual of the American Psychological Association* (APA). When MLA or APA conventions differ from those of the CMS, those alternatives are also listed.

' Apostrophe

To mark omissions An apostrophe is used to mark an omission in a contraction, number, or word mimicking speech.

> we will → we'll   class of 2008 → class of '08   you all → y'all

Contractions are not appropriate for all rhetorical situations. In formal contexts, your audience may expect you to use full words and numbers.

To form the possessive case of singular and plural nouns An apostrophe is commonly used to indicate possession, ownership, or origin.

> Sandra's dog   Sandra's car   Sandra's idea

It can also signal other types of relationships.

Relationship between people:	Sandra's friend
Traits or features of humans, plants, and animals:	Sandra's tenacity, the cat's yowl, the plant's stem
Features of objects:	the fabric's sheen, the room's lighting
Features of abstract nouns:	greed's hold
Identification of buildings:	St. John's Cathedral
Identification of illnesses:	Huntington's disease
Identification of holidays:	Valentine's Day, Presidents' Day
Type of certification:	bachelor's degree, driver's license
Measurement:	a month's vacation, ten dollars' worth of gas

An apostrophe and the letter *s* indicate the possessive case of singular nouns, indefinite pronouns, abbreviations, and acronyms.

the director's office   Dr. Seuss's stories   everyone's hope

the UN's announcement   NAFTA's history

A noun may end with the letter *s* in both its singular and plural forms. In such a case, only an apostrophe is added.

politics' attraction   physics' contribution

Rules vary regarding the possessive form of a name ending in the letter *s,* so be sure to consult the style guide preferred by your instructor or employer. According to CMS, an apostrophe and *s* should be added unless the final syllable is pronounced "eez": *Sophocles' poetry,* but *Alexis's laptop.* The MLA recommends always using an apostrophe and *s,* regardless of the pronunciation.

WAIT A MINUTE . . .

The words *its* and *it's* are often confused. *Its* is a possessive pronoun; *it's* is a contraction for "it is." The words *whose* and *who's* are also frequently confused. *Whose* is a pronoun; *who's* is a contraction for "who is."

Possessive Pronoun	**Contraction**
Its roof is steep.	It's a steep roof.
Whose is it?	Who's in charge?

Only an apostrophe is added to indicate the possessive case of a plural noun ending in the letter *s.*

the students' petition   the Lopezes' company

However, both an apostrophe and the letter *s* are needed to indicate the possessive case of an irregular plural not ending in *s.*

children's activities   men's health   women's programs

To show joint ownership or collaboration An apostrophe and the letter *s* are added to the second noun to indicate shared ownership or collaboration on a project.

> David Ayo and Jill Michelucci's studio
>
> the director and the producer's decision

To show separate ownership or individual contributions An apostrophe and the letter *s* are added to each noun to indicate that ownership is separate or that contributions have been made independently.

> David Ayo's and Jill Michelucci's apartments
>
> the director's and the producer's ideas

For possessive forms of compound nouns An apostrophe and the letter *s* are added to the last word of a compound noun to make it possessive.

> sister-in-law's job, the attorney general's report [singular]
>
> sisters-in-law's jobs, the attorneys general's reports [plural]

The awkwardness of making plural compounds possessive can be eliminated by using a prepositional phrase beginning with *of* instead of an apostrophe and *s*.

> the jobs of my sisters-in-law, the reports of the attorneys general

Before gerunds A noun used before a gerund should be in the possessive case.

> Jeff's <u>objecting</u> caused many members to feel uncomfortable.
>
> We were awakened by the neighbors' <u>shouting</u>.

WAIT A MINUTE . . .

If a noun precedes a participle, no apostrophe is needed.

I remember my aunt <u>telling</u> me stories about my parents.

A good way to tell the difference between a gerund and a participle is to ask whether the emphasis is on an action or on a person. In a phrase or clause containing a gerund, the emphasis is on the action (in *Jeff's objecting*, the emphasis is on the objecting). In a phrase or clause containing a participle, the emphasis is on the person (in *my aunt telling me,* the emphasis is on the aunt).

[ ]   Brackets

In quotations Brackets indicate that a clarification or explanation has been added to a quotation. In other words, the brackets indicate that the enclosed text was not written by the original author of the quoted passage.

> Three years after the death of Joseph Stalin, President Dwight D. Eisenhower asked, "Is it [the Soviet Union] prepared to allow other nations, including those of Eastern Europe, the free choice of their own forms of government?"

Within parentheses Brackets, instead of another set of parentheses, are used inside a parenthetical remark.

> (According to Stewart, the Battle of Little Bighorn [Custer's last stand] was a poorly planned attack.)

:   Colon

To introduce a list In academic writing, a colon is used after a complete independent clause to introduce a list.

> Musicians producing the neo-soul sound have been inspired by artists from the seventies: James Brown, Isaac Hayes, Curtis Mayfield, and Stevie Wonder, to mention a few.

For formal writing assignments, lists not preceded by a full independent clause must be revised, either by removing the colon or by using *as follows* or *the following* to fill out the clause.

> The books that most influenced Mario Puzo, author of *The Godfather,*
> included : *The Brothers Karamazov, The House by the Medlar Tree, Madame Bovary,*
>   *the following*
> and *Vanity Fair.*

In less formal contexts (as in an article in a popular magazine or newspaper), a full introductory clause may not be needed. Arian Camp-Flores (writing for the magazine *Newsweek*) does not use one in her description of a Christian nightclub.

> The price tag for all the renovations: $3 million, raised through donations and loans guaranteed by the club's founder, the Living Word Christian Center.

In academic writing, a complete independent clause precedes a colon, but a word or a phrase can follow it.

> She had only one word on her mind: success.

To direct attention to an explanation, an example, or a summary A colon is used between two independent clauses when the second clause expands, exemplifies, or summarizes the idea expressed in the first. Unless the second clause is a quotation, rule, or principle, the first letter of the second clause is not capitalized. Of the two sentences that follow, the second contains a general rule.

> After several reports of elephants being overworked and then attacking humans, government officials took action: they sent the fatigued animals to a wildlife sanctuary for a short vacation.

> The trainer wrote the first rule on the board: Never promise what you cannot deliver, and always deliver what you promise.

APA style for this kind of colon usage differs. According to APA guidelines, the first letter of the second clause should always be capitalized.

To introduce a quotation A quotation is often introduced by an introductory independent clause followed by a colon.

> In "High-Tech Bibliophilia," Paul Goldberger praises the newest building in downtown Seattle: "The complex polygonal form of the Seattle library, which is sheathed almost entirely in glass set in a diamond-shaped grid, has a dazzling energy; it's the most alluring architectural object to arrive in this city's downtown since the Space Needle."

After a salutation in a formal letter A colon is used in formal letters after the salutation.

> To Whom It May Concern:

> Dear Dr. Elmore:

, Comma

One of the most important punctuation marks to learn to use effectively is the comma. It can be difficult to decide whether to use a comma because this mark has so many functions. But commas are essential: they give sentences clarity and rhythm. See if you agree as you read the following passage—first with the commas removed and then in the original form.

WITHOUT COMMAS

Eighty years ago when I was about thirteen my elder brother Edwin was about eighteen and in his freshman year at Columbia College commuting from our home in Brooklyn. He was taking a survey course in English literature. He decided because I was interested in books to give me the same course at home that he was taking in college. So every day when he came home he would sit down with me and tell me what the assignment was for the next day. I had to read everything he read and take all the tests he took. I also had to write the papers he had to write. So what I got was a thorough survey course in English literature based on a textbook which I remember as being titled *Century Readings in English Literature*. I'm not sure that was the exact title but I think so because it was published by the Century Company. The editors however I do remember: Cunliffe Pyre and Young.

WITH COMMAS (ORIGINAL)

Eighty years ago, when I was about thirteen, my elder brother, Edwin, was about eighteen and in his freshman year at Columbia College, commuting from our home in Brooklyn. He was taking a survey course in English literature. He decided, because I was interested in books, to give me the same course at home that he was taking in college. So every day, when he came home, he would sit down with me and tell me what the assignment was for the next day. I had to read everything he read and take all the tests he took. I also had to write the papers he had to write. So what I got was a thorough survey course in English literature based on a textbook which I remember as being titled *Century Readings in English Literature*. I'm not sure that was the exact title but I think so, because it was published by the Century Company. The editors, however, I do remember: Cunliffe, Pyre, and Young.

—**Clifton Fadiman,** *For the Love of Books*

Knowing a few basic functions of commas will help you use them to clarify the meaning and enhance the rhythm of your sentences.

WAIT A MINUTE . . .

Some novice writers believe that they should place a comma wherever they would pause if they were speaking. The result of holding such a notion is the overuse or misplacement of commas. As you can hear when you read a sentence aloud, a comma indicates more than mere hesitation; it also affects intonation and stress and causes lengthening of certain words.

Two or more elements

To separate items in a series A comma separates words, phrases, and clauses in a series. A comma has not always been considered necessary before a conjunction (*and* or *or*) in a series; however, its use is now strongly recommended to ensure clarity.

Words: Diplomats from England, France, and Spain met on Tuesday.

Phrases: He worked before school, after school, and on weekends.

Clauses: We should support this candidate because she supports higher funding for education, because she has a plan for improving health care, and because her economic policies are sound.

If a pair of words combined with *and* are considered a single item, a comma should not separate them.

> The children's menu included hamburgers, hot dogs, and <u>macaroni and cheese</u>.

To separate coordinate adjectives Two or more adjectives that modify the same noun are called **coordinate adjectives**. To test whether adjectives are coordinate, either interchange them or put *and* between them. If the meaning does not change, the adjectives are coordinate and so should be separated by a comma or commas.

> The company honored their dedicated, energetic interns.

> [COMPARE: energetic, dedicated interns OR dedicated and energetic interns]

The adjectives in the following sentence are not separated by a comma. Notice that they cannot be interchanged or joined by *and*.

> The old wooden bridge was featured in a documentary.

> [NOT the wooden old bridge OR the old and wooden bridge]

To separate independent clauses A comma is generally used between two independent clauses in a compound sentence when they are linked by a coordinating conjunction. The comma appears before the conjunction.

> *Two clauses:* The ultraviolet rays used in tanning beds differ from those produced by the sun, but they are still dangerous.

If there are more than two clauses, each clause is followed by a comma.

> *Four clauses:* Responding to a flood of adrenaline, your heart pounds faster, your breathing quickens, your muscles contract, and your eyes dilate.

If the clauses are short and closely related in meaning, the comma is not always necessary.

> I collect pottery and my sister collects jewelry.

Introductory elements

After introductory words and phrases A comma usually follows a word or phrase that precedes the subject of a sentence. It indicates that the typical sentence structure has been altered.

> Rapidly, I calculated the total cost.

> In contrast, a counterculture defines itself by opposing the dominant culture.

> Backed by a bass and a keyboard, the guitarist played a familiar song.

A comma is not required after a single word or short prepositional phrase as long as there is no chance of misreading.

> On Monday we will discuss the new design.

After introductory attributive tags A comma follows an attributive tag, a short phrase that signals the source of a remark or quoted information. Although these tags may appear in the middle or at the end of a sentence, they often appear at the beginning in order to introduce the material.

> She replied, "Yeah, right."

> As Bill would say, "Where there's no hope, there's no hurry."

> According to Azar Nafisi, "What we search for in fiction is not so much reality but the epiphany of truth."

A comma is not used with indirect questions.

> He asked me when I would be able to finish the report.

After introductory dependent clauses A comma follows an introductory dependent clause.

> Even though traffic was heavy, we arrived on time.

Parenthetical elements

To set off parenthetical expressions A comma is used to set off a **parenthetical expression**—words, phrases, or clauses that make a transition in thought or add emotive details. When the parenthetical expression is placed in the middle of the sentence, two commas are used (before and after it) to indicate that it is a transition, an interruption, an interjection, an aside, or an additional but unnecessary detail.

> We all laughed, in nervous titters, as we introduced ourselves.

When the parenthetical expression is placed at the end of the sentence, just one comma is used to set off the element from the rest of the sentence.

> He did not mention his destination, however.

To set off nonessential verbal phrases Commas are used to set off nonessential verbal phrases. The term *nonessential* means that these phrases are not necessary for their referents to be specifically identified. These verbal phrases begin with either a present participle (*laughing, walking*) or a past participle (*offered, written*).

> Fans waited in line at the box office, hoping to get tickets to the evening concert.

> *nonessential*
>
> The annual Ellensburg Rodeo, held on Labor Day weekend, will attract many tourists.

When the information in the verbal phrase is essential for the referent to be identified, commas are not used.

> The rodeo planned for Labor Day weekend will attract many tourists.

To set off nonessential appositives A **nonessential appositive** is a word or phrase that provides extra information about an adjacent noun or pronoun. Because this type of appositive is not necessary for the identification of a referent, it

Grammar and Style

is set off from the rest of the sentence—by two commas when it occurs in the middle of a sentence or by a single comma when it appears at the end of a sentence.

> Suzanne Dittmer, president of the company, announced the opening of a new factory in Greenville.

> Delegates met in Hanoi, the capital of Vietnam.

To set off nonessential dependent clauses A nonessential dependent clause may be an adverbial clause, an adjectival clause, or a noun clause. These clauses add extra details rather than providing essential information for completing the meaning of a sentence, so they are set off by commas.

Adverbial clauses that begin with *although, even though,* or *while* are usually set off by commas because they provide nonessential, contrasting information.

> Sea Biscuit, although the odds were against him, won the race by a nose.

Adverbial clauses indicating time, cause, or purpose are usually not set off by commas.

> She studied in Tokyo for a year so that she could improve her Japanese.

A nonessential adjectival clause begins with a relative pronoun, most commonly *who* or *which*. The information conveyed in the clause adds details about a referent that has already been identified.

> Many families enjoy hiking on the Scout Trail, which is located at the end of Bay Road.

> Joel Cavanaugh, who reported the accident, was on his way home from work.

Adjectival clauses that are necessary for the identification of the referent are not set off by commas.

> The person who reported the accident was on his way home from work.

A nonessential noun clause adds information about or renames a preceding noun.

> His suggestion, that the application deadline be extended, resulted in a larger pool of candidates.

The exact content of the suggestion referred to here would have been mentioned earlier in the passage. The nonessential noun clause, then, is a repetition of that old information and is thus set off by commas. If the sentence were introducing the suggestion for the first time, no commas would be used.

> His suggestion that the application deadline be extended resulted in a larger pool of candidates.

If you read both versions of this sentence aloud, you should be able to hear a difference in rhythm.

To set off contrasting information Commas set off contrasting information. The phrase that is set off often contains the word *not*.

> The business owners, not the employees, were responsible for the accident.

With attributive tags Commas separate the words in a quotation or dialogue from an attributive tag (see pages 544–545).

"Being a hippie," explains DiFilippo, "means approaching life's obstacles in a way that promotes freedom, peace, love, and respect for our earth and all of humankind."

No one was injured, according to the sheriff's report.

Special uses

To indicate the omission of words When two or more adjacent parts of a sentence have similar structures (that is, they are parallel in form), a comma can be used in the element(s) after the first to indicate the omission of a word or words. The missing words should be easily retrievable from the context.

In June, there were two storms; in July, three; in August, four.

If there is no chance of misreading, no commas are needed to indicate omitted words.

I played the piano, my sister the trumpet, and my brother the saxophone.

With the more, the less, *and other comparatives* When comparative forms (e.g., *the more* or *the less*) are followed by clauses, a comma is used to separate the clauses.

The more we study this topic, the more complicated it becomes.

The less time I spend worrying about baseball, the better I feel.

To set off state or year A comma is used to set off the name of a state when it follows the name of a city. It is also used to set off the year in a complete date.

My parents moved to Athens, Vermont, on January 1, 1954.

A comma is not used between a month or specific day (without numerical date) and year.

My parents moved there in January 1954.

My parents moved to their new home on New Year's Day 1954.

Unnecessary or misplaced commas

Separating a subject and its verb or a verb and its object Although speakers often pause after the subject or before the object of a sentence, such a pause should not be indicated by a comma.

In this climate, rain at frequent intervals, produces mosquitoes. [no separation between subject (*rain*) and verb (*produces*)]

Following a coordinating conjunction Avoid using a comma after a coordinating conjunction (*and, but, for, nor, or, so,* or *yet*).

We worked very hard on her campaign for state representative, but, the incumbent was too strong in the northern part of the district.

Separating elements in a compound predicate Avoid using a comma between two elements of a compound predicate.

She picked up her baby, and ran out the door.

Occasionally, a comma is used in a compound predicate to provide emphasis. Use this option sparingly, however, or it will lose its effectiveness.

> I looked around the room at all the boxes of junk, and despaired.

Setting off words, phrases, and clauses that are clearly essential In the following sentences, the elements in boldface are clearly essential and so should not be set off by commas. (See also pages 705–706.)

> Kelly was born, **in Chicago in 1987.**

> Everyone, **who has a mortgage,** is required to have fire insurance.

— Dash

After an introductory list A dash follows an introductory list of nouns. No spaces are used before or after the dash.

> Frodo, Sam, Pippin, and Merry—these were the hobbits who left the Shire together.

Notice that a pronoun follows the dash; it refers to the list of nouns.

To set off comments Dashes are used to set off comments that interrupt or conclude a sentence.

> My story—it is a long one, so bear with me—begins in 1959.

> They had never been in trouble before—as far as we knew.

To indicate faltering speech A dash is used to indicate that a speaker is struggling to find the right word.

> May I—would you—is it possible for us to disagree and still be friends?

To set off nonessential appositives A nonessential appositive can be set off by dashes instead of commas. However, the dash, because it suggests a longer pause, emphasizes the content of the appositive.

> Sylvia—an avid videogame player—also likes to read books.

> He never tired of watching his favorite movie—*The Matrix*.

WAIT A MINUTE . . .

Which punctuation is better to use with a nonessential appositive—commas, dashes, or a colon? Any of these marks can be used. As a guide, though, consider the comma as neutral, the dash as semiformal and emphatic, and the colon as formal.

> He always had the same lunch, a turkey sandwich.
> He always had the same lunch—a turkey sandwich.
> He always had the same lunch: a turkey sandwich.

. . . Ellipsis points

To indicate omitted words in a quotation Ellipsis points—three periods separated from each other and adjacent words by spaces—indicate the omission of words from quoted sentences. An omission may occur within a quoted sentence or at the end of a quoted sentence. The examples of the use of ellipsis points that follow are based on this excerpt.

> Within months of their 1st birthday, most kids start attaching names to things. And whether they're learning Swahili or Swedish, they go about it in much the same way. Instead of proceeding by trial and error—unsure whether "doggie" refers to a part of a dog, to one dog in particular, or to anything with four legs—children start with a set of innate biases. They assume that labels refer to wholes instead of parts (the creature, not the tail) and to classes instead of items (all dogs, not one dog). They also figure that one name is for any class of object (if it's a dog, it's not a cow). These assumptions are not always valid—there's only one Lassie, after all, and any dog qualifies as a mammal—but they enable kids to catalog new words with breathtaking efficiency. A typical child is socking away a dozen words a day by 18 months, and may command 2,000 of them by the age of 2.
> —**Geoffrey Cowley,** "For the Love of Language"

Within a quoted sentence

> According to Geoffrey Cowley, "Instead of proceeding by trial and error . . . children start with a set of innate biases."

End of a quoted sentence Ellipsis points that replace words at the end of a sentence must be followed by an end punctuation mark (a period, a question mark, or an exclamation point).

> According to Geoffrey Cowley, "A typical child is socking away a dozen words a day by 18 months . . . ."

Beginning of a quoted sentence No ellipsis points are needed to indicate an omission at the beginning of a sentence.

> According to Geoffrey Cowley, children learn "a dozen words a day by 18 months, and may command 2,000 of them by the age of 2."

Omission of a sentence or more For an omission of a sentence or more, the ellipsis points should follow the end punctuation of the preceding sentence.

> Geoffrey Cowley explains how young children learn language:
>
> > Within months of their 1st birthday, most kids start attaching names to things. . . . They assume that labels refer to wholes instead of parts (the creature, not the tail) and to classes instead of items (all dogs, not one dog). They also figure that one name is for any class of object (if it's a dog, it's not a cow). These assumptions are not always valid—there's only one Lassie, after all, and any dog qualifies as a mammal—but they enable kids to catalog new words with breathtaking efficiency. A typical child is socking away a dozen words a day by 18 months, and may command 2,000 of them by the age of 2.

To indicate pauses or hesitation in speech Ellipsis points are used to indicate interrupted speech.

I talked to her once . . . twice . . . maybe three times.

! Exclamation Point

To indicate strong feeling Because an exclamation point signals an emphatic comment, it should be used sparingly. Academic writing rarely calls for an exclamation point.

What an incredible day!

- Hyphen

To form compound words A hyphen is used in some compound words.

father-in-law   nurse-practitioner   president-elect

A hyphen is used in a compound number.

sixty-three   seventy-eight   forty-two

A hyphen is also used with certain prefixes and suffixes.

self-confidence   self-reliance

ex-mayor   ex-president

cross-cultural   cross-reference

e-greeting   e-commerce

toll-free   debt-free

A hyphen in a compound adjective indicates that words in the compound should be considered as a single unit.

fifteenth-century church   fourth-floor apartment

six-year-old child   two-hour delay

down-and-dirty campaign   tit-for-tat response

Notice that when these modifiers do not come before a noun, they are not hyphenated.

The church was built in the fifteenth century.

The child is six years old.

A dictionary is a helpful source when trying to decide which compound words include hyphens. A compound consisting of an adverb that ends in -*ly* and an adjective never has a hyphen.

The rarely used church was finally abandoned.

In fractions A hyphen is used between the numerator and the denominator when a fraction is written as words.

two-thirds   eight-tenths

( ) Parentheses

To enclose numbers or letters in a list Parentheses enclose numbers or letters used in lists within paragraphs.

Use insect repellent carefully: (1) apply repellent just to clothing and shoes if possible, (2) wash off repellent applied to the skin when you go indoors, and (3) avoid putting repellent on your hands.

To enclose source information Parentheses enclose dates, authors' names, page numbers, and other types of source information.

Around this time, the first Penn State student donned a "furry lion outfit" for athletic events (Bezilla 30).

To enclose explanatory or supplementary material Parentheses enclose words, phrases, or sentences that explain or supplement the information in the main text.

Paragraphs can be organized chronologically (along a time line) or emphatically (starting or ending with the most important point).

If a complete sentence enclosed in parentheses appears within a sentence, the first letter is not capitalized, nor is end punctuation included within the parentheses.

Nosebleeds are common throughout childhood (see page 23 for common causes). You can usually stop a nose from bleeding by squeezing the soft part of the nose against the center wall. However, if the bleeding does not stop after you have applied pressure for twenty minutes, you should call your pediatrician.

If a complete sentence enclosed in parentheses is separate from other sentences, the first letter of the sentence is capitalized, and end punctuation is used.

Nosebleeds are common throughout childhood. (See page 23 for common causes.) You can usually stop a nose from bleeding by squeezing the soft part of the nose against the center wall. However, if the bleeding does not stop after you have applied pressure for twenty minutes, you should call your pediatrician.

. Period

To mark the end of a sentence A period signals the end of a sentence.

Both teachers and students attended the forum.

Be prepared to explain your answers.

Be careful not to use a period at the end of a phrase or clause. Although occasional sentence fragments may be effective, their use is generally discouraged in academic contexts. (See pages 717–718 and 719 for more information on sentence fragments.)

After initials and some abbreviations A period, followed by a space, is used after each initial in a person's name.

A. A. Milne   B. B. King

Some abbreviations commonly include periods, regardless of which style manual you refer to.

Mr.   Mrs.   Ms.   Dr.

et al.   e.g.   i.e.   etc.   a.m.   p.m.

Other types of abbreviations, such as those created by the U.S. Postal Service for the names of states, do not include periods (see page 722). MLA and CMS now recommend omitting periods from abbreviations such as *MA, PhD,* and *MD.*

?   Question mark

At the end of a direct question A question mark is used at the end of a direct question—that is, one that is not embedded in a statement.

Who will present the report?

A question that is embedded within a statement does not require a question mark.

Everyone wondered when the war would end.

In quotations A question mark is placed within quotation marks unless it does not belong with the quoted material.

He asked simply, "Why are we here?"

When the question mark is not part of the quoted material, it is placed outside the quotation marks.

Do you agree with James Surowiecki's claim that "collective intelligence relies on a certain degree of innocence"?

" "   Quotation marks

For direct quotations Double quotation marks appear before and after a direct quotation—the exact words from a source.

I remember my teacher saying, "Be good to your sentences, and they will be good to you."

According to the research reported by Natalie Angier, "There is a reason children are perpetually yearning for the flour-dusted, mythical figure called grandma or granny or oma or abuelita."

See pages 554–555 for information on capitalizing within direct quotations.

For titles of short works Quotation marks are used around titles of short works, such as essays, short stories, articles, short poems, songs, and episodes in a television series. Short works usually appear within larger works—a poem in a collection of poems, an article in a magazine.

> In "It's Easy Being Green," Bill McKibben argues that politicians should be encouraging the car industry to develop and produce more hybrid electric cars.

> "Outlaws" is just one of several episodes of *Lost* that rely on flashback techniques. [Note that the name of the program is italicized or underlined.]

For special uses of words or phrases Quotation marks around a word or phrase signal that the word is being used in an unusual way—ironically or informally, for example. Quotation marks used for such a purpose are often called **scare quotes.**

> His "health kick" consisted of eating cereal instead of doughnuts for breakfast.

Notice the change in intonation of words or phrases placed between quotation marks. Overuse of scare quotes distracts readers because it results in constant and abrupt changes in intonation and because it suggests that the writer has not put enough effort into finding more suitable words or phrases.

WAIT A MINUTE . . .

You may be wondering about single quotation marks. CMS, MLA, and APA recommend not using single quotation marks around words or phrases used in special ways. However, you should use single quotation marks when a word or phrase in a passage you are quoting was placed between double quotation marks by the original author.

> According to the author, some work "the 'optimizers' do is reasonable."

; Semicolon

To connect independent clauses A semicolon is used to link two independent clauses that are not already connected by a coordinating conjunction (*and, but, or, yet, so, nor,* or *for*).

> Sweet basil is essential in many Mediterranean foods; Thai basil is equally important in many Asian and East Indian recipes.

With transitional words and phrases A semicolon is often accompanied by a transitional word or phrase to establish a specific type of connection between ideas. For example, *however* and *on the contrary* signal contrast, and *thus* and *as a result* signal consequence.

> Rap music was once considered a fad; however, it has now lasted over twenty years.

> I just found out that funding is not forthcoming; as a result, we will have to postpone the project.

The following are common transitional words and phrases:

however	therefore	thus	then
instead	also	besides	as a result
at any rate	for example	for instance	in addition
in fact	in other words	on the contrary	

When these words and phrases are placed within a clause, a semicolon is not used. They are set off by two commas instead.

Voter registration, however, has been above normal.

WAIT A MINUTE . . .

Most transitional words and phrases are followed by a comma. However, the comma may be omitted after a transitional word such as *thus* or *then* when no pause is desired and no risk of misreading exists.

Turn right at the corner; then go straight for six miles.

To separate items in a series that contain commas A semicolon separates items in a series that also contain commas.

The student teacher focused on the bottom half of the food pyramid, including the vegetable group; the fruit group; and the bread, cereal, rice, and pasta group.

/ Slash

To signal alternatives A slash between two words indicates that either is acceptable.

Sometimes oppositions such as good/evil and right/wrong are hard to distinguish.

Slashes are rarely used in formal writing, especially when the word *or* would suffice.

The form must be signed by the patient or a guardian.

To indicate line breaks in quoted poetry A slash with a space on either side is used to indicate line breaks in poetry quoted within a sentence.

A secret message is introduced in the first lines of Tess Gallagher's "Under Stars": "The sleep of this night deepens / because I have walked coatless from the house / carrying the white envelope."

The following excerpt consists of just one sentence. Circle, or highlight, all punctuation marks in the sentence and explain their functions.

> If you sit on the periphery of a group of men telling jokes and you listen for a while and laugh appropriately and don't thrust yourself into the group but wait an appropriate length of time until there is a lull and then offer your joke and if it's a joke that is new to them and if you tell it well and don't flounder around in the setup, the crucial part of the joke, but tell it cleanly and simply with no missteps and not too much topspin, remembering this is Minnesota and we like it dry, no wheezing and chortling, and then you get to the elaboration where you can embroider a little and draw it out, if they're in the mood, and you do this gracefully, not overselling the joke, read your audience and just when they're ready for it you feed them the fat part, and then the punch line, and not laugh at the joke yourself until they do—then you'll be welcome here.
>
> —**Garrison Keillor,** *A Prairie Home Companion Pretty Good Joke Book*

Circle, or highlight, all punctuation marks in the following passage and explain their functions.

> The founding fathers of modern environmentalism, Henry David Thoreau and John Muir, promised "that in wildness is the preservation of the world." The presumption was that the wilderness was out there, somewhere, in the western heart of America, awaiting discovery, and that it would be the antidote for the poisons of industrial society. But of course the healing wilderness was as much the product of culture's craving and culture's framing as any other imagined garden. Take the first and most famous American Eden: Yosemite. Though the parking is almost as big as the park and there are bears rooting among the McDonald's cartons, we still imagine Yosemite the way Albert Bierstadt painted it or Carleton Watkins and Ansel Adams photographed it: with no trace of human presence. But of course the very act of identifying (not to mention photographing) the place presupposes our presence, and along with us all the heavy cultural backpacks that we lug with us on the trail.   —**Simon Schama,** *Landscape and Memory*

Find two passages that consist of no more than 250 words each and were written in response to widely different rhetorical situations. Circle, or highlight, every punctuation mark; then count the number of times each punctuation mark is used in each passage. Discuss your findings in terms of the rhetorical situation within which each author was writing.

Punctuation Trouble Spots

For most of the rhetorical situations you'll respond to, you'll be expected to use complete, accurately punctuated sentences. Incorrect punctuation of sentences often results in one of these common errors: a sentence fragment, a comma splice, or a fused sentence. When you edit your writing, check to make sure you have not made these typical mistakes. You may be able to help yourself notice these errors by reading your work aloud or having someone else read it aloud to you. Other helpful hints for finding trouble spots and making effective revisions are described in the following subsections.

Sentence fragments

A **sentence fragment** is only a piece of a sentence. It is missing either a complete subject, a complete predicate, or both. Phrases are often mispunctuated as complete sentences.

Prepositional phrase:	They live in northeastern Iowa. ~~Near~~ the Mississippi River. *(, near)*
Verbal phrase:	The fullback scored the final points. ~~Twisting~~ past and leaping over would-be tacklers to reach the goal line. *(, twisting)*
Appositive phrase:	The discussion bounced between two topics. ~~How~~ to increase the amount of oil available and how to avoid damaging the environment. *(: how)*

Mispunctuated dependent clauses are also sentence fragments.

Adverbial clause:	New buildings were continually constructed. ~~While~~ old buildings sat empty. *(, while)*
Adjectival clause:	The library changed its lending policy in January. ~~Which~~ resulted in much confusion at the end of the term. *(, which)*

Sentence fragments can be revised by either joining the fragment to an adjacent sentence, as above, or making it a complete sentence. When you recast a sentence fragment as a full sentence, you elevate the importance of the information it conveys.

The library changed its lending policy in January. This change resulted in much confusion at the end of the term.

In most academic rhetorical situations, sentence fragments are not appropriate. However, when a rhetorical situation calls for an intimate or playful tone, sentence fragments can be used judiciously to emphasize ideas, add surprise, or improve the rhythm of a paragraph.

My pity for Mrs. Cullinan preceded me the next morning like the Cheshire cat's smile. Those girls, who could have been her daughters, were beautiful. They didn't have to straighten their hair. Even when they were caught in the rain, their braids still hung down straight like tamed snakes. Their mouths were pouty little cupid's bows. Mrs. Cullinan didn't know what she missed. Or maybe she did. *Poor Mrs. Cullinan.* —Maya Angelou, "Finishing School"

See page 719 for help in determining whether you have written a sentence fragment.

Comma splices

A **comma splice**, or **comma fault**, is the incorrect use of a comma between two independent clauses. This problem can be corrected either by including a coordinating conjunction (usually *and* or *but*) or by using a stronger mark of punctuation, such as a period or a semicolon.

> *but*
> Color filters can reduce the atmospheric haze in a photograph, ʌ they can also increase it.

> Many millennia ago, human groups started evolving into complex societies, most of these groups settled in villages.

Comma splices often occur in the following situations:

- The second independent clause begins with a transition word or phrase, such as *however* or *for example*.

    > All nurses care for patients, however their responsibilities and working conditions vary according to the shift they work.

- The second independent clause provides an explanation or an example.

    > *. My*
    > I became obsessive about programming, my desire to be at the computer blocked out all other concerns.

- The second independent clause presents an alternative, usually negative.

    > A written argument is an opportunity to explore various perspectives and
    > *. It*
    > reach an informed position, it is not just a quarrel.

- The second independent clause begins with a pronoun whose antecedent is in the first clause.

    > *but*
    > Earth's atmosphere lets light in, ʌ it also keeps dangerous levels of ultraviolet light out.

Although they sometimes appear in pieces of fiction, comma splices are not used in most academic contexts. See page 720 for help in determining whether you have written a comma splice.

Fused sentences

A **fused sentence**, also called a **run-on sentence**, is actually two sentences (independent clauses) joined together without adequate punctuation. This type of problem can be corrected by adding appropriate punctuation and any necessary connecting words.

>   *. First,*
> They spent a great deal of time socializing their puppy ˄ they held "people-puppy
>   *later*
> parties" and ˄ "puppy-puppy parties."

Fused sentences occur in the same situations that comma splices do.

▌ The second independent clause begins with a transition word or phrase, such as *however* or *for example*.

>   Some historians claim that Andrew Carnegie was a benevolent
>   *;*   *,*
> philanthropist ˄ however ˄ others consider him a pitiless taskmaster.

▌ The second independent clause provides an explanation or an example.

>   *. Light*
> Myopia is a condition of the eye that results in blurry vision ˄ light rays entering the eye come together in front of the retina.

▌ The second independent clause presents an alternative.

>   *. It*
> The vote was not just an instance of majority rule ˄ it was an act of tyranny.

▌ The second independent clause begins with a pronoun whose antecedent is in the first clause.

>   *. They*
> Some people expect others to solve their problems ˄ they ignore their own responsibility to come up with a solution.

The following box can help you determine whether you have written a fused sentence.

WAIT A MINUTE . . .

If you suspect that you have written a sentence fragment, comma splice, or fused sentence but you are not sure, try placing the words in the following test-sentence frame.

They do not understand the idea that _____.

Sentence Fragment

A complete sentence will make sense when embedded in the test-sentence frame because it is an independent clause.

Test sentence fails: They do not understand the idea that <u>near the Mississippi River</u> (The underlined phrase is a sentence fragment.)

Test sentence succeeds: They do not understand the idea that <u>the town is located in northeastern Iowa, near the Mississippi River.</u> (This independent clause fits into the test-sentence frame and therefore could be written as a sentence.)

continued

Comma Splice

A comma splice will not make sense when embedded in the test-sentence frame because the second independent clause will sound tacked on.

Test sentence fails: They do not understand the idea that <u>Earth's atmosphere lets light in, it also keeps dangerous levels of ultraviolet light out.</u> (The underlined test sentence is a comma splice. The second clause sounds tacked on.)

Test sentence succeeds: They do not understand the idea that <u>Earth's atmosphere lets light in but also keeps dangerous levels of ultraviolet light out.</u> (The test sentence fits into the frame and therefore could be written as a sentence.)

Fused Sentence

A fused sentence will not make sense when embedded in the test-sentence frame because it will sound muddled. The boundary between the two independent clauses will be indistinct.

Test sentence fails: They do not understand the idea that <u>myopia is a condition of the eye that results in blurry vision light rays entering the eye come together in front of the retina.</u> (The underlined test sentence is a fused sentence. It is difficult to determine the boundary between the two independent clauses.)

Test sentence succeeds: They do not understand the idea that <u>myopia makes vision blurry because light rays entering the eye come together in front of the retina.</u> (The test sentence fits into the frame and therefore could be written as its own sentence.)

EXERCISE 25.7

Identify sentence fragments in an essay in this book (or in one assigned by your instructor) and explain their rhetorical effects.

EXERCISE 25.8

Find two or three advertisements that include sentence fragments and explain their rhetorical effects.

EXERCISE 25.9

Look for comma splices in the following excerpt from a novel. Why do you think writers of fiction sometimes use comma splices, while writers of academic prose generally do not?

> [1]When she didn't show up for several days on end to play the organ, it was known that Ms. DeWitt was suffering from nerves again. [2]Incrementally, tortuously, unnecessarily, she was unblessed by tiny fragments of memory. [3]Berndt materialized, cruelly, touch by touch, until he was all there but not there. [4]A word and a look, a moment they had spent together, had apparently entered the heart of Agnes to be kept sealed and safe until, for no particular reason, she was to be tormented by an elusive recovery. [5]She shut herself away. [6]Some people grieve by holding fast to the love of others, some by rejecting all companionship. [7]Some grieve with tears and some with dry howls. [8]Some grieve like water, some burn. [9]Some are fuel for the fire of sorrow and some are stone. [10]Agnes was pure slate, dark and impenetrable.
>
> —**Louise Erdrich,** *The Last Report on the Miracles at Little No Horse*

EXERCISE 25.10

Revise all fragments, comma splices, and fused sentences in the following paragraph. Change the wording, if necessary.

> [1]Traditionally an instrument used to accompany a vocalist. [2]The guitar has a humble origin. [3]Once plugged in, though, it gained center stage. [4]Along with the person playing it. [5]Any fan of jazz, blues, or rock can state an all-time favorite guitar player when I asked my office mates which guitar players they revered, they mentioned Charlie Christian, B. B. King, and Jimi Hendrix. [6]Without even pausing to consider my question. [7]The need for amplified guitars arose during the 1920s and 1930s when the public was listening and dancing to big-band jazz, the guitar had to match the sounds of the other, louder instruments and voices. [8]Coincidentally, a new style of guitar and guitar playing gained popularity the Hawaiian guitar, a flat guitar with six to eight strings, was played while resting in the player's lap. [9]As early as 1923, experiments were being conducted in an attempt to amplify the sound of the Hawaiian guitar however it was not until 1932 that the first electric guitar was created. [10]Built by Harry Watson and sold by the company Ro-Pat-In, the new Hawaiian-style electric guitar was nicknamed the frying pan. [11]More than seventy years have passed since the guitar was electrified. [12]And began to electrify audiences. [13]It has evolved tremendously since its conception. [14]Even influencing the kinds of music it is used to produce.

Guide to Mechanics

The conventions listed here are based on those presented in *The Chicago Manual of Style* (CMS), fifteenth edition. MLA or APA conventions that differ from those of CMS are mentioned.

Abbreviations, acronyms, and initialisms

Standard abbreviations An **abbreviation** is the shortened form of a word or phrase. Some abbreviations are acceptable in both formal and informal writing:

Mr. Mrs. Ms. Dr. Jr. Sr. a.m. p.m.

Correspondence abbreviations Words such as *Street, Road,* and *Corporation* are written out when they appear in sentences, but they are usually abbreviated when used in addresses on envelopes.

Sentence: Ben & Jerry's Foundation is located on Community Drive in South Burlington, Vermont.

Address: Ben & Jerry's Foundation

30 Community Dr.

S. Burlington, VT 05403

When addressing correspondence within the United States, use the abbreviations designated by the U.S. Postal Service for the names of the states. (No period follows these abbreviations.)

Documentation abbreviations *The Chicago Manual of Style,* the *MLA Handbook for Writers of Research Papers,* and the *Publication Manual of the American Psychological Association* all mention specific abbreviations to use in citations and bibliographies. Abbreviations common to all styles include the following:

anon.	anonymous
c.	circa, about (for example, c. 1840)
ch., chs.	chapter, chapters
fig.	figure
illus.	illustrated by, illustrator, illustration
intl.	international
ms., mss.	manuscript, manuscripts
natl.	national
n.d.	no date
n.p.	no page number
p., pp.	page, pages
trans.	translation, translated by
vol., vols.	volume, volumes
Jan.	January
Feb.	February
Mar.	March
Apr.	April
Aug.	August
Sept.	September
Oct.	October
Nov.	November
Dec.	December

cf. compare

e.g. for example

et al. and others

etc. and so forth, and others of the same kind

i.e. that is

v., vs. versus

Abbreviations of people's names When first and middle names are abbreviated as initials, they should be followed by a space.

 E. B. White J. R. R. Tolkien H. G. Wells

Acronyms An **acronym** is a shortened form of a name pronounced as a word. It is formed from the first letters or successive parts of words in a multiword name. Each letter is a capital, and no periods are required.

  AIDS acquired immunodeficiency syndrome
  NASA National Aeronautics and Space Administration
  NATO North Atlantic Treaty Organization
  OSHA Occupational Safety and Health Administration
  SWAT special weapons and tactics

The words an acronym stands for should be spelled out the first time the entity is mentioned; the acronym should follow in parentheses. This convention ensures that readers unfamiliar with the acronym will understand the reference.

 The Federal Emergency Management Administration (FEMA) issued revised
 evacuation guidelines for coastal cities.

Initialisms An initialism is similar to an acronym in that each letter is a capital. However, unlike the letters constituting acronyms, the letters of initialisms are pronounced individually.

  CIA Central Intelligence Agency
  FBI Federal Bureau of Investigation
  UN United Nations
  SUV sport-utility vehicle

The first time an initialism is used, the words it stands for should be spelled out.

Capitalization

Proper nouns All proper nouns are capitalized.

Buildings, bridges, monuments	Empire State Building, Golden Gate Bridge, World War II Memorial
Course titles	History of the Civil War
	[BUT history, the general subject]
Days, months, holidays	Monday, May, Memorial Day
	[NOT the names of the seasons: fall, winter, spring, summer]
Ethnic groups and languages	Latinos/Latinas, Spanish, Chinese
Geographical names	North America, Canada, Minnesota, Boston, Interstate 90, the Southwest, Lake Michigan, the Mississippi River, Central Park
	[NOT a direction, as in south of the park]
Historical documents, events, movements, and periods	Declaration of Independence, Allentown Fair, Renaissance, Stone Age
Military terms	Eighth Air Force, United States Army, Gulf War, Battle of the Bulge, Silver Star
	[NOT general military terms: the air force, the army, the war, the battle]
Names of people	Rosa Vargas, Dr. Lee, Alexander the Great
Organizations, agencies, companies, institutions	National Endowment for the Arts, Internal Revenue Service, Ford Motor Company, Yakima Valley Community College
	[BUT a university in New York]
Religious terms	Buddha, God, Allah, Yahweh, Buddhism, Christianity, Islam, Judaism, Buddhist, Christian, Muslim, Jew, Sutras, Bible, Koran, Talmud
	[NOT adjectives, such as biblical, talmudic]
Trade names	Nike, Oscar Mayer, Chevrolet

Earth, sun, and moon Except in technical contexts, the words *earth, sun,* and *moon* are not capitalized.

The earth, the sun, and the moon appear in many myths.

The Sun contains more than 99.8 percent of the total mass of the Solar System.

Words derived from names and trade names Adjectives and verbs that are derived from names of people or places are capitalized.

Whitmanesque   Americanize

Trade names are capitalized unless such a name has become the term for a general class of objects or ideas, such as *zipper* (which was originally a trademark).

Words used as names or proper nouns When words are used as names or parts of names, they are capitalized.

Mom   Uncle Tom   Senator Wellston   Professor Brown

WAIT A MINUTE . . .

Sometimes words such as *mom* and *dad* are capitalized, and sometimes they are not. The key to knowing when to use an uppercase letter and when to use a lowercase letter is understanding the difference between proper nouns and common nouns. Proper nouns can be replaced by a person's actual name.

Every Saturday, Mom [Catherine] took me to the park.

Such a substitution cannot be made if the word is a common noun.

Every Saturday, my mom [NOT my Catherine] took me to the park.

Titles of literary and artistic works All major words in titles and subtitles of literary and artistic works mentioned within a text are capitalized. Minor words, unless they are the first or last word in the title, are not. Minor words include articles (*a, an,* and *the*), coordinating conjunctions (see pages 689–690), prepositions (see pages 635–637), and the infinitive marker *to*.

Reading Lolita *in Tehran*

The Return of the King

"Once More to the Lake"

APA style for capitalizing titles of works differs. According to APA style, any word of four or more letters should be capitalized.

All words in a hyphenated compound are capitalized unless they are minor words such as prepositions and conjunctions.

"The Texas-Mexico Border"

"Touch-and-Go Decisions"

WAIT A MINUTE . . .

You'll sometimes notice that the title of a source has only the first word capitalized. Titles found in databases are often listed this way.

A meeting of minds

Nonetheless, if you use such a source in your paper, you should capitalize all major words.

The authors of "A Meeting of Minds" discussed cross-cultural similarities.

First words of sentences The first word of every sentence, and of every complete quoted sentence, is capitalized.

> Based on his experience as a cub reporter, James Alexander Thom asserts, "Human suffering has become a spectator sport."

Words related to the Internet Some words connected with the Internet are considered proper nouns and are thus capitalized.

> Internet   World Wide Web   Web site   Web address

Italics

The use of italics lets readers know that a word or a group of words is being used in a special way. CMS, APA, and MLA allow the use of italics. However, in handwritten or typewritten documents, underlining can be used instead of italics. On the Internet, underlining often indicates a hyperlink. In e-mail messages that cannot include italicized words, an underscore should be placed before and after words normally italicized.

> _The Novel of the Future_ was published in 1968.

For emphasis Italics indicate that a word is being given extra stress.

> She *is* our only hope.

Italics can also emphasize emotional content.

> We have to act *now*.

Italicized words should be used sparingly; otherwise, they will lose their impact.

Foreign words Italics indicate foreign words.

> I respect and serve my parents, prepare food for the family, eat rice and stew, *Iyan* and *Eba* with *egusi* stew.   —**Omotayo Banjo,** "Under My Skin"

Latin words used to identify genus and species are also italicized. The genus name is capitalized.

> *Stenella frontalis* (Atlantic spotted dolphin)
>
> *Raphus cucullatus* (dodo)

Legal cases The names of legal cases are italicized.

> *Roe v. Wade*   *Brown v. Board of Education*   *Miranda v. Arizona*

The shortened name of a well-known legal case is also italicized.

> The *Miranda* decision gave criminal suspects the right to remain silent and the right to legal advice.

Names of transporting vehicles The names of ships, submarines, aircraft, spacecraft, and satellites are italicized.

Titanic   USS *Hawkbill*   *Spirit of St. Louis*   *Atlantis*

However, the names of trains and the trade names of aircraft are not italicized.

Orient Express   Boeing 747   Concorde

Titles Works published or produced as a whole rather than as a part of a larger work are italicized. Thus, the name of a newspaper is italicized, but the title of an editorial is not. The titles of the following types of works are italicized.

Book	*Cold Mountain*
Magazine	*Wired*
Newspaper	*Wall Street Journal*
Play or film	*Monster*
Television or radio program	*American Idol*
Music recording	*Kind of Blue*
Work of art	*The Thinker*
Long poem	*Paradise Lost*
Pamphlet	*Saving Energy*
Comic strip	*Doonesbury*

When one title is embedded in another title, the embedded title is not italicized.

The main character in *The Making of* Kind of Blue is a young bass player.

Words, letters, or numbers referred to as such A word, letter, or number is italicized when it represents the word, letter, or number itself.

The *k* in words such as *knight* and *knock* was pronounced in Old English.

Who decided that the number *911* should be used for emergencies?

Numbers

For general purposes, numbers from one through one hundred are spelled out.

forty-five points   sixty-two pages

If the words *thousand, million,* or *billion* follow whole numbers from one through one hundred, the numbers should still be spelled out. For any other number, a numeral is used unless the number begins a sentence.

They earned 145 extra points.

According to APA style, words should be used only for numbers below ten.

Addresses The numbers in addresses do not need to be spelled out.

> For years, they lived at 25 East 45th Street.

Dates and times of day Numbers are used to indicate dates and times of day.

> The meeting is scheduled for 9:00 a.m. on June 7, 2007.

Except for specific years, dates and times may be spelled out.

> 3 p.m.   OR   three o'clock in the afternoon
>
> the first of March   OR   March 1
>
> the sixties   OR   the 1960s

Decimals and percentages Decimals and percentages are expressed in numbers.

> a 3.0 grade point average   80 percent

Identification numbers Numbers are used for identification of specific people and places.

> Henry IV   Interstate 90   Room 415

Large fractional numbers Large fractional numbers can be expressed numerically.

> 3.5 billion years   2.3 million inhabitants

Monetary amounts When monetary amounts are frequently mentioned, they can be written as numbers. However, if they are mentioned only rarely, they should be spelled out.

> $6,000   OR   six thousand dollars

Page numbers and divisions in books and plays Numerals are used for page numbers and for book or play divisions.

> page 82   chapter 16   act 1, scene 2   OR   Act II, Scene I

EXERCISE 25.11

Underline or highlight seven different uses of capital letters, italics, abbreviations, acronyms, or numbers in an essay in this book (or in one assigned by your instructor). Explain their functions.

EXERCISE 25.12

Describe the functions of capitalization and italics in an essay in this book (or in one assigned by your instructor). Are any of these uses unconventional? If so, are they still effective?

EXERCISE 25.13

Edit the following paragraph so that it follows the conventions for academic writing.

[1]On october first, nineteen fifty-eight, congress and president eisenhower created the national aeronautics and space administration (nasa). [2]The creation of nasa was related to national defense. [3]After world war two, political tensions and rivalry divided the united states and the soviet union. [4]Although no full-scale battles occurred, the friction was so intense that this period was called the cold war. [5]space exploration became a major arena for competition. [6]When the soviets launched sputnik one, americans feared that they were at a technological disadvantage and immediately directed more effort and funding to space exploration. [7]Nasa began its operation with 8,000 employees and an annual budget of $100,000,000. [8]Within months of its conception, nasa conducted space missions. [9]By the time it was 20 years old, apollo eleven had been launched, and a human being had actually walked on the moon.

EXERCISE 25.14

In an essay you have written recently, circle and number all capital letters, abbreviations, acronyms, initialisms, numbers, and italicized words. Identify the mechanics conventions covered in this chapter that you followed.

As the overview of part 5 explains, Standardized English is the stylistic option you'll most often choose when working in an academic context. This glossary presents many of those standardized usages and spellings, as well as usages and spellings considered to be conversational (or informal) and even unconventional (or nonstandardized). Using the information in this glossary, you'll be able to make informed decisions about the words you use.

The following labels will help you choose appropriate words for your rhetorical situation.

Conventional Words or phrases listed in dictionaries without special usage labels; generally considered appropriate in academic and professional writing.

Conversational Words or phrases that dictionaries label *informal, slang,* or *colloquial;* although often used in informal speech and writing, not generally appropriate for formal writing assignments.

Unconventional Words or phrases not generally considered appropriate in academic or professional writing and often labeled *nonstandard* in dictionaries; best avoided in formal contexts.

a half a, a half an Unconventional; instead use *half a, half an,* or *a half:* He commutes **a half an** hour to work.

a lot of A conversational expression for *many, much,* or *a great deal of:* **A lot of** Many people attended the concert. *A lot* is spelled as two words.

a while, awhile *A while* means "a period of time" and most frequently follows the preposition *after, for,* or *in:* They stopped for **a while.** *Awhile* means "a short time." It is not used after a preposition: We rested **awhile.**

accept, except *Accept* is a verb meaning "to receive": He will **accept** the offer. *Except* can be a verb meaning "to exclude": Her criminal record will **except** her from consideration for this job. However, *except* is more commonly used as a preposition meaning "other than": No one knew **except** us. Other forms: *acceptable, acceptance; exception*

adapt, adopt *Adapt* means "to adjust or change": He will **adapt** to the new climate. Adopt means "to take as one's own": The board of directors will **adopt** a new policy. Other forms: *adaptable, adaptation; adoption*

adverse, averse *Adverse* means "unfavorable": The storm had **adverse** effects on the county's economy. Usually followed by *to, averse* means "reluctant" or "opposed": They are not **averse** to negotiating a compromise. Other forms: *adversity; aversion*

advice, advise *Advice* is a noun: They asked an expert for **advice.** *Advise* is a verb: He should be able to **advise** us.

affect, effect *Affect* is a verb that means either "to influence" or "to touch the emotions": The threatened strike did not **affect** the company's decision to keep the factory open. The news **affected** us deeply. Psychologists use *affect* as a noun (with the stress on the first syllable) meaning "emotional expression": She noted the patient's lack of **affect.** As a noun, *effect* means "a result": Maren discussed the **effects** of secondhand smoke. When used as a verb, *effect* means "to bring about": They hoped to **effect** real political change. Other forms: *affective; effective*

agree on, agree to, agree with *Agree on* means "to be in accord with others about something": We **agreed on** the arrangments. *Agree to* means "to accept something" or "to consent to do something": They **agreed to** our terms. They **agreed to** discuss the matter. *Agree with* means "to share an opinion with someone" or "to approve of something": Everyone **agreed with** the chair of the committee. No one **agreed with** my position.

all ready, already *All ready* means "completely prepared": The documents are **all ready** for the meeting. *Already* means "by or before a specified time": We have **already** submitted our final report.

all right Two of the most common meanings of *all right* are "permissible" and "safe." They asked whether it was **all right** to arrive a few minutes late. Everyone in the accident was **all right.** The spelling *alright* is not a generally accepted alternative for *all right,* although it is frequently used in popular writing.

all together, altogether *All together* means "as a group": We sang **all together.** *Altogether* means "wholly, thoroughly": This song is **altogether** too difficult to play.

allude, elude *Allude* means "to refer to indirectly": She **alluded** to the poetry of Elizabeth Bishop. *Elude* means "to evade" or "to escape from": For months, the solution **eluded** the researchers.

allusion, illusion *Allusion* means "a casual or indirect reference": Her **allusion** was to Elizabeth Bishop's poetry. *Illusion* means "a false idea or an unreal image": The magician's trick was based on **illusion.**

among, between According to traditional usage, *among* is used when three or more individuals or entities are discussed: He must choose **among** several good job offers. *Between* is used when referring to only two entities: We studied the differences **between** the two proposals. Current dictionaries also mention the use of *between* to refer to more than two entities when the relationships between these entities are considered distinct: Connections **between** the four coastal communities were restored.

amoral, immoral *Amoral* means "not caring about right or wrong": The prosecutor in the case accused the defendent of **amoral** acts of random violence. *Immoral* means "not moral": Students discussed whether abortion should be considered **immoral.** Other forms: *amorality; immorality*

amount of, number of Use *amount of* before nouns that cannot be counted: The **amount of** rain that fell last year was insufficient. Use *number of* with nouns that can be counted: The **number of** students attending college has increased. *A number of* means "many" and thus takes a plural verb: **A number of** opportunities **are** listed. *The number of* takes a singular verb: **The number of** opportunities available to students **is** rising.

angry at, angry with *Angry* is commonly followed by either *at* or *with,* although according to traditional usage, *with* should be used when the cause of the anger is a person: She was **angry at** the school for denying her admission. He was **angry with** me because I corrected him in public.

anxious, eager *Anxious,* related to *anxiety,* means "worried" or "nervous": They are **anxious** about the test results. *Eager* means "keenly interested" or "desirous": We were **eager** to find a compromise. Current dictionaries report that *anxious* is often used as a synonym for *eager,* but such usage is still considered conversational.

anymore, any more *Anymore* means "any longer" or "now" and most frequently occurs in questions or nega-

tive sentences: We do not carry that product **anymore.** Its use in positive sentences is considered conversational; *now* is generally used instead: All they do **anymore** **now** is fight. *Any more* means "additional": Do you need **any more** help?

anyone, any one *Anyone* means "anybody": I did not see **anyone** familiar. *Any one* means "one from a group": **Any one** of them will suffice.

anyplace, everyplace, someplace As synonyms for *anywhere, everywhere,* and *somewhere,* these words are considered informal.

as, like According to traditional usage, *as,* not *like,* should begin a clause: Her son talked **like** **as** she did. When used as a preposition, *like* can introduce a phrase: He looks **like** his father. That scarf feels **like** silk.

as regards See **regard, regarding, regards.**

assure, ensure, insure *Assure* means "to state with confidence": He **assured** us that the neighborhood was safe. *Ensure* and *insure* can often be interchanged to mean "to make certain," but only *insure* means "to protect against loss": The researcher **ensured** [OR **insured**] the accuracy of the test results. Homeowners **insure** their houses and furnishings.

averse See **adverse, averse.**

awhile See **a while, awhile.**

bad Unconventional as an adverb; use *badly* instead: Some fans behaved **bad** **badly** during the game. However, as an adjective, *bad* can be used after sensory verbs (*feel, look, sound, smell,* and *taste*): I felt **bad** that I could not attend her recital.

being as, being that Unconventional; use *because* instead: **Being as** **Because** it was Sunday, many of the stores were closed.

better, had better *Better* is conversational. Use *had better* instead: They **better** **had better** buy their tickets tomorrow.

between See **among, between.**

breath, breathe *Breath* is a noun: I was out of **breath.** *Breathe* is a verb: It was hard to **breathe.**

bunch Conversational to refer to a group: A **bunch** **group** of students gathered in front of the student union.

busted Unconventional. Use *broken* instead: The printer was **busted** **broken,** so none of us had our papers ready on time.

can, may According to traditional definitions, *can* refers to ability, and *may* refers to permission: He **can** read music. You **may** not read the newspaper during class. According to current dictionaries, *can* and *may* are sometimes used interchangeably to denote permission, though *may* is generally preferred in formal contexts.

can't hardly, can't scarcely Both are examples of a double negative, used in some regions of the United States but unconventional. Use *can hardly* or *can scarcely* instead: I **can't hardly** believe it happened.

capital, capitol, Capitol A *capital* is a governing city; it also means "funds": The **capital** of California is Sacramento. They invested a large amount of **capital** in the organization. As an adjective, *capital* means "chief" or "principal": This year's election is of **capital** importance. It may also refer to the death penalty: In some countries, espionage is a **capital** offence. A *capitol* is a statehouse; the *Capitol* is the U.S. congressional building in Washington, DC.

censor, censure, sensor As a verb, *censor* means "to remove or suppress material that is deemed objectionable or classified": In some countries, the government **censors** the news. As a noun, *censor* refers to a person authorized to remove material considered objectionable or classified: The **censor** cleared the report. The verb *censure* means "to blame or criticize": The committee **censured** her. The noun *censure* is an expression of disapproval or blame: She received a **censure** from the committee. A *sensor* is a device that responds to a stimulus: The motion **sensor** detected an approaching car.

center on, center around *Center around* is conversational. Use *center on* or *revolve around* for formal occasions. The critic's comments **centered around** on health care.

cite, sight, site *Cite* means "to mention": She could easily **cite** several examples of altruism. *Sight,* as a verb, means "to see": The crew **sighted** land. As a noun, *sight* refers to a view: We had never seen such a **sight!** *Site,* as a verb, means "to situate": They **sited** their new house near the river. As a noun, *site* means "a location": The **site** for the new library was approved. Other forms: *citation, citing; sighting.*

climactic, climatic *Climactic* refers to a high point (a climax): The film's **climactic** scene riveted the viewers to their seats. *Climatic* refers to the climate: Global warming is creating **climatic** changes.

coarse, course *Coarse* means "rough" or "ill-mannered": Several people objected to his **coarse** language. A *course* is "a route" or "a plan of study": Because of the bad weather, we had to alter our **course.** She must take a **course** in anatomy. *Course* is used in the expression *of course.*

compare to, compare with *Compare to* means "to consider as similar": The film critic **compared** the actor **to** Humphrey Bogart. *Compare with* means "to examine to

discover similarities or differences": He **compared** early morning traffic patterns **with** late afternoon ones.

complement, compliment *Complement* means "to balance" or "to complete": Their voices **complement** each other. *Compliment* means "to express praise": After the reading, several people **complimented** the author. Other forms: *complementary* (they have **complementary** personalities); *complimentary* (her remarks were **complimentary**). *Complimentary* may also mean "provided free of charge": I received two **complimentary** books.

compose, comprise *Compose* means "to form by putting together": The panel is **composed** of several experts. *Comprise* means "to consist of": The course package **comprises** a textbook, a workbook, and a CD-ROM.

conscience, conscientious, conscious, consciousness *Conscience* means "a sense of right and wrong": His questionable actions weighed on his **conscience.** *Conscientious* means "careful": She appreciated her **conscientious** research assistant. A *conscientious objector* is a person who refuses to join the military for moral reasons. *Conscious* means "awake": For a few minutes, I wasn't **conscious.** I lost **consciousness** for a few minutes. *Conscious* may also mean "aware": I was **conscious** of the risks involved in starting a new business.

consequently, subsequently *Consequently* means "as a result": They exceeded their budget and **consequently** had little to spend during the holidays. *Subsequently* means "then" or "later": He was arrested and **subsequently** convicted of fraud.

continual, continuous *Continual* means "recurring": **Continual** work stoppages delayed progress. *Continuous* means "uninterrupted": The high-pitched **continuous** noise distracted everyone. Other forms: *continually; continuously*

convince, persuade *Convince* means "to make someone believe something": She **convinced** us that she was the best candidate for the office. *Persuade* means "to motivate someone to act": They **persuaded** me to write a letter to the editor. According to current dictionaries, many speakers and writers now use *convince* as a synonym for *persuade.*

could of See *of.*

council, counsel A *council* is a committee that advises or makes decisions: The library **council** proposed a special program for children. A *counsel* is a legal adviser: The **counsel** said he would appeal the case. *Counsel* also means "advice": They sought her out for her wise

counsel. As a verb, *counsel* means "to give advice": The adviser **counsels** people considering career changes.

course See **coarse, course.**

criteria, criterion A *criterion* is "a standard": The most important **criterion** for judging the competition was originality. *Criteria* is the plural form of *criterion:* To pass, the students had to satisfy three **criteria** for the assignment.

data, datum *Datum* means "fact"; *data,* the plural form, is used more often: The **data were** difficult to interpret. Some current dictionaries note that *data* is frequently used as a mass entity (like the word *furniture*), appearing with a singular verb.

desert, dessert *Desert,* with the stress on the first syllable, is a noun meaning "a barren land": Cacti grow in the **deserts** of Arizona. As a verb, with the second syllable stressed, *desert* means "to leave": Because of his behavior, his research partners **deserted** him. *Dessert* means "something sweet eaten at the end of a meal": I ordered chocolate ice cream for **dessert.**

device, devise *Device* means "mechanism": The **device** indicates whether a runner has made a false start. *Devise* means "to create": They **devised** a new way of packaging juice.

differ from, differ with *Differ from* means "to be different": His managament style **differs from** mine. *Differ with* means "to disagree": We **differed with** each other on just one point.

different from, different than *Different from* is normally used before a noun, a pronoun, a noun phrase, or a noun clause: His technique is **different from** yours. The results were **different from** what we had predicted. *Different than* is used to introduce an adverbial clause, with *than* serving as the conjunction: The style is **different than** it was ten years ago.

discreet, discrete, discretion *Discreet* means "tactful": Because most people are sensitive to this issue, you must be **discreet.** Related to *discreet, discretion* means "caution or self-restraint": Concerned about their privacy, the donors appreciated the fundraiser's **discretion.** *Discrete* means "distinct": The course was presented as three **discrete** units.

disinterested, uninterested *Disinterested* means "neutral": Scientists are expected to be **disinterested.** *Uninterested* means "lacking interest": Knowing nothing about the sport, I was **uninterested** in the score.

distinct, distinctive *Distinct* means "well-defined" or "easily perceived": We noticed a **distinct** change in the weather. *Distinctive* means "characteristic": The **distinctive** odor of chlorine met us in the entryway to the pool.

dyeing, dying *Dyeing,* from *dye,* means "coloring something, usually by soaking it": They are **dyeing** the wool today. *Dying,* from *die,* means "losing life" or "fading": We finished our hike just as the light was **dying.**

eager See **anxious, eager.**

effect See **affect, effect.**

elicit, illicit *Elicit* means "to draw out": Her joke **elicited** an unexpected response from the audience. *Illicit* means "illegal": The police searched for **illicit** drugs.

elude See **allude, elude.**

emigrate from, immigrate to *Emigrate* means "to move from one's own country": His ancestors **emigrated from** Norway. *Immigrate* means "to move to a different country": They **immigrated to** Australia. Other forms: *emigrant; immigrant*

eminent, imminent *Eminent* means "well-known and respected": An **eminent** scientist from the University of Montana received the award. *Imminent* means "about to happen": As conditions worsened, a strike was **imminent.**

ensure See **assure, ensure, insure.**

especially, specially *Especially* means "remarkably": The summer was **especially** warm. *Especially* also means "particularly": Tourists flock to the island, **especially** during the spring and summer months. *Specially* means "for a particular purpose": The seeds were **specially** selected for this climate.

etc. Abbbreviation of *et cetera,* meaning "and others of the same kind" or "and so forth." In academic writing, it is generally used only within parentheses. Avoid using *and etc.:* A noise forecast is based on several factors (time of day noise occurs, frequency of noise, duration of noise, **and etc.**).

everyday, every day *Everyday* means "routine": They took advantage of **everyday** opportunities. *Every day* means "each day": He practiced **every day.**

everyplace See **anyplace, everyplace, someplace.**

except See **accept, except.**

explicit, implicit *Explicit* means "expressed directly": The **explicit** statement of her expectations left little room for misinterpretation. *Implicit* means "expressed indirectly": Our **implicit** agreement was to remain silent.

farther, further *Farther* usually refers to geographic distance: They drove **farther** than they had planned. *Further* indicates additional effort or time: Tomorrow they will discuss the issue **further.**

fewer, less *Fewer* is used before nouns referring to people or objects that can be counted: **fewer** students,

fewer printers. *Less* is used before noncount or abstract nouns: **less** water, **less** interest. *Less than* may be used with measurements of distance or time: **less than** ten miles, **less than** two years.

first, firstly, second, secondly Although *first* and *second* are generally preferred, current dictionaries state that *firstly* and *secondly* are well-established forms.

foreword, forward A *foreword* is a preface or introduction to a book: In the **foreword,** the author discussed his reasons for writing the book. *Forward* means "in a frontward direction": The crowd lunged **forward.**

former, latter *Former* refers to the first and *latter* refers to the second of two people or items mentioned in the previous sentence: Employees could choose between a state pension plan or a private pension plan. The majority chose the **former,** but a few believed the **latter** would provide them with more retirement income.

further See **farther, further.**

good, well Use *well* instead of *good* to modify a verb. You played ~~good~~ well today. *Good* and *well* can be used interchangeably to mean "in good health": I did not feel **well** [OR **good**] when I woke up.

had better See **better, had better.**

hanged, hung *Hanged* means "executed by hanging": They were **hanged** at dusk. *Hung* means "suspended" or "draped": She **hung** a family photo in her office.

herself, himself, myself, yourself Unconventional when not used as reflexive or intensive pronouns. Jean and ~~myself~~ I prepared the presentation. I **myself** led the discussion.

hopefully Conversational for "I hope": ~~Hopefully,~~ I hope the weather will improve.

hung See **hanged, hung.**

i.e. Abbreviation of *id est,* meaning "that is." In academic writing, it is generally used only within parentheses and is followed by a comma: Everyone donated the same amount (**i.e.,** fifty dollars). Outside of parentheses, use *that is* rather than *i.e.:* The office will be closed for the autumn holidays, **that is,** Labor Day, Columbus Day, Veterans' Day, and Thanksgiving.

illicit See **elicit, illicit.**

illusion See **allusion, illusion.**

immigrate to See **emigrate from, immigrate to.**

imminent See **eminent, imminent.**

immoral See **amoral, immoral.**

impact Considered unconventional in academic writing when used as a verb to mean "to affect": The hurricane will **impact** affect coastal residents. However, according to current dictionaries, this usage is common in business writing.

implicit See **explicit, implicit.**

imply, infer *Imply* means "to suggest indirectly": I did not mean to **imply** that you were at fault. *Infer* means "to conclude or deduce": Given his participation at the meeting, I **inferred** that he would support the proposal.

in regards to Unconventional. See **regard, regarding, regards.**

ingenious, ingenuous *Ingenious* means "creative": This **ingenious** plan will satisfy everyone. *Ingenuous* means "innocent or naive": No one knew for sure whether she was truly **ingenuous** or just shrewd.

inside of, outside of Delete *of* when unnecessary: They met **outside of** the fortress.

insure See **assure, ensure, insure.**

irregardless A double negative (*ir-* means "not" and *-less* means "not having") that is used in some regions of the United States for *regardless* but is unconventional.

its, it's *Its* indicates possession: The Republican Party concludes **its** convention today. *It's* is a contraction of *it is*: **It's** difficult to predict the outcome. Confusion over *its* and *it's* is responsible for many usage errors.

kind, sort, type Use *this* or *that* to refer to one *kind, sort,* or *type;* avoid using the word *a*: **This kind** [OR **sort** OR **type**] of **a** leader is most effective. Use *these* or *those* to refer to more than one: **These kinds** [OR **sorts** OR **types**] of leaders are most effective.

kind of, sort of Conversational to mean "somewhat": The rock-climbing course was ~~kind of~~ somewhat difficult.

later, latter *Later* means "afterward": The concert ended **later** than we had expected. *Latter* refers to the second of two people or items mentioned in the previous sentence. See also **former, latter.**

lay, lie *Lay* (*laid, laying*) means "to put" or "to place": I will **lay** the book on your desk. *Lie* (*lay, lain, lying*) means "to rest" or "to recline": She **lay** perfectly still, trying to hear what they were saying. *Lay* takes an object (to **lay** something), but *lie* does not. The present tense of *lay* and the past tense of *lie* (which is *lay*) are often confused because they are spelled the same way.

lead, led The noun *lead* is a kind of metal: The gas had **lead** added to it. The verb *lead* means "to show the way" or "to go in front": The director will **lead** the campaign. The past tense of the verb *lead* is *led*: He **led** a discussion on the origins of abstract art.

less, less than See **fewer, less.**

liable *Liable* generally means "likely" but with a negative connotation: If they do not wear the appropriate gear, they are **liable** to harm themselves. Because of her experience, she is ~~liable~~ likely to win easily.

lie See **lay, lie.**

like See **as, like.**

literally Used in conversation for emphasis. In academic writing, *literally* indicates that an expression is not being used figuratively: My friend **literally** took the cake—at least the few pieces that were left after the party.

lose, loose *Lose* means "to misplace" or "to fail to succeed": She hates to **lose** an argument. *Loose* means "unfastened" or "movable": One of the boards had come **loose.**

lots, lots of Conversational for *many* or *much:* ~~Lots of~~ Many fans traveled to see the championship game. You will have ~~lots~~ much to do this year. See also **a lot of.**

may See **can, may.**

may of, might of See **of.**

maybe, may be *Maybe* means "possibly": **Maybe** we will have better luck next year. *May* and *be* are both verbs: I **may be** late.

media, medium *Media*, the plural form of *medium*, should be followed by a plural verb. The **media** ~~is~~ are covering the event. However, current dictionaries note the frequent use of *media* as a collective noun taking a singular verb.

morale, moral *Morale* means "confidence" or "spirits": **Morale** was always high. *Moral* means "ethical": She confronted a **moral** dilemma. *Moral* may also mean "the lesson of a story": The **moral** of the story is live and let live.

myself See **herself, himself, myself, yourself.**

number of See **amount of, number of.**

of Often mistakenly used for the unstressed auxiliary verb *have:* They must ~~of~~ have [OR could **have,** might **have,** may **have,** should **have,** would **have**] left early.

OK, O.K., okay All three spellings are acceptable, but usage of any of the forms is considered conversational: The teacher gave her ~~O.K.~~ permission to the students. Did the manager **okay** agree to the expense?

outside of See **inside of, outside of.**

passed, past *Passed* is the past tense of the verb *pass:* I **passed** city hall on my way to work. *Past* means "beyond": The band marched **past** the bleachers.

persecute, prosecute *Persecute* means "to harass" or "to oppress": The group had been **persecuted** because of its religious beliefs. *Prosecute* means "to take legal action against": They decided not to **prosecute** because of insufficient evidence. Other forms: *persecution; prosecution*

perspective, prospective *Perspective* means "point of view": Our **perspectives** on the issue differ. *Prospective* means "potential": **Prospective** graduate students must take an entrance exam.

persuade See **convince, persuade.**

plus *Plus* joins nouns or noun phrases to make a sentence seem like an equation: Supreme talent **plus** rigorous training **makes** this runner hard to beat. Note that a singular form of the verb is required. Avoid using *plus* to join clauses: She takes classes Monday through Friday, ~~plus~~ and she works on weekends.

precede, proceed To *precede* is to "go before": A determiner **precedes** a noun. To *proceed* is to "go on": After a layover in Chicago, we will **proceed** to New York. Other forms: *precedence, precedent; procedure, proceedings*

prejudice, prejudiced *Prejudice* can be a noun or a verb: Because of his **prejudice,** he was unable to make a fair decision. Be aware of your own bias so that you do not **prejudice** others. *Prejudiced* is an adjective: The authorities were racially **prejudiced.**

principal, principle *Principal* is a noun meaning "head" or an adjective meaning "main": The **principal** met the students at the door. The state's **principal** crop is wheat. *Principle* is a noun meaning "standard or belief": The doctrine was derived from three moral **principles.**

proceed See **precede, proceed.**

prosecute See **persecute, prosecute.**

prospective See **perspective, prospective.**

quotation, quote In academic writing, use *quotation*, rather than *quote*, to refer to a copied sentence or passage: Her introduction included a ~~quote~~ quotation from *Rebecca*. *Quote* expresses an action: My friend likes to **quote** lines from recent movies.

raise, rise *Raise* (*raised, raising*) means "to cause to increase or move upward": The Federal Reserve Board **raised** interest rates. *Rise* (*rose, risen, rising*) means "to get up" or "to increase": Prices **rose** sharply. *Raise* takes an object (to **raise** something); *rise* does not.

regard, regarding, regards These words are used appropriately in the expressions *with regard to, as regards, in regard to,* and *regarding:* I am writing **with regard to** [OR **as regards** OR **in regard to** OR **regarding**] your purchasing my computer. (*As regarding, in regards to,* and *with regards to* are unconventional.)

respectfully, respectively *Respectfully* means "considerately": The scholars **respectfully** disagreed with each other. *Respectively* means "in that order": The diplomat introduced her to the representative, the senator, and the governor, **respectively.**

rise See **raise, rise.**

second, secondly See **first, firstly, second, secondly.**

sensor See **censor, censure, sensor.**

sensual, sensuous *Sensual* refers to physical pleasure, especially sexual pleasure or indulgence of an appetite: The band's lead singer was renowned for his **sensual** movements. *Sensuous* refers to aesthetic pleasure, for example, in response to art: She found the **sensuous** colors of the painting very soothing. Other forms: *sensuality; sensuousness.*

set See **sit, set.**

should of See **of.**

sight See **cite, sight, site.**

sit, set *Sit* means "to take a seat": The judges of the competition **sat** on the left side of the stage. *Set* means "to place" or "to establish": We **set** the date for the meeting: May 4. *Set* takes an object (to **set** something), but *sit* does not.

site See **cite, sight, site.**

so *So* emphasizes another word that is followed by a *that* clause: We arrived **so** late **that** we could not find a place to stay. Avoid using *so* without a *that* clause; find a more precise modifier instead: She was ~~so~~ spectacularly successful.

someplace See **anyplace, everyplace, someplace.**

sometime, sometimes, some time *Sometime* means "at an unspecified time": We will move **sometime** in June. *Sometimes* means "every so often": **Sometimes** the weather changes abruptly. *Some time* means "a short period": After **some time** had passed, they were able to reach a compromise.

sort See **kind, sort, type.**

sort of See **kind of, sort of.**

specially See **especially, specially.**

stationary, stationery *Stationary* means "at a standstill": The planes on the runway were **stationary** for two hours. *Stationery* means "writing paper and envelopes": He objected to the new logo on the **stationery.**

subsequently See **consequently, subsequently.**

than, then *Than* links both parts of a comparison: The game lasted longer **than** we had expected. *Then* means "after that": Read the contract closely; **then** sign it.

that, which *Which* introduces nonessential (nonrestrictive) clauses and is preceded by a comma: The world's tiniest fish, **which** is *Hippocampus denise,* was found in Indonesia. *That* generally introduces essential (restrictive clauses): He wants to develop a bar code **that** can be used to identify animals. *Which* can be used in an essential clause introduced by a preposition: The legal battle **in which** we find ourselves seems endless.

that, who In essential (restrictive) clauses, *who* is generally used to refer to people: They did not know the protestors **who** [OR **that**] organized the rally.

their, there, they're *Their* is a possessive form: **Their** donation was made anonymously. *There* refers to location: We worked **there** together. *There* can also be used as an expletive: **There** are some unanswered questions. *They're* is a contraction of *they are:* **They're** performing on Wednesday.

theirself, theirselves Unconventional for *themselves.* They discussed the topic among ~~theirselves~~ themselves.

then See **than, then.**

there See **their, there, they're.**

they're See **their, there, they're.**

thru Use *through* in academic writing: He lived ~~thru~~ through two world wars.

to, too, two *To* is a preposition, usually signaling a direction: They sent the petition **to** everyone in the neighborhood. *To* is also an infinitive marker: They planned **to** finish their work by Friday. *Too* means "also": She goes to school and works **too.** *Too* also means "excessively": We have made **too** many commitments. *Two* is a number: She moved here **two** months ago.

toward, towards *Toward* is preferred in American English.

type See **kind, sort, type.**

uninterested See **disinterested, uninterested.**

unique *Unique* means "one of a kind" and thus is not preceded by a word such as *most* or *very:* San Francisco is **very** unique. However, according to current dictionaries, *unique* is frequently used to mean "extraordinary."

weather, whether *Weather* refers to the condition of the atmosphere: The **weather** report is usually accurate. *Whether* introduces alternatives: He must decide **whether** to sell now or wait for the market to improve.

well See **good, well.**

whether See **weather, whether.**

which See **that, which.**

who, whom *Who* is the subject or subject complement of a clause: Leon Bates, ~~whom~~ who I believe has great potential, will soon be competing in international events. (*Who* is the subject of *who has great potential.*) *Whom* is used as an object: Anna Holmes, **who** whom I met at a convention three years ago, has agreed to speak to our study group. (*Whom* is the object of *I met.*) According to current dictionaries, *who* is frequently used in the object position when it does not follow a preposition. See also **that, who.**

whose, who's *Whose* is a possessive form: The procedure was developed by a researcher **whose** mother will benefit from the innovation. *Who's* is the contraction of *who is:* **Who's** responsible for writing the report?

with regards to Unconventional. See **regard, regarding, regards.**

would of See **of.**

your, you're *Your* is a possessive form: **Your** review was chosen for publication. *You're* is the contraction of *you are:* **You're** almost finished.

yourself See **herself, himself, myself, yourself.**

Appendix of Academic Writing

Essay Exams and the Rhetorical Situation

You will not always have the luxury of planning, drafting, revising, getting feedback on, and editing a piece of writing over a stretch of days or weeks. Frequently, your college instructor or your employer will ask you to produce an essay or a report during a class period or within a day or two. No matter when a deadline falls, most writers feel some pressure. But when they are asked to write quickly or on demand, that pressure intensifies. This section will help you write well when faced with the constraints of time and place that come with essay examinations.

Using exam answers to address an exigence

You can begin preparing for an essay exam by thinking of answers as responses to specific exigencies. In an exam, the exigence has been provided for you by your instructor, although you may not know immediately just how you'll proceed. A good way to begin is to skim through the questions, if the exam has more than one, to be sure you understand them. If you don't, ask your instructor for clarification.

Once you can clearly identify the exigence posed by each question, figure out how much time to allot to answering each one. If you are faced with two questions that are worth the same number of points, give half the time to one and half to the other. When certain questions are weighted more heavily than others, however, you need to divide your time accordingly. However you allocate your time, allow ten minutes for final revising and proofreading.

Stick to your time allotment for each question. If you do not finish, leave room to complete it later and move on to the next question. Partial answers to *all* questions usually gain you more points than complete answers to only *some* questions. Besides, you can use the ten minutes you saved to put the finishing touches on any incomplete answers, even if you have to draw arrows to the margins or to the back of the page, or if you have to supply rough notes. Your instructor will probably appreciate the extra effort.

Using exam answers to address an audience and fulfill a purpose

Unlike most rhetorical situations, an essay exam usually has an audience that is easy to identify: your instructor. The questions on an exam offer big clues about what that audience wants to see in your responses and what kind of purpose you should have in writing; be sure to read all instructions and questions carefully. Invest a few minutes in studying each question, putting that question in your own words, and then jotting down a few notes in the margin next to it. If you have been given a choice of questions to answer, choose those that best suit your knowledge yet do not overlap.

Most questions contain specific instructions about how, as well as what, to answer. Be alert for words such as *compare, define,* and *argue,* which identify the writing task and provide specific cues for organizing your response. Other words, such as *discuss* and *explain,* are less specific, so try to determine exactly what it is your instructor wants you to do. When these more general directions appear, be tuned in to such accompanying words as *similar* or *different* (which signal, respectively, a comparison or a contrast), *identify* (which signals a definition or description), and *why* (which signals the need to identify causes). You will also want to be clear as to whether you are being asked to call up course-related information from memory or to respond with your own ideas. Words such as *think, defend,* and *opinion* signal that you are to frame a thesis and support it.

Most essay exam questions begin with or contain one of the words in the following list and end with a reference to the information you are to discuss. Understanding these terms and framing your answer in response to them will help you focus on what is being asked.

TERMS USED IN ESSAY QUESTIONS

Compare	Examine the points of similarity (compare) or difference (contrast) between two ideas or things.
Define	State the class to which the item to be defined belongs, and clarify what distinguishes it from the others of that class.
Describe	Use details in a clearly defined order to give the reader a clear mental picture of the item you are being asked to describe.
Discuss	Examine, analyze, evaluate, or state pros and cons. This word gives you wide latitude in addressing the topic and thus makes your task more difficult than do some of the others in this set, since you must choose your own focus. It is also the one that appears most frequently on exam questions.
Evaluate	Appraise the advantages and disadvantages of the idea or thing specified.
Explain	Clarify and interpret, reconcile differences, or state causes.
Illustrate	Offer concrete examples or, if possible, create figures, charts, or tables that provide information about the item.
Summarize	State the main points in a condensed form; omit details and curtail examples.
Trace	Narrate a sequence of events that show progress toward a goal or comprise a process.

Using exam answers as a fitting response

Preparing a fitting response to the exigence is another consideration (along with satisfying a specific audience) as you compose essay exam answers. You'll need to decide how to present your ideas and organize your responses in a way that fits the problem, can be delivered in a medium that will reach your audience, and successfully satisfies that audience.

Even under time constraints, you should be able to draft a rough outline or jot down a few phrases for an informal list. Identify your thesis; then list the most important points you plan to cover. You might decide to rearrange ideas later, but the first step is to get some down on paper. Before you begin to write the answer, quickly review the list, deleting any irrelevant or unimportant points and adding any better ones that come to you (keeping in mind how much time you have allotted to the specific question). Number the points in a logical sequence determined by chronology (reporting events in the order in which they occurred), by causation (showing how one thing led to another), or by order of importance (going from the most important point to the least important). Although arranging points in order of increasing importance is often effective, it can be risky in an exam situation because you might run out of time and not get to your most important point.

Following is a thesis statement and a list of supporting points that was quickly composed and edited during the first few minutes of an essay exam.

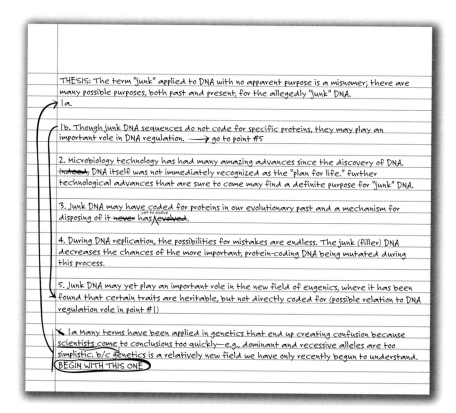

THESIS: The term "junk" applied to DNA with no apparent purpose is a misnomer; there are many possible purposes, both past and present, for the allegedly "junk" DNA.

1a.

1b. Though junk DNA sequences do not code for specific proteins, they may play an important role in DNA regulation. ⟶ go to point #5

2. Microbiology technology has had many amazing advances since the discovery of DNA. ~~Indeed,~~ DNA itself was not immediately recognized as the "plan for life." Further technological advances that are sure to come may find a definite purpose for "junk" DNA.

3. Junk DNA may have coded for proteins in our evolutionary past and a mechanism for disposing of it ~~never~~ has ∧evolved. _(yet to evolve)_

4. During DNA replication, the possibilities for mistakes are endless. The junk (filler) DNA decreases the chances of the more important, protein-coding DNA being mutated during this process.

5. Junk DNA may yet play an important role in the new field of eugenics, where it has been found that certain traits are heritable, but not directly coded for (possible relation to DNA regulation role in point #1)

1a Many terms have been applied in genetics that end up creating confusion because scientists come to conclusions too quickly—e.g., dominant and recessive alleles are too simplistic. b/c genetics is a relatively new field we have only recently begun to understand. (BEGIN WITH THIS ONE)

Biology major Trish Parsons was responding to the following question: "Discuss whether the term 'junk DNA' is an appropriate name for the nucleic DNA that does not code for proteins."

Sometimes, the language of the question will tell you how you should organize your answer. Consider this example:

> Discuss how the two-party political system of the United States influenced the outcome of the Bush-Gore presidential election.

At first glance, this exam question might seem to state the topic without indicating how to organize a discussion of it. *To influence*, however, is to be responsible for certain consequences. In this case, the two-party political system is a cause, and you are being asked to identify its effects. Once you have recognized this, you might decide to discuss different effects in different paragraphs. Here is another example:

> Consider Picasso's treatment of the human body early and late in his career. How did his concept of bodily form persist throughout his career? How did it change?

The reference to two different points in the artist's career, along with the words *persist* and *change*, indicates that your task is to compare and contrast. You could organize your response to this question by discussing Picasso's concept of the bodily form when his paintings were realistic and when they were cubist—preferably covering the same points in the same order in each part of the response. Or you could begin by establishing similarities and then move on to discuss differences. There is almost always more than one way to organize a thoughtful response. Devoting at least a few minutes to organizing your answer can help you better demonstrate what you know.

Once you have identified and organized your main points, try to make them stand out from the rest of the answer to the exam question. For instance, you can make a main point be the first sentence of each paragraph. Or you can use transitional words such as *first*, *second*, and *third*. You might even create headings to separate your points. By the time you have outlined your essay exam answer, you should know which points you want to highlight, even if the points change slightly as you begin writing. Use your conclusion to summarize your main points. If you tend to make points that differ from those you had in mind when you started, try leaving space for an introduction at the beginning of the answer and then writing it after you have written the rest. Or simply draw a line pointing into the margin (or to the other side of the paper), and write the introduction there.

Using exam answers as an available means

Finally, the success of your answers on an essay exam depends on your strategic employment of the available means. In most cases, the physical means available to you for delivering the required information are fairly limited and mostly predetermined. But what are the resources and constraints of your rhetorical situation?

As you already know, one major constraint is time. However, a time limit can also be seen as a resource to help keep you on track, focused clearly on the particular question you're trying to answer. It's critical while completing an essay exam to stick to the question at hand. Always answer each question as precisely and directly as you can, perhaps using some of the instructor's language in your thesis statement. If your thesis statement implies an organizational plan, follow that plan as closely as possible. If you move away from your original thesis because better ideas occur to you as you write, simply go back and revise your thesis statement. If you find yourself drifting into irrelevant material, stop and draw a line through it.

If you find yourself facing a vague or truly confusing question, construct a clear(er) question and then answer it. Rewriting the instructor's question can seem like a risky thing to do, especially if you have never done it before. But figuring out a reasonable question that is related to what the instructor has written is actually a responsible move if you can answer the question you have posed.

Since you'll have reserved time to reread your answers after you've drafted the last one, use this time as a resource to help you improve what you've already written. You can make whatever deletions and corrections you think are necessary. If time allows, ask yourself if there is anything you have left out that you can still manage to include (even if you have to write in the margins or on the back of the page). Unless you are certain that your instructor values neatness more than knowledge, do not hesitate to make additions and corrections. Simply draw a caret (∧), marking the exact place in the text where you want an addition or correction to be placed. Making corrections will allow you to focus on improving what you have already written, whereas recopying your answer just to make it look neat is an inefficient use of time (and you may have recopied only half your essay when the time is up). Finally, check spelling, punctuation, and sentence structure.

Oral Presentations and the Rhetorical Situation

In nearly every course you'll take, your grade will be based in part on participation, a term that is defined according to the subject, the course level, and the instructor. But regardless of the range of expectations this term implies, it nearly always includes oral presentations to the class. You might be expected to contribute to ongoing class discussions or a group project, as a way to demonstrate that you've done your homework and can engage productively with the subject matter and your classmates. Or you might be required to lead a class discussion, teach a lesson, or present research results.

Whether you're someone who feels confident participating in class discussions and who speaks regularly and knowledgeably in class or one of many people who cite public speaking as their greatest fear (even greater than the fear of dying), you can learn some ways to make oral presentations easier on you and better for your audience. Like preparing for an essay examination, preparing for an oral presentation means just that: preparing!

Using oral presentations to address an exigence

You can begin preparing by considering your oral presentation as a response to a specific exigence. For instance, you may have identified a problem that you can address by way of research, a public controversy that you want to investigate, or a personal problem that you want to resolve. If, however, the exigence has been provided for you by your instructor, you may not know immediately just how to proceed. In either situation (you've identified your own exigence or an exigence has been provided for you), you'll need to begin to gather information right away. As soon as you have your assignment and due date, start keeping a computer or paper file for your ideas and information. That way, as the term moves forward, you'll continually bank ideas and materials. Even if you don't know for sure what you'll end up speaking about (you may have in mind a general subject but not a more specific topic), your accumulation of ideas and materials will help you when it's time to begin addressing the specific exigence.

Using oral presentations to address an audience

As you consider the exigence to be addressed, you'll also need to consider your audience. First, you need to consider to whom you'll be speaking: Will you be speaking to your entire class, a smaller group, or several sections of the same course? Or will you have the opportunity to seek out the specific audience you most want to reach with your information? As you begin to envision an audience for your presentation, you'll need to consider the level of expertise of that audience so that you can shape your material and your oral presentation accordingly. In order to do so, you'll want to consider the following questions: How much (if anything) does your intended audience know about your subject? What opinions do members of the audience hold, if any? What role will you take in delivering your information? Will you deliver the information as an expert, a novice, a careful observer or researcher, or a peer? And, of course, you'll need to consider how you're going be evaluated. Finally, you'll need to consider the audience's role in evaluating your presentation. Will the audience evaluate or help evaluate your presentation, or will your instructor be the only one making an evaluation?

Using oral presentations with a rhetorical purpose

You know by now that it's impossible to separate purpose from audience. After all, your purpose is dependent on your audience. Do you want to gather, arrange, and deliver your information (assertions and detailed support) in order to help those in your audience make a decision, change their attitude or behavior, enrich their understanding, or give them pleasure? Your in-class oral presentations will usually be informative, but you'll occasionally be required to provide information that is argumentative or entertaining.

Using oral presentations as a fitting response

Offering a fitting response to the exigence is another consideration (along with satisfying a specific audience) for your oral presentation. You'll need to decide whether the information you've gathered and organized fits the problem, can be delivered in a medium that will reach your audience, and successfully satisfies that audience. You'll need to make decisions about whether you'll deliver your information in spoken words only or with spoken words and visuals. You'll want to make sure that the words you'll be speaking will sound as though they should be spoken. To that end, you'll want to read aloud slowly what you've written, making changes in sentence structure and word choices as you go along, so that the final presentation moves along smoothly and sounds natural. Another benefit of reading aloud is that you'll hear assertions that need support. You'll probably find yourself simplifying your sentence structure (by breaking long, complex sentences into two or more simpler sentences) and following each of your assertions with explicit examples. You may be able to add the type of sensory details that are elemental to narration, description, and definition. You'll also want to make sure that you emphasize transitional words and phrases, so your audience can hear the movement of your words: "first," "second," and so on. If audience members expect to hear three reasons or five main parts, then they will listen for those reasons or parts and be able to follow your words more easily—and with better comprehension. Finally, you can decide whether your presentation might benefit from visuals or audios: items that you bring in to show (sometimes referred to as realia), a handout, a flip chart, a transparency, a poster, a film clip, a podcast or an audio stream, or a PowerPoint presentation.

None of these items will automatically improve your presentation, but all of them hold the potential for bringing your points to life. Nothing can be more persuasive than a series of powerful visuals and audios (realia, photographs, graphs, tables, music, and so on) that complement (or complete) a speaker's argument. Nothing can be more aggravating than a series of bulleted points that a speaker reads to the audience while the audience is reading it from a display. Thus, as you consider the use of visuals and audios, keep in mind that they should complement your words—not mirror them. Some of the most effective PowerPoint presentations are cascades of visuals that accompany—and enhance—a speaker's words.

Using oral presentations as an available means

Finally, the success of an oral presentation depends on your strategic employment of the available means. What are the physical means available to you for delivering the information you want to deliver? Where will you be presenting your information? And what are the resources and constraints of your rhetorical situation?

An oral presentation by definition requires the use of spoken words—your own spoken words. Therefore, you need to practice by reading and/or reciting your information aloud several times. You want to be sure that you are presenting your information loudly, clearly, and slowly enough for all of the audience members to hear you. If you've ever left a presentation thinking "I don't listen as quickly as that speaker speaks," you know why practicing the delivery of your words is important: if you're going to all the trouble of putting together an oral presentation, you want your audience to be able to follow it. Another reason for practicing aloud is to ensure that your presentation comes in at a little less than the maximum time your instructor has allotted you. (It's always better for a presentation to be slightly shorter than slightly longer. Nothing is more annoying than listening to a speaker who has gone over time.) If you need to trim your presentation, consider which parts could be delivered through another means, such as a handout that lists additional resources or a URL for a Web site that supports your presentation. You'll also want to practice using your audios or visuals to make sure that all of your equipment (even something as simple as a flip chart) actually works.

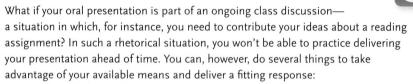

WAIT A MINUTE . . .

What if your oral presentation is part of an ongoing class discussion—
a situation in which, for instance, you need to contribute your ideas about a reading assignment? In such a rhetorical situation, you won't be able to practice delivering your presentation ahead of time. You can, however, do several things to take advantage of your available means and deliver a fitting response:

▌ It may sound obvious, but be sure to keep up with your assigned reading and take notes as you read so that you're familiar with the main subject under discussion. Responding to the text by "talking back" to the author in the margins of your book is one way of preparing for in-class discussions.

▌ Listen to what your classmates have said so that you can frame your ideas in terms of that larger conversation, making clear the relevance of your point. Listening carefully can also help you avoid repeating a point that has already been made.

▌ Jot down a couple of key words so that you remember what you want to say when it comes time for you to speak.

▌ Don't hesitate to offer a response that is inconclusive or that raises more questions than it answers: class discussions are a time to clarify your understanding of the subject, not just demonstrate what you already know.

Be sure to consider the resources and constraints of the physical location in which your presentation is to be delivered. If you're speaking in front of a classroom, you'll reach all of your classmates if you speak clearly and take time to look up from your notes as often as possible. If you're speaking in a lecture hall, however, you may find yourself dependent on a microphone, and you may want to practice with it beforehand. A lecture hall offers a few other challenges as well, not the least of which is the need to ensure that audience members who are hearing impaired or visually impaired can follow your presentation. You may want to make printed handouts available so that hearing-impaired individuals can follow along more easily. And you'll want to concentrate on facing your audience so that they can see your facial expressions and even read your lips, all the better to "hear" your words.

Again, you'll want to practice presenting your words aloud to make sure that your voice is clear enough, that your ideas move forward logically (with lots of transitional flags), and that your visuals or audios work to bring alive your words. You cannot overpractice or overprepare an oral presentation.

For many speakers, the problem isn't researching a topic, writing a text, or translating it into an oral presentation. The problem is getting up in front of a group and delivering the results of their hard work. The best prevention for overcoming this problem is practice, practice, practice—and preparation. The better you know your information, the more familiar your words are as you speak them, the more familiar you are with your speaking space and with any electronic equipment you're using, the easier time you'll have with oral presentations.

Portfolios and the Rhetorical Situation

Many instructors have undoubtedly asked you to keep a portfolio of your work—whether your work consists of drawings, blueprints, or writing. Student writers are asked to keep portfolios that include both works in progress and final projects so that their instructors can review the writing and rewriting that has been done over the course of a term. Rather than grade each formal paper individually, an instructor can look at a student's performance and progress in a variety of writing situations. Portfolios reveal the strengths and weaknesses of any student writer, the kinds of risks the student is willing to take, and the progress the student has made. Perhaps most important, portfolios give students the opportunity to declare what they see and value in their own writing.

Using portfolios to address an exigence

If your instructor requires an end-of-term portfolio, then the exigence for your portfolio is his or her evaluation. The basis of evaluation might be your ability to accomplish a sequence of challenging and complex writing tasks; to use writing as a means for in-depth learning; to write for different audiences, with different purposes, and with different kinds of responses; or to assess your own progress and to set your own goals as a writer. Your job, then, is to put together a portfolio that addresses the exigence of evaluation.

Using portfolios to address an audience

The audience for a portfolio is most often someone who will judge it, whether that person is you (as you decide what to include or take out of the portfolio) or your instructor. Of course, you're always an audience for your portfolio, for you are the one who writes the cover letter that introduces and reflects on the work included. Your instructor is the primary audience, however, in terms of evaluation, so you'll want to be sure to include the materials that your instructor has required and will most value.

Using portfolios with a rhetorical purpose

The purpose of your portfolio becomes clear as you select the materials you want to include (unless, of course, your instructor asks you to include every word you've written all term). Your purpose is to demonstrate how well your writing and critical thinking has progressed, how much you've learned about meeting the demands of any rhetorical situation, and what goals you have already achieved and plan to achieve. In your portfolio, you are making an argument about your development as a writer and using your writing as support for that argument (for strategies for writing arguments, see chapter 15). Thus, you'll want to decide not only what materials to include in your portfolio but also how to organize those materials.

Using portfolios as a fitting response

Many instructors ask for writing samples that best represent you as a writer. If all the samples must come from the course taught by that instructor, then your selection task is simplified. You include what the instructor has asked for and concentrate on your cover letter, describing the contents of the portfolio, commenting on the strengths and weaknesses of each piece of your writing, and explaining why you believe you've earned a specific grade in the course.

However, if your instructor wants you to choose the contents of the portfolio, you'll need to decide whether all your samples will come from the course or you should include materials from outside the course. (In either case, check with your instructor to make sure that your decision about what to include is acceptable.) If your writing portfolio is to represent you as a writer, you'll want to include both academic and nonacademic pieces: a course essay that argues a point, a personal essay that reveals your self-insight, a group or collaborative project and your evaluation of how the group worked, a successful writing assignment from another academic course, a sample of professional writing (perhaps your résumé or a job application letter), and a piece of writing that you simply like. Again, you'll want to reflect on the writing samples in your cover letter, showing your instructor that you understand your progress and have set reasonable goals for yourself throughout the term and for the future. Together, then, the contents of the portfolio, the arrangement of those contents, and the cover letter make a fitting response to the exigence at the same time as they satisfy your audience.

Using portfolios as an available means

Finally, the success of your portfolio ultimately depends on your means of delivery. Whether you deliver your portfolio on paper or electronically, you'll want to take advantage of the features that can be used to present your work more effectively. To that end, you'll want to include a title page and a table of contents, allowing your reader to decide which materials he or she will read. Your cover letter should include an explanation of your choices as well as an evaluation of each of those choices. It should also describe your perceived progress, your achievements, and your goals. If your writing includes a good deal of online and multimedia work (Web pages, multimedia presentations, PDF files, and the like), you might be better off delivering your portfolio electronically so that it can feature visuals, graphics, and audios. Some students create a link to their writing portfolio from their home page or print the URL on their résumé.

Like all important writing you do, you'll want your portfolio to reflect you at your best. So be sure to organize it effectively, proofread and edit it carefully, and showcase your most persuasive and engaging writing in your cover letter.

CREDITS

This page constitutes an extension of the copyright page. We have made every effort to trace the ownership of all copyrighted material and to secure permission from copyright holders. In the event of any question arising as to the use of any material, we will be pleased to make the necessary corrections in future printings. Thanks are due to the following authors, publishers, and agents for permission to use the material indicated.

TEXT

p. 13: *The Santa Fe New Mexican* newspaper.

p. 15: Judy Brady, "Why I Want a Wife," *Ms.* magazine, inaugural issue, 1971. Used by permission of the author.

p. 25: DOONESBURY © 2003 G. B. Trudeau. Distributed by Universal Press Syndicate. Reprinted with permission. All rights reserved.

pp. 26–29: From "Letter from Birmingham Jail," by Martin Luther King, Jr. Reprinted by arrangement with The Heirs to the Estate of Martin Luther King, Jr., c/o Writers House as agent for the proprietor, New York, NY. Copyright 1961 Dr. Martin Luther King, Jr.; Copyright renewed 1991 Coretta Scott King.

pp. 30–31: "Speech Is My Hammer" from *Open Mike: Reflections on Philosophy, Race, Sex, Culture and Religion*, by Michael Eric Dyson, pp. 289–304 (New York: Basic Books, 2003). Reprinted by permission of CIVITAS, a member of Perseus Books Group.

p. 35: Christopher Cokinos, from *Hope Is the Thing with Feathers: A Personal Chronicle of Vanished Birds* (New York: Grand Central Publishing, 2001).

pp. 36, 37–40: Margaret Spellings, "An Action Plan for Higher Education" (address, National Press Club, Washington, DC, September 26, 2006), http://www.ed.gov/news/speeches/2006/09/09262006.html.

p. 42: Board of Directors, Association of American Colleges and Universities, "AAC&U Statement on Spellings Commission Draft Report," August 2006, http://www.aacu.org/About/statements/Spellings.cfm.

p. 44: Academic Senate of San Francisco State University, "Resolution Regarding the Rodney King Verdict," http://sfsu.edu/~senate/documents/resolutions/RS92-107.pdf.

pp. 46, 47: Barbara Smith, from *The Truth That Never Hurts*, pp. 102–105 (New Brunswick, NJ: Rutgers University Press, 1998).

p. 53: Sojourner Truth, from speech given at 1851 Women's Rights Convention in Akron, Ohio.

p. 57: "Susan Orlean Delivers 2001 Johnston Lecture," *Flash: Newsletter of the School of Journalism and Communication*, vol. 16, no. 3 (2001), http://flash.uoregon.edu/S01/orlean.html.

pp. 58–59: From "The American Man, Age Ten," in *The Bullfighter Checks Her Makeup* by Susan Orlean, copyright © 2001 by Susan Orlean. Used by permission of Random House, Inc.

pp. 60–61: From *Life As We Know It* by Michael Bérubé, copyright © 1996 by Michael Bérubé. Used by permission of Pantheon Books, a division of Random House, Inc. and by The Doe Coover Literary Agency.

p. 66: Joyce Carol Oates, "To Invigorate Literary Mind, Start Moving Literary Feet," in *Writers on Writing: Collected Essays from The New York Times* (New York: Times Books/Holt, 2001), 165–71.

p. 67: Susan Sontag, in *Writers on Writing: Collected Essays from The New York Times* (New York: Times Books/Holt, 2001), 223–9.

pp. 69–73, 74–75, 76, 77–78, 81, 83–88: Courtesy of Anastasia Simkanin.

p. 92: Taryn Plumb, *Boston Globe*, May 4, 2006.

pp. 92–93: Jonathan Kibera, from "Fond Memories of a Congenital Glutton," http://www.epinions.com/educ-review-229A-80FFD6-388E720C-bd3, January 5, 2000.

p. 93: From http://www.chowhound.com/topics/312682.

p. 94: From "College Campus Food Carts," http://www.roadfood.com/Forums/topic.asp?TOPIC_ID=6915&SearchTerms=food+truck, March 15, 2005.

p. 94: Clotilde Dusolier, "Happiness (A Recipe)," http://chocolateandzucchini.com/archives.2003/10/happinessarecipe.

p. 95: Ruth Reichl, "The Queen of Mold," from *Tender at the Bone*, copyright © 1998 by Ruth Reichl. Used by permission of Random House, Inc. and Random House, UK.

pp. 95–96: Eric Schlosser, *Fast Food Nation* (Boston: Houghton Mifflin, 2001).

p. 98: Julia Silverman, from "Abu-Jaber Finally Pens Food Novel," *The Nashua Telegraph*, May 29, 2005, http://www.nashuatelegraph.com/apps/pbcs.dil/article?AID=/20050529/BOOKS/105.

p. 98: Katherine Powers, *Boston Globe*, November 5, 2006, p. D7.

pp. 99–100: Julie Powell, from "The Julie/Julia Project," July 8, 2003, http://blogs.salon.com/0001399/2003/07/08.html.

pp. 100–101: Jessica Thomson, "Blogs Add a New Ingredient to Food Writing," from *The Boston Globe*, January 24, 2007, p. E3. Used by permission of the author.

p. 103: Margaret Mead, from "The Wider Food Situation," *Food Habits Research: Problems of the 1960s*, National Research Council's Committee for the Study of Food Habits Update.

pp. 104, 105: Margaret Mead, from "The Changing Significance of Food," *American Scientist* 58 (March/April 1970): 176–81.

pp. 106–107: Corby Kummer, from "Good-bye Cryovac," *The Atlantic Monthly*, vol. 294, no. 3 (October 2004): p. 197+. Copyright 2004 The Atlantic Monthly Group, as first published in *The Atlantic Monthly*. Distributed by Tribune Media Services.

pp. 109–113, 120, 121: Pooja Makhijani, "School Lunch," from *Women Who Eat*, edited by Leslie Miller, pp. 41–49 (New York: Seal Press, 2003). Reprinted by permission of Seal Press, a member of Perseus Books Group.

pp. 114–115: Excerpt from *Fried Butter* © 2003 by Abe Opincar, used by permission of Soho Press, Inc.

pp. 122–126: Courtesy of Anna Seitz Hickey.

p. 129: Martin Luther King, Jr., from "I Have a Dream." Copyright 1963 Martin Luther King Jr., copyright renewed 1991 Coretta Scott King.

p. 132: From Dorothy Carnegie, *The Quick and Easy Way to Effective Public Speaking*, a revision of Dale Carnegie, *Public Speaking and Influencing Men in Business* (Garden City, NY: Dale Carnegie & Associates, 1962).

p. 132: Lowell Thomas, "A Shortcut to Distinction," in Dale Carnegie, *How to Win Friends and Influence People*, rev. ed. (New York: Simon & Schuster, 1981), p. 283.

pp. 134, 135: Robert Dallek, *Flawed Giant: Lyndon B. Johnson, 1960–1973* (New York: Oxford University Press, 1998), pp. 86, 125.

pp. 135, 136–138: From *The Years of Lyndon Johnson: Means of Ascent*, © 1990 by Robert A. Caro. Reprinted with the permission of Alfred A. Knopf, a division of Random House, Inc.

pp. 138–140: From *What I Saw at the Revolution*, by Peggy Noonan, copyright © 1989 by Peggy Noonan. Used by permission of Random House, Inc. and the William Morris Agency.

p. 141: James H. Costen, "Rev. Jesse L. Jackson," *Ebony*, 1993.

pp. 142–145: Michael Eric Dyson, "Gardner Taylor: The Poet Laureate of the American Pulpit." From *The Michael Eric Dyson Reader*, pp. 192–201 (Basic Books, 2004). Reprinted by permission of CIVITAS, a member of Perseus Books Group.

p. 146: From *Talkin and Testifyin: The Language of Black America* by Geneva Smitherman (Detroit: Wayne State University Press, 1977). Copyright © Wayne State University Press.

pp. 148–150, 158: "For Bush's Speechwriter, Job Grows Beyond Words, 'Scribe' Helps Shape, Set Tone for Evolving Foreign Policy" by Mike Allen (*Washington Post* [Final edition]): Oct. 11, 2002, p. A35. © 2002, The Washington Post, reprinted with permission.

pp. 151–153, 158–159: Marisa Lagos, "Successes Speak Well for Debate Coach" (*Los Angeles Times*, October 6, 2004, Home edition, p. B2).

pp. 160–166: Courtesy of Matthew Glasgow.

pp. 175–176: Don Hammonds, "Honda Challenges Students to Market Its Latest Car to Younger Buyers." From the *Pittsburgh Post-Gazette*, March 31, 2006.

pp. 177–178: Eyal Press and Jennifer Washburn, from "The Kept University," *The Atlantic Monthly*, vol. 285 (March 1, 2000), p. 39. Copyright 2000 The Atlantic Monthly Group, as first published in *The Atlantic Monthly*. Distributed by Tribune Media Service.

pp. 179–180: "Building a Buzz on Campus" by Sarah Schweitzer from *The Boston Globe* (October 24, 2005). Used by permission of author.

pp. 182–183: "Riding the Trojan Horse" by Mike Fish, ESPN, Inc. (1/11/06).

p. 184: "Corporate America Takes on the Care and Clothing of Public Education" by Paul Boyer from the *Wisconsin State Journal* (December 15, 1995).

pp. 186–189, 197: Robert Cwiklik, "How UPS Tried to Buy into the Ivory Tower." From *The Wall Street Journal* (Eastern edition), New York, NY: February 6, 1998, p. B1.

pp. 189–192: "They're Baaaaack: Card Marketers on Campus" by Kate Fitzgerald from *Credit Card Management* 16.3 (June 1, 2003), pp. 18–23. Copyright © 2003 www.cardforum.com.

pp. 199–204: Courtesy of Kelly E. McNeil.

pp. 206–207: Barbara Wallraff, "Word Court," *The Atlantic Monthly*, vol. 295, no. 3 (2005), p. 136. Copyright 2007 The Atlantic Monthly Group, as first published in *The Atlantic Monthly*. Distributed by Tribune Media Services.

p. 208: Zitkala-Ša, "Impressions of an Indian Childhood," *The Atlantic Monthly*, vol. 85, no. 507 (January 1900), pp. 37–47.

p. 209: From "Not Neither" by Sandra Mariá Esteves, quoted in Juan Flores, *From Bamboo to Hip-Hop: Puerto Rican Culture and Latino Identity* (New York: Columbia University Press, 2000), p. 56.

p. 210: Statistics on federal court proceedings from Marijke van der Heide, "Present and Future Needs for Language Skills in the U.S. Federal Courts." National Language Conference: A Call to Action, Adelphi, Maryland, June 22, 2004.

p. 212: Lines from "Nuestro Himno" ("Our Anthem") by Adam Kidron and comment from Pitbull, quoted in Laura Wides-Munoz, "Outcry Greets Spanish Anthem" (Associated Press), April 28, 2006.

p. 212: From "Sen. Alexander to Introduce Resolution on Singing National Anthem in English," press release, April 28, 2006, http://alexander.senate.gov/index.cfm?FuseAction=PressReleases.Det.

pp. 215–217: S. I. Hayakawa, "One Nation . . . Indivisible? The English Language Amendment." From *Language Loyalties: A Source Book on the Official English Controversy*, edited by James Crawford (Berkeley: University of California Press), pp. 94–100. Used by permission of The Regional Oral History Office, Berkeley, CA.

p. 217: From "Inhofe to Senate: 'Make English Our National Language,'" press release, May 8, 2007, http://infhofe.senate.gov/public/index.cfm?FuseAction=PressRoom.Pr.

p. 217: Quote from EPIC on English Plus from "The English Plus Alternative," in James Crawford (ed.), *Language Loyalties: A Source Book on the Official English Controversy* (Chicago: University of Chicago Press, 1992), pp. 151–3.

pp. 217, 218: Victor Villanueva, "On English Only." From *Language Ideologies: Critical Perspectives on the Official English Movement*, Volume 1, *Education and the Social Implications of Official Language*, edited by Roseann Dueñas Gonzáles and Ildikó Melis, pp. 333–342 (Urbana, IL: National Council of Teachers of English, 2000).

pp. 219, 220: Geoffrey Nunberg, "The Official English Movement: Reimagining America." From *Language Loyalties: A Source Book on the Official English Controversy*, edited by James Crawford (Chicago: University of Chicago Press, 1992), pp. 479–494.

pp. 220–221: Hyon B. Shin, with Rosalind Bruno, from *Language Use and English-Speaking Ability: Census 2000 Brief*. Washington, DC: U.S. Dept. of Commerce, 2003.

pp. 222–224, 226: "Los Olvidados: On the Making of Invisible People" by Juan F. Perea, 70 *N.Y.U. Law Review*, 965 (1995).

pp. 224–225: "Hunger of Memory" by Richard Rodriguez, from *Hunger of Memory: The Education of Richard Rodriguez* (New York: Bantam Books, 1982) pp. 19–20.

pp. 227–229, 236–237: Gabriela Kuntz, "My Spanish Standoff," *Newsweek*, May 4, 1998, p. 22. © Newsweek, Inc. All rights reserved. Used by permission and protected by the Copyright Laws of the United States. The printing, copying, redistribution, or retransmission of the Material without express written permission is prohibited.

pp. 229–230, 236, 237: "A Language Is a Terrible Thing to Lose" by Augustin Garza, from the *Los Angeles Times*, May 18, 1999, p. B1.

pp. 239–246: Courtesy of the author.

pp. 254–255, 259: "We Are Rebuilding New York" from *Working for the People* by Robert Moses (New York: Harper, 1956), pp. 557–560.

pp. 256–258: From *The Power Broker: Robert Moses and the Fall of New York* by Robert A. Caro. © 1974 by Robert A. Caro. Used by permission of Alfred A. Knopf, a division of Random House, Inc.

pp. 259–260: From *The Death and Life of Great American Cities* by Jane Jacobs, published by Jonathan Cape. Copyright © 1961, 1989 by Jane Jacobs. Reprinted by permission of Random House, Inc. and The Random House Group Ltd.

p. 261: Adina Levin, "Ants and Jane Jacobs," February 18, 2003, http://alevin.com/weblog/archives/000966.html.

p. 263: Quote from guidelines for World Trade Center site memorial competition, http://www.wtcsitememorial.org/p1.

pp. 264–265, 272: "Reflecting Absence" by Michael Arad and Peter Walker (World Trade Center Site Memorial Competition, http://www.wtcsitememorial.org/fin7.html). Reprinted with permission of LMDC.

pp. 265–267, 271, 272: "A More Civic Response to Loss" by Paula Deitz from *The New York Sun* (December 18, 2003), p. 17. Used by permission of *The New York Sun*.

pp. 273–278: Courtesy of Rupali Kumar.

p. 284: Charles A. Hill, *Intertexts: Reading Pedagogy in College Writing Classrooms* (Mahwah, NJ: Lawrence Erlbaum, 2003), p. 123.

p. 286: Jane Dark, "Reloaded Questions: Hacking the 'Matrix' Master Code," *The Village Voice*, May 14–20, 2003.

p. 287: Joshua Clover, "The Matrix," *British Film Institute Modern Classics Series* (London: BFI Publishing, 2004), p. 15.

pp. 288–289: "An Apocalypse of Kinetic Joy" by Kenneth Turan from the *Los Angeles Times*, (March 31, 1999): 1.

pp. 289–290: "Techno Prisoner" by Lisa Schwarzbaum, *Entertainment Weekly*, April 9, 1999: p. 45. © 2008 Time, Inc. All rights reserved. Reprinted from *Entertainment Weekly Magazine* with permission.

p. 291: Excerpt from *The Matrix*, from the British Film Institute Modern Classics Series, pp. 15, 26–29 (London: BFI Publishing, 2004).

p. 294: Eliot Noyes, quoted in Dung Ngo and Eric Pfeiffer, *Bent Ply: The Art of Plywood Furniture* (Princeton, NJ: Princeton Architectural Press, 2003), p. 49.

p. 294: Library of Congress, "The Work of Charles & Ray Eames: A Legacy of Invention," exhibition, http://www.loc.gov/exhibits/eames/furniture.html.

pp. 294–295: Pat Kirkham, "The Evolution of the Eames Lounge Chair and Ottoman," *The Eames Lounge Chair: An Icon of Modern Design* (Grand Rapids, MI: Grand Rapids Art Museum, 2006), p. 57.

p. 296: Rob Forbes, "The Endurance of an Icon," *Design Within Reach Newsletter*, "Design Notes," May 17, 2006, http://www.dwr.com/images/newsletter/eames0506.html.

pp. 296, 297: The Eames Office, http://www.eamesoffice.com/vintage/index.php?vintage=vintage.

p. 298: Thomas Hine, "Half a Century of Lounging: Sightings and Reflections." From *The Eames Lounge Chair: An Icon of Modern Design* by Martin Eidelberg, Thomas Hine, Pat Kirkham, and David A. Hanks (New York: Merrell Publishers, 2006). Used by permission of Merrell Publishers, in association with Grand Rapids Art Museum.

pp. 300–302, 307–308: Mike D'Angelo, "Unreally, Really Cool: Stop-Motion Movies May Be Old School, but They Still Eat Other Animation for Breakfast," *Esquire*, October 2005, pp. 72–73. Used by permission of the author.

pp. 302–303, 308: Susan Beatty, "Logo Logic: Professors Give "A" to the "Swoosh" but Flunk Giant." From The *Wall Street Journal* (Eastern edition), New York, NY: May 18, 1998, P1.

pp. 310–313: Courtesy of Alexis Walker.

p. 317: Global Village Voices, http://news.bbc.co.uk/1/hi/talking-point/3660971.stm.

p. 318: Jeffrey T. Grabill, "Community Computing and Citizen Productivity," *Computers and Composition*, vol. 20 (2003), p. 144.

p. 320: From interview with Marshall McLuhan by Eric Norden, in Marshall McLuhan, Eric McLuhan, and Frank Zingrone, *Essential McLuhan* (New York: Basic Books, 1996), p. 236.

p. 321: From interview with Marshall McLuhan on *Explorations*, video, http://archives.cbc.ca/IDC-1-74-342-1818/people/mcluhan/clip2.

pp. 321, 322: From Marshall McLuhan, *Understanding Media: the Extensions of Man*, Critical edition, W. Terrence Gordon, ed. (Corte Madera, CA: Gingko Press, 2003), foreword.

p. 323: Philip Marchand, *Marshall McLuhan: The Medium and the Messenger* (Boston: Ticknor & Fields, 1989), p. xi.

p. 324: From *Marshall McLuhan* by Jonathan Miller, Modern Masters Series (New York: The Viking Press, 1971), pp. 115–6, 117–9.

p. 327: From TIME, 2006 Person of the Year Issue. Copyright © 2006 Time, Inc. All rights reserved. Reprinted by permission.

pp. 329–330: Copyright 2005 from *Race, Rhetoric, and Technology: Searching for Higher Ground*, 1/e, by Adam J. Banks. Reproduced by permission of Lawrence Erlbaum Assciates, Inc., a division of Taylor & Francis.

pp. 332–333, 342, 343: "Global Village Idiocy" by Thomas L. Friedman. From *The New York Times*, 5/12/2002. Copyright © 2002 The New York Times. All rights reserved. Used by permission and protected by the Copyright Laws of the United States. The printing, copying, redistribution, or retransmission of the Material without express written permission is prohibited.

pp. 334–336, 342: "When Words Are the Best Weapon" by Russell Watson. From *Newsweek*, February 27, 1995, p. 36. © 1995 Newsweek, Inc. All rights reserved. Used by permission and protected by the Copyright Laws of the United States. The printing, copying, redistribution, or retransmission of the Material without express written permission is prohibited.

pp. 344–348: Courtesy of Anna Seitz Hickey.

p. 351: Jonathan Franzen, quote from interview with Terry Gross, *Fresh Air*, WHYY, Philadelphia, October 15, 2001.

p. 351: Sonny Mehta, quoted in Edward Wyatt, "Oprah's Book Club Reopening to Writers Who'll Sit and Chat," *New York Times*, September 23, 2006, p. A2.

p. 352: Maya Angelou, quoted in "Literary Legend Lends Name and Creates Original Poetry for New Hallmark Product Line; 'The Maya Angelou Collection from Hallmark' Will Feature Inspirational Greeting Cards and Specialty Products," *PR Newswire*, November 14, 2000. Hallmark Cards, Inc. http://www.prnewswire.com.

p. 353: Harold Bloom, "The Man in the Back Row Has a Question VI," *Paris Review*, vol. 42, no. 154 (Spring 2000): p. 379.

pp. 358–360: Mortimer Adler, "How to Mark a Book," in *The Sundance Writer*, 3rd ed. (Boston: Thomson/Wadsworth). Originally published in *Saturday Review of Literature* in 1940.

pp. 360–362: Sherman Alexie, "Superman and Me," essay for the *Times'* series "The Joy of Reading and Writing" (*Los Angeles Times*, 1998).

pp. 362–363: Marianne Gingher, "The Most Double-D-Daring Book I Read." From *Remarkable Reads: 34 Writers and Their Adventures in Reading* (New York: W.W. Norton & Co., 2004), pp. 95–104. Used by permission of the author.

p. 364: Elaine Oswald and Robert L. Gale, "On Marianne Moore's Life and Career," *Modern American Poetry 2000*. The Department of English, University of Illinois at Urbana-Champaign, July 10, 2007. http://www.english.uiuc.edu/maps/poets/m_r/moore/life.htm.

pp. 364–365: Marianne Moore, "Poetry." Reprinted with the permission of Scribner, an imprint of Simon & Schuster Adult Publishing Group, from THE COLLECTED POEMS OF MARIANNE MOORE by Marianne Moore. Copyright © 1935 by Marianne Moore; copyright renewed © 1963 by Marianne Moore & T. S. Eliot. Permission also granted, © 2003 Faber and Faber, Ltd., by Marianne Craig Moore, Literary Executor. All rights reserved.

p. 368: Quote from Hisaye Yamamoto, "Las Vegas Charley," in *Seventeen Syllables* (New Brunswick, NJ: Rutgers University Press, 1994).

p. 368: Quote from Alice Walker, *To Hell with Dying* (San Diego, CA: Harcourt, 1988).

pp. 370–373: Ralph Rees, "The Reality of Imagination in the Poetry of Marianne Moore." Originally published in *Twentieth Century Literature*, vol. 30, nos. 2–3 (Summer–Autumn 1988): pp. 231–41.

p. 375: Barbara T. Christian, *Everyday Use by Alice Walker* (New Brunswick, NJ: Rutgers University Press, 1994), introduction, p. 9.

pp. 375–381: "Everyday Use" from IN LOVE & TROUBLE: STORIES OF BLACK WOMEN, copyright © 1973 by Alice Walker, reprinted by permission of Harcourt, Inc. and The Wendy Weil Agency, Inc.

p. 382: Joy Harjo, quoted at http://www.joyharjo.org.

pp. 382–383: "Perhaps the World Ends Here" by Joy Harjo, from THE WOMAN WHO FELL FROM THE SKY by Joy Harjo. Copyright ©1994 by Joy Harjo. Used by permission of W.W. Norton & Company, Inc. and the author.

p. 383: Quote from Fishbowl Theatre's Web site, http://fishbowltheatre.com/jane_martin.html.

p. 383: Quote from Jon Jory, http://www.hartnell.cc.ca.us/westernstage/press_releases/Anton/antonarticle.htm.

pp. 383–387: *Beauty*, by Jane Martin. Used by permission of Alexander Speer, Trustee. Caution: Professionals and amateurs are hereby warned that Beauty © 2001 by Alexander Speer, Trustee, is subject to royalty. It is fully protected under copyright laws of the United States of America, British Commonwealth including Canada and all countries of the Copyright Union. All rights including professional, amateur, motion picture, recitation, lecturing, public reading, radio broadcasting, television, internet and other forms of electronic media and the rights of translation into foreign languages are strictly reserved. No part of this work may be reproduced, stored in a retrieval system or transmitted in any form, by any means, now known or yet to be invented, including mechanical, electronic, photocopying, recording, videotaping or otherwise without written permission of the Trustee. Particular emphasis is laid on the question of amateur or professional readings, permissions and terms for which must be secured in writing from Alexander Speer, Trustee, P. O. Box 66, Goshen, KY 40026.

p. 388: Raymond Carver, quoted in William L. Stull, "Raymond Carver," http://whitman.edu/english/carver/biography.html. Originally published in *Dictionary of Literary Biography*.

pp. 394–399: Courtesy of Matthew Marusak.

p. 405 (top): Britannica definition of "primates," http://www.britannica.com/eb/article-9105977/primate.

p. 405 (middle): Primate Conservation, Inc., http://www.primate.org/about.htm.

pp. 405–406: ChimpanZoo: Research, Education and Enrichment 2003, www.chimpanzoo.org/history%20of%20primates.html.

p. 406: "Primates," *Oxford English Dictionary*, 22nd ed. (Oxford, England: Oxford University Press, 1982).

p. 407: W. E. Le Gros Clark, *The Antecedents of Man*, 3rd ed. (Chicago: Quadrangle Books, 1971).

p. 408 (top): Katz, Jon, "Finding the Perfect Dog," from slate.com, Tuesday, May 18, 2004.

pp. 408–409: William Styron, *Darkness Visible* (New York: Random House, 1990), p. 52.

p. 409: Burciaga, José Antonio, "I Remember Masa" from *Weedee Peepo*. Published by Pan American University Press, Edinburgh, TX (1988).

p. 410: From *The American Heritage® Book of English Usage* (Houghton Mifflin Company, 1996).

p. 411: © The New Yorker Collection 2002 Leo Cullum from cartoonbank.com. All Rights Reserved.

p. 412: Dottie Indyke, "Mother's Day Exhibition of *Retablos* and *Bultos*," *Santa Fean*, May 2004, p. 63.

pp. 412–413: Gloria Yamato, "Something about the Subject Matter Makes It Hard to Name," *Race, Class and Gender: An Anthology*, 3/e, eds. Margaret C. Anderson and Patricia Hill Collins (Belmont, CA: Wadsworth, 1998), p. 89.

p. 413: Quote about POPS program run by Robert Carmona, from Susan Horsburgh, "Building a Better Dad," *People*, June 21, 2004, p. 85.

pp. 413–414: From "This World" in the *San Francisco Chronicle* (August 20, 1989). Copyright © 1989 by Rose Del Castillo Guilbault. Used by permission of the author.

p. 415: From *Sunrise with Seamonsters* by Paul Theroux. Copyright © 1985 by Cape Cod Scriveners Company.

p. 416: Courtesy of The Partnership for a Drug-Free America.

p. 417: From "Letter from Birmingham Jail" by Martin Luther King, Jr. Reprinted by arrangement with The Heirs to the Estate of Martin Luther King, Jr., c/o Writers House as agent for the proprietor, New York, NY. Copyright 1961 Dr. Martin Luther King, Jr.; Copyright renewed 1991 Coretta Scott King.

pp. 421–422: State College, PA *Centre Daily Times* (January 29, 2004), p. A8.

p. 422: From Catton, Bruce, "Grant and Lee: A Study in Contrasts." Copyright ©1956 by U.S. Capitol Historical Society.

p. 423: Mukherjee, Bharati, "Two Ways of Belonging in America" from *The New York Times*, September 22, 1996.

p. 423: Sedaris, David, from "Get Your Ya-Ya's Out," in *Naked* (Boston: Back Bay Books, 1997), pp. 35–6. Copyright © 1997 by David Sedaris.

p. 424: "Supermarket Showdown," *Consumer Reports*, September 2003, p. 29.

p. 427: Karen R. Rosenberg and Wenda R. Trevathan, "The Evolution of Human Birth," *Scientific American Special Edition: A New Look at Human Evolution*, August 25, 2003, p. 82.

p. 428: "Coalition of the Differing" by Patrick Cooke. *Smithsonian* (June 2003): 112.

p. 429: Robert Struckman, "Pass It On," National Museum of the American Indian (Summer 2004), pp. 11–14.

pp. 429–430: Sedaris, David, from "The Drama Bug," in *Naked* (Boston: Back Bay Books, 1997). Copyright © 1997 by David Sedaris.

pp. 430–431: "Gender, Class, and Terrorism" by Michael Kimmel. http://chronicle.com/weekly/v48/i22/22b01101.htm.

p. 431: "Word Up" by YiLing Chen-Josephson. Posted Thursday, December 4, 2003. http://slate.msn.com/toolbar.aspx?action +print&id+2091949.

p. 440: From Franz Beard, "Myth Dispelled: It Started in the Trenches," http://www.gatorcountry.com/interim/article/myth _dispelled_it_started_in_the_trenches, January 10, 2007.

p. 440–441: From *Car Talk*, http://www.washingtonpost.com/ac2/ wp-dyn/A63703-2004May28?language+printer.

p. 442: Jason Silverman, "Billions Unnerved: Super Size Diet Crisis," *The New Mexican, Pasatiempo*, June 11–17, 2004, p. 69.

p. 442: Melissa Nelson, from "Becoming Métis," in *The Colors of Nature*, edited by Alison H. Deming and Lauret E. Savoy (Minneapolis: Milkweed, 2002), p. 147.

pp. 442–443: From Francis Fukuyama, *Our Posthuman Future* (New York: Farrar & Straus, 2002), p. 8.

p. 444: Georgette Mosbacher, quoted in Nancy Collins, "The World of Georgette Mosbacher," *Harper's Bazaar* (July 2004), pp. 112–7.

p. 444: Dianne Hales and Dr. Robert E. Hales, "Too Tough to Seek Help?" *Parade* (June 20, 2004), p. 4.

p. 446: "Safe-Sex Lies" by Meghan Daum. Copyright © 1996 by Meghan Daum.

pp. 448–449: From Scünci International Web site: www.scunci .com/celebrity_style2.aspx?h=4&s=2.

pp. 449–450: From Michael McGarrity, *Everyone Dies* (New York: Dutton-Penguin), pp. 169–71.

p. 451: Peggy Post, from *Good Housekeeping* (July 2004), p. 28. Hearst Communications, Inc.

pp. 452, 453, 454: Julia Alvarez, from "Writing Matters," in *Something to Declare* (New York: Plume-Penguin, 1999), p. 277.

p. 454: Editor Bob, "Disc Doctorin," *Honda Tuning* (July 2004), p. 90.

pp. 455, 456: Mortimer Adler, *How to Read a Book: The Art of Getting a Liberal Education* (New York: Simon & Schuster, 1940).

p. 455: David Sedaris, from "Chicken in the Henhouse," in *Dress Your Family in Corduroy and Denim* (New York: Little Brown, 2004), p. 215.

p. 457: "The Memory Artist," from *O, The Oprah Magazine* (July 2003), p. 183. Hearst Communications, Inc. Hearst Magazines.

p. 460: Sherman Alexie, from "Indian Education," in *The Lone Ranger and Tonto Fistfight in Heaven* (Grove/Atlantic, 1993). Copyright © 1993 by Sherman Alexie.

p. 461: From "A Crime of Compassion." First published in *Newsweek* magazine in 1983. Copyright © 1983 Barbara Huttman.

p. 461: From "Entertaining Angels," Ed Madden original essay, maddene@gwm.sc.edu.

p. 464: "Bobby Hatfield: One Half of the Righteous Brothers, 63" by David Wild. From *Rolling Stone* (11 Dec. 2003), p. 46. © Rolling Stone LLC (2003). All Rights Reserved. Reprinted by Permission.

pp. 466–467: Susan Orlean, from "Fans," in *The Bullfighter Checks Her Makeup* (New York: Random House, 2001), p. 144.

p. 467: Dorothy Allison, from *One or Two Things I Know for Sure* (New York: Plume-Penguin), p. 15. Copyright © Dorothy Allison, 1995.

p. 468: "Tears for a Legend" by Jason Fine. From *Rolling Stone* (11 Dec. 2004), p. 50. © Rolling Stone LLC (2004). All Rights Reserved. Reprinted by Permission.

pp. 475, 476, 477, 478: Teresa Heinz Kerry, excerpts from speech at 2004 Democratic National Convention, http://www .presidentialrhetoric.com/campaign/dncspeeches/thkerry _print.html.

p. 480: Kevin Wall, quoted in Evan Serpick, "Live from Planet Rock," *Rolling Stone*, March 8, 2007, p. 13.

p. 484: Martin Luther King, Jr., excerpt from "Letter from Birmingham Jail." Reprinted by arrangement with The Heirs to the Estate of Martin Luther King, Jr., c/o Writers House as agent for the proprietor, New York, NY. Copyright 1961 Dr. Martin Luther King, Jr.; Copyright renewed 1991 Coretta Scott King.

pp. 484–485: From *Sex, Art, and American Culture* by Camille Paglia (New York: Vintage Books, 1992). Copyright © 1992 by Camille Paglia.

p. 485: PETA statement from www.peta.org/about.

pp. 485–487: From *Rumbles Left and Right* by William F. Buckley, Jr. Copyright © 1963. Wallace Literary Agency, Inc.

p. 488: Peter Gomes, "Homophobic? Re-read Your Bible." From *The New York Times*, 8/17/1992. Copyright © 1992 The New York Times. All rights reserved. Used by permission and protected by the Copyright Laws of the United States. The printing, copying, redistribution, or retransmission of the Material without express written permission is prohibited.

pp. 489, 490, 491: James Agee and Walker Evans, from *Let Us Now Praise Famous Men*, Reissue edition (Mariner Books, 1989).

p. 494: "Clues to Compulsive Collecting: Separating Useless Junk from Objects of Value" by Richard A. Lovett. REPRINTED WITH PERMISSION FROM PSYCHOLOGY TODAY MAGAZINE (March/April 2004), p. 29. Copyright © 2004 Sussex Publishers, LLC.

p. 499: "Ablow's Objets d'Art," *Bostonia* magazine, Winter 2003–2004, p. 16.

pp. 502–503: Timothy Quinn, excerpt from "Coyote (*Canis latrans*) Food Habits in Three Urban Habitat Types of Western Washington," *Northwest Science*, vol. 71, no. 1 (1997), p. 1.

p. 506: Margaret G. Zackowitz, "British Cool on Hot Tea," in *National Geographic*, December 2003.

p. 509: "What is NPR?" from www.npr.org/about/.

p. 520: Deborah Tannen, *You're Wearing That? Understanding Mothers and Daughters in Conversation* (New York: Random House, 2006), pp. 5, 6.

pp. 521, 522–523, 526–527: Mike Rose, from *The Mind at Work* (New York: Viking, 2004), pp. 31–32, 85–86, 219–20.

p. 524: Krista Ratcliff, *Rhetorical Listening: Identification, Gender, Whiteness* (Carbondale, IL: Illinois University Press, 2005), p. xiii.

pp. 524–526: Courtesy of Bethanie Orban.

p. 527: Diane Ackerman, *A Natural History of the Senses* (New York: Random House, 1990), p. xv.

pp. 535, 537, 541: Courtesy of Matthew Marusak.

p. 543: From interview with Debra Dickerson, author of *The End of Blackness: Returning the Souls of Black Folks to Their Rightful Owners*, in Sharifa Rhodes-Pitts, "Getting Over Race," *The Atlantic*, vol. 293, no. 1 (February 27, 2004).

pp. 545–546: William Lutz, "Doubts about Doublespeak." From *State Government News* (July 1993), pp. 22–24. Used by permission of the author.

pp. 549–550, 551: Courtesy of Jacob Thomas.

p. 554: William Byers, *How Mathematicians Think: Using Ambiguity, Contradiction, and Paradox to Create Mathematics* (Princeton, NJ: Princeton University Press, 2007), p. 29.

pp. 568, 569: Pantheon, 2005.

p. 573: Published by Duke University Press for the American Dialect Society. Used by permission of the American Dialect Society.

p. 578: *Journal of Aesthetic Education*, 2003 .

pp. 582–596: Courtesy of Matthew Marusak and Bethanie Orban.

p. 602 (left and right): Crown, 2005.

P. 605: National Council of Teachers of English (NCTE), May, 2006.

pp. 613–620, 623: Courtesy of Catherine L. Davis.

p. 622: Jack Finney, *Invasion of the Body Snatchers* (New York: Prion Books, 1997), p. 1.

p. 623: Joan Didion, from "Marrying Absurd," in *Slouching Towards Bethlehem* (New York: Farrar, Straus, & Giroux, 1990).

p. 634: James Thurber, from "A Snapshot of Rex," in *The Dog Department: James Thurber on Hounds, Scotties, and Talking Poodles* (New York: HarperCollins, 2001), p. 90.

p. 636: Philip Lopate, in *For the Love of Books* (New York: Putnam, 1992), edited by Ronald B. Schwartz.

p. 640: Jonathan Weiner, *The Beak of the Finch: A Story of Evolution in Our Time* (New York: Vintage Books, 1995).

p. 641: Marshall Jon Fisher, "Memoria ex Machina," in *The Best American Essays 2003*, eds. Anne Fadiman and Robert Atwan (Boston: Mariner Books, 2003), p. 64.

p. 643: James Baldwin, "Notes of a Native Son," in Collected Essays, ed. Toni Morrison (New York: Library of America, 1998).

p. 643: Barry Lopez, "Wide-Eyed in Galapagos," http://dir.salon.com/story/travel/feature/1998/06/25/pass, March 4, 2008.

p. 648: Dave Eggers, *A Heartbreaking Work of Staggering Genius*, (New York: Simon & Schuster, 2000), p. 48.

p. 649: William Zinsser, "College Pressures," *Blair and Ketchum's Country Journal* (April 1970).

p. 656: William O'Grady, Michael Dobrovolsky, and Mark Aronoff, eds., *Contemporary Linguistics: An Introduction*, 3rd ed. (New York: St. Martin's, 1997).

p. 657: Anne Fadiman, "Mail," in *At Large and At Small: Familiar Essays* (New York: Farrar, Straus, & Giroux, 2007).

pp. 666–667: Robert Boswell, in *The Place of Grammar in Writing Instruction: Past, Present, Future* (Portsmouth, NH: Boynton/Cook, 1995), edited by Susan Hunter and Ray Wallace.

p. 667: "Loud," *Heinle's Newbury House Dictionary of American English*, 4th ed. (Boston: Thomson/Heinle, 2004), p. 557.

p. 667: Susan Gubar, *Rooms of Our Own* (Champaign, IL: University of Illinois Press, 2006).

p. 668: Peter Schjeldahl, "Those Nasty Brits," *The New Yorker*, October 11, 1999, p. 104.

p. 670: Mark Twain, *The Tragedy of Pudd'nhead Wilson and the Comedy of Those Extraordinary Twins* (New York: Oxford University Press, 1894/1996).

p. 681: Paul K. Humiston, "Small World," in *I Thought My Father Was God* by Paul Auster (New York: Henry Holt, 2001), p. 183.

p. 682: James Gorman, "Finding a Wild, Fearsome World Beneath Every Fallen Leaf," in *The Best American Science and Nature Writing 2003*, ed. Richard Dawkins (Boston: Houghton Mifflin, 2003), p. 67.

p. 685: Michael Ventura, "Taboo: Don't Even Think About It," *Psychology Today* (January/February, 1998).

p. 685: Jody M. Roy, "The Case of the Cowboy," in *Love to Hate: America's Obsession with Hatred and Violence* (New York: Columbia University Press, 2002).

p. 685: John F. Kennedy, inaugural address, Washington, DC, January 1961.

p. 693: Louise Rafkin, *Other People's Dirt: A Housecleaner's Curious Adventures* (Chapel Hill, NC: Algonquin Books, 1998), p. 34.

p. 695: Joe Theismann, *The Complete Idiot's Guide to Football* (Royersford, PA: Alpha, 2001).

p. 696: Parker Palmer, *The Courage to Teach: Exploring the Inner Landscape of a Teacher's Life* (San Francisco: Jossey-Bass, 2007).

pp. 697, 702: Arian Camp-Flores, from "Get Your Praise On," *Newsweek*, April 19, 2004, p. 57.

p. 697: Karen R. Rosenberg and Wenda R. Trevathan, "The Evolution of Human Birth," *Scientific American Special Edition: A New Look at Human Evolution*, August 25, 2003, p. 82.

p. 702: Paul Goldberger, "High-Tech Bibliophilia," *The New Yorker* (May 24, 2004).

p. 703: Clifton Fadiman, in *For the Love of Books* (New York: Putnam, 1992), edited by Ronald B. Schwartz, p. 85.

p. 709: Geoffrey Cowley, "For the Love of Language," *Newsweek* (Fall/Winter, 2000), pp. 12–15.

p. 715: Garrison Keillor, ed., *A Prairie Home Companion Pretty Good Joke Book* (St. Paul, MN: High Bridge, 2000), p. 8.

p. 715: Simon Schama, *Landscape and Memory* (New York: Alfred A. Knopf, 1995), p. 7.

p. 717: Maya Angelou, "Finishing School," in *Heritage: African American Readings for Writers*, 2nd ed., by Joyce M. Jarrett, Doreatha D. Mbalia, and Margaret G. Lee (Upper Saddle River, NJ: Prentice Hall, 2002).

p. 721: Louise Erdrich, *The Last Report on the Miracles at Little No Horse* (New York: HarperCollins, 2001), p. 34.

p. 726: From a paper written by Omatayo Banjo during an internship with Professor Cheryl Glenn, 2007.

PHOTOS AND ILLUSTRATIONS

pp. 1–8 (visual preface): © Digital Vision/VEER.

p. 1: © Masterfile, Royalty-Free.

p. 2: © 2007 Steven Lunetta Photography.

p. 8: Provided by Rosalyn Marie Collings and Daniel Jacob Eves.

p. 11: Courtesy of Library of Congress.

p. 12: © AGC, Inc. American Greetings Corporation. Reproduced by permission.

p. 16: © Adbusters.

p. 18: © www.myspace.com.

p. 19: Provided courtesy of National Center for Missing Adults.

p. 21: © Barnes & Noble, 2007.

p. 22: Courtesy of General Motors Corporation.

p. 23 (top): © AP Photo/HO.

p. 23 (bottom): © Steven Lunetta Photography, 2007.

p. 27: © Bettmann/Corbis.

p. 31: © Lisa Godfrey from *Penn Arts & Sciences Magazine*, Spring 2003

p. 34: © Academy of Natural Sciences of Philadelphia/CORBIS.

p. 37: Courtesy of Department of Education Photo Archives.

p. 42: © 2006 Association of American Colleges and Universities, www.aacu.org/about/statements/Spellings9_26_06.cfm, accessed 10/01/2007.

p. 45: © Nick Ut/Associated Press.

p. 48 (left): © Pierre Vauthey/CORBIS SYGMA.

p. 48 (right): © Steven Lunetta Photography, 2007.

p. 50: Photo © Suzi Altman.

p. 51: Used courtesy of Bill Richardson, 2007.

p. 352: "Out Beyond Ideas of Wrongdoing and Rightdoing" by Jelaluddin Rumi, translated by Coleman Barks and John Moyne from *The Essential Rumi*. Copyright © 1995 by Coleman Barks. Used by permission of Poetry in Motion, Metropolitan Transit Authority and Barnes & Noble.

p. 353 (top): © AP Photo/Mark Lennihan.

p. 353 (bottom): © AP Photo/China Jorrin.

p. 354: © Nicole Bengiveno/The New York Times/Redux.

p. 355 (top): © AP Photo/Eddy Palumbo.

p. 355 (bottom): © Dailylit.com, 2007.

p. 358: © Bettmann/CORBIS.

p. 360: © AP Photo/Jim Cooper.

p. 364: © Gordon Converse / © 1955 The Christian Science Monitor (<http://www.csmonitor.com/>www.csmonitor.com). All rights reserved.

p. 375: © AP Photo/Noah Berger.

p. 382: © Paul Abdoo/MPI/Getty Images.

p. 401: © Masterfile, Royalty-Free.

p. 403: Courtesy of Cheryl Glenn.

p. 405: © Noel Rowe/All the World's Primates.

p. 410: Copyright © 1996 by Houghton Mifflin Company. Reproduced by permission.

p. 415: © Partnership for a Drug-Free America.

p. 419: © Steven Lunetta Photography, 2007.

p. 424: © 2003 by Consumers Union of U.S., Inc. Yonkers, NY 10703-1057, a nonprofit organization. Reprinted with permission from the September 2003 issue of CONSUMER REPORTS® for educational purposes only. No commercial use or reproduction permitted. <http://www.consumerreports.org/>www.ConsumerReports.org.

p. 428 (top): © Bettmann/Corbis.

p. 428 (bottom): © Photo by Keystone/Hulton Archive/Getty Images.

p. 429: © Sara Wiles. Used with permission.

pp. 434, 436: Images courtesy of NOAA.

p. 445: © ALLIANCE ATLANTIS/DOG EAT DOG/UNITED BROADCASTING/THE KOBAL COLLECTION.

p. 448: © Mindy Schauer/Orange County Register/Corbis.

p. 450: © Justin Kase/Alamy.

p. 453: From *Automotive Technology, A Systems Approach*, 4th edition, by ERJAVEC, 2005. Reprinted with permission of Delmar Learning, a division of Cengage Learning: www.cengagerights.com. Fax 800 730-2215.

p. 459: Courtesy of Cheryl Glenn.

p. 464: Photo © Bill Ray/Time & Life Pictures/Getty Images.

p. 465: © The J. Peterman Company.

p. 466: Marjane Satrapi, *Persepolis: The Story of a Childhood*. Copyright © 2005 Marjane Satrapi. Published by Pantheon, a division of Random House, Inc.

p. 468: © AP Photo/Mark Humphrey.

p. 470: © Steven Lunetta Photography, 2007.

p. 472: © Northampton Community College. www.northampton.edu.

p. 474: © AP Photo/Ron Edmonds.

p. 475: © AP Photo/J. Scott Applewhite.

p. 482: Photograph by Ansel Adams. Provided courtesy of Library of Congress.

p. 483: Image from National Archives and Records Administration.

pp. 486, 487: © PETA. Used with permission.

p. 489 (top): Cover from LET US NOW PRAISE FAMOUS MEN by Walker Evans and James Agee. Copyright © Penguin Ltd.

p. 489 (bottom), 490: Courtesy of Library of Congress.

p. 493: Courtesy of the Boston Public Library.

p. 494: Photo © WR Publishing/Alamy.

p. 499: *Large Still Life Frieze*, Joseph Ablow. Copyright © Joseph Ablow. Reprinted by permission of Pucker Gallery.

p. 500: © Pucker Gallery, 2007.

p. 506: Photo © Owen Franken/Corbis.

pp. 510, 511: Courtesy of Central Washington University, Brooks Library.

p. 512: © 2007 EBSCO Publishing.

p. 517: © AP Photo/David Kohl.

p. 519: Image by farwellphotography.com. Used courtesy of the author.

p. 533: © BYU Broadcasting, 2007. www.byubroadcasting.org.

p. 538: © Michelle Malven/iStockphoto.

p. 561: © Steven Lunetta Photography, Inc.

pp. 584, 586, 588, 589, 593: Courtesy of Bethanie Orban.

p. 621: © Chip Forelli/The Image Bank/Getty Images.